Frommer's

POSTCARDS FROM

Bahamas 2003

Eleuthera is an island of gorgeous white- and pink-sand beaches. See chapter 8. © Bob Krist Photography.

Paradise Island is home to the biggest, splashiest resort in The Bahamas, the Atlantis. See chapter 4. © Bob Krist Photography.

Some Paradise Island resorts boast multiple pools, tennis courts, golf courses, and waterfalls. See chapter 4. © M. Timothy O'Keefe Photography.

The Atlantis Resort has an incredible marine park, where visitors can observe tropical fish, sharks, and stingrays from catwalks above and from glassed-in observatories below. See chapter 4. © Mark E. Gibson Photography.

The Bahamian parrot, a colorful local character. © Michael Defreitas Photography.

Old-fashioned horse-drawn surreys are a fun, leisurely way to explore Nassau. See chapter 3. © Bob Krist Photography.

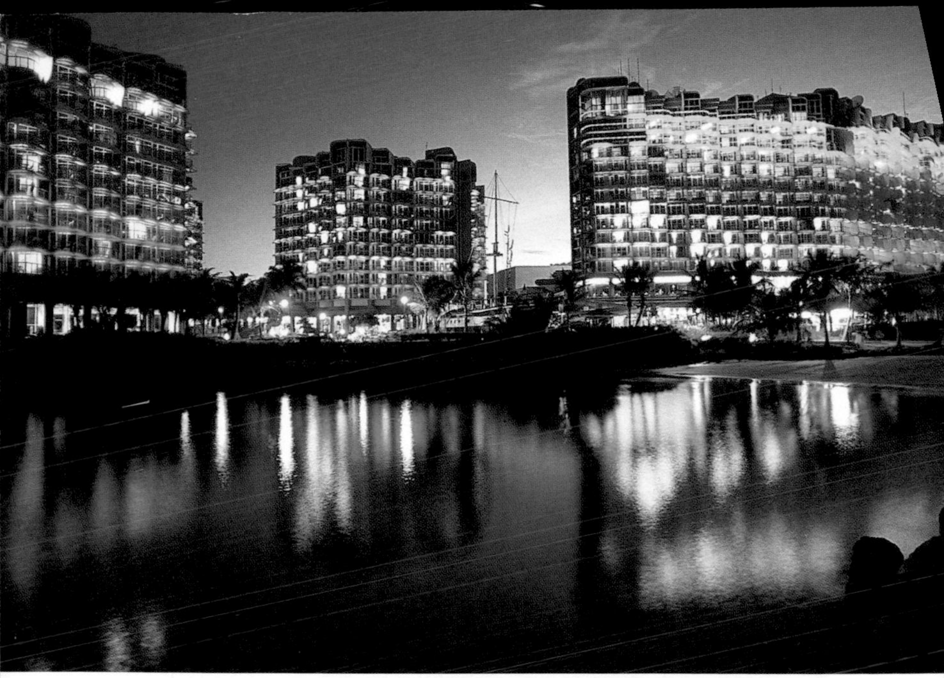

The Crystal Palace Casino on Cable Beach is one of the best places in the Bahamas to roll the dice or try your luck at the slot machines. If you're interested in gambling, head for Nassau, Cable Beach, Paradise Island, or Freeport/Lucaya. See chapters 3, 4, and 5. © *Michael Ventura/International Stock.*

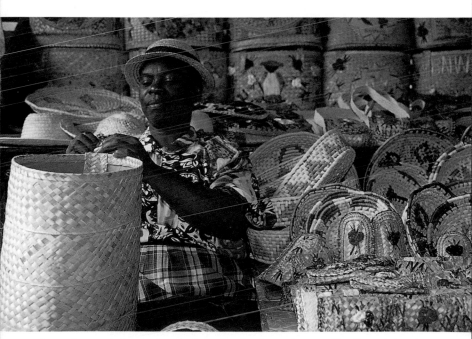

Nassau is a great place to shop for both duty-free luxury items and locally made handcrafts. See chapter 3. © *Bob Krist Photography.*

High-energy Junkanoo parades and celebrations are held throughout the islands on December 26, and many of these activities are repeated on New Year's Day. See chapters 2 and 3 for details. *© Darrell Jones Photography.*

A scene from one of the colorful Junkanoo celebrations. See chapters 2 and 3. *© Michael Ventura/International Stock.*

One of the most unforgettable adventures you can have in Lucaya is the chance to meet a friendly dolphin through UNEXSO's "Dolphin Experience." See chapter 5. *© M. Timothy O'Keefe Photography.*

Tens of thousands of pink flamingos nest in a nature preserve on Great Inagua Island. See chapter 10. © Bob Krist Photography.

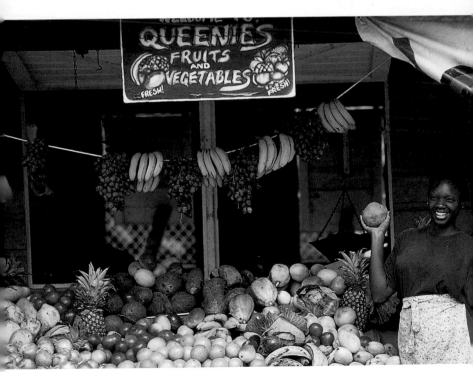

Lots of locally run farmstands offer a taste of The Bahamas. © Bob Krist Photography.

A New Star-Rating System & Other Exciting News from Frommer's!

In our continuing effort to publish the savviest, most up-to-date, and most appealing travel guides available, we've added some great new features.

Frommer's guides now include a new **star-rating system.** Every hotel, restaurant, and attraction is rated from 0 to 3 stars to help you set priorities and organize your time.

We've also added **seven brand-new features** that point you to the great deals, in-the-know advice, and unique experiences that separate travelers from tourists. Throughout the guide, look for:

Finds	Special finds—those places only insiders know about
Fun Fact	Fun facts—details that make travelers more informed and their trips more fun
Kids	Best bets for kids—advice for the whole family
Moments	Special moments—those experiences that memories are made of
Overrated	Places or experiences not worth your time or money
Tips	Insider tips—some great ways to save time and money
Value	Great values—where to get the best deals

We've also added a **"What's New"** section in every guide—a timely crash course in what's hot and what's not in every destination we cover.

Here's what the critics say about Frommer's:

"Amazingly easy to use. Very portable, very complete."

—*Booklist*

"Detailed, accurate, and easy-to-read information for all price ranges."

—*Glamour Magazine*

"Hotel information is close to encyclopedic."

—*Des Moines Sunday Register*

"Frommer's Guides have a way of giving you a real feel for a place."

—*Knight Ridder Newspapers*

Frommer's®

Bahamas 2003

by Darwin Porter & Danforth Prince

Wiley Publishing, Inc.

Published by:

Wiley Publishing, Inc.
909 Third Ave.
New York, NY 10022

ISBN 0-7645-6650-4
ISSN 1068-9338

Editor: Paul Karr
Production Editor: Heather Wilcox
Photo Editor: Richard Fox
Cartographer: John Decamillis
Production by Wiley Indianapolis Composition Services

For information on our other products and services or to obtain technical support, please contact our Customer Care Department within the U.S. at 800-762-2974, outside the U.S. at 317-572-3993 or fax 317-572-4002.

Wiley also publishes its books in a variety of electronic formats. Some content that appears in print may not be available in electronic formats.

Manufactured in the United States of America

5 4 3 2 1

Contents

4 Paradise Island 126

5 Grand Bahama (Freeport/Lucaya) 146

6 Bimini, the Berry Islands & Andros 181

7 The Abaco Islands 207

8 Eleuthera 233

List of Maps

About the Author

Darwin Porter, while still a teenager, began writing about The Bahamas for the *Miami Herald* and has been a frequent visitor ever since. His writing partner is Ohio-born Danforth Prince, formerly of the Paris bureau of the *New York Times,* who has co-authored numerous *Frommer's* bestsellers with Darwin, including the *Caribbean, Bermuda, Puerto Rico, Jamaica,* and the *Virgin Islands.* Together, they share their secrets, discoveries, and opinions about The Bahamas with you.

An Invitation to the Reader

In researching this book, we discovered many wonderful places—hotels, restaurants, shops, and more. We're sure you'll find others. Please tell us about them, so we can share the information with your fellow travelers in upcoming editions. If you were disappointed with a recommendation, we'd love to know that, too. Please write to:

Frommer's Bahamas 2003
Wiley Publishing, Inc. • 909 Third Ave. • New York, NY 10022

An Additional Note

Please be advised that travel information is subject to change at any time—and this is especially true of prices. We therefore suggest that you write or call ahead for confirmation when making your travel plans. The authors, editors, and publisher cannot be held responsible for the experiences of readers while traveling. Your safety is important to us, however, so we encourage you to stay alert and be aware of your surroundings. Keep a close eye on cameras, purses, and wallets, all favorite targets of thieves and pickpockets.

New! Frommer's Star Ratings & Icons

Every hotel, restaurant, and attraction listing in this guide has been ranked for quality, value, service, amenities, and special features using a star-rating scale. In country, state, and regional guides, we also rate towns and regions to help you narrow down your choices and budget your time accordingly. Hotels and restaurants in the Very Expensive and Expensive categories are rated on a scale of one (highly recommended) to three stars (exceptional). Those in the Moderate and Inexpensive categories rate from zero (recommended) to two stars (very highly recommended). Attractions, towns, and regions are rated according to the following scale: zero stars (recommended), one star (highly recommended), two stars (very highly recommended), and three stars (must-see).

In addition to the rating system, we also use seven icons to highlight insider information, useful tips, special bargains, hidden gems, memorable experiences, kid-friendly venues, places to avoid, and other useful information:

Finds ***Fun Fact*** ***Kids*** ***Moments*** ***Overrated*** ***Tips*** ***Value***

The following abbreviations are used for credit cards:

AE	American Express	DISC	Discover	V	Visa
DC	Diners Club	MC	MasterCard		

FROMMERS.COM

Now that you have the guidebook to a great trip, visit our website at **www.frommers.com** for travel information on nearly 2,500 destinations. With features updated regularly, we give you instant access to the most current trip-planning information available. At Frommers.com, you'll also find the best prices on airfares, accommodations, and car rentals—and you can even book travel online through our travel booking partners. At Frommers.com, you'll also find the following:

- Online updates to our most popular guidebooks
- Vacation sweepstakes and contest giveaways
- Newsletter highlighting the hottest travel trends
- Online travel message boards with featured travel discussions

What's New in The Bahamas

After major developments in the resorts of Cable Beach and Paradise Island (part of New Providence, real estate also shared with Nassau), the resorts and dining options are better than ever.

Even sleepy Grand Bahama Island (Freeport/Lucaya) is coming out of its doldrums and reconstructing and renovating resorts at record levels. The Out Islands remain relatively quiet, as always, except for a few hideaways that have opened.

NASSAU Dining The opening of **Chez Willie,** West Bay Street (© **242/322-5364**), has given the Paradise Island and Cable Beach crowd reason to go to the center of Nassau after dark. Elegant and romantic, this is a regal citadel of French and Bahamian cuisine and service often called "old-world." A long time standby, **Green Shutters Restaurant & Pub,** Parliament Street (© **242/322-3701**), is back in business again, with the best selection of beers in town and a respectable Bahamian and British cuisine. There's pub grub, too.

Seeing the Sights Long a landmark in the center of Nassau, **Balcony House,** Trinity Place and Market Street (© **242/302-2621**), is now open for tours. This pink, two-story structure is almost like a bit of 18th-century architecture, picked up from the American Southeast and dropped down intact in the islands. The **Central Bank of The Bahamas,** Trinity Place and Frederick Street (© **242/322-2193**), invites the public in to view a year-round exhibition of paintings that showcase some of the best and brightest young Bahamian artists.

After Dark The **601 Nightclub,** 601 East Bay Street, (© **242/322-3041**), has emerged as the "hot spot" for Nassau after dark. In some ways, it evokes the old Studio 54 in New York and offers the best live bands on the island.

For more information see chapter 3 "New Providence (Nassau/Cable Beach).

GRAND BAHAMA ISLAND (FREEPORT/LUCAYA) Accommodations On the inappropriately named Deadman's Reef (it teems with marine line), the small hideaway of **Paradise Cove** (© **242/349-2677**), has opened right on a good beach. Units have kitchens for your own housekeeping and are secluded and situated away from the glitz and glitter of Freeport. It's for escapists.

Dining Silvano's, Ranfurly Circus (© **242/352-5111**), has opened to challenge all other competitors with its finely honed Italian cuisine. Only "Mama Mia" can do it better. The new hot spot for dining is **Kokonuts Beach Bar & Restaurant,** St. Andrews Drive (© **242/351-5656**), right on the ocean and fronting miles of white sand. It's a family favorite, offering Bahamian cuisine in which the natural flavors of the food are emphasized.

Opening onto Count Basie Square at the Port Lucaya Marketplace, the new **Pub at Lucaya** (© **242/373-8450**) is all the rage. With its English and Bahamian cuisine, it lures diners with the likes of cracked conch or grilled catches of the day.

After Dark The most action-oriented club on island is the newly emerging **Prop Club,** Our Lucaya, Royal Palm Way (© **242/373-1333**), which uses remnants of an old airplane and propellers for its decor. Every night something different is happening, ranging from Sumo wrestling to Junkanoo shows.

For more information see chapter 5 "Grand Bahama."

ANDROS Long infamous for offering up some of the most raffish and bare-boned digs in The Bahamas, Andros Island swallowed several Viagra capsules with the opening of the posh and exclusive **Kamalame Cay** at Staniard Creek (© **242/368-6281**). The finest and most luxurious haven in the archipelago nation, this secluded complex of cottages and suites attracts those who can afford only the best.

The laid-back Emerald Pines-by-the-Sea is still laid-back, but it's got a fancy new name now: **Ritz Beach Resort,** Driggs Hill (© **800/742-4276** or 242/369-2661). Whether you're an ex-Enron accountant or just a weary working stiff needing a place to seriously hide out, this is it, in a setting of 10,000 palm trees and 8km (5 miles) of beachfront.

For more information see chapter 6 "Bimini, the Berry Islands & Andros."

THE ABACOS In the area of Marsh Harbour, a favorite of yachters, **Sunset Point Resort** (© **242/367-5333**), is the island's newest holiday complex, overlooking Bustick Bay. Its freshly decorated bedrooms are especially popular with bonefishermen, and its Lazy Parrot dining room is becoming increasingly known for the Bahamian and continental cuisine.

For more information see chapter 7 "The Abaco Islands."

THE EXUMAS Accommodations At long last, after a sleep of centuries, major tourism is on the way to the Southern Bahamas with the projected opening of the upmarket **Four Seasons Resort** (© **800/819-5053**). The Southern Bahamas have never seen the likes of luxury like this, except maybe at the Club Med on San Salvador island; a special feature will be the 18-hole golf course designed by Greg Norman. The giant, 500-acre oceanfront complex is currently scheduled to open sometime in 2003.

For more details, see chapter 9 "The Exuma Islands."

1

The Best of The Bahamas

The Bahamas (that's with a capital "T") is one of the most geographically complicated nations of the Atlantic. A coral-based archipelago, it is composed of more than 700 islands, 2,000 cays (pronounced "keys," from the Spanish word for small islands), and hundreds of rocky outcroppings that have damaged the hulls of countless ships since colonial days.

The Commonwealth of The Bahamas came into being in 1973 after centuries of colonial rule. After Great Britain granted The Bahamas internal self-rule in 1964, the fledgling nation adopted its own constitution but chose not to sever its ties with its motherland. It has remained in the Commonwealth, with the British monarch as its head of state. In the British tradition, The Bahamas has a two-house Parliament, a ministerial cabinet headed by a prime minister, and an independent judiciary. The queen appoints a Bahamian-general to represent the Crown.

As The Bahamas moves deeper into the new millennium, the government and various investors continue to pump money into the tourism infrastructure, especially on Paradise Island, across from Nassau, as well as Freeport/Lucaya on Grand Bahama Island. Cruise ship tourism continues to increase, and a more upscale crowd is coming back after abandoning The Bahamas for many years in favor of other Caribbean islands such as St. Barts and Anguilla.

When Hubert Ingraham became prime minister in 1992, he launched the country down the long road toward regaining its market share of tourism, which under Prime Minister Lynden Pindling had seen a rapid decline. Exit polls revealed some first-time visitors vowing never to return to The Bahamas under the administration of the notorious Pindling, whose government had taken over a number of hotels and failed to maintain them properly.

When Ingraham took over as new prime minister, however, he wisely recognized that the government wasn't supposed to be in the hospitality business and turned many properties back over to the professionals. After a painful slump, tourism in the post-Pindling era is booming again in The Bahamas, and more than 1.6 million visitors from all over the world now flock here annually. In the capital of Nassau, it's easy to see where money is being spent: on new air terminals, widened roads, repaved sidewalks, underground phone cables, massive landscaping, sweeping esplanades, a cleanup campaign, and additional police officers walking the beat to cut down on crime.

Unlike Haiti and Jamaica, The Bahamas has remained politically stable and made the transition from minority white rule to black majority rule with relatively little tension.

And economic conditions have slowly improved here. You do not see the wretched poverty in Nassau that you see in, say, Kingston, Jamaica, though many poor residents do still live on New Providence Island's "Over-the-Hill" section, an area where few tourists venture to visit (although the neighborhood is gritty and fascinating).

The Bahamas

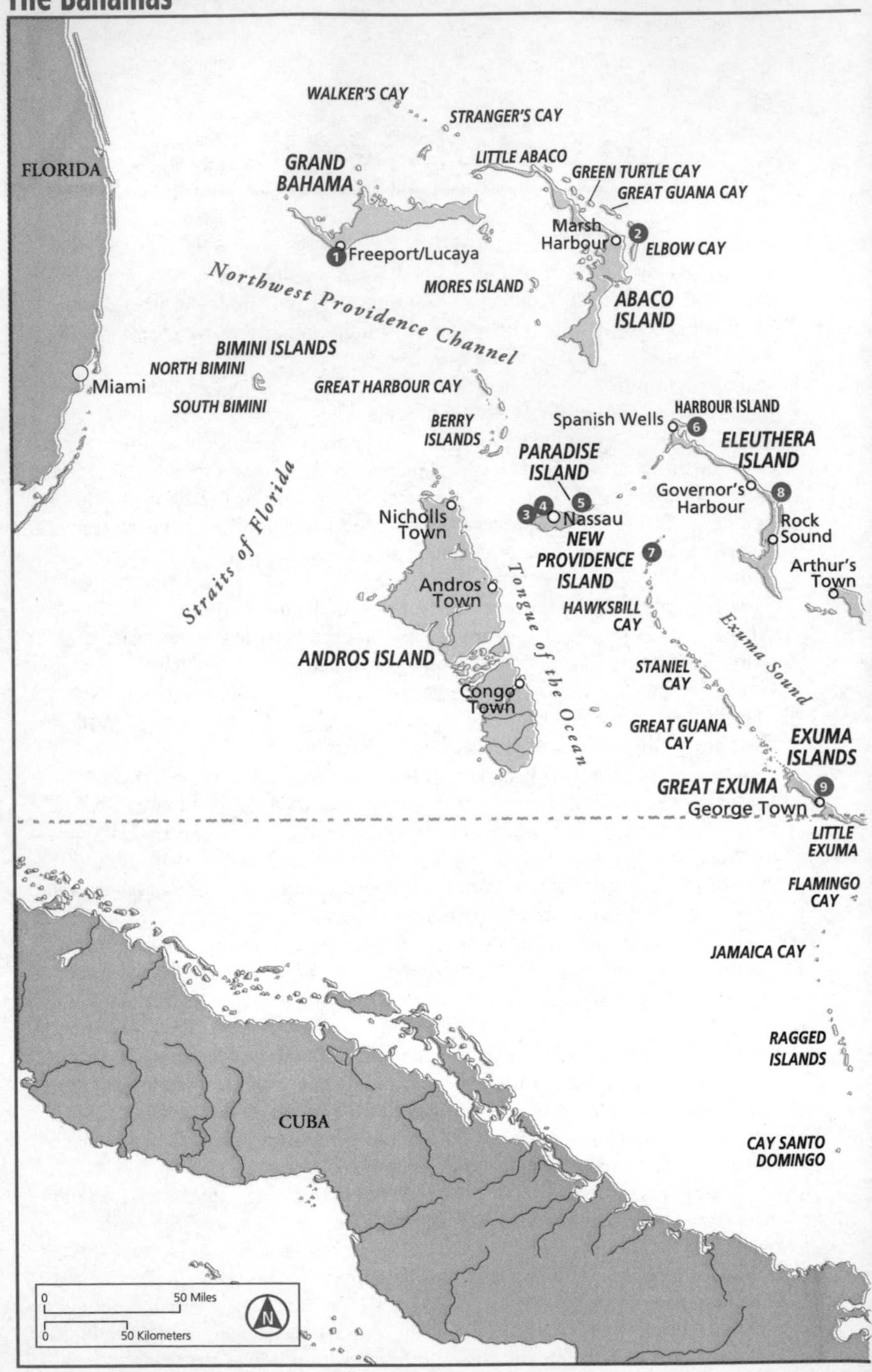
WALKER'S CAY
STRANGER'S CAY
FLORIDA
GRAND BAHAMA
LITTLE ABACO
GREEN TURTLE CAY
GREAT GUANA CAY
Marsh Harbour
2
ELBOW CAY
1 Freeport/Lucaya
Northwest Providence Channel
MORES ISLAND
ABACO ISLAND
BIMINI ISLANDS
NORTH BIMINI
Miami
SOUTH BIMINI
GREAT HARBOUR CAY
BERRY ISLANDS
Spanish Wells
HARBOUR ISLAND
6
ELEUTHERA ISLAND
PARADISE ISLAND
Governor's Harbour
8
Nicholls Town
3
4
5
Nassau
Rock Sound
Straits of Florida
NEW PROVIDENCE ISLAND
7
Arthur's Town
Andros Town
Tongue of the Ocean
HAWKSBILL CAY
Exuma Sound
ANDROS ISLAND
STANIEL CAY
Congo Town
GREAT GUANA CAY
EXUMA ISLANDS
GREAT EXUMA
9
George Town
LITTLE EXUMA
FLAMINGO CAY
JAMAICA CAY
RAGGED ISLANDS
CUBA
CAY SANTO DOMINGO
0
50 Miles
0
50 Kilometers
N

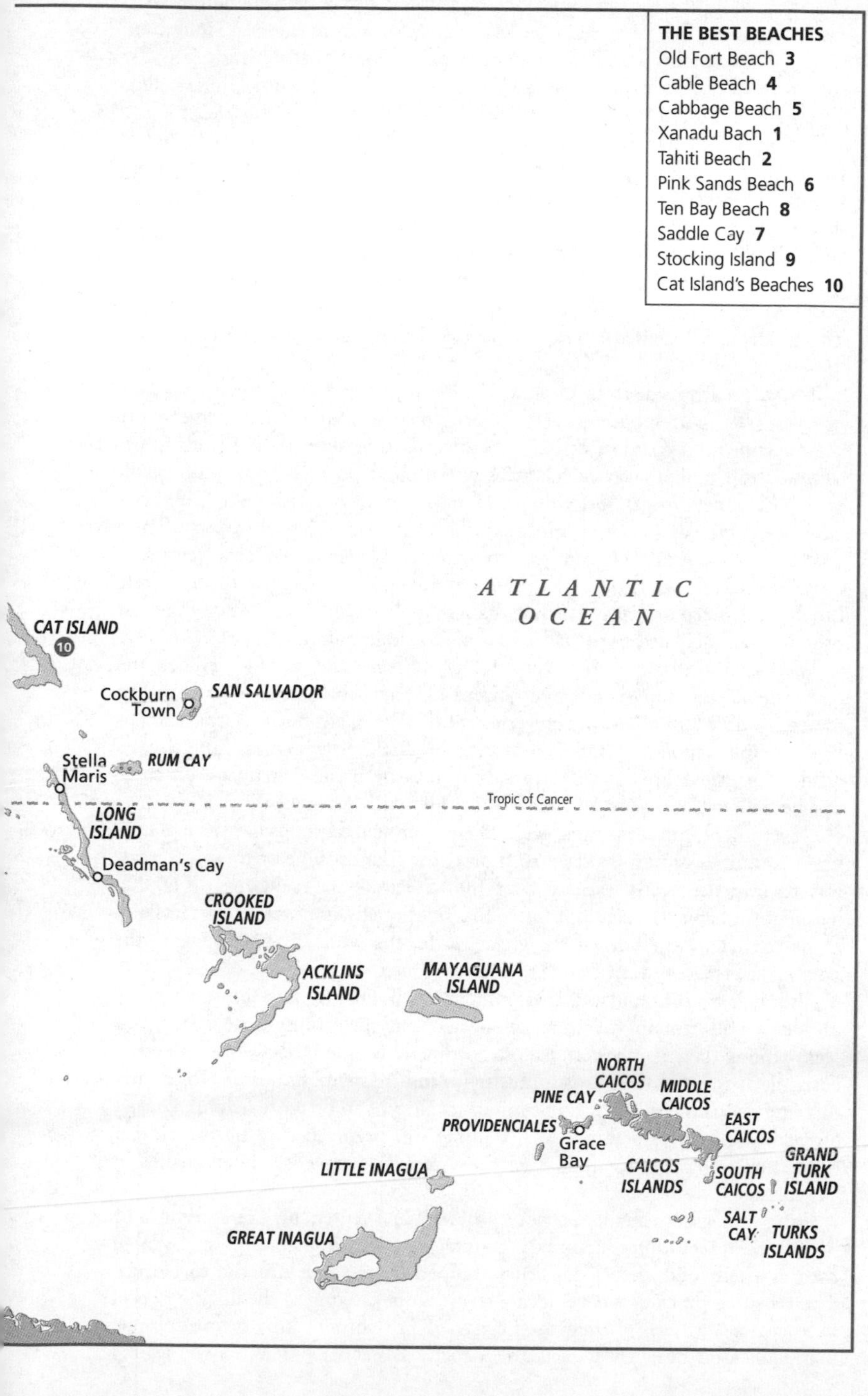

THE BEST BEACHES
Old Fort Beach **3**
Cable Beach **4**
Cabbage Beach **5**
Xanadu Bach **1**
Tahiti Beach **2**
Pink Sands Beach **6**
Ten Bay Beach **8**
Saddle Cay **7**
Stocking Island **9**
Cat Island's Beaches **10**

Nassau really is the true The Bahamas. You'd think a city so close to the U.S. mainland would have been long since overpowered by American culture. Yet, except for some fast-food chain outlets, American pop music and Hollywood films, Nassau retains a surprising amount of its traditionally British feel. (By contrast, Freeport/Lucaya on Grand Bahama Island has become almost completely Americanized, with little British aura or Bahamian tradition left.)

The biggest changes have occurred in the hotel sector. Sun International has vastly expanded its Atlantis property on Paradise Island, turning it into a virtual waterworld. Several new restaurants have opened, replacing older establishments that had grown tired over the years. The Hilton interests have developed the decaying old British Colonial in Nassau, restoring it to life.

And Grand Bahama Island is in an interesting state of flux. Hotels along the entire Lucayan strip are being either built from scratch or upgraded; the fabled The Resorts at Bahamia in Freeport is experiencing a renaissance under new owners.

If there's a downside to this boom, it's the emphasis on megahotels and casinos—and the corresponding lack of focus on the Out Islands. Large resort chains, with the exception of Four Seasons, have ignored these islands; most continue to slumber away in relative seclusion and poverty. Four Seasons will open a huge new megaresort with an 18-hole golf course as soon as 2003, but other development has been minor, so the Out Islands remain drowsy. Their very lack of progress will continue to attract a certain breed of adventurous explorer, the one who shuns the resorts and casinos of Paradise Island, Cable Beach, and Freeport/Lucaya. Little change in this Out Islands-versus-the-rest situation is anticipated until well into the new millennium.

There's another interesting trend to note here. After a long slumber, the government and many concerned citizens of The Bahamas have awakened to eco-tourism. More than any government in the Caribbean except perhaps Bonaire, this nation is trying to protect its natural heritage. If nothing else, its residents realize doing this will be good for tourism, because many visitors come to The Bahamas precisely for a close encounter with nature.

Government, private companies, and environmental groups have drawn up a national framework of priorities to protect the islands. One of their first goals was to save the nearly extinct West Indian flamingo. Today, nearly 60,000 flamingos inhabit the Island of Great Inagua. Equally important programs aim to prevent the extinction of the green turtle, the white-crowned pigeon, the Bahamian parrot, and the New Providence iguana.

Although tourism and the environment are bouncing back, however, many problems still remain for this archipelago nation. While some Bahamians seem among the friendliest and most hospitable people in the world, others—particularly those in the tourist industry—can be downright hostile. To counter this, the government is working to train its citizens to be more helpful, courteous, and efficient. Sometimes this training has been taken to heart; at other times, however, it still clearly has not. Service with a smile is still not assured in The Bahamas.

Drug smuggling remains a serious problem, and regrettably there seems to be no immediate solution. Because the country is so close to U.S. shores, it is often used as a temporary depot for drugs shipped from South America to Florida. The Bahamas previously developed a tradition of catering to the illicit habits of U.S. citizens, as well; during the heyday of Prohibition, long before cocaine, marijuana, and heroin were outlawed, many Bahamians grew rich smuggling rum into the United States. Things have improved recently, but you'll still see stories in the newspapers about floating bales of marijuana turning up in the sea just off The Bahamas' coastline and such.

Though this illicit trade rarely affects the casual tourist, it's important to know that it is a factor here—and so, armed with this knowledge, don't agree to carry any packages to or from the U.S. for a stranger while you're visiting. You could end up taking a much longer vacation on these islands than you had ever imagined!

1 The Best Beaches

- **Old Fort Beach** (New Providence Island): With pristine white sands and turquoise water, this is the least developed major beach on New Providence Island, near the relatively unpopulated western tip of The Bahamas' most crowded island. Many of its biggest fans are homeowners from nearby Lyford Cay, whose homes are among the most expensive in The Bahamas. The beach is least crowded on weekdays, and windiest throughout the winter. There's great water-skiing in summer, when waters are the calmest. See "Beaches, Watersports & Other Outdoor Pursuits," in chapter 3.
- **Cable Beach** (New Providence Island): The glittering shoreline of Cable Beach has easy access to shops, casinos, restaurants, watersports, and bars. It's a sandy 6.5km- (4-mile-) long strip, with a great array of facilities and activities. See chapter 3.
- **Cabbage Beach** (Paradise Island): Think Vegas in the tropics. It seems as if most of the sunbathers dozing on the sands here are recovering from the previous evening's partying, and it's likely to be crowded near the megahotels, but you can find a bit more solitude on the beach's isolated northwestern extension (Paradise Beach)—which is accessible only by boat or on foot. Lined with palms, sea grapes, and casuarinas, the sands are broad and stretch for at least 3km (2 miles). See "Beaches, Watersports & Other Outdoor Pursuits," in chapter 4.
- **Xanadu Beach** (Grand Bahama Island): Grand Bahama has 97km (60 miles) of sandy shoreline, but Xanadu Beach is most convenient to Freeport's resort hotels, several of which offer shuttle service to Xanadu. There's more than a kilometer of white sand and (usually) gentle surf. Don't expect to have Xanadu to yourself, but if you want more quiet and privacy, try any of the beaches that stretch from Xanadu for many miles in either direction. See "Beaches, Watersports & Other Outdoor Pursuits," in chapter 5.
- **Tahiti Beach** (Hope Town, the Abacos): Since the beach is so isolated at the far end of Elbow Cay Island, you can be sure that only a handful of people will ever visit these cool waters and white sands. The crowds stay away because you can't drive to Tahiti Beach: To get there, you'll have to walk or ride a rented bike along sand and gravel paths from Hope Town. You can also charter a boat to get there, which isn't too hard, since the Abacos are the sailing capital of The Bahamas. See "Elbow Cay (Hope Town)," in chapter 7.
- **Pink Sands Beach** (Harbour Island): Running the entire length of the island's eastern side, these pale pink sands stretch for 5km (3 miles) past a handful of low-rise

hotels and private villas. A coral reef protects the shore from breakers, making for some of the safest swimming in The Bahamas. See chapter 8.

- **Ten Bay Beach** (Eleuthera): Ten Bay Beach lies a short drive south of Palmetto Point, just north of Savannah Sound. Once upon a time, the exclusive Cotton Bay Club chose to build a hotel here because of the fabulous scenery. There may not be facilities here, but now that the hotel has closed, the white sands and turquoise waters here are more idyllic and private than ever. See "Harbour Island," in chapter 8.
- **Saddle Cay** (the Exumas): Most of the Exumas are oval-shaped islands strung end to end like links in a 209km (130-mile) chain. One notable exception is Saddle Cay, with its horseshoe-shaped curve near the Exumas's northern tip. It can be reached only by boat, but once achieved offers an unspoiled setting without a trace of the modern world—and plenty of other cays and islets where you can play Robinson Crusoe for a few hours if you like. See "Exumas Essentials," in chapter 9.
- **Stocking Island** (the Exumas): One of the finest white sandy beaches in The Bahamas lies off Elizabeth Harbour, the main harbor of the archipelago, close to the little capital of George Town. You can reach Stocking Island easily by boat from Elizabeth Harbour, and the sands of this offshore island are rarely crowded; snorkelers and divers love to explore its gin-clear waters. In addition to its beach of powdery white sand, the island is also known for its "blue holes," coral gardens, and undersea caves. See "Beaches, Watersports & Other Outdoor Pursuits," in chapter 9.
- **Cat Island's Beaches:** The white sandy beaches ringing this island are pristine, opening onto crystal-clear waters and lined with coconut palms, palmettos, and casuarina trees—and best of all, you'll practically have the place to yourself. One of our favorite beaches here, near Old Bight, has a beautiful, lazy curve of white sand. Another fabulous beach lies 5km (3 miles) north of New Bight, site of the Fernandez Bay Village resort. This curvy white sandy beach is set against another backdrop of casuarinas, and is idyllic and unusually tranquil. One more good beach here is the long, sandy stretch that opens onto Hawk's Nest Resort and Marina on the southwestern side. None of the Cat Island beaches has any facilities (bring anything you need from your hotel), but they do offer peace, quiet, and seclusion. See "Cat Island," in chapter 10.

2 The Best Diving

- **New Providence Island:** Many ships have sunk near Nassau in the past 300 years, and all the dive outfitters here know the most scenic wreck sites. Other attractions are underwater gardens of elkhorn coral and dozens of reefs brimming with underwater life. The most spectacular dive site is the **Shark Wall,** 16km (10 miles) off the southwest coast of New Providence; it's blessed with incredible, colorful sea life and the healthiest coral offshore. You'll even get to swim with sharks (not as bait, of course). See "Beaches, Watersports & Other Outdoor Pursuits," in chapter 3.

- **Grand Bahama Island:** The island is ringed with reefs, and dive sites are plentiful, including the Wall, the Caves (site of a long-ago disaster known as Theo's Wreck), and Treasure Reef. Other popular dive sites include Spit City (yes, that's right), Ben Blue Hole, and the Rose Garden (no one knows how this one got its name). What makes Grand Bahama Island a cut above the others is the presence of a world-class dive operator, **UNEXSO** (the Underwater Explorer's Society; ✆ **888/365-3483** or 242/373-1250). See "Beaches, Watersports & Other Outdoor Pursuits," in chapter 5.
- **Andros:** Marine life abounds in the barrier reef off the coast of Andros, which is one of the largest in the world and a famous destination for divers. The reef plunges 1,800m (6,000 ft.) to a narrow drop-off known as the Tongue of the Ocean. You can also explore mysterious blue holes, formed when subterranean caves fill with seawater, causing their ceilings to collapse and exposing clear, deep pools. See "The Islands in Brief," in chapter 2, and "Andros," in chapter 6.
- **Bimini:** Although Bimini is most famous for its game fishing, it boasts excellent diving, too. Five kilometers (3 miles) of offshore reefs attract millions of colorful fish. Even snorkelers can see black coral gardens, blue holes, and an odd configuration on the sea floor that is reportedly part of the lost continent of Atlantis (a fun legend, at any rate). Divers can check out the wreck of a motorized yacht, the *Sapona* (owned by Henry Ford), which sank in shallow waters off the coast in 1929. See "Bimini," in chapter 6.
- **Eleuthera:** In addition to lovely coral and an array of colorful fish, divers can enjoy some unique experiences here, such as the "Current Cut," an exciting underwater gully that carries you on a swiftly flowing underwater current for 10 minutes. Four wrecked ships also lie nearby, at depths of less than 12m (40 ft.), including a barge that was transporting the engine of a steam locomotive in 1865, reportedly after the American Confederacy sold it to raise cash for its war effort. See "Harbour Island," in chapter 8.
- **Long Island** (the Southern Bahamas): Snorkeling is spectacular on virtually all sides of the island. But experienced divers venturing into deeper waters offshore can visit underwater cages to feed swarms of mako, bull, and reef sharks. Dive sites abound, including the Arawak "green hole," a blue hole of incomprehensible depth. See "Long Island," in chapter 10.

3 The Best Snorkeling

- **New Providence Island/Paradise Island:** The waters that ring densely populated New Providence Island and nearby Paradise Island are easy to explore. Most people head for the Rose Island Reefs, the Gambier Deep Reef, Booby Rock Channel, the Goulding Reef Cays, and some easily seen, well-known underwater wrecks that lie in shallow water. Virtually every resort hotel on the island offers equipment and can book you onto a snorkel cruise to sites further offshore. See "Beaches, Watersports & Other Outdoor Pursuits," in chapter 3, and "Beaches, Watersports & Other Outdoor Pursuits," in chapter 4.

- **Bimini:** Snorkelers are enthralled with the offshore black coral gardens, which are easily accessible from shore, and the colorful marine life around the island. Sometimes when conditions are right, snorkelers enjoy frolicking with a pod of spotted dolphins. Off North Bimini, snorkelers are attracted to a cluster of huge, flat rocks that jut from 6m to 9m (20–30 ft.) out of the water at Paradise Point. The most imaginative snorkelers claim these rocks, which seem hand-hewn, are part of a road system that once traversed the lost continent of Atlantis. See "Bimini," in chapter 6.
- **Long Island:** Shallow bays and sandy beaches offer many possibilities for snorkeling, and the staffs at both major resorts will direct you to the finest conditions near their stretches of beach. The southern end of the island is especially dramatic because of its unique sea cliffs. Many east-coast beach coves also offer fantastic snorkeling opportunities. See "Long Island," in chapter 10.

4 The Best Fishing

- **Bimini:** Big-game fish can still be caught in the deep waters around Bimini, but the most sought-after trophy is the marlin, whose image appears on the Bahamian $100 bill. As many as 40 annual fishing tournaments are held every year in The Bahamas, many of which transform Bimini into a mini-Olympic village where the elusive fish are hunted by a daunting armada of well-equipped fishing boats. Bimini was Ernest Hemingway's favorite place to fish when the oceans were not nearly so depleted as they are now. See "Bimini," in chapter 6.
- **Andros:** Bonefish thrive in the shallow, sunlit waters off Andros Island. It isn't the best-tasting fish in the islands (as you might guess, it consists mostly of cartilage and bones), but serious anglers say that it puts up one of the strongest fights of any fish in the world. Other islands good for bonefishing include Bimini, Walker's Cay, Abaco, Eleuthera, Exuma, and Long Island. See "Andros," in chapter 6.
- **The Abacos:** In the Marsh Harbour area, you'll find bonefish in the flats, marlin in the deep, and yellowtail on the reefs—and many of the world's greatest anglers will be in hot pursuit. In Elbow Cay, you can arrange to head out with the local fishermen. Another good place for deep-sea charters in the Abacos is Green Turtle Cay, which hosts a hugely popular fishing tournament each May. See chapter 7.

5 The Best Sailing

- **The Abacos:** Known among yachties for their many anchorages, sheltered coves, and plentiful marine facilities, the Abacos are considered one of the most perfect sailing areas in the world. You can charter boats of all shapes and sizes for a week or longer, with or without a crew. Major charter centers are located in Marsh Harbour and Hope Town. Arrange for rentals with **The Moorings** (© **800/535-7289** or 242/367-4000), in Marsh Harbour. See "The Active Vacation Planner," in chapter 2, and

"Marsh Harbour (Great Abaco Island)," in chapter 7.

- **The Exumas:** Each April, the Exumas host the famed Family Island Regatta, the most popular sailing event in The Bahamas. Elizabeth Harbour is a Mecca for yachters, who explore nearby deserted islands and cays, secluded bays, safe anchorage harbors, and secret coves. Even in winter, unless the weather turns unexpectedly bad (and foul weather is usually short-lived), the seas are balmy and the temperatures ideal. *Yachting* magazine praise the Exumas for having the finest cruising areas in The Bahamas. See "The Active Vacation Planner," in chapter 2, and "George Town," in chapter 9.

6 The Best Golf Courses

- **South Ocean Golf Course** (New Providence Island; © **242/362-4391**): This course, designed by Joe Lee with four challenging water holes, is so isolated from the congestion of Nassau that you can imagine yourself on a remote island. The rolling terrain is hilly and dotted with palm trees; from this relatively high elevation, you'll enjoy views over the "Tongue of the Ocean." We think this course is better and more demanding than the other major choice on New Providence Island at Cable Beach (see below). See "Beaches, Watersports & Other Outdoor Pursuits," in chapter 3.
- **Cable Beach Golf Course** (New Providence Island; © **242/327-6000**): The oldest golf course in The Bahamas, this par-72 green was the private retreat of British expatriates in the 1930s. Today, it's managed by a corporate namesake of Arnold Palmer and owned by Cable Beach casino marketers. Small ponds and water traps heighten the challenge, amid more than 7,000 yards of well-maintained greens and fairways. Despite these assets, however, we still prefer the competition: the Ocean Club Golf Club and the South Ocean Golf Course. See "The Active Vacation Planner," in chapter 2, and "Beaches, Watersports & Other Outdoor Pursuits," in chapter 3.
- **Ocean Club Golf Club** (Paradise Island; © **242/363-3925**): Tom Weiskopf designed this 18-hole, par-72 course, and it's a stunner. With its own pitfalls, including the world's largest sand trap and water hazards (mainly the Atlantic Ocean) on three sides, Jack Nicklaus and Gary Player have endorsed this course. For the best panoramic ocean view—good enough to take your mind off your game—play the par-3 14th hole. See "The Active Vacation Planner," in chapter 2, and "Beaches, Watersports & Other Outdoor Pursuits," in chapter 4.
- **The Reef Course** (Grand Lucaya, Grand Bahama Island; © **242/373-2002**): Designed by Robert Trent Jones Jr., this is the first golf course to open in The Bahamas in 3 decades. The course boasts 6,920 yards of links-style playing grounds. See "Beaches, Watersports & Other Outdoor Pursuits," in chapter 5.
- **The Resorts at Bahamia** (Grand Bahama Island; © **242/350-7000**): This megaresort offers two golf courses, Bahamia's Ruby and Bahamia's Emerald. Both are par 72, with rolling, sandy terrain, but they're not as challenging as the South Ocean Golf Course. See p. 151.

Eco-Tourism Highlights of The Bahamas

The Bahamas spreads over 100,000 square miles of the Atlantic Ocean—this is the largest oceanic archipelago nation in the tropical Atlantic Ocean, with miles of crystal-clear waters rich with fish and other marine resources—and thus is home to countless natural attractions, including a series of underwater reefs that stretch 1,224km (760 miles) from the Abacos in the northeast to Long Island in the southeast. It has the most extensive systems of blue holes and limestone caves in the world.

And, unlike Puerto Rico, Jamaica, Barbados, and other Caribbean island nations, The Bahamas also possesses large areas of undeveloped natural mainland.

It all adds up to plenty of opportunity for getting up-close and personal with nature.

Start with the reefs. Lying off the coast of Andros, The Bahamas includes approximately 900 square miles of coral reef, comprising the third-largest barrier reef system in the world. Rich with diverse marine life, the reef attracts green moray eels, cinnamon clownfish, and Nassau grouper. When officials realized that long-line fishing threatened this fragile ecology, The Bahamas became one of the first Caribbean countries to outlaw the practice.

7 The Best Tennis Facilities

- **Paradise Island:** Paradise Island has the best courts and the best players in The Bahamas. If you're really serious about your game, consider checking into **Club Med Paradise** (✆ **242/363-2640**), which has the largest court complex on the island, with 20 clay composition courts (eight of them lit for night games), ball machines, a full staff of instructors who offer expert advice, and an instant-replay TV. The tennis complex at the **Atlantis** (✆ **242/363-3000**) is more accessible to the general public, with a dozen asphalt courts, some lit for night games. See "Beaches, Watersports & Other Outdoor Pursuits," in chapter 4.
- **Freeport** (Grand Bahama Island): Freeport is another top choice for tennis buffs. **The Resorts at Bahamia** (✆ **242/350-7000**) has nine state-of-the-art courts, three of them clay and eight lit for night games. You don't have to be a guest to play here, but you should call ahead for a reservation. See "The Active Vacation Planner," in chapter 2, and p. 151.
- **Lucayan National Park:** This park on Grand Bahama Island is the site of a 9.5km- (6-mile-) long, underground, freshwater cave system, the longest of its type in the world. The largest cave contains spiral staircases that lead visitors into a freshwater world inhabited by shrimp, mosquito fish, fruit bats, freshwater eels, and a species of crustacean (*Spelionectes lucayensis*) that has never been documented elsewhere. On the 40-acre preserve you'll find examples of the island's five

The nation's Parliament also passed the Wild Birds Protection Act to ensure the preservation of rare bird species. That law has made a significant difference: Great Inagua Island now shelters more than 60,000 pink flamingos, Bahamian parrots, and a large portion of the world's population of reddish egrets. These birds live in the government-protected, 287-square-mile Inagua National Park.

And that's not all. The islands of The Bahamas are home to more than 1,370 species of plant life, plus 13 species of mammals; the majority of them, it must be said, are bats, but wild pigs, donkeys, raccoons, and the Abaco wild horse also roam the interiors of the nation's islands. You'll see whales and dolphins, including humpback and blue whales and the spotted dolphin, swimming in the sea.

To keep an eye on all this natural wealth, and share it with the public, the **Bahamas National Trust** administers 12 national parks and more than 240,000 acres of protected land. Its headquarters, with one of the finest collections of wild palms in the western hemisphere, are located in Nassau at **The Retreat** on Village Road (**© 242/328-6849**). Guided 30-minute tours are conducted Tuesday through Thursday. Volunteers at The Retreat can also help arrange visits to the national parks on the various islands, the best of which are previewed below.

ecosystems—pine forests, rocky coppice, mangrove swamps, whiteland coppice, and sand dunes. Pause to sunbathe on a lovely stretch of sandy beach, or hike along paths where you can spot orchids, hummingbirds, and barn owls. See p. 173.

- **Pelican Cays Land and Sea Park:** Known for its undersea caves, seemingly endless coral reefs, and abundant plant and marine life, this park, 13km (8 miles) north of Cherokee Sound at Great Abaco Island, is a highlight for scuba divers. See "Marsh Harbour (Great Abaco Island)," in chapter 7.
- **Exuma Cays National Land and Sea Park:** A major attraction of The Bahamas, this park is the first of its kind anywhere on the planet. The 35km- (22-mile-) long, 13km- (8-mile-) wide natural preserve attracts scuba divers to its 175 square miles of sea gardens with spectacular reefs, flora, and fauna. Inaugurated in 1958, it lies some 35km (22 miles) northwest of Staniel Cay or 64km (40 miles) southeast of Nassau and is accessible only by boat. See "Exumas Essentials," in chapter 9.
- **Great Inagua:** This sleepy island in the Southern Bahamas is internationally famous for its colony of wild West Indian flamingos, the world's largest. In local dialect, these birds are sometimes called "fillymingos" or "flamingas." See "Great Inagua," in chapter 10.
- **Union Creek Reserve:** This 7-square-mile enclosed tidal creek on Great Inagua serves as a captive breeding research site for giant sea turtles, with special emphasis on green turtles, which have been overhunted and are now an endangered species. See "Great Inagua," in chapter 10.

8 The Best Honeymoon Resorts

- **Sandals Royal Bahamian Hotel** (Cable Beach, New Providence Island; ✆ **800/SANDALS** or 242/327-6400): This Jamaican chain of male-female couples-only, all-inclusive hotels is a honeymooners' favorite. The Bahamas's branch of the chain is more upscale than many of its Jamaican counterparts, and it offers 27 secluded honeymoon suites with semiprivate plunge pools. Staff members lend their experience and talent to on-site wedding celebrations; Sandals will provide everything from a preacher to flowers, as well as champagne and a cake. It's more expensive than most Sandals resorts, but you can usually get better rates through a travel agent or a package deal. See p. 90.
- **Nassau Marriott Resort & Crystal Palace Casino** (New Providence Island; ✆ **800/222-7466** or 242/327-6200): If you're bored with the idea of honeymooning in an isolated village, with just you, your loved one, the moon, and the stars, head to this flashy, high-tech megacomplex, where bright lights and a mind-boggling assortment of diversions will help you while away your time. See p. 88.
- **Compass Point** (New Providence Island; ✆ **800/688-7678** or 242/327-4500): This choice is the charming and personalized statement of record-company impresario Christopher Blackwell; it's purely for those who shun megaresorts. The accommodations are found in floridly painted huts or cottages, some of which have kitchenettes and some of which are raised on stilts. Completely in harmony with the lovely natural setting, it's nevertheless state-of-the-art. See p. 92.
- **Ocean Club** (Paradise Island; ✆ **800/321-3000** in the U.S. only, or 242/363-2501): It's elegant, low-key, and low-rise, and it feels exclusive. The guests are likely to include many older couples celebrating honeymoons. With waterfalls, fountains, reflecting pools, and a stone gazebo, the Ocean Club's formal terraced gardens were inspired by the club's founder (an heir to the A&P fortune) and are the most impressive in The Bahamas. At the center is a French cloister, with carvings from the 12th century. See p. 130.
- **Old Bahama Bay** (Grand Bahama Island; ✆ **800/572-5711** or 242/350-6500). Honeymooners seeking a quiet hideaway boutique-style hotel with cottages adjacent to a marina. The casinos, entertainment, shopping, and dining of Freeport/Lucaya are 40km (25 miles) away, but here you can sneak away to luxury, solitude, and romance. See p. 159.
- **Kamalame Cay** (Staniard Creek, Andros; ✆ **242/368-6281**). You'll need deep pockets to afford one of the most exclusive resorts in the Out Islands, a perfect honeymoon retreat for the couple who want to escape casinos and resorts. With its 5km (3 miles) of white-sand beaches in both directions, this pocket of posh is a citadel of luxury and comfort. It's also recommended for a second or even a third honeymoon. See p. 199.
- **Green Turtle Club** (Green Turtle Cay, the Abacos; ✆ **242/365-4271**): Romantics appreciate this resort's winning combination of yachting atmosphere and well-manicured comfort. It's small (31 rooms) and civilized in an understated way; the charming, clapboard-covered village of New Plymouth is nearby, accessible by motor launch or, even better, a

45-minute walk across windswept scrublands. See p. 227.

- **Bluff House Club Beach Hotel** (Green Turtle Cay, the Abacos; ✆ **242/365-4247**): This place was named because of its location high atop an 80-foot cliff towering over a pink sand beach. Its 12 acres front the Sea of Abaco on one side and the harbor of White Sound on the other. The accommodations are very private, with a rustic, seafaring decor that has its own kind of elegance. In addition to rooms, the hotel offers beach and hillside villas, and colonial suites with private balconies that overlook the water. See p. 226.
- **Pink Sands** (Harbour Island, Eleuthera; ✆ **800/OUTPOST** or 242/333-2030). You can have a spectacular getaway at this elite retreat on a 28-acre beachfront estate owned by Chris Blackwell, the famous founder of Island Records. Its location on a 5km (3-mile) stretch of private pink sand, sheltered by a barrier reef, is just one of its assets. You can ask for a bedroom that evokes an upscale bordello in Shanghai to put you in a romantic mood, and you can also enjoy the best meals on the island. See p. 247.
- **Stella Maris Resort Club** (Long Island, the Southern Bahamas; ✆ **800/426-0466,** 242/338-2051, or 954/359-8236): Right on the Atlantic, built on the grounds of an old plantation, Stella Maris has become a social hub on Long Island. Sailing is important here, as are diving and getting away from it all. Many of the guests hail from Germany, and they lend the place a European flair. The sleepy island itself is one of the most beautiful in The Bahamas, and honeymooners fit into the grand scheme of things perfectly. See p. 283.

9 The Best Family Vacations

- **Radisson Cable Beach Hotel** (Cable Beach, New Providence Island; ✆ **800/333-3333** or 242/327-6000): A family could spend their entire vacation on the grounds of this vast resort. There's a pool area that features the most lavish artificial waterfall this side of Tahiti; a health club at the nearby Crystal Palace that welcomes both guests and their children; Camp Junkanoo, with supervised play for children 3 through 12; and a long list of in-house activities that includes dancing lessons. See p. 89.
- **Atlantis Paradise Island Resort & Casino** (Paradise Island; ✆ **800/ATLANTIS** in the U.S., or 242/363-3000): This is one of the largest hotel complexes in the world, with endless rows of shops and watersports galore. Both children and adults will enjoy the 14-acre sea world with water slides, a lagoon for watersports, white sandy beaches, and underground grottoes plus an underwater viewing tunnel and 240m (800 ft.) of cascading waterfalls. Its children's menus and innovative, creative children's programs are the best in The Bahamas and perhaps even in the Caribbean. See p. 129.
- **The Resorts at Bahamia** (Grand Bahama Island; ✆ **800/545-1300** or 242/350-7000): Many guests come here just to gamble and work on their tans, but others bring their kids. To divert them, the hotel maintains a pair of playgrounds and a swimming pool inspired by a tropical oasis, and offers children's platters in some of the restaurants. The architecture features lots of "Aladdin and His Lamp" accessories, such

as minarets above a decidedly non-Islamic setting. See p. 151.

- **Castaways Resort & Suites** (Grand Bahama Island; ✆ **242/352-6682**): Here's a good choice for families on a budget. The pagoda-capped lobby is set a very short walk from the ice-cream stands, souvenir shops, and fountains of the International Bazaar. Children under 12 stay free in their parents' room, and the in-house lounge presents limbo and fire-eating shows several evenings a month. The hotel offers a baby-sitting service and a free shuttle to Xanadu Beach. See p. 154.
- **Regatta Point** (George Town, Great Exuma; ✆ **800/688-0309** in the U.S., or 242/336-2206): This resort offers efficiency apartments at moderate prices. On a palm-grove cay, it is family-friendly, with its own little beach. Bikes are available, and Sunfish boats can be rented. There's also a grocery store nearby where you can pick up supplies. Many units are suitable for families of four or five. See p. 262.

10 The Best Places to Get Away from It All

- **Green Turtle Club** (Green Turtle Cay, the Abacos; ✆ **242/365-4271**): Secluded and private, this sailing retreat consists of tasteful one- to three-bedroom villas with full kitchens. It opens onto a small private beach with a 35-slip marina, which is the most complete yachting facility in the archipelago. Many rooms open onto poolside, and there's a dining room decorated in Queen Anne style. See p. 227.
- **Dunmore Beach Club** (Harbour Island, off the coast of Eleuthera; ✆ **877/891-3100**): Dunmore is one of the least expensive all-inclusive resorts in The Bahamas. Because it's relatively small, the atmosphere feels like a private party in a New England summer house. Each of the dozen or so lodgings is positioned for privacy. For complete solitude, you can escape to the nether regions of the local beach. See p. 246.
- **Club Med-Columbus Isle** (San Salvador, the Southern Bahamas; ✆ **800/CLUB-MED** or 242/331-2000): This was the first large resort to be built on one of The Bahamas's most isolated islands, site of Columbus's first landfall in the New World. It's unusually luxurious, and unusually isolated, for a Club Med, and it occupies a gorgeous beach. The sheer difficulty of reaching it adds to the get-away-from-it-all mystique. See p. 277.
- **Fernandez Bay Village** (Cat Island, the Southern Bahamas; ✆ **800/940-1905,** or 242/342-3043): The dozen stone and timber villas of Fernandez Bay Village are the closest thing to urban congestion Cat Island ever sees. There's a funky, thatch-roofed beach bar that'll make you feel like you're in the South Pacific, enjoying a cold beer each afternoon after you leave the stunning sands and turquoise waters behind for the day. There's only one phone at the entire resort, and your bathroom shower will probably open to a view of the sky. See p. 274.

11 The Best Restaurants

- **Chez Willie** (Nassau, New Providence Island; © **242/322-5364**): This is one of the newest, but also the classiest, restaurants on New Providence Island, overshadowing its competitors on Cable Beach. It's a throwback to the grandeur of Old Nassau in its Duke and Duchess of Windsor cafe society heyday. Your host, Willie Armstrong, oversees a smoothly run operation serving some of the best French and Bahamian cuisine found on island. See p. 96.
- **Sun And . . .** (Nassau, New Providence Island; © **242/393-1205**): This is a favorite haunt of visiting celebrities. Most importantly, the restaurant serves top-notch food. As you cross a drawbridge to enter a soothing world with a fountain and rock pool, you'll begin to hear tantalizing sizzling sounds from the kitchen, which is always cooking up an array of vividly flavored fresh seafood, the hallmark of a master French chef. Try to save room for a soufflé—they can hold their own with anything this side of France. See p. 97.
- **The Restaurant at Compass Point** (Love Beach, New Providence Island; © **242/327-4500**): The California/Caribbean cuisine here has made this a hot spot for savvy foodies; it's one of The Bahamas's finest eateries. The menu is innovative, with many exotic touches: Everybody around here serves conch, but here it appears with agnolotti, sun-dried tomatoes, and spinach in a tomato-basil cream sauce. Or try a Bahamian maki roll with conch, mango, and cucumber served with wasabi and pickled ginger. See p. 104.
- **Dune** (in the Ocean Club, Paradise Island; © **242/363-2000**): The most cutting-edge restaurant in either Paradise Island or Nassau is this creation of French-born restaurant guru Jean-Georges Vongerichten, he of several of New York City's leading lights. Every dish served here is something special—from shrimp dusted with orange powder to chicken and coconut milk soup with shiitake cakes. See p. 135.
- **Five Twins** (in the Atlantis Paradise Island Resort and Casino, Paradise Island; © **242/363-3000**): This trendy, upscale restaurant has generated more excitement than any other that opened during the 1990s. Located on a chic island across from Nassau and featuring Pacific Rim cuisine, it serves flavorful dishes with a flair that even James Bond might have appreciated. (Yes, 007 himself was seen dining on Paradise Island in *Thunderball.*) The chefs create refined dishes that justify the high prices. See p. 136.
- **Villa d'Este** (in the Atlantis Paradise Island Resort and Casino, Paradise Island; © **242/363-3000**): This is the finest Italian restaurant on Paradise Island, with nothing in Nassau to top it, either. The setting is gracious, tasteful, and Old World, but it's the food that keeps visitors and locals alike clamoring for reservations. All the old favorites are here, including veal parmigiana and fettuccine Alfredo as fine as any you'd find in Rome. Fresh herbs add zest to many dishes, and the pasta dishes are particularly good. See p. 136.
- **Mangoes Restaurant** (Marsh Harbour, the Abacos; © **242/367-2366**): For the best and most authentic Bahamian food in the Abaco chain, head for this

welcoming spot, where both visiting yachties and locals flock for the fine cuisine. Order up a "conch burger" for lunch, then return in the evening for the catch of the day—straight from the sea and grilled to your specifications. The namesake mango sauce really dresses up a plate of grilled pork tenderloin. See p. 213.

- **The Landing** (Harbour Island, Eleuthera; © **242/333-2707**): This attractive restaurant at the ferry dock has awakened the sleepy taste buds of Eleuthera. Brenda Barry and daughter Tracy feed you well from a choice of international cuisines, often prepared from recipes gathered during world travels. Under mature trees in their garden, you feast on delicious pasta dishes, freshly made gazpacho, pan-fried grouper, or a warm duck salad. See p. 249.

12 The Best Nightlife

- **Cable Beach:** Cable Beach has a lot more splash and excitement than Nassau, its neighbor on New Providence Island, and wandering around Cable Beach is also much safer than exploring the back streets of Nassau at night. The main attraction is the **Nassau Marriott Resort & Crystal Palace Casino** (© **242/327-6200**), with an 800-seat theater known for staging glitzy extravaganzas and a gaming room that will make you think you're smack dab in the middle of Vegas. One of the largest casinos on the islands, the Crystal Palace features 750 slot machines, 51 blackjack tables, nine roulette wheels, seven craps tables, and a baccarat table (we think the Paradise Island casino has more class, though). Despite all the glitter, you can still find cozy bars and nooks throughout the resort if you'd prefer a tranquil evening. See p. 88.
- **Atlantis Paradise Island Resort & Casino:** Paradise Island has the flashiest nightlife in all of The Bahamas, hands down. Not even nearby Nassau and Cable Beach can come close. Nearly all of the action takes place at the incredible **Atlantis Paradise Island Resort & Casino** (© **242/363-3000**), where you'll find high rollers from Vegas and Atlantic City alongside grandmothers from Iowa who play the slot machines when family isn't looking. It's all gloss, glitter, and show biz, with good gambling (though savvy locals say your odds of beating the house are better in Vegas). For a quieter night out, you can also find intimate bars, discos, a comedy club, and lots more in this sprawling behemoth of a hotel. See p. 129.
- **Freeport:** Although the giant casino in **The Resorts at Bahamia** (© **242/350-7000**) ranks third behind Paradise Island and Cable Beach, most of the nightlife in Freeport/Lucaya revolves around this glittering Moroccan-style palace, one of the largest casinos in either The Bahamas or the Caribbean. You get not only high- and low-stakes gambling, but also a splashy Vegas-like (well, maybe Reno-like) ambience. See p. 151.

2

Planning Your Trip to The Bahamas

You can be in The Bahamas sipping a Goombay Smash after a quick 35-minute jet-hop from Miami. And it's never been easier to take advantage of great package deals that can make these islands a terrific value.

1 The Islands in Brief

The Bahamian chain of islands, cays, and reefs stretches from Grand Bahama Island, 121km (75 miles) almost due east of Palm Beach, Florida, to Great Inagua, the southernmost island, which lies about 97km (60 miles) northeast of Cuba and fewer than 161km (100 miles) north of Haiti.

The most developed islands for tourism in The Bahamas are **New Providence Island,** site of Nassau (the capital) and Cable Beach; **Paradise Island;** and **Grand Bahama,** home of Freeport and Lucaya. If you're after glitz, gambling, bustling restaurants, nightclubs, and a beach-party scene, these big three islands are where you'll want to be. Package deals are easily found here.

Set sail (or hop on a short commuter flight) for one of the **Out Islands,** such as Andros, the Exumas, or the Abacos, and you'll find fewer crowds—and often lower prices, too. Though some of the Out Islands are accessible mainly (or only) by boat, it's still worth your while to make the trip if you like the idea of having an entire beach to yourself. This is really getting away from it all.

NEW PROVIDENCE ISLAND (NASSAU/CABLE BEACH) New Providence isn't the largest of the Bahamian Islands, but it's the historic heart of the nation, with a strong maritime tradition and the largest population in the country. Home to about 125,000 residents, it offers groves of pines and casuarinas; sandy, flat soil; the closest thing in The Bahamas to urban sprawl; and superb anchorages sheltered from rough seas by the presence of nearby Paradise Island. New Providence has the country's busiest airport and is dotted with hundreds of villas owned by foreign investors. Its two major resort areas are Cable Beach and Nassau.

The resort area of **Cable Beach** is a glittering beachfront strip of hotels, restaurants, and casinos; only Paradise Island has been more developed. Its center is the Marriott Resort & Crystal Palace Casino. Often, deciding between Cable Beach and Paradise Island isn't so much a choice of which island you prefer as a choice of which hotel you prefer. But it's easy to sample both, since it takes only about 30 minutes to drive between the two.

Nassau, the Bahamian capital, isn't on a great stretch of shoreline and doesn't have as many first-rate hotels as either Paradise Island or Cable Beach—with the exception of the Bahama Hilton, which has a small private beach. The main advantages of

Nassau are colonial charm and price. Its hotels may not be ideally located, but they are relatively inexpensive; some offer very low prices even during the winter high season. You can base yourself here and commute easily to the beaches at Paradise Island or Cable Beach. Some travelers even prefer Nassau because it's the seat of Bahamian culture and history—not to mention the shopping Mecca of The Bahamas.

PARADISE ISLAND If high-rise hotels and glittering casinos are what you want, along with some of the best beaches in The Bahamas, there is no better choice than Paradise Island, directly off the coast of Nassau. It has the best food, the best entertainment, terrific beaches, casinos, and the best hotels. Its major drawbacks are that it's expensive and often overcrowded. Boasting a colorful history, yet a host of unremarkable architecture, Paradise Island remains perhaps the most intensely marketed piece of real estate in the world. The sands and shoals of the elongated and narrow island protect the wharves and piers of Nassau, which rise across a narrow channel only 180m (600 ft.) away.

Owners of the 685-acre island have included brokerage mogul Joseph Lynch (of Merrill Lynch) and Huntington Hartford, heir to the A&P supermarket fortune. More recent investors have included Merv Griffin. The island today is a carefully landscaped residential and commercial complex with good beaches, lots of glitter (some of it tasteful, some of it way too over-the-top), and many diversions.

GRAND BAHAMA ISLAND (FREEPORT/LUCAYA) The island's name derives from the Spanish term *gran bajamar* ("great shallows"), which refers to the shallow reefs and sandbars that, over the centuries, have destroyed everything from Spanish galleons to English clipper ships on Grand Bahama's shores. Thanks to the tourist development schemes of U.S. financiers such as Howard Hughes, Grand Bahama boasts a well-developed tourist infrastructure. Casinos, beaches, and restaurants are now plentiful here.

Grand Bahama's **Freeport/Lucaya** resort area is another popular destination for American tourists, though it has a lot more tacky development than Paradise Island or Cable Beach. The compensation for that is a lower price tag on just about everything. Freeport/Lucaya offers plenty of opportunities for fine dining, entertainment, and gambling. Grand Bahama also offers the best hiking in The Bahamas and has some of the finest sandy beaches. Its golf courses attract players from all over the globe, and the island hosts major tournaments several times a year. You'll find some of the world's best diving here, as well as UNEXSO, the internationally famous diving school. Grand Bahama Island is especially popular with families.

BIMINI One of the smallest islands in The Bahamas and close enough to Miami (just 81km/50 miles away) to be distinctly separate from the other islands of the archipelago, Bimini is actually a pair of islands with a total area of 9 square miles; smaller North Bimini is better developed than South Bimini. Luxurious yachts and fishing boats are always docked at the island's marinas. Throughout Bimini, there's a slightly run-down Florida-resort atmosphere mingled with some small-town charm (think old-time Key West, before the cruise-ship crowds ruined the town).

Once the setting for Ernest Hemingway's *Islands in the Stream* (Papa was a frequent guest; see below), Bimini attracts big-game fishers for big-league fishing tournaments. It has only minor appeal for the casual sightseer, but if you'd like to follow in the footsteps of such famous anglers as Zane Grey and Howard Hughes, this

Fun Fact Hemingway in Bimini

It's one of the oddest pieces of real estate in the Atlantic. Less than a few hundred feet wide in many places, with a surface area of only 9 square miles, Bimini has always floated like a magic lure, only 81km (50 miles) from some of the most crowded seashores in the United States. Even during the 1930s, it was famous as an alter ego to Key West. Soaked with liquor during U.S. Prohibition (Bimini served as a depot for outlawed contraband) and widely recognized today as a storage depot for illegal drugs, the place has always found itself bathed in controversy. And thanks to novelist Ernest Hemingway, its raunchy, no-holds-barred lifestyle became infamous throughout North America.

Hemingway's first boat (the *Pilar*) was a diesel-powered tub he skippered with fellow writer John Dos Passos for the express purpose of reaching Bimini. One of the bloodiest of his many self-destructive acts occurred off the coast of Bimini when, struggling to aim a revolver at the thrashing jaws of a captured mako shark, he accidentally shot himself in both legs. But don't let that fool you: Hemingway did some serious and successful fishing here. Among the most impressive catches of his life were a 785-pound mako and a 514-pound tuna, both hauled in off the coast of Bimini.

Some of Hemingway's most famous fistfights happened on Bimini, too—one with wealthy publisher Joseph Knapp, others with a series of black contenders who stood to earn $250 if they could stay in the ring with him for three 3-minute rounds. (No one ever collected the money.)

Hemingway revised the manuscript of *To Have and Have Not* on Bimini in 1937. His evocative description of the seaport in *Islands in the Stream* was Alice Town, Bimini's still-seedy capital.

is your island: Sportfishing here is among the best in the world, and the scuba diving among the very best in The Bahamas.

THE BERRY ISLANDS Lying between Nassau and the coast of Florida, these 30-odd islands—which contain only about 30 square miles of dry land among them—attract devoted yachters and serious fishermen. A series of islets, cays, and rows of barely submerged rocks, they have extremely limited tourist facilities and are geared mostly toward well-heeled anglers, many of whom hail from Florida. Most of the full-time population (about 700 people) lives on Great Harbour. We find these islands a lot classier and charming than Bimini.

ANDROS Andros is actually two islands, connected by a series of canals and cays called *bights*. It's the largest landmass in The Bahamas and attracts divers, fishing enthusiasts, and sightseers.

Most of the island is uninhabited and unexplored. The main villages are Nicholl's Town, Andros Town, and Congo Town; all are accessible by frequent boat and plane connections from Miami and Nassau. Lodgings range from large resorts to small, plain guesthouses that cater mainly to fishermen.

The world's third-largest barrier reef lies off the coast of Andros, and divers come from all over the world to explore it. The reef plunges 1,800m (6,000 ft.) to a narrow drop-off known as the Tongue of the Ocean. Bonefishing here is among the best on earth, and Andros is also known for its world-class marlin and bluefin tuna fishing.

Known as the "Big Yard," the central portion of Northern Andros is largely a dense forest of mahogany and pine where more than 50 varieties of orchids bloom. Southern Andros boasts a 40-square-mile forest and mangrove swamp. Any hotel can arrange a local guide to give a tour.

THE ABACO ISLANDS Though this "island" is often called Abaco, it is actually a cluster of islands and islets. It is a Mecca for yachters and other boaters who flock here year-round—particularly in July when the Regatta Time in Abaco race is held at the Green Turtle Yacht Club. For hundreds of years the residents of the Abacos have been boat builders, although tourism is now the main industry.

With the exception of Harbour Island in Eleuthera, there is more New England charm here than anywhere else in The Bahamas. Loyalists who left New England after the American Revolution settled here and built Cape Cod–style clapboard houses with white picket fences. The best places to experience this old-fashioned charm are Green Turtle Cay and Elbow Cay, which are accessible from Marsh Harbour. Marsh Harbour itself houses an international airport and a shopping center, although its hotels aren't as good as those on Green Turtle Cay and Elbow Cay (Hope Town).

Many of the Abaco islands are undeveloped and uninhabited. For the best of both worlds, visitors can stay at resorts on Walker's, Green Turtle, or Treasure cays, then charter a boat to tour the more remote areas.

ELEUTHERA Long and slender, this most historic of the Out Islands (the first English settlers arrived here in 1648) is actually a string of islands that includes Spanish Wells and Harbour Island, a chic destination. The length of the island (177km/110 miles) and the distances between Eleuthera's communities require access via three airports. The island lies about 97km (60 miles) west of Nassau; frequent flights connect the two. Eleuthera is similar to Abaco, and visitors are drawn to the miles of barrier reef and fabulous, secluded beaches.

Gregory Town is the pineapple capital of the island chain. A bit farther south is Surfers Beach, one of the best surfing spots in The Bahamas. Several accommodations are available in this sleepy, slightly budget-oriented section of Eleuthera. The only major resort along the entire stretch of Eleuthera is the Club Med at Governor's Harbour. Other inns are more basic.

Moments Slow Boat to the Out Islands

Delivering goats, chickens, hardware, and food staples along with the mail, Bahamian mail boats greatly improve the quality of life for the scattered communities of the Out Islands. You can book passage on one to at least 17 different remote islands. All 30 boats leave from Nassau, and the round-trip takes a full day. For more information, consult an office of **The Bahamas Tourist Office** (see "Visitor Information," below) or the dockmaster at the Nassau piers at ✆ **242/393-1064**. See "Getting Around," later in this chapter, for additional details.

At the southern end of the island, **Rock Sound** is in a slump, waiting to see whether the fabled Cotton Bay Club will ever reopen.

Off the coast of Eleuthera, **Harbour Island** offers excellent hotels and food, picket fences, and pastel-colored houses that evoke Cape Cod. The beaches on Harbour Island are famed for their pink sand, tinted that color by crushed coral and shells. Another offshore island near Eleuthera, **Spanish Wells** has extremely limited accommodations, and the residents—descendants of long-ago Loyalists—aren't very welcoming to visitors.

THE EXUMA ISLANDS Just 56km (35 miles) southeast of Nassau, this 588km- (365-mile-) long string of islands and keys—most of them uninhabited—is the great yachting hub of The Bahamas, rivaling or even surpassing Abaco. These waters, some of the prettiest in The Bahamas, are also ideal for fishers (bonefishers especially). Many secluded beaches open onto tranquil cays. Daily flights service the Exumas from both Nassau and Miami.

This island chain's commercial center is **George Town** on **Great Exuma,** while the Exuma National Land and Sea Park—protected by The Bahamas National Trust—encompasses much of the coastline. The park is accessible only by boat and is one of the major natural wonders and sightseeing destinations of The Bahamas, with an abundance of undersea life, reefs, blue holes, and shipwrecks. Portions of the James Bond thriller *Thunderball* were filmed at **Staniel Cay.** Each year in April, George Town hosts the interisland Family Island Regatta, a major event on the yachting calendar. A few good inns are centered mainly at George Town, and the locals are very hospitable. Otherwise, you'll practically have the archipelago to yourself.

THE SOUTHERN BAHAMAS This cluster of islands on the southern fringe of The Bahamas is known for its remoteness. Yet most of the islands have excellent beaches, good fishing, and dive sites. With a skinny, eel-like shape, **Cat Island** is only a few miles wide and 77km (48 miles) long. It's a lush, sleepy island in the southern Bahamian backwater, a great place to get away from it all.

Tradition holds that **San Salvador** was the first landmass that Christopher Columbus reached during his voyage to the New World in 1492. With its history and good beaches, the island is sure to undergo further development.

The appropriately named **Long Island** stretches for 93km (58 miles) and, despite a beautiful landscape—there are high cliffs in the north, wide shallow beaches, historic plantation ruins, and native caves—it has remained thoroughly off the beaten track. It's not always easy to get here; there are two minor airports with arrivals from Nassau, but flights do not occur daily. Both the Stella Maris Resort Club and the luxurious Cape Santa Maria Beach offer fishing and watersports.

Acklins Island & Crooked Island are hard to reach, have very limited tourist facilities, and appeal to people who want to escape civilization. The clear waters offshore offer good snorkeling and diving, and you'll have the sandy beaches to yourself. These islands are populated by only a mere 1,000 souls; lodging is available on Crooked Island only.

Set very close to the eastern tip of Cuba, **Inagua Island** is the most southerly island of The Bahamas and the third largest in the nation. Pink flamingos thrive here: For the serious bird-watcher, there is no place else like it in the Caribbean. A handful of no-frills inns provide accommodations.

2 Visitor Information

The "Planning Your Trip Online" section that begins on p. 59 is packed with invaluable advice about how to search for late-breaking information on the Web.

However, travel conditions are ever changing, and you'll want to marshal other resources as well. The two best sources to try before you leave home are your travel agent and **The Bahamas Tourist Office** nearest you. The nation's official tourism office can be located on the Web at www.bahamas.com, or by phone if you dial ✆ **800/BAHAMAS.** There are also walk-in branch offices at the following locations:

Chicago: 8600 W. Bryn Mawr Ave., Suite 820, Chicago, IL 60631 (✆ **773/ 693-1500**)

Miami: 1 Turnberry Place, 19495 Biscayne Blvd., Aventura, FL 33180 (✆ **800/224-3681,** or 305/932-0051)

Los Angeles: 3450 Wilshire Blvd., Suite 1204, Los Angeles, CA 90010 (✆ **800/439-6993**)

New York: 150 E. 52nd St., New York, NY 10022 (✆ **212/758-2777**)

Toronto: 121 Bloor St. E., Suite 1101, Toronto, ON M4W 3M5 (✆ **416/ 968-2999**)

United Kingdom: 3 The Billings, Walnut Tree Close, Guildford, Surrey SE1 8XP (✆ **01483/ 448900**)

You may also want to contact the U.S. State Department for background bulletins, which supply up-to-date information on crime, health concerns, import restrictions, and other travel matters. Write the **Superintendent of Documents,** U.S. Government Printing Office, Washington, DC 20402 (✆ **202/512-1800**).

A good travel agent can be a source of information. Make sure your agent is a member of the American Society of Travel Agents (ASTA). If you get poor service from an ASTA agent, you can write to the ASTA Consumer Affairs Department, 1101 King St., Alexandria, VA 22314 (✆ 703/739-8739; www. astanet.com).

SEARCHING THE WEB

Bahamas websites include:

The Bahamas Ministry of Tourism (www.bahamas.com): Official tourism site.

The Bahamas Out Islands Promotion Board (www.bahama-out-islands.com): Focuses on remote isles.

Bahamas Tourist Guide (www.interknowledge.com/bahamas): Travelers' opinions.

Bahamas Vacation Guide (www.bahamasvg.com): Service listings.

Virtual Voyages Bahamas Directory (www.virtualvoyages.com): Links to other websites. Click on "Bahamas."

3 Entry Requirements & Customs

ENTRY REQUIREMENTS

DOCUMENTS

To enter The Bahamas, **citizens of the United States, Britain, and Canada** coming in as visitors for a period of less than 8 months need to bring proof of citizenship, such as a passport, a birth certificate with photo ID, or an official photo ID. (We strongly recommend that you bring a passport anyway, since you're traveling to a foreign country.)

Onward or return tickets must be shown to immigration officials in The Bahamas. Citizens of other countries, including Australia, Ireland, and New Zealand, should carry a valid passport.

The Commonwealth of The Bahamas does not require visas. On entry to The Bahamas, you'll be given an Immigration Card to complete and sign. The card has a carbon copy that you must keep until departure, at which time it must be turned in. You'll also have to pay a departure tax before you can exit the country (see "Taxes" under "Fast Facts: The Bahamas," later in this chapter).

It's good policy to make copies of your most valuable documents, including your passport, before you leave home. Make a photocopy of the inside page of your passport, the one with your photograph. In case of loss or theft abroad, you should also make copies of your driver's license, airline tickets, hotel vouchers, and so on. You should also make copies of any prescriptions you take. Place one copy in your luggage and carry the original with you. Leave another copy at home.

CUSTOMS

WHAT YOU CAN BRING INTO THE BAHAMAS

Bahamian Customs allow you to bring in 200 cigarettes, 50 cigars, or 1 pound of tobacco, plus 1 quart of wine and a quart of "spirits" (that is, hard liquor). You can also bring in items classified as "personal effects," and all the money you wish.

WHAT YOU CAN TAKE HOME

Visitors leaving Nassau or Freeport/Lucaya for most U.S. destinations clear U.S. Customs and Immigration before departing The Bahamas. Charter companies can make special arrangements with the Nassau or Freeport flight services and U.S. Customs and Immigration for pre-clearance. No further formalities are required upon arrival in the United States once the pre-clearance has taken place in Nassau or Freeport.

Collect receipts for all the purchases you make in The Bahamas. *Note:* If a merchant suggests giving you a false receipt, misstating the value of the goods, beware—the merchant might be an informer to U.S. Customs. You must also declare all gifts received during your stay abroad.

If you purchased an item during an earlier trip abroad, carry proof that you have already paid Customs duty on the item at the time of your previous reentry. To be extra careful, compile a list of expensive carry-on items and ask a U.S. Customs agent to stamp your list at the airport before your departure.

Returning U.S. citizens who have been away for 48 hours or more are allowed to bring back, once every 30 days, $600 worth of merchandise duty-free. You'll be charged a flat rate of 10% duty on the next $1,000 worth of purchases. Be sure to have your receipts handy. On gifts, the duty-free limit is $100. You cannot bring fresh foodstuffs into the United States; canned or packaged foods, however, are allowed, and you can bring back 1 liter of alcohol. For more information, contact the **U.S. Customs Service,** 1301 Constitution Ave. (P.O. Box 7407), Washington, DC 20044 (© **202/354-1000**), and request the free pamphlet *Know Before You Go.* It's also available on the Web at **www.customs.us treas.gov**.

For a clear summary of Canadian rules, write for the booklet *I Declare,* issued by the **Canada Customs and Revenue Agency** (© **800/461-9999** in Canada, or 204/983-3500; www.ccra-adrc.gc.ca). Canada allows its citizens a Can$750 exemption, and you're allowed to bring back duty-free one carton of cigarettes, 1 can of tobacco, 40 imperial ounces of liquor, and 50 cigars. In addition, you're allowed to mail gifts to Canada valued at less than Can$60 a day, provided they're unsolicited and don't contain alcohol or tobacco (write on the package "Unsolicited gift, under $60 value"). All valuables should be declared on the Y-38 form before departure from Canada, including serial numbers of valuables you already own, such as expensive foreign cameras. *Note:* The Can$750 exemption can only be used once a year and only after an absence of 7 days.

U.K. citizens returning from The Bahamas have a customs allowance of 200 cigarettes; 50 cigars; 250g of smoking tobacco; 2 liters of still table wine; 1 liter of spirits or strong liqueurs (over 22% volume); 2 liters of fortified wine, sparkling wine or other liqueurs; 60cc (ml) perfume; 250cc (ml) of toilet water; and £145 worth of all other goods, including gifts and souvenirs. People under 17 cannot have the tobacco or alcohol allowance. For more information, contact **HM Customs & Excise,** Passenger Enquiry Point, 2nd Floor Wayfarer House, Great South West Road, Feltham, Middlesex, TW14 8NP (✆ **0181/910-3744,** or from outside the U.K. 44/181-910-3744), or consult their website: www.open.gov.uk.

The duty-free allowance in **Australia** is A$400, or A$200 for those under 18. Personal property mailed home should be marked "Australian goods returned" to avoid payment of duty. Upon returning to Australia, you can bring 250 cigarettes or 250g of loose tobacco and 1,125ml of alcohol. If you're returning with valuable goods you own, such as foreign-made cameras, file form B263. A helpful brochure, available from Australian consulates or Customs offices, is *Know Before You Go.* For more information, contact **Australian Customs Services,** GPO Box 8, Sydney NSW 2001 (✆ **02/9213-2000**).

The duty-free allowance for **New Zealand** is NZ$700. Citizens over 17 can bring in 200 cigarettes, or 50 cigars, or 250g of tobacco (or a mixture of all three if their combined weight doesn't exceed 250g); plus 4.5 liters of wine and beer, or 1.125 liters of liquor. New Zealand currency does not carry import or export restrictions. Fill out a certificate of export, listing valuables you're bringing with you; you can bring them home later without paying duty. Learn more in the free pamphlet available at consulates and Customs offices: *New Zealand Customs Guide for Travellers, Notice no. 4.* For more information, contact **New Zealand Customs,** 50 Anzac Ave., P.O. Box 29, Auckland (✆ **09/359-6655**).

4 Money

The currency is the **Bahamian dollar (B$1),** pegged to the U.S. dollar so that they're always equivalent. (In fact, U.S. dollars are accepted widely throughout The Bahamas.) There is no restriction on bringing foreign currency into The Bahamas. Most large hotels and stores accept traveler's checks, but you may have trouble using a personal check.

ATMS

ATMs are linked to a network that most likely includes your bank at home. **Cirrus** (✆ **800/424-7787;** www.mastercard.com) and **PLUS** (✆ **800/843-7587;** www.visa.com) are the two most popular networks in the U.S.; call or check online for ATM locations at your destination. Be sure you know your four-digit PIN access number before you leave home and be sure to find out your daily withdrawal limit before you depart. You can also get cash advances on your credit card at an ATM. Keep in mind that credit-card companies try to protect themselves from theft by limiting the funds someone can withdrawn away from home. It's therefore best to call your credit-card company before you leave and let them know where you're going and how much you plan to spend. You'll get the best exchange rate if you withdraw money from an ATM, but

What Things Cost in The Bahamas	U.S.$/B$
Taxi from airport to Nassau's center	20.00
Local phone call	.25
Double room at Graycliff (deluxe)	290.00
Double room at Holiday Inn Junkanoo Beach (moderate)	149.00
Dinner for one at Chez Willie (expensive)	75.00
Dinner at Avery's Restaurant (inexpensive)	20.00
Bottle of beer in a bar/hotel	2.00–4.50
Rolls of ASA 100 color film, 36 exposures	8.00–10.00
Movie ticket	6.00

keep in mind that many banks impose a fee every time a card is used at an ATM in a different city or bank. On top of this, the bank from which you withdraw cash may charge its own fee.

On New Providence Island and Paradise Island, there are plenty of ATMs, some three dozen or so, including one at the Nassau International Airport. There are far fewer ATMs on Grand Bahama Island (Freeport/Lucaya), but those that are here are strategically located—including ones at the airport and the casino (of course).

There are very few ATMs in the Out Islands, so don't count on using this form of cash withdrawal when traveling beyond the major tourist centers. If you must have cash on your Out Island trip, make arrangements before you leave Nassau or Freeport; outside of Freeport, we counted just seven ATMs in the entire remaining chain of Out Islands, including the one at the post office in Marsh Harbour. It's very likely you won't one on most of these islands.

This situation is fluid, however, and more ATMs may be added in the future. Fortunately, you can always rely on old-fashioned traveler's checks.

TRAVELER'S CHECKS

Traveler's checks are something of an anachronism from the days before the ATM (automated-teller machine) made cash accessible at any time. Traveler's checks used to be the only sound alternative to traveling with dangerously large amounts of cash. They were as reliable as currency, but, unlike cash, could be replaced if lost or stolen.

These days, traveler's checks seem less necessary because most cities have 24-hour ATMs that allow you to withdraw small amounts of cash as needed. However, you're likely to be charged an ATM withdrawal fee if the bank is not your own, so if you're withdrawing money every day, you might be better off with traveler's checks—provided that you don't mind showing identification every time you want to cash one.

You can get traveler's checks at almost any bank. **American Express** offers denominations of $20, $50, $100, $500, and (for cardholders only) $1,000. You'll pay a service charge ranging from 1% to 4%. You can also get American Express traveler's checks over the phone by calling ✆ **800/221-7782;** Amex gold and platinum cardholders who use this number are exempt from the 1% fee. AAA members can obtain checks without a fee at most AAA offices.

Visa offers traveler's checks at Citibank locations nationwide, as well as at several other banks. The service charge ranges between 1.5% and 2%; checks come in denominations of $20, $50, $100, $500, and $1,000.

Call ✆ **800/732-1322** for information. **MasterCard** also offers traveler's checks. Call ✆ **800/223- 9920** for a location near you.

CREDIT CARDS

Credit cards are invaluable when traveling. They are a safe way to carry money and provide a convenient record of all your expenses. You can also withdraw cash advances from your credit cards at any bank (though you'll start paying hefty interest on the advance the moment you receive the cash). At most banks, you don't even need to go to a teller; you can get a cash advance at the ATM if you know your PIN access number. If you've forgotten yours, or didn't even know you had one, call the number on the back of your credit card and ask the bank to send it to you. It usually takes 5 to 7 business days, though some banks will provide the number over the phone if you tell them your mother's maiden name or pass some other security clearance.

In Nassau, Paradise Island, Freeport/Lucaya, and all the big resorts—even some (though certainly not all) of the smaller inns—credit cards are accepted. However, if you intend to patronize small, out-of-the-way establishments, it's wise to carry sufficient amounts of U.S. cash as a backup.

WHAT TO DO IF YOUR WALLET GETS STOLEN

Crime is, indeed, a problem in parts of The Bahamas, particularly in Nassau. Should the unthinkable happen, be sure to block charges against your account the moment you discover a card has been lost or stolen. Then be sure to file a police report.

Almost every credit-card company has an emergency toll-free number to call if your card is stolen. They may be able to wire you a cash advance off your credit card immediately, and in many places they can deliver an emergency credit card within a day or 2. The issuing bank's toll-free number is usually printed on the back of your credit card—though of course, if the card has been stolen, that won't help you much unless you also recorded the number elsewhere.

Citicorp **Visa**'s U.S. emergency number is ✆ **800/336-8742. American Express** cardholders and traveler's check holders should call ✆ **800/221-7282. MasterCard** holders should call ✆ **800/307-7309.** Otherwise, call the toll-free number directory at ✆ **800/555-1212.**

It's worth informing the authorities if theft happens: Your credit-card company or insurer may later require a police report of the incident.

If you choose to carry traveler's checks, be sure to keep a record of your serial numbers separate from your checks. You'll get a refund faster if you know the numbers.

If you need emergency cash over the weekend when all banks and American Express offices are closed, you can have money wired to you from **Western Union** (✆ **800/325-6000;** www.westernunion.com/). You must present valid ID to pick up the cash at the Western Union office. However, in most countries, you can pick up a money transfer even if you don't have valid identification, as long as you can answer a test question provided by the sender. Be sure to let the sender know in advance that you don't have ID. If you need to use a test question instead of ID, the sender must take cash to his or her local Western Union office, rather than transferring the money over the phone or online.

MONEYGRAMS

Sponsored by American Express, **Moneygram** (✆ **800/926-9400**) is the fastest-growing money-wiring service in the world. Funds can be transferred from one individual to another in less than 10 minutes between thousands of locations throughout the world. An American Express phone representative will give you the names of four or five offices near you. (You don't always have to go to an American Express office; some locations are pharmacies and convenience stores in smaller communities.) Acceptable forms of payment include cash, Visa, MasterCard, or Discover, and occasionally, a personal check. Service charges collected by American Express are $40 for the first $500 sent, with a sliding scale of commissions for larger sums. Included in the transfer is a 10-word telex-style message. The deal also includes a free 3-minute phone call to the recipient. Funds are transferred within 10 minutes, and can then be retrieved by the beneficiary at the most convenient location with a proper photo ID.

5 When to Go

THE WEATHER

The temperature in The Bahamas varies surprisingly little, averaging between 75°F and 85°F in both winter and summer, although it can get chilly in the early morning and at night. The Bahamian winter is usually like a perpetual May, so that's naturally the high season for North Americans rushing to escape snow and ice in their own hometowns. Summer brings broiling hot sun and humidity. There's a much greater chance of rain during the summer and fall.

THE HURRICANE SEASON

The curse of Bahamian weather, the hurricane season, lasts (officially) from June 1 to November 30. But there is no cause for panic. More tropical cyclones pound the U.S. mainland than The Bahamas. Hurricanes are actually fairly infrequent here, and when one does come, satellite forecasts generally give adequate advance warning so that precautions can be taken.

If you're heading for The Bahamas during the hurricane season, you might phone the nearest branch of the National Weather Service. Look it up under the U.S. Department of Commerce listing.

If you want to know how to pack just before you go, check the Weather Channel's online 5-day forecast at www.weather.com. You can get the same information by calling ✆ **900/WEATHER,** though it does cost 95¢ per minute.

THE "SEASON"

In The Bahamas, hotels charge their highest prices during the peak winter period from mid-December to mid-April, when visitors fleeing from cold north winds flock to the islands. Winter is the driest season.

So take heed: If you plan to visit during the winter, make reservations at least 2 to 3 months in advance if possible. And bear in mind that, at certain hotels, it's sometimes impossible to book accommodations for Christmas and the month of February without even more lead time.

Note that these numbers are daily averages, so expect temperatures to climb significantly higher in the noonday sun and to cool off a good deal in the evening.

Average Temperatures & Rainfall (in.) in The Bahamas

Month	Jan	Feb	Mar	Apr	May	June	July	Aug	Sept	Oct	Nov	Dec
Temp. °F	70	70	72	75	77	80	81	82	81	78	74	71
Temp. °C	21	21	22	24	25	27	27	28	27	26	23	22
Rainfall (in.)	1.9	1.6	1.4	1.9	4.8	9.2	6.1	6.3	7.5	8.3	2.3	1.5

Avoiding Spring Break

Throughout March and into mid-April, it's spring break season in the Caribbean for hell-raising vacationing college and high school students. This season is filled with beach parties, sports events, and musical entertainment, but if the idea of hundreds of partying fraternity kids doesn't appeal to you, beware. When you make your reservations, ask if your hotel is planning to host any big groups of kids.

SAVING MONEY IN THE OFF-SEASON

The Bahamas is a year-round destination. The island's "off-season" runs from late spring to late fall, when tolerable temperatures (see "The Weather," above) prevail throughout most of the region. Trade winds ensure comfortable days and nights, even in accommodations without air-conditioning. Although the noonday sun may raise temperatures to uncomfortable levels, cool breezes usually make the morning, late afternoon, and evening more pleasant here than in many parts of the U.S. mainland.

Dollar for dollar, you'll spend less money by renting a summer house or fully equipped unit in The Bahamas than you would on Cape Cod, Fire Island, Laguna Beach, or the coast of Maine.

The off-season—roughly from mid-April to mid-December (rate schedules vary from hotel to hotel)—amounts to a summer sale. In most cases, hotel rates are slashed from 20% to a startling 60%. It's a bonanza for cost-conscious travelers, especially families who like to go on vacations together. In the chapters ahead, we'll spell out in dollars the specific amounts hotels charge during the off-season.

OTHER OFF-SEASON ADVANTAGES

Although The Bahamas may appear inviting in the winter to those who live in northern climates, there are many reasons why your trip may be much more enjoyable if you go in the off-season:

- After the winter hordes have left, a less-hurried way of life prevails.
- Swimming pools and beaches are less crowded—perhaps not crowded at all.
- To survive, resort boutiques often feature summer sales.
- You can often appear without a reservation at a top restaurant and get a table for dinner.
- The endless waiting game is over: no waiting for a rented car, no long wait for a golf course tee time, and quicker access to tennis courts and watersports.
- The atmosphere is more cosmopolitan in the off-season than it is in winter, mainly because of the influx of Europeans.
- Some package-tour fares are as much as 20% lower, and individual excursion fares may be reduced from 5% to 10%.
- Accommodations and flights are much easier to book.
- Summer is an excellent time for family travel, which is not always possible during the hectic winter season.
- Finally, the best Bahamian attractions—sea, sand, surf, and lots of sunshine—remain absolutely undiminished during the off-season.

OFF-SEASON DISADVANTAGES

Let's not paint too rosy a picture, however. Although the advantages of off-season travel far outweigh the disadvantages, there are nevertheless some drawbacks to traveling here in summer:

- You might be staying at a construction site. Hoteliers save their serious repairs and their major renovations until the off-season. You might wake up to the sound of hammers.
- Single tourists find the dating scene better in winter when there are more visitors, especially unattached ones.
- Services are often reduced. In the peak of winter, everything is fully operational. But in summer, many programs (such as watersports) might be curtailed in spite of fine weather.

THE BAHAMAS CALENDAR OF EVENTS

For specific events, you can call your nearest branch of **The Bahamas Tourist Office** (see "Visitor Information," earlier in this chapter) at © **800/BAHAMAS** or check their website at **www.bahamas.com**.

January

Junkanoo. This Mardi Gras–style festival begins 2 or 3 hours before dawn on New Year's Day. Throngs of cavorting, costumed figures prance through Nassau, Freeport/Lucaya, and the Out Islands. Jubilant men, women, and children wear elaborate headdresses and festive apparel as they celebrate their African heritage with music and dance. Mini-Junkanoos, in which visitors can participate, are regular events. Local tourist offices will advise the best locations to see the festivities, or call © **242/356-2691.**

New Year's Day Sailing Regatta, Nassau and Paradise Island. Three dozen or more sailing sloops, ranging from 5m to 8.5m (17–28 ft.), converge off Montagu Bay in a battle for bragging rights organized by The Bahamas Boat Owners Association. For information, contact the **Regatta Desk at the Ministry of Youth, Sports & Culture** (© **242/325-9370**). January 1 and 6, 2003.

Annual Bahamas Wahoo Championships, the Abacos. Anglers from all over America take up the tough challenge to bait one of the fastest fish in the ocean reaching speeds up to 70 mph. This fete takes place at Abaco Beach Resort and Boat Harbour (© **800/468-4799** or 242/367-2158).

February

The Mid-Winter Wahoo, Bimini. The Bimini Big Game Fishing Club draws Hemingway look-alikes and other anglers to this winter event that is heavily attended by Floridians. For more information, call © **800/737-1007** or contact the tournament director, Raul Miranda, at the Big Game Fishing Club at © **242/347-3391.** February 5 to 9, 2003.

Farmer's Cay Festival. This festival is a rendezvous for yachtsmen cruising The Exuma Islands and a homecoming for the people of Farmer's Cay, Exuma. Boat excursions will depart Nassau at Potter's Cay for the festival at 8pm on February 6, then return to Nassau at 8pm on February 7 from the Farmer's Cay Dock. For information contact Terry Bain in Little Farmer's Cay, Exuma at © **242/355-4006/2093;** or the Exuma Tourist Office at © **242/336-2430.** February 7, 2003.

March

Bacardi Billfish Tournament, Bimini. A prestigious weeklong tournament attracting the *Who's*

Who of deep-sea fishing. Headquarters is the Bimini Big Game Fishing Club & Marina. For more information, call ✆ **800/737-1007** or 242/347-3391. March 17 to 21, 2003.

April

The Bahamas Family Island Regatta, George Town, the Exumas. Featuring Bahamian craft sloops, these celebrated boat races are held in Elizabeth Harbour. There's also a variety of onshore activities including basketball, a skipper's party, and a Junkanoo parade. Call ✆ **242/336-2430** for exact dates and information. Usually last week of April.

Bahamas Billfish North Abaco Championship, Walker's Cay in the Abacos. Six action-packed tournaments draw anglers in pursuit of the big one, and they are highly competitive. Call the **Bahamas Billfish Championship** at ✆ **954/920-5577** for more information. April to June.

May

Treasure Cay Billfish Championship, the Abacos. The Treasure Cay Hotel-Resort & Marina is one of the finest in the Out Islands, and its marina attracts fishing boats from throughout Florida, especially during this May billfish championship. Dates vary, but you can call ✆ **242/365-8535** for more information.

Bimini Break Blue Marlin Rendezvous. This is a rendezvous off Bimini drawing anglers seeking an action-packed billfish tournament. The headquarters is the Bimini Big Game Fishing Club & Marina. For more information, call ✆ **800/737-1007** or 242/347-3391. May 11 to 14, 2003.

Bimini Billfish Championship. The same participants seem to show up year after year to the big-game-fishing capital of the world. Headquarters for the event is the **Bimini Big Game Fishing Club & Marina** at ✆ **800/737-1007** or 242/347-3391.

June

Eleuthera Pineapple Festival, Gregory Town, Eleuthera. This celebration devoted to the island's succulent pineapple features a Junkanoo parade, craft displays, dancing, a pineapple recipe contest, tours of pineapple farms, and a "pineathalon"—a .5km (¼-mile) swim, 5.5km (3½-mile) run, and 6.5km (4-mile) bike ride. For more information, call ✆ **242/332-2480.** June 5 to 9, 2003.

Long Island Regatta, Salt Pond, Long Island, sees some 40 to 50 sailing sloops from throughout The Bahamas compete in three classes for trophies and cash prizes. Onshore, there are dancing to indigenous "rake and scrap" music, sporting events, and local food specialties for sale, all of which makes for a carnival-like atmosphere. For more information, call ✆ **242/394-1535.** June 17 to 20, 2003.

July

Annual Racing Time in Abaco, Marsh Harbour. This weeklong regatta features a series of five sailboat races in the Sea of Abaco. Onshore festivities include nightly entertainment, cocktail parties, beach picnics, cultural activities, and a grand finale party. For registration forms and information, contact **Dave or Kathy Ralph** at ✆ **242/367-2677.** July 4 to 11, 2003.

Independence Week. Independence celebrations are marked throughout the islands by festivities, parades, and fireworks. It all culminates on Independence Day, July 10.

Bahamas Summer Boating Fling/Flotilla. Boating enthusiasts and yachters make the 5-day crossing from Florida to The Bahamas (Port Lucaya's marina on Grand Bahama Island) in a flotilla of boats guided by a lead boat. All "flings" depart from the Radisson Bahia Mar Resort & Yacht Center in Fort Lauderdale. For more information, contact the **Bahamas Tourism Center** in Florida at © **800/224-3681** or 305/932-0051. July 31 to August 4, 2003.

August

Emancipation Day. The first Monday in August commemorates the emancipation of slaves in 1834. A highlight of this holiday is an early-morning "Junkanoo Rushout" starting at 4am in Fox Hill Village in Nassau, followed by an afternoon of "cook-outs," cultural events such as climbing a greased pole, and the plaiting of the Maypole. First Monday in August.

Cat Island Regatta, Southern Bahamas. Sleepy Cat Island comes alive in the weekend of festive events, including sloop races, live "Rake 'n' Scrape" bands, quadrille dancing, old-fashioned contests and games, and the sale of indigenous dishes. Contact the **Regatta Desk** at © **242/394-0445** in Nassau or **Allen Gilbert** at © **242/342-3011** on Cat Island. August 4 to 7, 2003.

September

Grand Bahama Junkanoo Carnival. This is an exciting weekend of cultural festivities, including a Junkanoo Carnival, a parade evocative of the famous carnival at Trinidad, and open-air concerts featuring the hottest bands. For more information, contact the **Grand Bahama Island Tourism Board** at © **242/352-8044.** Last week in September.

October

Discovery Day. The New World landing of Christopher Columbus, traditionally said to be the island of San Salvador, is celebrated throughout The Bahamas. Naturally, San Salvador town has a parade every year on October 12.

North Eleuthera Sailing Regatta. Native sailing sloops take to the waters of North Eleuthera, Harbour Island, and Spanish Wells in a weekend of championship races. For information contact the **Eleuthera Tourist Office** at © **242/332-2142** or **Glenroy Aranha** at © **242/333-2281.** Mid-October.

All Abaco Sailing Regatta. Local sailing sloops rendezvous at Treasure Cay Harbour for a series of championship races and onshore festivities. Contact the **Regatta Desk** in Nassau at © **242/394-04445** or **Everette Hart** in Abaco at © **242/367-2344.**

Great Bahamas Seafood and Heritage Festival. This October festival is a combination of the Great Seafood Festival and Heritage festival. A cultural affair, showcasing authentic Bahamian cuisine, traditional music, and storytelling. Location: Heritage Village, Arawak Cay. For more information, exact time, and schedule of events, contact the Ministry of Tourism at © **242/302-2072.**

November

Guy Fawkes Day. The best celebrations are in Nassau. Nighttime parades through the streets are held on many of the islands, culminating in the hanging and burning of Guy Fawkes, an effigy of the British malefactor who was involved in the Gunpowder Plot of 1605 in London. It usually takes place around November 5, but check with island tourist offices.

Bimini Big Game Fishing Club All Wahoo Tournament. Anglers take up the tough challenge of baiting one of the fastest fishes in the ocean. Headquarters is the Bimini

Big Game Fishing Club & Marina. For information, contact ✆ **800/737-1007** or 242/347-3391. Mid-November.

Annual One Bahamas Music & Heritage Festival. This 3-day celebration is staged at both Nassau and Paradise Island to celebrate national unity. Highlights include concerts featuring top Bahamian performing artists. Events include "fun walks" on the island and other activities. For more information, contact the **Nassau/Paradise Island Tourist Office** at ✆ **242/326-0633, ext. 4100.** Last week of November.

December

Junkanoo Boxing Day. High-energy Junkanoo parades and celebrations are held throughout the islands on December 26. Many of these activities are repeated on New Year's Day (see "January," above).

6 Insurance, Health & Safety

TRAVEL INSURANCE AT A GLANCE

Check your existing insurance policies before you buy travel insurance to cover trip cancellation, lost luggage, medical expenses, or car-rental insurance. You're likely to have partial or complete coverage. But if you need some, ask your travel agent about a comprehensive package. The cost of travel insurance varies widely, depending on the cost and length of your trip, your age and overall health, and the type of trip you're taking. Insurance for extreme sports or adventure travel, for example, will cost more than coverage for a cruise.

For information, contact one of the following popular insurers:

Access America (✆ **800/284-8300;** www.accessamerica.com/)
Travel Guard International (✆ **800/826-1300;** www.travelguard.com)
Travel Insured International (✆ **800/243-3174;** www.travelinsured.com)
Travelex Insurance Services (✆ **800/228-9792;** www.travelex-insurance.com)

TRIP-CANCELLATION INSURANCE (TCI)

There are three major types of trip-cancellation insurance—one, in the event that you prepay a cruise or tour that gets canceled, and you can't get your money back; a second when you or someone in your family gets sick or dies, and you can't travel (but beware that you may not be covered for a pre-existing condition); and a third, when bad weather such as a hurricane makes travel impossible. Some insurers provide coverage for events like jury duty; natural disasters close to home, like floods or fire; even the loss of a job. A few have added provisions for cancellations because of terrorist activities. Always check the fine print before signing on, and don't buy trip-cancellation insurance from the tour operator that may be responsible for the cancellation; buy it only from a reputable travel insurance agency. Don't overbuy. You won't be reimbursed for more than the cost of your trip.

Some credit cards (American Express and certain gold and platinum Visa and MasterCards, for example) offer automatic flight insurance against death or dismemberment in case of an airplane crash if you charged the cost of your ticket.

If you require additional insurance, try one of the following companies:

MEDEX International, 9515 Deereco Rd., Timonium, MD 21093-5375 (✆ **888/MEDEX-00** or 410/453-6300; fax 410/453-6301; www.medexassist.com).

Travel Assistance International (✆ **800/821-2828;** www.travelassistance.com), 9200 Keystone Crossing, Ste. 300, Indianapolis, IN 46240 (for general information on services, call the company's Worldwide Assistance Services, Inc., at ✆ **800/777-8710**).

For diving trips, you can also contact **The Divers Alert Network** (DAN; ✆ **800/446-2671** or 919/684-8181; www.diversalertnetwork.org).

The cost of travel medical insurance varies widely. Check your existing policies before you buy additional coverage. Also, check to see if your medical insurance covers you for emergency medical evacuation: If you have to buy a one-way same-day ticket home and forfeit your nonrefundable round-trip ticket, you may be out big bucks.

LOST-LUGGAGE INSURANCE

On domestic flights, including those going to The Bahamas, checked baggage is covered up to $2,500 per ticketed passenger. If you plan to check items more valuable than the standard liability, you may purchase "excess valuation" coverage from the airline, up to $5,000. Be sure to take any valuables or irreplaceable items with you in your carry-on luggage. If you file a lost luggage claim, be prepared to answer detailed questions about the contents of your baggage, and be sure to file a claim immediately, as most airlines enforce a 21-day deadline. Before you leave home, compile an inventory of all packed items and a rough estimate of the total value to ensure you're properly compensated if your luggage is lost. You will only be reimbursed for what you lost, no more. Once you've filed a complaint, persist in securing your reimbursement; there are no laws governing the length of time it takes for a carrier to reimburse you. If you arrive at a destination without your bags, ask the airline to forward them to your hotel or to your next destination; they will usually comply. If your bag is delayed or lost, the airline may reimburse you for reasonable expenses, such as a toothbrush or a set of clothes, but the airline is under no legal obligation to do so.

Lost luggage may also be covered by your homeowner's or renter's policy. Many platinum and gold credit cards cover you as well. If you choose to purchase additional lost-luggage insurance, be sure not to buy more than you need. Buy in advance from the insurer or a trusted agent (prices will be much higher at the airport).

CAR-RENTAL INSURANCE (LOSS/DAMAGE WAIVER OR COLLISION DAMAGE WAIVER)

If you hold a private auto insurance policy in the U.S., check to see if you are covered in The Bahamas for loss or damage to the car, and liability in case a passenger is injured. The credit card you used to rent the car also may provide some coverage.

Car-rental insurance probably does not cover liability if you caused the accident. Check your own auto insurance policy, the rental company policy, and your credit card coverage for the extent of coverage: Is your destination covered? Are other drivers covered? How much liability is covered if a passenger is injured? (If you rely on your credit card for coverage, you may want to bring a second credit card with you, as damages may be charged to your card and you may find yourself stranded with no money.)

Car-rental insurance costs about $20 a day.

THE HEALTHY TRAVELER

The Bahamas has excellent medical facilities. Physicians and surgeons in private practice are readily available in Nassau, Cable Beach, and Freeport/Lucaya. In the Out Islands there are a dozen or so health centers. Medical

Tips Quick I.D.

Tie a colorful ribbon or sturdy piece of yarn around your luggage handle, or slap a distinctive sticker on the side of your bag. This makes it less likely that someone else will mistakenly appropriate it. And if your luggage gets lost, it will be easier to find when it does eventually turn up.

personnel hold satellite clinics periodically in small settlements, and there are about 35 other clinics, adding up to a total of approximately 50 health facilities throughout the outlying islands. (We've listed the names and telephone numbers of specific clinics in the individual island coverage that follows throughout this book.) If intensive or urgent care is required, patients are brought by the Emergency Flight Service to **Princess Margaret Hospital** (© **242/322-2861**) in Nassau. Some of the big resort hotels have in-house physicians or can quickly secure one for you.

There is also a government-operated hospital, **Rand Memorial** (© **242/352-6735**), in Freeport, and several government-operated clinics on Grand Bahama Island. Nassau and Freeport/Lucaya also have private hospitals.

Dentists are plentiful in Nassau, somewhat less so on Grand Bahama. You'll find dentists on Great Abaco Island, at Marsh Harbour, at Treasure Cay, and on Eleuthera. There are no dentists on some of the remote islands, especially those in the southern Bahamas, but hotel staff should know where to send you for dental emergencies.

WHAT TO DO IF YOU GET SICK AWAY FROM HOME

If you worry about getting sick away from home, consider purchasing **medical travel insurance** and carry your ID card in your purse or wallet. In most cases, your existing health plan will provide the coverage you need. See the section on insurance earlier in this chapter for more information.

If you suffer from a chronic illness, consult your doctor before your departure. For conditions like epilepsy, diabetes, or heart problems, wear a **Medic Alert Identification Tag** (© **800/825-3785**; www.medicalert.org), which will immediately alert doctors to your condition and give them access to your records through Medic Alert's 24-hour hot line.

Pack **prescription medications** in your carry-on luggage, and carry prescription medications in their original containers. Also bring along copies of your prescriptions in case you lose your pills or run out. Carry the generic name of prescription medicines, in case a local pharmacist is unfamiliar with the brand name.

Don't forget sunglasses and an extra pair of contact lenses or your glasses.

Contact the **International Association for Medical Assistance to Travelers** (**IAMAT**; © **716/754-4883** or 416/652-0137; www.sentex.net/~iamat) for tips on travel and health concerns in Puerto Rico and lists of local, English-speaking doctors. If you get sick, consider asking your hotel concierge to recommend a local doctor—even his or her own. You can also try the emergency room at a local hospital; many have walk-in clinics for emergency cases that are not life threatening. You may not get immediate attention, but you won't pay the high price of an emergency room visit (usually a minimum of $300 just for signing your name).

THE SAFE TRAVELER

In general, The Bahamas, unlike Jamaica, are considered a safe destination, although you should take the same precautions you would when traveling anywhere. That means not flashing your jewelry, your cash, or your wallet, of course, or leaving valuables lying about unguarded. In other words, if you have it, don't flaunt it, as your mama might advise you.

If your hotel doesn't have an in-room safe, ask to check valuables at the front desk. All hotels have safety-deposit boxes, except for the small inns and guesthouses.

Nassau at night is the most dangerous place to go walking in all of The Bahamas, especially in the slums away from the port. Paradise Island and Cable Beach are far safer places for walking and exploring after dark. If you wish to visit a place in the center of Nassau at night, it's best to take a taxi to the door.

Freeport/Lucaya is, in general, a safe destination. Even so, it's best to avoid deserted areas at night, including (unfortunately) romantic walks along deserted beaches. Traveling around the island is also reasonably safe, though there have been a few sporadic reports of hijacking cars.

The Out Islands, save for Bimini (with its persistent drug-smuggling connections), are usually quite safe destinations for the traveler who is discreet and takes the usual precautions.

7 Tips for Travelers with Special Needs

TRAVELERS WITH DISABILITIES

A disability shouldn't stop anyone from traveling. There are more resources out there than ever before.

Because the Bahamian islands are relatively flat, it is fairly easy to get around, even for persons with minor disabilities.

You can obtain a free copy of Air Transportation of Handicapped Persons, published by the U.S. Department of Transportation. Write for Free Advisory Circular No. AC12032, Distribution Unit, U.S. Department of Transportation, Publications Division, 3341Q 75 Ave., Landover, MD 20785 (✆ **301/322-4961;** fax 301/386-5394; http://isddc.dot.gov). Only written requests are accepted.

AGENCIES/OPERATORS

Flying Wheels Travel (✆ **800/535-6790;** www.flyingwheelstravel.com) offers escorted tours and cruises that emphasize sports and private tours in minivans with lifts.

Access Adventures (✆ **716/ 889-9096**), a Rochester, New York–based agency, offers customized itineraries for a variety of travelers with disabilities.

Accessible Journeys (✆ **800/TINGLES** or 610/521-0339; www.disabilitytravel.com) caters specifically to slow walkers and wheelchair travelers and their families and friends.

ORGANIZATIONS

The Moss Rehab Hospital (✆ **215/456-5995;** www.mossresourcenet.org)

Tips **Finding an Accessible Hotel**

You can call the **Bahamas Association for the Physically Disabled** (✆ **242/322-2393**) for information about accessible hotels in The Bahamas. This agency will also send a rented van to the airport to transport you to your hotel for a fee and can provide ramps.

---

provides helpful phone assistance through its Travel Information Service.

The Society for Accessible Travel and Hospitality (✆ **212/447-7285;** fax 212/725-8253; www.sath.org) offers a wealth of travel resources for all types of disabilities and informed recommendations on destinations, access guides, travel agents, tour operators, vehicle rentals, and companion services. Annual membership costs $45 for adults; $30 for seniors and students.

The American Foundation for the Blind (✆ **800/232-5463;** www.afb.org) provides information on traveling with Seeing Eye dogs.

PUBLICATIONS

Mobility International USA (✆ **541/343-1284;** www.miusa.org) publishes A World of Options, a 658-page book of resources, covering everything from biking trips to scuba outfitters, and a biannual newsletter, Over the Rainbow. Annual membership is $35.

Twin Peaks Press (✆ **360/694-2462**) publishes travel-related books for travelers with special needs.

Open World for Disability and Mature Travel magazine, published by the Society for Accessible Travel and Hospitality (see above), is full of good resources and information. A year's subscription is $13 ($21 outside the U.S.).

TIPS FOR BRITISH TRAVELERS WITH DISABILITIES The Royal Association for Disability and Rehabilitation (RADAR), Unit 12, City Forum, 250 City Rd., London, EC1V 8AF (✆ **020/7250-3222;** fax 020/7250-0212; www.radar.org.uk), publishes holiday "fact packs," three in all, which sell for £2 each or all three for £5.

GAY & LESBIAN TRAVELERS

Think twice before choosing The Bahamas. Although many gay people visit or live here, the country has very strict anti-homosexual laws. Relations between homosexuals, even when between consenting adults, are subject to criminal sanctions carrying prison terms. Sexual intercourse (either homosexual or heterosexual) in a public place, which would include a beach late at night, is punishable by up to 20 years in prison.

Of course, the big resorts—with one exception—welcome one and all. That exception is the all-inclusive Sandals Royal Bahamian on Cable Beach, which refuses to accept same-sex couples and does so without apology. You must be heterosexual and arrive in a man-woman combination, or else you'll be forbidden entry.

If you would like to make visiting gay beaches, gay bars, or gay clubs part of your vacation, consider South Miami Beach, Key West, or Puerto Rico instead.

Nevertheless, in the wake of the travel-industry disaster in which the government of the Cayman Islands refused a cruise ship permission to land with its gay passenger, government officials of The Bahamas took an opposite position. When word reached tourist authorities that protests were being organized against the arrival of gay cruises, some government officials actually went aboard to welcome these gay passengers to Nassau. Of course, cynics would claim they welcomed their dollars more than their sexual orientation, because the laws are still on the books. Yet, we still applaud this welcoming attitude in the wake of the Cayman Islands debacle.

Nevertheless, The Bahamas cannot at all be considered a gay-friendly destination. Single gays or gay couples should travel here with great discretion.

The International Gay & Lesbian Travel Association (IGLTA; ✆ **800/448-8550** or 954/776-2626; fax 954/776-3303; www.iglta.org) links travelers up with gay-friendly hoteliers, tour operators, and airline and cruise-line representatives. It offers monthly newsletters, marketing mailings, and a membership directory that's updated once a year. Membership is $150 yearly, plus a $100 administration fee for new members.

AGENCIES/OPERATORS

Above and Beyond Tours (✆ **800/397-2681**; www.abovebeyondtours.com)offers gay and lesbian tours worldwide and is the exclusive gay and lesbian tour operator for United Airlines.

Now, Voyager (✆ **800/255-6951**; www.nowvoyager.com) is a San Francisco-based gay-owned and operated travel service.

Olivia Cruises & Resorts (✆ **800/631-6277** or 510/655-0364; http://oliviatravel.com) charters entire resorts and ships for exclusive lesbian vacations all over the world.

PUBLICATIONS

Out and About (✆ **800/929-2268** or 415/644-8044; www.outandabout.com) offers guidebooks and a newsletter 10 times a year packed with solid information on the global gay and lesbian scene.

Spartacus International Gay Guide and Odysseus are good, annual Englishlanguage guidebook focused on gay men, with some information for lesbians. You can get them from most gay and lesbian bookstores, or order them from Giovanni's Room bookstore, 1145 Pine St., Philadelphia, PA 19107 (✆ **215/923-2960**; www.giovannisroom.com).

Gay Travel A to Z: The World of Gay & Lesbian Travel Options at Your Fingertips, by Marianne Ferrari (Ferrari Publications; www.ferrariguides.com), is a very good gay and lesbian guidebook series.

SENIOR TRAVEL

Mention the fact that you're a senior citizen when you first make your travel reservations. All major airlines and many Bahamian hotels offer discounts for seniors.

Members of AARP (formerly known as the American Association of Retired Persons), 601 E St. NW, Washington, DC 10049 (✆ **800/424-3410** or 202/434-2277; www.aarp.org), gets discounts on hotels, airfares, and car rentals. AARP offers members a wide range of benefits, including Modern Maturity of My Generation magazine and a monthly newsletter. Anyone over 50 can join.

The Alliance for Retired Americans, 8403 Colesville Rd., Ste. 1200, Silver Spring, MD 20910 (✆ **301/578-8422**; www.retiredamericans.org), offers a newsletter six times a year and discounts on hotel and auto rentals; annual dues are $13 per person or couple. *Note:* Members of the former National Council of Senior Citizens receive automatic membership in the Alliance.

The U.S. National Park Service offers a Golden Age Passport that gives seniors 62 years or older lifetime entrance to U.S. national parks for a one-time processing fee of $10, which must be purchased in person at any NPS facility that charges an entrance fee. Besides free entry, a Golden Age Passport also offers a 50% discount on federal-use fees charged for such facilities as camping, swimming, parking, boat launching, and tours. For more information, call ✆ **888/GO-PARKS.**

AGENCIES/OPERATORS

Grand Circle Travel (✆ **800/221-2610** or 617/350-7500; www.gct.com) offers package deals for the 50-plus market, mostly of the tour-bus variety, with free trips thrown in for those who organize groups of 10 or more.

SAGA Holidays (✆ **800/343-0273**; www.sagaholidays.com) offers inclusive tours and cruises for those 50 and older. SAGA also offers a number of single-traveler tours and sponsors the

Zero Cost Lodging

Elder Travelers, 1615 Smelter Ave., Black Eagle, MT 59414 (editor@eldertravelers.com), aids those who are more than 50 years old, like to travel and to meet people. Their stated purpose is to provide members with "zero cost lodging" anywhere in the world, as senior citizens are hooked up with their counterpart hosts in the lands in which they travel. For $40 annually, subscriptions are given to their informative newsletter, which provides links to the best travel data sites worldwide. For more information on this unique group, seek them out at www.eldertravelers.com.

"Road Scholar Tours" (© **800/621-2151;** sales@sagaholidays.com), vacations with an educational bent. Order a free brochure from the website.

PUBLICATIONS

The Book of Deals is a collection of more than 1,000 senior discounts on airlines, lodging, tours, and attractions around the country; it's available for $9.95 by calling © **800/460-6676.**

101 Tips for the Mature Traveler is available from Grand Circle Travel (© **800/221-2610** or 617/350-7500; fax 617/346-6700).

The 50+ Traveler's Guidebook (St. Martin's Press).

Unbelievably Good Deals and Great Adventures That You Absolutely Can't Get Unless You're Over 50 (Contemporary Publishing Co.).

FAMILY TRAVEL

The Bahamas is one of the top family-vacation destinations in North America. The smallest toddlers can spend blissful hours on sandy beaches and in the shallow seawater or in swimming pools constructed with them in mind. There's no end to the fascinating pursuits offered for older children, ranging from boat rides to shell collecting to horseback riding, hiking, or even dancing. Some children are old enough to learn to snorkel and to explore an underwater wonderland. Some resorts will even teach kids to swim or windsurf.

Most families with kids head for New Providence (Nassau), Paradise Island, or Grand Bahama Island (Freeport). See the "Family-Friendly Hotels" boxes in those chapters for our recommendations of the best hotels for parents traveling with kids. See also "The Best Family Vacations," in chapter 1, for additional recommendations in the Out Islands.

AGENCIES/OPERATORS

Familyhostel (© **800/733-9753;** www.learn.unh.edu/familyhostel) takes the whole family on moderately priced domestic and international learning vacations. All trip details are handled by the program staff, and lectures, field trips, and sightseeing are guided by a team of academics. For kids ages 8 to 15 accompanied by their parents and/or grandparents.

PUBLICATIONS

How to Take Great Trips with Your Kids (The Harvard Common Press) is full of good general advice that can apply to travel anywhere.

WEBSITES

Family Travel Network (www.familytravelnetwork.com) offers travel tips and reviews of family-friendly destinations, vacation deals, and thoughtful features such as "What to Do When

Tips **Entertaining Your Kids**

Many of the island's resorts realize that Mom and Dad's idea of fun may not be quite what the kids had in mind. So they offer extras like daily supervised children's activities, babysitters, family discounts, and kids' meals, helping your children to have a great vacation while their parents gain some freedom to relax, too.

Your Kids Are Afraid to Travel" and "Kid-Style Camping."

Travel with Your Children (www.travelwithyourkids.com) is a comprehensive site offering sound advice for traveling with children.

The Busy Person's Guide to Travel with Children (http://wz.com/travel/TravelingWithChildren.html) offers a "45-second newsletter" where experts weigh in on the best websites and resources for tips for traveling with children.

8 Getting There: Flying to The Bahamas

Lying right off the east coast of Florida, the archipelago of The Bahamas is the easiest and most convenient foreign destination you can fly to unless you live next to the Canadian or Mexican borders.

Nassau is the busiest and most popular point of entry (this is where you'll fly if you're staying on Paradise Island). From here, you can make connections to many of the more remote Out Islands. If you're headed for one of the Out Islands, refer to the "Getting There" section that appears at the beginning of each island's coverage later in this book for details. Freeport, on Grand Bahama, also has its own airport, which is served by flights from the U.S. mainland, too.

Flight time to Nassau from Miami is about 35 minutes; from New York, 2½ hours; from Atlanta, 2 hours and 5 minutes; from Philadelphia, 2 hours and 45 minutes; from Charlotte, 2 hours and 10 minutes; from central Florida, 1 hour and 10 minutes; and, from Toronto, 3 hours.

THE MAJOR AIRLINES

From the U.S. mainland, about a half dozen carriers fly nonstop to the country's major point of entry and busiest airline hub, **Nassau International Airport** (✆ **242/377-1759**). Some also fly to the archipelago's second-most-populous city of Freeport. Only a handful (see below) fly directly to any of the Out Islands.

American Airlines's subsidiary **American Eagle** (✆ **800/433-7300;** www.aa.com) flies to Nassau nonstop from Miami, with more than a dozen daily departures. There is no nonstop flight between New York and Nassau on American (you'll have to fly to Miami and change planes there). American Eagle also offers about 10 daily flights between Miami and Freeport.

Delta (✆ **800/221-1212;** www.delta.com) has several connections to The Bahamas, with service from Atlanta, Orlando, and New York's LaGuardia.

The national airline of The Bahamas, **Bahamasair** (✆ **800/222-4262;** www.bahamasair.com), flies to The Bahamas from Miami, landing at either Nassau (with seven nonstop flights daily) or Freeport (with two nonstop flights daily).

US Airways (✆ **800/428-4322;** www.usairways.com) offers daily direct flights to Nassau from Philadelphia and Charlotte, North Carolina.

TWA (✆ **800/892-4141;** www.twa.com) has one daily flight from New York's JFK to Nassau.

Smaller carriers include **Continental Airlines** (✆ **800/525-0280;** www.continental.com), with daily flights to North Eleuthera from both Fort Lauderdale and Miami, plus **Twin Air** (✆ **954/359-8266;** www.flytwinair.com), flying from Fort Lauderdale three times a week to Rock Sound and Governor's Harbour and four times a week to North Eleuthera.

Air Canada (✆ **800/268-7240** in Canada, or 888/247-2262 in the U.S.; www.aircanada.ca) is the only carrier offering scheduled service to Nassau from Canada. A direct flight from Toronto leaves once weekly on Sunday; other flights from both Toronto and Montréal, as well as other Canadian cities, make connections in the U.S.

British travelers opt for transatlantic passage aboard **British Airways** (✆ **800/247-9297** in the U.S., or 0845/773-3377 toll-free from anywhere in the U.K.; www.britishairways.com), which offers four weekly direct flights from London to Nassau. The airline also has at least one flight daily to Miami. From here, a staggering number of connections are available to Nassau and many other points within the archipelago on several carriers.

FLYING TO THE OUT ISLANDS

Many frequent visitors to The Bahamas do everything they can to avoid the congestion, inconvenience, and uncertain connections of the Nassau International Airport. A couple of U.S.-based airlines offer service directly to some of the Out Islands. **American Eagle** (✆ **800/433-7300;** www.aa.com) offers frequent service from Miami's International Airport to the Abacos, Eleuthera, and the Exumas. **US Airways** (✆ **800/428-4322;** www.usairways.com) flies nonstop every day from Fort Lauderdale to Eleuthera, usually making stops at both Governor's Harbour and North Eleuthera. US Airways also flies every day from West Palm Beach to the Abacos, stopping in both Treasure Cay and Marsh Harbour.

Chalk's Ocean Airways (✆ **800/424-2557** or 242/363-1687) operates 17-passenger amphibious aircraft that take off and land in waters near the company's portside terminals. From the Florida mainland, a nonstop flight departs for Bimini from Miami's Watson Island Airport. The flight then continues on to Paradise Island. There's also a one-stop flight from Fort Lauderdale's International Airport to Bimini. (The airline also offers charter flights to virtually anywhere in The Bahamas.)

NEW AIR TRAVEL SECURITY MEASURES

In the wake of the terrorist attacks of September 11, 2001, the airline industry began implementing sweeping security measures in airports. Expect a lengthy check-in process and extensive delays. Although regulations vary from airline to airline, you can expedite the process by taking the following steps:

Arrive early. Arrive at the airport at least 2 hours before your scheduled flight.

Try not to drive your car to the airport. Parking and curbside access to the terminal may be limited. Call ahead and check.

Don't count on curbside check-in. Some airlines and airports have stopped curbside check-in altogether, whereas others offer it on a limited basis. For up-to-date information on specific regulations and implementations, check with the individual airline.

Be sure to carry plenty of documentation. A government-issued photo ID (federal, state, or local) is

Tips What You Can Carry On—And What You Can't

The Federal Aviation Administration (FAA) has devised new restrictions on carry-on baggage, not only to expedite the screening process but to prevent potential weapons from passing through airport security. Passengers are now limited to bringing just one carry-on bag and one personal item onto the aircraft (previous regulations allowed two carry-on bags and one personal item, like a briefcase or a purse). For more information, go to the FAA's website www.faa.gov. The agency has released a new list of items passengers are not allowed to carry onto an aircraft.

Not permitted: knives and box cutters, corkscrews, straight razors, metal scissors, metal nail files, golf clubs, baseball bats, pool cues, hockey sticks, ski poles, and ice picks.

Permitted: nail clippers, tweezers, eyelash curlers, safety razors (including disposable razors), syringes (with documented proof of medical need), walking canes, and umbrellas (must be inspected first).

The airline you fly may have additional restrictions on items you can and cannot carry on board. Call ahead to avoid problems.

now required. You may need to show this at various checkpoints. With an E-ticket, you may be required to have with you printed confirmation of purchase, and perhaps even the credit card with which you bought your ticket (see "All About E-Ticketing," below). This varies from airline to airline, so call ahead to make sure you have the proper documentation. And be sure that your ID is **up-to-date;** an expired driver's license, for example, may keep you from boarding the plane altogether.

Prepare to be searched. Expect spot-checks. Electronic items, such as a laptop or cellphone, should be readied for additional screening. Limit the metal items you wear on your person.

It's no joke. When a check-in agent asks if someone other than you packed your bag, don't decide that this is the time to be funny. The agents will not hesitate to call an alarm.

No ticket, no gate access. Only ticketed passengers will be allowed beyond the screener checkpoints, except for those people with specific medical or parental needs.

FLYING FOR LESS: TIPS FOR GETTING THE BEST AIRFARE

Passengers within the same airplane cabin are rarely paying the same fare. Business travelers who need to purchase tickets at the last minute, change their itinerary at a moment's notice, or get home for the weekend pay the premium rate. Passengers who can book their ticket long in advance, who can stay over Saturday night, or who are willing to travel on a Tuesday, Wednesday, or Thursday after 7pm, will pay a fraction of the full fare. Here are a few other easy ways to save.

Airlines periodically lower prices on their most popular routes. Check the travel section of your Sunday newspaper for advertised discounts or call the airlines directly and ask if any **promotional rates** or special fares are available. You'll almost never see a sale during the peak winter season in The Bahamas, or during the Thanksgiving

Tips All About E-Ticketing

Only yesterday **electronic tickets (E-tickets)** were the fast and easy ticket-free alternative to paper tickets. E-tickets allowed passengers to avoid long lines at airport check-in, all the while saving the airlines money on postage and labor. With the increased security measures in airports, however, an E-ticket no longer guarantees an accelerated check-in. You often can't go straight to the boarding gate, even if you have no bags to check. You'll probably need to show your printed E-ticket receipt or confirmation of purchase, as well as a photo I.D., and sometimes even the credit card with which you purchased your E-ticket. That said, buying an E-ticket is still a fast, convenient way to book a flight; instead of having to wait for a paper ticket to come through the mail, you can book your fare by phone or on the computer, and the airline will immediately confirm by fax or e-mail. In addition, airlines often offer frequent flier miles as incentive for electronic bookings.

---

or Christmas seasons. If your schedule is flexible, say so, and ask if you can secure a cheaper fare by staying an extra day, by flying midweek, or by flying at less-trafficked hours. If you already hold a ticket when a sale breaks, it may even pay to exchange your ticket, which usually incurs a $100 to $150 surcharge. *Note:* The lowest-priced fares are often nonrefundable, require advance purchase of 1 to 3 weeks and a certain length of stay, and carry penalties for changing dates of travel.

Search **the Internet** for cheap fares. Great last-minute deals are available through free weekly e-mail services provided directly by the airlines. See "Planning Your Trip Online," later in this chapter, for more information.

Book a seat on a **charter flight.** Discounted fares have pared the number available, but they can still be found. Most charter operators advertise and sell their seats through travel agents, thus making these local professionals your best source of information for available flights. Before deciding to take a charter flight, however, check the restrictions on the ticket. You may be asked to purchase a tour package, to be amenable if the day of departure is changed, to pay a service charge, to fly on an airline you're not familiar with (this usually is not the case), and to pay harsh penalties if you cancel—but be understanding if the charter doesn't fill up and is canceled up to 10 days before departure.

The most prominent charter operator in The Bahamas is **Nassau/Paradise Island Freeport/Lucayan Express,** P.O. 1004, 284 Millburn Ave., Millburn, NJ 07041 (✆ **800/722-4262;** fax 973/467-4933). The company contracts for the entire aircraft. No advance booking is required, and there are no restrictions on travel dates. You can stay for a day or as long as you like. The company contracts an entire Continental Airlines aircraft, which operates daily from both Newark and Houston. Airfare can be sold alone or in conjunction with hotel packages at New Providence, Paradise Island, and Freeport/Lucaya.

Join a travel club such as **Moment's Notice** (✆ **718/234-6295;** www.moments-notice.com) or **Sears Discount Travel Club** (✆ **800/433-9383** or 800/255-1487 to join; www.travelersadvantage.com), which supply unsold tickets at discounted prices. You pay an annual membership fee to get the club's hot-line number. Of course, you're limited to what's available, so you have to be flexible.

Join **frequent-flier clubs.** It's best to accrue miles on one program, so you can rack up free flights and achieve elite status faster. But it makes sense to open as many accounts as possible, no matter how seldom you fly a particular airline. It's free, and you'll get the best choice of seats, faster response to phone inquiries, and prompter service if your luggage is stolen, your flight is canceled or delayed, or if you want to change your seat.

9 Package Deals

Before you start your search for the lowest airfare on your own (see above), you may want to consider booking your flight as part of a package, since there are so many good-value packages often available to The Bahamas.

A package deal is primarily a way of traveling independently but paying group rates.

A package tour is not the same as an escorted tour. An escorted tour where you're hauled around by a guide is not the way one visits The Bahamas, unless you consider cruise ships an escorted tour. An escorted tour is for those who want to see—say, "all of Europe" in 13 days. Except by cruise ships visiting certain islands, the option of being escorted around six or so Bahamian islands on an escorted tour does not exist.

Packages are simply a way to buy airfare and accommodations at the same time. For popular destinations like The Bahamas, they are a smart way to go, because in many cases, they can save you a lot of money. Often, a package that includes airfare, hotel, and transportation to and from the airport will cost you less than just the hotel alone would have had you booked plane tickets, hotels, and car rentals independently. That's because packages are sold in bulk to tour operators who resell them to the public at a cost that drastically undercuts standard rates.

Packages, however, vary widely. Some offer a better class of hotels than others. Some offer the same hotels for lower prices. Some offer flights on scheduled airlines, while others book charters. In some packages, your choice of accommodations and travel days may be limited. Some packages let you choose between escorted vacations and independent vacations; others will allow you to add on just a few excursions or escorted day trips (also at lower prices than you could locate on your own) without booking an entirely escorted tour. Each destination usually has one or two packagers that are usually cheaper than the rest because they buy in even greater bulk. It's important to spend a little time shopping around; just be sure to compare apples to apples, since the offerings can vary. You can use the reviews and rack rates given in this book to evaluate whether a package is really a good deal.

Here are a few tips to help you tell one package from another, and figure out which one is right for you:

- **Read the fine print.** Make sure you know *exactly* what's included in the price you're being quoted, and what's not. Are hotel taxes and airport transfers included, or will you have to pay extra? Conversely, don't pay for a rental car you don't need. Before you commit to a package, make sure you know how much flexibility you have, say, if your child gets sick or your boss suddenly asks you to adjust your vacation schedule. Some packagers require ironclad commitments, whereas others will go with the flow, charging only minimal fees for changes or cancellations.

- **Use your best judgment.** Stay away from fly-by-nights and shady packagers. If a deal appears to be too good to be true, it probably is. Go with a reputable firm with a proven track record. This is where your travel agent can come in handy; he or she should be knowledgeable about different packagers.

The best place to start your search is the travel section of your local Sunday newspaper. Also check the ads in the back of national travel magazines like *Travel & Leisure, National Geographic Traveler, Travel Holiday,* and *Condé Nast Traveler. Arthur Frommer's Budget Travel* always has lots of ads and frequent articles about good-value packages.

Online Vacation Mall (© **800/839-9851;** www.onlinevacationmall.com) allows you to search for and book packages offered by a number of tour operators and airlines. The **United States Tour Operators Association**'s website (www.ustoa.com) has a search engine that allows you to look for operators that offer packages to a specific destination.

RECOMMENDED PACKAGE-TOUR OPERATORS

Liberty Travel (© **888/271-1584;** www.libertytravel.com) is one of the biggest packager in the Northeast, and it usually boasts a full-page ad in Sunday papers.

One good source of package deals is the airlines themselves. Most major airlines offer air/land packages, including **American Airlines Vacations** (© **800/321-2121;** http://aav1.aavacations.com), **Delta Vacations** (© **800/221-6666;** www.deltavacations.com), and **US Airways Vacations** (© **800/455-0123** or 800/422-3861; www.usairwaysvacations.com), and **Continental Airlines Vacations** (© **800/301-3800;** www.coolvacations.com).

The biggest hotel chains and resorts also offer package deals. If you already know where you want to stay, call the resort itself and ask if it can offer land/air packages.

There's also **TourScan, Inc.,** P.O. Box 2367, Darien, CT 06820 (© **800/962-2080** in the U.S., or 203/655-8091; fax 203/655-6689; www.tourscan.com), which researches the best value vacation at each hotel and condo. Two catalogs are printed each year. Each lists a broad choice of hotels on most of the islands in The Bahamas, in all price ranges. Catalogs cost $4 each, the price of which is credited to any TourScan vacation. Prices are based on travel from New York, Newark, Baltimore, Philadelphia, and Washington, D.C., although the company will arrange trips originating from any location in the United States or abroad on request.

For one-stop shopping on the Web, go to **www.vacationpackager.com**, a search engine that will link you to many different package-tour operators offering Bahamas vacations, often with a company profile summarizing the company's basic booking and cancellation terms.

ALL-INCLUSIVE TOURS

Horizon Tours (© **877/TRIPSAI** or 202/393-8390; www.horizontours.com) specializes in all-inclusive resorts on the islands of The Bahamas, plus other destinations in the Caribbean including Barbados, Jamaica, Aruba, St. Lucia, and Antigua.

Club Med (© **800/258-2633;** www.clubmed.com) has various all-inclusive options throughout the Caribbean and The Bahamas.

SPECIAL TOURS FOR FISHERMEN

Frontiers International (© **800/245-1950,** or 724/935-1577 in Pennsylvania; www.frontierstrvl.com) features fly- and spin-fishing tours of The Bahamas and is a specialist in saltwater-fishing destinations.

FOR BRITISH TRAVELERS

Package tours to The Bahamas can be booked through **Harlequin Worldwide Connoisseurs Collection,** 2 North Rd., South Ockendon, Essex RM15 6QJ (© **01708/850-300**). This agency offers both air and hotel packages not only to Nassau, but to most of the Out Islands as well. The company also specializes in scuba-diving and golf holidays.

Another specialist is **Kuoni Travel,** Kuoni House, Dorking, Surrey RH5 4AZ (© **01306/742-222;** www.kuoni.co.uk), which offers both land and air packages to The Bahamas, including such destinations as Nassau and Freeport, and to some places in the Out Islands. They also offer packages for self-catering villas on Paradise Island.

10 For the Cruise-Ship Traveler

Cruises to The Bahamas are usually either 3- or 4-day weekend getaways or weeklong itineraries in which the ship may stop at Nassau, Freeport, and/or one of several privately owned Bahamian islands for a day at the beach en route to Caribbean ports farther south. If you've never been to The Bahamas, consider a cruise to Nassau, where you can also enjoy Paradise Island and Cable Beach on the same visit. It has better shopping possibilities, better restaurants, and more entertainment than any other site in The Bahamas, including Freeport/ Lucaya on Grand Bahama Island.

A summary of cruise lines that offer diversions in The Bahamas is outlined below, but for much more detailed information, and reviews of each of the ships spending significant time in either the Caribbean or The Bahamas, consider picking up a copy of ***Frommer's Caribbean Cruises & Ports of Call 2003.***

Regardless of the ship you choose, there's a strong possibility that your cruise will depart from the cruise capital of the world, Miami. A handful of vessels also depart for Bahamian waters from Port Everglades (adjacent to Fort Lauderdale), Port Canaveral, and, in very rare instances, from New York. Many cruise-ship passengers combine a 3- or 4-day cruise with visits to Orlando's theme parks, Miami's South Beach, the Florida Everglades, or the Florida Keys and Key West.

Nearly all cabins aboard ships today have two twin beds that can be pushed together, plus storage space (of varying size), a shower and a toilet (ditto), and sometimes a TV showing a rotating stock of programs. If you want to keep costs to a minimum when booking, ask for one of the smaller, inside cabins (one without windows). If you're the type who likes to be active all day and then stay out late enjoying the ship's bars and nightclubs, you won't miss the sunshine anyway. On the other hand, passengers of means are being offered suites today that have an amazing array of pampering options (including hot tubs on their own private verandas!).

Because they buy in such bulk, cruise lines typically offer some of the best deals on airfare to your port of embarkation, and also typically offer extension packages that allow pre- or post-cruise stays at a hotel or resort.

Because getting around Freeport/ Lucaya or Nassau is relatively easy, and the official shore excursions offered by most ships are dull and

Tips It's Not Easy Being Green

Cabins situated on low decks in the middle of the ship are the most stable, and thus the best choices for those susceptible to seasickness. Various medications are also available, including Dramamine, Bonine, ginger capsules, and time-release Transderm patches (worn behind the ear), plus acupressure wristbands.

sometimes restrictive, it's best to decide what you want to do (shopping, swimming, snorkeling, or gambling) and head off on your own during your stop at each port of call. You'll certainly have time to relax at the beach if you choose, or to enjoy watersports (the chapters that follow will give you details on what companies or outfitters to contact for equipment, so you needn't feel dependent on the cruise line for everything). See chapter 3, for more details about sports in Nassau, or chapter 5, for information about sports in Freeport/Lucaya.

In Nassau, cruise ships anchor at piers along Prince George Wharf. Taxi drivers meet all arrivals and will transport you into the heart of Nassau, center of most shopping and sightseeing activities. Duty-free shops also lie just outside the dock area, but for that, you'd do better to go inside the city's commercial and historic core.

As you disembark, you'll find a tourist information office in a tall pink tower, where you can pick up maps of New Providence Island or of Nassau itself. One-hour walking tours are conducted from here if you'd like an overview of the city, with a guide pointing out historic monuments. Outside this office, an ATM will supply you with U.S. dollars if your cash is running low.

THE MAJOR CRUISE LINES

Here's a rundown of the major cruise lines that serve The Bahamas. Most of them focus on either Nassau or Freeport (or maybe both).

- **Carnival Cruise Line** (**© 800/327-9501**; or 305/599-2200; fax 305/406-4740; www.carnival.com): The cruise line everyone's heard of offers a big, loud, flashy cruise party with lots of gambling, glitz, and crowds, so if you're looking for some quiet, reflective time, this might not be your cup of rum.

  Carnival's best bet for The Bahamas is aboard the *Fantasy,* which sails on 3-night loops to Nassau and 4-night excursions to both Freeport and Nassau, and also manages to include the activity-loaded day at sea mentioned above. The *Fantasy* departs throughout the year from Port Canaveral rather than from the more southerly port of Miami. Refurbished in 2000, this vessel has at its centerpiece an entertainment complex that attempts to evoke the heyday of Pompeii. If you like theme decor, such as a piano bar where Cleopatra would feel at home, sail on the *Fantasy.*

  Similar in appeal, the *Fascination* visits The Bahamas year-round from a base in Miami. These cruises especially appeal to passengers seeking a "long weekend" at sea and in port. Movie buffs like the *Fascination* because of its backdrop featuring legends from Hollywood or Broadway (Marilyn Monroe, among others). The average on-board age of most passengers on these Bahamian jaunts is a relatively youthful mid-40s, although ages range from 3 to 95 and usually include lots of children.

- **Celebrity Cruises** (✆ **800/327-6700** or 305/539-6000; www.celebrity-cruises.com): Celebrity, a more upscale sibling company to Royal Caribbean, maintains eight medium- to large-size ships that offer Caribbean cruises of between 7 and 10 nights. This line is unpretentious but classy, several notches above mass-market, but with pricing that's pretty competitive. Cabins are roomy and well-equipped, and the cuisine is among the best of any of the cruise lines.

  However, *Celebrity* rarely features The Bahamas in most of its itineraries, which concentrate heavily on the Caribbean instead. The exception is the *Century,* which includes a stopover in Nassau as part of a greater itinerary that leaves year-round from Fort Lauderdale, visiting such islands as Nassau as mentioned, San Juan, St. Thomas, and the Dutch island of Sint Maarten. Celebrity vessels attract passengers who want elegance without stuffiness, fun without bad taste, and pampering without a high price tag. The line focuses on middle- to upper-middle-income cruisers, although a handful of discreetly wealthy patrons might be on any given cruise or, conversely, a small business owner, school teacher, or computer consultant. Most of the clientele give the impression of being prosperous but not obscenely rich, well behaved but not necessarily obsessed with the nuances of international protocol.

- **Costa Cruise Lines** (✆ **800/462-6782** or 305/358-7325; fax 305/375-0676; www.costacruises.com): Similar to Celebrity and unlike Carnival, Costa Cruises doesn't spend much time in The Bahamas, but does feature a stopover in Nassau on some of its cruises. This old Italian cruise outfit offers virtually identical 7-night jaunts through the western and eastern Caribbean on two of its larger, newer ships (*CostaAtlantica* and *CostaVictoria*), departing from Fort Lauderdale. Of the two, *CostaVictoria* includes a stopover in its 7-night sails through the Eastern Caribbean, with visits to San Juan and St. Thomas, with a special stopover in Catalina Island, a private island off the coast of the Dominican Republic that's owned by the line. These cruises are possible only from December to April. This line attracts passengers who want to pay a reasonable price and who avoid all-American megaships like those of Carnival. Costa passengers are impressed with Italian style, appreciate a sense of cultural adventure and fun, and like the atmosphere of casual elegance at which the Italians excel. The ship features tame versions of ancient Roman Bacchanalia, as well as such celebrations as toga nights and focaccia and pizza parties by the pool.

- **Disney Cruise Line** (✆ **800/951-3532** or 407/566-7000; fax 407/566-7353; www.disney.go.com/DisneyCruise): Launched with lots of publicity in 1999, the *Disney Wonder* is saturated with the total Disney vibe and is specifically marketed to families. It succeeds in mingling state-of-the-art technology and audio-visuals with lots of Disney razzle-dazzle. Disney's ships also offer the best-designed family cabins of any cruise ship, the biggest children's facilities, and even a number of adults-only areas, including one swimming pool, a piano bar, a comedy club, and various social venues.

Disney Wonder itineraries begin and end in Port Canaveral, last between 3 and 4 days, and include daylong visits (8am–3am) to Nassau and Castaway Cay (8am–5pm), the latter a privately owned Bahamian island featuring extensive children's facilities, an adults-only beach area, a family beach area, and all the sports and recreation choices you could want.

Most Disney cruises are sold as 7-night packages that include either 3 days at Disney World and 4 days at sea or vice versa. The 4-night cruise offers a full day at sea as well as visits to the ports.

A day at Walt Disney World and you'll see the kind of people Disney attracts to its ships—families, honeymooners, adults without children, and seniors. Just about everybody, actually. Although Disney is certainly family-oriented, it's estimated that 30% of the passengers are child-free married couples or singles. Also, 10% to 15% of Disney's passengers are Europeans eager to experience that patented Disney magic.

- **Holland America Line-Westours** (**© 800/426-0327;** www.hollandamerica.com): HAL is the most high-toned of the mass-market cruise lines, with eight respectably hefty and good-looking ships serving a clientele of generally mature travelers. Late-night revelers and serious party people might want to book cruises on other lines, such as Carnival. Throughout the winter, three of these vessels include daylong stopovers in Nassau and/or full-day stopovers at the line's privately owned island (Half Moon Cay, in the Exumas) as part of 5- to 8-night cruises to such Caribbean ports as San Juan, St. Thomas, St. John, Antigua, Grand Cayman, Sint Maarten, Dominica, St. Kitts, Martinique, and St. Lucia. Fort Lauderdale is the point of embarkation for all three of the ships that make stops in The Bahamas.

  The *Maasdam* includes Nassau or Half Moon Cay on its 7-night sails through the Eastern or Western Caribbean. These trips are year-round, and stop at Nassau, San Juan, St. Thomas, and Half Moon Cay on its Eastern Caribbean jaunts, with only Half Moon Cay featured on its Western Caribbean sails. The *Veendam* features both Nassau and Half Moon Cay on its 7-night Eastern Caribbean trips that run between October and April. Finally, the *Westerdam* visits both Nassau and Half Moon Cay on its 5-night Eastern Caribbean itineraries and also on its 8-night sails through the Eastern Caribbean. Five-night tours are possible from November to April, with 8-night sailings from October to April. HAL is simply too decorous and modest an outfit to ever define itself as a mass-market line in the sense of Carnival. Its allure and amenities fall into the "premium" category, a euphemism that implies a middle-market niche that's far from being the lowest but still has a long climb before ever making it to the top. Corporate priorities for shipboard ambience include an unstuffy lack of pretension, relaxed friendliness, good value for the money, and absolutely no illusions that its vessels fall into the loftiest tiers of the luxury market.

- **Norwegian Cruise Line** (**© 800/327-7030** or 305/436-4000; www.ncl.com): NCL offers 3-night Miami–Bahamas transits aboard the *Norwegian Sea,* visiting Nassau and either Great Stirrup Key (NCL's private island) or Key West. Generally inexpensive and emphasizing sports, NCL's ships attract a lot of active travelers in the 24-to-45 age bracket. Activities and cuisine are routine but adequate enough for short cruises.

The fleet's *Norwegian Sky* includes only Great Stirrup Cay (not Nassau) on its 7-night voyages through the Eastern Caribbean, with departures from Miami October to March. Of the vessels, the *Norwegian Sky* is the largest and most glitzy, with a total of six restaurants and such deluxe features as a sports deck.

Passengers who book on NCL want to travel to a hot weather destination in winter, but don't want to spend lavish sums for the experience. The line offers a wide variety of cabins at a range of prices to cater to a fairly diverse clientele than those usually found aboard HAL or Celebrity ships.

- **Royal Caribbean International** (© **800/327-6700** or 305/539-6000; fax 800/722-5329; www.royalcaribbean.com): This cruise line vies with Carnival (see above) in offering The Bahamas as a specific destination instead of including the archipelago as a 1-night stopover with most of the cruise devoted to other destinations south toward the Caribbean. Things run smoothly on this middle-of-the-road cruise line, which has a less frenetic atmosphere than that aboard Carnival's megaships but is more lively than Celebrity or Holland America. The company is well run, and there are enough on-board activities to suit virtually any taste and age level. Though accommodations and facilities are more than adequate, they're not upscale, and cabins aboard some of the line's older vessels tend to be a bit more cramped than the industry norm.

  Your best bet if you want The Bahamas only (not the Caribbean) is to sail aboard the *Majesty of the Seas* or the *Sovereign of the Seas.* Majesty sails on 3-night Bahamian jaunts going round-trip from Miami year-round, visiting Nassau with a stopover at Coco Cay. The latter is a private Bahamian island that RCCL has filled with such facilities as beach barbecues and watersports. This vessel also features year-round 4-night trips from Miami that include Nassau and Coco Cay but with a day in Key West as well.

  For those who'd like the same itinerary but will find departures from Port Canaveral more convenient, *Sovereign of the Seas* offers 3- to 4-night sails year-round that call on Nassau and Coco Cay. Two other RCCL vessels, *Enchantment of the Seas* and *Explorer of the Seas,* include Nassau as part of 7-night itineraries going through either the Western or Eastern Caribbean.

  Defining the typical passenger aboard a line that is noted for its broad-based, mass-market appeal is about as treacherous as sailing a megaship over a shallow Bahamian reef. Forced to generalize, though, we'd define Royal Caribbean's typical passengers as couples (and, to a lesser extent, singles) aged 30 to 60. There are a good number of families, sometimes with children, thrown into the mix as well.

HOW TO GET THE BEST DEAL ON YOUR CRUISE

Cruise lines operate like airlines, setting rates for their cruises and then selling them in a rapid-fire series of discounts, offering almost whatever it takes to fill their ships. Because of this, great deals come and go in the blink of an eye, and most are available only through travel agents.

If you have a travel agent you trust, leave the details to him or her. If not, try contacting a travel agent who specializes in booking cruises. Some of the most likely contenders include the following: **Cruises, Inc.,** 1415 NW 62 St., Ste. 205, Fort Lauderdale, FL 33009 (✆ **800/854-0500** or 954/958-3700); **Cruise Masters,** Century Plaza Towers, 2029 Century Park E., Ste. 950, Los Angeles, CA 90067 (✆ **800/ 242-9000** or 310/556-2925); **The Cruise Company,** 10760 Q St., Omaha, NE 68127 (✆ **800/289-5505** or 402/339-6800); **Kelly Cruises,** 1315 W. 22nd St., Ste. 105, Oak Brook, IL 60523 (✆ **800/837-7447** or 630/990-1111); **Hartford Holidays Travel,** 129 Hillside Ave., Williston Park, NY 11596 (✆ **800/828-4813** or 516/746-6670); and **Mann Travel** and **Cruises American Express,** 4400 Park Rd., Charlotte, NC 28209 (✆ **800/849-2301** or 704/556-8311).

A FEW MONEY-SAVING TIPS

- **Book early:** You can often receive considerable savings on a 7-day cruise by booking early. Ask a travel agent or call the cruise line directly.
- **Book an inside cabin:** If you're trying to keep costs down, ask for an inside cabin (one without a window). They're often the same size and offer the same amenities as the more expensive outside cabins. If you're planning on using the space only to sleep, who needs natural light during the day?
- **Take advantage of senior discounts:** The cruise industry offers some discounts to seniors (usually defined as anyone 55 or older), so don't keep your age a secret. Membership in AARP, for example, can net you substantial discounts; always ask your travel agent about these types of discounts when you're booking.
- **Don't sail alone:** Cruise lines base their rates on double occupancy, so solo passengers usually pay between 150% and 200% of the per-person rate. If you're traveling alone, most lines have a program that allows two solo passengers to share a cabin.

SAILING INTO NASSAU

With three stars as the top rating, we'd give Nassau three stars for the overall experience, for activities close to port, and for its beaches and watersports. Shopping and dining would get two stars.

With its adjoining Cable Beach and Paradise Island (linked by bridge to the city), Nassau has luxury resorts set on powdery-soft beaches; all the watersports, golf, and tennis you could want; and so much duty-free shopping that its stores outdraw its museums. Yet historic Nassau hasn't lost its British colonial charm—it just boasts up-to-date tourist facilities to complement them.

Many people come on 3- to 4-day cruises leaving from Miami, Fort Lauderdale, and Port Canaveral.

COMING ASHORE

Cruise ships dock at Prince George Wharf near Rawson Square, the very center of the city and its main shopping area. The Straw Market, at Market Plaza, is nearby (its restoration is in progress after a devastating fire), as is the main shopping artery of Bay Street. The Nassau International Bazaar is at the intersection of Woodes Rogers Walk and Charlotte Street.

If you want to make long-distance calls, go to the BATELCO center of Bahamas Telecommunication, along East Street, lying 4 blocks up the street from the landmark Rawson Square.

INFORMATION & GETTING AROUND Visitor information is readily available near the cruise-ship docks, as are several means of transport, ranging from taxis to buses. For a detailed description, refer to "Visitor Information" and "Getting Around" in chapter 3.

SHORE EXCURSIONS

Shore excursions in Nassau are relatively minor and aren't really necessary, as you can easily get around on your own. The most heavily booked tour visits **the heart of Nassau and Ardastra Gardens** (see "Seeing the Sights," in chapter 3). You're taken along Bay Street, the main shopping district, and later treated to the famous marching flamingo review in the gardens. Other stops include the Queen's Staircase and Fort Charlotte. This jaunt lasts 2½ hours and costs $25 per person. Another 2-hour tour visits **Fort Fincastle** for the view, the Queen's Staircase, and some of the most beautiful homes of Nassau. It also takes passengers across the bridge to view the highlights of Paradise Island, including the Cloisters and its side gardens. This tour costs $22. See chapter 3 for more details.

These two tours are rather standardized. For something more offbeat, take one of the **Goombay Guided Walking Tours** (p. 116). In less than an hour, you can visit most of the city's major landmarks. It's a lot of a fun and great orientation as well. Consider also taking our own walking tour of Nassau landmarks (p. 112).

If you want a close encounter with the sea, a real adventure for devotees of marine life, join **Hartley's Undersea Walk** (p. 108). This adventure take about 3½ hours, some 20 minutes of which are spent walking along the ocean bottom.

To escape from the tourist hordes descending on Nassau, join a tour offered by **Majestic Tours Ltd.** (p. 106). These 3-hour cruises on large catamarans take you to secluded beaches and the best of the offshore reefs.

SEEING THE SIGHTS

The best way to see some of the major public buildings of Nassau is to take a walk, which will give you not only an overview of the historical monuments, but a feel for the city and its history.

Begin your stroll around Nassau at **Rawson Square,** the once and future home of Nassau's Straw Market stalls. (A fire swept away the market in fall 2001, but rebuilding has begun; officials say the new version will be open by summer 2003.) We also enjoy the native market along the waterfront, a short walk past the Straw Market; this is where Bahamian fishermen unload a variety of fish and produce—crates of mangoes, oranges, tomatoes, and limes, plus lots of crimson-lipped conch. For a look, it's best to go any Monday to Saturday morning before noon.

Women might consider a visit to the **Hair Braiding Centre** at Woodes Rogers Walk. It costs about $2 to braid a single strand, although we've seen some women get an elaborate braided coiffure for as much as $100.

For a look at local market life, head over to **Potter's Cay** at the foot of the bridge leading to Paradise. When you see sloops unloading their catch from the Out Islands, you'll realize at once that conch is the favorite food of the Bahamians—that and grouper. You can even eat lunch here providing you like conch soup, conch fritters, or raw conch marinated in lime juice. It's a colorful introduction to Nassau.

It's quite likely you'll miss the Junkanoo parade beginning at 2am on Boxing Day, December 26, but you can relive the Bahamian Junkanoo carnival at the **Junkanoo Expo,** Prince George Wharf (p. 111) in the old Customs Warehouse. All the glitter and glory of Mardi Gras comes alive in this museum, with its fantasy costumes used for the holiday bacchanal.

A VISIT TO PARADISE

Actually part of New Providence Island like Nassau, Paradise Island is a world apart from bustling Nassau and well worth a visit to see the following attractions. See chapter 4 for more details.

The Cloister, in front of the Ocean Club, Ocean Club Drive, Paradise Island (p. 142), is a real 14th-century cloister, built in France by Augustinian monks and reassembled here stone by stone. Huntington Hartford, the A&P grocery heir, purchased the cloister from the estate of William Randolph Hearst at Sam Simeon in California. This is one of only four cloisters that have ever been removed stone by stone from France. The gardens, extending over the rise to Nassau Harbour, are filled with tropical flowers and classic statuary.

The second major attraction luring cruise-ship passengers to Paradise Island is actually a hotel. "City" would be a better word than hotel. **Atlantis Paradise Island Resort & Casino** (p. 129) is a world unto itself. Lying just across the Paradise Island Bridge, the resort complex invites you to "Discover Atlantis" on self-guided tours. You wander through walk-in aquariums, shopping malls, a bevy of drinking and dining choices, the area's biggest casino, and even the re-created ruins of the Lost Continent of Atlantis itself.

GAMBLING THE DAY AWAY

Many cruise-ship passengers spend almost their entire time ashore at one of the casinos on Cable Beach or Paradise Island.

All gambling roads eventually lead to the extravagant **Atlantis Resort's Casino** (p. 143). For sheer gloss, glitter, and show-biz extravagance, this mammoth 30,000-square-foot casino, with adjacent attractions, is the place to go. It's the only casino on Paradise Island, and is superior to the Crystal Palace Casino. Some 1,000 whirring and clanging slot machines operate 24 hours a day.

The dazzling **Crystal Palace Casino,** West Bay Street, Cable Beach (p. 123)—the only one on New Providence Island—is run by Nassau Marriott Resort. The 35,000-square-foot casino is also filled with flashing lights. The gaming room features 750 slot machines in true Las Vegas style.

SHOPPING

The Bahamas has abolished import duties on 11 categories of luxury goods, including china, crystal, fine linens, jewelry, leather goods, photographic equipment, watches, fragrances, and other merchandise. Antiques are exempt from import duty worldwide. Even though prices are duty-free, you can still end up spending more on an item in The Bahamas than you would back home. If you're contemplating buying a good Swiss watch or some expensive perfume, it's best to look in your hometown discount outlets before making serious purchase here.

The principal shopping area is a stretch of **Bay Street,** the main drag, and its side streets. There are also shops in the hotel arcades. In lieu of street numbers along Bay Street, look for signs advertising the various stores.

MARKETS We've recommended the best of the specialty shops in chapter 3 under "Shopping," but a few places are good for one-stop browsing. The **Nassau International Bazaar** is comprised of some 30 shops selling goods from around the globe. The bazaar runs from Bay Street down to the waterfront near the Prince George Wharf. The alleyways here have been cobbled and storefronts are garreted, evoking the villages of old Europe. **Prince George Plaza,** Bay Street can be crowded with cruise-ship passengers. Many fine shops here sell Gucci and other quality merchandise. You can also patronize an open-air rooftop restaurant overlooking the street. The presently-being-reconstructed **Straw Market** in Straw Market Plaza on Bay Street seems to be on every shopper's itinerary. Even those who don't want to buy anything come here to look around (assuming it reopens on schedule in 2003). You can watch the Bahamian craftspeople weave and pleat straw hats, handbags, dolls, place mats, and other items, including straw shopping bags.

BEACHES

The allure of New Providence Island for sun lovers is **Cable Beach,** one of the best-equipped in the Caribbean, with all sorts of watersports as well as easy access to shops, casinos, bars, and restaurants. Cable Beach runs for some 4 miles and is incredibly varied. Keep searching until you find a spot that suits you. Waters can be rough and reefy, then turn calm and clear. The beach is about 6.5km (2 miles) from the port and can be reached by taxi or bus no. 10. See p. 86.

Cable Beach is far superior to the meager one in town, the **Western Esplanade,** which sweeps westward from the British Colonial hotel. But Western Esplanade is closer and more convenient for those arriving in a cruise ship. It has restrooms, changing facilities, and a snack bar. See p. 105.

Even Cable Beach buffs like **Paradise Beach** on Paradise Island. It's convenient to Nassau—all visitors have to do is walk or drive across the bridge or take a boat from the Prince George Wharf. See p. 105.

Paradise Island has a number of smaller beaches, including **Cabbage Beach** (p. 140) on the north shore. Bordered by casuarinas, palms, and sea grapes, Cabbage Beach's broad sands stretch for at least 3km (2 miles). It's likely to be crowded with guests of the island's megaresorts. Escapists find something approaching solitude on the northwestern end, accessible only by boat or foot.

SPORTS

Both New Providence and Paradise Island offer a wealth of sports. For the best selection, refer to "Beaches, Watersports & Other Outdoor Pursuits" in chapter 3, or the same named section in chapter 4 on Paradise Island.

Cruise-ship passengers should reserve space as soon as possible for any activity that requires a reservation, including scuba diving and golf.

DINING

IN NASSAU **Bahamian Kitchen,** Trinity Place, off Market Street (next to Trinity Church; ✆ **242/325-0702**), is one of the best places for good, down-home Bahamian food at modest prices. Specialties include lobster Bahamian style, fried red snapper, conch salad, stewed fish, curried chicken, okra soup, and pea soup and dumplings.

Café Matisse, Bank Lane at Bay Street (✆ **242/356-7012**), is one of the best restaurants convenient to cruise-ship passengers. Serving an international and Italian cuisine, it is set directly behind Parliament House north of Parliament Square. An array of Nassau favorites such as mixed grill of seafood and other delights are prepared fresh daily.

Far removed from the well-trodden tourist path, the **Shoal Restaurant and Lounge,** Nassau Street (✆ **242/323-4400**), is a steadfast local favorite. We rank it near the top for authentic flavor. After all, where can you get a good bowl of okra soup these days?

Green Shutters Restaurant, 48 Parliament St. (2 blocks south of Rawson Sq.; ✆ **242/322-3701**), is an English pub transplanted to the tropics. It offers three imported English beers along with pub grub favorites such as steak-and-kidney pie, bangers and mash, shepherd's pie, and fish and chips. **Gaylord's,** Dowdeswell Street at Bay Street (✆ **242/356-3004**), is the only Indian restaurant in the country, and as such, is now a culinary staple of Nassau, serving a wide range of Punjabi, tandoori, and curried dishes. Recently, such concessions to local culture as curried or tandoori-style conch have cropped up on the menu.

Poop Deck, at the Nassau Yacht Haven Marina, East Bay Street (✆ **242/393-8175**), draws the visiting yachter and is a favorite with cruise-ship passengers who enjoy its open-air terrace overlooking the harbor and Paradise Island. The Bahamian seafood is also fresh and well prepared.

For more details about these restaurants, plus a selection of other dining favorites, refer to chapter 3.

AT CABLE BEACH **Café Johnny Canoe,** in the Nassau Beach Hotel, West Bay Street (✆ **242/327-3373**), serves burgers, all kinds of steaks, seafood, and chicken dishes. The best items on the menu are blackened grouper and barbecued fish.

For a fine Italian and international cuisine, at very modest prices, especially at lunch, head for **Capriccio,** West Bay Street (✆ **242/327-8547**), with its indoor terrace. Much like a luncheonette, the kitchen here turns out such local favorites as "cracked conch," which is actually breaded conch much like a breaded veal cutlet.

For more details on Cable Beach restaurants, refer to chapter 3.

ON PARADISE ISLAND **The Cave,** at the Atlantis, Paradise Drive (✆ **242/363-3000**), is a burger and salad joint located near the beach of the most lavish hotel and casino complex on Paradise Island. It caters to the bathing suit and flip-flops crowd. To reach the place, you pass beneath a simulated rock-sided tunnel illuminated with flaming torches. It seems like a pirate rendezvous. **Seagrapes Restaurant,** in the Atlantis, Casino Drive (✆ **242/363-3000**), serves buffet-style tropical food, including Cuban, Caribbean, and Cajun dishes.

Convenient for cruise-ship passengers, **Columbus Tavern,** Paradise Island Drive (✆ **242/363-2534**), serves from 7am to 3pm for visitors coming over from their ships. It offers a continental and Bahamian cuisine, and does so exceedingly well. Try for an outside table overlooking the harbor.

SAILING INTO GRAND BAHAMA ISLAND (FREEPORT)

With three stars as our top rating, we'd award Freeport/Lucaya on Grand Bahama Island two stars for overall experience, beaches and watersports, shopping, and dining, but only one star for shore excursions, and no stars for activities close to port.

A bit of a comedown after the glamour of Nassau and Paradise Island, Freeport/Lucaya on Grand Bahama Island is the second most popular tourist destination in The Bahamas. Its cosmopolitan glitz may be too much for some visitors, but there are alternatives to the glamour—sun, surf, and excellent golf, tennis, and watersports. And because the island is so big and relatively unsettled, there are plenty of places to get close to nature. Or else you can gamble the day away or shop until you drop.

COMING ASHORE Unlike some ports of call, where you land in the heart of everything, on Grand Bahama Island you're deposited in what cruisers call the middle of nowhere—the west end of the island. You'll want to take a $10 taxi ride (for two passengers) over to Freeport and its International Bazaar, the center of most of the action. As you'll quickly learn after leaving the dreary port area, everything on this island is spread out. Grand Bahama doesn't have the compactness of Nassau. In the Port

Terminal, you'll find phones where you can make long-distance calls.

VISITOR INFORMATION & GETTING AROUND A branch office of the **Grand Bahama Tourist Board** (✆ **800/823-316** or 242/352-8044) is found at the cruise-ship docks. Plenty of taxis are available to take you where you want to go on Grand Bahama Island. For more detailed transportation information, refer to chapter 5, "Getting Around."

SHORE EXCURSIONS

The offerings here are weak. You can often manage better on your own. Most cruise ships tout a 40km (25-mile) round-trip sightseeing trip, during which you spend about 30 minutes at the Garden of the Groves and then are led like cattle around the International Bazaar. This latter is better explored on your own. The 3-hour trip costs $25 per passenger.

SEEING THE SIGHTS

None of the island's major attractions are close to the cruise-ship docks. To reach the center of the action, you'll have to taxi over to the Freeport or Lucaya area.

The prime attraction is the 12-acre **Parrot Jungle's Garden of the Groves,** at the intersection of Midshipman Road and Magellan Drive (p. 173). Eleven kilometers (7 miles) east of the International Bazaar, this scenic preserve of waterfalls and flowering shrubs has some 10,000 trees. The **Palmetto Café** (✆ **242/373-5668**) serves snacks and drinks, and a Bahamian straw market sits at the entrance gate.

Hydroflora Garden, on East Beach at Sunrise Highway (p. 173), is an artificially created botanical wonder, featuring 154 specimens of indigenous Bahamian plants. A special section is devoted to bush medicine.

Filled with mangrove, pine, and palm trees, the 40-acre **Lucayan National Park,** Sunrise Highway (for information, contact Rand Memorial Nature Centre; p. 173), is about 19km (12 miles) from Lucaya. The park contains one of the loveliest, most secluded beaches on Grand Bahama. A wooden path winding through the trees leads to this long, wide-dune-covered stretch. You'll cross Gold Rock Creek, fed by a spring from what is said to be the world's largest underground freshwater cavern system. You can enter two caves, exposed when a portion of ground collapsed. The pools there are composed of 2m (6 ft.) of freshwater atop a heavier layer of saltwater.

Located 3km (2 miles) east of Freeport's center, the **Rand Memorial Nature Centre,** East Settlers Way (p. 174), is the regional headquarters of The Bahamas National Trust, a nonprofit conservation organization. Forest nature trails highlight native flora and bush medicine in this 100-acre pineland sanctuary. Wild birds abound. Other features include native animal displays, an education center, and a gift shop.

GAMBLING THE DAY AWAY

Even though there are casinos aboard ships, many passengers head immediately for a land-based casino once they hit shore.

Most of the daylife/nightlife in Freeport/Lucaya centers on **The Casino at Bahamia,** the Mall at West Sunrise Highway (✆ **242/350-7000**), a glittering, giant, Moroccan-style palace. The casino is open daily from 10am to 3am.

SHOPPING

THE INTERNATIONAL BAZAAR

There's no place for shopping in The Bahamas quite like the **International Bazaar,** at East Mall Drive and East Sunrise Highway. It's one of the world's most unusual shopping marts—Bahamian kitsch in poured concrete and plastic, 10 acres of born-to-shop theme park tastelessness—but in the nearly 100 shops, you're bound to find something that is both a discovery and a bargain. Displayed here are African handcrafts, Chinese jade, British china, Swiss watches, Irish linens, and Colombian emeralds—and that's just for starters. Continental cafes and dozens of shops loaded with merchandise await visitors. Buses marked INTERNATIONAL BAZAAR will take you right to the much-photographed Toril Gate, a Japanese symbol of welcome.

At the **Straw Market,** beside the International Bazaar—presently being reconstructed after a devastating 2001 fire—you could long find items with a special Bahamian touch—colorful baskets, hats, handbags, and place mats—all of which make fine gifts and souvenirs of a trip. The market is scheduled to reopen in the summer of 2003.

PORT LUCAYA MARKETPLACE

The first of its kind in The Bahamas, Port Lucaya on Seahorse Road was named after the original settlers of Grand Bahama. This is a shopping and dining complex set on 6 acres. Free entertainment, such as steel-drum bands and strolling musicians, adds to a festival atmosphere.

Full advantage is taken of the waterfront location. Many of the restaurants and shops overlook a 50-slip marina. A variety of charter vessels are also based at the Port Lucaya Marina, and dockage at the marina is available to visitors coming by boat to shop or dine. A boardwalk along the water makes it easy to watch the frolicking dolphins and join in other activities at the Underwater Explorers Society (UNEXSO).

Merchandise in the shops of Port Lucaya ranges from leather to lingerie to wind chimes. Traditional and contemporary fashions are featured for men, women, and children.

For more details on these sprawling markets, plus a detailed list of recommendations for the best specialty shops, refer to "Shopping" under chapter 5.

BEACHES

Grand Bahama has some 97km (60 miles) of white-sand beaches rimming the blue-green waters of the Atlantic. The 1.5km- (1-mile-) long **Xanadu Beach,** at the Xanadu Beach Resort, is the premier beach in the Freeport area. Most beaches are in the Lucaya area, site of the major resort hotels. The resort beaches, with a fairly active program of watersports, tend to be the most crowded in winter, of course.

Other island beaches include **Taíno Beach,** lying to the east of Freeport, plus **Smith's Point** and **Fortune Beach,** the latter one of the finest on Grand Bahama. Another good beach, about a 20-minute ride east of Lucaya, is **Gold Rock Beach,** a favorite picnic spot with the locals, especially on weekends.

SPORTS

Even for the cruise-ship passenger with very limited time on the island, Grand Bahama offers a wealth of sporting activities ranging from golf to sailing. It is especially known for its golf courses, but passengers should make reservations as early as possible, especially if arriving in the winter months when they have to compete for time with land-based passengers.

The island is also known for its snorkeling and scuba diving. For complete details of the offerings, refer to "Beaches, Watersports & Other Outdoor Pursuits" in chapter 5.

DINING

If you want to eat where the Grand Bahama locals dine, head for **Geneva's,** Kipling Lane, the Mall at West Sunrise Highway (✆ **242/352-5085**), where the food is the way it was before the hordes of tourists invaded. **The Pepper Pot,** East Sunrise Highway at Coral Road (a 5-min. drive east of the International Bazaar, in a tiny shopping mall; ✆ **242/373-7655**), serves takeout portions of the best carrot cake on the island, as well as a savory conch chowder, the standard fish and pork chops, chicken souse (an acquired taste), cracked conch, sandwiches and hamburgers, and an array of daily specials. **The Pub on the Mall,** Ranfurly Circus, Sunrise Highway (opposite the International Bazaar; ✆ **242/352-5110**), is three different themed eating areas, each with a separate theme, serving English, Italian, and island favorites. **Safari Restaurant,** East Mall Drive (✆ **242/352-2805**), is one of the few restaurants in the neighborhood that's as popular at breakfast as it is at dinner. Items include such international and relatively straightforward staples as New York strip steaks, lamb, broiled or grilled snapper, broiled chicken, or seafood platters.

Cooking time-tested recipes from the Out Islands, **Beckey's,** East Sunrise Highway. and East Beach Drive (✆ **242/352-5247**), is another local favorite. It does excellent Bahamian specialties including fish platters and minced lobster, though it doesn't "fare" as well with its American offerings.

AT THE INTERNATIONAL BAZAAR Café Michel (✆ **242/352-2191**) is a good place for refueling when you're shopping the bazaar, offering coffee, platters, salads, and sandwiches throughout the day. **China Temple** (✆ **242/352-5610**) is the dining bargain of the bazaar, dishing out a standard menu of chop suey or chow mein.

PORT LUCAYA MARKETPLACE Restaurants here are infinitely superior to those at the International Bazaar (see above). **Fatman's Nephew** (✆ **242/373-8520**) is an island legend, turning out a savory Bahamian cuisine, including eight kinds of game fish. Another favorite is **Ferry House** beside Bell Channel (✆ **242/373-1595**), with its bar floating on a pontoon. It features a more refined continental cuisine. **Pisces** (✆ **242/373-5192**), is another good bet for lunch, offering a Bahamian and international cuisine, specializing in fish and chips and pizzas at lunch. If you like to soak up the suds at lunch, head for **Shenanigan's Irish Pub** (✆ **242/373-4734**). It also serves a respectable continental cuisine.

11 Planning Your Trip Online

Researching and booking your trip online can save time and money. Sites such as **Frommers.com**, **Travelocity.com**, **Expedia.com**, and **Orbitz.com** allow consumers to comparison shop for airfares, access special bargains, book flights, and reserve hotel rooms and rental cars.

But don't fire your travel agent just yet. Although online booking sites can help you bargain-shop, they cannot endow you with the hard-earned experience that makes a seasoned, reliable travel agent an invaluable resource, even in the Internet age. For consumers with a complex itinerary, a trusty travel agent is still the best way to arrange an itinerary.

Some sites, like Expedia.com, send **e-mail notification** when low fares pop up, and some notify you when fares to a destination become low.

TRAVEL-PLANNING & BOOKING SITES

Keep in mind that because several airlines are no longer willing to pay commissions on tickets sold by online travel agencies, these agencies may either add a $10 surcharge to your bill if you book on that carrier—or neglect to offer those carriers' schedules.

The list of sites below is selective, not comprehensive. Some sites may have evolved or disappeared by the time you read this.

- **Travelocity** (www.travelocity.com or www.frommers.travelocity.com) and **Expedia** (www.expedia.com) are among the most popular sites, each offering an excellent range of options. Travelers search by destination, dates and cost.
- **Orbitz** (www.orbitz.com) is a popular site launched by United, Delta, Northwest, American, and Continental airlines.
- **Qixo** (www.qixo.com) is another powerful search engine that allows you to search for flights and accommodations from some 20 airline and travel-planning sites (such as Travelocity) at once. Qixo sorts results by price.

12 Getting Around

If your final destination is Paradise Island, Freeport, or Nassau (Cable Beach) and you plan to fly, you'll have little trouble in reaching your destination. However, if you're heading for one of the Out Islands, you face more exotic choices, not only of airplanes but also of other means of transport, including a mail boat, the traditional connecting link in days of yore.

As mentioned, each section on one of the Out Island chains has specific transportation information, but in the meantime, we'll give you a general overview.

For "Chartering a Boat," see below.

BY PLANE

The national airline of The Bahamas, **Bahamasair** (✆ **800/222-4262;** www.bahamasair.com), serves 19 airports on 12 Bahamian islands, including Abaco, Andros, Cat Island, Eleuthera, Long Island, and San Salvador. Many of the Out Islands have either airports or airstrips, or are within a short ferry ride's distance of one. You can usually make connections to these smaller islands from Nassau.

BY RENTAL CAR

Many travelers don't really need to rent a car in The Bahamas, especially those who are coming for a few days of soaking in the sun at their resort's own beach. In Nassau and Freeport, you can easily rely on public transportation or taxis. In some of the Out Islands, there are a few car-rental companies, but most rental cars are unusually expensive and in poor condition (the roads are often in the same bad state as the rental cars).

Most visitors need transportation only from the airport to their hotel; perhaps you can arrange an island tour later, and an expensive private car won't be necessary. Your hotel can always arrange a taxi for you if you want to venture out.

You may decide that you want a car to explore beyond the tourist areas of New Providence Island, and you're very likely to want one on Grand Bahama Island.

Just remember: Road rules are much the same as those in the U.S., but you *drive on the left.*

For the Out Islands, turn to the relevant "Getting Around" sections of the chapters that follow to determine if you'll want a car (you may want one on Eleuthera, or to explore on Great Abaco Island); perhaps you'll stay put at your resort but rent a car for only 1 day of exploring.

The major U.S. car-rental companies operate in The Bahamas, but not on all the remote islands. There are also a handful of local car-rental companies, some of which may charge a few dollars less. We always prefer to do business with one of the major firms if they're present because you can call ahead and reserve from home via a toll-free number; they tend to offer better-maintained vehicles; and it's easier to resolve any disputes after the fact. Call **Budget** (✆ **800/527-0700;** www.budgetrentacar.com), **Hertz** (✆ **800/654-3131;** www.hertz.com), **Dollar** (✆ **800/800-4000;** www.dollar.com), or **Avis** (✆ **800/331-1212;** www.avis.com). Budget rents only in Nassau. Liability insurance is compulsory.

"Petrol" is easily available in Nassau and Freeport, though quite expensive. In the Out Islands, where the cost of gasoline is likely to vary from island to island, you should plan your itinerary based on where you'll be able to get fuel. The major towns of the islands have service stations. You should have no problems on New Providence or Grand Bahama Island unless you start out with a nearly empty tank.

Visitors may drive with their home driver's license for up to 3 months. For longer stays, you'll need to secure a Bahamian driver's license.

As you emerge at one of the major airports, including those of Nassau (New Providence) and Freeport (Grand Bahama Island), you can pick up island maps that are pretty good for routine touring around those islands. However, if you plan to do extensive touring in the Out Islands, you should go first to a bookstore in either Nassau or Freeport and ask for a copy of ***Atlas of The Bahamas.*** It provides touring routes (outlined in red) through all the major Out Islands. Once you arrive on these remote islands, it may be hard to obtain maps.

BY TAXI

Once you've reached your destination, you'll find that taxis are plentiful in the Nassau/Cable Beach/Paradise Island area and in the Freeport/Lucaya area on Grand Bahama Island. These cabs, for the most part, are metered—but they take cash only, no credit cards. See "Getting Around" in the chapters on each island that follow for further details.

In the Out Islands, however, it's not so easy. In general, taxi service is available at all air terminals, at least if those air terminals have "port of entry" status. They can also be hailed at most marinas.

Taxis are usually shared, often with the local residents. Out Island taxis aren't metered, so you must negotiate the fare before you get in. (Expect to pay a rate of around $20 per hr.) Cars are often old and badly maintained, so be prepared for a bumpy ride over some rough roads if you've selected a particularly remote hotel.

BY MAIL BOAT

Before the advent of better airline connections, the traditional way of exploring the Out Islands—in fact, about the only way unless you had your own craft—was by mail boat. This service is still available, but it's recommended only for those who have lots of time and a sense of adventure. You may ride with cases of rum, oil drums, crawfish pots, live chickens, or even an occasional piano.

The boats—19 of them composing the "Post Office Navy"—under the direction of the Bahamian Chief of Transportation are often fancifully colored, high-sided, and somewhat clumsy in appearance, but the little motor vessels chug along, serving the 30 inhabited islands of The Bahamas. Schedules can be thrown off by weather and other causes, but most morning mail boats depart from Potter's Cay (under the Paradise Island Bridge in Nassau) or from Prince George Wharf. The voyages last from 4½ hours to most of a day, sometimes even overnight. Check the schedule of the particular boat you wish to travel on with the skipper at the dock in Nassau.

This is a cheap way to go: The typical fare from Nassau to Marsh Harbour is $45 per person, one-way. Many of the boats offer two classes of passenger accommodations, first and second. In first class you get a bunk bed; in second, you may be entitled only to deck space. (Actually, the bunk beds are usually reserved for the seasick, but first-class passengers on larger boats sit in a reasonably comfortable enclosed cabin.)

For information about mail boats to the Out Islands, contact the **Dockmasters Office** in Nassau, under the Paradise Island Bridge on Potter's Cay (✆ **242/393-1064**).

BY CHARTERED BOAT

For those who can afford it, this is the most luxurious way to see The Bahamas. On your private boat, you can island-hop at your convenience. Well-equipped marinas are on every major island and many cays. There are designated ports of entry at Great Abaco (Marsh Harbor), Andros, the Berry Islands, Bimini, Cat Cay, Eleuthera, Great Exuma, Grand Bahama Island (Freeport/Lucaya), Great Inagua, New Providence (Nassau), Ragged Island, and San Salvador.

Vessels must check with Customs at the first port of entry and receive a cruising clearance permit to The Bahamas. Carry it with you and return it at the official port of departure.

You might buy ***The Yachtsman's Guide to The Bahamas*** (Tropic Isle Publishers), the only guide covering the entire Bahamas. Copies of the book are available at major marine outlets and bookstores, and by mail direct from the publisher for $39.95, U.S. post-paid: Tropic Island Publishers, Inc., P.O. Box 610938, North Miami, FL 33261-0938 (✆ **305/893-4277**; www.yachtsmansguide.com).

Experienced sailors with a sea-wise crew can charter **"bareboat"** (a fully equipped boat with no crew). You're on your own, and you'll have to prove you can handle it before you're allowed to take out such a craft. You may want to take along an experienced yachter familiar with local waters, which may be tricky in some places.

Most yachts are rented on a weekly basis. Contact **Abaco Bahamas Charters** (✆ **800/626-5690,** or 242/366-0131; www.abacocharters.com), the **Moorings** (✆ **800/535-7289,** or 242/367-4000; www.moorings.com), **Charter Cats of The Bahamas** (✆ **800/446-9441**), or **Tropical Diversions** (✆ **800/343-7256**; www.tropicaldiversions.com).

13 The Active Vacation Planner

The more than 700 islands in the Bahamian archipelago (fewer than 30 of which are inhabited) are surrounded by warm, clear waters that are ideal for fishing, sailing, and scuba diving. (Detailed recommendations and the costs of these activities are previewed under the individual destinations listings.) The country's perfect weather and its many cooperative local entrepreneurs allow easy access to more than 30 sports throughout the islands. For sports-related information about any of the activities listed below, call ✆ **800/32-SPORT.**

WATERSPORTS

FISHING The shallow waters between the hundreds of cays and islands of The Bahamas are some of the most fertile fishing grounds in the world. Even waters where marine traffic is relatively congested have yielded impressive catches in the past, although overfishing has depleted schools of fish, especially big game fish. Grouper, billfish, wahoo, tuna, and dozens of other species thrive in Bahamian waters, and dozens of charter boats are available for deep-sea fishing. Reef fishing, either from small boats or from shorelines, is popular everywhere, with grouper, snapper, and barracuda being the most commonly caught species. Specialists, however, or serious amateurs of the sport, often head for any of the following destinations.

The island of **Bimini** is known as the "Big-Game Fishing Capital of the World." Here anglers can hunt for the increasingly elusive swordfish, sailfish, and marlin, and there are frequent tournaments (see the "Calendar of Events," earlier in this chapter). Bimini maintains its own Hall of Fame, where many a proud angler has had his or her catch honored. World records for the size of catches don't seem to last long here; they are usually quickly surpassed.

Walker's Cay in the Abacos and **Chub Cay** in the Berry Islands are famous for both deep-sea and shore fishing. Some anglers return to these cays year after year. Grouper, jacks, and snapper are plentiful. Even spearfishing without scuba gear is common and popular.

Andros boasts the world's best bonefishing. Bonefish (also known as "gray fox") are medium-size fish that feed in shallow, well-lit waters. Known as some of the most tenacious fish in the world, they struggle ferociously against anglers who pride themselves on using light lines from shallow-draft boats. **Andros Island Bonefishing Club** in North Andros (© **242/368-5167**; www.androsbonefishing.com) specializes in fishing adventures off some of the most remote and sparsely populated coastlines in the country.

SAILING The Bahamas, rivaled only by the Virgin Islands and the Grenadines, is one of the top yachting destinations in the Atlantic. Its more than 700 islands and well-developed marinas provide a spectacular and practical backdrop for sailing enthusiasts, and there are frequent regattas (see the "Calendar of Events," earlier in this chapter). The mini-archipelago of the **Abacos** is called "The Sailing Capital of the World." You might think it deserves the title until you've sailed the **Exumas,** which we think are even better.

Don't be dismayed if you don't own a yacht. All sizes and types of crafts, from dinghies to blue-water cruisers, are available for charter, and crew and captain are optional. If your dreams involve experiencing the seagoing life for an afternoon or less, many hotels offer sightseeing cruises aboard catamarans or glass-bottomed boats, often with the opportunity to snorkel or swim in the wide-open sea.

The Abacos have many marinas. The best arrangements for boating can be made at **Abaco Bahamas Charters** (© **800/626-5690** or 242/366-0151) and at **The Moorings** (© **800/535-7289** or 242/367-4000). In the Exumas it's difficult to rent boats, because most yachters arrive with their own. However, take a chance and contact **Happy People Marina** (© **242/355-2008**) on Staniel Cay.

SCUBA DIVING The unusual marine topography of The Bahamas

Tips **A Warning to Poachers**

It is illegal to take sponges or turtles from Bahamian waters. The Ministry of Agriculture, Fisheries, and Local Government also keeps a close eye on crayfish (spiny lobster) and prohibits the export of conch meat. Stone crab cannot be caught within 3km (2 miles) off Bimini or Grand Bahama.

Moments Meet Flipper

Oceanic Society Expeditions, Fort Mason Center, Building E, San Francisco, CA 94123 (✆ **800/326-7491** or 415/441-1106; www.oceanic-society.org), organizes research trips involving close encounters with dolphins in the wild in the waters of The Bahamas. Note that some studies, contrary to popular belief, claim that dolphins do not liked to be touched, as was once thought.

offers an astonishing variety of options for divers. Throughout the more than 700 islands, there are innumerable reefs, drop-offs, coral gardens, caves, and shipwrecks. In many locations, you may feel that you are the first human ever to explore the site. Since fewer than 30 of the Bahamian islands are inhabited, you can usually dive in pristine and uncrowded splendor.

Andros Island boasts the third-largest barrier reef in the world. Chub Cay in the Berry islands, and Riding Rock, San Salvador, also offer premium spots to take a plunge in an underwater world teeming with aquatic life. The intricate layout of the Exumas includes virtually every type of underwater dive site, very few of which have ever been explored. The Abacos, famous for its yachting, and the extensive reefs off the coast of Freeport are also fabulous dive sites.

Freeport, incidentally, is home to the country's most famous and complete diving operation, **UNEXSO** (✆ **800/992-DIVE;** www.unexso.com). It offers a 5.5m- (18-ft.-) deep training tank where divers can work toward certification, and the popular "Dolphin Experience," in which visitors are allowed to pet, swim, snorkel, and dive with these remarkable animals.

You can easily learn to dive for the first time in The Bahamas. Lots of Bahamian hotels offer resort courses for novices, usually enabling a beginner to dive with a guide after several hours of instruction. You'll probably start out in the swimming pool for your initial instruction, then go out with a guide from the beach. A license proving the successful completion of a predesignated program of scuba study is legally required for solo divers. Many resort hotels and dive shops offer the necessary training as part of a 5-day training course. Participants who successfully complete the courses are awarded PADI- or NAUI-approved licenses.

For useful information, check out the website of the Professional Association of Diving Instructors (PADI) at www.padi.com. You'll find a description of the best dive sites and a list of PADI-certified dive operators. *Rodale's Scuba Diving Magazine* also has a helpful website at www.scubadiving.com. Both sites list dive-package specials and display gorgeous color photos of some of the most beautiful dive spots in the world.

SEA KAYAKING If you want to explore the pristine Exumas National Land and Sea Park, a spectacular natural area consisting of 365 mostly uninhabited cays that may be more impressive than anything in the Caribbean, **Ecosummer Expeditions** is your best bet. They'll take you on sea-kayaking itineraries that will allow you lots of time to enjoy the area's white-sand beaches and numerous reefs. You can also snorkel along the way. A 1-week trip leaving from Nassau costs $1,500. The 2-week trip leaves from George Town, the capital of the Exumas, and goes for $2,200.

For more information, call **Ecosummer Expeditions,** P.O. Box 1765, Clearwater, BC, Canada V0E 1NO (✆ **800/465-8884;** www.ecosummer.com).

Another sea-kayaking outfit is **Ibis Tours.** They also take you through the Exumas, at $1,695 for an 8-day adventure, depending on the time of year. The trips include guides, all meals, the boat, equipment (including camping gear), and waterproof bags. The kayaks come with sails to shorten travel time and to make paddling easier. To make reservations, contact **Ibis Tours** at P.O. Box 208, Pelham, NY 10803 (✆ **800/525-9411;** www.ibistours.com).

SNORKELING WITH THE PROS Jean-Michel Cousteau, son of famed oceanographer Jacques Cousteau, has teamed up with the Out Islands of The Bahamas, American Airlines/ American Eagle, and US Divers to create a snorkeling program that emphasizes marine conservation and education. Jean-Michel Cousteau's Out Islands Snorkeling Adventures, located in eight resorts on eight islands, takes visitors through Bahamian reefs from $99 a trip. The fee includes instruction, two guided tours, snorkeling gear, waterproof ID charts and reference books, and a T-shirt. They even send you a set of snorkeling gear after you've returned home. For more information, contact **The Bahamas Out Island Promotion Board** at ✆ **800/688-4752,** or 305/ 931-6611 in Miami.

OTHER ACTIVITIES

BIKE & SCOOTER RENTALS Most biking or scooter riding is done either on New Providence Island (Nassau) or on Grand Bahama Island; both have relatively flat terrain. Biking is best on Grand Bahama Island because it's bigger, with better roads and more places to go. Getting around New Providence Island is relatively easy once you're out of the congestion of Nassau and Cable Beach. In Nassau many hotels will rent you a bike or motor scooter.

On Grand Bahama Island, you can rent bikes at most big hotels (see chapter 5, for phone numbers and addresses of hotels). You can also rent motor scooters starting at about $35 per day. The tourist office at Freeport/ Lucaya will outline on a map the best biking routes.

In the Out Islands, roads are usually too bumpy and potholed for much serious biking or scooter riding. Bike-rental places are almost nonexistent unless your hotel has some vehicles.

GOLF The richest pickings are on Grand Bahama Island, home to three courses that have been designated as potential PGA tour stops. The **Bahamia** boasts two challenging and spectacular courses: the Princess Ruby and the Princess Emerald, site of The Bahamas National Open. The big news here is the opening of **The Reef Course,** the first new golf course to open in The Bahamas since 1969. Designed by Robert Trent Jones, Jr., it features water along 13 of its 18 holes. The oldest course on Grand Bahama Island is the **Lucayan Park Golf & Country Club,** a heavily wooded course with elevated greens and numerous water hazards designed for precision golf. See chapter 5, for more information, and also refer to "The Best Golf Courses," in chapter 1.

Quality golf in The Bahamas, however, is not restricted to Grand Bahama Island. The **Cable Beach Golf Course,** part of the Radisson Cable Beach Hotel on New Providence, is the oldest golf course in the country, although not as good as the **South Ocean Golf Resort** in the secluded southern part of New Providence. The widely publicized **Ocean Club Golf Club** has unusual obstacles—a lion's den and a windmill—which have challenged the skill of both Gary Player and Jack Nicklaus. It also boasts the world's largest sand trap. After restoration, the course opened in 2000. See chapters 3 and 4, for more information, and also refer to "The Best Golf Courses," in chapter 1.

Note that a prime new Greg Norman-designed course is slated to open in the Exumas in 2003, as part of the massive new Four Seasons resort and it likely will be very impressive (and expensive). See chapter 9 or call ✆ **800/819-5053** for an update.

Golf is also available at a course in the Abacos on Treasure Cay. The design is challenging, with many panoramic water views and water obstacles. See chapter 7, for more information.

HIKING The Bahamas isn't the greatest destination for serious hikers. The best hiking is on Grand Bahama Island, especially in **Lucayan National Park,** which spreads across 40 acres and is located some 32km (20 miles) from Lucaya. A large map at the entrance to the park outlines the trails. The park is riddled with trails and elevated walkways. The highlight of the park is what may be the largest underground cave system in the world, some 11km (7 miles) long. Spiral steps let you descend into an eerie underground world.

Also on Grand Bahama Island, the **Rand Memorial Nature Centre** is the second-best place for hiking. It offers some 100 wooded acres that you can explore on your own or with a tour guide. A .75km (½-mile) of winding trails acquaints you with the flora and fauna that call Grand Bahama home, everything from a native boa constrictor to the Cuban emerald hummingbird, whose favorite food is the nectar of the hibiscus.

HORSEBACK RIDING The best riding possibilities are at Pinetree Stables on Grand Bahama Island (✆ **242/373-3600**). Its beach rides are especially interesting. Both trail and beach rides are offered two times a day, Tuesday through Sunday; be sure to book rides a few days in advance. See chapter 5, for more information.

Virtually the only place on New Providence Island (Nassau) that offers horseback riding is **Happy Trails Stables,** Carl Harbour (✆ **242/362-1820**), which features both morning and afternoon trail rides and requires a reservation. These tours include transportation to and from your hotel. The trail rides are guided through the woods and along the beach. See chapter 3, for more information.

Horseback riding is hardly a passion on the other islands.

TENNIS Most tennis courts are part of large resorts and are usually free during the day for the use of registered guests. Charges are imposed to light the courts at night. Nonguests are welcome but are charged a player's fee; they should call in advance to reserve. Larger resorts usually offer on-site pro shops and professional instructors. Court surfaces range from clay or asphalt to such technologically advanced substances as Flexipave and Har-Tru.

New Providence, with more than 80 tennis courts, wins points for offering the greatest number of choices. At least 21 of these lie on Paradise Island. Also noteworthy are the many well-lit courts at the Radisson Cable Beach Hotel. See chapters 3 and 4. After New Providence, Grand Bahama has the largest number of courts available for play—almost 40 in all. See chapter 5. Within the Out Islands, tennis courts are available on Eleuthera, the Abacos, the Berry Islands, and the Exumas. See chapters 6, 7, 8, and 9, for more information.

14 Tips on Accommodations

The Bahamas offers a wide selection of accommodations, ranging from small private guesthouses to large luxury resorts. Hotels vary in size and facilities, from deluxe (offering room service, sports, swimming pools, entertainment, and so on) to fairly simple inns.

There are package deals galore, and they are always cheaper than "rack rates." (A rack rate is what an individual pays if he or she literally walks in from the street; these are the rates we've listed in the chapters that follow, though you can almost always do better at the big resorts.) So it's sometimes good to go to a reliable travel agent to find out what, if anything, is available in the way of a land-and-air package before booking into a particular accommodation. See section 9, "Package Deals," earlier in this chapter, for details on a number of companies that usually offer good-value packages to The Bahamas.

There is no rigid classification of hotel properties in the islands. The word "deluxe" is often used (or misused) when "first class" might have been a more appropriate term. "First class" itself often isn't. For that and other reasons, we've presented fairly detailed descriptions of the properties so that you'll get an idea of what to expect. However, even in the deluxe and first-class resorts and hotels, don't expect top-rate service and efficiency. When you go to turn on the shower, sometimes you get water and sometimes you don't. You may even experience power failures.

The winter season in The Bahamas runs roughly from the middle of December to the middle of April, and hotels charge their highest prices during this peak period. Winter is generally the dry season in the islands, but there can be heavy rainfall regardless of the time of year. During the winter months, make reservations 2 months in advance if you can. You can't book early enough if you want to travel over Christmas or in February.

The off-season in The Bahamas—roughly from mid-April to mid-December (although this varies from hotel to hotel)—amounts to a sale. In most cases, hotel rates are slashed a startling 20% to 60%. It's a bonanza for cost-conscious travelers, especially for families who can travel in the summer. Be prepared for very strong sun, though, plus a higher chance of rain. Also note that hurricane season runs through summer and fall.

MAP VERSUS AP OR DO YOU WANT TO GO EP?

All Bahamian resorts offer a **European Plan** (EP) rate, which means that you pay for the price of a room. That leaves you free to dine around at night at various other resorts or restaurants without restriction. Another plan preferred by many is the **Continental Plan** (CP), which means you get a

What the Hotel Symbols Mean

As you're shopping around for your hotel, you may see the following terms used:

- **AP (American Plan):** Includes three meals a day (sometimes called full board or full pension).
- **EP (European Plan):** Includes only the room—no meals.
- **MAP (Modified American Plan):** Sometimes called half board or half pension, this room rate includes breakfast and dinner (or lunch instead of dinner if you prefer).

continental breakfast of juice, coffee, bread, and jam included in a set price. This plan is preferred by those who don't like to "dine around" at breakfast time.

Another major option is the **Modified American Plan,** which includes breakfast and one main meal of the day, either lunch or dinner. The final choice is the **American Plan** (AP), which includes breakfast, lunch, and dinner. At certain resorts you will save money by booking in on either MAP or AP, because discounts are granted. If you dine a la carte often for lunch and dinner, your dining costs will be much higher than if you stay on the MAP or AP.

Dining at your hotel at night cuts down on transportation costs. Taxis especially are expensive. Nonetheless, if dining out and having many different culinary experiences is your idea of a vacation, and you're willing to pay the higher price, avoid AP plans or at least make sure the hotel where you're staying has more than one dining room (see above).

One option is to ask if your hotel has a dine-around plan. You might still keep costs in check, but you can avoid a culinary rut by taking your meals in some other restaurants if your hotel has such a plan. Such plans are rarer in The Bahamas, which does not specialize in all-inclusive resorts the way that Jamaica or some other islands do.

Before booking a room, check with a good travel agent or investigate on your own what you are likely to save by booking on a dining plan. Under certain circumstances in winter you might not have a choice if MAP is dictated as a requirement for staying there. It pays to investigate, of course.

A RIGHT ROOM AT THE RIGHT PRICE

Ask detailed questions when booking a room. Don't just ask to be booked into a certain hotel, but specify your likes and dislikes. There are several logistics of getting the right room in a hotel. Entertainment in The Bahamas is often alfresco, so light sleepers obviously won't want a room directly over a steel band. In general, back rooms cost less than oceanfront rooms, and lower rooms cost less than upper-floor units. Therefore, if budget is a major consideration with you, opt for the cheaper rooms. You won't have a great view, but you'll pay less and save your money for something else. Just make sure that it isn't next to the all-night drummers.

Of course, all first-class or deluxe resorts feature air-conditioning, but many Bahamian inns do not, especially in the Out Islands. Cooling might be by ceiling fans or, in more modest places, the breeze from an open window, which also brings the mosquitoes. If sleeping in a climate-controlled environment is important to your vacation, ascertain this in advance.

If you're being your own travel agent, it pays to shop around by calling the local number given for a hotel and its toll-free number if it has one. You can check online and call a travel agent to see where you can obtain the best price.

Another tip. Ask if you can get an upgrade or a free night's stay if you stay an extra few days. If you're traveling during the marginal periods between low and high season, you can sometimes delay your travel plans by a week or 10 days and get a substantial reduction. For example, a $300 room booked on April 12 might have been lowered to $180 by April 17, as mid-April marks the beginning of the low season in The Bahamas.

Tip for senior citizens: Ask if an AARP card will get you a discount.

Transfers from the airports or the cruise dock are included in some hotel bookings, most often in a package plan but usually not in ordinary bookings.

This is true of first-class and deluxe resorts but rarely of medium-priced or budget accommodations. Always ascertain whether transfers (which can be expensive) are included.

When using the facilities at a resort, make sure that you know exactly what is free and what costs money. For example, swimming in the pool is nearly always free, but you might be charged for use of a tennis court. Nearly all watersports cost extra, unless you're booked on some special plan such as scuba package. Some resorts seem to charge every time you breathe and might end up costing more than a deluxe hotel that includes most everything in the price.

Some hotels are right on the beach. Others involve transfers to the beach by taxi or bus, so factor in transportation costs, which can mount quickly if you stay 5 days to a week.

THE ALL-INCLUSIVES

A hugely popular option in Jamaica, the all-inclusive resort hotel concept finally has a foothold in The Bahamas. At most resorts, everything is included—sometimes even drinks. You get your room and all meals, plus entertainment and many watersports (although some cost extra). Some people find the cost of this all-inclusive holiday cheaper than if they'd paid individually for each item, and some simply appreciate knowing in advance what their final bill will be.

The first all-inclusive resort hotel in The Bahamas was **Club Med** (✆ **800/258-2633**) at its property on Paradise Island. This is not a swinging-singles kind of place; it's popular with everybody from honeymooners to families with kids along. There's another mammoth Club Med at Governor's Harbour on Eleuthera. Families with kids like it a lot here, and the resort also attracts scuba divers. There's a third branch in San Salvador, in the southern Bahamas, which has more of a luxurious hideaway atmosphere.

The biggest all-inclusive of them all, **Sandals** (✆ **800/SANDALS**), came to The Bahamas in 1995 on Cable Beach. This Jamaican company is now walking its sandals across the Caribbean, having established firm beachheads in Ocho Rios, Montego Bay, and Negril. The most famous of the all-inclusives (but not necessarily the best), it caters only to male-female couples, having long ago rescinded its initial policy of "Any two people in love."

RENTAL VILLAS & VACATION HOMES

You might rent a big villa, a good-size apartment in someone's condo, or even a small beach cottage (more accurately called a cabana).

Private apartments come with or without maid service (ask up front exactly what to expect). This is more of a no-frills option than the villas and condos. The apartments may not be in buildings with swimming pools, and they may not have a front desk to help you.

Many cottages or cabanas ideally open onto a beach, although others may be clustered around a communal swimming pool. Most of them are fairly simple, containing no more than a plain bedroom plus a small kitchen and bathroom. In the peak winter season, reservations should be made at least 5 or 6 months in advance.

VHR Worldwide (✆ **800/633-3284** or 201/767-9393) offers the most comprehensive portfolio of luxury villas, condominiums, resort suites, and apartments for rent not only in The Bahamas, but also in the Caribbean, Mexico, the United States, and Europe.

Hideaways International (✆ **888/843-4433** in the U.S., or 603/430-4433; www.hideaways.com) publishes ***Hideaways Guide,*** a 148-page pictorial directory of home rentals throughout the world, with full descriptions so you know what you're renting. Rentals range from cottages to staffed villas to whole islands! On most rentals you deal directly with owners. At condos and small resorts, Hideaways offers member discounts. Other services include specialty cruises, yacht charters, airline ticketing, car rentals, and hotel reservations. Annual membership is $129; a 4-month trial membership is $49.

Sometimes local tourist offices will also advise you on vacation-home rentals if you write or call them directly.

THE BAHAMIAN GUESTHOUSE

The guesthouse is where many Bahamians themselves stay when they're traveling in their own islands. In The Bahamas, however, the term "guesthouse" can mean anything. Sometimes so-called guesthouses are really like simple motels built around swimming pools. Others are small individual cottages, with their own kitchenettes, constructed around a main building in which you'll often find a bar and restaurant serving local food.

FAST FACTS: The Bahamas

American Express Representing American Express in The Bahamas is **Playtours,** on Shirley Street (between Charlotte and Parliament sts.), Nassau (✆ **242/322-2931**). Hours are 9am to 5pm Monday through Friday. The travel department is also open Saturday 9am to 1pm. If you present a personal check and an Amex card, you can buy traveler's checks here.

Business Hours In Nassau, Cable Beach, and Freeport/Lucaya, commercial banking hours are 9:30am to 3pm Monday through Thursday, 9:30am to 5pm on Friday. Hours are likely to vary widely in the Out Islands. Ask at your hotel. Most government offices are open Monday through Friday from 9am to 5pm, and most shops are open Monday through Saturday from 9am to 5pm.

Camera & Film Purchasing film in Nassau/Paradise Island or Freeport/Lucaya is relatively easy, if a little expensive. But stock up if you're going to the Out Islands and need a special kind.

Car Rentals See "Getting Around," earlier in this chapter. We do not recommend renting a car in The Bahamas.

Climate See "When to Go," earlier in this chapter.

Crime See "Safety," below.

Currency See "Money," earlier in this chapter.

Drug Laws Importing, possessing, or dealing in unlawful drugs, including marijuana, is a serious offense in The Bahamas, with heavy penalties. Customs officers may at their discretion conduct body searches for drugs or other contraband goods.

Drugstores Nassau and Freeport are amply supplied with pharmacies (see individual listings). However, if you're traveling in the Out Islands, it is always best to carry your prescribed medication with you, since pharmacies are harder to find.

Electricity Electricity is normally 120 volts, 60 cycles, AC. American appliances are fully compatible; British or European appliances will need both converters and adapters.

Embassies & Consulates The U.S. embassy is on Queen Street, P.O. Box N-8197, Nassau (✆ **242/322-4753**), and the Canadian consulate is on Shirley Street Shopping Plaza, Nassau (✆ **242/393-2123**). The British High Commission is in the BITCO Building (third floor), East Street, Nassau (✆ **242/325-7471**).

Emergencies Throughout The Bahamas, the number to call for a medical, dental, or hospital emergency is ✆ **911.** To report a fire, however, call ✆ **411.**

Holidays Public holidays observed in The Bahamas are New Year's Day, Good Friday, Easter Sunday, Easter Monday, Whitmonday (7 weeks after Easter), Labour Day (the first Fri in June), Independence Day (July 10), Emancipation Day (the first Mon in Aug), Discovery Day (Oct 12), Christmas, and Boxing Day (the day after Christmas). When a holiday falls on Saturday or Sunday, stores and offices are usually closed on the following Monday.

Hospitals See "Insurance, Health & Safety," earlier in this chapter.

Internet Access Access is limited on the islands, but it can be obtained. Cybercafe, in The Mall at Marathon in Nassau (✆ **242/394-6254**), is open daily from 8:30am to 8pm, charging 15¢ per minute; there are six computers available. There's another Internet cafe in Nassau, the Internet Café at the Downtown Mall on Bay Street (✆ **242/356-2217**), open the same hours, charges just 5¢ per minute. In Freeport, try the Cyberclub, Seventeen Center (✆ **242/351-4560**), open Monday to Saturday 9am to 8pm and charging 15¢ per minute; there are 30 computers available. In the Out Islands, you most often will be able access the Web at your hotel.

Language In The Bahamas, locals speak English, but sometimes with a marked accent that provides the clue to their ancestry—African, Irish, Scottish, or whatever.

Liquor Laws Liquor is sold in liquor stores and various convenience stores; it's readily available though not sold on Sundays. The legal drinking age is 18.

Mail & Postage Rates You'll need Bahamian (not U.S.) postage stamps to send postcards and letters. Most of the kiosks selling postcards also sell the stamps you'll need to mail them, so you probably won't need to visit the post office. Sending a postcard or an airmail letter (up to a half-oz. in weight) from The Bahamas to anywhere outside its borders (including the U.S., Canada, and the U.K.) costs 45¢ and 65¢, respectively, with 65¢ charged for each additional half-ounce of weight. Postcards and letters mailed within The Bahamas to anywhere else within The Bahamas cost 20¢ and 25¢ per half-ounce, respectively.

Mail to and from the Out Islands is sometimes slow. Airmail may go by air to Nassau and by boat to its final destination. If a resort has a U.S. or Nassau address, it is preferable to use it.

Newspapers & Magazines Three newspapers are circulated in Nassau and Freeport: the *Nassau Guardian,* the *Tribune,* and the *Freeport News.* Circulation in the Out Islands is limited and likely to be slow. You can find such papers as *The New York Times, Wall Street Journal, USA Today, The Miami Herald, Times of London,* and *Daily Telegraph* at newsstands in your hotel and elsewhere in Nassau.

Passports See "Entry Requirements & Customs," above.

Pets You'll have to get a valid import permit to bring any animal into The Bahamas. Application for such a permit must be made in writing, accompanied by a $10 processing fee and a $5 fax fee, to the **Director of Agriculture,** Department of Agriculture, P.O. Box N-3028, Nassau, The Bahamas (✆ **242/325-7413**), at least 4 weeks in advance.

Police Dial ✆ **911.**

Safety When going to Nassau (New Providence), Cable Beach, Paradise Island, or Freeport/Lucaya, exercise the kind of caution you would if visiting Miami. Whatever you do, if people peddling drugs approach you, steer well clear of them.

Women, especially, should take caution if walking alone on the streets of Nassau after dark, particularly if those streets appear to be deserted. Pickpockets (often foreigners) work the crowded casino floors of both Paradise Beach and Cable Beach. See that your wallet, money, or other valuables are secured.

If you're driving a rental car, always make sure your car door is locked, and never leave possessions in view in an automobile. Don't leave valuables, such as cameras and purses, lying unattended on the beach while you go for a swim. If you have valuables with you, especially jewelry, don't leave them unguarded in hotel rooms. Many of the bigger hotels will provide safes. Keep your hotel-room doors locked. Bahamian tourist officials often warn visitors, "If you've got it, don't flaunt it."

You're less likely to get mugged in the Out Islands, where life is generally more peaceful. There are some resort hotels that, even today, don't have locks on the doors.

Taxes Departure tax is $20 ($22 from Grand Bahama Island) for visitors ages 7 and up. International airline and steamship tickets issued in The Bahamas are subject to a nominal tax, which is written into the cost of the ticket. An 8% tax is imposed on hotel bills. There is no sales tax in The Bahamas.

Telephone Communications have improved recently, although some of the Out Islands are still difficult to reach. In recent years, virtually every hotel in The Bahamas seems to have installed a fax machine. Direct long-distance dialing between North America and Nassau, Grand Bahama, the Abacos, Andros, the Berry Islands, Bimini, Eleuthera, Harbour Island, Spanish Wells, the Exumas, and Stella Maris on Long Island is available.

To call The Bahamas from the U.S. or Canada, dial 1-242 plus the seven-digit local number. From the U.K., dial 001-242 plus the local seven-digit number.

To make a direct international call from The Bahamas to the U.S. or Canada, dial 1 plus the area code and local number. To call other countries, dial 011 plus the country code (the U.K. is 44, for example), the area code (usually without its initial zero), and the local number.

For local calls within The Bahamas, simply dial the seven-digit number. To call from one island to another within The Bahamas, dial 1-242 and then the seven-digit local number.

Note that the old coin-operated phones are still prevalent and still swallow coins. Each local call costs 25¢; you can use either Bahamian or U.S. quarters. Those old phones, however, are gradually being replaced by phones that use calling cards (debit cards), similar in appearance to a credit card, that come in denominations of $5, $10, $20, and $50. They can be bought from any office of BATELCO (Bahamas Telephone Co.).

BATELCO's main branch is on Kennedy Drive, Nassau (© **242/302-7000**), although a popular local branch lies in the commercial heart of Nassau, on East Street off Bay Street.

To get **directory assistance** within The Bahamas, dial © **916.** To reach an international or a domestic operator within The Bahamas, dial **0.** There is no distinction made in The Bahamas between the two types of operators.

To reach the major international services of **AT&T,** dial © **800/CALLATT** from any phone, or head for any phone with AT&T or USA DIRECT marked on the side of the booth. Picking up the handset will connect you with an AT&T operator. These phones are often positioned beside cruise-ship docks to help passengers disembarking on shore leave for the day. **MCI** can be reached at © **800/888-8000** or 800/624-1000.

Time Eastern Standard Time is used throughout The Bahamas, and daylight savings time is observed in the summer.

Tipping Many establishments add a service charge, but it's customary to leave something extra if service has been especially fine. If you're not sure whether service has been included in your bill, don't be shy—ask.

Bellboys and porters, at least in the expensive hotels, expect a tip of $1 per bag. It's also customary to tip your maid at least $2 per day—more if she or he has performed special services such as getting a shirt or blouse laundered. Most service personnel, including taxi drivers, waiters, and the like, expect 15% (20% in deluxe restaurants).

Tourist Offices See "Visitor Information," earlier in this chapter, and also specific island chapters.

Water Technically, tap water is drinkable throughout The Bahamas. But we still opt for bottled because it tastes better, and because your holiday isn't worth being shortchanged by a queasy stomach. Resorts tend to filter and chlorinate water more aggressively than most other establishments; anywhere else, bottled water is available at stores and supermarkets.

On many of the Out Islands, rainfall is the main source of water. Definitely drink bottled water when you're on them.

Weddings To marry here, bride and groom must both be in The Bahamas at the moment they apply for the $40 wedding license. If both are single and U.S. citizens, they must obtain an affidavit to that effect from the U.S. embassy in Nassau. The fee is $55 per person; you'll need to appear in person with ID such as a passport (and, if applicable, proof of divorce). If all of these requirements are met, you can then get married after staying for 24 hours in The Bahamas. No blood test is necessary. Contact the **Ministry of Tourism** at P.O. Box N-3701, Nassau, The Bahamas (© **242/302-2034**) for more details.

3

New Providence (Nassau/Cable Beach)

One million visitors a year have cast their vote: They want to visit Nassau, adjoining Cable Beach, or Paradise Island (which is covered separately in chapter 4). This is the center of all the action: the best shopping, the best entertainment, the most historic attractions—plus some of the best beaches in The Bahamas.

The capital of The Bahamas, the historic city of Nassau is a 35-minute flight from Miami. Despite the development and the modern hotels, a laid-back tropical atmosphere still hangs over the city, and it still offers a good dose of colonial charm. The commercial and banking hub of The Bahamas, as well as a mecca for shoppers, Nassau lies on the north side of New Providence, which is 34km (21 miles) long and 11km (7 miles) wide at its greatest point.

Cable Beach, a stretch of sand just west of the city, is lined with luxury resorts—in fact, the Nassau/Cable Beach area has the largest tourist infrastructure in The Bahamas, though there's another concentration of luxury hotels on Paradise Island. (If you want to stay right on the sands, don't choose a hotel in downtown Nassau itself. Head for Cable Beach or Paradise Island. You can easily reach the beach from a base in Nassau, but it won't be right outside your window.)

When you're based in Nassau/Cable Beach, you have an array of watersports, golf, tennis, and plenty of duty-free shopping nearby—and that's not to mention those fine, powdery beaches. In addition, the resorts, restaurants, and beaches of Paradise Island, discussed in the next chapter, are just a short distance away. (Paradise Island, which lies just opposite Nassau, is connected to New Providence Island by a toll bridge that costs $2 for cars, 25¢ for pedestrians; there's also frequent ferry and water-taxi service between Nassau and Paradise Island.)

As the sun goes down, Cable Beach and Paradise Island heat up, offering fine dining, glitzy casinos, cabaret shows, moonlight cruises, dance clubs, and romantic evening strolls. (We'd confine that evening stroll to Cable Beach or Paradise Island, though, and not the streets of downtown Nassau, which can be dangerous at night.)

The shops might draw a lot more business than the museums, but no city in The Bahamas is as rich in history as Nassau. You can take a "royal climb" up the Queen's Staircase to Fort Fincastle. These 66 steps lead to a fort said to have been cut in the sandstone cliffs by slaves in the 1790s. Other Nassau attractions include Ardastra Gardens, which feature 5 acres of landscaping and more than 300 exotic birds, mammals, and reptiles. (Most popular are the trained pink flamingos that march for audiences daily to their trainer's commands.)

It's surprising that Nassau has retained its overlay of British colonial charm despite its proximity to Florida. Yet, it truly hasn't become Americanized; despite new development, traffic,

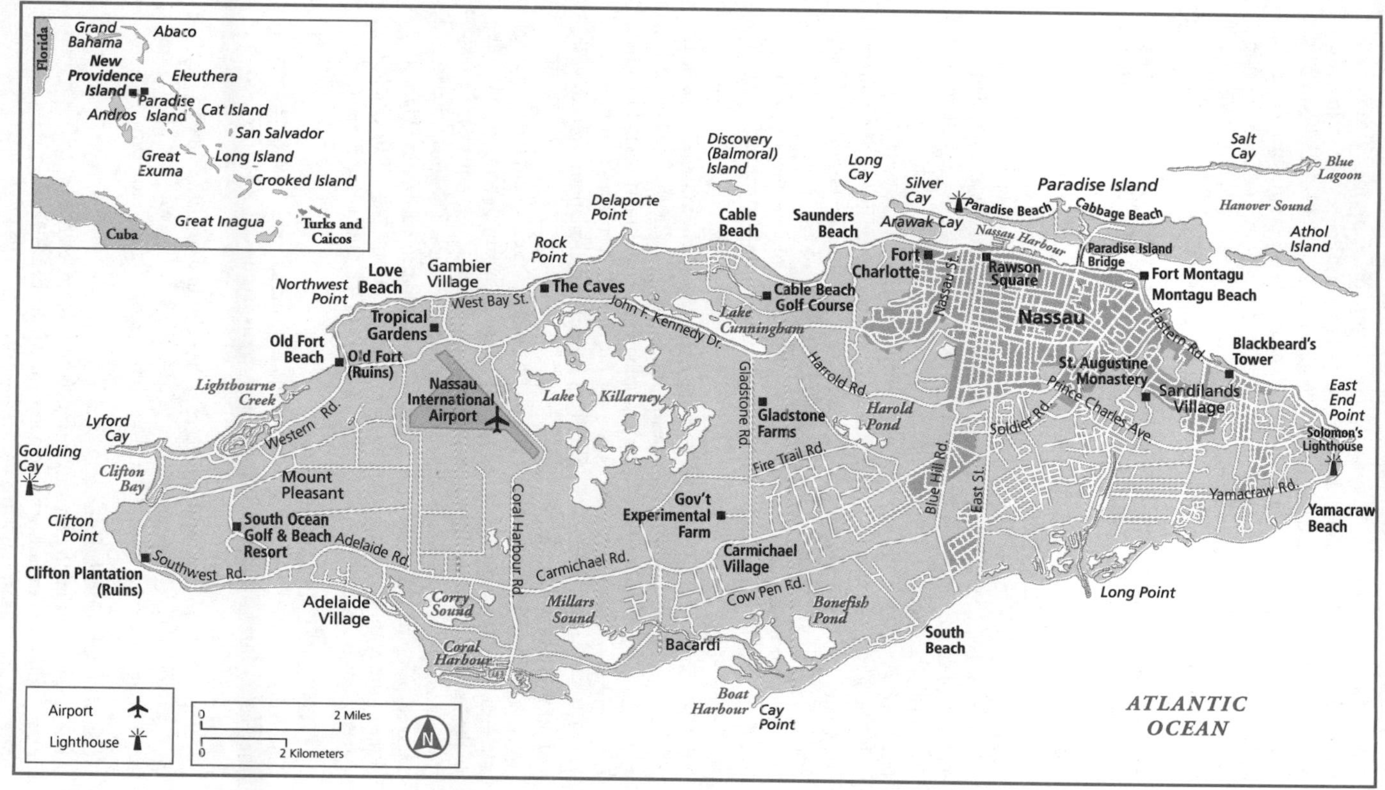

Florida
Grand Bahama
Abaco
New Providence Island
Paradise Island
Andros
Eleuthera
Cat Island
San Salvador
Great Exuma
Long Island
Crooked Island
Great Inagua
Turks and Caicos
Cuba
Discovery (Balmoral) Island
Long Cay
Silver Cay
Salt Cay
Blue Lagoon
Paradise Island
Paradise Beach
Cabbage Beach
Hanover Sound
Athol Island
Delaporte Point
Cable Beach
Saunders Beach
Arawak Cay
Nassau Harbour
Paradise Island Bridge
Rock Point
Fort Charlotte
Rawson Square
Fort Montagu
Montagu Beach
Northwest Point
Love Beach
Gambier Village
The Caves
West Bay St.
John F. Kennedy Dr.
Cable Beach Golf Course
Lake Cunningham
Nassau St.
Nassau
Eastern Rd.
Blackbeard's Tower
Tropical Gardens
Old Fort Beach
Old Fort (Ruins)
Lightbourne Creek
Nassau International Airport
Lake Killarney
Gladstone Rd.
Gladstone Farms
Harrold Rd.
Harold Pond
St. Augustine Monastery
Prince Charles Ave.
Soldier Rd.
Sandilands Village
East End Point
Solomon's Lighthouse
Lyford Cay
Western Rd.
Goulding Cay
Clifton Bay
Mount Pleasant
Fire Trail Rd.
Blue Hill Rd.
East St.
Yamacraw Rd.
Clifton Point
South Ocean Golf & Beach Resort
Adelaide Rd.
Coral Harbour Rd
Gov't Experimental Farm
Yamacraw Beach
Clifton Plantation (Ruins)
Southwest Rd.
Carmichael Rd.
Carmichael Village
Adelaide Village
Corry Sound
Millars Sound
Cow Pen Rd.
Bonefish Pond
Long Point
Coral Harbour
Bacardi
South Beach
Boat Harbour
Cay Point
Airport
Lighthouse
0
2 Miles
0
2 Kilometers
N
ATLANTIC OCEAN

and cruise-ship crowds, Nassau's a long way from becoming another Miami. Stately old homes and public buildings still stand proudly among the modern high-rises and bland government buildings. Tropical foliage lines streets where horse-drawn surreys still trot by, carrying visitors on leisurely tours. Police officers in white starched jackets and colorful pith helmets still direct traffic on the main streets as they have long done. It could almost be England—but for the weather, that is.

1 Orientation

ARRIVING

BY PLANE Planes land at **Nassau International Airport** (© **242/377-1759**), which lies 13km (8 miles) west of Nassau by Lake Killarney.

There is no bus service from the airport to Cable Beach, Nassau, or Paradise Island. Your hotel may provide airport transfers if you've made arrangements in advance; these are often included in package deals. There are also any number of car-rental offices here if you plan to have a car while on New Providence Island (see "Getting Around," below, though we don't really think you need one).

If you don't have a lift arranged, take a taxi to your hotel. From the airport to the center of Nassau, expect to pay around $20; from the airport to Cable Beach, $15; from the airport to Paradise Island, $25 to $27 including toll. Drivers expect to be tipped 15%, and some will remind you should you "forget." You don't need to stop at a currency exchange office before departing the airport: U.S. currency is fine for these (and any other) transactions.

BY CRUISE SHIP In recent years, Nassau has spent millions of dollars expanding its port so that 11 cruise ships. Sounds great in theory. Practically speaking, however, facilities in Nassau, Cable Beach, and Paradise Island become extremely overcrowded as soon as the big boats dock. You'll have to stake out your space on the beach, and you will find shops and attractions overrun with visitors every day you're in port.

Cruise ships dock near Rawson Square, the heart of the city and the shopping area—and the best place to begin a tour of Nassau. Unless you want to go to one of the beach strips along Cable Beach or Paradise Island, you won't need a taxi. You can go on a shopping expedition near where you dock: The site of the Straw Market (being rebuilt at the moment after a fire) is nearby, at Market Plaza; Bay Street—the main shopping artery—is also close; and the Nassau International Bazaar is at the intersection of Woodes Rogers Walk and Charlotte Street.

VISITOR INFORMATION

The Bahamas Ministry of Tourism maintains a **tourist information booth** at the Nassau International Airport in the Arrivals terminal (© **242/377-6806**). Hours are from 8:30am to 11:30pm daily.

Information can also be obtained from the Information Desk at the **Ministry of Tourism's Office,** Rawson Square (© **242/328-7810**), which is open Monday through Saturday from 8:30am to 5pm, Sunday 8:30am to 3pm.

THE LAY OF THE LAND

Most of the hotels in Nassau are city hotels and are not on the water. If you want to stay right on the sands, choose a hotel in Cable Beach (later in this chapter) or on Paradise Island (see chapter 4).

Rawson Square is the heart of Nassau, lying just a short walk from **Prince George Wharf,** where the big cruise ships, usually from Florida, berth. Here

Favorite New Providence Experiences

Listening to the Sounds of Goombay. At some local joint, you can enjoy an intoxicating beat and such island favorites as "Goin' Down Burma Road," "Get Involved," and "John B. Sail."

A Ride in a Horse-Drawn Surrey. If you'd like to see Nassau as the Duke of Windsor did when he was governor, consider this unique form of transportation. It's elegant, romantic, and nostalgic. Surreys await passengers at Rawson Square, in the exact center of Nassau.

A Glass-Bottom Boat Ride. Right in the middle of Nassau's harbor, numerous boats wait to take you through the colorful sea gardens off New Providence Island. In the teeming reefs offshore, you'll meet all sorts of sea creatures that inhabit this underwater wonderland.

An Idyllic Day on Blue Lagoon Island. It's like an old Hollywood fantasy of a tropical island. Located off the eastern end of Paradise Island, this Blue Lagoon has seven sandy beaches. Boats from Nassau Harbour take you there and back.

you'll see the Churchill Building, which contains the offices of the Bahamian prime minister along with other government ministries.

Busy **Bay Street,** the main shopping artery, begins on the south side of Rawson Square. This was the street of the infamous "Bay Street Boys," a group of rich, white Bahamians who once controlled all political and economic activity on New Providence.

On the opposite side of Rawson Square is **Parliament Square,** with a statue of a youthful Queen Victoria. Here are more government houses and the House of Assembly. These are Georgian and neo-Georgian buildings, some dating from the late 1700s.

The courthouse is separated by a little square from the **Nassau Public Library and Museum,** which opens onto Bank Lane. It was the former Nassau Gaol. South of the library, across Shirley Street, are the remains of the **Royal Victoria Hotel,** which opened the year the American Civil War was launched (1861) and once hosted blockade runners and Confederate spies.

A walk down Parliament Street leads to the post office, and philatelists may want to stop in, since some Bahamian stamps are collector's items.

Going south, moving farther away from the water, Elizabeth Avenue takes you to the **Queen's Staircase,** one of the major landmarks of Nassau, leading to Bennet's Hill and Fort Fincastle.

If you return to Bay Street, you'll discover the **Straw Market,** a former emporium where you could buy all sorts of souvenirs; check with local officials for the status of this landmark as its restoration continues. At the intersection of Charlotte Street is another major shopping emporium, the **Nassau International Bazaar.**

In Nassau, and especially in the rest of The Bahamas, you will seldom, if ever, find street numbers on hotels or other businesses. Sometimes in the more remote places, you won't even find street names. Get directions before heading somewhere in particular. Of course, you can always ask along the way, as Bahamians tend to be very helpful.

2 Getting Around

BY TAXI

You can easily rely on taxis and skip renting a car. The rates for New Providence, including Nassau, are set by the government. Working meters are required in all taxis, although you will also find gypsy cabs without meters. When you get in, the fixed rate is $2.20, plus 30¢ for each additional .5km (¼ mile). Each passenger over two pays an extra $3. Taxis can also be hired at the hourly rate of $20 to $23 for a five-passenger cab. Luggage is carried at a cost of 50¢ per piece, although the first two pieces are transported free. The radio-taxi call number is **© 242/323-4555.** It's also easy to get a taxi at the airport or at one of the big hotels.

BY CAR

You don't need to rent a car. It's a lot easier to rely on taxis when you're ready to leave the beach and do a little exploring.

However, if you choose to drive anyway, perhaps for a day of touring the whole island, some of the biggest U.S. car-rental companies maintain branches at the airport, downtown, and on Paradise Island. **Avis** (**© 800/228-0668;** www.avis.com) operates at the airport (© 242/377-7121 locally), and also has branches at the cruise-ship docks at Bay Street and Marlborough Street, behind the British Colonial Hilton (© 242/326-6380), and in the Paradise Island Shopping Plaza (© 242/363-2061). **Budget Rent-a-Car** (**© 800/527-0700;** www.budgetrentacar.com) has a branch at the airport (© 242/377-9000), and another on Paradise Island, at Hurricane InnSun Spree next to the police station (© 242/363-3095). **Dollar Rent-a-Car** (**© 800/800-4000,** or 242/377-7231 locally; www.dollarcar.com) rents at the airport. **Hertz** (**© 800/654-3131;** www.hertz.com) has an airport location (© 242/377-8684) and is also in downtown Nassau at East Bay Street (© 242/393-2326).

Again, we remind you: Drive on the left!

BY JITNEY

The least-expensive means of transport is by jitney—medium-size buses that leave from the downtown Nassau area to outposts on New Providence. The fare is 75¢, and exact change is required. They operate daily from 6:30am to 7pm. Some hotels on Paradise Island and Cable Beach run their own free jitney service. Buses to the Cable Beach area leave from the Navy Lion Road depot. Buses to the eastern area depart from the Frederick Street North depot, and buses to the malls leave from Marlborough Street East.

Moments A Surrey with a Fringe on Top

The elegant, traditional way to see Nassau is in a horse-drawn surrey—the kind with the fringe on top and a wilted hibiscus stuck in the straw hat shielding the horse from the sun. Before you get in, you should negotiate with the driver and agree on the price. The average charge is $5 per person for a 25-minute ride. The maximum load is three adults plus one or two children under the age of 12. The surreys are available daily from 9am to 4:30pm, except when the horses are resting (that's 1–3pm from May–Oct, and 1–2pm from Nov–Apr). You'll find the surreys at Rawson Square, off Bay Street.

Tips On Your Own Sturdy Feet

This is the only way to see Old Nassau, unless you rent a horse and carriage. All the major attractions and the principal stores are close enough to walk to. You can even walk to Cable Beach or Paradise Island, although it's a hike in the hot sun. Confine your walking to the daytime, and beware of pickpockets and purse-snatchers. In the evening, avoid walking the streets of downtown Nassau, where muggings occur.

BY BOAT

Water-taxis operate daily from 9am to 5:30pm at 20-minute intervals between Paradise Island and Prince George Wharf at a round-trip cost of $2 per person. There is also ferry service from the end of Casuarina Drive on Paradise Island across the harbor to Rawson Square for a round-trip fare of $2 per person. The ferry operates daily from 9:30am to 4:15pm, with departures every half hour from both sides of the harbor.

BY SCOOTER OR BICYCLE

Lots of visitors like to rent mopeds to explore the island. Unless you're an experienced moped rider, stay on quiet roads until you feel at ease. (Don't start out in all the congestion on Bay St.!) Many hotels have rentals on the premises. If yours doesn't, try **Knowles** (© **242/356-0741**), outside the British Colonial Hotel, which rents scooters for $50 per day. Included in the rental price are insurance and mandatory helmets for both drivers and passengers.

FAST FACTS: New Providence

American Express The local representative is **Playtours,** 303 Shirley St., between Charlotte and Parliament streets, Nassau (© **242/322-2931**). Hours are Monday through Friday from 9am to 5pm.

Climate See "When to Go," in chapter 2.

Dentist Try the dental department of the **Princess Margaret Hospital** on Sands Road (© **242/322-2861**).

Doctor For the best service, use a staff member of the **Princess Margaret Hospital** on Sands Road (© **242/322-2861**).

Drugstores Try **Lowes Pharmacy,** Palm Dale (© **242/322-8594**), open Monday through Saturday from 8am to 6:30pm. They also have two branches: **Harbour Bay Shopping Center** (© **242/393-4813**), open Monday through Saturday 8am to 8:30pm and Sunday from 9am to 5pm; and **Town Center Mall** (© **242/325-6482**), open Monday through Saturday 10am to 9pm. Nassau has no late-night pharmacies.

Embassies & Consulates See "Fast Facts: The Bahamas," in chapter 2.

Emergencies For any major emergency, call © **911.**

Eyeglass Repair The **Optique Shoppe,** 22 Parliament St. at the corner of Shirley Street (© **242/322-3910**), is convenient to the center of Nassau. Hours are Monday through Friday from 9am to 5pm and on Saturday from 9am to noon.

Hospitals The government-operated **Princess Margaret Hospital** on Sands Road (✆ **242/322-2861**) is one of the major hospitals in The Bahamas. The privately owned **Doctors Hospital,** 1 Collins Ave. (✆ **242/322-8411**), is the most modern private healthcare facility in the region.

Information See "Visitor Information," above.

Laundry & Dry Cleaning **The Laundromat Superwash** (✆ **242/323-4018**), at the corner of Nassau Street and Boyd Road, offers coin-operated machines; it's open 24 hours a day, 7 days a week. In the same building is the **New Oriental Dry Cleaner** (✆ **242/323-7249**). Another dry cleaner a short drive north of the center of town is the **Jiffy Quality Cleaner** (✆ **242/323-6771**) at the corner of Blue Hill Road and Cordeaux Avenue.

Photographic Needs The largest camera store in Nassau is **John Bull,** Bay Street (✆ **242/322-3328**), a block east of Rawson Square.

Police Dial ✆ **911** or ✆ **919.**

Post Office **The Nassau General Post Office,** at the top of Parliament Street on East Hill Street (✆ **242/322-3344**), is open Monday through Friday from 9am to 5:30pm and on Saturday from 8:30am to 1pm. Note that you can buy stamps from most postcard kiosks.

Safety Avoid walking in downtown Nassau at night, where there are sometimes robberies and muggings. (Most tourists are never affected, and Nassau is certainly safer than Kingston, Jamaica, or Port of Spain, Trinidad, but better safe than sorry.) Cable Beach and Paradise Island are much safer places to be in the evening.

Taxes There is no sales tax, though there is an 8% hotel tax. All visitors leaving The Bahamas pay a $15 departure tax.

3 Where to Stay

In the hotel descriptions that follow, we've listed regular room prices or "rack rates," but these are simply for ease of comparison. They are likely to be accurate for smaller properties, but you can almost always do better at the larger hotels and resorts. *Read the section "Package Deals" in chapter 2 before you book a hotel separately from your airfare,* and if you do book yourself, always inquire about honeymoon specials, golf packages, summer weeks, and other discounts. In many cases, too, a travel agent can get you a package deal that would be cheaper than these official rates.

Hotels add an 8% tax "resort levy" to your rate. Sometimes this is quoted as part of the price; at other times, it's added to your final bill. When you are quoted a rate, always ask if the tax is included. Many hotels also add a 15% service charge to your bill. Ask about these charges in advance so you won't be shocked when you receive the final tab.

Taxes and service are not included in the rates listed below. We'll lead off with a selection of hotels within the heart of Nassau, followed by accommodations in Cable Beach. Most visitors prefer to stay at Cable Beach since the resorts here are right on the sand. But it is possible to stay in Nassau and commute to the beaches at Cable Beach or Paradise Island; it's cheaper but less convenient. Those who prefer the ambience of Old Nassau's historic district and being near the best shops may decide to stay in town.

NASSAU

VERY EXPENSIVE

Graycliff ★★ Now in a kind of nostalgic decay, Graycliff remains the grande dame of downtown Nassau hotels even though her tiara is a bit tarnished and her age showing. In spite of its drawbacks, this place still has its devotees, especially among older readers. Originally an 18th-century private home and an example of Georgian colonial architecture, it's now an intimate inn, with an old-fashioned atmosphere. Even though the inn isn't on the beach, people who can afford to stay anywhere often choose Graycliff because it epitomizes the old-world style and grace that evokes Nassau back in the days when the Duke and Duchess of Windsor were in residence. Churchill, of course, can no longer be seen paddling around in the swimming pool with a cigar in his mouth, and the Beatles are long gone, but the three-story Graycliff continues without the visiting celebs, who today head for Paradise Island. Beach lovers usually go by taxi to either nearby Goodman's Bay or to the Western Esplanade Beach, nearly adjacent to Arawak Cay. The bigger British Colonial Hilton is Graycliff's main competitor; they both have a rather staid, deliberately unflashy ambience.

The historic garden rooms in the main house, are large and individually decorated with antiques, though the better units are the more modern garden rooms. The Yellow Bird, Hibiscus, and Pool cottages are ideal choices, but the most luxurious accommodation of all is the Mandarino Suite, with Asian decor, a king-size bed, an oversize bathroom, and a private balcony overlooking the swimming pool. Bathrooms are spacious, with shower-tub combinations deluxe toiletries and robes.

W. Hill St. (P.O. Box N-10246), Nassau, The Bahamas. ✆ **800/688-0076** in the U.S., or 242/322-2796. Fax 242/326-6110. www.graycliff.com. 20 units. Winter $290–$400 double, $310 poolside cottage for 2; off-season $200 double, $250 poolside cottage for 2. AE, MC, V. Free parking. Bus: 10 or 21A. **Amenities:** 2 restaurants, 2 bars; 3 swimming pools; health club; Jacuzzi; sauna; room service (8am–11:30pm); concierge; laundry service; dry cleaning; babysitting; massage. *In room:* A/C, TV, minibar, hair dryer, safe.

EXPENSIVE

British Colonial Hilton ★★ In the newly refurbished British Colonial Hilton, there's a palpable air of the long-ago days when The Bahamas was firmly within the political and social orbit of Britain. This landmark seven-story hotel has seen its share of ups and downs over the years. Plush and glamorous when it was built in 1900, it burned to the ground in 1920, and was rebuilt 3 years later before deteriorating into a flophouse. Between 1996 and 1999, a Canadian entrepreneur poured $68 million into its restoration.

Don't expect the glitz and glitter of Cable Beach or Paradise Island here—the Hilton is after business travelers rather than the casino crowd. It also lacks the aristocratic credentials of Graycliff (see above). Nonetheless, it's a dignified and friendly, but rather sedate, hotel with a discreetly upscale decor (no Disney-style themes or gimmicks). Bedrooms are a bit on the small side, but capped with rich crown moldings and accessorized with tile or stone-sheathed bathrooms with shower-tub combinations. The staff, incidentally, is superbly trained and motivated; we've found them upbeat and hardworking. There's a small beach a few steps away, but it's not very appealing (it's on the channel separating New Providence from Paradise Island, with no "cleansing" wave action at all).

The cuisine at the British Colonial is good standard fare, which doesn't even try to compete with the deluxe viands at Graycliff (see above). The most upscale restaurant is Wedgwood (see "Where to Dine," later in this chapter). Less formal is Portofino, a casual Italian trattoria. The Patio Grill offers light lunches

Nassau Accommodations

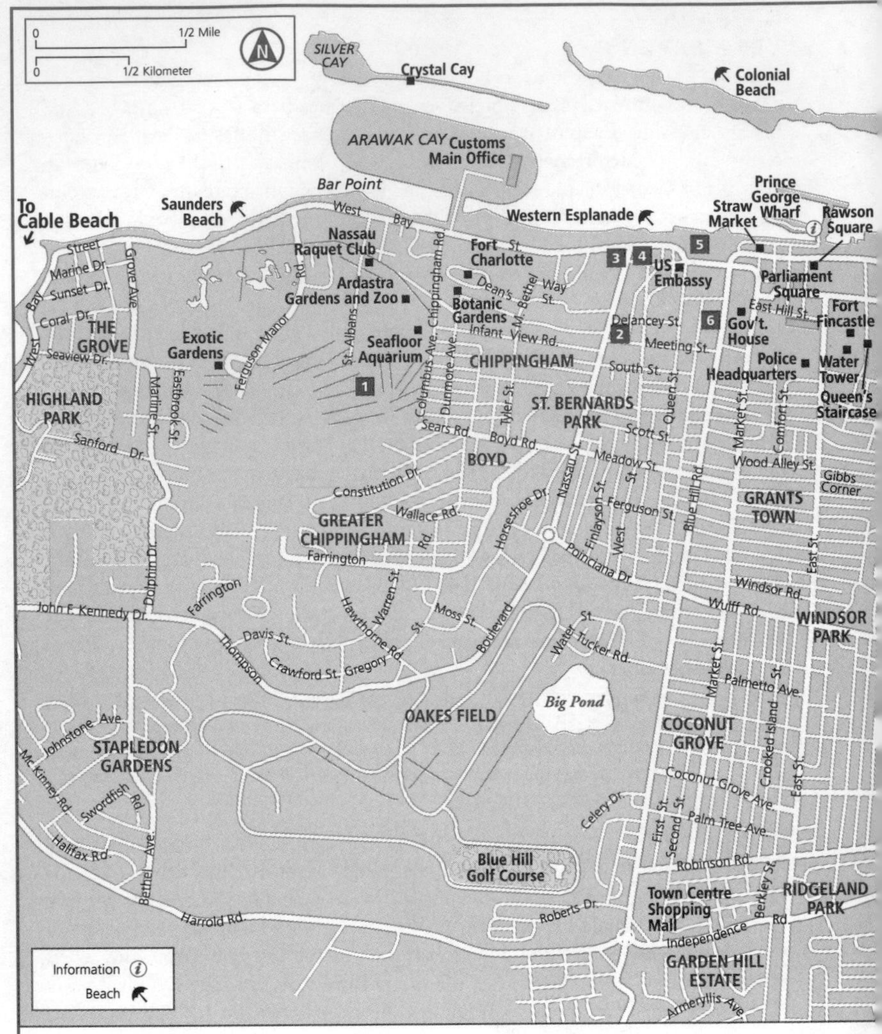

British Colonial Hilton **5**
Buena Vista Hotel **2**
Dillet's Guest House **1**
El Greco Hotel **4**
Graycliff **6**
Holiday Inn Junkanoo Beach **3**
Nassau Harbour Club **7**
Ocean Spray Hotel **4**

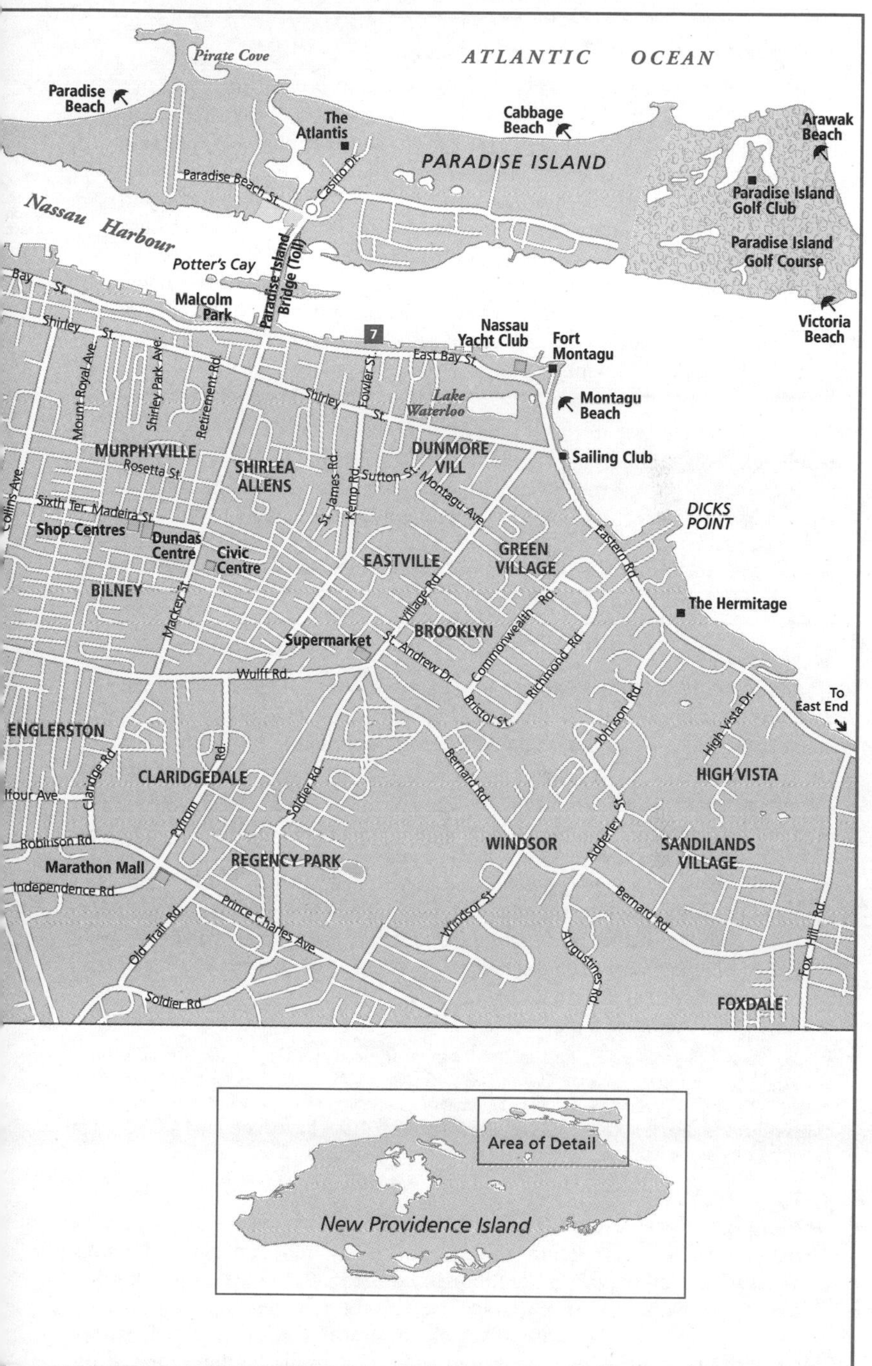

ATLANTIC OCEAN
Pirate Cove
Paradise Beach
The Atlantis
Cabbage Beach
Arawak Beach
PARADISE ISLAND
Paradise Beach St.
Casino Dr.
Paradise Island Golf Club
Paradise Island Golf Course
Nassau Harbour
Potter's Cay
Paradise Island Bridge (Toll)
Bay St.
Malcolm Park
Victoria Beach
Shirley St.
7
Nassau Yacht Club
Fort Montagu
East Bay St.
Mount Royal Ave.
Shirley Park Ave.
Retirement Rd.
Fowler St.
Lake Waterloo
Montagu Beach
MURPHYVILLE
Rosetta St.
SHIRLEA ALLENS
St. James Rd.
Kemp Rd.
Sutton St.
DUNMORE VILL
Montagu Ave.
Sailing Club
Collins Ave.
Sixth Ter. Madeira St.
Shop Centres
Dundas Centre
Civic Centre
BILNEY
Mackey St.
EASTVILLE
Village Rd.
GREEN VILLAGE
Eastern Rd.
DICKS POINT
Commonwealth Rd.
The Hermitage
BROOKLYN
Supermarket
St. Andrew Dr.
Richmond Rd.
Wulff Rd.
Bristol St.
Johnson Rd.
High Vista Dr.
To East End
ENGLERSTON
Claridge Rd.
CLARIDGEDALE
Pyfrom Rd.
Soldier Rd.
Bernard Rd.
HIGH VISTA
lfour Ave.
Robinson Rd.
Marathon Mall
Independence Rd.
REGENCY PARK
WINDSOR
Adderley St.
SANDILANDS VILLAGE
Bernard Rd.
Old Trail Rd.
Prince Charles Ave.
Windsor St.
Augustines Rd.
Fox Hill Rd.
Soldier Rd.
FOXDALE
Area of Detail
New Providence Island

Fun Fact In Suite Double O, A "License to Kill"

In both *Thunderball* and *Never Say Never Again,* James Bond, or secret agent 007, was served shaken martinis at the British Colonial. To commemorate that historic event, the Hilton-owned property now has a "Double-O" suite filled with Bond memorabilia, including posters, books, CDs, movie stills, and all the best Bond flicks, including *Goldfinger* and *Live and Let Die.* Guests can take a Bond book from the suite, perhaps *Tomorrow Never Dies,* and curl up on a chaise lounge at the beach. The suite is a one-bedroom unit with living room and ocean views. When you get tired of the movie Bond, you can stroll over and meet the real Bond, namely, Sean Connery who is often at his island home on nearby Lyford Cay—that is, if 007 is kind enough to extend an invite.

beside the pool. A woodsy-looking bar, Blackbeard's Cove, evokes a private club in London, and attracts the local suit-and-tie crowd for after-work drinks.

1 Bay St. (P.O. Box N-7148), Nassau, The Bahamas. ✆ **800/HILTONS** in the U.S. and Canada, or 242/322-3301. Fax 242/302-9009. www.hilton.com. 291 units. Winter $239–$299 double, $340–$1,133 suite; off-season $203–$254 double, $320–$1,133 suite. AE, DC, MC, V. Bus: 10. **Amenities:** 2 restaurants, 3 bars; pool; health club; Jacuzzi; 24-hr. room service; babysitting; laundry/dry cleaning; bike rentals. *In room:* A/C, TV, minibar, coffeemaker, hair dryer, safe.

MODERATE

Holiday Inn Junkanoo Beach West of downtown Nassau and overlooking Junkanoo Beach, the hotel lies exactly between the Atlantis and Crystal Palace casinos. Although not as fine as Cable Beach, Junkanoo is also a safe beach with tranquil waters, white sands, and a lot of shells; the hotel offers lounge chairs on the beach but no waiter service for drinks. This place is a good value for those who don't want to pay the higher prices charged by the more deluxe hotels along Cable Beach. All the motel-style bedrooms have a view of either the beach or Nassau Harbour, and they come with extras you don't always find in a moderately priced choice, such as alarm clocks, two-line phones, and a working desk. All come with well-maintained bathrooms containing shower-tub combinations.

The on-site Bay Street Grille is not reason enough to stay here, although you can dine outside in a tropical courtyard overlooking the pool. The West Coast Bar and Grill is another dining option.

W. Bay St. (P.O. Box SS-19055), Nassau, The Bahamas. ✆ **800/465-4329** or 242/356-0000. Fax 242/323-1408. www.basshotels.com/holiday-inn. 183 units. Winter $149 double, $179 suite; off-season $99 double, $129 suite. AE, DISC, MC, V. Bus: 10 or 17. **Amenities:** 2 restaurants, bar; 2 heated swimming pools; fitness center; tour desk; laundry/dry cleaning; room service (7am–11pm); boutiques. *In room:* A/C, TV, minibar, fridge, coffeemaker, hair dryer, iron/ironing board, safe.

INEXPENSIVE

Buena Vista Hotel Although this place really revolves around its restaurant (reviewed in "Where to Dine," below), it rents a few spacious bedrooms upstairs. It's a good bargain if you don't mind the lack of resort-style facilities. The building, with a pale pink facade, started out a century ago as a private home, and stands 1km (½-mile) west of downtown Nassau. Expect a pastel decor, with a tasteful mix of antiques and reproductions. Each room comes with a small bath containing a shower-tub combination. The staff might be a bit distracted because of the demands of the busy restaurant downstairs. Bus no. 16

carries you on a short eastbound trek into downtown Nassau, and you're about 10 minutes from the nearest beach.

Delancy and Augusta sts. (P.O. Box N-564), Nassau, The Bahamas. © **242/322-2811.** Fax 242/322-5881. www.buenavista-restaurant.com. 5 units. Mid-Apr to mid-Dec $70 double, $80 triple; mid-Dec to mid-Apr $100 double, $110 triple. AE, MC, V. Bus: 16. **Amenities:** Restaurant, bar; limited room service; laundry. *In room:* A/C, TV, refrigerator, coffeemaker.

Dillet's Guest House *Value* This is New Providence's only B&B. It is not for everyone, however, as it suffers from some drawbacks; it does not really achieve the quality level of, say, a similarly priced B&B in an American city. In the 1920s, local contractor Edward Dillet built the house just off West Bay and welcomed family, friends, and acquaintances to spend time here. Later, he expanded his home into a small inn; now his daughter Iris invites travelers to do the same. Each room has such amenities as cable TV, a ceiling fan, a clock radio, a good bed, and a minibar stocked with soda (no alcohol) and chips. Five of the rooms have full kitchenettes, though the bathrooms are small, each with a shower-tub combination. The house is informal and homey—nothing fancy, but spotless and charming. The building's focal point is a gracefully appointed living room, with a large, striking coral-stone fireplace. No smoking.

One of the main drawbacks is that the Chippingham section in which the B&B lies is not entirely safe at night. Dillet's posts an armed guard outside at night. To reach the nearest beach is an unpleasant 7-minute walk, often past roadkill. After you come to the bus stop, it's still a 5- to 10-minute bus ride to the nearest beach. You can catch the no. 10 or 38 bus to Cable Beach for $1. You can also rent a bike at Dillet's and tour the area for $15 a day. A well-known artist and relative of the Dillet family, John Cox, lives in a cottage in the garden, and he welcomes visits from guests to see whatever painting he's working on at the moment.

After a breakfast of freshly baked pastries, you might request an authentic Bahamian dinner that night for around $30 per person; Iris can also arrange a picnic for you to take to the beach.

Dunmore Ave. and Strachan St., Chippingham, Nassau, The Bahamas. © **242/325-1133.** Fax 242/325-7183. www.islandeaze.com/dillets/. 7 units. Winter $125 double; off-season $100 double. Extra person $35. Rates include continental breakfast. No credit cards. Free parking. Bus: 10. **Amenities:** Restaurant, bar; pool; art gallery; laundry. *In room:* A/C, TV, minibar, no phone.

El Greco Hotel Across the street from Lighthouse Beach, and a short walk from the shops and restaurants of Bay Street, El Greco is a well-managed bargain choice that attracts many European travelers. The Greek owners and staff genuinely seem to care about their guests—in fact, the two-story hotel seems more like a small European B&B than your typical Bahamian hotel.

The midsize rooms aren't that exciting, but they're clean and comfortable, with decent beds and small tile bathrooms, containing shower-tub combinations.

Moments What to Do on a Rainy Day?

To cheer your spirits, head first for the **Pink Pearl** (p. 97) and order local conch drizzled with a tamarind-flavored barbecue sauce. Hopefully, it'll be a weekend when a jazz combo plays on a side porch. Tearing yourself away, head over to the **Café Matisse** (p. 97) and ask for an order of apple semifreddo with kiwi sauce. After downing this touch of heaven, you'll be walking the streets outside *Singin' in the Rain.*

After an extensive post-hurricane refurbishment in 1999, the bedrooms have a brighter decor—a sort of Mediterranean motif, each with two ceiling fans and carpeted floors. Accommodations are built around a courtyard that contains statues crafted in the Italian baroque style, draped with lots of bougainvillea. There is no on-site restaurant, but you can walk to many places nearby for meals.

W. Bay St. (P.O. Box N-4187), Nassau, The Bahamas. ✆ **242/325-1121.** Fax 242/325-1124. www.bahamasnet.com. 27 units. Winter $109 double, $150 suite; off-season $89 double, $125 suite. AE, DISC, MC, V. Free parking. Bus: 10. **Amenities:** Restaurant, bar; pool; babysitting. *In room:* A/C, TV.

Nassau Harbour Club Don't expect lush and sprawling gardens, or much peace and privacy here—this hotel is in the heart of Nassau's action and is usually overrun in March and early April with college kids on spring break. A compound of two-story pink buildings from the early 1960s arranged like a horseshoe around a concrete terrace, it occupies a bustling strip of land between busy Bay Street and the edge of the channel that separates New Providence from Paradise Island. From your room, you'll have views of yachts and boats moored at a nearby marina, and there is easy access to the shops, bars, and restaurants of downtown Nassau and within the Harbour Bay Shopping Centre, a few steps away. Throughout, it's down-to-earth and just a bit funky—a huge contrast with the glitter of such megaresorts as the Atlantis. Bedrooms are simple and small but comfortable and equipped with bathrooms containing shower-tub combinations. However, they are a little worn and located near the animated hubbub of the busy bar.

E. Bay St. (P.O. Box SS-5755), Nassau, The Bahamas. ✆ **242/393-0771.** Fax 242/393-5393. www.thetrip.onlinevacationmall.com. 50 units. Winter $100–$130 double, $140 suite; off-season $90–$110 double, $120 suite. Extra person $25. AE, MC, V. Free parking. Bus: 11 or 19. **Amenities:** Restaurant; swimming pool; bar; laundry. *In room:* A/C, TV, fridge.

Ocean Spray Hotel This modest four-story corner hotel is a short stroll from the shopping district and across the street from a good beach. Midsize bedrooms have comfortable twin beds, carpeting, and your basic Miami-motel decor. Although furnishings show some wear, they're clean and reasonably comfortable, though bathrooms are small, each with a shower-tub combination. Students on spring break would be happy here.

This hotel is better known for its on-site restaurant and bar, Europe, than it is for its rooms.

W. Bay St. (P.O. Box N-3035), Nassau, The Bahamas. ✆ **242/322-8032.** Fax 242/325-5731. www.oceansprayhotel.com. 30 units. Winter $110 double; off-season $85 double. AE, MC, V. Free parking. Bus: 10. **Amenities:** Restaurant, bar; babysitting; laundry. *In room:* A/C, TV, refrigerator.

CABLE BEACH

The glittering shoreline of Cable Beach, located west of Nassau, is topped only by Paradise Island (see chapter 4). It has loyal fans, many of whom think Paradise Island is too snobbish. Cable Beach has for years attracted visitors with its broad stretches of beachfront, a wide array of sports facilities, and great nightlife, including casino action. Deluxe or first-class resorts, two of which are all-inclusive, line the shoreline.

VERY EXPENSIVE

Breezes ★ SuperClubs, which competes successfully with Sandals (see below) in Jamaica, spent $125 million transforming a tired old relic, the Ambassador Beach Hotel, into this all-inclusive resort. The nearby Sandals is more imposing, elegant, stylish, and upscale, with better amenities and views. Rowdier and more

Cable Beach Accommodations & Dining

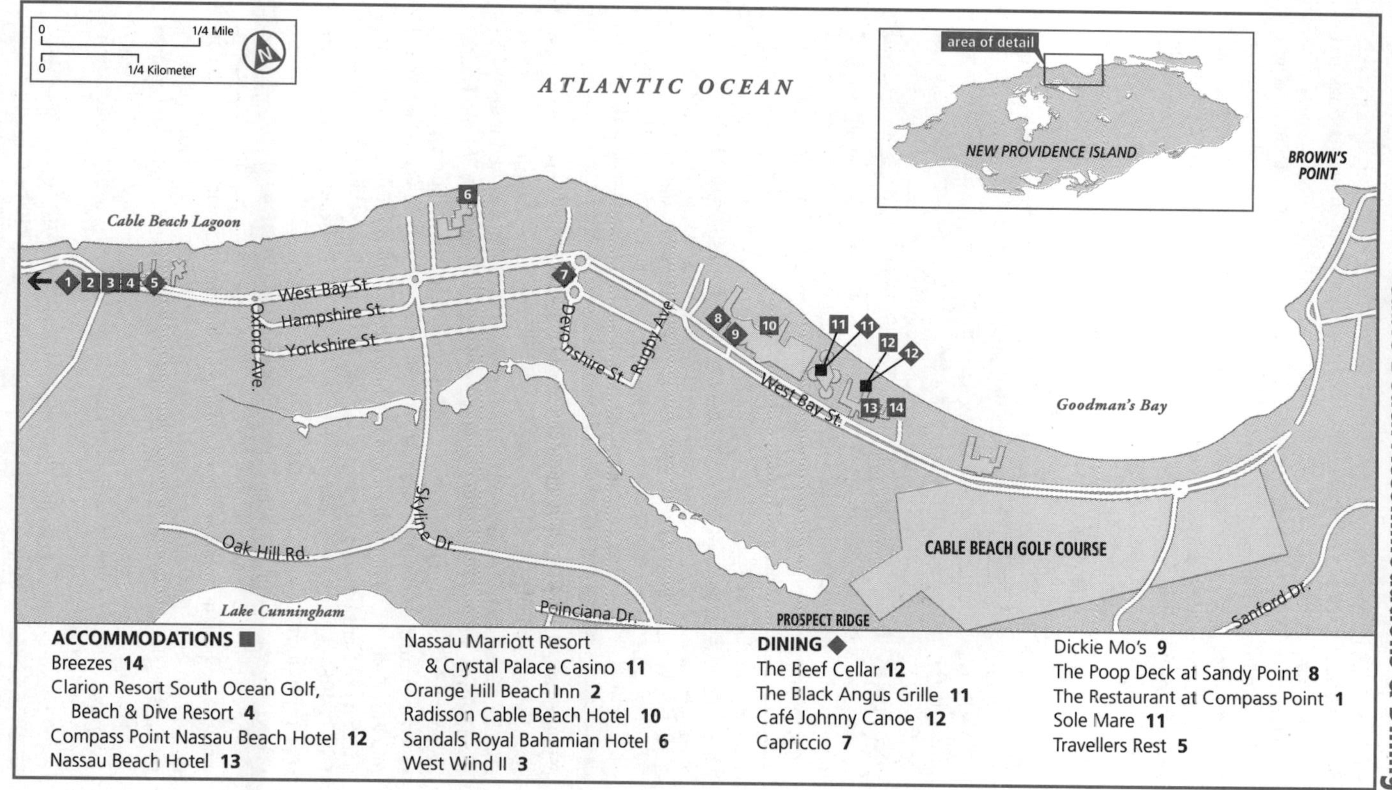
0
1/4 Mile
0
1/4 Kilometer
ATLANTIC OCEAN
area of detail
NEW PROVIDENCE ISLAND
BROWN'S POINT
Cable Beach Lagoon
West Bay St.
Hampshire St.
Yorkshire St.
Oxford Ave.
Devonshire St.
Rugby Ave.
Goodman's Bay
Skyline Dr.
Oak Hill Rd.
CABLE BEACH GOLF COURSE
Lake Cunningham
Poinciana Dr.
PROSPECT RIDGE
Sanford Dr.
ACCOMMODATIONS ■
Breezes 14
Clarion Resort South Ocean Golf, Beach & Dive Resort 4
Compass Point Nassau Beach Hotel 12
Nassau Beach Hotel 13
Nassau Marriott Resort & Crystal Palace Casino 11
Orange Hill Beach Inn 2
Radisson Cable Beach Hotel 10
Sandals Royal Bahamian Hotel 6
West Wind II 3
DINING ◆
The Beef Cellar 12
The Black Angus Grille 11
Café Johnny Canoe 12
Capriccio 7
Dickie Mo's 9
The Poop Deck at Sandy Point 8
The Restaurant at Compass Point 1
Sole Mare 11
Travellers Rest 5

raucous, and located on a prime 450m (1,500-ft.) beachfront along Cable Beach, Breezes attracts a more middle-of-the-road crowd; it's unpretentious and more affordable (though it ain't exactly cheap, and we think it's rather overpriced for what it is). This U-shaped beachfront resort has two wings of rooms plus a main clubhouse facing a large pool area. Except between March and May, when no one under 21 is admitted, both couples and single travelers over 16 are accepted here (unlike at Sandals, which accepts only heterosexual couples in love). Everything is included—the room, meals, snacks, unlimited wine (not the finest) with lunch and dinner, even premium brand liquor at the bars, plus activities and airport transfers.

The refurbished hotel rooms contain pastel-painted wooden furniture with Formica tops, and an air-conditioning system that actually works. Rooms, however, are not as luxurious as those at Sandals. Bathrooms are medium-size but well-equipped and are tiled with a shower and bathtub.

Diners can sample unremarkable international fare at the food court, although the Italian restaurant serves a better dinner. A beachside grill and snacks are available throughout the day. Entertainment includes a high-energy disco, a piano bar, and a nightclub. Karaoke is inevitable, but the professional "Junkanoo" live shows, which are presented every Saturday night, are better, and local bands often perform. The social centerpiece is a sometimes-overcrowded terrace with a swimming pool. The resort offers a first for The Bahamas—ice-skating in a 149-square-m (1,600-sq.-ft.) outdoor rink open 24 hours. Equipment is complimentary.

P.O. Box CB-13049, Cable Beach, Nassau, The Bahamas. ✆ **800/GO-SUPER** or 242/327-5356. Fax 242/327-5155. www.breezes.com. 391 units. Winter $580–$680 double, $780 suite; off-season $430–$540 double, $660 suite. Rates include all meals, drinks, most activities, and airport transfers. No tipping allowed. AE, DISC, MC, V. Free parking. Bus: 10. No children under 16 year-round; no one under 21 Mar–May. **Amenities:** 4 restaurants, 4 bars; 2 pools; 3 tennis courts; fitness center; aerobics classes; nonmotorized watersports; ice-skating; rock-climbing wall; basketball court. *In room:* A/C, TV, hair dryer, safe.

Nassau Marriott Resort & Crystal Palace Casino ★★ This is the biggest and flashiest megaresort on the lovely sands of Cable Beach, and it's undergone a lot of changes since Marriott took it over from Carnival Cruise Lines. When Carnival ran it, it was shamelessly glitzy and nicknamed "The Purple Palace" because of its glaring color scheme. Although you still shouldn't expect understated elegance, Marriott has already toned it down a notch and has added touches of class. It's a great place for an action-packed honeymoon, complete with an excellent beach, swaying palm trees, and good snorkeling right offshore. It's so self-contained that you don't have to leave the premises during your entire stay. If you have a choice, stay here and not at Radisson's Cable Beach Hotel (see below), where food, service, and maintenance are not as good.

The complex incorporates five high-rise towers, a futuristic central core, and a cluster of gardens and beachfront gazebos—all connected with arcades, underground passages, and minipavilions. Bedrooms are modern, spacious, and comfortable, cozier and more low-key than the flashy exterior might lead you to believe. Most have ocean views. Units have one king-size bed or two doubles, along with tiny combination bathrooms (shower and tub) with spacious dressing areas and dual basins.

Aside from a massive casino (the largest in The Bahamas), the complex contains eleven restaurants, and a cabaret theater (the Palace Theater, recommended under "New Providence After Dark," later in this chapter). The restaurants run a wide culinary gamut. The best and most expensive (also the most formal) is the

Moments Junkanoo Festivals

No Bahamian celebration is as raucous as the Junkanoo (which is also the name of the music associated with this festival). The special rituals originated during the colonial days of slavery, when African-born newcomers could legally drink and enjoy themselves only on certain strictly predetermined days of the year. In its celebration, Junkanoo closely resembles Carnival in Rio and Mardi Gras in New Orleans. Its major difference lies in the costumes and the timing (the major Junkanoo celebrations occur the day after Christmas, a reminder of the medieval English celebration of Boxing Day on Dec 26 and New Year's Day).

In the old days, Junkanoo costumes were crafted from crepe paper, often in primary colors, stretched over wire frames. (One sinister offshoot of the celebrations was that the Junkanoo costumes and masks were used to conceal the identity of anyone seeking vengeance on a white or on another slave.) Locals have more money to spend on costumes and Junkanoo festivals today than they did in decades past. Today the finest costumes can cost up to $10,000 and are sometimes sponsored by local bazaars, lotteries, and charity auctions, though everyday folks from all walks of Bahamian life join in, too, usually with their own homemade costumes, many of which are sensual or humorous. The best time and place to observe Junkanoo is New Year's Day in Nassau, when throngs of cavorting, music-making, and costumed figures prance through the streets. Find yourself a good viewing position on Bay Street. Less elaborate celebrations take place in major towns on the other islands, including Freeport.

Sole Mare, serving Italian food (see "Where to Dine," below). The Black Angus Grille (also see "Where to Dine") has some of the best steaks on Cable Beach.

W. Bay St. (P.O. Box N-8306), Cable Beach, Nassau, The Bahamas. ✆ **800/222-7466** in the U.S., or 242/327-6200. Fax 242/327-6818. www.marriott.com. 867 units. Winter $179–$249 double, $299–$500 suite for 2; off-season $145–$195 double, $295–$400 suite for 2. AE, DC, DISC, MC, V. Free self-parking, valet parking $5. Bus: 10. **Amenities:** 6 restaurants, 6 bars; casino; pool shaped like tropical lagoon; 10 tennis courts; 18-hole golf course; health club; gym; 24-hr. room service; laundry/valet; babysitting. *In room:* A/C, TV, minibar, hair dryer, safe.

Radisson Cable Beach Hotel ★ *Kids* Right in the middle of Cable Beach (its best asset) this high-rise is connected by a shopping arcade to the Crystal Palace Casino. The nearby Nassau Marriott is glitzier and has better facilities, but the Radisson is still one of the most desirable choices for families, as it has the best children's programs in the area, and because many of its bedrooms contain two double beds, suitable for a family of four. The nine-story property has an Aztec-inspired facade of sharp angles and strong horizontal lines, built in a horseshoe-shaped curve around a landscaped beachfront garden. You'll think of Vegas when you see the rows of fountains in front, the acres of marble sheathing inside, and the four-story lobby with towering windows. Big enough to get lost in, but with plenty of intimate nooks, the hotel offers an almost endless array of things to do. Note, however, that readers constantly complain of staff attitude and slow service at this sprawling resort.

Bedrooms are modern and comfortable if rather standard, with big windows that open onto views of the garden or the beach. Units are equipped with one king-size bed or two doubles, along with phones with voice mail, plus tiled combination baths (tub and shower).

The hotel contains six restaurants, the most glamorous of which is the Amici, serving a traditional Italian cuisine in a two-story garden setting. You can also spice up your evening at Islands, which sometimes has karaoke and other entertainment. We try to avoid the overpriced Avocado's or Bimini's, both of which have poor service and an uninspired cuisine. The Mini-Market Grill serves Caribbean/continental breakfast and lunch buffets, and the Forge is a steak and seafood restaurant where guests are seated around a tabletop grill to prepare their own steaks, seafood, or chicken. Beach parties and revues are often staged.

W. Bay St. (P.O. Box N-4914), Cable Beach, Nassau, The Bahamas. ✆ **800/333-3333** or 242/327-6000. Fax 242/327-6987. www.radisson.com. 691 units. Winter $285–$350 double; off-season $220–$255 double. Year-round $625–$1,250 suite. AE, DC, DISC, MC, V. Free parking. Bus: 10. **Amenities:** 6 restaurants, 3 bars; 6 pools; 18 tennis courts; 3 racquetball and 3 squash courts; room service (7am–10pm); concierge; babysitting at Camp Junkanoo for children 3–12; laundry; dry cleaning; beauty salon; boutiques. *In room:* A/C, TV, minibar, hair dryer, safe.

Sandals Royal Bahamian Hotel ★★★ This is the most upscale Sandals resort in the world. It's shockingly expensive, though you can often get special promotional rates that make it more reasonable. It originated as a very posh hotel, the Balmoral Beach, in the 1940s. In 1996, the Jamaica-based Sandals chain poured $20 million into renovating and expanding the property, which lies on a sandy beach a short walk west of the more glittery megahotels of Cable Beach. Everywhere, you'll find manicured gardens, rich cove moldings, hidden courtyards tastefully accentuated with sculptures, and many of the trappings of Edwardian England in the tropics. Note that only heterosexual couples—and no children at all—are admitted to this resort.

A favorite for honeymoon getaways, Sandals offers well-furnished and often elegant rooms, all classified as suites. Some are in the Manor House, while others are in outlying villas. The villas are preferred because they have romantic, secluded settings and easy access to nearby plunge pools. Some units have Jacuzzis and private pools, and some of the bathrooms are as spacious as many big-city apartments. The bedrooms have thick cove moldings, formal English furniture, and shower-tub combination bathrooms loaded with perfumed soaps and cosmetics. The rooms that face the ocean offer small, curved terraces with ornate iron railings and views of an offshore sand spit, Sandals Key.

Bahamian and international fare is offered in generous portions in the property's restaurants. In addition to spectacular buffets, the options include white-glove service and continental dishes in the Baccarat Dining Room. The two latest additions include Kimono's, offering Japanese cuisine, and Casanova, specializing in Italian fare. Other choices are The Royal Café for southwestern grilled specialties, and Spices, for upscale buffets at breakfast, lunch, and dinner. The pool here is one of the most appealing on Nassau, with touches of both Vegas and ancient Rome (outdoor murals and replicas of ancient Roman columns jutting skyward above the water). There is complimentary shuttle bus service to casino and nightlife options at the nearby Marriott Crystal Palace complex, plus concierge service in suites and upper-tier doubles.

W. Bay St. (P.O. Box CB-13005), Cable Beach, Nassau, The Bahamas. ✆ **800/SANDALS** or 242/327-6400. Fax 242/327-6961. www.sandals.com. 405 units. Winter $4,870–$10,290 per couple for 7 days ($1,450–$2,710 per couple for 2 days); off-season $4,550–$8,540 per couple for 7 days ($1,300–$2,440 per couple for 2 days). Rates include meals, drinks, and activities. Always ask for special promotional rates or see what a travel agent can get you. AE, DISC, MC, V. Free parking. Bus: 10. Couples only; no children or singles allowed. **Amenities:** 8 restaurants, 6 bars; 5 pools; 2 tennis courts; exercise center; spa; watersports; access to golf facilities. *In room:* A/C, TV, hair dryer.

MODERATE

Nassau Beach Hotel *Kids* This place has been somewhat overshadowed by the glitzy properties a short walk away, but a crowd of loyal fans—often families—comes every year, enjoying a 900m (3,000-ft.) white-sand beach. Guests here avoid the carnival at such neighboring megaresorts as the Nassau Marriott (although this place is now also part of the Marriott family). A good value, the Nassau Beach is a conservative, moderately priced choice with a lively but restrained atmosphere.

The hotel was built in the 1940s, with three separate wings in a pink-and-white twin-towered design, and it features modified Georgian detailing and tile- and marble-covered floors. In the early 1990s, it was restored by new owners, and in 1999, $12 million was spent on upgrading the bedrooms and the public areas. Today, the place has been enhanced by new landscaping and touches that include ceiling fans and mahogany, English-inspired furniture. Each of the mid-size accommodations contains summery rattan pieces, comfortable beds, and a marble bathroom with a tub and shower combination.

On-site are seven restaurants (including the Beef Cellar, which is reviewed under "Where to Dine"), plus entertainment in the evening (including live bands and dancing). It's also near the Crystal Palace Casino.

P.O. Box N-7756, Cable Beach, Nassau, The Bahamas. ✆ **888/NASSAUB** in the U.S., or 242/327-7711. Fax 242/327-8829. www.nassaubeachhotel.com. 400 units. $145–$377 double; $300–$350 1-bedroom suite, $400–$450 2-bedroom suite; $550–$600 2-bedroom penthouse. AE, DISC, MC, V. Free parking. Bus: 10. **Amenities:** 6 restaurants, 3 bars; 6 tennis courts; health club; babysitting; laundry; watersports. *In room:* A/C, TV, hair dryer, safe.

West Wind II *Kids* Set on the western edge of Cable Beach's hotel strip, 9.5km (6 miles) from the center of Nassau, the West Wind II is a cluster of two-story buildings that contain two-bedroom, two-bathroom timeshare units, each with a full kitchen (there's a grocery store nearby). The size and facilities of these units make them ideal for traveling families. These units are available to the public whenever they're not otherwise occupied by investors. All the diversions of the megahotels are close by and easily reached, but in the complex itself, you can enjoy a low-key, quiet atmosphere and privacy. (A masonry wall separates the compound from the traffic of West Bay Street and the hotels and vacant lots that flank it.) Each unit has a pleasant decor that includes white tiled floors, rattan furniture, bathrooms with shower-tub combinations, and either a balcony or a terrace. Since units are identical, price differences depend on whether the units face the beach, the pool, or the garden. The manicured grounds feature palms, flowering hibiscus shrubs, and seasonal flower beds. Don't stay here if you expect any of the luxuries or facilities of the nearby Nassau Beach Hotel (see above). West Wind II is more for do-it-yourself types.

W. Bay St. (P.O. Box CB-11006), Cable Beach, Nassau, The Bahamas. ✆ **866/369-5921**, or 242/327-7019. Fax 242/327-7529. www.westwindIIclub.com. 54 apts. Nov–Apr $1,500–$2,000 per week for up to 4 persons; May–Oct $1,250–$2,000 per week for up to 4 persons. MC, V. Bus: 10. **Amenities:** 2 pools; 2 tennis courts; laundromat; babysitting. *In room:* A/C, TV, kitchen, refrigerator, coffeemaker, safe.

WEST OF CABLE BEACH

Clarion Resort South Ocean Golf, Beach, and Dive Resort ★ Set in an isolated position near the extreme western tip of New Providence, this is the only hotel in this area, which mostly consists of scrubland dotted with some upscale private villas. Centered around a well-known golf course, it's divided into two distinctly different sections. The larger and older of the two, with 152 rooms, lies across the coastal road from the sea, adjacent to the golf course, with low-rise, comfortable, but not particularly dramatic accommodations. Newer and better are the 111 oceanfront rooms, which seem like an upscale condominium complex built in Bahamian style, with large bathrooms containing showers and whirlpool baths. Clients run the gamut here between young married couples and more sedate older folk. Most are relatively conservative, enjoying golf and the beach, and not minding the resort's isolation and lack of flashiness. A talented team of social directors keeps a stream of wholesome activities flowing, organizing lots of group activities like volleyball games on the beach.

Both sections of this resort have their own swimming pools, but other than the beach, most of the services for the hotel are in the older section, including two of the three restaurants. Most upscale of the lot is Papagayos; the others are alfresco snack bars and grills. There's live music most evenings; game nights are every Friday, with prize giveaways and trivia contests.

P.O. Box N-8191, South Ocean Rd. ✆ **242/362-4391** or 877/766-2326. Fax 242/362-4810. www.clarionnassau.com. 253 units. Winter $165–$405 double; off-season $130–$175 double. AE, DISC, MC, V. **Amenities:** 3 restaurants, 3 bars; 4 tennis courts; 2 pools; watersports; dive shop; babysitting. *In room:* A/C, TV, hair dryer, safe.

Compass Point ★★ Charming, personalized, and casually upscale, this is an alternative to the megahotels of Cable Beach, which lie about 9.5km (6 miles) to the east. It's part of the Island Records empire of music-industry mogul Chris Blackwell. Think British colonial hip, with guests straight out of Soho (either London or New York) and a smattering of music-industry types. The place isn't as snobby as Graycliff, but for those who want an intimate inn and like the vibrant Bahamian colors, there is no other place like it on the island. Scattered over 2 acres of some of the most expensive terrain in The Bahamas, the property lies beside one of the few sandy coves along the island's northwest coast, about 20 minutes from downtown Nassau and near a great snorkeling beach. The beach is very small, a sandy crescent that virtually disappears at high tide.

Each unit is a private, fully detached "hut" or cottage painted in pulsating, vivid colors. Everything larger than a studio has a kitchenette. Designed for privacy, all the units have exposed rafters, high ceilings with ceiling fans, and a half-dozen windows facing the ocean breezes. Some units are raised on stilts, others hug the ground. They all have king-size beds covered in bright batik, sundecks, spacious shower-only bathrooms with herbal toiletries, and CD players and a selection of music. Those few of the units without natural cross ventilation (about five) are air-conditioned. The most deluxe accommodations are the two-story cottages, each with a small outdoor kitchen and dining area. The Restaurant at Compass Point is recommended separately in "Where to Dine," below. There's also a bar that frequently hosts live music.

W. Bay St., Gambier, Love Beach, New Providence, The Bahamas. ✆ **800/688-7678** in the U.S., or 242/327-4500. Fax 242/327-3299. www.islandoutpost.com. 19 units. Winter $245 studio double, $280–$310 1-bedroom cottage, $355–$600 2-bedroom cottage for 4. Rates usually 20% lower in off-season. AE, DC, MC, V. Free parking. Bus: Western Bus. **Amenities:** Restaurant, bar; pool; laundry. *In room:* TV, minibar, coffeemaker, iron/ironing board, safe.

Orange Hill Beach Inn This hotel, set on 3½ landscaped hillside acres, lies about 13km (8 miles) west of Nassau and 1.5km (1 mile) east of Love Beach, which has great snorkeling. It's perfect for those who want to escape the crowds and stay in a quieter part of New Providence Island; it's easy to catch a cab or jitney to Cable Beach or downtown Nassau. The welcoming owners, Judy and Danny Lowe, an Irish-Bahamian partnership, jokingly refer to their operation as "Fawlty Towers Nassau."

This place was built as a private home in the 1920s and became a hotel in 1979 after the Lowes added more rooms and a swimming pool. Rooms and apartments come in a variety of sizes, although most are small. The bathrooms, likewise, are small but well-maintained, each with a shower unit. Each has a balcony or patio, and a few apartments are equipped with kitchenettes. Many of the guests are European, especially in summer.

On-site is a bar serving sandwiches and salads throughout the day, and a restaurant that offers simple but good dinners. Diving excursions to the rich marine fauna of New Providence's southwestern coast are among the most popular activities here.

W. Bay St. just west of Blake Rd. (P.O. Box N-8583), Nassau, The Bahamas. ✆ **242/327-7157.** Fax 242/327-5186. www.orangehill.com. 32 units. Winter $117–$130 double, $157 apt; off-season $99–$110 double, $114–$140 apt. AE, MC, V. Free parking. Bus: Western Bus. **Amenities:** Restaurant, bar; pool; coin laundry. *In room:* A/C, TV, no phone.

4 Where to Dine

IN NASSAU

Nassau restaurants open and close with alarming regularity. Even if reservations aren't required, it's a good idea to call first just to see that a place is still functioning. European and American cuisine are relatively easy to find in Nassau. Surprisingly, it used to be difficult to find Bahamian cuisine, but in recent years, more places have begun to offer authentic island fare.

VERY EXPENSIVE

Buena Vista ★ CONTINENTAL/BAHAMIAN/SEAFOOD Although it's not quite up there with Graycliff or Sun And . . . , this is definitely third runner-up in Nassau's culinary sweepstakes. It's a block west of Government House (Delancy St. is opposite the cathedral close off St. Francis Xavier, and only a short distance from Bay St.). It opened back in the 1940s in a colonial mansion set on 5 acres of tropical foliage. Traditional elegance and fine preparations have always characterized this place.

You're likely to be shown to the main dining room, unless you request the cozy and intimate Victoria Room or, even better, the Garden Patio, which has a greenhouse setting and a ceiling skylight. The chef scours Nassau's markets to collect the freshest and finest ingredients, which he puts together in menus bursting with flavor and full of originality. Look for impromptu daily specials such as breaded veal chop or Long Island duckling. There is not only nouvelle cuisine here but also a respect for tradition. The rack of lamb Provençale is a classic, but you might want to try instead some of the lighter veal dishes. The cream of garlic soup has plenty of flavor but never overpowers. Instead of wildly fanciful desserts, Buena Vista sticks to the classics—say, cherries jubilee or baked Alaska flambé au cognac. Service is deft, efficient, and polite. Calypso coffee finishes the meal off nicely as you listen to soft piano music.

Delancy and Meeting sts. ✆ **242/322-2811.** Reservations recommended. Main courses $32–$40; fixed-price dinner $43. AE, MC, V. Mon–Sat 7–9:30pm. Bus: Western Bus.

Nassau Dining

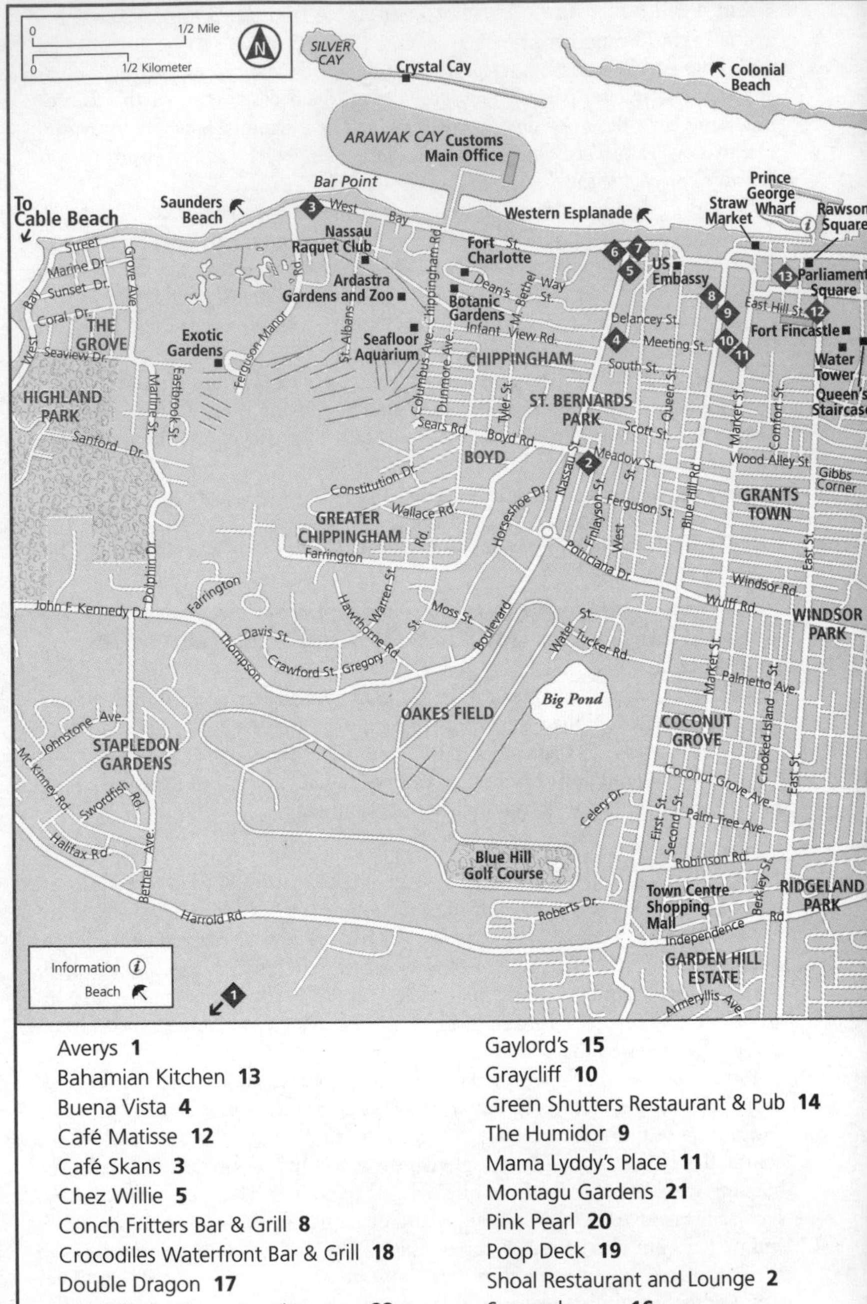

Averys **1**
Bahamian Kitchen **13**
Buena Vista **4**
Café Matisse **12**
Café Skans **3**
Chez Willie **5**
Conch Fritters Bar & Grill **8**
Crocodiles Waterfront Bar & Grill **18**
Double Dragon **17**
East Villa Restaurant and Lounge **22**
Europe **7**
Gaylord's **15**
Graycliff **10**
Green Shutters Restaurant & Pub **14**
The Humidor **9**
Mama Lyddy's Place **11**
Montagu Gardens **21**
Pink Pearl **20**
Poop Deck **19**
Shoal Restaurant and Lounge **2**
Sun and........ **16**
Wedgewood Restaurant **6**

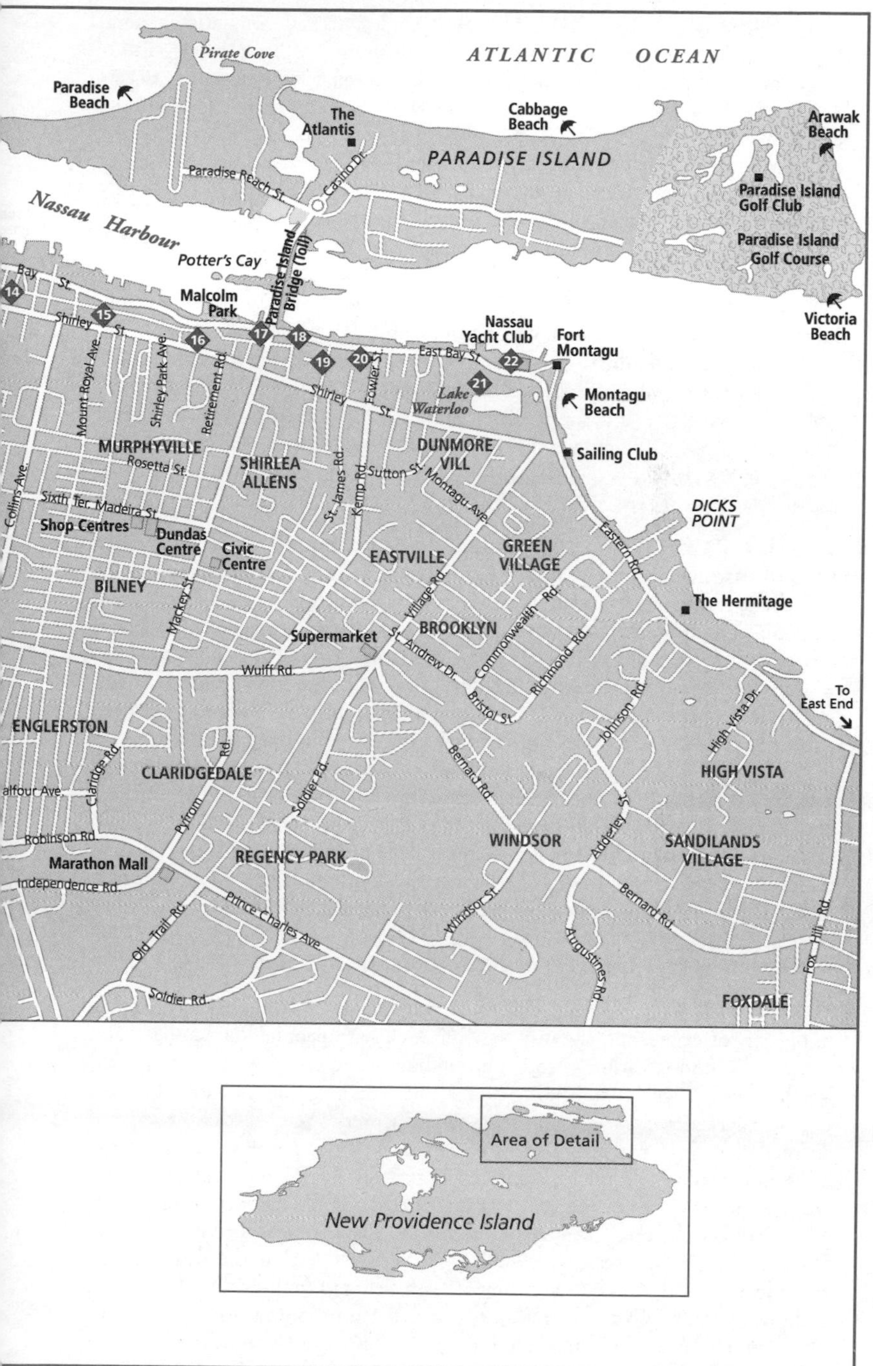

ATLANTIC OCEAN
Pirate Cove
Paradise Beach
The Atlantis
Cabbage Beach
Arawak Beach
PARADISE ISLAND
Paradise Island Golf Club
Paradise Island Golf Course
Victoria Beach
Paradise Beach St.
Casino Dr.
Nassau Harbour
Potter's Cay
Paradise Island Bridge (Toll)
Bay St.
Malcolm Park
Shirley St.
Nassau Yacht Club
Fort Montagu
East Bay St.
Lake Waterloo
Montagu Beach
Sailing Club
Mount Royal Ave.
Shirley Park Ave.
Retirement Rd.
Fowler St.
MURPHYVILLE
Rosetta St.
SHIRLEA ALLENS
DUNMORE VILL
St. James Rd.
Kemp Rd.
Sutton St.
Montagu Ave.
Collins Ave.
Sixth Ter.
Madeira St.
Shop Centres
Dundas Centre
Civic Centre
EASTVILLE
GREEN VILLAGE
DICKS POINT
Eastern Rd.
BILNEY
Mackey St.
Village Rd.
Commonwealth Rd.
The Hermitage
Supermarket
BROOKLYN
St. Andrew Dr.
Richmond Rd.
Wulff Rd.
Bristol St.
Johnson Rd.
High Vista Dr.
To East End
ENGLERSTON
Claridge Rd.
CLARIDGEDALE
Pyfrom Rd.
Soldier Rd.
Bernard Rd.
HIGH VISTA
Balfour Ave.
Robinson Rd.
WINDSOR
Adderley St.
SANDILANDS VILLAGE
Marathon Mall
REGENCY PARK
Independence Rd.
Prince Charles Ave.
Old Trail Rd.
Windsor St.
Augustines Rd.
Fox Hill Rd.
Soldier Rd.
FOXDALE
Area of Detail
New Providence Island

Chez Willie ★★ FRENCH/BAHAMIAN Elegant and romantic in aura, Chez Willie is now a hot new dinner reservation along Bay Street, luring visitors at night. Up to now many patrons had no real reason to visit at night. Jackets are preferred for men, and you can dine alfresco, listening to live piano music. Somehow this place recaptures some of the grandeur of Nassau in its cafe society days. In this relaxing atmosphere, you are likely to meet Willie Armstrong himself, the host. You'll recognize him by his bow tie with jeweled clip, kissing the hand of female guests. In the courtyard is a fountain and regal statuary.

The food is exquisite. Launch into your repast with the stone crab claws with a Dijon mustard sauce or perhaps a fresh Bahamian tuna and crab mousse in a light sauce. The main courses are prepared with first-rate ingredients. Much of it is familiar fare but beautifully prepared, ranging from lobster thermidor to sautéed Dover sole in a tarragon and tomato-laced sauce. We often opt for the broiled seafood platter in a sauce made with fresh herbs. The chef's special is grouper in puff pastry with crabmeat, served with a coconut cream sauce. Special dinners for two, taking an hour, feature beef Wellington, a delicate chateaubriand, or roast rack of lamb.

W. Bay St. ✆ **242/322-5364.** Reservations required. Main courses $36.50–$48.50. Set menu for 2 $55 per person. AE, MC, V. Daily 7–10pm.

Graycliff ★ CONTINENTAL Part of the Graycliff hotel, an antiques-filled colonial mansion located opposite Government House, this restaurant is the domain of connoisseur and bon vivant Enrico Garzaroli. The chefs use local Bahamian products whenever available and turn them into an old-fashioned, heavy cuisine that still has a lot of appeal for tradition-minded visitors, many of whom return here year after year. Young diners with more contemporary palates might head elsewhere, though, as the food as fallen off a bit of late. The chefs, neither completely traditional nor regional, produce such dishes as grouper soup in puff pastry, and plump, juicy pheasant cooked with pineapples grown on Eleuthera. Lobster is another specialty, half in beurre blanc and the other sided with a sauce prepared with the head of the lobster. Other standard dishes include escargots, foie gras, and tournedos d'agneau. The pricey wine list is the finest in the country, with more than 175,000 bottles. The collection of Cuban cigars here—almost 90 types—is said to be the most varied in the world.

W. Hill St. ✆ **242/322-2796.** Reservations required. Jacket advised for men. Lunch main courses $20–$27; dinner main courses $35–$44. AE, MC, V. Mon–Fri noon–2:45pm; daily 7–9:30pm. Bus: 10 or 17.

The Humidor ★★ INTERNATIONAL Its theme derives from the growing popularity of cigars, and the way they mix well with people, liquors, beer, and food. You'll find it within a stone outbuilding of the previously recommended hotel, Graycliff, where two dining rooms and a highly accommodating bar area present a large selection of cigars from virtually everywhere. Part of the space is devoted to a factory, where a team of carefully trained "rollers" produced the house brand (Graycliff) of cigars. Drop in just for a drink and a smoke if you wish. Head to either of the two elegantly decorated dining rooms for a meal where patrons often puff away between courses. The cuisine is the kind of hearty fare types like Jackie Gleason or Frank Sinatra enjoyed back in the '50s—that is, well-prepared and unfussy selections of fresh fish and high-quality meat, even such bistro fare as lobster or crab cakes, stuffed mushroom ravioli and a decent roast lamb with the inevitable mint sauce. Fresh oysters and clams—often washed down by champagne—are savory delights as well.

At the Graycliff Hotel, West Hill St. ✆ **242/322-2796.** Reservations recommended. Main courses $20–$39. AE, DC, MC, V. Mon–Sat dinner seatings at 7, 7:30, 9, and 9:30pm. Bar Mon–Sat 7–10pm. Bus: 10 or 21A.

Sun And . . . ★★ FRENCH/SEAFOOD Near Fort Montagu, this place seems to have been here forever and can name-drop better than anyplace but Graycliff. Sun And . . . is the classic Nassau restaurant, a citadel of top-notch cuisine and service with a hearty dose of British colonial charm. To get to this hard-to-find place, you pass over a drawbridge between two pools and then enter a Spanish-style courtyard, complete with fountains. In this fine old Bahamian home, you can order drinks in the patio bar and then dine cozily inside or alfresco around the rock pool.

Start with the spicy conch chowder; there's none better in Nassau. The chef shines with ingeniously prepared dishes such as braised duckling with sweet and sour sauce. Sure, it's been done before, but it's prepared ever so well here. The grilled veal chop with portobello mushrooms is another of the more admirably executed dishes, as is the classic roast spring lamb, almost melt-in-your-mouth tender and perfectly seasoned without being overpowered with herbs and garlic. Local foodies always praise Ronny Deryckere's incomparable soufflés (even better than the Grand Marnier soufflé at Graycliff, and that's saying a lot). Our favorite is prepared with rum raisins and Black Label Bacardi. More than 100 wines complement the well-thought-out menu.

Lake View Rd., off Shirley St. ✆ **242/393-1205.** Reservations required. Jacket preferred for men. Main courses $32–$40. AE, DISC, MC, V. Tues–Sun 6:30–9:30pm. Closed Aug–Sept. Bus: 10 or 17.

EXPENSIVE

Pink Pearl ★ BAHAMIAN/CONTINENTAL This winning restaurant is set across from the Nassau Yacht Haven Marina in a dark pink colonial building with a wraparound porch. Some of the restaurants nearby, such as the Poop Deck, do lots more business and become a lot more animated, but this place stands in stark contrast, simply because it's relatively uncrowded and relatively formal, though there is after-hours dancing every Friday and Saturday night. The menu mingles Bahamian staples with continental flair. The best examples include creamy conch chowder with chives; angel-hair pasta with crabmeat and fresh cream and green onions; grilled breast of chicken with mango glaze and sweet mango mash; and filet of snapper and plantain with sautéed spinach.

E. Bay St. ✆ **242/394-6413.** Reservations recommended. Main courses $17.95–$29.95. MC, V. Daily 11:30am–3:30pm and 6:30–10:30pm. Bus: 11 or 19.

Wedgwood Restaurant INTERNATIONAL This is a very appealing relative newcomer to downtown Nassau, ensconced in a hotel that's known for a thoroughly British atmosphere. Hilton pays a royalty to England's Wedgwood pottery company for the right to use the name and the right to outfit the place with a combination of gleaming mahogany and Wedgwood's trademark blue-gray color. Most of the guests here, many of them conducting business with local banks or manufacturers, begin their meal with a drink at the formal bar before heading into the dining room for seamless service and well-prepared food. Examples include tenderloin of beef, veal chop with exotic mushrooms, a succulent rock lobster with lime and garlic butter, and a savory loin of pork with onion marmalade. Everything here seems to taste better when it's accompanied by side orders like mushroom casserole with fresh chives.

In the British Colonial Hilton, 1 Bay St. ✆ **242/322-3301.** Reservations recommended. Main courses $28–$42. AE, MC, V. Mon–Sat 5–11:30pm. Bus: 10.

MODERATE

Café Matisse ★ INTERNATIONAL/ITALIAN Set directly behind Parliament House, in a beige building that was built a century ago as a private home, this restaurant is on everybody's short list of downtown Nassau favorites. It serves well-prepared Italian and international cuisine to businesspeople, workers from nearby government offices, and all kinds of deal-makers. There are dining areas within an enclosed courtyard, as well as on two floors of the interior, which is decorated with colorful Matisse prints. It's run by the sophisticated Bahamian-Italian team of Greg and Gabriella Curry, who prepare menu items that include an enticing cannelloni with lobster sauce; mixed grill of seafood; grilled rack of lamb with grilled tomatoes; a perfect filet mignon in a green pepper sauce; and a zesty curried shrimp with rice. There are also meal-size pizzas.

Bank Lane at Bay St., just north of Parliament Sq. ✆ **242/356-7012.** Lunch main courses $24–$20; dinner main courses $17–$30. AE, MC, V. Mon–Sat noon–3pm and 6–10pm. Bus: 17 and 21.

East Villa Restaurant and Lounge CHINESE/CONTINENTAL You might imagine yourself in Hong Kong during the 1980s in this well-designed modern house across the road from the headquarters of the Nassau Yacht Club. It's somewhat upscale, sometimes attracting rich Florida yachties to its dimly lit precincts, where aquariums bubble in a simple but tasteful contemporary setting. Zesty Szechwan flavors appear on the menu, but there are less spicy Cantonese alternatives, including sweet-and-sour chicken and steamed vegetables with cashews and water chestnuts. Lobster tail in the spicy Chinese style is one of our favorites. Dishes can be ordered mild, medium, or zesty hot.

E. Bay St. ✆ **242/393-3377.** Reservations required. Main courses $8.75–$29.50. AE, MC, V. Sun–Fri noon–3pm and daily 6–11pm. Bus: 11 or 19.

Europe GERMAN/CONTINENTAL Attached to an inexpensive hotel, Europe offers the best German specialties in Nassau. Admittedly, that may not be the kind of food you came to Nassau for, and it's a little heavy for the tropics; but the dishes are properly rendered and politely served, and the price is fair. This is where you go when you think you can't stare another grouper or conch in the face. Robust flavors have traveled across the ocean rather well—at least the horde of German visitors on our last visit agreed. When the waiter suggests hearty soups to begin with, he means it—perhaps lima bean and sausage. Naturally, there is bratwurst and quite good sauerbraten. If you don't opt for the Wiener schnitzel, you might settle for a perfectly done pepper steak cognac. The chef will also prepare two kinds of fondue: bourguignon and cheese. Everybody's favorite dessert is the meltingly moist German chocolate cake. All right, we said it was heavy. Diet tomorrow.

In the Ocean Spray Hotel, W. Bay St. ✆ **242/322-8032.** Lunch main courses $8–$21; dinner main courses $12–$22. AE, MC, V. Mon–Fri 8:30am–11pm. Bus: 10.

Gaylord's NORTHERN INDIAN The Indian owners of this restaurant arrived in The Bahamas via Kenya and then England, and they are wryly amused at their success "in bringing India to The Bahamas." Within a room lined with Indian art and artifacts, you'll dine on a wide range of savory and zesty Punjabi, tandoori, and curried dishes. Some of the best choices are the lamb selections, although recently such concessions to local culture as curried or tandoori-style conch have cropped up on the menu. If you don't know what to order, consider a tandoori mixed platter, which might satisfy two of you with a side dish or two. Any of the korma dishes, which combine lamb, chicken, beef, or vegetables in a creamy curry sauce, are very successful. Takeout meals are also available.

Dowdeswell St. at Bay St. ✆ **242/356-3004.** Main courses $13.95–$29.95; fixed-price lunch $17.95–$20.95; fixed-price dinner $22.95–$49.95; vegetarian dinner $22.95. AE, MC, V. Mon–Fri noon–3pm and daily 6:30–11pm. Bus: 10 or 17.

Green Shutters Restaurant & Pub BAHAMIAN/BRITISH Almost 2 centuries old, this landmark British-inspired pub with an adjoining restaurant is still a Nassau favorite, patronized by locals and visitors alike. Green Shutters features the best selections of beers in town, and the food is good, too. You can sip a pint of Guinness in the pub and enjoy such grub as steak-and-kidney pie, or else go into the restaurant and peruse the menu. Appetizers are savory, including tomatoes stuffed with minced lobster and mozzarella. Bahamian conch chowder appears daily on the menu, given zest by a tomato base, and Cuban black-bean soup is also a regular feature. Main dishes are very familiar fare—nothing innovative or experimental here. We usually select the grilled Nassau grouper, or else you can go fancy and order the fish stuffed with minced lobster and topped with a spicy sweet glaze. The fresh catch of the day is always sold at market price. Beef lovers get a wide array of offerings, everything from beef Wellington to pan-seared New York sirloin. On Friday and Saturday nights a calypso band entertains.

Parliament St., off Bay St. ✆ **242/322-3701.** Reservations recommended in restaurant. Main courses $14.95–$30.95; pub platters $8.95–$22.95. AE, MC, V. Daily 11:30am–midnight.

Montagu Gardens STEAKS/SEAFOOD/CONTINENTAL At the edge of Lake Waterloo, this restaurant is installed in an old mansion at the eastern end of Bay Street. The dining room is in a courtyard garden. The chefs get some of the best seafood and beef on the island, and they are especially noted for their Angus beef, which they carve into succulent T-bones, filet mignons, and rib-eyes, all prepared to order. In addition, they also offer baby back ribs and, on most occasions, a perfectly seasoned and cooked rack of lamb. The stuffed lobster tail is a mite ordinary, but they do wonders with that old Bahamian standby, grouper, and also serve some moist and well-seasoned dolphinfish. If you eat too much here, you can dance the night away (and the calories) at the adjoining Club Waterloo.

E. Bay St. ✆ **242/394-6347.** Reservations recommended. Lunch main courses $4–$17; dinner main courses $14.50–$26. AE, MC, V. Mon–Sat 11:30am–3pm and 6–11pm.

Poop Deck BAHAMIAN/SEAFOOD This is a favorite with yachties and others who find a perch on the second-floor, open-air terrace, which overlooks the harbor and Paradise Island. If you like your dining with a view, there is no better place in the heart of Nassau. At lunch, you can order conch chowder (perfectly seasoned) or some juicy beef burgers. The waiters are friendly, the crowd is convivial, and the festivities continue into the evening with lots of drinking and good cheer. Native grouper fingers served with peas 'n' rice is the Bahamian soul food dish on the menu. Two of the best seafood selections are the fresh lobster and the stuffed mushrooms with crabmeat. The creamy homemade lasagna with crisp garlic bread is another fine choice.

Nassau Yacht Haven Marina, E. Bay St. ✆ **242/393-8175.** Lunch $7.75–$20; main courses $17–$39. AE, MC, V. Daily noon–4pm and 5–10:30pm. Bus: 10 or 17.

Shoal Restaurant and Lounge BAHAMIAN Many of our good friends in Nassau swear that this is the best joint for authentic local food. We're not entirely convinced this is true, but we rank it near the top. The place is a beehive of activity on Saturday mornings, when seemingly half of Nassau shows up for the chef's specialty, boiled fish and johnnycake. This may or may not be your fantasy, but if you're Bahamian, it is like pot liquor and turnip greens with cornbread to a Southerner. Far removed from the well-trodden tourist path, this restaurant is a real local favorite. After all, where else can you get a good bowl of okra soup these days? Naturally, conch chowder is the favorite opener. Many diners follow the chowder with more conch, "cracked" this time. But you can also order more unusual dishes such as Bahamian-style mutton using native spices and herbs. The seafood platter, with lobster, shrimp, and fried grouper, is more international in appeal. Peas 'n' rice accompanies everything. The restaurant even offers to transport you to and from the restaurant from your hotel free of charge.

Nassau St. ✆ **242/323-4400.** Main courses $12–$30. AE, DISC, MC, V. Daily 7:30am–midnight.

INEXPENSIVE

Avery's Restaurant ★ *Finds* BAHAMIAN There is not a more authentic or native dining spot in all of New Providence. Occupying a pink-painted, two-story cinderblock house and set beside the main road passing through Adelaide Village, this is the hamlet's prominent bar and restaurant. Avery Ferguson, the owner, is likely to be tending her own bar or taking orders at the time of your arrival. Menu items focus on fresh seafood and imported meat items such as pork chops and steaks. Snapper and grouper are likely to be available either fried, grilled, or smothered (stewed) with onions, spices, and tomatoes. No one here will mind if you opt for a drink or two at any hour of the afternoon. The local brew (Kalik) is always available, as is virtually any drink you can think of that's made with Bahamian rum.

Adelaide Rd. ✆ **242/362-1547.** Main courses $10–$35. MC, V. Daily noon–11pm.

Bahamian Kitchen *Value* *Kids* BAHAMIAN Next to Trinity Church, this is one of the best places for good Bahamian food at modest prices. Down-home dishes, full of local flavor, include lobster Bahamian style, fried red snapper, conch salad, stewed fish, curried chicken, okra soup, and pea soup and dumplings. Most dishes are served with peas 'n' rice. You can order such old-fashioned Bahamian fare as stewed fish and corned beef and grits, all served with johnnycake. If you'd like to introduce your kids to Bahamian cuisine, this is an ideal choice. There's takeout service if you're planning a picnic.

Trinity Place, off Market St. ✆ **242/325-0702.** Lunches $5–$12; main courses $12–$22. AE, DC, MC, V. Mon–Sat 11am–10pm. Bus: 10 or 17.

Café Skans *Value* INTERNATIONAL This is a straightforward, Formica-clad diner with an open kitchen, offering flavorful food that's served without fanfare in generous portions. It's next door to the Straw Market site, attracting local residents and office workers from the government buildings nearby. Menu items include Bahamian fried or barbecued chicken; bean soup with dumplings; souvlakia or gyros in pita bread; and burgers, steaks, and various kinds of seafood platters. This is where workaday Nassau comes for breakfast.

W. Bay St., adjacent to the Straw Market. ✆ **242/322-2486.** Reservations not accepted. Breakfast $3.45–$9.50; sandwiches $4.95–$8.95; main-course platters $5.95–$15. MC, V. Daily 8am–6pm.

Conch Fritters Bar & Grill BAHAMIAN/INTERNATIONAL A true local hangout with real island atmosphere, this light-hearted restaurant changes its focus several times throughout the day. In the morning, folks stop in for a quick breakfast before heading off to work in downtown Nassau. Lunches and dinners are high-volume, high-turnover affairs mitigated only by attentive staff who seem genuinely concerned about the well-being of their guests. Live music is presented every day except Monday from 7pm until closing, when the place transforms again into something of a singles bar. Food choices are rather

Finds **The Secret Garden**

The Retreat, Village Road (✆ **242/393-1317**), consists of 11 acres of the most unspoiled gardens on New Providence, even more intriguing than the Botanical Gardens. They're home to about 200 species of exotic palm trees. You'll think you've wandered into *1001 Arabian Nights* in this true oasis in the heart of Nassau. Half-hour tours of the grounds are given Tuesday through Thursday at noon. This is the home of The Bahamas National Trust, and the grounds (without the tours) can be visited Monday through Friday from 9am to 5pm for a $2 admission for adults or 50¢ for children.

standard but still quite good, including cracked conch, fried shrimp, grilled salmon, six different versions of chicken, blackened rib-eye steak, burgers, and sandwiches. Specialty drinks from the active bar include a Goombay Smash.

Marlborough St. (across the st. from the British Colonial Hilton). ✆ **242/323-8801.** Burgers, sandwiches, and platters $9.95–$36. AE, MC, V. Daily 7am–midnight.

Crocodiles Waterfront Bar & Grill INTERNATIONAL/BAHAMIAN One of the most appealing, funky bar/restaurants in Nassau lies about a 2-minute walk from the Nassau side of the Paradise Island Bridge, with a view over the water. Set on a deck that's partially protected with thatched parasols but mostly open to the sky and a view of the channel, it's completely casual. (You'll recognize the place by the hundreds of stenciled crocodiles happily cavorting on the wall that separates the place from the dense traffic of E. Bay St.) After one of the rum concoctions from the bar, you might get into the swing of things. If you're hungry, order up cracked or grilled conch, a grilled 10-ounce sirloin steak, teriyaki-marinated tuna, grilled lobster tail, a mushroom and melted cheese chicken breast, crab cakes, or a standard but creamy lasagna. A particularly good sandwich choice is blackened mahimahi. There's a lounge on the premises with frequent live entertainment.

E. Bay St. ✆ **242/323-3341.** Main courses $14.50–$33.95. AE, MC, V. Daily 11am–5pm and 6–10:30pm. Bus: 10 or 17.

Double Dragon *Kids* CANTONESE/SZECHWAN The chefs hail from the province of Canton in mainland China, and that's the inspiration for most of the food here. If you've ever really wondered about the differences between Cantonese and Szechwan cuisine, a quick look at the menu here will highlight the differences. Lobster, chicken, or beef, for example, can be prepared Cantonese style, with a mild black-bean or ginger sauce; or in spicier Szechwan formats of red peppers, chilis, and garlic. Honey-garlic chicken and orange-flavored shrimp are always popular and succulent. Overall, this place is a fine choice if you're eager for a change from grouper and burgers.

Bridge Plaza Commons, Mackey St. ✆ **242/393-5718.** Main courses $8–$13. AE, DISC, MC, V. Mon–Fri noon–10pm; Sat 4–11pm; Sun 5–10pm. Bus: 10 or 17.

Mama Lyddy's Place ★ *Value* BAHAMIAN/AMERICAN This restaurant occupies the homestead of a Bahamian matriarch, Lydia Russell, who died in the 1980s and never had a hand in actually establishing the place. That honor belongs to her children, who used their extensive experience at a neighboring takeout place (**The Palm Tree Restaurant;** ✆ **242/322-4201**) to re-create a sense of wholesomeness and The Bahamas the way it used to be. This place is set within a white-and-tangerine-colored stucco house in the heart of Nassau. Inside, you'll find lots of exposed wood, a color scheme of hot pink and black, and lots of local paintings inspired by Junkanoo. Menu items are as down-home as you can get (cracked conch, baked pork chops, fried or steamed grouper, minced or broiled lobster, and baked chicken) and are served with two of at least seven side dishes like potato salad, creamed corn, beets, coleslaw, macaroni and cheese, peas 'n' rice, or fried plantain.

Corner of Market St. at Cockburn St. ✆ **242/328-6849.** Main courses $8–$15. No credit cards. Mon–Sat 8am–6pm; Sun 8am–3pm. Bus: 18.

CABLE BEACH

VERY EXPENSIVE

The Black Angus Grille ★ INTERNATIONAL/STEAKS/SEAFOOD This is your best bet for dining if you're testing your luck at the Crystal Palace Casino nearby (and you may need to win to pay the hefty bill here). The Rotisserie in the Sheraton Grand Resort Paradise Island has the edge and is also more reasonably priced, but this is a close runner-up. Serving some of the best beef and steaks along Cable Beach, it's the favorite of hundreds of casino-goers. Set one floor above the gambling tables, it has a boldly geometric decor of brightly colored tilework and comfortable banquettes.

Although steaks are frozen and flown in from the mainland, they are well-prepared—succulent, juicy, and cooked to your specifications. The filet mignon is especially delectable, although the T-bone always seems to have more flavor. Prime rib is a nightly feature. The kitchen also prepares a number of sumptuous seafood platters, and Bahamian lobster tails here are fresh and flavorful.

In the Nassau Marriott Resort and Crystal Palace Casino, W. Bay St. ✆ **242/327-6200.** Reservations recommended. Main courses $28–$39.50. AE, DC, DISC, MC, V. Mon–Sat 6–11pm (though hours can vary, so call in advance). Bus: 10.

Sole Mare ★★ NORTHERN ITALIAN This is our top choice for elegant dining along Cable Beach, and it also serves the best Northern Italian cuisine along the beach strip. The chefs are well-trained and inventive. A filet of whatever fresh fish is available that day appears on the menu and is the keynote of many a delectable meal here. Many of the other ingredients have to be imported from the mainland, but the chefs still work their magic with them. Their apple-scented lobster bisque laced with cream and cognac is so velvety smooth it's worth the calorie overload. Veal sautéed with endive is something usually encountered in a little upmarket tavern in northern Italy, but it appears here perfectly prepared and with some extra flavor from white wine and capers. The dessert soufflés are hardly the equal of those served at Sun And . . . , but they're still excellent, especially when served with a vanilla sauce.

In the Nassau Marriott Resort & Crystal Palace Casino, W. Bay St. ✆ **242/327-6200.** Reservations required. Main courses $21–$39. AE, DC, DISC, MC, V. Wed–Sun 6–11pm (though hours can vary slightly, so call ahead). Bus: 10.

EXPENSIVE

The Beef Cellar ★ STEAKS/SEAFOOD If you like steak, look no farther than Cable Beach and its Nassau Beach Hotel. The steaks here are juicy, succulent, and tender—and cooked just as you like. Located downstairs from the hotel's lobby, within a short walk of the casino at the neighboring Nassau Marriott Resort, the Beef Cellar features a warmly masculine decor of exposed stone and leather, two-fisted drinks, and tables that have individual charcoal grills for diners who prefer to grill their own steaks. The prices here are more reasonable than those at the Black Angus Grille in the Marriott Resort.

In the Nassau Beach Hotel. ✆ **242/327-7711.** Main courses $16.95–$32.50. AE, DC, MC, V. Daily 6–10:30pm. Bus: 10 or 38.

MODERATE

Capriccio ITALIAN/INTERNATIONAL Set beside a prominent roundabout, about .5km (¼-mile) west of the megahotels of Cable Beach, this restaurant lies within a grandly Italian building with Corinthian columns and an outdoor terrace. Inside, it's a lot less formal, outfitted like a luncheonette, but with lots of exposed granite, busy espresso machines, and kindly Bahamian staff who have been trained in their understanding of Italian culinary nuance. At lunch you get pretty ordinary fare such as fresh salads, sandwiches, and a few hot platters like cracked conch. But the cooks shine at night, offering dishes such as chicken breast with sage and wine sauce, spaghetti with pesto and pine nuts, and seafood platters.

W. Bay St. ✆ **242/327-8547.** Reservations recommended. Lunch items $9.75–$14.50; dinner main courses $9.75–$24.75. MC, V. Mon–Sat 11am–10pm; Sun 5–10pm.

Dickie Mo's SEAFOOD/CONTINENTAL Set on Cable Beach's main road, 2 blocks west of the Radisson Hotel, this restaurant is a well-maintained place that has managed to hold its own against the better-financed restaurants in the nearby megahotels. The decor is nautical, with fishnets, wide-plank flooring, weathered driftwood, and sailing memorabilia; there are three separate dining rooms plus an outside terrace. Enjoy such dishes as barbecued chicken or ribs, grilled salmon or mahimahi in garlic-flavored butter sauce, yellowfin tuna with onion and sweet-pepper sauce, and shark filet. The most expensive items include stone crabs and broiled and stuffed lobsters. Good cooking, without fancy artifice, keeps diners coming back for more.

Next door, under the same ownership, is a red-and-black-fronted restaurant named **The Japanese Steak House,** which usually operates at about the same hours and prices.

Cable Beach Hwy., Cable Beach. ✆ **242/327-7854.** Main courses $10.95–$35.95. AE, MC, V. Wed–Mon 4am–midnight.

The Poop Deck at Sandy Point INTERNATIONAL/SEAFOOD This is the largest and most imposing restaurant west of Cable Beach, convenient for the owners of the many upscale villas and condos that surround it. It's set within a pink concrete building that's highly visible from West Bay Street—but despite its impressive exterior, it's a bit sterile-looking on the inside. This simple island restaurant evolved from a roughneck bar that occupied this site during the early 1970s. Lunch is usually devoted to well-prepared burgers, pastas, sandwiches, and salads. Dinners are more substantial, featuring filet mignon, "surf-and-turf" (seafood and steak combo), cracked conch, and fried shrimp caught off the Bahamian Long Island. The house drink is a Bacardi splish-splash, containing Bacardi Select, Nassau Royal Liqueur, pineapple juice, cream, and sugar-cane syrup.

Poop Deck Dr., off W. Bay St. ✆ **242/327-DECK.** Reservations recommended. Lunch main courses $11–$30; dinner main courses $14–$70. AE, MC, V. Tues–Sun noon–3pm and 5:30–10:30pm.

INEXPENSIVE

Café Johnny Canoe *Kids* INTERNATIONAL/BAHAMIAN There's absolutely nothing stylish about this place (it was originally a Howard Johnson's), but because of its good value and cheerful staff, it's almost always filled with satisfied families. Within a yellow-painted interior that's accented with junkanoo memorabilia, you can order filling portions of diner-style food with a Bahamian twist: cracked conch and lobster, grilled mahimahi, grouper fingers with tartar sauce, homemade soups, and fried fish. Sandwiches always come with one side order; platters always come with two. The place is named after the legend of a Bahamian slave who escaped in the canoe of a junkanoo band. Every Friday night between 8 and 10pm, there's live junkanoo music, accented with goatskin drums and synchronized cowbells.

In the Nassau Beach Hotel, W. Bay St. ✆ **242/327-3373.** Breakfast $5–$7; salads, sandwiches, and lunch and dinner platters $8.95–$23.95. AE, DISC, MC, V. Daily 7:30am–midnight.

WEST OF CABLE BEACH

The Restaurant at Compass Point ★★ CALIFORNIAN/CARIBBEAN/INTERNATIONAL This is one of the best restaurants on New Providence, and the only one to join the stellar ranks of Graycliff and Sun And . . . in years. It's not as formal as either of those, but instead it has a low-key, casually hip style that attracts lots of entertainment-industry types and local foodies. The dining room is indoor/outdoor, outfitted in island colors; the interior is capped with slowly spinning ceiling fans.

The cuisine is a combination of California and Caribbean, with many innovative dishes, some of which even show a Thai influence. Lunch offerings include warm grilled-chicken sandwiches, salade niçoise garnished with strips of grilled mahimahi, and tandoori fried calamari and jerk chicken salad. At night, many of the chef's dishes exhibit touches of whimsy, as in the case of agnolotti filled with conch (a masterful, original dish), snails in puff pastry, seafood fish cakes, a delectable rack of lamb with a guava-roasted garlic glaze, and grilled or blackened snapper. The risotto with a variety of mushrooms and fresh herbs is the best we've ever sampled on the island.

In the Hotel at Compass Point, W. Bay St., Gambier, Love Beach. ✆ **242/327-4500.** Reservations required. Lunch main courses $11.75–$22; dinner main courses $19–$45. AE, MC, V. Daily 7am–10:30pm.

Travellers Rest ★ *Value* BAHAMIAN/SEAFOOD Set in an isolated spot about 2.5km (1½ miles) west of the megahotels of Cable Beach, this restaurant feels far away from it all. Its owners will make you feel like you're dining on a remote Out Island. Travellers Rest is set in a cozy cement-sided house that stands in a grove of sea-grape and palm trees facing the ocean. It was established by Winnipeg-born Joan Hannah in 1972, and since then has fed ordinary as well as famous folks like Stevie Wonder, Gladys Knight, spy novelist Robert Ludlum, Julio Iglesias, Eric Clapton, and Rosa Parks. You can dine outside, but if it's rainy (highly unlikely), you can go inside the tavern with its small bar decorated with local paintings. Many diners use the white-sand beach across from the restaurant; others pull up in their own boats. In this laid-back atmosphere, you can feast on well-prepared grouper fingers, barbecue ribs, curried chicken, steamed or cracked conch, or minced crawfish, and finish perhaps with guava cake, the best on the island. The conch salad served on the weekends is said to increase virility in men.

W. Bay St., near Gambier (14km/9 miles west of the center of Nassau). ✆ **242/327-7633.** Lunch main courses $9–$24.50; dinner main courses $12–$28.50. AE, MC, V. Daily noon–10pm. Western Transportation bus to and from Nassau $2 each way.

5 Beaches, Watersports & Other Outdoor Pursuits

One of the great sports centers of the world, Nassau and the islands that surround it are marvelous places for swimming, sunning, snorkeling, scuba diving, boating, water-skiing, and deep-sea fishing, as well as tennis and golf.

You can learn more about most of the available activities by calling **The Bahamas Sports and Aviation Information Center** (© **800/32-SPORT** or 305/932-0051) from anywhere in the continental United States. Call Monday through Friday from 9am to 5pm, EST. Or write the center at 19495 Biscayne Blvd., Suite 809, Aventura, FL 33180.

HITTING THE BEACH

Lovely **Cable Beach** ★★, is the most popular beach on New Providence Island, which offers all sorts of watersports, as well as easy access to shops, casino action, bars, and restaurants. The beach offers 6.5km (4 miles) of soft white sand, and the different types of food, restaurants, snack bars, and watersports offered at the hotels lining the waterfront are incredibly varied. You can arrange snorkeling or scuba diving, order fresh fruit juices or cold beer, or get your hair braided by one of the locals. The beach also functions as a kind of bazaar, with many Bahamians parading up and down, hawking various crafts. You'll need to hunt for a spot on the strip that's suitable for you. Waters can be rough and reefy, then calm and clear a little farther along the shore.

Cable Beach is far superior to the meager beach in Nassau, the **Western Esplanade** (also called **Junkanoo Beach**), which sweeps westward from the British Colonial. But if you're staying in a Nassau hotel and don't want to make the trip to Cable Beach, you might use the local beach instead; it has restrooms, changing rooms, and a snack bar.

At some point in a visit, even Cable Beach beach buffs like to desert the sands here in favor of **Paradise Beach** on Paradise Island (see chapter 4). Paradise Beach is even more convenient to residents of Nassau hotels, because all they have to do is walk, drive, or take a boat to nearby Paradise Island. Paradise Beach can be reached by boat from the Prince George Wharf. Round-trip tickets cost $4 per person. It's also possible to drive to the beach across the Paradise Island Bridge for a toll of $2, or you can walk across for only 25¢.

To reach **Saunders Beach,** where many of the local people go on weekends, take West Bay Street toward Coral Island. This beach lies across from Fort Charlotte.

On the north shore, past the Cable Beach Hotel properties, **Caves Beach** lies some 11km (7 miles) west of Nassau. It stands near Rock Point, right before the turnoff along Blake Road that leads to the airport. Since visitors often don't know of this place, it's another good spot to escape the hordes. It's also a good beach with soft sands.

Finds A Beach for Lovers

Continuing west along West Bay Street, you reach **Love Beach,** across from Sea Gardens, a good stretch of sand lying east of Northwest Point. Love Beach, although not big, is a special favorite with lovers. The snorkeling is superb, too. It's technically private, though no one bothers visitors who come, and locals fervently hope it won't ever become overrun like Cable Beach.

We often head for **Old Fort Beach** ★ when we want to escape the crowds on weekdays, a 15-minute drive west of the Nassau International Airport (take W. Bay St. toward Lyford Cay). This lovely sandy beach opens onto the turquoise waters of Old Fort Bay near the western part of New Providence. The least developed of the island's beaches, it attracts many homeowners from swanky Lyford Cay nearby. In winter, the beach can be quite windy, but in summer it's as calm as the Caribbean Sea.

BOAT CRUISES

Cruises from the harbors around New Providence Island are offered by a number of operators, with trips ranging from daytime voyages for snorkeling, picnicking, sunning, and swimming, to sunset and moonlight cruises.

Barefoot Sailing Cruises, Sugar Reef Marina (© **242/393-0820**) runs the *Wind Dance,* which leaves for all-day cruises from this dock, offering many sailing and snorkeling possibilities. This is your best bet if you're seeking a more romantic cruise and don't want 100 people aboard. The cruises usually stop at Rose Island, which is a charming, picture-perfect spot, with an uncrowded white sandy beach and palm trees. You can also sail on a ketch, the 16m (54-ft.) *Riding High,* which is bigger than the 12m (41-ft.) *Wind Dance.* Another vessel, the 65-passenger catamaran *Big Foot,* has also joined the fleet. Cruise options are plentiful, ranging from a half day of sailing, snorkeling, and exploring ($39) to a full day ($59) to private dinner cruises of 3 moonlit hours ($500 for two). If the cruise becomes a party, $500 is charged for the first two guests, then $55 for each additional person.

Flying Cloud, Paradise Island West Dock (© **242/393-1957**), features catamaran cruises carrying 50 people on day and sunset trips, or a maximum of 30 for dinner. It's a good bet for people who want a more intimate cruise and shy away from the heavy volume carried aboard Majestic Tours catamarans (see below). Snorkeling equipment is provided free. A half-day charter costs $40 per person; a 2½-hour sunset cruise goes for $35. The 3½-hour dinner cruise at 7pm is $55 per person (half price for children).

Majestic Tours Ltd., Hillside Manor (© **242/322-2606**), will book 3-hour cruises on two of the biggest catamarans in the Atlantic, offering views of the water, sun, sand, and outlying reefs. This is the biggest and most professionally run of the cruise boats, and it's an affordable option; but we find that there are just too many other passengers aboard. The *Yellow Bird* is suitable for up to 250 passengers. It departs from Prince George's Dock; ask for the exact departure point when you make your reservation. The cost is $15 per adult, $7.50 for children under 10, and snorkeling equipment is $10 extra. The outfitter has recently added another boat, the *Robinson Crusoe,* holding 350 passengers. This boat offers daily cruises from 10am to 4pm, costing $45 for adults or half price for children 11 and under. Sunset dinner cruises Tuesday and Friday cost $50 per adult, again half price for children.

FISHING

May through September are the best months for the oceanic bonito and the blackfin tuna; June and July for blue marlin; and November through May for the amberjack found in reefy areas.

Arrangements can be made at any of the big hotels, and unfortunately, there's a hefty price tag. Prices are usually $350 for a half-day boat rental for parties of two to six or $700 for a full day's fishing.

One of the most reliable companies, **Born Free Charters** (© **242/393-4144**), offers a fleet of 8 to 10 vessels that can seat six comfortably; they can be rented for a half-day ($400) or a full day ($800). Each additional person is charged $60 depending on boat size. Fishing choices are plentiful: You can troll for wahoo, tuna, and marlin in the deep sea or cast in the shallows for snapper, amberjack, grouper, and yellowtail. Anchoring and bottom-fishing are calmer options. We recommend this charter because they offer so many types of fishing and give you a lot of leeway regarding where you want to fish and how much time you want to spend.

The best charter operator, **Nassau Yacht Haven** (© **242/393-8173**), has both a 11m (35-ft.) boat and a 13m (42-ft.) boat. Fishing is mainly close to shore. It takes 15 to 20 minutes to reach a drop-off where wahoo and barracuda abound. This charter is recommended not only for its quality fishing, but also for its convenience, since you don't have far to travel before you start fishing.

GOLF

Some of the best golfing in The Bahamas is found in Nassau. The following courses are open to the public, not just to guests of the hotels that operate the properties.

Cable Beach Golf Course ★★ on West Bay Road, Cable Beach (© **242/327-6000**), is a spectacular 18-hole, 7,040-yard, par-72 championship golf course, but it's not as challenging as the one at the South Ocean Golf Course (see below). The Cable Beach course is under the management of the Radisson Cable Beach Hotel, but it's often used by guests of the other hotels nearby. Greens fees are $45 for residents of Radisson, $100 for all other players. Carts are included.

South Ocean Golf Course ★★★ on Southwest Bay Road (© **242/362-4391**), the best course on New Providence Island and one of the best in The Bahamas, is a 30-minute drive from Nassau on the southwest edge of the island. The course has palm-fringed greens and fairways. Overlooking the ocean, the 6,706-yard beauty has some first-rate holes amid trees, shrubs, ravines, and undulating hills. The 18-hole, USPGA-sanctioned course has a par of 72. The lofty elevation of this course offers panoramic water views, including an area of the Atlantic called Tongue of the Ocean. Golf architect Joe Lee designed the course with four challenging water holes and made very effective use of the rolling terrain. Guests at the South Ocean Golf and Beach Resort next to the course pay $65 for 18 holes; nonguests are charged $110 for 18 holes and a golf cart. It's best to phone ahead in case a golf tournament is scheduled for the day you had planned to play.

HORSEBACK RIDING

Happy Trails Stables, Coral Harbour, on the southwest shore (© **242/362-1820**), offers a 90-minute horseback trail ride for $85, including free transportation to and from your hotel. Riders must weigh less than 200 pounds. The stables are signposted from the Nassau International Airport, which is 3km (2 miles) away. Children must be 9 or older, and reservations are required, especially during the holiday season.

SNORKELING, SCUBA DIVING & UNDERWATER WALKS

There's great snorkeling off most of the beaches on New Providence, especially **Love Beach.** Most any of the hotels and resorts will rent or loan you snorkeling equipment. Several of the companies mentioned above under "Boat Cruises" also offer snorkel trips, as does Bahamas Divers, below. See also "Easy Side Trips to Nearby Islands," below, for additional snorkeling excursions.

There are more dive sites around New Providence than you can see in one visit, so we've included a few of our favorites. **Shark Wall** ★★ is the most intriguing, which is a diving excursion 16km (10 miles) off the coast; others include the Rose Island Reefs, the Southwest Reef, the Razorback, and Booby Rock Reef. All dive outfitters feature one or more of these sites.

Bahama Divers, East Bay Street (✆ **242/393-5644**), has packages that range from a half-day of snorkeling to offshore reefs for $30 per person, to a half-day scuba trip with preliminary pool instruction for beginners, for $70 for two tanks or $45 for one tank, including all equipment. Half-day excursions for certified divers to deeper outlying reefs, drop-offs, and blue holes can be arranged.

Participants receive free transportation from their hotel to the boats. Children must be 12 or older, and reservations are required, especially during the holiday season.

Hartley's Undersea Walk, East Bay Street (✆ **242/393-8234**), offers an exciting and educational experience. They take you out from Nassau Harbour aboard the yacht *Pied Piper.* On the 3½-hour cruise, you're submerged for about 20 minutes, descending through shallow water until you walk along the ocean bottom through a "garden" of tropical fish, sponges, and other undersea life. As you're guided through the underwater world, you'll wear a helmet that allows you to see and breathe with ease. Entire families can go on this safe adventure, which costs $75. You don't even have to be able to swim. Two trips run per day, at 9:30am and 1:30pm, Tuesday through Saturday. Arrive 30 minutes before departures, and make reservations 2 to 3 days in advance.

Stuart Cove's Dive Bahamas, Southwest Bay Street, South Ocean (P.O. Box CB13137, Nassau; ✆ **800/879-9832** in the U.S., or 242/362-4171), is about 10 minutes from top dive sites, including the coral reefs, wrecks, and an underwater airplane structure used in filming James Bond thrillers. The Porpoise Pen Reefs, named for Flipper, and steep sea walls are also on the diving agenda. A two-tank dive in the morning costs $80, or an all-day program goes for $125. All prices for boat dives include tanks, weights, and belts. An open-water certification course starts at $695. Bring along two friends, and the price drops to $395 per person. Escorted boat snorkeling trips cost $40. A special feature is a series of shark-dive experiences priced from $125. In one outing, Caribbean reef sharks swim among the guests. In one dive, called "Shark Arena," divers kneel down while a dive master feeds the sharks off a long pole. Another experience, a "Shark Buoy" in 1,800m (6,000 ft.) of ocean, involves a dive among silky-skinned sharks at about 9m (30 ft.). They swim among the divers while the dive master feeds them. Another popular outing is the Shark Wall dive along an 24m (80-ft.) coral wall, with shark feedings at 15m (50 ft.).

The outfitter has recently generated much excitement with its introduction of yellow "submarines," actually jet bikes called Scenic Underwater Bubbles. An air-fed bubble covers your head as these self-contained and battery-powered jet bikes propel you through an underwater wonderland. The subs are popular with nondivers, and they're viewed as safe for kids as well (that is, those older than 12). An underwater armada is escorted along to view the reefs, all for a cost of $95. The whole experience, from pickup at your hotel or cruise ship to return, takes about 3 hours.

TENNIS

Courts are available at only some hotels. Guests usually play free or for a nominal fee, whereas visitors are charged.

Most of the courts at Cable Beach are under the auspices of the **Radisson Cable Beach Hotel,** West Bay Street (© **242/327-6000**), which offers 18 courts. Residents of Radisson play free until sunset. After that, illumination costs $15 per hour. Non-Radisson guests pay $15 per person.

Other hotels offering tennis courts include the **Nassau Beach Hotel,** West Bay Street, and Cable Beach (© **242/327-7711**), with six Flexipave night-lit courts.

6 Seeing the Sights

Most of Nassau can be explored on foot, beginning at Rawson Square in the center near the stalls of the Straw Market, the country's largest native market (currently being rebuilt after a fire), which spills over to the waterfront. Here is where Bahamian fishers unload a variety of produce and fish—crates of mangoes, oranges, tomatoes, and limes, plus lots of crimson-lipped conch. To experience this slice of Bahamian life, go any morning Monday through Saturday before noon.

The best way to see some of the major public buildings of Nassau is to take our walking tour (see below), which will give you not only an overview of the historic sights, but also a feel for the city as a whole. Then you can concentrate on specific sights you'd like to take in, notably Ardastra Gardens and Coral Island Bahamas.

THE TOP ATTRACTIONS

Ardastra Gardens ★ The main attraction of the Ardastra Gardens, almost 5 acres of lush tropical planting about 1.5km (1 mile) west of downtown Nassau near Fort Charlotte, is the parading flock of **pink flamingos.** The Caribbean flamingo, national bird of The Bahamas, had almost disappeared by the early 1940s but was brought back to significant numbers through the efforts of the National Trust. They now flourish in the rookery on Great Inagua. A flock of these exotic feathered creatures has been trained to march in drill formation, responding to the drillmaster's commands with long-legged precision and discipline. The Marching Flamingos perform daily at 11am, 2, and 4pm.

Other exotic wildlife at the gardens include boa constrictors (very tame), kinkajous (honey bears) from Central and South America, green-winged macaws, peacocks and peahens, blue-and-yellow macaws, capuchin monkeys, iguanas, ring-tailed lemurs, red-ruff lemurs, margays, brown-headed tamarins (monkeys), and a crocodile. There are also numerous waterfowl to be seen in Swan Lake, including black swans from Australia and several species of wild ducks.

You can get a good look at Ardastra's flora by walking along the signposted paths. Many of the more interesting and exotic trees bear plaques with their names.

Chippingham Rd. © **242/323-5806.** Admission $12 adults, $6 children. Daily 9am–4pm. Bus: 10.

Seaworld Explorer ★ If you are curious about life below the waves but aren't a strong swimmer, hop aboard this submarine, which holds about 45 passengers. It's doubtful that the military will ever press this particular craft into service in wartime, but for a quick jaunt into the deep to see colorful fish and coral, it has no equal within The Bahamas. Tours last 90 minutes and include 45 minutes of actual underwater travel at depths of about 3.5m (12 ft.) below

Finds Going Over-the-Hill

Few visitors take this trip any more, but it used to be a tradition to go "Over-the-Hill" to Nassau's most colorful area. Over-the-Hill is the actual name of this poor residential district, where the descendants of former slaves built compact, rainbow-hued houses, leaving the most desirable lands around the harbor to the rich folks. This, not the historic core of Nassau around Rawson Square, is truly the heart of Bahamian-African culture.

The thump of the Junkanoo-Goombay drum can be heard here almost any time of the day or night. The area never sleeps, or so it is said. Certainly not on Sunday morning, when you can drive by the churches and hear hell and damnation promised to all sinners and backsliders.

This fascinating part of Nassau begins .5km (¼-mile) south of Blue Hill Road, which starts at the exclusive Graycliff hotel. But once you're Over-the-Hill, you're a long way from the vintage wine and expensive Cuban cigars of Graycliff. Some people—usually savvy store owners from abroad—come here to buy local handcrafts from individual vendors. The area can be explored on foot (during the day only), but many visitors prefer to drive.

the waves. Big windows allow big views of a protected ecology zone offshore from the Paradise Island Airport. About 20 minutes are devoted to an above-water tour of landmarks on either side of the channel that separates Nassau from Paradise Island.

Deveaux St. Docks. ✆ **242/356-2548.** Reservations required. Tours daily at 11:30am year-round; additional departure at 1:30pm Dec–June. $37 adults, $19 children ages 2–2.

MORE ATTRACTIONS

Balcony House The original design of this landmark house is a transplant of late-18th-century southeast American architecture. The pink, two-story structure is named for its overhanging and much photographed balcony. Restored in the 1990s, the House has been returned to its original design, recapturing a historic period. The mahogany staircase inside was thought to have been salvaged from a wrecked ship in the 1800s. You visit the house on a guided tour.

Trinity Place and Market St. ✆ **242/302-2621.** Free admission but donation advised. Mon–Wed and Fri 10am–4:30pm; Thurs 10am–1pm.

Blackbeard's Tower These crumbling remains of a watchtower are said to have been used by the infamous pirate Edward Teach in the 17th century. The ruins are only mildly interesting—there isn't much trace of buccaneering. What's interesting is the view: With a little imagination, you can see Blackbeard peering out from here at unsuspecting ships. Blackbeard also purportedly lived here, but this is hardly well-documented.

Yamacraw Hill Rd. (8km/5 miles east of Fort Montagu). Free admission. Open all day. Reachable by jitney.

Botanical Gardens More than 600 species of tropical flora are found in this 18-acre park, located within a former rock quarry near Fort Charlotte. The garden features vine-draped arbors, two freshwater ponds with lilies, water plants, tropical fish, and a small cactus garden. After viewing them, you can take a leisurely walk along one of the trails.

Chippingham Rd. ✆ **242/323-5975.** Admission $1 adults, 50¢ children under 12. Mon–Fri 8am–4pm; Sat–Sun 9am–4pm. Bus: 10 or 17.

Central Bank of The Bahamas The nerve center that governs the archipelago's financial transactions is also the venue for a year-round exhibition of paintings that represent some of the emerging new artistic talent of the island. The cornerstone of the building itself was laid by Prince Charles on July 9, 1973, when the country became independent from Britain. His mother in February of 1975 officially inaugurated the bank.

Trinity Place and Frederick St. ✆ **242/322-2193.** Free admission. Mon–Fri 9:30–am–4:30pm.

Fort Charlotte Begun in 1787, Fort Charlotte is the largest of Nassau's three major defenses, built with plenty of dungeons. It used to command the western harbor. Named after King George III's consort, it was built by Gov. Lord Dunmore, who was also the last royal governor of New York and Virginia. Its 42 cannons never fired a shot, at least not at an invader. Within the complex are underground passages and a waxworks, which can be viewed on free tours. Tour guides at the fort are free but are very happy to accept a tip.

Off W. Bay St. on Chippingham Rd. ✆ **242/325-9186.** Free admission. Mon–Sat 8am–4pm. Bus: 10 or 17.

Fort Fincastle Reached by climbing the Queen's Staircase, this fort was constructed in 1793 by Lord Dunmore, the royal governor. You can take an elevator ride to the top and walk on the observation floor (a 38m-/126-ft.-high water tower and lighthouse) for a panoramic view of the harbor. The tower is the highest point on New Providence.

Although the ruins of the fort can hardly compete with the view, you can walk around on your own. Be wary, however, of the very persistent young men who will try to show you the way here. They'll try to hustle you, but you really don't need a guide to see some old cannons on your own.

The so-called bow of this fort is patterned like a paddle-wheel steamer, the kind used on the Mississippi. It was built to defend Nassau against a possible invasion, though no shot was ever fired.

Elizabeth Ave. No phone. Free admission to fort; 50¢ for water tower. Mon–Sat 9am–4pm. Bus: 10 or 17.

Fort Montagu Fort Montagu was built in 1741 and stands guard at the eastern entrance to the harbor of Nassau. It's the oldest fort on the island. The Americans captured it in 1776 during the War of Independence. Less interesting than Fort Charlotte and Fort Fincastle, the ruins of this place are mainly for fort buffs. Many visitors find the nearby park, with well-maintained lawns and plenty of shade, more interesting than the fort. Several vendors peddle local handcrafts in the park, so you can combine a look at a ruined fort with a shopping expedition if you're interested.

Eastern Rd. Free admission. No regular hours. Bus: 10 or 17.

Junkanoo Expo This museum is dedicated to Junkanoo, that colorful, musical, and surreal festival that takes place on December 26 when Nassau explodes into a riot of sounds, festivities, celebrations, and masks. It is the Bahamian equivalent of the famous Mardi Gras in New Orleans. If you can't visit Nassau for Junkanoo, this exhibition is the next best thing. You can see the lavish costumes and floats, which the revelers use during this annual celebration. The bright colors and costume designs are impressive if for no other reason than the sheer size of the costumes themselves. Some of the costumes are nearly as big as one of the small parade floats, but they are worn and carried by one person. The Expo has been installed in an old customs warehouse at the entrance to the Nassau wharf. The Expo also includes a souvenir boutique with Junkanoo paintings and a variety of Junkanoo handcrafts.

Prince George Wharf. © **242/356-2731.** Admission $2 adults, 50¢ children. Daily 9am–5:30pm.

Pirates of Nassau *Kids* This museum celebrates the dubious "golden age of piracy" (from 1690–1720). Nassau was once a bustling and robust town where pirates grew rich from plundered gold and other goods robbed at sea. Known as a paradise for pirates, it attracted various rogues and the wild women who flooded into the port to entertain them—for a price, of course. This newly opened museum re-creates those bawdy, lusty days in a series of exhibits illustrating pirate lore. You can walk through the belly of a pirate ship (the *Revenge*) as you hear "pirates" plan their next attack. You can smell the dampness of a dungeon, and you'll even hear the final prayer of an ill-fated victim before he walks the gangplank. It's fairly cheesy, but fun for kids. Exhibits also tell the saga of Captain Woodes Rogers, who was sent by the English crown to suppress pirates in The Bahamas and the Caribbean.

Marlborough and George sts. © **242/356-3759.** Admission $12 adults, $6 children 3–18, free 2 and under. Mon–Sat 9am–5pm. Bus: 10 or 17.

Pompey Museum Vendue House was built of cut limestone blocks around 1769. The property served as the island's commodity market, where palm and coconut oil, lumber, dried fish, hardware, and slaves were bartered and sold. The slavery aspect of the place continued until 1834, when an act of Parliament outlawed the practice throughout the British Empire. Full emancipation was activated in 1838. Named after the leader of a 19th-century slave revolt in the Exumas, the museum houses an exhibition on Bahamian life and culture, including many mementos on what the museum refers to as "the enslavement experience," 19th-century agriculture and sea trading, and 19th-century Bahamian culture.

At Vendue House, Bay St. at George St. © **242/326-2566.** Admission $1 adults, 50¢ children. Mon–Fri 10am–4:30pm; Sat 10am–1pm. Bus: 10 or 17.

WALKING TOUR HISTORIC NASSAU

Start: Rawson Square.
Finish: Prince George Wharf.
Time: 2 hours.
Best Times: Monday through Saturday between 10am and 4pm.
Worst Times: Sunday when many places are closed, and any day lots of cruise ships are in port.

Begin your tour at:

1 Rawson Square

The center of Nassau, Rawson Square lies directly inland from Prince George Wharf, where many of the big cruise ships dock. It is the crossroads of the city, and everyone seems to pass through here, from the prime minister to bankers and local attorneys, to cruise-ship passengers, to shoppers from Paradise Island, to Junkanoo bands. On the square is the Churchill Building, where the controversial prime minister Lynden Pindling

Walking Tour: Historic Nassau

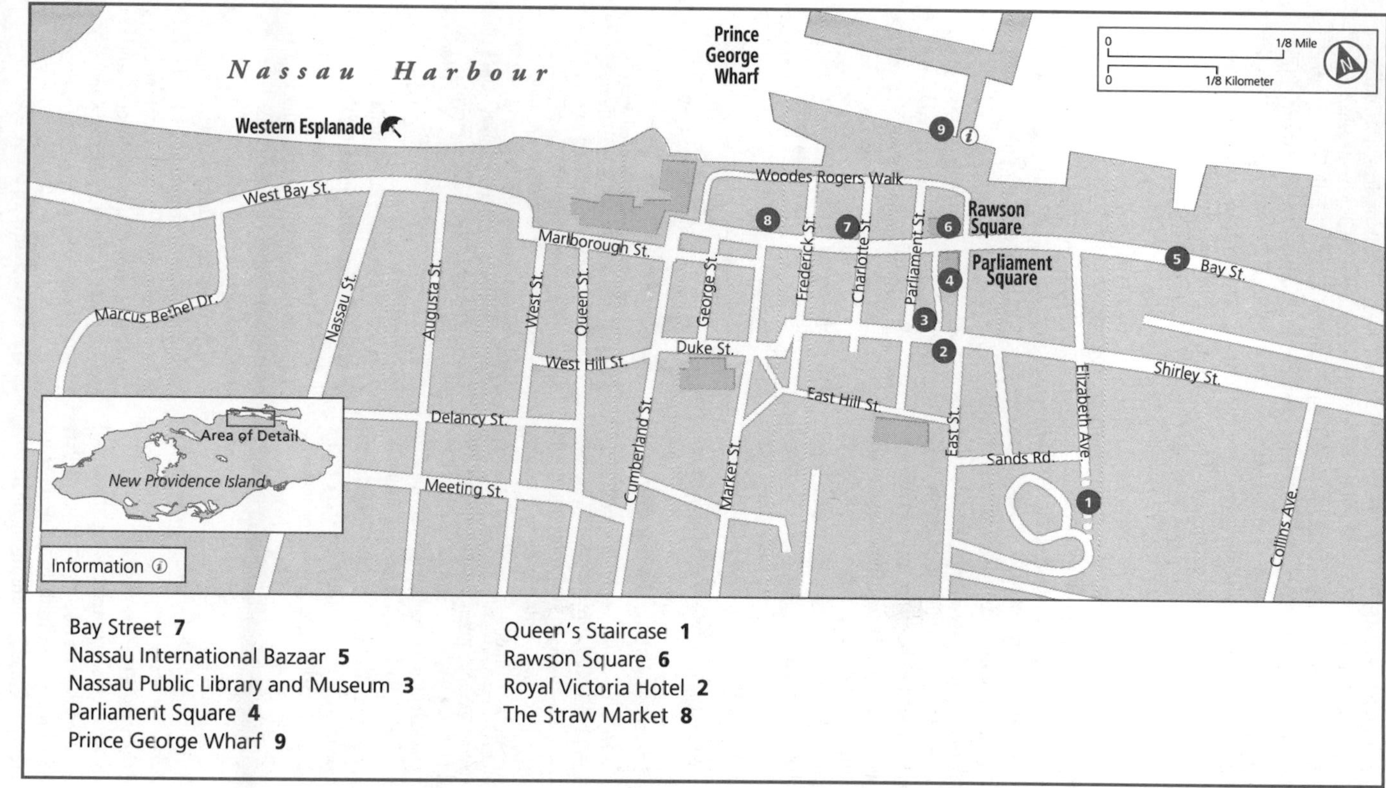

conducted his affairs for 25 years before his ouster in 1992. The current prime minister and some other government ministries use the building today. Look for the statue of Sir Milo Butler, a former shopkeeper who became the first governor of The Bahamas after Britain granted independence in 1973.

Across Rawson Square is:

❷ Parliament Square

A statue of a youthful Queen Victoria dominates the square. To the right of the statue stand more Bahamian government office buildings, and to the left is the House of Assembly, the oldest governing body in continuous session in the New World. In the building behind the statue, the Senate meets; this is a less influential body than the House of Assembly. Some of these Georgian-style buildings date from the late 1700s and early 1800s.

The Supreme Court building stands next to the:

❸ Nassau Public Library and Museum

This 1797 building was once the Nassau Gaol (jail). If you want to pop in here for a look, you can do so Monday through Thursday from 10am to 8pm, Friday from 10am to 5pm, and Saturday from 10am to 4pm. Chances are you will have seen greater libraries in your day. What's amusing is that the small prison cells are now lined with books. Another item of interest is the library's collection of historic prints and old documents dating from colonial days. It became the public library in 1873.

Across from the library on Shirley Street is the former site of the:

❹ Royal Victoria Hotel

In its day, the hotel was the haunt of Confederate spies, royalty, smugglers of all sorts, and ladies and gentlemen. Horace Greeley pronounced it "the largest and most commodious hotel ever built in the tropics," and many agreed with this American journalist. The hotel experienced its heyday during the American Civil War. At the Blockade Runners' Ball, some 300 guests reportedly consumed 350 magnums of champagne. Former guests have included two British prime ministers, Neville Chamberlain, and his replacement, Winston Churchill. Prince Albert, consort of Queen Victoria, also stayed here once. The hotel closed in 1971. After it was destroyed by fire, it was demolished and razed to the ground. Today, on its former site sits one of Nassau's showcase parking lots. Ironically, the parking lot seems to be such a source of pride to the city that it is unlikely the Royal Victoria will ever be rebuilt, at least in that spot.

After imagining the former splendor of the Royal Victoria, head south along Parliament Street.

TAKE A BREAK
If you'd like to relax, try **Café Matisse,** Bank Lane and Bay Street, behind Parliament Square (✆ **242/356-7012**). Although this cafe is also a full-fledged restaurant, it's an ideal place to stop for a drink, especially during happy hour, Monday to Saturday from 5 to 7pm. The house specialty is pizza topped with *frutti di mare,* or fresh local seafood.

At the end of Parliament Street stands:

❺ Nassau General Post Office

If you're a collector, you may want to purchase Bahamian stamps, which can be valuable. You can also mail letters and packages.

Armed with your colorful purchases, walk east (right) on East Hill Street and turn left onto East Street, then right onto Shirley Street, and head straight on Elizabeth Avenue. This will take you to the landmark:

❻ Queen's Staircase

The stairway leads to Bennet's Hill. In 1793, slaves cut these 66 steps out of sandstone cliffs. They provided access from the center of Old Nassau to:

❼ Fort Fincastle

Lord Dunmore built this fort in 1793. Designed in the shape of a paddle-wheel steamer, the fort was a place to look out for marauders who never came. It was eventually converted into a lighthouse, because it occupied the highest point on the island. The tower is more than 60m (200 ft.) above the sea, providing a panoramic view of Nassau and its harbor.

A small footpath leads down from the fort to Sands Road. Once you reach it, head west (left) until you approach East Street again, then bear right. When you come to East Hill Street (again), go left, because you will have returned to the post office.

Continue your westward trek along East Hill Street, which is the foothill of:

❽ Prospect Ridge

This was the old dividing line between Nassau's rich and poor. The rich people lived along the waterfront, often in beautiful mansions. Black Bahamians went "over-the-hill" to work in these rich homes during the day but returned to Prospect Ridge to their own homes (most often shanties) at night.

Near the end of East Hill Street, you come to:

❾ Gregory Arch

This tunnel was cut through the hill in 1850; after it opened, working-class black Bahamians didn't have to go "over-the-hill"—and steep it was—but could go through the arch to return home.

At the intersection with Market Street, turn right. On your right rises:

❿ St. Andrew's Kirk (Presbyterian)

Called simply "the Kirk," the church dates from 1810 but has seen many changes over the years. In 1864, it was enlarged, and a bell tower was added along with other architectural features. This church had the first non-Anglican parishioners in The Bahamas.

On a steep hill, rising to the west of Market Street, you see on your left:

⓫ Government House

This house is the official residence of the governor-general of the archipelago, the queen's representative to The Bahamas. (The post today is largely ceremonial, as an elected prime minister does the actual governing.) This pink-and-white neoclassical mansion dates from the early 19th century. Poised on its front steps is a rather jaunty statue of Christopher Columbus.

Opposite the road from Government House on West Hill Street rises:

⓬ Graycliff

A Georgian-style hotel and restaurant from the 1720s, this stamping ground of the rich and famous was constructed by Capt. John Howard Graysmith in the 1720s. In the 1920s, it achieved notoriety when it was run by Polly Leach, a pal of gangster Al Capone. Later, under royal ownership, it attracted such famous guests as the Duke and Duchess of Windsor and Winston Churchill.

Upon leaving Graycliff, you will see a plaque embedded in a hill. The plaque claims that this site is the spot where the oldest church in Nassau once stood.

On the corner of West Hill Street and West Street is Villa Doyle, former home of William Henry Doyle, chief justice of the Bahamian Supreme Court in the 1860s and 1870s.

Opposite it stands:

⓭ St. Francis Roman Catholic Church

Constructed between 1885 and 1886, it was the first Catholic church in The Bahamas. The Archdiocese of New York raised the funds to construct it.

Continue along West Street until you reach Marlborough. Walk the short block that leads to Queen Street and turn right, passing the front of the American embassy. At the corner of Queen Street and Marlborough rises:

14 British Colonial Hilton

Built in 1923, the most famous hotel in The Bahamas was once run by Sir Harry Oakes, who was at the time the most powerful man on the islands and a friend of the Duke of Windsor. Oakes's murder in 1943, still unsolved, was called "the crime of the century." A set for several James Bond thrillers, this historic location was also the site of Fort Nassau. In the summer of 1999, it became a Hilton hotel.

One part of the hotel fronts George Street, where you'll find:

15 Vendue House

One of the oldest buildings in Nassau, Vendue House was once called the Bourse (Stock Exchange) and was the site of many slave auctions. It is now a museum.

Not far from Vendue House on George Street is:

16 Christ Church Cathedral

Dating from 1837, this Gothic Episcopal cathedral is the venue of many important state ceremonies, including the opening of the Supreme Court: a procession of bewigged, robed judges followed by barristers, accompanied by music from the police band.

If you turn left onto Duke Street and proceed along Market Street, you reach:

17 The Straw Market

The market—largely destroyed by fire in the fall of 2001, but currently being rebuilt by the Bahamian government—opens onto Bay Street and was long a favorite of cruise-ship passengers. Assuming it is back up and running as something like its former self by 2003, you'll find not only straw products but all sorts of souvenirs and gifts, as well. Bahamian women here weave baskets and braid visiting women's hair with beads as another sidelight.

Next, take the narrow little Market Range, leading to:

18 Woodes Rogers Walk

The walk was named for a former governor of the colony who was thrown into debtors' prison in London before coming back to Nassau as royal governor. Head east along this walk for a panoramic view of the harbor, with its colorful mail and sponge boats. Markets here sell vegetables, fish, and lots of conch. The walk leads to:

19 Prince George Wharf

The wharf was constructed in the 1920s, the heyday of American Prohibition, to provide harbor space for hundreds of bootlegging craft defying the American blockade against liquor. The yacht of Queen Elizabeth II, the HMS *Britannia,* has been a frequent visitor over the years. Cruise ships also dock here.

ORGANIZED TOURS

There's a lot to see in Nassau, and many tour options to suit your taste and take you through the colorful historic city and outlying sights of interest.

Goombay Guided Walking Tours, arranged by the Ministry of Tourism, leave from the Tourist Information Booth on Rawson Square at 10, 11:30am, 1, 2:30, and 3:45pm daily. Tours last for 45 minutes and include descriptions of some of the city's most venerable buildings, with commentaries on Nassau's history, customs, and traditions. The hour-long tours require advance reservations, as schedules may vary. The cost is $5, $2.50 for children under 12. Call © **242/326-9772** to confirm that tours are on schedule.

Majestic Tours, Hillside Manor, Cumberland Street, Nassau (© **242/322-2606**), offers a number of trips, both night and day, to many sites. A 2-hour city-and-country tour leaves daily at 2:30pm and goes to all points of interest in Nassau, including the forts, the Queen's Staircase, the water tower, and the Straw Market (passing but not entering it). The tour costs $20 per person, but ask for summer specials. An extended city-and-country tour also leaves daily at 2:30pm and includes the Ardastra Gardens. The charge is $28 per person, half price for children. Combination tours depart Tuesday, Wednesday, and Thursday at 10am and combine all the sights you see on the first tour listed above, plus the Retreat Gardens and lunch. It costs $36 per person, half price for children. Many hotels have a Majestic Tours Hospitality Desk in the lobby, for information about these tours, as well as for reservations and tickets. Other hotels can supply brochures and tell you where to sign up.

EASY SIDE TRIPS TO NEARBY ISLANDS

A short boat trip will take you to several small islands lying off the north coast of New Providence. One of these, **Blue Lagoon Island,** has become so popular that several cruise ships offer their passengers day trips here. Just 5km (3 miles) north of the Narrows at the eastern end of Paradise Island, Blue Lagoon has seven beaches. Although the name recalls images of Brooke Shields, barely clad, cavorting on a desert isle, the reality is quite different. Visitors can dance to a live band, dive with sea creatures at Stingray City, parasail, snorkel, kayak, shop, and lunch at a buffet, among many other things. They also have hammocks and a children's play area with toys.

Blue Lagoon Island has had several owners, including the British Navy, cartoonist John McCutcheon, and the author of *Sophie's Choice,* William Styron. McCutcheon built a watchtower in the 1940s to replace one that was destroyed by an earlier hurricane, and added his own special touch to the structure. He covered the walls of the first floor with his collection of rocks from famous places around the world, including a brick from the Great Wall of China.

Now Ludwig Meister owns the island, and **Nassau Cruises Ltd.** ★★★, Paradise Island Bridge, (© **242/363-3333**) leases it and provides the transportation. Nassau Cruises maintains three motorized yachts, the *Calypso I,* the *Calypso IV,* and the *Islander.* These are the most luxurious cruises you can book. Their trip to uninhabited Blue Lagoon Island (see "Easy Side Trips to Nearby Islands," below) is reason enough just to sail with them. Equipped with bars, their yachts depart from a point just west of the tollbooth on the Paradise Island Bridge. Daytime trips depart every day for the scheduled beaches of Blue Lagoon Island, a 6.5km (4-mile) sail east of Paradise Island. The day sails leave at 10 and 11:30am and come back from the island at 2, and 4:30pm. The Day Pass is $25 for adults and $15 for children and covers for the boat ride only. The all-inclusive Day Pass is $65 for adults and $35 for children (3–12) and covers transportation, the boat ride, lunch, two daiquiris for adults, and all nonmotorized watersports, including snorkeling.

Remote **Rose Island** is a sliver of land poking up out of the sea northeast of the Prince George waterfront docks of Nassau. Shelling is one of the lures of this little islet. If you want to escape the crowds of Nassau, you can take a boat, the *Robinson Crusoe,* which leaves daily at 9am from Nassau and returns at 4:45pm. The cost is $50, $25 for children ages 5 through 11, and free for kids under 5. You can relax in a hammock, snorkel among the coral reefs, and enjoy the white-sand beach before and after your sizzling barbecue lunch with unlimited white wine (included in the price). Bookings for this island retreat trip are available through **Majestic Tours** (© **242/322-2606**).

If you want to see the Exuma island chain on a daylong excursion, try **The Fantastic Exuma Powerboat Adventure.** The name may sound silly, but the trip provides an excellent overview of the area. The boat departs Nassau Harbour at 9am and arrives in the Exuma Cays about an hour later. There are several stops, with snorkeling at a private cay (Ship Channel), a visit with the iguanas on Allan's Cay, feeding stingrays along the shore, and a barbecue lunch. A full bar is available all day, and the drinks are free. The cost is $175 per adult or $99 for children 2 through 12. For more information and prices, contact **Powerboat Adventures** (**© 242/327-5385**).

7 Shopping

The major change occurring in Nassau shopping is that it is going more upscale than decades past. Swanky jewelers and a burgeoning fashion scene have appeared. There are still plenty of T-shirts claiming that "It's Better in The Bahamas," but in contrast you can also find platinum watches and diamond jewelry.

The range of goods in recent years is staggering, in the midst of all the junk souvenirs, you'll find an increasingly array of china, crystal, or whatever watches from such names as Bally, Herend, Lalique, Baccarat, and Ferragamo.

But can you really save money on prices stateside? The answer is "yes" on some items, "no" on others. To figure on what's a bargain and what's not, you've got to know the price of everything back in your hometown, turning yourself into a human calculator about prices—well, almost (see below).

There are no import duties on 11 categories of luxury goods, including china, crystal, fine linens, jewelry, leather goods, photographic equipment, watches, fragrances, and other merchandise. Antiques, of course, are exempt from import duty worldwide. But even though prices are "duty-free," you can still end up spending more on an item in The Bahamas than you would back in your hometown. It's a tricky situation.

If you're contemplating a major purchase, such as a good Swiss watch or some expensive perfume, it's best to do some research in your hometown discount outlets before making a serious purchase in The Bahamas. While the alleged 30% to 50% discount off stateside prices might apply in some cases, it's not true in most cases. Certain cameras and electronic equipment, we have discovered, are listed in The Bahamas at, say, 20% or more below the manufacturer's "suggested retail price." That sounds good, except the manufacturer's suggested price might be a lot higher than what you'd pay in your hometown. You aren't getting the discount you think you are. Some shoppers even take along department-store catalogs from the States to determine if they are indeed getting a bargain.

A lot of price-fixing seems to be going on in Nassau. For example, a bottle of Chanel is likely to sell for pretty much the same price regardless of the store.

Tips **To Bargain or Not to Bargain**

Don't try to bargain with the salespeople in Nassau stores as you would with merchants at the Straw Market (see "Markets," below). The price asked in the shops is the price you must pay, but you won't be pressed to make a purchase. The salespeople here are courteous and helpful in most cases.

Do You
Yahoo!
?

How much you can take back home depends on your country of origin. For more details, plus Customs requirements for some other countries, refer to "Entry Requirements & Customs," in chapter 2.

The principal shopping areas are **Bay Street** and its side streets downtown, as well as the shops in the arcades of hotels. Not many street numbers are used along Bay Street; just look for store signs.

ANTIQUES

Marlborough Antiques This store carries the type of antiques you'd expect to find in a shop in London: antique books, antique maps and engravings, English silver (both sterling and plate), and unusual table settings (fish knives and so on). Among the most appealing objects is the store's collection of antique photographs of the islands. Also displayed are works by Bahamian artists Brent Malone and Maxwell Taylor. Corner of Queen and Marlborough sts. ✆ **242/328-0502.**

ART

Kennedy Gallery Although many locals come here for custom framing, the gallery also sells original artwork by well-known Bahamian artists, including limited-edition prints, handcrafts, pottery, and sculpture. Parliament St. ✆ **242/325-7662.**

BRASS & COPPER

Brass and Leather Shop With two branches on Charlotte Street, this shop offers English brass, handbags, luggage, briefcases, attachés, and personal accessories. Shop no. 2 has handbags, belts, scarves, ties, and small leather goods from such famous designers as Furla, Bottega Veneta, Pierre Balmain, and others. If you look and select carefully, you can find some good buys here. 12 Charlotte St., between Bay and Shirley sts. ✆ **242/322-3806.**

CIGARS

Remember, U.S. citizens are prohibited from bringing Cuban cigars back home because of the trade embargo. If you buy them, you're supposed to enjoy them in The Bahamas.

Tropique International Smoke Shop Many cigar aficionados come here to indulge their passion for Cubans, which are handpicked and imported by Bahamian merchants. The staff at this outlet trained in Havana, so they know their cigars. In Nassau Marriott Resort & Crystal Palace Casino, W. Bay St. ✆ **242/327-7292.**

COINS & STAMPS

Bahamas Post Office Philatelic Bureau Here you'll find beautiful Bahamian stamps slated to become collector's items. One of the most sought-after stamps has a seashell motif. In the General Post Office, at the top of Parliament St. on E. Hill St. ✆ **242/322-1112.**

Coin of the Realm This family-run shop is in a lovely building that was hewn out of solid limestone over 200 years ago. The shop offers not only fine jewelry, but also Bahamian and British postage stamps, mint and used, and rare (and not-so-rare) Bahamian silver and gold coins. It also sells old and modern paper Bahamian currency. Bahama pennies that were minted in 1806 and 1807 are now rare and expensive items. Charlotte St., just off Bay St. ✆ **242/322-4497.**

FASHION

Barry's Limited One of Nassau's more formal and elegant clothing stores, this shop sells garments made from lamb's wool and English cashmere. Elegant sportswear (including Korean-made Guayabera shirts) and suits are sold here. Most of the clothes are for men, but women often stop in for a look at the fancy handmade Irish linen handkerchiefs and the stylish cuff links, studs, and other accessories. Bay and George sts. ✆ **242/322-3118.**

Bonneville Bones The name alone will intrigue, but it hardly describes what's inside. This is the best men's store we've found in Nassau. You can find everything here, from standard T-shirts and designer jeans to elegant casual clothing, including suits. Bay St. ✆ **242/328-0804.**

Cole's of Nassau This boutique offers the most extensive selection of designer fashions in Nassau. Women can be outfitted in everything from swimwear to formal gowns, from sportswear to hosiery. Cole's also sells gift items, sterling-silver designer and costume jewelry, hats, shoes, bags, scarves, and belts. Parliament St. ✆ **242/322-8393.**

Fendi This is Nassau's only outlet for the well-crafted Italian-inspired accessories endorsed by this famous leather-goods company. With handbags, luggage, shoes, watches, cologne, wallets, and portfolios to choose from, the selection may well solve some of your gift-giving quandaries. Charlotte St. at Bay St. ✆ **242/322-6300.**

Mademoiselle, Ltd. The store specializes in the kinds of resort wear that looks appropriate at either a tennis club or a cocktail party. It features locally made batik garments by Androsia. Swimwear, sarongs, jeans, and halter tops are the rage here, as are the wonderfully scented soaps and lotions. Their on-site "Body Shop" boutique supplies all the paraphernalia you need for herbal massages and beauty treatments. Bay St. at Frederick St. ✆ **242/322-5130.**

HANDICRAFTS

Island Tings Everything inside "Tings" pays homage to Bahamian artisans and their ability to craft worthwhile pieces from humble and sometimes-unlikely materials. Expect a minilibrary of books on the archipelago's culture and cuisine, as well as sculptures crafted from driftwood and conch shells, utilitarian jewelry, straw goods such as baskets, natural sea sponges, wall hangings, and Junkanoo masks made from all-natural traditional materials as well as newfangled versions molded from fiberglass. The collection also includes aloe-based skin lotions and perfumes distilled from local plants and flowers. Bay St., between East St. and Elizabeth Ave. ✆ **242/326-1024.**

Sea Grape Boutique This is the finest gift shop on New Providence, with an inventory of exotic decorative items that you'll probably find fascinating. It includes jewelry crafted from fossilized coral, sometimes with sharks' teeth embedded inside, beadwork from Guatemala, Haitian paintings, silver from India, hairbrushes shaped like parrots, and clothing that's well-suited to the sometimes-steamy climate of The Bahamas. There's a second branch of this outfit, Sea Grape Too, in the Radisson Hotel's Mall, on Cable Beach (✆ 242/327-5113). W. Bay Rd. (next to Travelers Restaurant). ✆ **242/327-1308.**

JEWELRY

John Bull The jewelry department here offers classic selections from Tiffany & Co.; cultured pearls from Mikimoto; the creations of David Yurman, Stephen Lagos, Carrera y Carrera, and Sea Life by Kanbana; Greek and Roman coin jewelry; and Spanish gold and silver pieces. It's the best name in the business. The store also features a wide selection of watches, cameras, perfumes, cosmetics,

Finds Goin' Local—Coconut Gin and a Fish Fry

Locals call the small artificial island of **Arawak Cay** "Fish Fry." It lies right in the heart of Nassau, across West Bay Street (from the Botanical Gardens, walk back along Chippingham Rd.). Early in the day, you'll be able to buy ultra-fresh conch; vendors will crack the mollusk before your eyes (this isn't everybody's favorite attraction). They'll give you some hot sauce and tell you to chow down. Beginning around noon, you'll find at least a half-dozen simple bars and kiosks dispensing cracked conch, fried fish, and grits garnished with either spicy corned beef or tuna salad. With it, you can sample a favorite drink of the islands, coconut milk laced with gin (an acquired taste, to say the least, but you'll feel like a real Bahamian). It's at its most crowded and popular every Sunday night, beginning around 5pm until around midnight, when hundreds of Bahamians gather together next to bonfires to gossip, flirt, raise hell, and generally hang out.

leather goods, and accessories. It is one of the best places in The Bahamas to buy a Gucci or Cartier watch. Corner of Bay and Charlotte sts. ✆ **242/322-4253.**

LEATHER

In addition to the stores mentioned below, another good store for leather goods is the **Brass and Leather Shop,** described under "Brass & Copper," above.

Gucci This shop, opposite Rawson Square, is the best place to buy leather goods in Nassau. The wide selection includes handbags, wallets, luggage, briefcases, gift items, scarves, ties, casual clothes, evening wear for men and women, umbrellas, shoes, sandals, watches, and perfume, all by Gucci of Italy. Saffrey Sq., Bay St., corner of Bank Lane. ✆ **242/325-0561.**

Leather Masters This well-known retail outlet carries an internationally known collection of leather bags, luggage, and accessories by Ted Lapidus, Lanvin, and Lancel of Paris; Etienne Aigner of Germany; and "i Santi" of Italy. Leather Masters also carries luggage by Piel and Marroquinera of Colombia, leather wallets by Bosca, and pens, cigarette lighters, and watches by Colibri. Silk scarves, neckties, and cigar accessories are also featured. Parliament St. ✆ **242/322-7597.**

LINENS

The Linen Shop This is the best outlet for linens in Nassau. It sells beautifully embroidered bed linens, Irish handkerchiefs, hand-embroidered women's blouses, and tablecloths. Look also for the most exquisite children's clothing and christening gowns in town. Ironmongery Bldg., Bay St., near Charlotte St. ✆ **242/322-4266.**

MAPS

Balmain Antiques This place offers a wide and varied assortment of 19th-century etchings, engravings, and maps, many of them antique and all reasonably priced. Other outlets have minor displays of these collectibles, but this outlet has the finest. Some items are 400 years old. It's usually best to discuss your interests with Mr. Ramsey, the owner, so he can direct you to the proper drawers. His specialties include The Bahamas, America during the Civil War, and black history. He also has a collection of military historical items. You'll find the shop on the second floor, three doors east of Charlotte Street. Mason's Bldg., Bay St., near Charlotte St. ✆ **242/323-7421.**

MARKETS

The **Nassau International Bazaar** consists of some 30 shops selling international goods in a new arcade. A pleasant place for browsing, the $1.8 million complex sells goods from around the globe. The bazaar runs from Bay Street down to the waterfront (near the Prince George Wharf). With cobbled alleyways and garreted storefronts, the area looks like a European village.

Prince George Plaza, Bay Street, is popular with cruise-ship passengers. Many fine shops (Gucci, for example) are found here. When you get tired of shopping, you can dine at the open-air rooftop restaurant that overlooks Bay Street.

The **Straw Market** in Straw Market Plaza on Bay Street seems to be on every shopper's itinerary, and hopefully the government will finish rebuilding it soon (a fall 2001 fire gutted nearly the entire facility). It may be operating again by the time you read this, though a 2003 reopening seems more likely. Even those who don't want to buy anything should come for a look around. Bahamian craftspeople weave and pleat straw hats, handbags, dolls, placemats, and other items—including straw shopping bags to hold your purchases. You can buy items ready-made (often from Taiwan) or order special articles, perhaps bearing your initials. You can also have fun bargaining for the lowest price. The Straw Market has traditionally been open daily from 7am to 7pm, though these times are subject to change pending the reopening.

MUSIC

Jam Productions One of the finest record stores in the Bahamas, Jam specializes in contemporary music from the Caribbean and abroad. The stores most intriguing service is its made-to-order tapes, a feature that allows you to customize a selection of your favorite music from any existing albums for sales. Shirley St. in the Island Plaza. ✆ **242/394-1789.**

PERFUMES & COSMETICS

Nassau has several good perfume outlets, notably **John Bull** and **Little Switzerland,** which also stock a lot of nonperfume merchandise.

The Beauty Spot The largest cosmetic shop in The Bahamas, this outlet sells duty-free cosmetics by Lancôme, Chanel, YSL, Elizabeth Arden, Estée Lauder, Clinique, Prescriptives, and Biotherm, among others. It also operates facial salons. Bay and Frederick sts. ✆ **242/322-5930.**

Lightbourn's A pharmacy 100 years ago, Lightbourn's is a family-owned and -operated business that today carries a wide selection of duty-free fragrances and cosmetics. It is known for the quality of its goods and its service. Bay and George sts. ✆ **242/322-2095.**

The Perfume Bar This little gem has exclusive rights to market Boucheron and Sublime in The Bahamas. It also stocks the Clarins line (but not exclusively). Bay St. ✆ **242/322-3785.**

The Perfume Shop In the heart of Nassau, within walking distance of the cruise ships, the Perfume Shop offers duty-free savings on world-famous perfumes. Treat yourself to a flacon of Eternity, Giorgio, Poison, Lalique, Shalimar, or Chanel. Those are just a few of the scents for women. For men, the selection includes Drakkar Noir, Polo, and Obsession. Corner of Bay and Frederick sts. ✆ **242/322-2375.**

STEEL DRUMS

Pyfroms If you've fallen under the Junkanoo spell and want to take home some steel drums, you've come to the right place. They'll always be useful if island fever overtakes you after you return home. Bay St. ✆ **242/322-2603.**

8 New Providence After Dark

Gone are the days when tuxedo-clad gentlemen and elegantly gowned ladies drank and danced the night away at such famous nightclubs as the Yellow Bird and the Big Bamboo. You can still find dancing, along with limbo and calypso, but for most visitors, the major attraction is gambling.

Cultural entertainment in Nassau is limited, however. The chief center for this is the **Dundas Center for the Performing Arts,** which sometimes stages ballets, plays, or musicals. Call ✆ **242/393-3728** to see if a production is planned at the time of your visit.

ROLLING THE DICE

Note that you also can easily head over to Paradise Island and drop into the massive, spectacular casino in the Atlantis resort. See chapter 4.

Nassau Marriott Resort & Crystal Palace Casino This dazzling casino—the only one on New Providence Island—is now run by Nassau Marriott Resort. Although some experienced gamblers claim you get better odds in Vegas, the Crystal Palace stacks up well against the major casinos of the Caribbean. The 3,252-square-m (35,000-sq.-ft.) casino is filled with flashing lights, and the gaming room features 750 slot machines, blackjack tables, roulette wheels, craps tables, a baccarat table, and a big six. W. Bay St., Cable Beach. ✆ **242/327-6200.** No cover.

THE CLUB & MUSIC SCENE

Club Waterloo They've seen it all over the years at the Club Waterloo, located in an old colonial mansion set beside a narrow saltwater estuary known as Lake Waterloo. To qualify for the $5 cover charge, you can purchase a visitors' pass from most taxi drivers, which will get you inside the door. If you're not registered at a hotel, the cover charge is $15 Sunday to Thursday, going up to $40 on Friday and Saturday. But despite these high prices, you'll get the feeling that very few people actually pay full price: It's management's way of screening out the bad drunks. The main bar is open nightly from 8pm to 4am, and the sports bar is open from midnight to 4am. Three other minor bars include the Shooters Bar, where shots go for $2, an open-air pool bar, and a Bacardi Bar, which specializes in its namesake. The crowd tends to be an eclectic mix of locals, Europeans, and American vacationers, both singles and couples. E. Bay St. ✆ **242/393-7324.** Cover $5–$40, including 1 or 2 drinks.

King & Knights This is the only folkloric Bahamian show on New Providence. Its linchpin is Eric Gibson ("King Eric"), a talented musician and calypso artist from Acklins Island. He has functioned as the semiofficial ambassador of Bahamian goodwill, conducting concert tours throughout North America, Europe, and Australia. A musical staple here since the late 1950s, his act includes a half-dozen musicians, four or five dancers, a "calypsonian" who might double as a comedian, and a limbo contortionist. The shows are a little short (only 75 min.), but end with a sequence that emulates the Junkanoo festival. If you opt for a dinner here, you can schedule it for whenever you want, before, during, or after the show. In the Nassau Beach Hotel, Cable Beach. ✆ **242/327-7711.** Reservations recommended. Cover charge $10–$30 including 1 drink. Tues–Sun 8:30 and 10:30pm; Sun–Mon 8:30pm.

601 Nightclub This is Nassau's leading nightclub, evocative of the "way it used to be." Don't show up in shorts or tennis shoes, but the dress code isn't what it used to be when women wore evening dresses and men came in black tie. The present decor evokes the heyday of Studio 54 without the glitter ball. The best live bands in Nassau are heard here. Thursday is ladies night when women are admitted free until 11pm (after that, a $5 cover). The club is closed Monday to Wednesday. 601 E. Bay St. ✆ **242/322-3041.** Cover $15–$20. After 8pm, or $5 5–8pm. Open Fri–Sun 5pm with no set closing.

The Zoo Set midway between Cable Beach and the western periphery of Nassau, this is the largest and best-known nightspot of its kind on New Providence. It's housed on two floors of what was once a warehouse, with five bars, an indoor/outdoor restaurant (Zoo Cafe), and a sometimes-crowded dance floor that attracts mainly an under-30 crowd. Each of the five bars has a different theme, including an underwater theme, a jungle theme, and a Gilligan's Island theme. The sports bar is complete with pool tables and wide-screen broadcasts. The most raucous area of the complex is on the street level, where a young crowd congregates to drink and dance. If you're looking for a respite from the brouhaha below, climb a flight of stairs to the "VIP Lounge," which offers stiff drinks and the chance for conversation. Most of the complex is open nightly from 8pm to 4am. W. Bay St. at Saunders Beach. ✆ **242/322-7195.** Cover $5–$40, sometimes including the 1st drink.

VEGAS-STYLE SHOWS

Palace Theater This 800-seat theater is one of The Bahamas's major nightlife attractions. With fake palm trees on each side and lots of glitz, it's an appropriate setting for the Las Vegas–style extravaganzas that are presented on its stage. Two shows are presented every Tuesday, Wednesday, Friday, and Saturday, at 8:45 and 11pm. On Thursday and Sunday, only one show is presented, at 8pm. Except during periods of exceptionally heavy demand, the theater is usually closed on Monday. Advance reservations are recommended, especially for shows on Tuesday and Saturday, when many of the seats might be filled with cruise-ship passengers. In the Crystal Palace Casino, W. Bay St., Cable Beach. ✆ **242/327-6200.** Admission to show plus dinner in any resort restaurant $59; admission to show with 2 drinks but without dinner $39.

THE BAR SCENE

Charlie's on the Beach/Cocktails 7 Dreams The focus within this sparsely decorated club is local gossip, calypso and reggae music, and stiff drinks, all of which can combine into a high-energy night out in Nassau. At press time, the setting was a simple warehouse-like structure a few blocks west of the British Colonial Hotel, although management warns that during some particularly active weekends (including spring break), the entire venue might move, short-term, to a larger, and as yet undetermined, location. Open only Wednesday and Friday to Sunday 9m to 4:30am. W. Bay St. near Long Wharf Beach. ✆ **242/328-3745.** Cover $10–$30.

Crocodiles Waterfront Bar & Grill Look for the hundreds of crocodiles stenciled into the wall that shields this watering hole from busy East Bay Street, and venture into this funky bar for a rum drink. There's a relaxed vibe on the deck, which offers a bit of shade under thatched parasols. You can order up moderately priced steak, seafood, or sandwiches (this place is reviewed under "Where to Dine," earlier in this chapter). There's another wooden building on the premises that is now the home of the America Cup Challenge, which for a fee of $89 per person will train you as a crew member on an 11m (36-ft.) racing yacht. The 4-hour excursion includes your participation in an actual race. You can contact them at ✆ 242/323-1143. The restaurant and bar are open daily 11am to midnight. E. Bay St. (a 2-min. walk from the Nassau side of the Paradise Island Bridge). ✆ **242/323-3341.**

The Drop Off Every harbor town has a rowdy, raucous, and sudsy dive with whiffs of spilled beer and ample doses of iodine from the nearby sea, and in Nassau, this is it. Most of its clients are either local residents, or workers aboard one of the fishing and cargo boats that bob at anchor in nearby Nassau Harbor. The setting is a cavernous room lined with murals of underwater life, all within a cellar that's usually several degrees cooler than the baking sidewalks outside. There's live music some evenings after 11pm, and a short list of two-fisted platters that includes grilled or fried snapper or grouper, steaks, burgers, and sandwiches. E. Bay St. at East St. ✆ **242/322-3444.**

Out Island Bar/The Beach Bar These bars, both within the same hotel, are used primarily by its guests, but both of them are open to all, attracting everybody from newlyweds to those who married when Eisenhower was in office. The more central of the two is the Out Island Bar, set adjacent to the lobby and outfitted in a breezy wicker and rattan theme that goes well with the party-colored drinks that are its specialty. If you want a view, head for the thatch-covered beach bar, set directly on the sands of one of the best beaches in the area. In the Nassau Beach Hotel, Cable Beach. ✆ **242/327-7711.**

4

Paradise Island

Located just 180m (600 ft.) off the north shore of Nassau, Paradise Island is a favorite vacation spot for East Coast Americans, who flee their icy winters for the stunning white sands of Paradise Beach. In addition to its gorgeous beaches, the island boasts beautiful foliage, including brilliant red hibiscus and a grove of casuarina trees sweeping down to form a tropical arcade.

Now the priciest real estate in The Bahamas, the island once served as a farm for Nassau and was known as Hog Island. Purchased for $294 by William Sayle in the 17th century, it cost A&P grocery chain heir Huntington Hartford $11 million in 1960. He decided to rename the 6.5km- (4-mile-) long sliver of land Paradise before selling out his interests. Long a retreat for millionaires, the island experienced a massive building boom in the 1980s. Its old Bahamian charm is now gone forever, lost to the high-rises, condos, second homes of the wintering wealthy, and gambling casino that have taken over. The centerpiece of Paradise Island is the mammoth Atlantis Paradise Island Resort & Casino, which has become a nightlife mecca and a sightseeing attraction in its own right.

For those who want top hotels, casino action, Vegas-type revues, some of the best beaches in The Bahamas, and a posh address, Paradise Island is the place to be. It's now sleeker and more upscale than Cable Beach, its closest rival, and Freeport/Lucaya. True, Paradise Island is overbuilt and overly commercialized, but its natural beauty still makes it a choice vacation spot, perfect for a quick 3- or 4-day getaway.

Although Paradise Island is treated as a separate entity in this guide, it is actually part of New Providence, to which it is connected by a bridge. (You must fly into Nassau to get to Paradise Island.) You can travel between the two on foot, by boat, or by car. So you have the option of staying in Nassau or Cable Beach and coming over to enjoy the beaches, restaurants, attractions, and casino on Paradise Island. You can also stay on Paradise Island and easily go into Nassau for a day of sightseeing and shopping. So view this section as a companion to chapter 3, on New Providence; refer to it for "Fast Facts: New Providence," transportation details, nearby sights, and a wider array of sports and recreation choices.

1 Orientation

ARRIVING

When you arrive at the **Nassau International Airport** (see chapter 3 for information on flying into Nassau), there is no bus service to take you to Paradise Island. Many package deals will provide hotel transfers from the airport. Otherwise, if you're not renting a car, you'll need to take a taxi. Taxis in Nassau are metered and take cash only, no credit cards. It will usually cost you $23 to $25

Paradise Island Accommodations

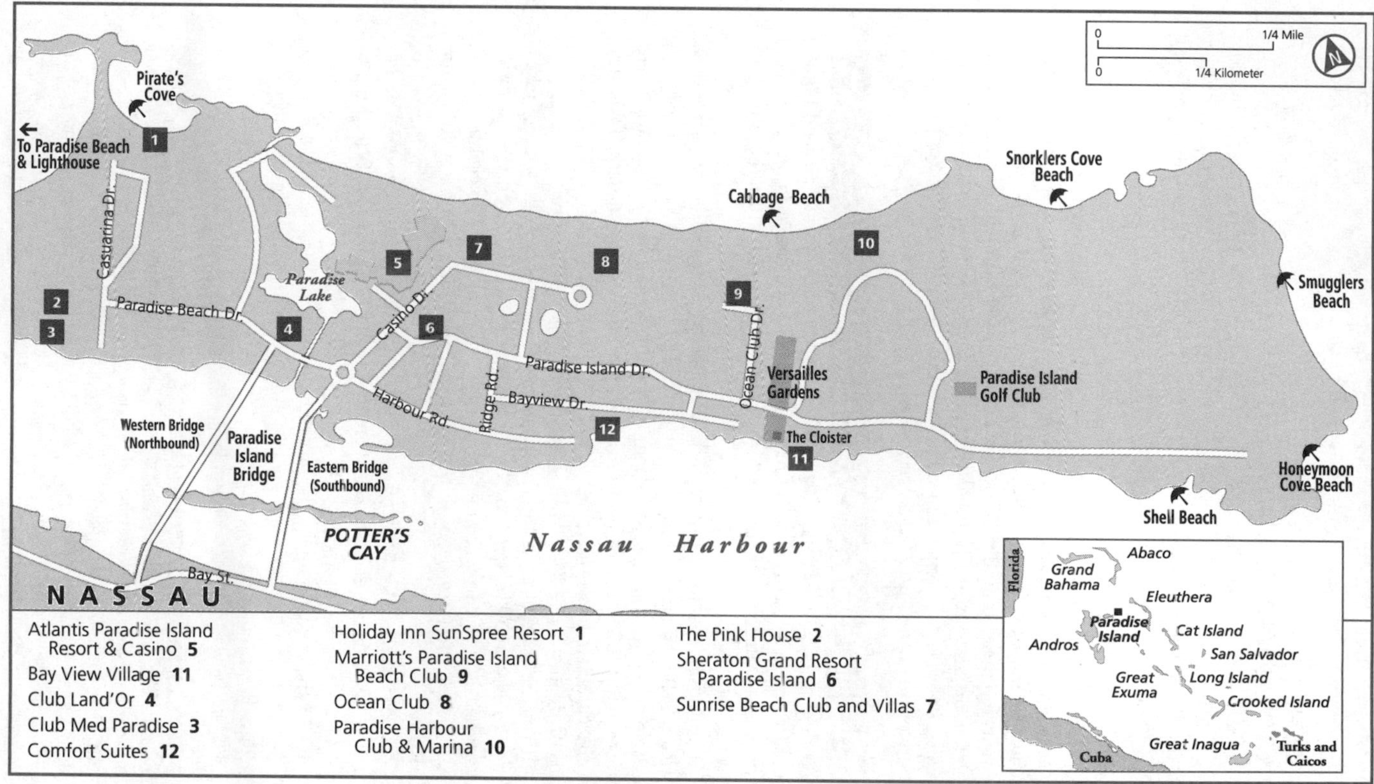

to go by cab from the airport to your hotel. The driver will also ask you to pay the one-way $2 bridge toll (this charge will be added onto your metered fare at the end).

VISITOR INFORMATION

Paradise Island does not have a tourist office of its own, so refer to the tourist facilities in downtown Nassau (see "Orientation," at the beginning of chapter 3). The concierge or the guest services staff at your hotel can also give you information about the local attractions.

ISLAND LAYOUT

Paradise Island's finest beaches lie on the Atlantic (northern) coastline; the docks, wharves, and marinas are located on the southern side. Most of the island's largest and glossiest hotels and restaurants, as well as the famous casino and a lagoon with carefully landscaped borders, lie west and north of the roundabout. The area east of the roundabout is less congested, with only a handful of smaller hotels, a golf course, the Versailles Gardens, the Cloister, the airport, and many of the island's privately owned villas.

2 Getting Around

You don't need to rent a car. Most visitors walk around Paradise Island's most densely developed sections and hire a taxi for the occasional longer haul. For information on renting a car, refer to "Getting Around," at the beginning of chapter 3.

The most popular way to reach nearby Nassau is to **walk across the toll bridge.** Pedestrians pay 25¢.

If you want to tour Paradise Island or New Providence by **taxi,** you can make arrangements with either the taxi driver or the hotel reception desk. Taxis wait at the entrances to all the major hotels. The going hourly rate is about $50 in cars or small vans.

If you are without a car and don't want to take a taxi or walk, you can take a **ferry to Nassau.** The ferry to Nassau leaves from the dock on Casino Drive every half hour, and the 10-minute ride costs $3 one-way. Quicker and easier than a taxi, the ferry deposits you right at Bay Street. Daily service is from 9:30am to 4:15pm.

Water-taxis also operate between Paradise Island and Prince George Wharf in Nassau. They depart daily from 8:30am to 6pm at 20-minute intervals. Round-trip fare is $6 per person.

If you are a guest at one of the properties of Atlantis Paradise Island Resort & Casino, you can take a complimentary tour of the island, leaving Monday and Wednesday through Friday at 2pm.

Unlike New Providence, no public buses are allowed on Paradise Island.

3 Where to Stay

In the off-season (mid-Apr to mid-Dec), prices are slashed by at least 20%—and perhaps a lot more, though the weather isn't as ideal. But because Paradise Island's summer business has increased dramatically, you'll never see some of the 60% reductions that you might find at a cheaper property in the Greater Nassau area. Paradise Island doesn't have to lower its rates to attract summer business. For inexpensive accommodations, refer to the recommendations on New Providence Island (see chapter 3). Paradise Island ain't cheap!

VERY EXPENSIVE

Atlantis Paradise Island Resort & Casino ★★★ Kids The megaresort of The Bahamas, the Atlantis is *massive,* opening onto a long stretch of white-sand beach with a sheltered marina. Think Vegas in the tropics, with a fairly interesting ancient mythology theme thrown in, and you'll get the picture. The advantage is that you'll never be bored; the downside is that it's sprawling and the service just can't keep up with the number of guests here. The Atlantis is a self-contained "water world," with the Lost Continent of Atlantis as its theme. It's a great choice for a family vacation, since kids love all the facilities and gimmicks, and the children's program is outstanding. Singles and young couples who want a lot of action like it, too, though some people find it too over-the-top and impersonal. The Atlantis proudly offers so many sports, dining, and entertainment options that many guests never set foot off the property during their entire vacation.

During 1998 and 1999, a $600-million face-lift was completed, adding more rooms and more wild design touches. A soaring "Royal Tower"—the tallest building in The Bahamas—was added, replete with decorative sea horses, winged dragons, and mega-size conch shells sprouting from cornices and rooflines. The casino and entertainment complex were moved to an area over the watery depths of a lagoon. The best and most plush accommodations are in this new Royal Tower. (Rooms in the Royal Tower's Imperial Club have a personal concierge and upgraded amenities.) But even in the older, less expensive sections, rooms have a comfortable tropical decor. Every one sports a balcony or terrace with water views, individually controlled air-conditioning, in-room movies, voice mail, and modem access, plus roomy bathrooms with tubs and showers. The most deluxe accommodation is the "Bridge Suite," renting for $25,000 a day and sometimes occupied by Michael Jordan while hosting his celebrity invitational at the on-site golf course.

Any old hotel might sport tropical gardens, but the Atlantis goes one better by featuring the world's largest collection of outdoor open-air marine habitats, each of them aesthetically stunning. A few of these were conceived for snorkelers and swimmers, but most were designed so guests could observe the marine life from catwalks above and from glassed-in underwater viewing tunnels. Even folks who don't stay here—including thousands of cruise-ship passengers—come to check out these 11 distinctly different exhibition lagoons containing millions of gallons of water and at least 200 species of tropical fish. They include a shark tank, a stingray lagoon, and separate holding tanks for lobsters, piranhas, and underwater exotica. Swimmers can meander along an underwater snorkeling trail (Paradise Lagoon) and explore a five-story, Disney-style replica of a Mayan temple complete with 18m (60-ft.) water slides.

The focal point of this extravagance is the massive **Paradise Island Casino,** the best-designed casino in The Bahamas. There are 13 bars, nightclubs, and lounges, including a cigar bar (see "Paradise Island After Dark," later in this chapter). There are also 20 restaurants, some reviewed under "Where to Dine"; expect to pay a lot to dine in most of them.

Casino Dr. (P.O. Box N-4777), Paradise Island, The Bahamas. ✆ **800/ATLANTIS** in the U.S., or 242/363-3000. Fax 242/363-6300. www.atlantisresort.com. 2,349 units. Winter $325–$450 double, from $725 suite; off-season $220–$310 double, from $525 suite. Many package deals available. AE, DC, DISC, MC, V. Self-parking free, valet-parking $5 day. **Amenities:** 20 restaurants, 13 bars; 10 tennis courts; marina with 63 megayacht slips; 2 theaters; 11 pools; watersports; 14-acre water park; salon; spa; sauna; massage; travel desk; 24-hr. room service; 24-hr. medical service; babysitting; laundry. *In room:* A/C, TV, minibar, refrigerator, hair dryer, iron/ironing board, safe.

Tips Make a Deal Before You Go

The rates given below are rack rates, and you should be able to avoid paying them. Always ask if special promotional rates are available, or see if a travel agent can help you do better. Package deals often greatly reduce the prices of these resorts, too. ***Be sure to read the section "Package Deals," in chapter 2, before you book a hotel yourself.***

Ocean Club ★★★ Sun International's Ocean Club is the most exclusive address on Paradise Island, with sky-high prices that match the pampering service (the best in The Bahamas) and refined ambience. The white-sand beach that lies adjacent to the hotel is the finest in the Nassau/Paradise Island area. This is also one of the best-developed tennis resorts in The Bahamas. In 1999, Sun International began a major expansion and renovation that was completed in 2000. A favorite honeymoon spot, it's more upscale than the megahotel Atlantis, which is really a fun family resort. Guests can revel in the casino and nightlife activities of Atlantis nearby, then retire to this more tranquil, secluded, and intimate retreat.

The tasteful and spacious rooms are plushly comfortable with king-size beds, gilt-framed mirrors, dark-wood armoires, and one king-size or two double beds. The marble bathrooms in the suites are massive, and each contains a bidet, twin basins, and both a tub and shower.

The real heart and soul of the resort lies in the surrounding gardens, which were designed by the island's former owner, Huntington Hartford. This resort, in fact, was once his private home. Formal gardens surround a French cloister set on 35 acres of manicured lawns. The 12th-century carvings of the Cloister are visible at the crest of a hill, across a stretch of terraced waterfalls, fountains, a stone gazebo, and rose gardens. Larger-than-life statues dot the vine-covered niches on either side of the gardens. Begin your tour of the gardens at the large swimming pool, which feeds a series of reflecting pools that stretch out toward the cloister.

The exciting news for dining on Paradise Island is the resort's opening of Dune, the creation of culinary legend Jean-Georges Vongerichten. In addition, a pair of fountains illuminates the Courtyard Terrace at night. See "Where to Dine," later in this chapter, for a review of both restaurants. Another option is a beachfront restaurant and bar where you can dine under cover but in the open air.

Ocean Club Dr. (P.O. Box N-4777), Paradise Island, The Bahamas. © **800/321-3000** in the U.S., or 242/363-2501. Fax 242/363-2424. www.oceanclub.com. 119 units, 5 private villas. Winter $695–$975 double, $1,250–$1,750 suite, $1,250–$1,350 villa; off-season $400–$645 double, $715–$1,100 suite, $810 villa. AE, DC, MC, V. Free parking. **Amenities:** 3 restaurants, 4 bars; pool; golf course; 9 tennis courts; spa and fitness center; babysitting; shuttle to casino. *In room:* A/C, TV, minibar, hair dryer, iron/ironing board, safe.

EXPENSIVE

Club Land'Or ★ Across the saltwater canal from Atlantis, these self-sufficient timeshare apartments are in three-story motel-like buildings set in a landscaped garden dotted with shrubs and reflecting pools. Although the club isn't located on the bay, the beach is a short drive away. There's a small freshwater swimming pool, as well as a walking path beside the canal where guests can take in a little salt air. If you're itching to try your luck at the casino, you'll have to drive there or take a taxi. Each of the accommodations includes a separate bedroom, a patio or balcony, and a fully equipped living room. Bathrooms are utilitarian, with showers but no tubs. Some apartments are said to be suitable for four, but we think you'd really have to be into togetherness. The rates depend on the view (garden or water). Facilities include the Blue Lagoon restaurant (see "Where to Dine," below).

Paradise Dr. (P.O. Box SS-6429), Paradise Island, The Bahamas. ✆ **242/363-2400.** Fax 242/363-3403. www.clublandor.com. (For reservations and information, contact the club's executive offices: 7814 Carousel Lane, Ste. 200, Richmond, VA 23294; ✆ **800/552-2839** in the U.S.) 69 units. Winter $225–$285 apt for 2; off-season $175–$195 apt for 2. AE, DISC, MC, V. Free parking. **Amenities:** Restaurant, 2 bars; pool; activities program; massage; babysitting; laundry. *In room:* A/C, TV, safe.

Club Med Paradise ★ This all-inclusive resort occupies 21 acres with lush gardens; its two wings of three-story pastel bungalows curve along 5km (3 miles) of white-sand beach. It appeals to visitors who like lots of activities and watersports. In 1996, Club Med began a $30-million renovation project that continued through 1998, turning the hotel into a "Finest Village," the most deluxe version of the club.

The midsize rooms feature a mix of furniture and art from Asia and the Caribbean, and the bathrooms were redone in white marble. They're small, with twin beds (the norm for Club Meds—but why?), comfortable white-cane furniture, and little else. The theory is that you're going to be outdoors all day. In the middle of the complex stands a Georgian-style mansion housing public rooms and restaurant facilities. A walk through the landscaped garden brings members harborside and to the main restaurant. The resort accepts children under 12, but there are no special facilities for them. The place is mostly for people without children. It attracts lots of honeymooners and singles in their 30s. The biggest draw is the tennis facilities, which are among the best in The Bahamas.

Casuarina Dr. (P.O. Box N-7137), Paradise Island, The Bahamas. ✆ **800/CLUB-MED** in the U.S., or 242/363-2640. Fax 242/363-3496. www.clubmed.com. 360 units. Winter $188–$278 per person daily, $1,316–$1,946 per person weekly; off-season $158–$188 per person daily, $1,106–$1,316 per person weekly. Yearly membership $50 per person. Prices are all-inclusive. AE, DC, MC, V. Free parking. **Amenities:** Restaurant (both indoor and outdoor), 2 bars; pool; 18 tennis courts; fitness center; disco; beach bar; open-air theater/dance floor/bar complex; aerobics classes; laundry. *In room:* A/C, TV, hair dryer, safe.

Holiday Inn SunSpree Resort ★ This older, 12-floor property adjacent to the waters of Nassau Harbour opens onto a marina with very little beach, although there is a large swimming pool. It was rescued from oblivion in the late 1990s when a Florida-based investment group, Driftwood Ventures, renovated it. This group turned it into an all-inclusive resort, which lies just a short stroll away from the popular Atlantis and all its attractions. Bedrooms are midsize with twins or king-size beds, plus well-maintained private bathrooms with tub and shower combinations. The decor is comfortable, airy and sunny, and outfitted with tropically inspired colors and upholstery. All third-floor rooms and select units on the fourth floor are designated for nonsmokers only. The food is palatable but needs much improvement, and service is very slow, so be duly warned.

Harbour Dr. (P.O. Box SS-6249), Paradise Island. ✆ **800/331-6471** in the U.S., or 242/363-2561. Fax 242/363-3803. www.basshotelandresorts.com. 246 units. Winter $358–$500 double; summer $198–$298 double. Rates include all drinks, meals, snacks, and most watersports. AE, DC, MC, V. **Amenities:** 2 restaurants overlooking the pool and harbor, poolside snack bar, lobby bar; tennis courts; pool; exercise room; fitness center; massage; sauna; supervised children's program; room service. *In room:* A/C, TV, refrigerator, coffeemaker, hair dryer, iron/ironing board, safe.

Marriott's Paradise Island Beach Club ★ Set near the eastern tip of Paradise Island, adjacent to a relatively isolated strip of spectacular beachfront, this two- and three-story timeshare complex was built in 1985. Managed by

Marriott, it's more of a self-catering condo complex than a full-fledged resort. Many guests cook at least some meals in their own kitchens and head elsewhere, often to bigger hotels, for restaurants, watersports, gambling, and entertainment. Views from the bedrooms are usually ocean panoramas; overall, the setting is comfortable and, at its best, even cozy. You'll feel like you have your own Florida apartment, with easy access to the beach. Apartments have two bedrooms, with wicker and rattan furnishings, and luxuries that include double basins in each bathroom, plus a tub and shower.

On the premises are both a round and a triangular-shaped swimming pool, one with a simple snack bar that's open only at lunchtime. The entertainment and casino facilities of the more densely developed sections of Paradise Island are just a short walk away. The major drawback here is the service, which is very laissez-faire.

Garden View Dr. (P.O. Box N-10600), Paradise Island, The Bahamas. © **800/845-5279** in the U.S., or 242/363-2814. Fax 242/363-2130. www.marriott.com. 44 units. $300 for up to 6. AE, DC, MC, V. **Amenities:** Snack bar; laundry/dry cleaning; 2 pools. *In room:* A/C, TV, kitchen, safe.

Sheraton Grand Resort Paradise Island ★ Kids Opening onto a 5km (3-mile) stretch of sandy beach, the first Sheraton in either The Bahamas or the Caribbean, this hotel was radically rebuilt and renovated to the tune of $10 million after substantial damage during the 1999 hurricanes. This 14-story pink high-rise offers some of the most comfortable recently renovated bedrooms on Paradise Island. This place is more understated than the Atlantis, a lot cheaper, and more user-friendly and manageable in terms of size and layout. Your kids will be happier with all the spectacular events at the Atlantis, but the Sheraton is a viable runner-up for the family trade. Guests can leave the shelter of the poolside terrace and settle almost immediately onto one of the waterside chaise lounges at the beach. The hotel is within walking distance of the casino, restaurants, and nightlife facilities of the Atlantis Paradise Island Resort & Casino properties.

Welcoming drinks are served while you relax on comfortable chairs in the lobby bar amid palm trees and tropical foliage. All the spacious accommodations here are deluxe and tastefully decorated, and equipped with medium-size bathrooms containing tub and shower combos. Many have spacious balconies that afford sweeping water views. Two floors are nonsmoking.

The premier restaurant is The Rotisserie, which serves excellent lobster, steak, and seafood. Other choices include the multilevel Verandah Restaurant, where you can have breakfast with a view of the sea. Julie's Ristorante Italiano is another good restaurant with moderate prices (see "Where to Dine," below).

Casino Dr. (P.O. Box SS-6307), Paradise Island, The Bahamas. © **800/782-9488** in the U.S., or 242/363-3500. Fax 242/363-3500. www.sheratongrand.com. 340 units. Winter $320–$350 double, from $700 suite; off-season $255–$285 double, from $270 suite. AE, DC, MC, V. **Amenities:** 4 restaurants, 4 bars; pool; 4 lighted tennis courts; fitness center; room service; laundry/dry cleaning; babysitting; valet, beauty salon; fleet of boats for various water pursuits such as parasailing or jet skiing; scuba and snorkeling lessons. *In room:* A/C, TV, minibar, coffeemaker, hair dryer, iron/ironing board, safe.

Sunrise Beach Club and Villas ★ Kids This cluster of Spanish-inspired low-rise town houses occupies one of the most desirable stretches of beachfront on Paradise Island. You'll find it midway between the Sheraton Grand and the Ocean Club, a short walk from the casino and a variety of sports and dining options. Accommodations are clustered within five separate groupings of red-roofed town houses, each with access to the resort's two swimming pools (one of which has a waterfall) and a simple snack bar. The hotel is usually full of lots of Germans, Swiss, and Austrians, many of whom stay for several weeks, preparing most of their own meals, since units have kitchens. Expect pastel colors, summery-looking furniture, and a private patio or veranda, plus king-size beds and floor-to-ceiling mirrored headboards, as well as average-size bathrooms with tub and shower. This is a good bet for "quieter" families who want a more subdued and relaxed vacation, and who want to avoid the "circus" going on 24 hours at the Atlantis.

P.O. Box SS-6519, Paradise Island, Nassau, The Bahamas. ✆ **242/363-2250.** Fax 242/363-2308. www.sunrisebeachvillas.com. 35 units. Winter $352–$470 1-bedroom apt for 1–4, $465 2-bedroom apt for 1–6, $726–$1,097 3-bedroom apt for 1–8; off-season $170 studio, $238 1-bedroom apt for 1–4, $416 2-bedroom apt for 1–6, $953–$1,097 3-bedroom apt for 1–8. AE, MC, V. **Amenities:** Restaurant, bar; 2 pools; laundry/dry cleaning; babysitting. *In room:* A/C, TV, kitchen.

MODERATE

Bay View Village ★ More than 20 kinds of hibiscus and many varieties of bougainvillea beautify this 4-acre condo complex. If you get the right nest here, you'll find the accommodations better than those at the more expensive Club Land'Or, its major competitor (see above). Although it is near the geographic center of Paradise Island, it's only a 10-minute walk to either the harbor or the white sands of Cabbage Beach (the complex has no beach of its own). The restaurants, nightlife, and casino of Atlantis are only a few minutes away.

We particularly recommend rooms near the center of the resort, because they are closest to the swimming pools and facilities. Each accommodation has its own kitchen with dishwasher, plus a patio or balcony and daily maid service. Some units open onto views of the harbor. A full-time personal cook can be arranged on request. The units come in a wide variety of sizes; the largest can hold up to six. Rates are slightly less for weekly rentals. Penthouse suites contain roof gardens that open onto views of the harbor. Bedrooms, come with king-, queen-, or twin-size beds. Bathrooms are medium in size, well-maintained, and equipped with tub and shower combos.

Bayview Dr. (P.O. Box SS-6308), Paradise Island, The Bahamas. ✆ **800/757-1357** in the U.S. and Canada, or 242/363-2555. Fax 242/363-2370. 30 units. www.bayviewvillage.com. Winter $210 1-bedroom suite for 2, $300 penthouse for 2, $350 town house for 4, $370–$385 villa for 4, $510 villa for 6; off-season $150 1-bedroom suite for 2, $220 penthouse for 2, $255 town house for 4, $265 villa for 4, $355 villa for 6. AE, MC, V. **Amenities:** Poolside cafe, bar; 3 swimming pools; tennis court; babysitting; 2 coin-operated laundry rooms; small market. *In room:* A/C, TV, kitchen, hair dryer, safe.

Comfort Suites *Value* A favorite with honeymooners and a good value, this three-story, all-suite hotel is across the street from the Atlantis. If the mammoth Atlantis seems too overpowering, Comfort Suites is a nice alternative. You get the splash and wonder of the Atlantis, but you don't have to stay there all night or when the cruise-ship crowds descend. Although there are both a pool bar and a restaurant on the premises, guests are granted signing privileges at each of the drinking-and-dining spots, as well as the pool, beach, and sports facilities of the nearby Atlantis. Accommodations are priced by their views, over the island, the pool, or the garden. The medium-size bathrooms have beach towels, and ample vanities. Bedrooms are standard motel size with two double beds or one king.

Paradise Island Dr. (P.O. Box SS-6202), Paradise Island, The Bahamas. ✆ **800/517-4000** or 242/363-3680. Fax 242/363-2588. www.comfortsuites.com/hotel/bs003. 228 units. Winter $245–$295 double; off-season $185–$235 double. Rates include continental breakfast. AE, DISC, MC, V. **Amenities:** Restaurant, bar; swimming pool; massage; babysitting; laundry. *In room:* A/C, TV, coffeemaker, hair dryer, safe, refrigerator, iron/ironing board.

INEXPENSIVE

Paradise Harbour Club & Marina The noteworthy thing about this place is its sense of isolation on heavily developed Paradise Island. Set near its extreme eastern tip, a few steps from the also-recommended Columbus Tavern, it was built in 1991. It's pale pink, with rambling upper hallways, terra-cotta tile floors, and clean, well-organized bedrooms. If available, opt for one of the top-floor accommodations so you can enjoy the view.

Paradise Island Dr. (P.O. Box SS-5804), Paradise Island, Nassau, The Bahamas. ✆ **800/HOTEL-411** in the U.S., or 242/363-2992. Fax 242/363-2840. www.phclub.com. 22 units. $150–$275 double; $180–$300 jr. suite; $250–$360 1-bedroom apt for 4, $350–$550 2-bedroom apt for 6. MC, V. **Amenities:** Restaurant, bar; limited room service; laundry/dry cleaning; babysitting; pool; hot tub; tennis court; bikes for guests. *In room:* A/C, TV, kitchenette, minibar, hair dryer, safe.

The Pink House ★ *Value* This place might remind you of a bed-and-breakfast in a verdant corner of England, thanks to its stately nature and the rigorous standards of its owner, Minnie Winn. It was built in the 1920s by Howard Major, the architect who designed many of the mansions of Palm Beach, Florida. Comfortable and commodious, it sports wide wraparound verandas, a brick facade, and a wood-paneled interior. Once part of an estate owned by the heirs to the Sears-Roebuck fortune, it sits on land that's now owned by Club Med (though neither Ms. Winn nor her house is associated with Club Med in any way). For access, you'll have to pass by a security guard at the entrance to the fenced-in Club Med Compound. And although Ms. Winn's establishment doesn't have any particular sports or entertainment facilities of its own, you can pay a fee between $35 and $50 per person for unlimited daylong access to Club Med's buffet tables, swimming pools, tennis courts, and watersports facilities. Many guests of Ms. Winn, however, skip Club Med and swim on the beach (a 5-min. stroll across the narrow island), rest on one of the covered verandas where views extend out over the channel between Paradise Island and Nassau, and read in their simple but dignified and slightly worn midsize bedrooms, each with a shower unit.

P.O. Box SS-19157, Casuarina Dr., Paradise Island, The Bahamas. ✆ **242/363-3363.** Fax 242/469-8102. www.bahamasnet.com/pinkhouse. 4 units. Dec–Apr $120 double; May–Nov $120 double. No credit cards. **Amenities:** Breakfast only; laundry. *In room:* A/C, TV.

4 Where to Dine

Paradise Island offers an array of the most dazzling, and the most expensive, restaurants in The Bahamas. If you're on a strict budget, cross over the bridge into downtown Nassau, which has far more reasonably priced places to eat. Meals on Paradise Island may be expensive, but they're often unimaginative. (Surf and turf appears on many a menu.) Unfortunately, you may not get what you pay for.

The greatest concentration of restaurants, all near the casino, is owned by Sun International. There are other good places outside this complex, however, including the Courtyard Terrace at the Ocean Club and The Rotisserie at the Sheraton Grand Resort, which is that hotel's showcase restaurant.

VERY EXPENSIVE

Bahamian Club ★ FRENCH/INTERNATIONAL Overall, this is our favorite restaurant at the Atlantis. With an upscale British colonial-era feel, it's a big but civilized and clubby spot, with spacious vistas, mirrors, gleaming mahogany, and forest green walls. The excellent food is served in two-fisted portions. Meat is king here, all those old favorites from roasted prime rib to Cornish hen, plus the island's best T-bone, along with a selection of veal and lamb chops. The retro menu also features the inevitable Dover sole, lobster, and salmon steak. All of these dishes are prepared only with top-quality ingredients imported from the mainland. Appetizers also harken back to the good old days, with fresh jumbo shrimp cocktail, baby spinach salad with a bleu cheese dressing, and onion soup. Side dishes are excellent here, especially the penne with fresh tomato sauce and the roasted shiitake mushrooms.

In the Atlantis. ✆ **242/363-3000.** Reservations required. Main courses $41–$45. AE, DC, DISC, MC, V. Thurs–Mon 6–10pm.

Blue Lagoon ★ SEAFOOD Lying across the lagoon from Atlantis, this restaurant is located two floors above the reception area of the Club Land'Or. Come here to escape the glitter and glitz of the casino and the restaurants along Bird Cage Walk. Views of the harbor and Paradise Lake, and music from an island combo, will complement your candlelight meal. Many of the fish dishes, including stone crab claws or the Nassau conch chowder, are excellent. The chef even whips up a good Caesar salad for two. The ubiquitous broiled grouper almandine is on the menu, or try some of the other dishes such as steak au poivre with a brandy sauce, or duck a l'orange. Yes, you will probably have had better versions of these dishes elsewhere, but they are competently prepared and served here, even though the meats are shipped in frozen.

In the Club Land'Or, Paradise Dr. ✆ **242/363-2400.** Reservations required. Main courses $24–$39.95. AE, DC, MC, V. Daily 5–10pm.

Courtyard Terrace ★ CONTINENTAL/BAHAMIAN Okay, so the food isn't the island's finest, which it ought to be for these prices. The on-site Dune is better. But when the moon is right, an evening meal here can be heavenly for people who don't have to watch their wallets. You dine amid palms, flowering shrubs, and a fountain in a flagstone courtyard surrounded by colonial verandas. Live music wafts from one of the upper verandas to the patio below. This isn't the most glittering dining room, but it's the most sophisticated. Women should bring some kind of evening wrap in case it becomes chilly.

The menu includes a strong showing of the classics: beefsteak tartare, prime sirloin, lobster quiche, and chateaubriand. Such a menu also calls for rack of lamb; though the shrimp Provençale or the calf's liver lyonnaise, if featured, may have more zest. With candles flickering in the breeze, music floating down, and tables set with Wedgwood china and crisp linen, you might not even mind the slow service.

In the Ocean Club, Ocean Club Dr. ✆ **242/363-3000.** Reservations required. Jacket and tie required for men. Main courses $42–$60 (highest price for a Maine lobster; most dishes under $45). AE, MC, V. Daily 6:30–9pm.

Dune ★★★ INTERNATIONAL The most sophisticated and cutting-edge restaurant on Paradise Island lies in the west wing, lobby level, of the previously recommended Ocean Club. Created (and still owned) by French-born restaurant guru Jean-Georges Vongerichten, it has a charcoal-gray and black decor that looks like it was plucked directly from a chic enclave in Milan, a sweeping view of the ocean, a teakwood floor that evokes a yacht, and very attentive service. If you approach the place from the grounds, rather than from the interior of the hotel, you'll pass by the herb garden from which many of the culinary flavorings are derived. The chefs here invariably select the very finest ingredients, which are then handled with a razor-sharp technique. Every dish has a special something, especially shrimp dusted with orange powder and served with artichokes and arugula. A splendid choice is tuna spring rolls with soybean salsa. Also charming to the palate is a chicken and coconut milk soup served with shiitake cakes. The goat cheese and watermelon salad is an unexpected delight. Filet of grouper—that standard throughout The Bahamas—is at its savory best here when served with a zesty tomato sauce.

At the Ocean Club, Ocean Club Dr. ✆ **242/363-2000, ext. 64739.** Reservations required. Lunch main courses $14–$38; dinner main courses $28–$65. AE, DC, DISC, MC, V. Daily 7–11am, noon–3pm and 6–9:30pm.

Fathoms ★ SEAFOOD You'll feel as if you're dining under the sea in this very dark seafood palace, with menus printed on stainless-steel sheets and an almost-mystical decor. Illuminating its glossy, metallic interior and four enormous plate-glass windows, sunlight filters through the watery aquariums that surround The Dig, Atlantis's re-creation of an archaeological excavation of the underwater ruins of the Lost Continent.

At first you'll think the best appetizer is a selection of raw seafood in season. But then you're tempted by the blackened sashimi flavored with red ginger as it passes by. The lobster gazpacho is the best on the island, and you can also dig into a bowl of steamy black mussels flavored with chardonnay, garlic, and tomato. The wood-grilled yellowtail appears perfectly cooked with a wasabi potato mash and caviar, and the grilled Atlantic salmon is made extra inviting with its side dish of Parmesan garlic fries, a first for many diners. Save room for dessert, and make it a light, feathery soufflé—a different one is served every night.

In the Atlantis Aquarium. ✆ **242/363-3000.** Reservations recommended. Main courses $33–$59. AE, DC, MC, V. Daily 5:30–10pm.

Five Twins ★ PACIFIC RIM This is one of the most dramatic, cutting-edge, and upscale restaurants in the Atlantis. It's conspicuous consumption all the way, very plush, with a high-tech maritime decor that includes lots of wrought iron and tones of metallic silver and gold. Five Twins offers a cigar bar, ventilated well enough to keep non-smokers content, a satay and sushi bar, and an urban club-style setting with a DJ booth suspended 4.5m (15 ft.) above the dance floor. Menu items fuse Indonesian satay with sushi and touches from California, Thailand, Japan, and other parts of the Pacific Rim.

Begin perhaps with the beluga caviar with cucumber refresh or pepper-cured salmon with vegetable tempura. The main courses are a savory kettle of goodies, especially the crispy fried jumbo shrimp or the steamed sea bass with oven-baked chicken given extra flavor by a shrimp truffle sauce. The sweet and spicy lamb is delectable, appearing with red chard, white beets, and fresh spinach.

In the Casino and Entertainment Complex of the Atlantis Resort. ✆ **242/363-3000.** Reservations required. Main courses $34–$38. AE, DC, MC, V. Daily 6–10pm, with a sushi and satay bar open daily 6:30–11pm.

Villa d'Este ★ ITALIAN Paradise Island's most elegant Italian restaurant offers classic dishes prepared with skill and served with flair. It's become less oriented to Tuscan dishes and is more Americanized Italian now. Italian murals decorate the walls.

Main dishes have flair, including pan-fried chicken breast with artichokes and mushrooms in a lemon-laced white-wine sauce, or a whole roasted rack of lamb coated with red-wine sauce and rosemary potatoes. The freshly made fettuccine tomato sauce and basil is almost perfect. The sea bass is quite delectable here, served with a perfect seafood broth.

In the Atlantis, Bird Cage Walk, Coral Tower, Casino Dr. ✆ **242/363-3000.** Reservations required. Main courses $28–$39. AE, DC, MC, V. Thurs–Tues 6–10pm.

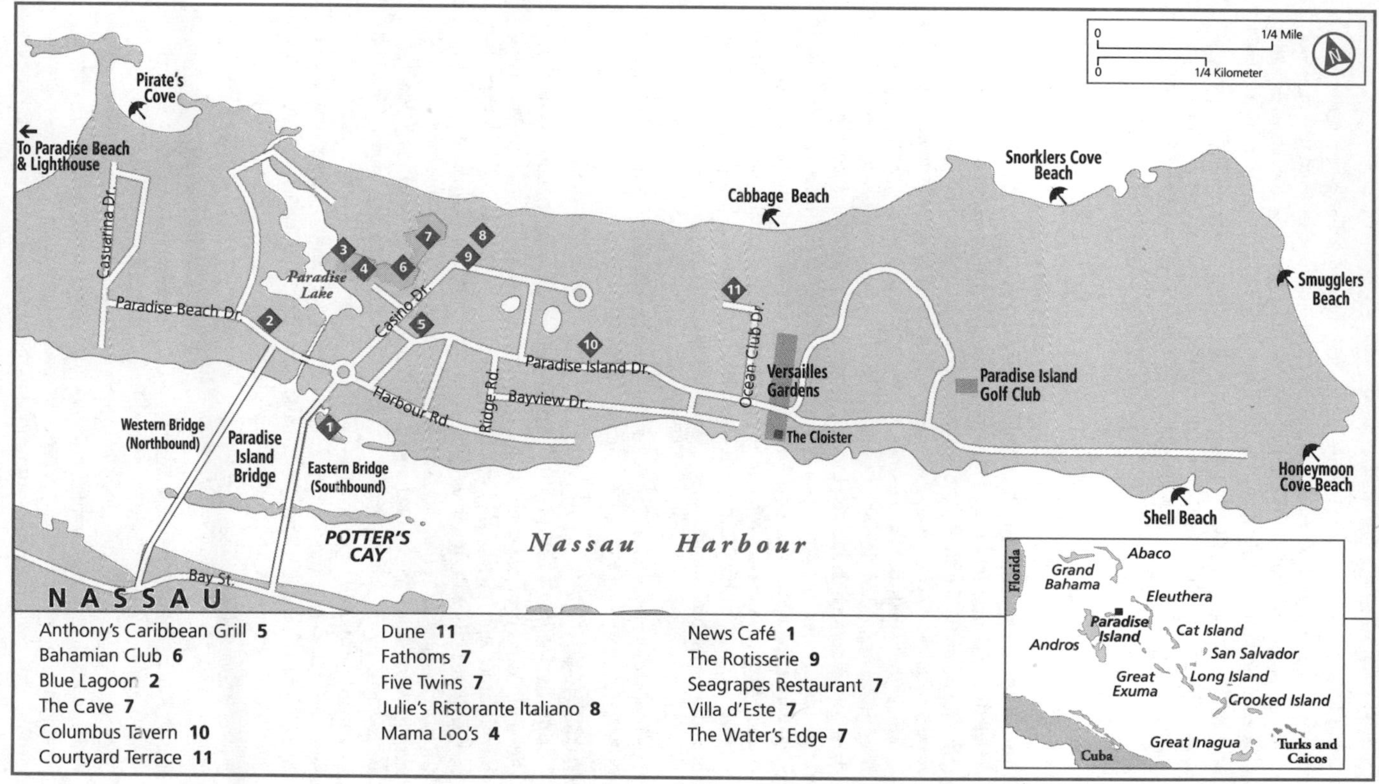
0
1/4 Mile
0
1/4 Kilometer
Pirate's Cove
To Paradise Beach & Lighthouse
Casuarina Dr.
Paradise Beach Dr.
Paradise Lake
Casino Dr.
Harbour Rd.
Ridge Rd.
Paradise Island Dr.
Bayview Dr.
Ocean Club Dr.
Versailles Gardens
The Cloister
Paradise Island Golf Club
Cabbage Beach
Snorklers Cove Beach
Smugglers Beach
Honeymoon Cove Beach
Shell Beach
Western Bridge (Northbound)
Paradise Island Bridge
Eastern Bridge (Southbound)
POTTER'S CAY
Nassau Harbour
Bay St.
NASSAU
Florida
Grand Bahama
Abaco
Eleuthera
Paradise Island
Andros
Cat Island
San Salvador
Great Exuma
Long Island
Crooked Island
Great Inagua
Turks and Caicos
Cuba
Anthony's Caribbean Grill 5
Bahamian Club 6
Blue Lagoon 2
The Cave 7
Columbus Tavern 10
Courtyard Terrace 11
Dune 11
Fathoms 7
Five Twins 7
Julie's Ristorante Italiano 8
Mama Loo's 4
News Café 1
The Rotisserie 9
Seagrapes Restaurant 7
Villa d'Este 7
The Water's Edge 7

EXPENSIVE

Mama Loo's ★ ASIAN Many people come here just to hang out in the bar, but if you're in the mood for a good Chinese meal, you'll be ushered to a table in a dining room with spinning ceiling fans, flaming torches from an overhead chandelier, and lots of potted palms. It evokes Shanghai during the British colonial age. The menu includes dishes from the Szechwan, Cantonese, Polynesian, and Caribbean repertoire. The best dish on the menu is Mama Loo's stir-fried lobster, beef, and broccoli with ginger. Two specialties we also like are shrimp in spicy chili sauce with a peanut sauce, and deep-fried chicken filets with honey-flavored garlic sauce.

In the Coral Tower, Atlantis, Casino Dr. ✆ **242/363-3000.** Reservations recommended. Main courses $21.50–$31. AE, DC, MC, V. Tues–Sun 6–10pm.

The Water's Edge ★ EURO/MEDITERRANEAN Three 4.5m (15-ft.) waterfalls splash into an artificial lagoon just outside the dining room's windows. Huge chandeliers illuminate the room, which has views of an open kitchen, where a battalion of chefs work to create such dishes as paella Valencia or grilled salmon with French beans, potatoes, olives, and artichokes. The oak-smoked and spit-roasted duckling with figs and braised cabbage may win your hearts. Many guests come here just to sample the pizza and pasta specialties. The pizzas are standard, but some of the pastas have a bit of zest, including penne a l'arrabbiata, with a spicy tomato sauce. The chef pays special attention to the antipasti, which evokes the tangy flavors of the Mediterranean, especially the *soup au pistou* (vegetables with basil and roasted garlic). Depending on the night, some of these dishes are better than others. The main problem here is that the food has a hard time competing with the ambience.

At the Atlantis, Casino Dr. ✆ **242/363-3000.** Reservations recommended. Main courses $28–$35. AE, DC, MC, V. Fri–Wed 7:30am–noon and 6–10pm.

MODERATE

Columbus Tavern CONTINENTAL/BAHAMIAN Far removed from the glitz and glamour of the casinos, the tavern seems relatively little known, even though Erika and Peter Kugler have been running it for years now. It deserves to be discovered, because it serves good food at reasonable (for Paradise Island) prices. The tavern has the typical nautical decor (don't come here for the setting), with tables placed both inside and outside overlooking the harbor. The bar is worth a visit in itself, with its long list of tropical drinks. You can go local by starting off with the conch chowder, or opt for cheese-stuffed mushrooms with foie gras. Even though they're imported frozen, both the chateaubriand and the rack of lamb are flawless. You can also order a decent veal cutlet and a quite good filet of grouper with a tantalizing lobster sauce.

Paradise Island Dr. ✆ **242/363-2534.** Reservations required for dinner. Lunch main courses $12–$18; dinner main courses $21–$40. MC, V. Daily 7am–3pm and 5:30–10:30pm.

Julie's Ristorante Italiano ★ *Value* ITALIAN For moderately priced, down-home Italian cooking, check out this place. The gimmick is that you get to create your own pasta dish, choosing from a wide selection of pastas and sauces. Veal and chicken dishes dominate the menu, and most, especially the chicken parmigiana, are quite acceptable. A house specialty is Bahamian lobster tail with shrimp, scallops, and mushrooms topped with Alfredo sauce. You can also order fish, various shrimp dishes, or the ubiquitous grouper, appearing this time decorated with tricolor peppers.

Finds Going Native with Conch

Just once in your life, you've got to sample a Nassau conch salad. The best we could find on the island is at the **Sundeck Bar and Grille,** at the Sheraton Grand Resort on Casino Drive (✆ **242/363-3500**). The uncooked conch is marinated in Old Sour, a hot pepper sauce, to break down its tissue and to add an extra tangy flavor. It's served with diced small red or green peppers along with chopped onions. Sundeck chefs make it fresh daily but only on a limited basis. They warn, "When it's gone, it's gone." You'd better go early.

In the Sheraton Grand Resort Paradise Island, Casino Dr. ✆ **242/363-2011.** Main courses $15.95–$34. AE, DC, DISC, MC, V. Daily 6–11pm.

The Rotisserie ★ AMERICAN This place competes with the better-known steakhouses on New Providence Island but does it at substantially lower prices. The setting includes lots of masculine dark paneling that's softened somewhat with a ring of hand-painted pink and red hibiscus borders. Enjoy sea views through the big open windows, or watch what's going on in the showcase-style glassed-in kitchen. Begin with a grilled chicken salad, conch fritters, or grouper coated with chopped plantain and served with a ginger-flavored butter sauce. Main courses include perfectly prepared roasted rack of lamb, spit-roasted chicken, filet mignon, and either sirloin or porterhouse steaks.

In the Sheraton Grand Resort Paradise Island, Casino Dr. ✆ **242/363-3500.** Reservations required. Main courses $17.95–$32.95. AE, MC, V. Wed–Mon 6–11pm.

INEXPENSIVE

Anthony's Caribbean Grill AMERICAN/CARIBBEAN Its owners think of this place as an upscale version of Bennigan's or TGI Fridays. But the decor is thoroughly Caribbean, thanks to psychedelic tropical colors, underwater sea themes, and jaunty maritime decorative touches. A bar dispenses everything from conventional mai tais to embarrassingly oversize, 48-ounce "sparklers"—with a combination of rum, amaretto, vodka, and fruit punch that is about all most serious drinkers can handle. Menu items include burgers, pizzas capped with everything from lobster to jerk chicken, barbecued or fried chicken, ribs with Caribbean barbecue sauce, and several meal-size salads.

Paradise Island Shopping Center, at the junction of Paradise and Casino drives. ✆ **242/363-3152.** Lunch platters and main courses $5.95–$14; dinner platters and main courses $10.95–$37.95. AE, DC, MC, V. Daily 11:30am–11pm.

The Cave *Kids* BURGERS/SALADS/SANDWICHES This burger-and-salad joint is near the Atlantis's beach, catering to the bathing-suit and flip-flops crowd, most often families. To reach the restaurant, you pass beneath a simulated rock-sided tunnel illuminated with flaming torches. The selection of ice cream will cool you off in the midafternoon sun.

At the Atlantis, Paradise Dr. ✆ **242/363-3000.** Lunch platters $7–$12. AE, DC, MC, V. Daily 11am–6pm.

News Café DELI Low-key and untouristy, this is where you'll find most of the island's construction workers, groundskeepers, and hotel staff having breakfast and lunch. They maintain a stack of the day's newspapers, so you can have something to read as you sip your morning cappuccino or latte. You can also stock up here on sandwiches for your beach picnic.

In the Hurricane Hole Shopping Centre, Paradise Island. © **242/363-4684.** Reservations not accepted. Pizzas, breakfast and lunch sandwiches, platters $6–$9. Assorted coffees $2–$3.50. AE, MC, V. Daily 7am–10pm.

Seagrapes Restaurant *Kids* INTERNATIONAL Buffet lunches and dinners are the specialty of this pleasantly decorated tropical restaurant. This is the most affordable and family-oriented choice in the Atlantis, offering Cuban, Caribbean, and Cajun dishes. It's pretty straightforward fare, but you get a lot of food for not a lot of money—a rarity on pricey Paradise Island. The restaurant, which can seat 200 to 300 diners at a time, overlooks the lagoon and has a marketplace look, with buffet offerings displayed in little stalls and stations.

In the Atlantis, Casino Dr. © **242/363-3000.** Breakfast buffet $19.49; lunch buffet $19.49; dinner buffet $32.14. AE, DC, MC, V. Daily 7–11am, 12:30–3pm, and 5:30–10pm.

5 Beaches, Watersports & Other Outdoor Pursuits

Visitors interested in something more than lazing on the beaches have only to ask hotel personnel to make the necessary arrangements. Guests at the **Atlantis** (© **242/363-3000**), for example, can have access to a surprising number of diversions without so much as leaving the hotel property. They can splash in private pools; play tennis, Ping-Pong, and shuffleboard; ride the waves; snorkel; or rent Sunfish, Sailfish, jet skis, banana boats, and catamarans from contractors located in kiosks.

HITTING THE BEACH

For comments about Paradise Beach, refer to "Beaches, Watersports & Other Outdoor Pursuits," in chapter 3. Paradise Island has a number of smaller beaches, as well. **Cabbage Beach** ★★ is among these, with broad sands that stretch for at least 3km (2 miles). Casuarinas, palms, and sea grapes border it. It's likely to be crowded, but you can find a little more elbowroom by walking on to the northwestern stretch of the beach.

FISHING

Anglers can fish close to shore for grouper, dolphinfish, red snapper, crabs, even lobster. Farther out, in first-class fishing boats fitted with outriggers and fighting chairs, they troll for billfish or giant marlin.

The best way to hook up with this pastime is to go to the activities desk of your hotel. All hotels have contacts with local charter operators who take their passengers out for a half or full day of fishing. For other possibilities, refer to "Beaches, Watersports & Other Outdoor Pursuits," in chapter 3.

GOLF

Ocean Club Golf Club ★★ on Paradise Island Dr. (© **242/363-3925**), at the east end of the island, is an 18-hole championship golf course, designed by Tom Weiskopf, and overlooks both the Atlantic Ocean and Nassau Harbour. Attracting every caliber of golfer, the par-72 course is known for its Hole 17, which plays entirely along the scenic Snorkelers Cove. Greens fees, including cart, are $245 per player, and rental clubs and shoes are available.

Golfers who want more variety will find two other courses on New Providence Island (see "Beaches, Watersports & Other Outdoor Pursuits," in chapter 3).

Favorite Paradise Island Experiences

Catching a Dazzling Stage Show. In the Las Vegas tradition, show-biz extravaganzas are staged at the Atlantis showroom of the Paradise Island Casino.

Watching the Sunset at the Cloister. Here, amid the reassembled remains of a 12th-century French stone monastery, once owned by William Randolph Hearst, you can enjoy one of the most beautiful pink and mauve sunsets in all The Bahamas.

A Day at Paradise Beach. It's one of the best beaches in the entire Caribbean. The beach is dotted with *chikees* (thatched huts) for when you've had too much of the sun.

A Night at the Casino. The Paradise Island Casino is one giant pleasure palace. Many visitors arrive on the island just to test their luck in this 2,787-square-m (30,000-sq.-ft.) casino. The nearby Bird Cage Walk is home to some of the finest restaurants in The Bahamas.

SNORKELING & SCUBA DIVING

For more scuba sites in the area, see "Snorkeling, Scuba Diving & Underwater Walks," in chapter 3.

Bahamas Divers, Sheraton Grand Resort, Casino Drive (© **242/393-8724**), is the best all-around center for watersports on the island, specializing in scuba diving and snorkeling. A one-tank dive, all equipment included, costs $61; a two-tank dive goes for $86. Snorkeling reef trips depart daily at 8am and 1pm, costing $30 with all equipment included.

TENNIS

If you're a true tennis buff, you'll head for the previously recommended **Club Med** ★★ (© **242/363-2640**), which has the largest court complex on the island, a total of 18 clay composition courts. Six of these courts are lit for night games. There are ball machines, plus a full staff of instructors who offer expert advice. There's also instant replay TV. Experienced tennis players who are residents of Club Med can sign up for the ATP (Advanced Tennis Player) program, where for a fee of $150 they'll be coached in tennis techniques for 6 hours a day over a period of 5 days. Nonguests who want to play tennis here should call ahead; they can buy an all-inclusive day pass ($40, valid any day from 8:30am–7pm) and then combine as much tennis as they want with access to all of Club Med's facilities, including its buffets and bars.

Well-heeled tennis buffs check into **Ocean Club,** Ocean Club Drive (© **242/363-3000**). Many visitors come to Paradise Island just for tennis, which can be played day or night on the 10 Har-Tru courts near the Ocean Club. Guests booked into the cabanas and villas of the club can practically roll out of bed onto the courts. Although beginners and intermediate players are welcome, the courts are often filled with first-class competitors. At least two major tennis championships a year are played at the Ocean Club courts, drawing players from the world's top 20. Tennis is free for guests of the Ocean Club. Racket rentals cost $5 per hour for both residents and nonresidents.

Other hotels with courts include the **Atlantis** ★ (✆ **242/363-3000**), with 10 hard-surface courts; and the **Sheraton Grand Resort** (✆ **242/363-2011**), with four night-lit Har-Tru courts and lessons available. These courts are open only to guests, with both hotels charging $20 per hour and the Atlantis $20 per hour.

6 Seeing the Sights

Most of the big hotels here have activity-packed calendars, especially for that occasional windy, rainy day that comes in winter. Hordes of Americans can be seen taking group lessons in such activities as backgammon, whist, tennis, and cooking and dancing Bahamian style. They're even taught how to mix tropical drinks, such as a Goombay Smash or a Yellow Bird. But to an increasing degree, hotels such as the Atlantis have configured themselves as destinations in their own right.

Atlantis Resort & Casino ★★ Regardless of where you're staying—even if it's at the most remote hotel on New Providence—you'll want to visit this lavish theme park, hotel, restaurant complex, casino, and entertainment center. It's Paradise Island's big attraction. You could spend all day here—and all night, too—wandering through the glitzy shopping malls; sampling the international cuisine of the varied restaurants; gambling at the roulette wheels, slot machines, and blackjack tables; or seeing Vegas-style revues. And once you're here, don't even think about leaving without a tour of The Dig, a Disney-style attraction that celebrates the eerie and tragic legend of the lost continent of Atlantis. During the day you can dress casually, but at night you should dress up a bit, especially if you want to try one of the better restaurants.

The most crowded time to visit Atlantis is between 9am and 5pm on days when cruise ships are berthed in the nearby harbor. (That's usually every Tues and Sat between 9am–5pm.) The most crowded time to visit the casino is between 8 and 11pm any night of the week. There is no cover to enter: You pay just for what you gamble away (and that could be considerable), eat, and drink. The big shows have hefty cover charges, although some entertainment in the bars is free, except for the price of the liquor.

Casino Dr. ✆ **242/363-3000.** No cover. Open 24 hr.

The Cloister ★ Located in the Versailles Gardens of the Ocean Club, this 12th-century cloister, originally built by Augustinian monks in southwestern France, was reassembled here stone by stone. Huntington Hartford, the A&P heir, purchased the cloister from the estate of William Randolph Hearst at San Simeon in California. Regrettably, after the newspaper czar originally bought the cloister, it was hastily dismantled in France for shipment to America, but the parts had not been numbered—they all arrived unlabeled on Paradise Island. The reassembly of the complicated monument baffled most conventional methods of construction, until artist and sculptor Jean Castre-Manne set about to reassemble it piece by piece. It took him 2 years, and what you see today, presumably, bears some similarity to the original. The gardens, which extend over the rise to Nassau Harbour, are filled with tropical flowers and classic statues. Unfortunately, although the monument retains a timeless beauty, recent buildings have encroached on either side, marring Huntington Hartford's original vision.

Ocean Club, Ocean Club Dr. ✆ **242/363-3000.** Free admission. Open 24 hr.

7 Shopping

For serious shopping, you'll want to cross over the Paradise Island Bridge into Nassau (see chapter 3). However, many of Nassau's major stores also have shopping outlets on Paradise Island.

The Shops at the Atlantis, in the Atlantis (✆ **242/363-3000**), is the largest concentration of shops and boutiques on Paradise Island, rivaling anything else in The Bahamas in terms of size, selection, and style. The boutiques lie within the recently rebuilt Crystal Court Arcade within the sprawling Atlantis. Most of them are set adjacent to the resort's casino, in a well-appointed arcade that meanders between the Royal Tower and the Coral Tower, although a handful, as noted below, are scattered strategically throughout the resort. It's all very upscale and all about conspicuous consumption, so if you want to do more than browse, bring your platinum card.

There are two separate branches of **Colombian Emeralds** (one in the Crystal Court arcade, another closer to the beach within the Atlantis's Beach Tower), where the colored gemstones far outnumber the relatively limited selection of diamonds. Other choices include **Mademoiselle,** with branches in both the Beach Tower and the Coral Tower, where chic but simple clothing for women focuses on festive beach and resort wear.

The richest pickings lie within the **Crystal Court arcade.** Here, 3,252 square m (35,000 sq. ft.) of merchandising space features **Lalique,** France-based purveyor of fine crystal and fashion accessories for men and women; **Cartier; Versace,** the late designer to the stars (this boutique also has a particularly charming housewares division); **Armani,** whose clothes make almost any woman look like Michelle Pfeiffer and any man at least a bit thinner; **Façonnable,** youthful, sporty designer for young and beautiful club-hoppers; **Bulgari,** purveyor of the most enviable jewels in the world, as well as watches, giftware, and perfumes; and **Gucci** and **Ferragamo,** in case you forgot your dancing shoes. And if you want a bathing suit, **Coles of Nassau** sells swimwear by Gottex, Pucci, and Fernando Sanchez. Finally, **John Bull,** known for its Bay Street store in Nassau and as a pioneer seller of watches throughout The Bahamas, also has an interesting assortment of watches, jewelry, and designer accessories at this outlet.

8 Paradise Island After Dark

Paradise Island has the best **nightlife** in The Bahamas, and most of it centers on the Atlantis.

The Atlantis Resort's Casino and Discothèque There's no other spot in The Bahamas, with the possible exception of the Crystal Palace complex on Cable Beach, with such a wide variety of after-dark attractions, and absolutely nothing that approaches its inspired brand of razzle-dazzle. Even if you stay in Nassau or Cable Beach, you'll want to drop into this artfully decorated, self-contained temple to decadence, even if gambling isn't really your passion. Love it or hate it, this place is simply a jaw-dropper.

The casino is the most lavishly planned, most artfully "themed" casino this side of Las Vegas. The only casino in the world built above a body of water, it was designed as an homage to the lost continent of Atlantis, and it appears to have risen directly from the waters of the lagoon. The gaming area is centered on buildings representing a Temple of the Sun and a Temple of the Moon with a painted replica of the zodiac overhead. Rising from key locations in and around the casino are five of the most elaborate sculptures in the world. Massive

Moments A Special Place of Beauty

If you head up Paradise Island Drive, you'll reach Ocean Club Drive and a garden of tranquillity known as the **Versailles Gardens at the Ocean Club.** This is the loveliest spot on Paradise Island, far removed from the glitz and faux-glamour of the casinos. Its seven terraces frequently host weddings. Statues of some of Hartford's favorite people are found in the gardens, including Mephistopheles, Franklin D. Roosevelt, and even Napoléon. The gardens are open any time, day or night—and there's no admission.

and complex, they were crafted by teams of artisans spearheaded by Dale Chihuly, the American-born resident of Venice whose glass-blowing skills are the most celebrated in the world. Other than the decor, the casino's gaming tables, open daily from 10am to 4am, provide the main attraction in this enormous place; in addition, about a thousand whirring and clanging slot machines operate 24 hours a day.

One side of the casino contains **Dragons,** a disco that manages to attract a few local hipsters as well as guests of the Atlantis. Come here anytime during casino hours for a drink. A sweaty, flirty crowd parties all night on the dance floor. Often, you can catch some of the best live music in The Bahamas, as bands take to the stage that's cantilevered above the dance floor. Live music begins around 9pm nightly. On Friday and Saturday, there's a cover charge of $25, payable by anyone not a guest of the Atlantis.

Ringing the casino are some 3,252 square m (35,000 sq. ft.) of retail shopping space (see "Shopping," above) and an impressive cluster of hideaway bars and restaurants.

Also in the same Atlantis complex, **Joker's Wild** (© **242/363-3000**) is the only real comedy club in The Bahamas, with a talented company of funny people who work hard to make their guests laugh. Show times are Tuesday through Sunday from 8:30 to 9:30pm and from 10:30pm to midnight. At least three comedians will appear on any given night, most of them hailing from The Bahamas, with occasional appearances of performers from London and New York. Midway between the Royal Tower and the Coral Tower. © **242/363-3000.** No cover charge for casino, but cover charges apply to clubs and shows.

THE BAR SCENE

Dune Bar Previously recommended as the number-one restaurant on Paradise Island, this deluxe dining room is also the setting for the island's most elegant and sophisticated bar. It's increasingly popular as a plush and appealing, permissive singles bar. It's centered on a translucent white marble bar that's skillfully illuminated from behind. At the Ocean Club, Ocean Club Dr. © **242/363-2000, ext. 64722.**

The Piranha Pub Overall, this is the most unusual and interesting bar in the entire Atlantis Resort. This mystical-looking pub lies within the hotel's replica of the archaeological excavations of the lost continent of Atlantis. Schools of South America piranhas glare menacingly behind thick plate-glass windows a few inches from your face, darting through a forest of toppled columns, ruined arches, and scattered paving stones. The preferred drink here is a Miami Vice, something midway between a strawberry daiquiri and a piña colada. In theory, this place is open daily from 11am to midnight, but it closes whenever there isn't enough business, so call before you drop by. In The Dig, Atlantis Resort. ✆ **242/363-3000.**

Plato's Lounge This is the hotel's most romantic bar, a sensual spot where you can escape the din of the slot machines. There's a glow from dozens of flickering candles set within lavish candelabras, and ocean views through the oversize windows. A pianist sets the mood during cocktail hour and early evening. In the morning, the site doubles as a cafe, serving pastries and snacks. On the lobby level of the Royal Towers, Atlantis Resort. ✆ **242/363-3000.**

5

Grand Bahama (Freeport/Lucaya)

B*ig, bold,* and *brassy* are the words that best describe Grand Bahama Island, where you'll find the resort area of Freeport/Lucaya. Though there's a ton of tourist development, it doesn't have the upscale chic of Paradise Island, but it does have fabulous white-sand beaches and a more reasonable price tag.

It may never return to its high-roller days with the gloss and glitz of the '60s, when everybody from Howard Hughes to Frank Sinatra and Rat Packers showed up, but recent renovations and massive development have brought a smile back to its face, which had grown wrinkled and tired over the latter part of the 20th century.

The second-most-popular tourist destination in The Bahamas (Nassau/Cable Beach/Paradise Island is first), Grand Bahama lies just 81km (50 miles) and less than 30 minutes by air off the Florida coast. That puts it just 122km (76 miles) east of Palm Beach, Florida. The island is the northernmost and fourth-largest landmass in The Bahamas (118km/73 miles long and 6.5–13km/4–8 miles wide).

Freeport/Lucaya was once just a dream—a low-lying pine forest that almost overnight in the 1950s turned into one of the world's major resorts. The resort was the dream of Wallace Groves, a Virginia-born financier who saw the prospect of developing the island into a miniature Miami Beach. Today, with the casino, the International Bazaar, high-rise hotels, golf courses, marinas, and a bevy of continental restaurants, that dream has been realized.

The Lucaya district was developed 8 years later, as a resort center along the coast. It has evolved into a blend of residential and tourist facilities. As the two communities grew, their identities became almost indistinguishable. But elements of their original purposes still exist today. Freeport is the downtown area and attracts visitors with its commerce, industry, and own resorts, whereas Lucaya is called the "Garden City" and pleases residents and vacationers alike with its fine sandy beaches.

Grand Bahama is more than an Atlantic City clone, however. If you don't care for gambling at one of the island's two casinos, or if you're not interested in Vegas-style cabaret revues, there are alternatives. Because the island is so big, most of it remains relatively unspoiled. There are plenty of quiet places where you can get close to nature, including the Rand Memorial Nature Centre (see below) and the Garden of the Groves. Lucayan National Park, with its underwater caves, forest trails, and secluded beach, is another major attraction. Just kilometers from Freeport/Lucaya are serene places where you can wander in a world of casuarina, palmetto, and pine trees. During the day, you can enjoy long stretches of open beach, broken by inlets and little fishing villages.

The reviews of Grand Bahama Island are definitely mixed. Some

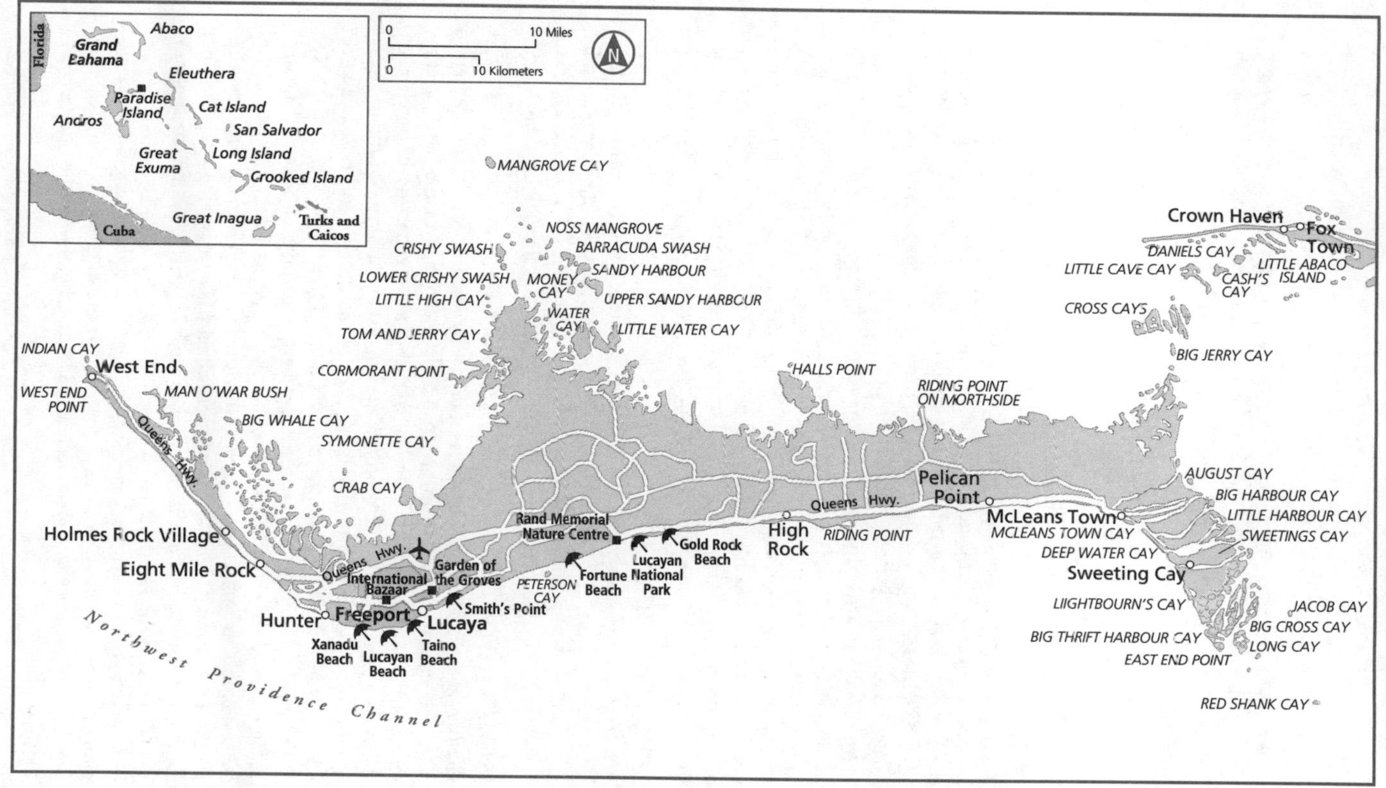
Florida
Grand Bahama
Abaco
Eleuthera
Paradise Island
Andros
Cat Island
San Salvador
Great Exuma
Long Island
Crooked Island
Great Inagua
Turks and Caicos
Cuba
0 10 Miles
0 10 Kilometers
N
MANGROVE CAY
NOSS MANGROVE
CRISHY SWASH
BARRACUDA SWASH
LOWER CRISHY SWASH
MONEY CAY
SANDY HARBOUR
LITTLE HIGH CAY
UPPER SANDY HARBOUR
WATER CAY
TOM AND JERRY CAY
LITTLE WATER CAY
INDIAN CAY
West End
CORMORANT POINT
WEST END POINT
MAN O'WAR BUSH
BIG WHALE CAY
SYMONETTE CAY
Queens Hwy.
CRAB CAY
Holmes Rock Village
Eight Mile Rock
Queens Hwy.
International Bazaar
Garden of the Groves
Hunter
Freeport
Lucaya
Xanadu Beach
Lucayan Beach
Taino Beach
Smith's Point
PETERSON CAY
Rand Memorial Nature Centre
Fortune Beach
Lucayan National Park
Gold Rock Beach
Northwest Providence Channel
HALLS POINT
High Rock
Queens Hwy.
RIDING POINT
RIDING POINT ON NORTHSIDE
Pelican Point
McLeans Town
MCLEANS TOWN CAY
DEEP WATER CAY
Sweeting Cay
LIIGHTBOURN'S CAY
BIG THRIFT HARBOUR CAY
EAST END POINT
Crown Haven
Fox Town
DANIELS CAY
LITTLE CAVE CAY
LITTLE ABACO ISLAND
CASH'S CAY
CROSS CAYS
BIG JERRY CAY
AUGUST CAY
BIG HARBOUR CAY
LITTLE HARBOUR CAY
SWEETINGS CAY
JACOB CAY
BIG CROSS CAY
LONG CAY
RED SHANK CAY

discerning travelers who could live anywhere have built homes here; others vow never to set foot on the island again, finding it "tacky" or "uninspired." Judge for yourself.

1 Orientation

For a general discussion on traveling to The Bahamas, refer to chapter 2.

ARRIVING

A number of airlines fly to Grand Bahama International Airport from the continental United States, including **American Eagle** (© **800/433-7300;** www.aa.com) and **Bahamasair** (© **800/222-4262;** www.bahamasair.com), both with daily flights from Miami. **Lynx Air International, Inc.,** a Fort Lauderdale–based commercial carrier (© **888/596-9247**), flies from Fort Lauderdale to Freeport. **GulfStream Continental Connection** (© **800/231-0856**) flies to Freeport from both Fort Lauderdale and Miami. **TWA** (© **800/221-2000**) flies in from New York's LaGuardia Airport about five times per week. **US Airway** (© **800/428-4322**) flies daily from New York's LaGuardia Airport, and also has a daily flight from Charlotte, North Carolina.

Many visitors arrive in Nassau, then hop a Bahamasair flight to Freeport. These 35-minute hops run about $128 round-trip.

No buses run from the airport to the major hotel zones. But many hotels will provide airport transfers, especially if you've bought a package deal. If yours does not, no problem; taxis meet arriving flights and will take you from the airport to one of the hotels in Freeport or Lucaya for about $11 to $14. The ride shouldn't take more than about 10 minutes.

VISITOR INFORMATION

Assistance and information are available at the **Grand Bahama Tourism Board,** International Bazaar in Freeport (© **242/352-6909**). Another information booth is at the **Freeport International Airport** (© **242/352-2052**). There's also a branch at the cruise-ship docks. Hours are 9am to 5pm Monday through Saturday.

ISLAND LAYOUT

Getting around Freeport/Lucaya is fairly easy because of its flat terrain. Although Freeport and Lucaya are frequently mentioned in the same breath, newcomers should note that Freeport is a landlocked collection of hotels and shops rising from the island's center, while Lucaya, about 4km (2½ miles) away, is a waterfront section of hotels, shops, and restaurants clustered next to a saltwater pond on the island's southern shoreline.

Freeport lies midway between the northern and southern shores of Grand Bahama Island. Bisected by some of the island's largest roads, it contains the biggest hotels, as well as two of the most-visited attractions in the country: the Resorts at Bahamia Casino and the International Bazaar shopping complex. The local straw market, where you buy inexpensive souvenirs, lies just to the right of the entrance to the International Bazaar.

To reach **Port Lucaya** from Freeport, head east from the International Bazaar along East Sunrise Highway, then turn south at the intersection with Seahorse Road. Within about 4km (2½ miles), it will lead to the heart of the Lucaya complex, Port Lucaya.

Set between the beach and a saltwater pond, Port Lucaya's architectural centerpiece is **Count Basie Square,** named for the great entertainer who used to have a home on the island. Within a short walk east or west, along the narrow strip of sand between the sea and the saltwater pond, rise most of the hotels of Lucaya Beach.

Heading west of Freeport and Lucaya, the West Sunrise Highway passes industrial complexes such as The Bahamas Oil Refining Company. At the junction with Queen's Highway, you can take the road northwest all the way to **West End,** a distance of some 45km (28 miles) from the center of Freeport. Along the way you pass Freeport Harbour, where cruise ships dock. Just to the east lies Hawksbill Creek, a village known for its fish market.

Much less explored is the **East End** of Grand Bahama. It's located some 72km (45 miles) from the center of Freeport and is reached via the Grand Bahama Highway, which, despite its name, is rather rough in parts. Allow about 2 hours of driving time. First you pass the **Rand Memorial Nature Centre,** about 5km (3 miles) east of Freeport. About 11km (7 miles) on is **Lucaya National Park,** and 8km (5 miles) farther lies the hamlet of **Free Town;** east of Free Town is **High Rock,** known for its Emmanuel Baptist Church. From here, the road becomes considerably rougher until it ends in **MacLean's Town,** which celebrates Columbus Day with an annual conch-cracking contest. From here, it's possible to take a water-taxi across Runners Creek to the exclusive Deep Water Cay club, catering to serious anglers.

In Freeport/Lucaya, but especially on the rest of Grand Bahama Island, you will almost never find a street number on a hotel or a store. Sometimes in the more remote places, you won't even find a street name. In lieu of numbers, locate places by prominent landmarks or hotels.

2 Getting Around

BY TAXI

The government sets the taxi rates, and the cabs are metered (or should be). If there's no meter, agree on the price with the driver in advance. The cost is $3 for the first kilometer (¾ mile), plus 40¢ for each additional half-kilometer (¼ mile).

You can call for a taxi, although most taxis wait at the major hotels or the cruise-ship dock to pick up passengers. One major taxi company is **Freeport Taxi Company,** Old Airport Road (✆ **242/352-6666**), open 24 hours. Another is **Grand Bahama Taxi Union** at the Freeport International Airport (✆ **242/352-7101**), also open 24 hours.

BY BUS

There is public bus service from the International Bazaar to downtown Freeport and from the Pub on the Mall to the Lucaya area. The typical fare is 75¢ for adults, 50¢ for children. Check with the tourist office (see "Visitor Information," above) for bus schedules. There is no number to call for information.

Tips Island Hopping

If you'd like to visit some other islands while on Grand Bahama, you can do so aboard a small commuter-type airline, **Major's Airlines,** Freeport International Airport (✆ **242/352-5778**), which offers regular flights to Bimini for $110 round-trip, or to Abaco for $140 round-trip. Most of its carriers transport 9 to 15 passengers. Flights are not available every day, so call for schedules, reservations, and more information.

BY CAR

If you plan to confine your exploration to the center of Freeport with its International Bazaar, and Lucaya with its beaches, you can rely on public transportation. However, if you'd like to branch out and explore the rest of the island (perhaps finding a more secluded beach), a rental car is the way to go. Try **Avis** (✆ **800/331-2112,** or 242/352-7666 locally; www.avis.com) or **Hertz** (✆ **800/654-3001,** or 242/352-9277 locally; www.hertz.com). Both of these companies maintain offices in small bungalows outside the exit of the Freeport International Airport.

One of the best local companies is **Star Rent-a-Car,** Old Airport Road (✆ **242/352-9325**), which rents everything from a new-style Volkswagen Beetle to a Toyota Corolla. Rates range from $49 per day with unlimited mileage, plus another $14 per day for a CDW (Collision Damage Waiver). Gas is expensive, usually costing about $7 per gallon.

BY SCOOTER

This is a fun way to get around as most of Grand Bahamas is flat with well-paved roads. Scooters can be rented at most hotels, or, for cruise-ship passengers, there are motor scooters for rent in the Freeport Harbour area. Helmets are required and provided by the outfitter. There are dozens of stands along the road in Freeport and Lucaya and also in the major parking lots. Rentals cost $40 per day, plus a $100 deposit, including insurance. Call ✆ **242/352-9661** (at the Resorts at Bahamia), for more information on scooters.

ON FOOT

You can explore the center of Freeport or Lucaya on foot, but if you want to venture into the East End or West End, you'll need to rent a car, hire a taxi, or try Grand Bahama's erratic public transportation.

FAST FACTS: Grand Bahama

Climate See "When to Go," in chapter 2.

Currency Exchange Americans need not bother to exchange their dollars into Bahamian dollars, because the currencies are on par. However, Canadians and Brits will need to convert their money, which can be done at local banks or sometimes at a hotel, though hotels tend to offer less favorable rates.

Dentists A reliable dentist is Dr. Larry Bain, Sun Alliance Building, Pioneer's Way, Freeport (✆ **242/352-8492**). Hours are Monday through Wednesday from 8:30am to 4pm and Thursday and Friday from 8:30am to noon.

Doctors For the fastest and best service, just head to Rand Memorial Hospital (see "Hospitals," below).

Drugstores For prescriptions and other pharmaceutical needs, go to Mini Mall, 1 West Mall, Explorer's Way, where you'll find **L.M.R. Prescription Drugs** (✆ **242/352-7327**), next door to Burger King. Hours are Monday through Saturday from 8am to 9pm and Sunday 8am to 3pm.

Embassies & Consulates See "Fast Facts: The Bahamas," in chapter 2.

Emergencies For all emergencies, call ✆ **911,** or dial 0 for the operator.

Eyeglass Repair The biggest specialist in eyeglasses and contact lenses is the **Optique Shoppe,** 7 Regent Centre, downtown Freeport (✆ **242/352-9073**).

Hospitals If you have a medical emergency, contact the **Rand Memorial Hospital,** East Atlantic Drive (✆ **242/352-6735,** or 242/352-2689 for ambulance emergency). This is a government-operated, 90-bed hospital.

Information See "Visitor Information," earlier in this chapter.

Laundry & Dry Cleaning Try **Jiffy Cleaners and Laundry,** West Mall at Pioneer's Way (✆ **242/352-7079**), open Monday through Saturday from 8am to 6pm.

Newspapers & Magazines *The Freeport News* is a morning newspaper published Monday through Saturday except holidays. The two dailies published in Nassau, the *Tribune* and the *Nassau Guardian,* are also available here, as are some New York and Miami papers, especially the *Miami Herald,* usually on the date of publication. American news magazines, such as *Time* and *Newsweek,* are flown in on the day of publication.

Police In an emergency, dial ✆ **911.**

Post Office The main post office is on Explorer's Way in Freeport (✆ **242/352-9371**).

Safety Avoid walking or jogging along lonely roads. There are no particular danger zones, but stay alert: Grand Bahama is no stranger to drugs and crime.

Taxes All visitors leaving The Bahamas from Freeport must pay an $18 departure tax—in cash. (Both U.S. and Bahamian dollars are accepted.) There is no sales tax, but there's an 8% hotel tax.

Taxis See "Getting Around," earlier in this chapter.

Weather Grand Bahama, in the north of The Bahamas, has temperatures in winter that vary from about 60°F to 75°F daily. Summer variations range from 78°F to the high 80s. In Freeport/Lucaya, phone ✆ **242/352-6675** for weather information.

3 Where to Stay

Your choices are the Freeport area, near the Bahamia Casino and the International Bazaar, or Lucaya, closer to the beach.

Remember: In most cases, a resort levy of 8% and a 15% service charge will be added to your final bill. Be prepared, and ask if it's already included in the initial price you're quoted.

FREEPORT

EXPENSIVE TO MODERATE

The Resorts at Bahamia ★ *Kids* This mammoth complex actually consists of two differently styled resorts combined under one umbrella: the 10-story Crowne Plaza at Bahamia and the less glamorous, three-story Holiday Inn Sun-Spree at Bahamia. Reinventing itself to stay competitive, the resort is said to be spending some $42 million on its once-tired, built-in-the-1960s properties, hoping to revive some of their old glitz and glamour.

Freeport/Lucaya Accommodations

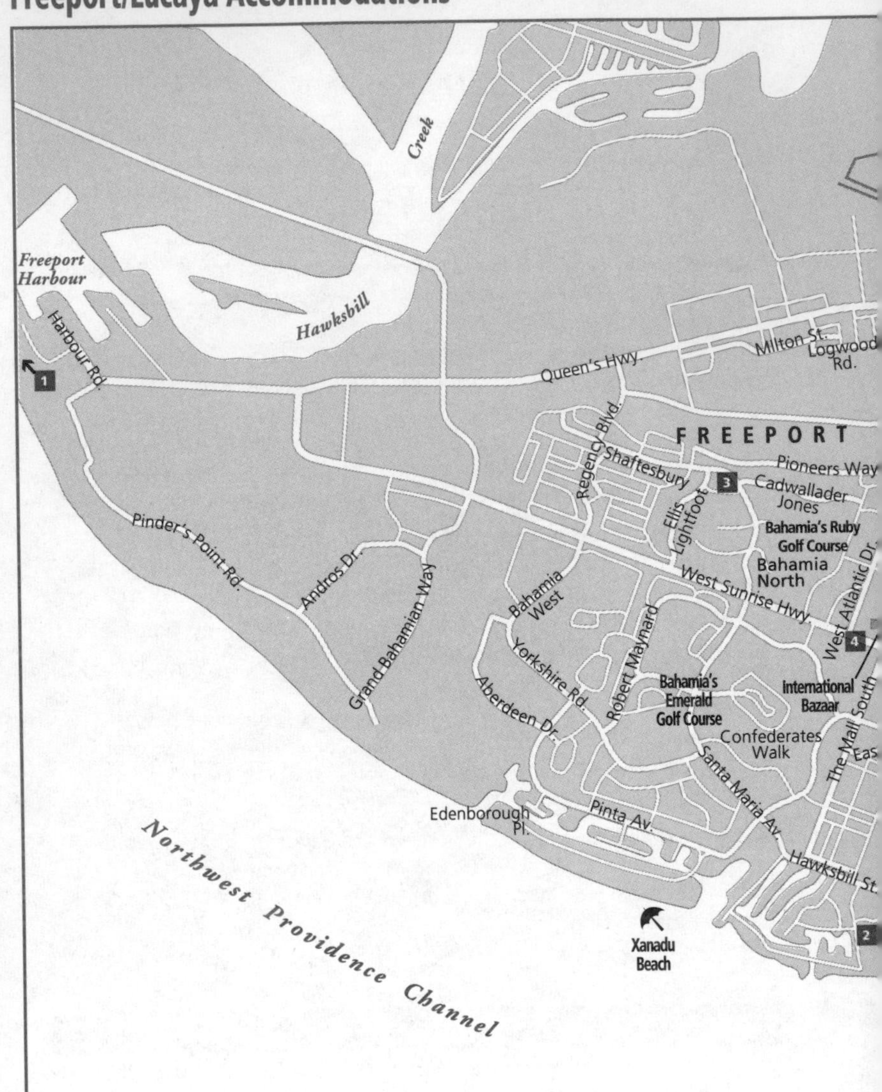

Castaways Resort **5**
Club Villa Fortuna **8**
Coral Beach **13**
Deep Water Cay **9**
Island Palm **7**
Lakeview Manor Club **3**
Old Bahama Bay **1**
Our Lucaya **10**
Pelican Bay at Lucaya **11**
Port Lucaya Resort & Yacht Club **12**
The Resorts at Bahamia **4**
Royal Islander **6**
Running Mon Marina & Resort **2**

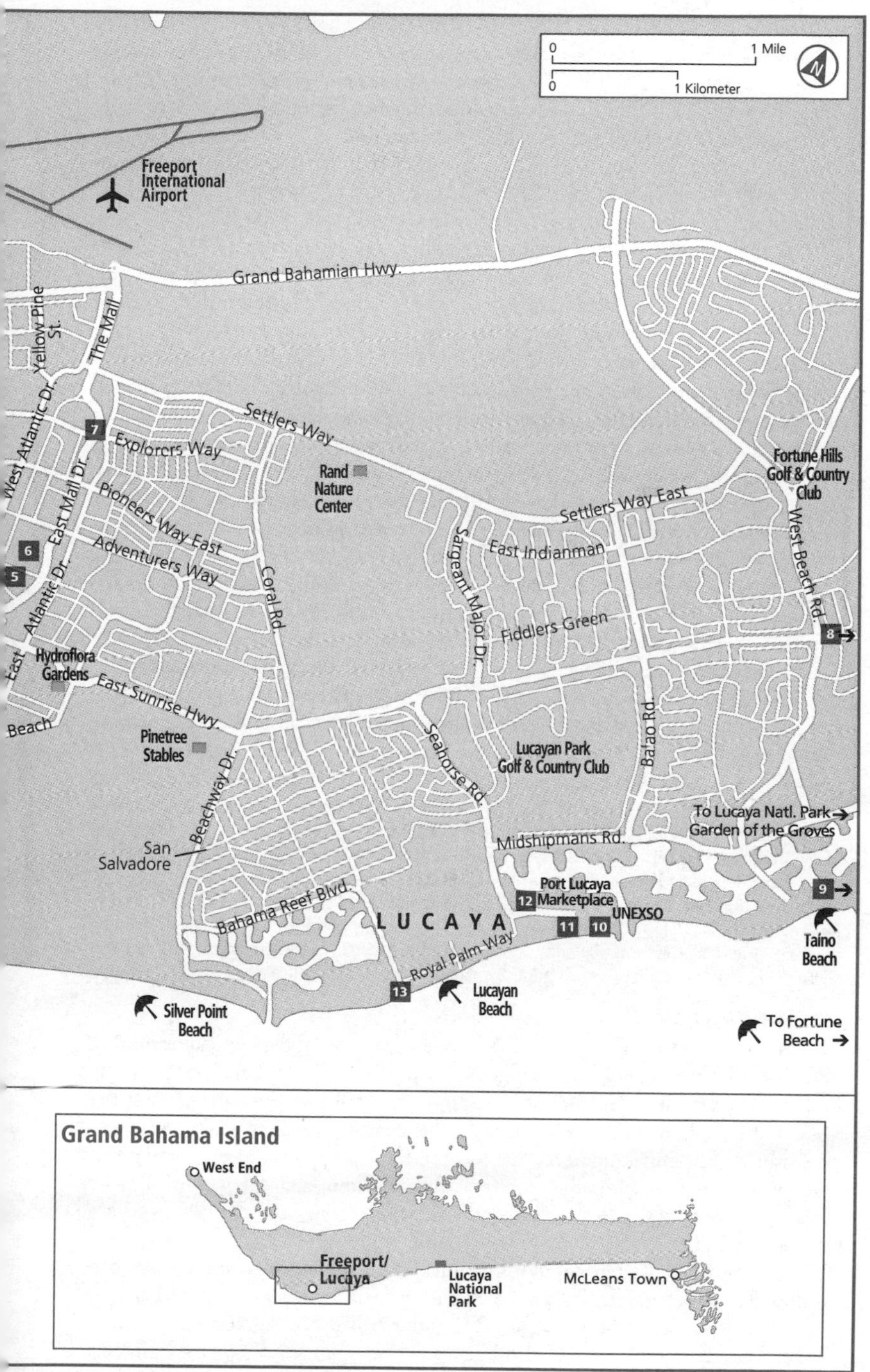
0
1 Mile
0
1 Kilometer
N
Freeport
International
Airport
Grand Bahamian Hwy.
Yellow Pine St.
The Mall
West Atlantic Dr.
East Mall Dr.
East Atlantic Dr.
Settlers Way
Explorers Way
Pioneers Way East
Adventurers Way
Rand
Nature
Center
Coral Rd.
Hydroflora
Gardens
East Sunrise Hwy.
Beach
Pinetree
Stables
Beachway Dr.
San
Salvadore
Bahama Reef Blvd.
LUCAYA
Royal Palm Way
Silver Point
Beach
Lucayan
Beach
Seahorse Rd.
Sargeant Major Dr.
East Indianman
Settlers Way East
Fiddlers Green
Lucayan Park
Golf & Country Club
Balao Rd.
Midshipmans Rd.
Port Lucaya
Marketplace
UNEXSO
Fortune Hills
Golf & Country
Club
West Beach Rd.
To Lucaya Natl. Park
Garden of the Groves
Taino
Beach
To Fortune
Beach
1
2
3
4
5
6
7
8
9
10
11
12
13
Grand Bahama Island
West End
Freeport/
Lucaya
Lucaya
National
Park
McLeans Town

Flanked by a pair of fine golf courses, and thus catering to the convention crowd, the resorts are set on 2,500 acres of tropical grounds. As it lies inland from the sea, the complex doesn't have its own natural beach. However, by the time you read this, a marine park and a man-made, landlocked beach may have been opened; otherwise, you can take frequent shuttle buses to good natural beaches nearby. The two "Bahamias" also jointly share one of the largest casinos in the entire country, a serviceable site that's functional—though nowhere near as flashy or cutting edge as, say, the Atlantis Casino on Paradise Island.

The Holiday Inn at Bahamia attracts families, honeymooners, frugal couples, golfers, and others who don't need or want luxury. The hotel's design is rather like an enormous low-rise wagon wheel, with a Disney-inspired minimountain surrounded by a swimming pool at its core. The hotel is so spread out, guests often complain that they need ground transport just to reach their bedrooms. (Nine wings radiate from the pool.) Some of the rooms have kitchenettes and are sold as timeshare units. Regular accommodations come in several classifications; even standard rooms are well-equipped, with two comfortable double beds, dressing areas, and full-size bathrooms. Rooms in the 900 wing are the largest and best furnished—and are usually the ones that sell out first. Both resorts also rent out a number of suites, each furnished in summery fabrics plus beachy but durable furniture.

Crowne Plaza, lying across the Mall from its larger sibling, is smaller and more tranquil, and a bit more posh, containing 22 suites and 352 luxuriously furnished large units. The tower structure adjoins the Casino and the International Bazaar. The somewhat passé and even vaguely campy Arabic motif, the crowning glory of which is the Moorish-style tower (with turrets, arches, and a white dome), continues through the octagon-shaped lobby. Lots of conventioneers and folks on quick getaways from Florida tend to stay here, as do high rollers.

The Mall at W. Sunrise Hwy. (P.O. Box F-207), Freeport, Grand Bahama, The Bahamas. ✆ **800/545-1300** in the U.S. and Canada, or 242/350-7000. Fax 242/350-7002. www.sunfinder.com. 965 units. Winter Holiday Inn $149–$159 double, $231 1-bedroom suite, $291 2-bedroom suite; Crowne Plaza $179–$189 double, $411 1-bedroom suite, $531 2-bedroom suite. Off-season Holiday Inn $115–$125 double, $180 1-bedroom suite, $240 2-bedroom suite; Crowne Plaza $145–$155 double, $256 1-bedroom suite, $360 2-bedroom suite. Rates are all-inclusive (all meals and drinks). Up to 2 children under 12 stay free in parents' room. AE, DC, MC, V. **Amenities:** 6 restaurants, 6 bars; safe; 2 pools; 2 18-hole championship golf courses nearby; 12 tennis courts (8 lit at night); Jacuzzi; nearby white-sand beach reached by shuttle-bus service; watersports, including deep-sea fishing; room service (7am–10pm); babysitting; massage. *In room:* A/C, TV, hair dryers.

INEXPENSIVE

Castaways Resort & Suites *Kids* Castaways is a modest and unassuming hotel despite its platinum location adjacent to the International Bazaar and the casino. You stay here because of its location and the low price. It's not on the beach, but a free shuttle will take you to nearby Williams Town Beach or Xanadu Beach. Surrounded by gardens, the four-story hotel has a pagoda roof and an indoor/outdoor garden lobby with a gift shop, a clothing shop, a game room, and tour desks. Rooms are your basic motel style, and the best units are on the ground.

The Flamingo Restaurant features unremarkable Bahamian and American dishes. There is a swimming-pool area with a wide terrace and a pool bar that offers sandwiches and cool drinks. The Yellow Bird Show Club (see "Grand Bahama After Dark," later in this chapter) stays open until 3am and features limbo dancers and fire-eaters Monday through Saturday.

International Bazaar (P.O. Box F-42629), Freeport, Grand Bahama, The Bahamas. ✆ **242/352-6682.** Fax 242/352-5087. www.grand-bahama.com/castaways. 130 units. Winter $119–$139 double, $154–$164 suites;

off-season $99–$129 double, $130–$140 suites. Children under 12 stay free in parents' room. AE, MC, V. **Amenities:** Restaurant, 2 bars, nightclub; pool; bike rentals; laundry; babysitting. *In room:* A/C, TV.

Island Palm Set within the commercial heart of Freeport, this simple three-story motel, completely renovated in 1999, consists of four buildings separated by parking lots and greenery. Within an easy walk from virtually everything in town, and 2km (1¼ miles) from the International Bazaar, it offers good value in no-frills, eminently serviceable rooms with well-kept bathrooms equipped with shower-tub combinations. Complimentary shuttle-bus service ferries anybody who's interested to nearby Williamstown Beach (also called Island Seas Beach), where you can use the beachfront facilities (including jet skis and snorkeling equipment) of its sibling resort, a timeshare unit known as Island Sea. The Safari Restaurant, under separate management next door, is recommended separately (see "Where to Dine," below).

E. Mall Dr. (P.O. Box F-40200), Freeport, Grand Bahama, The Bahamas. ✆ **242/352-6648.** Fax 242/352-6640. www.islandpalm.tripod.com. 150 units. Year-round $89–$119 double. AE, DISC, MC, V. **Amenities:** Restaurant next door, bar, snack bar; pool; shuffleboard court. *In room:* A/C, TV.

Lakeview Manor Club Today this 1970s-era resort is a timeshare, but it was originally built as private apartments. It's a good bargain for those who want peace and privacy, but the staff seems a bit lax. Catering to self-sufficient types, it offers midsize one-bedroom and studio apartments, each with tropical furniture, a private balcony, plus small bathrooms with shower stalls. The club overlooks the fifth hole of the PGA-approved Princess Ruby Golf Course. It's 8km (5 miles) from the beach, but it's ideal for golfers or for anyone to whom a sea view isn't important. A complimentary shuttle bus travels to International Bazaar and beach areas.

Cadwallader Jones Dr. (P.O. Box F-42699), Freeport, Grand Bahama, The Bahamas. ✆ **242/352-9789.** Fax 242/352-2283. www.bahamasvg.com/lakeview. 52 units. $75 double studio, $450 double studio weekly; $100 double 1-bedroom apt, $600 double 1-bedroom apt weekly. MC, V. Closed 1 week in Nov. **Amenities:** Pool; 2 tennis courts; reduced greens fees at nearby golf courses; laundry. *In room:* A/C, TV.

Royal Islander Don't be fooled by the corny-looking, storm-battered exterior of this place. It was built during an unfortunate Disney-style period in Freeport's expansion, during the early 1980s, with an improbable-looking pyramidal roof inspired by a cluster of Mayan pyramids. Inside, it's a lot more appealing than you might think, with rooms arranged around a verdant courtyard that seems far, far removed from the busy traffic and sterile-looking landscape outside. Rooms have white-tile floors and bathrooms that are on the small side, with tiny sinks and shower stalls. Otherwise, the motif is Florida/tropical, with some pizzazz.

There's a coffee-shop-style snack bar on the premises, but other than that, you'll have to wander a short distance, perhaps to the International Bazaar just across the street, to find diversions and dining.

E. Mall Dr., Freeport, Grand Bahama, The Bahamas. ✆ **242/351-6000.** Fax 242/351-3546. www.bahamasvg.com. 100 units. Winter $124 double; off-season $82–$92 double. AE, MC, V. **Amenities:** Coffee shop, bar; pool; Jacuzzi; laundry. *In room:* A/C, TV.

Running Mon Marina & Resort ★ *Kids* Renovated in 2000, this is a small-scale, family-friendly resort that caters to yachties and anyone seeking peace and quiet. Originally built in 1991, it's ringed by canals and waterways, the focal point for which is a 66-slip marina. Rising two stories above a mostly flat landscape covered with sand, wispy trees, and scrub, it consists of well-designed, midsize bedrooms face the marina, and each is simply but comfortably outfitted with an unstocked refrigerator and wicker furniture, plus good beds and smallish bathrooms, each with a shower stall.

The complex includes a diving facility (if it's not opened in time for your arrival, the hotel will make alternative arrangements with an outside associate), plus a rather ordinary restaurant (the Mainsail) that's open for breakfast, lunch, and dinner. A free shuttle bus will take you to and from the International Bazaar and the beach.

208 Kelly Court (P.O. Box F-42663), Freeport, Grand Bahama, The Bahamas. ✆ **242/352-6834.** Fax 242/352-6835. www.runningmonbahamas.com. 32 units. Winter $128 double, $249 suite; off-season $98 double, $198 suite. AE, MC, V. **Amenities:** Restaurant, 2 bars; pool; laundry; children's playground; bike rentals; deep-sea fishing arranged; shopping center. *In room:* A/C, TV, refrigerator, hairy dryer, safe.

LUCAYA

EXPENSIVE

Our Lucaya ★★★ This massive resort, one of the largest in The Bahamas, is firmly anchored at the center of two of the best white sandy beaches in The Bahamas—Lucayan Beach and Taino Beach. Expect nearly 8 acres of soft white sand. Freeport/Lucaya, which had been losing tourist business to Paradise Island, got a big boost in 1999 when this sprawling metropolis opened its doors. Prior to that, this was the site of two battered, past-their-prime hotels (the Atlantik Beach Hotel and the Lucayan Beach Resort & Casino). Accompanied by fireworks and brass bands, with the entire island looking on, the Atlantik Beach was imploded to make room for the vision of things to come. The Hong Kong–based Hutchison-Whampoa Group committed themselves to a total investment of at least $290 million. The radically redesigned resort was completed in 2000, when all three of its hotel components were fully operational and functional.

The first of the three sections was completed late in 1998 under the name **The Reef Village.** It's the only one of the three branches of Our Lucaya to focus exclusively on all-inclusive holidays, whereby all meals, drinks, and most activities are included in one set price. With a vague South Beach Art Deco design, it's a massive, open-sided hexagon, with rooms facing the beach and the swimming pool. The resort is contemporary but relaxed; the developers have created a young vibe that draws a high number of families. Bedrooms are whimsical and fun, thanks to fabrics you'd expect on a loud Hawaiian shirt from the Elvis era and maple-veneered furniture, all put together with the kind of artful simplicity you'd expect in a California beach house.

In 2000, two newer subdivisions of Our Lucaya were opened, neither of which is marketed as an all-inclusive property. The smaller and somewhat more private of the two is **Lighthouse Pointe,** a 221-unit, low-rise complex that focuses specifically on an adult clientele. Its larger counterpart is the 550-unit **Breakers Cay,** a grand, 10-story, white-sided tower. The three sections stretch in a glittering profile along a narrow strip of beachfront, allowing residents to drop into any of the bars, restaurants, and gardens. A complex this big contains a staggering diversity of restaurants, each designed with a different theme and ambience. The best of the resort's 14 cuisine selections will be reviewed under "Where to Dine," later in this chapter. And consistent with the broad themes, each of the subdivisions has a dramatic and/or unconventional swimming pool. For example, the Reef Village's pool is designed around a replica of a 19th-century sugar mill, complete with an aqueduct that might be worthy of the ancient Romans. During the lifetime of this edition, look for the opening of a spa and fitness center, a quartet of tennis courts, a convention center, a state-of-the-art

Tips **Never Pay Top Price**

Before you try to book your hotel on your own, be sure to read the section in chapter 2 on "Package Deals" and the tips on how to lower hotel costs. Never pay the rack rate! Use the rates given in this section as a point of comparison only.

casino, and a shopping mall, and an increasing emphasis on golf thanks to the opening of the spectacular Reef Course (separately recommended later in this chapter); most or all of these additions were expected to be completed by summer 2002. Children aged 2 to 12 can be amused and entertained throughout daylight hours every day at Camp Lucaya, whose headquarters lie adjacent to the pool at the Reef Village.

P.O. Box F-42500, Royal Palm Way, Lucaya, Grand Bahama, The Bahamas. ✆ **800/LUCAYAN** in the U.S., or 242/373-1333. Fax 242/373-8804. www.ourlucaya.com. 1,251 units. Reef Village (all-inclusive) winter $165–$205 double; off-season $140–$180 double; $30 extra per day for 3rd and 4th occupant. Lighthouse Pointe or Breakers Cay winter $230–$325 double; off-season $130–$200 double; $30 extra for 3rd and 4th occupant. AE, DC, DISC, MC, V. **Amenities:** These will change as new additions open, but you can count on the following: 14 restaurants and lounges; 2 championship 18-hole golf courses; 3 pools; 5 tennis courts; watersports; children's programs; 24-hr. room service; babysitting; laundry. *In room:* A/C, TV, minibar, iron. Suites: A/C, TV, kitchen, refrigerator, minibar, iron.

MODERATE

Pelican Bay at Lucaya ★★ Here's a good choice for travelers with champagne tastes and beer budgets, a hotel with more architectural charm than any other small property on Grand Bahama. It's built on a peninsula jutting into a labyrinth of inland waterways, with moored yachts on virtually every side. Pelican Bay evokes a Danish seaside village, with rows of "town houses," each painted a different color and sporting whimsical trim, and each overlooking the harbor. The hotel opened in the fall of 1996 and later expanded with a new wing in 1999. Its location couldn't be better, right next to Port Lucaya Marketplace, where restaurants and entertainment spots abound. Lucayan Beach, one of the best stretches of white sand on the island, is just across the street, and Taino Beach, with equally good sands, lies immediately to the east of the hotel. UNEXSO, providing some of the best dive facilities in The Bahamas, is next door.

The spacious accommodations have Italian tile floors and whitewashed furniture, with either a king-size bed or twin beds. The end rooms have cross ventilation and are the ideal choices for those who don't want to rely entirely on air-conditioning. No-smoking accommodations can also be requested. Each unit comes with a wet bar and satellite TV, as well as a balcony with a view of the nearby waterway and marina. Bathrooms, although of standard size, contain oversize cotton robes and tub and shower combos.

The hotel has one main restaurant, the Ferry House, which specializes in American and Bahamian food and serves breakfast, lunch, and dinner daily. The Yellow Tail Pool Bar offers drinks and snacks all day.

Royal Palm Way (P.O. Box F-42654), Lucaya, Grand Bahama, The Bahamas. ✆ **800/600-9192** in the U.S., or 242/373-9550. Fax 242/373-9551. www.pelicanbayhotel.com. 69 units. Winter $150–$195 double; off-season $120–$160 double. AE, MC, V. **Amenities:** Restaurant, bar; pool; hot tub. *In room:* A/C, TV, minibar, coffeemaker, hair dryer, safe.

Port Lucaya Resort & Yacht Club ★ With its own 50-slip marina lying next to the Port Lucaya Marketplace, this is an even better choice than the

Running Mon Marina & Resort, its major competitor. Opened in 1993, the resort consists of a series of pastel-colored two-story structures that guests reach via golf cart after checking in. The wings of guest rooms separate the piers—site of some very expensive marine hardware—from a verdant central green space with a gazebo-style bar and a swimming pool. All of this is in the heart of the Port Lucaya restaurant, hotel, and nightlife complex. Although set back inland on a waterway, Lucayan Harbour, this resort lies within a few minutes' walk of Lucayan Beach, one of the island's finest, and is also close to Taino Beach. Even though it's not right on the beach, it's such an easy walk that no one seems to complain. Some guests actually prefer the nautical, yachting look of the place and the nearness to Port Lucaya Marketplace.

The medium-size rooms have tile floors and are attractively and comfortably furnished with rattan pieces and big wall mirrors. The rooms are divided into various categories, ranging from standard to deluxe, and open onto the marina (preferred by yachting guests), the Olympic-size swimming pool, or the well-landscaped garden. (If you don't want to hear the sounds coming from the lively marketplace, request units 1 through 6, which are more tranquil and away from the noise. Nonsmokers can reserve a room in units 5 or 6.) Bathrooms with new shower-tub combinations are tidy and well-maintained, with adequate shelf space.

The hotel's restaurant, Tradewinds Cafe, offers standard Bahamian, American, and international dishes.

Bell Channel Bay Rd. (P.O. Box F-42452), Lucaya, Grand Bahama, The Bahamas. ✆ **800/582-2921** or 242/373-6618. Fax 242/373-6652. www.bahamasnet.com/portlucayaresort. 160 units. Winter $100–$145 double, $175–$250 suite; off-season $80–$120 double, $125–$200 suite. Extra person $25. AE, MC, V. **Amenities:** Restaurant, 2 bars; limited room service; babysitting; pool; Jacuzzi; laundry. *In room:* A/C, TV.

INEXPENSIVE

Coral Beach Built in 1965 as privately owned condominiums, this peacefully isolated property near a sandy beach sits amid gardens and groves of casuarinas in a residential neighborhood. Some of the apartments and rooms have verandas, and four contain kitchenettes. More suitable for older travelers, the complex rents large but rather sparsely furnished units. The Garden Cafe provides international food at reasonable prices and is open daily for breakfast and dinner. You're also within walking distance of the Port Lucaya Marketplace.

Coral Rd. at Royal Palm Way (P.O. Box F-42468), Lucaya, Grand Bahama, The Bahamas. ✆ **242/373-2468.** Fax 242/373-5140. 10 units. Winter $113 double, $122 triple; off-season $91 double, $100 triple. MC, V. **Amenities:** Restaurant, 2 bars; pool; exercise room. *In room:* A/C, TV.

OUTSIDE FREEPORT/LUCAYA

Club Viva Fortuna ★ Think of this as an Italian Club Med. It caters to a mostly European, relatively young crowd, who appreciate the 35 secluded acres of beachfront and the nonstop sports activities that are included in the price. Some guests like to go topless, not the norm in The Bahamas. Established in 1993, Club Fortuna lies 9.5km (6 miles) east of the International Bazaar in the southeastern part of the island, amid an isolated landscape of casuarinas and scrubland. Midsize bedrooms lie in a colorful group of two-story outbuildings. About three-quarters have ocean views; the others overlook the garden. Each has a private balcony, and two queen-size beds, with a small bathroom with shower stalls. Singles can book one of these rooms, but they are charged 40% more than the per-person double-occupancy rate.

All meals, which are included in the rates, are served buffet-style in a pavilion near the beach, and the Italian cuisine is actually some of the best on Grand

Bahama Island. In addition to the buffets, there is a casual Italian restaurant, La Trattoria, where you can order sit-down dinners within a candlelit setting. Bahamian and Italian performers provide nightly entertainment.

1 Dubloon Rd. (P.O. Box F-42398), Freeport, Grand Bahama, The Bahamas. ✆ **242/373-4000.** Fax 242/373-5555. www.vivaresorts.com. 276 units. Winter $162–$324 double, $231–$312 triple, $284–$484 quad; off-season $178–$270 double, $231–$312 triple, $284–$432 quad. Children under 7 stay free. Children 7–11 50% off per day in parents' room (maximum of 2). Rates include meals, and land and watersports. AE, MC, V. **Amenities:** 2 restaurants, bar, snack bar, nightclub; Italian language lessons; babysitting; laundry; exercise room; pool; watersports; land sports; aerobics classes; outings to a nearby golf course; children's playground. *In room:* A/C, TV, safe, no phone.

Deep Water Cay Club ★ *Finds* The ultimate hideaway, even more so than Paradise Cove, this is a secret address passed around privately by bonefish devotees. Bahamian-style cottages are strung along a pristine beach of white sand on a private island. The bonefishing is first-rate among these saltwater flats. The club has been a tradition since it was established in 1958 by Gilbert Drake, a sportsman and avid fisherman. The club continues today as the premier bonefishing lodge in The Bahamas. Bonefish here average 4 to 5 pounds, and licensed guides head a fleet of customized Dolphin Super Skiffs. Bedrooms are exceedingly spacious and well-furnished, with private entrances and roomy bathrooms with tub and shower. Some 22 guests at a time are housed here in an intimate, relaxed setting.

Everyone dines together on a well-prepared but simple continental and island cuisine. Naturally the favorite dish is the catch of the day.

Deep Water Cay (1100 Lee Wagener Blvd., Ste. 352, Fort Lauderdale, FL 33315). ✆ **242/353-3073** or 954/359-0488. Fax 242/353-3095. www.deepwatercay.com/About.html. 11 units. Dec–Feb $1,375 per person double occupancy; Mar–Nov $1,457–$1,530 per person double occupancy. Rates all-inclusive for 3 nights and 2½ days of fishing. No credit cards. **Amenities:** Dining room, self-service bar; pool; babysitting; snorkeling, boating, and fishing; 2 tennis courts. *In room:* A/C, refrigerator, coffeemaker, no phone.

Old Bahama Bay ★★ A cottage-style resort, this former Jack Tar Village is the centerpiece of a 28-acre site with home sites and a marina. Its opening is hailed as part of the overall renaissance of Grand Bahama Island. In an oceanfront setting, the boutique hotel has cottages adjacent to the marina complex; a private beach is only steps away. The colonial-style architecture graces a setting 40km (25 miles) west of Freeport, consisting of suites set in six two-story beach houses and three spacious buildings overlooking the marina. The living space is the most generous on the island, with custom-designed furnishings along with private beachfront terraces. Bathrooms are luxurious with deluxe toiletries, and a tub and shower combo. Dockside Grill serves quite good Bahamian and American dishes at three meals a day.

West End (P.O. Box F-42546), Grand Bahama Island, The Bahamas. ✆ **800/572-5711** in the U.S., or 242/350-6500. Fax 242/346-6546. 47 units. May–Dec 22 $290 double; Dec 23–Apr $495 double. $8 extra per child. AE, MC, V. **Amenities:** Restaurant, bar; 2 all-weather tennis courts; pool; exercise facilities; massage; dive shop; watersports; snorkeling. *In room:* A/C, TV, fax and modem lines, refrigerator, coffeemaker, safe.

Paradise Cove ★ *Finds* Deadman's Reef sounds unappetizing but teems with rainbow-hued tropical marine life and a vast array of coral to delight the snorkeler in you. This is a secluded hideaway on a beach, an informal series of one-bedroom apartments and two-bedroom cottages rented to those who like to escape the glitz and glam of Freeport or Lucaya. Away from the crowds, Paradise Cove is like Grand Bahama used to be before the tourist hordes invaded. Yet you are only a 20-minute drive east of West End. Snorkeling, swimming, kayaking, and sunbathing fill the day here. All units are good-size and have full kitchens for those who want to cook their own grub.

Deadman's Reef (P.O. Box F-42771), Freeport, Grand Bahama Island. ✆ **242/349-2677.** Fax 242/352-5471. www.bahamasnet.com/paradise cove. 5 units. Nov–Apr $100 apt for 2, $125 cottage, $175 2-bedroom villa; off-season $75 apt for 2, $105 cottage, $150 2-bedroom villa. Extra person $12.50 daily. **Amenities:** Bar, snack bar; snorkeling; boating. *In room:* A/C, kitchen, no phone.

4 Where to Dine

Foodies will find that the cuisine on Grand Bahama Island doesn't match the more refined fare served at dozens of places on New Providence (Nassau/Paradise Island). However, a few places in Grand Bahama specialize in fine dining; others get by with rather standard fare. The good news is that the dining scene is much more affordable here.

FREEPORT

EXPENSIVE

Crown Room ★ CONTINENTAL The Crown Room offers stylish casino dining. It evokes an Art Deco ocean liner, with pink-marble accents, brass-trimmed walls, and rose-colored mirrors. As you peruse the menu, light jazz is played in the background. Whatever you whisper to your dining partner is likely to be overheard, because tables are a little too closely placed. Prices are high for Freeport, but this Crown Room tries to be regal, and the service and the fine ingredients seem to justify the high tabs.

It's quite easy to fill up on the selection of hot and cold appetizers, ranging from paté to smoked salmon to snow crab claws. The best of the main dishes is the perfectly roasted rack of lamb, with the medallions of veal coming in a close second. Pasta dishes are also quite succulent. Sometimes the chef will have something more unusual on the menu, but for the most part, it's elegant country-club fare from a standard international repertoire.

In the Resorts at Bahamia, the Mall at W. Sunrise Hwy. ✆ **242/352-6721.** Reservations required. Jackets required for men. Main courses $21.95–$42.95. AE, DC, MC, V. Wed–Sat 6:30–11pm.

The Rib Room ★ SEAFOOD/STEAKS The Rib Room serves the island's best steaks, in huge portions. Everything is served in the atmosphere of a British hunting lodge. If you don't want one of the steaks, opt instead for the blue-ribbon prime rib of beef with a passable Yorkshire pudding. Special praise goes to the broiled Bahamian lobster, but steer clear of the grouper. Shrimp can be succulent when it's not overcooked, and steak Diane, although rather fully flavored, is meltingly textured. The wine list is reasonably priced.

In the Resorts at Bahamia, the Mall at W. Sunrise Hwy. ✆ **242/352-6721.** Reservations recommended. Jackets required for men. Main courses $19.95–$33.95. AE, DC, MC, V. Thurs–Mon 6–11pm.

MODERATE

Silvano's ★ ITALIAN This is the only authentic Italian dining spot in Freeport. The 80-seat restaurant with its Mediterranean decor serves a worthy but not exceptional cuisine. The standard repertoire from Mama Mia's kitchen is presented here with quality ingredients, most often shipped in from the United States. Service is polite and helpful. The grilled veal steak is our favorite, although the home pastas are equally alluring. They're served with a wide variety of freshly made sauces. The chef also works his magic with fresh shrimp. Other traditional Italian dishes round out the menu.

Ranfurley Circus. ✆ **242/352-5111.** Reservations recommended. Main courses $12–$36. MC, V. Daily noon–3pm and 5:30–11pm.

INEXPENSIVE

Beckey's Restaurant BAHAMIAN/AMERICAN This pink-and-white restaurant offers authentic Bahamian cuisine prepared in the time-tested style of the Out Islands. Go here to rev up before a day of serious shopping at the International Bazaar, which is right at hand. Owned by Beckey and Berkeley Smith, the place offers a welcome dose of down-to-earth noncasino reality. Breakfasts are either all-American or Bahamian and are available all day. Also popular are minced lobster, curried mutton, fish platters, baked or curried chicken, and conch salads. Stick to the local specialties instead of the lackluster American dishes.

E. Sunrise Hwy. and E. Beach Dr. ✆ **242/352-5247.** Breakfast $4.50–$9.95; lunch items $6.95–$16.95; dinner main courses $7.95–$23.95 AE, MC, V. Daily 7am–11pm.

Geneva's BAHAMIAN/SEAFOOD If you want to eat where the locals eat, head for Geneva's, where the food is made the old-fashioned way. This restaurant is one of the best places to sample conch, which has fed and nourished Bahamians for centuries. The Monroe family will prepare it for you stewed, cracked, or fried, or in a savory conch chowder that makes an excellent starter. Grouper also appears, prepared in every imaginable way. The bartender will get you into the mood with a rum-laced Bahama Mama.

Kipling Lane, the Mall at W. Sunrise Hwy. ✆ **242/352-5085.** Lunch sandwiches and platters $4–$10; dinner main courses $9–$25.90. No credit cards. Daily 7am–11pm.

Kokonuts Beach Bar & Restaurant BAHAMIAN *Kids* This relatively new restaurant is fast emerging as an island spot for both visitors and islanders. With picnic tables placed outside to take advantage of, it is beautifully situated on the ocean before kilometers of white sand stretching in either direction. The menu is wisely limited, the chef preferring to concentrate on grilled seafood. The catch of the day is usually done to perfection. Nothing is too fancy or elaborate here. The place is also a real family favorite because of its location on the beach. It lies about a 10-minute drive from the center of Freeport.

St. Andrew Dr. ✆ **242/351-5656.** MC, V. Main courses $7.95–$23. MC, V. Daily 11am–1am.

The Pepper Pot BAHAMIAN This might be the only place on Grand Bahama that specializes in Bahamian takeout food. You'll find it after about a 5-minute drive east of the International Bazaar, in a tiny shopping mall. You can order takeout portions of the best guava duff on the island, as well as a savory conch chowder, the standard fish and pork chops, chicken souse (an acquired taste), cracked conch, sandwiches and hamburgers, and an array of daily specials. The owner is Ethiopian-born Wolansa Fountain.

E. Sunrise Hwy. (at Coral Rd.). ✆ **242/373-7655.** Breakfast $3–$5; main courses $4–$7.50; vegetarian plates $5.50. No credit cards. Daily 24 hr.

The Pub on the Mall INTERNATIONAL Located on the same floor of the same building and under the same management, three distinctive eating areas lie across the boulevard from the International Bazaar and attract many locals. The **Prince of Wales** serves such Olde English staples as shepherd's pie, fish and chips, platters of roast beef or fish, and real English ale. One end of the room is devoted to the **Red Dog Sports Bar,** with a boisterous atmosphere and at least three TV screens blasting away for dedicated sports fans. **Silvano's** is an Italian restaurant serving lots of pasta, usually with verve, as well as veal, chicken, beefsteaks, and such desserts as tiramisu. The Bahamian-themed **Islander's Roost**

Freeport/Lucaya Dining

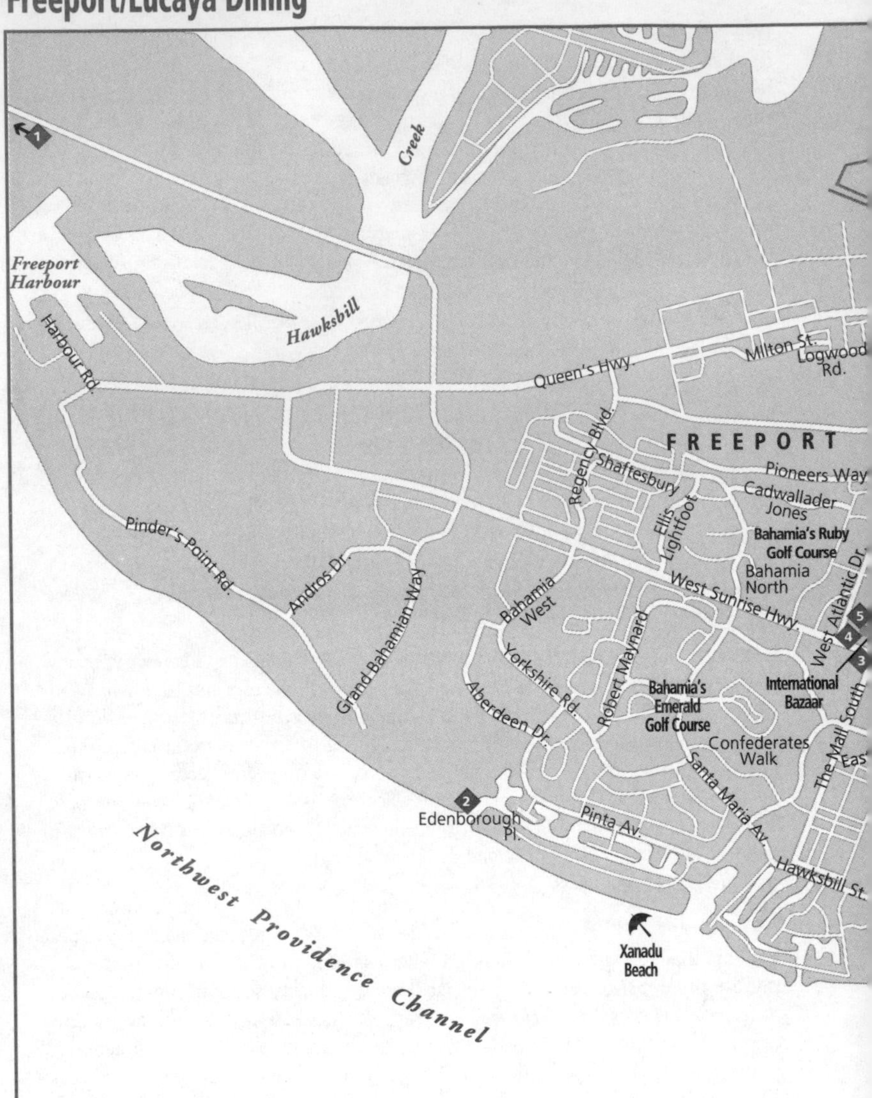

Arawack Restaurant **15**
Barracuda's **16**
Becky's Restaurant **5**
Café Michel **5**
Captain's Charthuse Restaurant **9**
China Temple **5**
Club Caribe **19**
Crown Room **4**
Fatman's Nephew **12**
Ferry House **13**
Geneva's **7**
Giovanni's Café **11**
Kokonuts **2**
La Dolce Vita **12**
Luciano's **12**
Outrigger's Native Restaurant / White Wave Club **18**
Paradise Cove **1**
The Pepper Pot **10**
Pisces **12**
Pub at Lucaya **14**
The Pub on the Mall **8**
The Rib Room **4**
Safari Restaurant **6**
Shenanigan's Irish Pub **12**
Silvano's **3**
Stoned Crab **17**

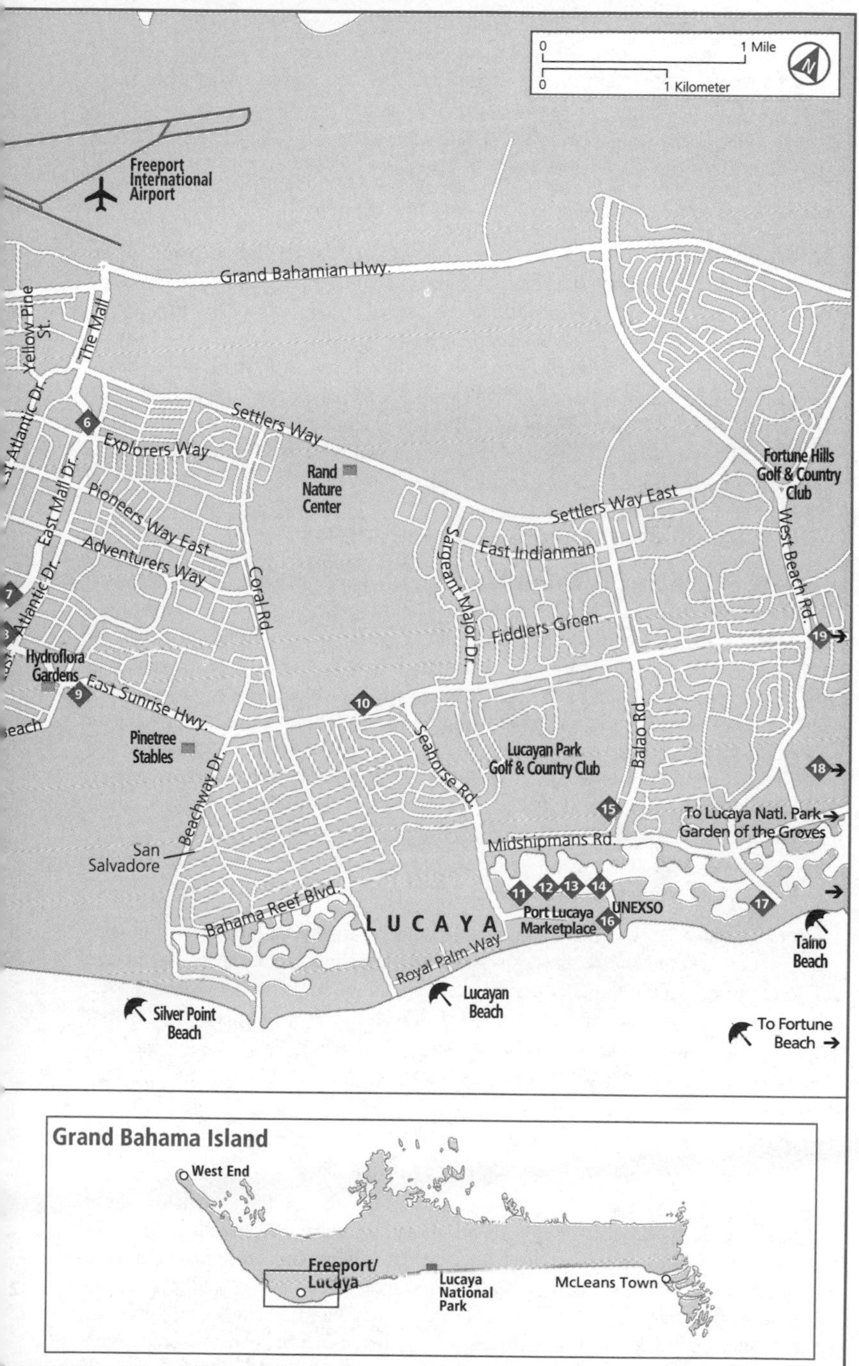

0
1 Mile
0
1 Kilometer
N
Freeport International Airport
Grand Bahamian Hwy.
Yellow Pine St.
The Mall
Settlers Way
Explorers Way
Pioneers Way East
Adventurers Way
East Mall Dr.
Atlantic Dr.
Rand Nature Center
Coral Rd.
Sargeant Major Dr.
Settlers Way East
East Indianman
Fiddlers Green
Fortune Hills Golf & Country Club
West Beach Rd.
Balao Rd.
Hydroflora Gardens
East Sunrise Hwy.
Pinetree Stables
Beachway Dr.
Seahorse Rd.
Lucayan Park Golf & Country Club
To Lucaya Natl. Park Garden of the Groves
Midshipmans Rd.
San Salvadore
Bahama Reef Blvd.
LUCAYA
Port Lucaya Marketplace
UNEXSO
Royal Palm Way
Lucayan Beach
Silver Point Beach
Taíno Beach
To Fortune Beach
Grand Bahama Island
West End
Freeport/ Lucaya
Lucaya National Park
McLeans Town

has a tropical decor of bright island color and a balcony overlooking the Bazaar. The food is good if not great; the main platters are a good value, usually very filling and satisfying. Menu items include sandwiches, salads, grilled fish, beefsteaks, and prime rib.

Ranfurley Circus, Sunrise Hwy. ✆ **242/352-5110.** Reservations recommended. Main courses in Prince of Wales Pub and Red Dog $5.95–$29; main courses in Silvano's $12.75–$36; main courses in Islander's Roost $15.50–$29. AE, MC, V. Prince of Wales and Red Dog Sports Bar daily noon–2am; Silvano's Italian Restaurant daily noon–3pm and 5–11pm; Islander's Roost Mon–Sat 5:30pm–midnight.

Safari Restaurant INTERNATIONAL At breakfast or lunch, you'll place your order at a kiosk-style snack bar and carry simple paper plates to an outdoor table near the pool. But at dinner, more formal meals are served in a large, conventional, sit-down restaurant, which has a bar and a stage for live music. The menu is full of straightforward staples like New York strip steaks, pork chops, hot roast beef, broiled or grilled snapper, broiled chicken, or seafood platters. After 10:30pm every Wednesday, Friday, Saturday, and Sunday, the place becomes a disco (with a $12 cover charge that includes the first drink). Locals often stop by for dinner and nightclubbing.

E. Mall Dr. ✆ **242/352-2805.** American breakfast $4.95; lunch main courses $3.75–$9.75; dinner main courses $9.75–$22.95. AE. Daily 7:30–11am, noon–4pm, and 5:30–11:30pm.

IN THE INTERNATIONAL BAZAAR

Cafe Michel BAHAMIAN/FRENCH The name implies that you've found a real French bistro set amid the bustle of the International Bazaar, but alas, it turns out to be a mere coffee shop. Nevertheless, it's a good place for refueling when you're shopping the bazaar. There are about 20 tables outside, placed under red umbrellas and bistro-style tablecloths. Inside are about a dozen more. Local shoppers know to come here not only for coffee, but also for platters, salads, and sandwiches throughout the day. Both American and Bahamian dishes are served, including seafood platters, steaks, and, of course, grouper. The house specialty is a Bahamian lobster platter with all the fixings.

International Bazaar. ✆ **242/352-2191.** Reservations recommended for dinner. Main courses $6.95–$35. AE, MC, V. Mon–Sat noon–8pm.

China Temple CHINESE This is a Chinese joint—not a lot more—that also does takeout. Over the years it's proved to be the dining bargain of the bazaar. The menu is familiar and standard: chop suey, chow mein, and sweet-and-sour. It's certainly not gourmet Asian fare, but it's cheap; and it might hit the spot when you're craving something different.

International Bazaar. ✆ **242/352-5610.** Lunch $6.50–$8.25; main courses $6.50–$17.25. AE, DISC, MC, V. Mon–Sat 11am–10pm.

LUCAYA

Arawak Restaurant INTERNATIONAL Set in the clubhouse of one of Freeport's largest golf courses, and managed by the Reef Village (which is about 1.5km/1 mile away), this restaurant boasts tall windows that overlook the fairways, lots of exposed wood, and an international menu that has occasional French touches. Lunch brings sandwiches, meal-size salads, and platters of grilled steaks and fish. Dinner is more substantial, with starters like a lobster-and-prawn cocktail, smoked salmon, and grilled portobello mushrooms with leeks and morels in Chablis sauce. Main courses such as breast of duck with honey sauce, surf and turf, rack of lamb, and chateaubriand are always popular and generally very well-prepared. Every Sunday from 11:30am to 3pm, there's a $35 brunch with unlimited champagne.

In the Lucaya Golf & Country Club, Bishop Lane. ✆ **242/373-1066.** Reservations recommended for dinner. Lunch main courses $10–$18; dinner main courses $17–$31. AE, DISC, MC, V. Daily 11:30am–3pm and 6:30–10pm.

Barracuda's ★ INTERNATIONAL With high ceilings and big windows, this space is the size of an airplane hanger, and it's done up with playful art and a whimsical, hip decor that would be at home in Miami's South Beach. The kitchen turns out light international dishes that are loaded with flavor. Examples include grilled grouper tuna and white-bean salad; stone crab claws; leek tart with mozzarella and apples; chicken breast with fresh ginger; and all manner of steaks, seafood, and pastas. If you want to drink your dessert, consider a China Beach, a chocolate-laced affair that's made with crème de cacao, Kahlúa, and Carolans Irish cream.

In the Reef Village Hotel at the Lucayan Beach & Golf Resort, Royal Palm Way, Lucaya. ✆ **242/373-1333.** Main courses $9.50–$22. AE, DC, MC, V. Daily 7–10:30am and 5:30–9:30pm.

Captain's Charthouse Restaurant INTERNATIONAL In a casual, treetop-level dining room, guests can select from a menu of 1950s favorites, such as prime rib of beef, teriyaki steak, and grouper filet, along with some other good seafood dishes. You don't come here for New Wave cooking; this is the place for the old standards that mom and pop enjoyed. Thc chunky lobster thermidor, baked in its shell, is a taste treat. Meals are served with tasty homemade bread and a do-it-yourself salad bar. Portions are large, but if you still have an appetite, the homemade desserts include Key lime pie. A happy hour is held in the Mates Lounge from 5 to 7pm, with complimentary hors d'oeuvres. In winter, there's nightly entertainment and courtcsy transportation to and from your hotel.

E. Sunrise Hwy. and Beach Dr. ✆ **242/373-3900.** Early-bird dinner $10.95 (5–6:30pm); main courses $16.95–$31. AE, DISC, MC, V. Daily 5–9:30pm (last seating).

Churchill's ★ AMERICAN One of the island's most elegant new restaurants, Churchill's now lures discerning palates to Our Lucaya—even guests staying in Freeport. We like to arrive early for drinks in the colonial-style bar with its dark wood floors, potted plants, and ceiling fans, even a grand piano. (All the setting needs to feel complete is a new Bogie-and-Ingrid Bergman combo willing to remake **Casablanca** on-site.) This is the island's best chophouse, featuring both succulent steaks flown over from the mainland and locally caught seafood. The manor house setting is a perfect foil for the finely honed service and top quality ingredients, deftly prepared.

At Our Lucaya Hotel, Royal Palm Way. ✆ **242/373-1333.** Reservations required. Main courses $19.95–$37.50. AE, DC, MC, V. Mon–Sat 6–11pm.

Pub at Lucaya ENGLISH/BAHAMIAN Opening onto Count Basie Square, this restaurant and bar lies at the center of the Port Lucaya Marketplace. Returning visitors might remember the joint when it was called Pusser's Pub, named after that popular brand of rum.

You can come here to eat, but many patrons visit just for the drinks, especially rum-laced Pusser's Painkillers. You can order predictable pub grub such as shepherd's pie or steak-and-ale pie. Juicy American-style burgers are another lure. But you can also dine on substantial Bahamian fare at night, especially Bahamian lobster tail, cracked conch, or the fresh grilled catch of the day. The tables outside overlooking the water are preferred, or else you can retreat inside under a wooden beamed ceiling, where the rustic are tables lit by *faux* Tiffany-style lamps.

Port Lucaya Marketplace. ✆ **242/373-8450.** Main courses $6.95–$10.95. Sandwiches and burgers $4.95–$10.95. AE, MC, V. Daily 11am–1am.

The Stoned Crab ★ SEAFOOD Tired of frozen seafood shipped in from the mainland? Come here for the sweet stone crab claws and the lobster, both caught in Bahamian waters. There's none better on the island. You can't miss this place—a circa-1968 triple pyramid whose four-story wood and steel framework is strong enough to withstand any hurricane. Swiss-born Livio Peronino is the manager and chef, preparing a seafood platter with everything on it, including grouper, conch fritters, and all kinds of shellfish. The best pasta on the menu is linguine al pesto with lobster and shrimp. For starters, try the zesty conch chowder. Have a salad and home-baked raisin bread with your meal, and finish with Irish coffee.

At Taino Beach, Lucaya. ✆ **242/373-1442.** Reservations recommended. Main courses $23–$39. AE, MC, V. Daily 5–10:30pm.

AT THE PORT LUCAYA MARKETPLACE

Fatman's Nephew ★ BAHAMIAN In another location, "Fatman" became a legend on Grand Bahama Island. Although he's no longer with us, the Fatman must have left his recipes and cooking skills to another generation of cooks. Today the place, which used to cater mainly to locals, has gone touristy, but much of the same traditional fare is still served with the same unflagging allegiance to Bahamian ways. The restaurant overlooks the marina at Port Lucaya from an eagle's-nest position on the second floor. You can enjoy drinks or meals inside, but we like to head out to an outdoor covered deck to watch the action below. There are usually at least eight kinds of game fish, including both wahoo and Cajun blackened kingfish, plus curried chicken, mutton, or beef. Bahamian-style shark soup, made from the flesh of hammerheads ("little tender ones," according to the chef), is sometimes featured on the menu.

Port Lucaya Marketplace. ✆ **242/373-8520.** Main courses $11–$32. DISC, MC, V. Daily 10am–midnight.

Ferry House ★ *Kids* CONTINENTAL This restaurant's bar floats on pontoons, beneath a canvas canopy, above the waters of Bell Channel, the waterway that funnels boats from the open sea into the sheltered confines of Port Lucaya Marina. On the waterside deck, you can order breakfast every day between 7 and 10am, joining a crowd of locals. Lunches are relatively simple affairs, consisting of pastas, catch of the day, and meal-size salads. Dinner might feature a seafood platter laden with calamari, fish, and shrimp; a delectable broiled chicken breast stuffed with crabmeat or shrimp; fresh salmon with hollandaise sauce; and savory grilled lamb chops with garlic sauce. But our favorite meal here is the ginger and honey glazed tiger shrimps with a lobster bisque.

Beside Bell Channel, Port Lucaya. ✆ **242/373-1595.** Reservations recommended for dinner. Lunch platters $6–$14.95; dinner main courses $19–$29. AE, MC, V. Daily 7–11am and noon–11:30pm. Closed Mon evenings.

Giovanni's Cafe ITALIAN/SEAFOOD Tucked away into one of the pedestrian thoroughfares of Port Lucaya Marketplace, you'll find a yellow-sided clapboard house that opens into a charming 38-seat Italian trattoria. The chefs (including head chef Giovanni Colo) serve Italian-influenced preparations of local seafood, specializing in seafood pasta (usually prepared only for two diners) and a lobster special. Giovanni stamps each dish with his Italian verve and flavor whether it be Bahamian conch, local seafood, or scampi. Dishes show off his precision and rock-solid technique.

In the Port Lucaya Marketplace. ✆ **242/373-9107.** Reservations recommended. Lunch main courses $5–$8.50; dinner main courses $11–$27.95. AE, MC, V. Mon–Sat 7am–10pm.

La Dolce Vita ★ ITALIAN Next to The Pub at Port Lucaya (see above) is a small upscale Italian restaurant with modern decor and traditional food. Enjoy freshly made pastas and Italian-style pizzas on a patio overlooking the marina or in the 44-seat dining room. Start with portobello mushrooms, fresh mozzarella with tomatoes, and a vinaigrette, or else carpaccio with arugula and spices. Homemade ravioli appears with different fillings such as cheese, lobster, or spinach. An excellent risotto flavored with black ink is served, or else you can order roast pork tenderloin or a crisp and perfectly flavored rack of lamb.

Port Lucaya Marketplace. ✆ **242/373-8652.** Reservations recommended. Main courses $11.95–$30. AE, MC, V. Daily 5–11pm. Closed Sept.

Luciano's ★ CONTINENTAL Its tables usually occupied by local government officials and deal makers, Luciano's is the grande dame of Freeport restaurants, with a very European atmosphere. It's the only restaurant in Port Lucaya offering caviar, foie gras, and bouillabaisse, all served with a flourish by a formally dressed waitstaff wearing black and white. You can go early and enjoy a cocktail in the little bar inside or on the wooden deck overlooking the marina. Lightly smoked and thinly sliced salmon makes a good opener, as do snails in garlic butter. Fresh fish and shellfish are regularly featured and delicately prepared, allowing their natural flavors to shine through, with no heavy, overwhelming sauces. Steak Diane is one of Luciano's classics, along with an especially delectable prime rib of beef.

Port Lucaya Marketplace. ✆ **242/373-9100.** Reservations required. Main courses $16.95–$31.95. AE, DISC, MC, V. Mon–Sat 5:30–10pm (last seating).

Outrigger's Native Restaurant/White Wave Club BAHAMIAN Cement-sided and simple, with a large deck extending out toward the sea, this restaurant was here long before the construction of the nearby Port Lucayan Marketplace, which lies only 4 blocks away. The restaurant area is the domain of Gretchen Wilson, whose kitchens produce a rotating series of dishes that include such lip-smacking dishes as lobster tails, minced lobster, steamed or cracked conch, pork chops, chicken, fish, and shrimp, usually served with peas 'n' rice and macaroni. Every Wednesday night, from 6pm to midnight, the restaurant is the venue for "Outrigger's Famous Wednesday Night Fish Fry," when as many as a thousand diners will line up for platters of fried or steamed fish, priced at $10 each, which are accompanied by live music. Drinks are served within the restaurant, but at any time of the week, you might consider stepping into the nearby ramshackle bar, the White Wave Club, which serves only drinks.

Smith's Point. ✆ **242/373-4811.** Main courses $7–$15. No credit cards. Daily 4pm–midnight.

Pisces ★ BAHAMIAN/INTERNATIONAL This is our favorite among the many restaurants in the Port Lucaya Marketplace, and we're seconded by a healthy mix of locals and yacht owners who pack the place every weekend. Decorated with Tiffany-style lamps and captain's chairs, it boasts the most charming waitstaff on Grand Bahama Island. Lunches are relatively simple affairs, with fish and chips, sandwiches, and salads. Pizzas are available anytime and come in 21 different types, including a version with conch, lobster, shrimp, and chicken. Dinners are more elaborate, with a choice of curries (including a version with conch); lobster in cream, wine, and herb sauce; all kinds of fish and shellfish; and several kinds of pasta.

Port Lucaya Marketplace. ✆ **242/373-5192.** Reservations recommended. Pizzas $15–$25; lunch main courses $8.95–$11.95; dinner main courses $15.95–$27. AE, MC, V. Mon–Sat 11am–2am.

Shenanigan's Irish Pub CONTINENTAL Dark and beer-stained from the thousands of pints of Guinness, Harp, and Killian's that have been served and spilled here, this is the premier Irish or Boston Irish hangout on Grand Bahama Island. Many visitors come just to drink, sometimes for hours at a time, soaking up the suds, and perhaps remembering to eventually order some food. If you get hungry, there's surf and turf, French-style rack of lamb for two, seafood Newburg, and several preparations of chicken.

Port Lucaya Marketplace. ✆ **242/373-4734.** Main courses $10.95–$39.95. AE, DC, MC, V. Mon–Thurs 10:30am–midnight; Fri–Sat 10:30am–2am.

OUTSIDE FREEPORT/LUCAYA

Club Caribe AMERICAN/BAHAMIAN Set about 11km (7 miles) east of the International Bazaar, beside a beach and an offshore reef that teems with underwater life, this restaurant is a funky and offbeat charmer. You can spend a day on the beach here, renting the club's snorkeling equipment, sunbathing or swimming, and perhaps enjoying one of the house-special cocktails (try a Caribe Delight, made with bananas, banana-flavored liqueur, and rum). When it's lunchtime, you might order up a heaping platter of cracked conch; barbecued ribs; snapper or grouper that's fried, steamed, or grilled; or a sandwich or salad. This place is simple, outdoorsy, and a refreshing change from the more congested parts of Grand Bahama.

Churchill Beach, Mather Town, off Midshipman Rd. ✆ **242/373-6866.** Sandwiches and platters $4.50–$12.95. AE, DISC, MC, V. Tues–Sun 11am–6pm.

5 Beaches, Watersports & Other Outdoor Pursuits

HITTING THE BEACH

Grand Bahama Island has enough beaches for everyone, the best ones opening onto Northwest Providence Channel at Freeport and sweeping east for some 97km (60 miles) to encompass Xanadu Beach, Lucayan Beach, Taino Beach, and others, eventually ending at such remote eastern outposts as Rocky Creek and McLean's Town. Once you leave the Freeport/Lucaya area, you can virtually have your pick of white sandy beaches all the way east. Once you're past the resort hotels, you'll see a series of secluded beaches used mainly by locals. If you like people, a lot of organized watersports, and easy access to hotel bars and rest rooms, stick to Xanadu, Taino, and Lucayan beaches.

Though there's fine snorkeling offshore, you should book a snorkeling cruise aboard one of the catamarans offered by Paradise Watersports (see below) to see the most stunning reefs.

Xanadu Beach ★★ is one of our favorite beaches, immediately east of Freeport and the site of the famed Xanadu Beach Resort. The beach may be crowded at times in winter, but that's because of those gorgeous, soft, powdery white sands, which open onto tranquil waters. The beach is set against a backdrop of coconut palms and Australian pines. You can hook up here with some of the best watersports on the island, including snorkeling, boating, jet skiing, and parasailing.

Immediately east of Xanadu is **Silver Point Beach,** a little white sandy beach, site of a timeshare complex where guests are out riding the waves on water bikes

Moments Private White Sands for You Alone

Once you head east from Port Lucaya and Taino, you'll discover so many splendid white sandy beaches that you'll lose count. Although these beaches have names, you'll never really know what beach you're on unless you ask a local because they are unmarked. If you like seclusion and don't mind the lack of any facilities, you'll find a string of local favorites. Directly east of Taino is **Churchill's Beach,** followed by **Smith's Point, Fortune Beach,** and **Barbary Beach.** Fortune Beach is a special gem because of its beautiful waters and white sands.

or playing volleyball on the beach. You'll see horseback riders from Pinetree Stables (see below) taking beach rides along the sands.

Most visitors will be found at **Lucayan Beach,** right off Royal Palm Way and immediately east of Silver Point Beach. This is one of the best beaches in The Bahamas, with kilometers of white sand. It might be crowded for a few weeks in winter, but in general there is beach-blanket space for all. At any of the hotel resorts along this beach, you can hook up with an array of watersports or get a frosty drink from a hotel bar. It's not for those seeking seclusion, but it's a fun beach-party scene.

Immediately to the east of Lucayan Beach is **Taino Beach,** a family favorite and a good place for watersports. This, too, is a fine, wide beach of white sands, opening onto generally tranquil waters.

Another choice not too far east is **Gold Rock Beach,** a favorite picnic spot with locals on weekends, although you'll usually have this beach to yourself on weekdays. Gold Rock Beach is a 19km (12-mile) drive from Lucaya. At Gold Rock you are at the doorstep to the **Lucayan National Park** (see below), a 40-acre park filled with some of the longest, widest, and most fabulous secluded beaches on the island.

BOAT CRUISES

Mermaid Kitty, Port Lucaya Dock (✆ **242/373-5880**), run by Reef Tours is supposedly the world's largest twin-diesel-engine glass-bottom boat. Any tour agent can arrange for you to go out on this vessel. You'll get a panoramic view of the beautiful underwater life that lives off the coast of Grand Bahama. Cruises depart from Port Lucaya behind the Straw Market on the bay side at 9:30, 11:15am, 1:15, and 3:15pm, except Monday and Friday, when only two tours leave at 9:30 and 11:15am. The tour lasts 1½ hours, costs $25 for adults and $15 for children 6 to 12, and is free for children 5 and under. When calling for a reservation, confirm the departure times mentioned above, because there may be seasonal variations.

Superior Watersports, P.O. Box F-40837, Freeport (✆ **242/373-7863**), on its *Bahama Mama,* a two-deck 22m (72-ft.) catamaran. Its Robinson Crusoe Beach Party, offered daily from noon to 5pm, costs $59 per person. There's also a sunset booze cruise that goes for $35. (In summer, these cruises are on Tues, Thurs, and Sat night from 6:30–8:30pm. In the off-season, they are on the same nights but sail from 6–8pm.)

For an underwater cruise, try the company's quasi-submarine, the *Seaworld Explorer.* The sub itself does not descend; instead, you walk down into the hull of the boat and watch the sea life glide by. The "sub" departs daily at 10 and

11:30am, and 1:30 and 3pm, and it costs $39 for adults and $25 for children 12 and under.

THE DOLPHIN EXPERIENCE

A pod of bottle-nosed dolphins is involved in a unique dolphin/human familiarization program at Dolphin Experience, located at **Underwater Explorers Society (UNEXSO),** next to Port Lucaya, opposite Lucayan Beach Casino (✆ **888/365-3483** or 242/373-1250). This "close encounter" program viewed as "politically incorrect" by some groups allows participants to observe these intelligent and friendly animals close up and to hear an interesting talk by a member of the animal-care staff. This project seems very eco-sensitive; this is the world's largest dolphin facility, so there are no cramped conditions. Dolphins can swim out to sea, and if they don't like the project, they could in theory never return to it. But they seem to enjoy interacting with humans and do return. You can step onto a shallow wading platform and interact with the dolphins; the experience costs $59 and is a highly educational, yet fun adventure for all ages. Children under 5 participate free. You'll want to bring your camera. An "Assistant Trainer" program is an all-day interactive experience in which a maximum of four people, ages 16 or older, learn about dolphins and marine mammals from behind the scenes. Participants help feed the animals and swim with them for a cost of $189. Dolphins also swim out from Sanctuary Bay daily to interact with scuba divers from UNEXSO in a "Dolphin Dive" program, costing $169.

FISHING

In the waters off Grand Bahama, you can fish for barracuda, snapper, grouper, yellowtail, wahoo, and kingfish, along with other denizens of the deep.

Reef Tours, Ltd., Port Lucaya Dock (✆ **242/373-5880**), offers one of the least expensive ways to go deep-sea fishing around Grand Bahama Island. Adults pay $80 if they fish, $45 if they only go along to watch. Four to six people can charter the entire craft for $480 per half day or $950 per whole day. Departures for the half-day excursion are at 8:30am and 1pm, 7 days a week. Bait, tackle, and ice are included in the cost.

GOLF

This island boasts more golf links than any other in The Bahamas. The courses are within 11km (7 miles) of one another, and you usually won't have to wait to play. All courses are open to the public year-round, and clubs can be rented from all pro shops on the island.

Moments Land & Sea Eco-tours

If you're a nature lover, escape from the casinos and take one of the **East End Adventures** (✆ **242/373-6662** or 242/373-1652) bush and sea safaris. You're taken through dense pine forests and along deserted beaches, going inland on hikes to such sites as blue holes, mangrove swamps, and underground caverns. You may even learn how to crack conch. A native lunch is served on a serene beach in Lightbourne's Cay, a remote islet in the East End. Most of the tour is laid-back, as you can snorkel in blue holes or shell hunt. Safaris are conducted daily between 8am and 5:30pm, costing adults $110 and kids $55.

Bahamia's Emerald Golf Course, the Mall South, at the Resorts at Bahamia (© **242/350-7000**), was the site of The Bahamas National Open some years back, and more recently, in conjunction with the Ruby course (see below), it's the site of the annual January Grand Bahama Pro-Am Tournament. The course has plenty of trees along the fairways, as well as an abundance of water hazards and bunkers. The toughest hole is the ninth, a par 5 with 545 yards from the blue tees to the hole. In winter, greens fees to either of these courses are $95 per day, reduced to $85 in summer.

The championship course **Bahamia's Ruby Golf Course,** Sunrise Highway, at the Resorts at Bahamia.(© **242/350-7000**), received a major upgrade in 2001 by Jim Fazio Golf Design, Inc. The Ruby course was lengthened to increase the rating and to enhance play. A fully automated irrigation system was installed. For greens fees, see the Emerald Golf Course, above. It's a total of 6,750 yards if played from the championship blue tees.

Fortune Hills Golf & Country Club, Richmond Park, Lucaya (© **242/373-4500**), was originally intended to be an 18-hole course, but the back 9 were never completed. You can replay the front 9 for 18 holes and a total of 6,916 yards from the blue tees. Par is 72. Greens fees are $31 for 9 holes, $43 for 18. Electric carts cost $34 and $44 for 9 and 18 holes, respectively.

The best-kept and most-manicured course on Grand Bahama is the **Lucayan Park Golf & Country Club,** Lucaya Beach (© **242/373-1066**). Recently made over, it is quite beautiful and is known for a hanging boulder sculpture at its entrance. Greens are fast, and there are a couple of par 5s more than 500 yards long, totaling 6,824 yards from the blue tees and 6,488 from the whites. Par is 72. Greens fees are $67 for 18 holes. This includes a mandatory shared golf cart. We'll let you in on a secret: Even if you're not a golfer, sample the food at the club restaurant—everything from lavish champagne brunches to first-rate seafood dishes.

The first golf course to open in The Bahamas since 1969 made its premiere late in 2000. **The Reef Course** ★★ at Royal Palm Way, Lucaya (© **242/373-2002**), was designed by Robert Trent Jones, Jr., who called it "a bit like a Scottish course but a lot warmer." The course requires precise shot-making to avoid its numerous lakes: There is water on 13 of its 18 holes and various types of long grass swaying in the trade winds. The course boasts 6,920 yards of links-style playing grounds. Residents of Our Lucaya, with which the course is associated, pay $100 for 18 holes or $66 for 9 holes. Nonresidents are charged $120 for 18 holes, but the same price, $66, for 9 holes.

HORSEBACK RIDING

The **Pinetree Stables,** North Beachway Drive, Freeport (© **242/373-3600**), are the best riding stables in The Bahamas, superior to rivals on New Providence Island (Nassau). Pinetree offers trail rides to the beach in winter Tuesday through Sunday at 9, 11:30am, and 2pm, but only at 9 and 11am off-season. The cost is $65 per person for a ride lasting 2 hours.

SEA KAYAKING

If you'd like to explore the waters off the island's north shore, call **Kayak Nature Tours,** (© **242/373-2485**), who'll take you on trips through the mangroves, where you can see wildlife as you paddle along. The cost is $69 per person, and trips are offered daily from 9am to 4pm, with a meal included. Both single and double kayaks are used on these jaunts, and children must be at least 5 years of age.

Finds A Sudsy Look at Grand Bahama

You don't think of Freeport as brewery country, but the island is known for its Hammerhead Ale, a favorite of connoisseurs. The Grand Bahama Brewing Co., Logwood Rd., Freeport (✆ **242/351-5191**), offers tours Monday to Friday of its brewery at 10am, 12:30, 4, and 4:40pm, and again on Saturday at 10:30am only. In addition to Hammerhead Ales, Lucayan Lager is also made here. Tours cost $5, but the fee is credited to any lager or ale purchases you might make.

SNORKELING & SCUBA DIVING

Serious divers are attracted to such Grand Bahama sites as the Wall, the Caves, Theo's Wreck, and Treasure Reef. Other sites frequented by UNEXSO include Spit City, Ben Blue Hole, and the Rose Garden. Keep in mind that UNEXSO's specialty is diving, while Paradise Watersports primarily entertains snorkelers.

Paradise Watersports, located at the Xanadu Beach Resort & Marina (✆ **242/352-2887**), offers a variety of activities. On the snorkeling trips, you cruise to a coral reef on a 14m (48-ft.) catamaran. The cost is $30 per person. Kayaks rent for $8 for a half hour, $12 per hour, and water-skiing is priced at $20 for a 2.5km (1½-mile) ride. Parasailing costs $40 for a 4-minute ride. See "Boat Cruises," above, for their offerings.

The **Underwater Explorers Society (UNEXSO)** ★★★ (✆ **888/365-3483** or 242/373-1250) is one of the premier dive outfitters in The Bahamas and the Caribbean. There are seven dive trips daily, including reef trips, shark dives, wreck dives, and night dives. This is also the only facility in the world where divers can dive with dolphins in the open ocean (see "The Dolphin Experience," above).

A popular 3-hour learn-to-dive course is offered daily. Over UNEXSO's 30-year history, more than 50,000 people have successfully completed this course. For $99, students learn the basics in UNEXSO's training pools. Then, the same day, they dive the beautiful shallow reef with their instructor.

TENNIS

The Resorts at Bahamia ★★, at the Mall at West Sunrise Highway (✆ **242/352-9661**), has a near monopoly on tennis courts on Grand Bahama, a total of nine. Guests and nonguests are charged $10 per hour, and lessons are also available. The courts are open daily from 9am to dusk. If you want to play at night, you have to call and reserve a special time. It costs $12 for the courts to be lighted.

6 Seeing the Sights

Several informative tours of Grand Bahama Island are offered. One reliable company is **H. Forbes Charter Co.,** the Mall at West Sunrise Highway, Freeport (✆ **242/352-9311**). From headquarters in the lobby of the Bahamas Princess Country Club, this company offers half- and full-day bus tours. The most popular option is the half-day Super Combination Tour, priced at $35 per adult and $25 per child under 12. It includes guided visits to the botanical gardens, drive-through tours of residential areas and the island's commercial center, and stops at the island's deep-water harbor. Shopping and a visit to a wholesale liquor store are also included on the tour. Departures are Monday through Saturday at 9am and 1pm; the tour lasts 3½ hours.

See also "Beaches, Watersports & Other Outdoor Pursuits," above, for details on UNEXSO's Dolphin Experience, and "Shopping," below, for coverage of the International Bazaar and the Port Lucaya Marketplace.

Hydroflora Gardens At this artificially created botanical wonder, you can see 154 specimens of plants that grow in The Bahamas. A special section is devoted to bush medicine, which is widely practiced by Bahamians (who have been using herbs and other plants to cure everything from sunburn to insomnia since the native Lucayans were here centuries ago). Guided tours cost at 11am $6 per person.

On East Beach at Sunrise Hwy. ✆ **242/352-6052.** Admission $3 adults, $1.50 children. Mon–Fri 9am–5pm; Sat 9am–4pm.

Lucayan National Park This 40-acre park, filled with mangrove, pine, and palm trees, contains one of the loveliest, most secluded beaches on Grand Bahama, a long, wide, dune-covered stretch of sandy beach that you'll reach by following a wooden path winding through the trees. There's a coral reef offshore; bring your snorkeling gear along so you can glimpse the colorful creatures that live beneath these turquoise waters. As you wander through the park, you'll cross Gold Rock Creek, fed by a spring from what is said to be the world's largest underground freshwater cavern system. Two of the caves can be seen, because they were exposed when a portion of ground collapsed. The pools in the caves are composed of 2m (6 ft.) of freshwater atop a heavier layer of saltwater. Spiral wooden steps have been built down to the pools, and there are 36,000 passages in the cavern system.

The freshwater springs once lured native Lucayans, those Arawak-connected tribes who lived on the island and depended on fishing for their livelihood. They would come inland to get fresh water for their habitats on the beach. Lucayan bones and artifacts, such as pottery, have been found in the caves, as well as on the beaches.

Midshipman Rd. ✆ **242/352-5438.** Admission $3; tickets available only at the Rand Memorial Nature Centre (see below). Daily 9am–4pm. Drive east along Midshipman Rd., passing Sharp Rock Point and Gold Rock.

Parrot Jungle's Garden of the Groves One of the island's major attractions is this 12-acre garden, which honors its founder, Wallace Groves, and his wife, Georgette. Eleven kilometers (7 miles) east of the International Bazaar, this scenic preserve of waterfalls and flowering shrubs has some 10,000 trees. Tropical birds flock here, making this a lure for bird-watchers and ornithologists. There are free-form lakes, footbridges, ornamental borders, lawns, and flowers. Parrot Jungle of Miami, the new managers, have introduced a number of animals to the site, including macaws, cockatoos, pygmy goats, potbelly pigs, and American alligators. Other species introduced include the park's first Bahamian raccoons and the white-crowned pigeon, the latter on the endangered species list. The park also has a children's playground. A lovely little nondenominational chapel, open to visitors, looks down on the garden from a hill. **The Palmetto Café** (✆ **242/373-5668**) serves snacks and drinks, and a Bahamian straw market is located at the entrance gate.

Midshipman Rd. and Magellan Dr. ✆ **242/373-5668.** Admission $9.95 adults, $6.95 children 3–10, free for children under 3. Garden daily 9am–4pm; Palmetto Café daily 9am–4pm.

Rand Memorial Nature Centre This 100-acre pineland sanctuary, located 3km (2 miles) east of the center of Freeport, is the regional headquarters of The Bahamas National Trust, a nonprofit conservation organization. Nature trails highlight native flora and "bush medicine" and provide opportunities for bird-watching; as you stroll, keep your eyes peeled for the lush blooms of tropical orchids or the brilliant flash of green and red feathers in the trees. Wild birds abound at the park, and a freshwater pond is home to a flock of West Indian pink flamingos, the national bird of The Bahamas. There is a bird-watching tour on the first Saturday of every month at 8am and a wildflower walk on the last Saturday of the month, also starting at 8am. Other features of the nature center include native animal displays, an education center, and a gift shop selling nature books and souvenirs.

E. Settlers Way. ✆ **242/352-5438.** Admission $5 adults, $3 children 5–12, free for children under 5. Mon–Fri 9am–4pm. Guided tours must call in advance to book.

7 Shopping

Shopping hours in Freeport/Lucaya are 9:30am to 3pm Monday through Thursday, 9:30am to 5pm on Friday. Many shops are closed on Saturday and Sunday. However, in the International Bazaar, hours vary widely. Most places there are open Monday through Saturday. Some begin business daily at 9:30am; others don't open until 10am, and closing time ranges from 5:30 to 6pm.

THE INTERNATIONAL BAZAAR

One of the world's most unusual shopping complexes, the International Bazaar, at East Mall Drive and East Sunrise Highway, covers 10 acres in the heart of Freeport. Although it remains one of the most visited sites in The Bahamas, it frankly is a bit tarnished today and is due for a makeover. Looking better every day is its rising competitor, the Port Lucaya Marketplace (see below). There is a major bus stop at the entrance of the complex. Buses aren't numbered, but those marked INTERNATIONAL BAZAAR will take you right to the gateway. Visitors walk through the much-photographed Torii Gate, a Japanese symbol of welcome, into a miniature World's Fair setting (think of it as a kitschy Bahamian version of Epcot). Continental cafes and dozens of shops loaded with merchandise await visitors. The bazaar blends architecture and cultures from some 25 countries, each re-created with cobblestones, narrow alleys, and authentically reproduced architecture. True, it's more theme-park-style shopping than authentic Bahamian experience, but it's fun nevertheless. In the nearly 100 shops, you're bound to find something that is both unique and a bargain. Here you'll find African handcrafts, Chinese jade, British china, Swiss watches, Irish linens, and Colombian emeralds—and that's just for starters.

On a street patterned after the Ginza in Tokyo, just inside the entrance to the bazaar, is the Asian section. A rich collection of merchandise from the Far East can be found here, including cameras, handmade teak furniture, fine silken goods, and even places where you can have clothing custom-made.

To the left you'll find the Left Bank of Paris, or at least a reasonable facsimile, with sidewalk cafes where you can enjoy a café au lait and perhaps a pastry under shade trees. In the Continental Pavilion, there are leather goods, jewelry, lingerie, and gifts at shops with names such as Love Boutique.

A narrow alley leads you from the French section to East India, where shops sell such exotic goods as taxi horns and silk saris. Moving on from the India

House, past Kon Tiki, you arrive in Africa, where you can purchase carvings or a colorful dashiki.

For a taste of Latin America and Iberia, make your way to the Spanish section, where serapes and piñatas hang from the railings, and imports are displayed along the cobblestone walks.

Many items sold in the shops here are said to cost 40% less than if you bought them in the United States, but don't count on that. If you were contemplating a big purchase, it's best to compare prices before you leave home. You can have purchases sent anywhere you wish.

The **Straw Market,** next door to the International Bazaar, contains items with a special Bahamian touch—colorful baskets, hats, handbags, and place mats—all of which make good gifts or souvenirs from your trip. (As with the Straw Market in Nassau, some items sold here are actually made in Asia.)

Here's a description of the various shops in the bazaar.

ART

Flovin Gallery This gallery sells original Bahamian and international art, frames, lithographs, posters, and Bahamian-made Christmas ornaments and decorated coral. It also offers handmade Bahamian dolls, coral jewelry, and other gift items. Another branch is at Port Lucaya Marketplace (see below). In the Arcade section of the International Bazaar. ✆ **242/352-7564.**

CRYSTAL & CHINA

Island Galleria There's an awesome collection of crystal here. Fragile, breakable, and beautiful, it includes works of utilitarian art in china and crystal by Waterford, Aynsley, Lenox, Dansk, Belleek, and Swarovski. Anything you buy can be carefully packed and shipped. Another branch is located in the Port Lucaya Marketplace (✆ **242/373-8400**). International Bazaar. ✆ **242/352-8194.**

FASHION

Cleo's Boutique This shop offers everything from eveningwear to lingerie, and all in between. A warm and inviting destination, Cleo's prides itself on capturing the Caribbean woman in all of her moods. You can also find a wide array of costume jewelry beginning at $20 a piece. International Bazaar. ✆ **242/351-3340.**

HANDCRAFTS & GIFTS

Bahamian Souvenir Outlet This place, just below the Ministry of Tourism, has lots of inexpensive souvenirs and gifts: the usual array of T-shirts, key rings, mugs, and all that stuff. International Bazaar. ✆ **242/352-2947.**

Bahamian Things This native art gallery sells an array of locally handcrafted items, including books on The Bahamas, Abaco ceramics, woodwork, and even handmade Christmas decorations. 15B Poplar Crescent, Freeport. ✆ **242/352-9550.**

Caribbean Cargo This is one of the island's best gift shops, specializing in such items as picture frames, candles, and clocks, and clothes. In the Arcade section of the International Bazaar. ✆ **242/352-2929.**

Far East Traders Look for Asian linens, hand-embroidered dresses and blouses, silk robes, lace parasols, smoking jackets, and kimonos. There's a branch location inside the Island Galleria at the Port Lucaya Marketplace. International Bazaar. ✆ **242/352-9280.**

Paris in The Bahamas This shop contains the biggest selection of luxury goods under one roof in the International Bazaar. The staff wears couture black dresses like you might have expected in Paris, and everywhere there's a sense of French glamour and conspicuous consumption. There are both Gucci and Versace leather goods for men and women; crystal from Lalique, Baccarat, Daum, Kosta Boda, and Örrefors; and a huge collection of cosmetics and perfumes. International Bazaar. ✆ **242/352-5380.**

Unusual Centre Where else can you get a wide array of items made of eel skin or goods made from exotic feathers such as peacock? There's another branch at the **Port Lucaya Marketplace** (✆ **242/352-3994**). International Bazaar. ✆ **242/352-3994.**

JEWELRY

Colombian Emeralds International This is a branch of the world's foremost emerald jeweler, offering a wide array of precious gemstone jewelry and one of the island's best watch collections. Careful shoppers will find significant savings over U.S. prices. The outlet offers certified appraisals and free 90-day insurance. There are two branches at the Port Lucaya Marketplace (✆ **242/373-8400**). South American Section of the International Bazaar. ✆ **242/352-5464.**

LEATHER GOODS

The Leather Shop This is another good outlet, carrying a much more limited Fendi line, but also many other designers including Land and HCL. Additional leather goods include shoes and gift items. Additional locations include the Port Lucaya Marketplace (✆ **242/373-2323**) and Regent's Centre (✆ **242/352-2895**). International Bazaar. ✆ **242/352-5491.**

MUSIC

Intercity Music This is the best music store on the island; you get not only Bahamian music, but soca, reggae, and all the music of the islands as well. CDs, records, and tapes are sold. You can also purchase Bahamian posters and flags, portable radios, Walkmans, and blank audiotapes, along with accessories for camcorders. There's a branch office at the Port Lucaya Marketplace (✆ **242/373-8820**). International Bazaar. ✆ **242/352-8820.**

PERFUMES & FRAGRANCES

Les Parisiennes This outlet offers a wide range of perfumes, including the latest from Paris, and it also sells Lancôme cosmetics and skin-care products. There's a branch office at the Port Lucaya Marketplace (✆ **242/373-2974**). In the French section of the International Bazaar. ✆ **242/352-5380.**

The Perfume Factory Fragrance of The Bahamas This is the top fragrance producer in The Bahamas. The shop is housed in a model of an 1800s mansion, in which visitors are invited to hear a 5-minute commentary and to see the mixing of fragrant oils. There's even a "mixology" department where you can create your own fragrance from a selection of oils. The shop's well-known products include Island Promises, Goombay, Paradise, and Pink Pearl (with conch pearls in the bottle). The shop also sells Guanahani, created to commemorate the 500th anniversary of Columbus's first landfall, and Sand, the leading Bahamian-made men's fragrance. At the rear of the International Bazaar. ✆ **242/352-9391.**

STAMPS & COINS

Bahamas Coin and Stamp Ltd. This is the major coin dealer on the island. It specializes in Bahamian coin jewelry, ancient Roman coins, and relics from sunken Spanish galleons. It also carries a vast selection of antique U.S. and English coins and paper money. International Bazaar. ✆ **242/352-8989.**

PORT LUCAYA MARKETPLACE

Port Lucaya Marketplace on Seahorse Road is a shopping and dining complex set on 6 acres. Free entertainment, such as steel-drum bands and strolling musicians, adds to a festival atmosphere. A boardwalk along the water makes it easy to watch the frolicking dolphins.

The complex rose on the site of a former Bahamian straw market, but the craftspeople and their straw products are back in full force after having been temporarily dislodged.

The waterfront location is a distinct advantage. Many of the restaurants and shops overlook a 50-slip marina, home of a "fantasy" pirate ship featuring lunch and dinner/dancing cruises. A variety of charter vessels are also based at the Port Lucaya Marina, and dockage at the marina is available to visitors coming by boat to shop or dine.

Bandolera The staff can be rather haughty here, but despite its drawbacks, this store carries a collection of chic women's clothing that's many, many cuts above the usual run of T-shirts and tank tops that are the norm within many of its competitors. Port Lucaya Marketplace. ✆ **242/373-7691.**

Coconits by Androsia This is the Port Lucaya outlet of the famous batik house of Andros Island. Its designs and colors capture the spirit of The Bahamas. Fabrics are handmade on the island of Andros. The store sells quality, 100%-cotton resort wear, including simple skirts, tops, jackets, and shorts for women, and it also offers a colorful line of children's wear. Port Lucaya Marketplace. ✆ **242/373-8387.**

Flovin Gallery II This branch of the art gallery located in the Port Lucaya Marketplace sells a collection of oil paintings (both Bahamian and international), along with lithographs and posters. In its limited field, it's the best in the business. It also features a number of gift items, such as handmade Bahamian dolls, decorated corals, and Christmas ornaments. Port Lucaya Marketplace. ✆ **242/373-8388.**

Harley-Davidson of Freeport This is one of only two registered and licensed Harley outlets in The Bahamas. You can special-order a motorcycle if you feel flush with funds from a casino, but it's more likely that you'll content yourself with T-shirts, leather vests, belts, caps, sunglasses, and gift items. Port Lucaya Marketplace. ✆ **242/373-8269.**

Jeweler's Warehouse This is a place for bargain hunters looking for good buys on discounted, closeout 14-karat gold and gemstone jewelry. Discounts range up to 50%, but the quality of many of these items remains high. Guarantees and certified appraisals are possible. Port Lucaya Marketplace. ✆ **242/373-8400.**

UNEXSO Dive Shop This is the premier dive shop of The Bahamas. It sells everything related to the water—swimsuits, wet suits, underwater cameras, and video equipment, shades, hats, souvenirs, state-of-the-art diver's equipment, and computers. Port Lucaya Marketplace. ✆ **242/373-1250.**

8 Grand Bahama After Dark

Many resort hotels stage their own entertainment at night, and these shows are open to the general public.

ROLLING THE DICE

The Casino at Bahamia Most of the nightlife in Freeport/Lucaya centers around this glittering, giant, Moroccan-style palace, one of the largest casinos in The Bahamas and the Caribbean. Under this Moorish-domed structure, visitors play games of chance and attend Las Vegas–inspired floor shows. They can also dine in a first-class restaurant, the Crown Room (see "Where to Dine," above), which is the only restaurant within the sprawling Resort at Bahamia that requires jackets and neckties for men. Slot machines operate daily from 8am to 3am; table games are conducted daily from 10am to 3am. Entrance is free. In the Resorts at Bahamia, the Mall at W. Sunrise Hwy. ✆ **242/350-7000.**

THE CLUB & BAR SCENE

Located in the center of the **Port Lucaya Marketplace** waterfront restaurant and shopping complex, **Count Basie Square** contains a vine-covered bandstand where the best live music on the island is performed on Tuesday, Friday, and Saturday evenings from about 7:30 to 8pm. And it's free! The square honors the "Count," who used to have a grand home on Grand Bahama. Steel bands, small Junkanoo groups, and even gospel singers from a local church are likely to be heard performing here, their voices or music wafting across the 50-slip marina. There are several bars in the complex where you can sip a beer or a tropical rum concoction. (See "Where to Dine," earlier in this chapter, for details on a few of these, including **Fatman's Nephew** and **Shenanigan's Irish Pub.**)

Club 2000/The Ruthnell Deck The setting is a sprawling green and white Bahamian-style house with a wraparound veranda, immediately adjacent to the International Bazaar. There's a large interior with a dance floor that offers a high-tech lighting system and lots of gyrating bodies, but lots of people gravitate to the wraparound deck, where beer and drinks are passed through open windows to the crowd outside. Frequent contests reward anyone who qualifies for the "sexiest black dress" or "most muscular male." It's open Tuesday to Sunday from 9pm until at least 1am. In the International Bazaar. ✆ **242/351-2692.** $10 cover for men only; women admitted free.

Prop Club This sports bar and dance club is the most action-oriented of them all at Lucaya, and you can also dine here on hearty fare. Each night something different is happening: karaoke on Tuesday, Sumo wrestling on Wednesday, cultural show nights on Thursday, island "jam nights" on Friday, and '70s revival

---

Finds **Bahamian Theater**

Instead of one of those Las Vegas leggy showgirl revues, you can call the 450-seat **Regency Theater** (✆ **242/352-5533**), and ask if one of its performances is being scheduled. This is the home of two nonprofit companies, The Freeport Players' Guild and Grand Bahama Players. The season runs from September to June, and you are likely to see works by both Bahamian and Caribbean playwrights. Some really intriguing shows are likely to be staged every year. Both groups are equally talented.

---

nights on Saturday. But also expect a "get down with the DJ" snooze-a-thon on Sundays, and game nights on slow Mondays. The highlight is the cultural show with a live Junkanoo finale. You can also dine here, enjoying the likes of beef and chicken fajitas and baby-back ribs, paying from $10 for a full meal. For decor, as the name suggests, remnants of an old airplane and antique propellers adorn the walls. Lunch is served daily from 11am to 3pm and dinner daily 6 to 9pm, but the bar is open 11am to 11pm. Our Lucaya, Royal Palm Way. ✆ **242/373-1333.**

9 A Side Trip to West End

If you're looking for a refreshing escape from the plush hotels and casinos of Freeport/Lucaya, head to West End, 45km (28 miles) from Freeport. At this old fishing village, you'll get glimpses of how things used to be before package-tour groups began descending on Grand Bahama.

To reach West End, you head north along Queen's Highway, going through Eight Mile Rock, to the northernmost point of the island. West End has several good restaurants, so you can plan to make a day (or a night) of it.

A lot of the old village buildings are now dilapidated, but they still have some charm and some legend. Many old-timers remember when rum boats were busy and the docks buzzed with activity day and night. This was from about 1920 to 1933, when Prohibition rather unsuccessfully reigned in the United States. West End was so close to the U.S. mainland that rumrunning became a lucrative business, with booze flowing out of West End into Florida at night. Al Capone is reputed to have been a frequent visitor.

Villages along the way to West End have colorful names, such as **Hawksbill Creek.** For a glimpse of local life, try to visit the fish market along the harbor here. You'll pass some thriving harbor areas, too, but the vessels you'll see will be oil tankers, not rumrunners.

Eight Mile Rock is a hamlet of mostly ramshackle houses that stretches along both sides of the road for—you guessed it—13km (8 miles). At **West End,** you come to an abrupt stop. You can enjoy a meal here at the Buccaneer Club or Pier One before heading back to Freeport/Lucaya to catch the last show at the casino.

WHERE TO DINE

Buccaneer Club ★ CONTINENTAL/BAHAMIAN The Buccaneer Club is a tropical version of a German beer garden and is the best place to eat in West End. Heinz Fischbacher and his Bahamian wife, Kitty, created the whimsical decor. The compound is ringed with stone walls; inside it, palm-dotted terraces and foot-stomping alpine music provide lots of fun for the yachting crowd that always packs this place. The collection of inner rooms contains mismatched crystal chandeliers and a beer-hall ambience that's unique in The Bahamas. Many of the dishes are from eastern Europe, including a decent Wiener schnitzel and an excellent veal Oskar. On Tuesday, the Fischbachers host Junkanoo beach parties, which cost $40 per person. The price includes transportation from hotels, an hour-long open bar, a buffet, a tequila-drinking contest, and limbo dancing.

Deadman's Reef. ✆ **242/349-3794.** Reservations required. Main courses $15–$30. AE, MC, V. Tues–Sun 5–11pm.

Pier One *Kids* BAHAMIAN/INTERNATIONAL Many people head to this restaurant because it is close to the cruise-ship dock, and it's also an ideal place to sample some fresh seafood. It rises on stilts a few steps from the water's edge, and a footbridge leads to an interior loaded with nautical artifacts. The high-ceilinged bar is a nice spot for a round of drinks before your meal. There are several dining rooms, the most desirable of which overlooks schools of fish. The lunch fare includes a delectable cream-based clam chowder, and fresh oysters are also available. The house specialty is actually baby shark, prepared in a number of ways. (There's a shark pool on-site.) We prefer ours sautéed with garlic; the stuffed version, with cheese and crabmeat, tends to overpower the natural shark flavor. A fresh fish of the day is also featured.

Freeport Harbour. © **242/352-6674.** Reservations recommended for dinner. Lunch main courses $4.95–$15; dinner main courses $16.95–$42.95. AE, MC, V. Mon–Sat 10am–10pm; Sun 4–10pm.

Star Restaurant & Bar *Finds* BAHAMIAN At the very western tip of Grand Bahama, about a 45-minute drive from the center of Freeport, this battered old restaurant and bar is housed in a two-structure building that is the island's oldest hotel. Since 1946 it has welcomed the likes of everyone from Ernest Hemingway to Martin Luther King, Jr. When other joints on the Island close, it is often still going strong. Conch, done in many lovely forms, is the specialty: The conch chowder and the fresh conch salad are the island's best. You can also order fried chicken and fish and chips, plus various seafood platters; just tell the cook how you like them cooked. And surely no one serves a better Bahama Mama!

Bayshore Rd., West End. © **242/346-6207.** Main courses $10–$16. No credit cards. Daily 10am–2pm.

6

Bimini, the Berry Islands & Andros

In this chapter, we begin a journey through the Out Islands—a very different world from that found in the major tourist developments of Nassau, Cable Beach, Paradise Island, and Freeport/Lucaya.

Bimini, the Berry Islands, and Andros are quite different. Bimini is famous and overrun with tourists, particularly in summer, but visitors will have the Berry Islands practically to themselves. These two island chains are to the north and west of Nassau and could be called the "westerly islands," because they, along with Grand Bahama, lie at the northwestern fringe of The Bahamas. They are the closest islands to the Florida coastline.

In contrast, much larger Andros is located southwest of Nassau. In many ways Andros is the most fascinating, because it is actually a series of islands laced with creeks and dense forests, said once to have been inhabited by mysterious creatures.

Each of the three island chains attracts a different type of visitor. **Bimini,** just 81km (50 miles) off the east coast of Florida (and the setting for Hemingway's *Islands in the Stream*) lures the big-game fisher, the yachter from Miami, and even the drug dealer from South Florida. (The proximity to the Florida mainland helps make drug smuggling big business here.) Bimini is home to world-famous sportfishing, excellent yachting and cruising, and some good scuba diving. Anglers will find seas swarming with tuna, dolphinfish, amberjack, white and blue marlin, swordfish, barracuda, and shark, along with many other varieties. Bonefish are also plentiful around the flats off the coast of Alice Town, the capital, but the blue marlin is the prize. (Bahamians think so highly of this fish that they even put it on their $100 bill.) Scuba divers can see black coral trees over The Bimini Wall and reefs off Victory Cay.

The **Berry Islands** are the kind of retreat that might attract weary Bill Gates or Steve Forbes types. It also draws fishermen, but this string of islands, which has only 700 residents, is mainly for escapists—*rich* escapists. The islands' very limited accommodations (some of which used to be private clubs) lie near the Tongue of the Ocean, home of the big-game fish.

Andros, the largest island in the nation, is mainly uninhabited. If The Bahamas still has an unexplored wilderness, this is it. The island's forest and mangrove swamps are home to a wide variety of birds and animals, including the nonpoisonous Bahamian boa constrictor and the 2m- (6-ft.-) long iguana. The Bahamian national bird, the West Indian flamingo, can also be spotted during migration in late spring and summer. The waters off Andros are home to a wondrous barrier reef, the third largest in the world and a diver's dream. The reef plunges 1,800m (6,000 ft.) to a narrow drop-off known as the Tongue of the Ocean. Andros's mysterious blue holes, another diver's delight, are formed when subterranean caves fill with seawater, causing the ceiling to collapse and expose clear, deep pools. Few come here anymore looking for Sir Henry Morgan's pirate treasure, said to have been buried in one of the caves off Morgan's Bluff on the north tip of the island. But Andros does attract anglers, because it is known for its world-class fishing for marlin and the bluefin tuna, and its bonefishing is perhaps the best in the world.

1 Bimini

Bimini is still known as the big-game fishing capital of the world, and fishermen still come here throughout the year to fish in flats, on the reefs, and in the streams. Ernest Hemingway came to write and fish, and here, he wrote much of *To Have and Have Not.* His novel *Islands in the Stream* put Bimini on the map. Regrettably, fishing isn't what it used to be in Papa's day, and such species as marlin, swordfish, and tuna have been dangerously overfished by commercial longline boats.

Located 81km (50 miles) east of Miami, Bimini consists of a number of islands, islets, and cays, including North and South Bimini, the main tourist areas. You'll most often encounter the word "Bimini," but it might be more proper to say "The Biminis," since North Bimini and South Bimini are two distinct islands, separated by a narrow ocean passage. Ferry-service shuttles between the two. The major development is on North Bimini, mostly in Alice Town. The western side of North Bimini is a long stretch of lovely beachfront.

Off North Bimini, in 9m (30 ft.) of water, are some large hewn-stone formations that some people claim to be from the lost continent of Atlantis. Divers find the reefs laced with conch, lobster, coral, and many tropical fish.

Bimini's location off the Florida coastline is at a point where the Gulf Stream meets the Bahama Banks. This fact has made Bimini a favorite cruising ground for America's yachting set, who follow the channel between North and South Bimini into a spacious, sheltered harbor, where they can stock up on food, drink, fuel, and supplies at well-equipped marinas. From here, they can set off to cruise the cays that begin south of South Bimini. Each has its own special appeal, beginning with Turtle Rocks and stretching to South Cat Cay (the latter of which is uninhabited). Along the way, you'll pass Holm Cay, Gun Cay, and North Cat Cay.

Hook-shaped North Bimini is 12km (7½ miles) long, and combined with South Bimini, it makes up a landmass of only 23 square km (9 sq. miles). That's why Alice Town looks so crowded. Another reason is that a large part of Bimini is privately owned; despite pressure from the Bahamian government, the landholders have not sold their acreage, and Bimini can't "spread out" until they do. At Alice Town, the land is so narrow that you can walk "from sea to shining sea" in just a short time. Most of Bimini's population of some 1,600 people lives in Alice Town; other hamlets include Bailey Town and Porgy Bay.

Although winter is usually high season in The Bahamas, visitors flock to Bimini's calmer summer waters, which are better for fishing. Winter, especially from mid-December to mid-March, is quieter, and Bimini has never tried to develop a resort structure that would attract more winter visitors. If you go to Bimini, you'll hear a lot of people mention **Cat Cay** (not to be confused with Cat Island, in the Southern Bahamas). You can stay overnight at Cat Cay's marina, which lies 13km (8 miles) off South Bimini. Transient slips are available to mariners. The island is the domain of **Cat Cay Yacht Club** (✆ **242/347-3565**), whose initiation fee is a cool $25,000. This is a privately owned island,

attracting titans of industry and famous families. It is for the exclusive use of Cat Cay Club members and their guests, who enjoy a golf course, tennis, a large marina, white-sand beaches, and club facilities such as restaurants and bars. Many wealthy Americans have homes on the island, which has a private airstrip.

GETTING THERE

Note: A passport or a birth certificate with picture ID is required for entry to Bimini (bring your passport to be on the safe side), and an outbound (return) ticket also must be presented to Bahamian Customs before you will be allowed entry. Passengers returning from Bimini to the United States must pay a $15 departure tax.

BY PLANE The island's only airstrip is at the southern tip of South Bimini, a time-consuming transfer and ferryboat ride away from Alice Town on North Bimini, site of most of the archipelago's hotels and yacht facilities.

The best way to avoid this transfer is to fly the small **Chalk's Ocean Airways,** based in Miami (✆ **800/424-2557**). The airline has a fleet of 17-passenger amphibious aircraft that land in the waters near Alice Town. Chalk's offers two daily flights from Miami, one of which originates in Fort Lauderdale. The 20- to 30-minute flights depart from the calm waters at Watson Island Terminal, near downtown Miami (about a $12 cab ride from Miami International Airport). Round-trip tickets start at $221. Chalk's sometimes flies in from Nassau;

call the airline for more details. There is a baggage allowance of only 30 pounds per passenger; if you're carrying heavy travel or fishing gear, you'll be hit with overweight charges. *Note:* Chalk's doesn't allow any hand luggage on board—every piece of your luggage must be weighed and checked in.

Also, **Island Air** (✆ **800/444-9904** or 954/359-9942) flies five times a week from Fort Lauderdale to South Bimini.

BY BOAT In the olden days, the traditional way to get from Nassau to Bimini was by a slow-moving boat; you can still do it, and it'll take you 12 hours. You can go by sea on the MV ***Bimini Mack,*** which leaves from Potter's Cay Dock in Nassau and stops at Cat Cay and Bimini. The vessel leaves Nassau weekly but with no set schedule. For details about departure, call the dockmaster at **Potter's Cay Dock** in Nassau (✆ **242/393-1064**).

GETTING AROUND

If you've taken our advice and traveled lightly to Bimini, you can walk to your hotel from the point where the seaplanes land in Alice Town. If not, a small minibus will transport you for $3 per person. If you arrive at the small airport on South Bimini, it is a $5 taxi and ferry ride to Alice Town.

You won't need a car on Bimini—in fact, there are no car-rental agencies. Most people walk to where they want to go (though your hotel may be able to arrange a minibus tour or rent you a bike or golf cart). The walk is up and down King's Highway, which has no sidewalks. It's so narrow that two automobiles have a tough time squeezing by. Be careful walking along this highway, especially at night when drivers might not see you.

This highway, lined with low-rise buildings, splits Alice Town on North Bimini. If you're a beachcombing type, stick to the side bordering the Gulf Stream. It's here you'll find the best beaches. The harborside contains a handful of inns (most of which are reviewed below), along with marinas and docks where supplies are unloaded. You'll see many Floridians arriving on yachts.

FAST FACTS: Bimini

Banks **The Royal Bank of Canada** has a branch office in Alice Town (✆ **242/347-3031**), open Monday and Friday 9am to 3pm and Tuesday, Wednesday, and Thursday from 9am to 1pm.

Clothing If you're going to Bimini in the winter months, you'd better take along a windbreaker for those occasional chilly nights.

Customs & Immigration The Chalk's flight from Miami stops right near the Alice Town office of **Customs and Immigration** (✆ **242/368-2030**) for The Bahamas. There's only one Immigration officer, plus another Customs official.

In Miami you will have been handed a Bahamian Immigration Card to fill out, and you must carry proof of your citizenship. Though it may be possible to use your voter-registration card or a birth certificate plus photo ID, we recommend that you just bring your passport to be on the safe side. Regrettably, many passengers cross over from Miami with only a driver's license, which will not be accepted by immigration. Customs may or may not examine your baggage.

Drugs The rumrunners of the Prohibition era have now given way to those smuggling illegal drugs into the United States from The Bahamas. Because of its proximity to the U.S. mainland, Bimini, as is no secret to anyone, is now a major drop-off point for drugs, many of which have found their way here from Colombia. If not intercepted by the U.S. Coast Guard, these drugs will find their way to the Florida mainland and eventually to the rest of the United States.

Buying and/or selling illegal drugs, such as cocaine and marijuana, is an extremely risky business in The Bahamas. You may be approached by pushers on Bimini, but make sure you don't get into trouble, because there are undercover agents everywhere. If caught with any illegal drugs on Bimini, or elsewhere in The Bahamas, you will face immediate imprisonment.

Emergencies To call the police or report a fire, dial ✆ **919.**

Mail If you're sending mail back to the United States, we suggest you skip the Bahamian postal service entirely and drop your letter off at Chalk's airline's special basket. You can use U.S. postage stamps, and your mail will reach its mainland target far quicker than by the usual route.

Medical Care There are nurses, a doctor, and a dentist on the island, as well as the **North Bimini Medical Clinic** (✆ **242/347-2210**). However, for a serious medical emergency, patients are usually airlifted to either Miami or Nassau. Helicopters can land in the well-lit baseball field on North Bimini.

Special Events The annual **Bacardi Rum Billfish Tournament** and the **Hemingway Billfish Tournament** bring world anglers to Bimini in March. Make hotel reservations well in advance. There are additional tournaments throughout the year; see "The Bahamas Calendar of Events," in chapter 2, for additional details. The Bahamas Tourist Office near you (see "Visitor Information," in chapter 2) can provide details if you'd like to enter a tournament.

Visitor Information There's a branch of **The Bahamas Ministry of Tourism** in Bimini, located in the Government Building, Kings Highway, Alice Town (✆ **242/347-3529**). It's open Monday to Friday from 9am to 5:30pm.

WHERE TO STAY

Accommodations in Bimini are extremely limited, and it's almost impossible to get a room during one of the big fishing tournaments unless you've reserved way in advance. Inns are cozy and simple; many are family-owned and -operated (chances are, your innkeeper's name will be Brown). Furnishings are often time-worn, the paint chipped. No one puts on airs here; the dress code, even in the evening, is very simple and relaxed. From wherever you're staying in Alice Town, it's usually easy to walk to another hotel for dinner or drinks.

Bimini Beach Hotel/Bimini Sands Condo Complex There are two distinctly different aspects to this complex; both of which lie at the edge of a sandy beach, a 5-minute drive from South Bimini's international airport. The less well-accessorized and comfortable of the two is the two-story motel, half of whose rooms overlook the sea, the other half of which front a marina. Originally built in the 1970s, it was radically overhauled and renovated in 1999. Expect something akin to a roadside motel in Florida, but with a beach a few steps away. The

Island in the Stream

Nevil Norton Stuart, a Bahamian, came to Bimini in the late 1920s and purchased the Fountain of Youth, a Prohibition-era bar, renaming it the **Bimini Big Game Fishing Club.** In 1940, Stuart reclaimed land in Bimini Harbor, constructed a marina, and added several cottages along with a desalination plant. Thus began the legend of one of the most highly publicized sportfishing meccas in the world.

Film stars, including Judy Garland and Sir Anthony Hopkins, among others, have lodged at the club, and Martin Luther King, Jr., visited twice. Of course, no one immortalized the island as much as Hemingway, who called it "My Island in the Stream."

Today the complex has grown to more than 50 rooms, including cottages and penthouses, and it's owned by the rum maker Bacardi International. In the 100-slip marina, you'll find enormous sportfishing boats, costing more than several million dollars, proudly standing alongside simple outboard-powered runabouts.

The club hosts many fishing tournaments throughout the year, including the **Bacardi Rum Billfish Tournament** in March. This week-long world-class event attracts the biggest names in sportfishing and is regarded by many fishermen as the event of the year to win.

condo complex is more elaborate, with many of the features you'd expect (balconies, patios, contemporary furniture, and so on) in a generic-looking apartment complex somewhere in South Florida. Like the motel section, half the rooms overlook the sea, the other half overlook a marina. Rooms in each of the two complexes do feature well-maintained bathrooms with tub and shower combinations.

South Bimini. ✆ **242/347-3500.** Fax 242/347-3501. 36 conventional motel units, 18 1- or 2-bedroom condos with kitchens. $130–$150 conventional double; $200 1-bedroom condo with kitchen, $300 2-bedroom condo with kitchen. 2-night minimum required in the condo complex. AE, MC, V. **Amenities:** 3 restaurants, 2 bars; 2 pools; volleyball court; tennis court; laundry/dry cleaning. *In room:* A/C.

Bimini Big Game Resort & Marina ★★ The chosen "watering hole" of the big-game fisherman since the 1950s, this resort was sold in 2002 and is now better than ever following multimillion-dollar renovations. With its 81-slip marina, it is often a favorite stopover with the yachting crowd from Florida's east coast. The resort's restoration has been called a rebirth, and the patrons have remained loyal—mainly boaters, divers, eco-adventurers, and the deep-sea and bonefishing elite. Both the resort and marina facilities have been improved, including a complete overhaul of the guest rooms and the dining and drinking facilities.

Accommodations are well furnished, both the guest units in the main building and those in surrounding cottages and penthouse apartments. All rooms have patios or porches opening onto the marina and the club's swimming pool. The ground-floor cottages are more spacious than the standard bedrooms and have tiny kitchenettes and refrigerators. If you want to charcoal-broil your catch of the day, you can use one of the outdoor grills. The small bathrooms are well maintained and come with shower stalls. The hotel staff can arrange fishing charters.

The hotel is the best place to go for food and entertainment on the island (see "Where to Dine" and "Bimini After Dark," below). The hotel will help you arrange all kinds of fishing charters.

King's Hwy. (P.O. Box 699), Alice Town, Bimini, The Bahamas, or P.O. Box 523238, Miami, FL 33152. © **800/737-1007** in the U.S., or 242/347-3391. Fax 242/347-3392. www.bimini-big-game-club.com. 35 units, 12 cottages, 4 penthouse apts. $165 double; $190 cottage for 2; $275 penthouse. Extra person $25. AE, MC, V. **Amenities:** Restaurant, 3 bars; pool; tennis court; laundry; babysitting; bike rentals. *In room:* A/C, TV, refrigerator, no phone.

Bimini Blue Water Resort Ltd. ★ This is essentially a resort complex for sportfishermen, with complete dockside services, containing 32 modern slips. It's one of the finest places of its kind in The Bahamas. The main building is a white-frame waterfront Bahamian guesthouse, the Anchorage, where Michael Lerner, the noted fisherman, used to live. It's at the top of the hill, with a dining room and bar from which you can look out onto the ocean (see "Where to Dine," below). The regular midsize bedrooms contain double beds, wood-paneled walls, white furniture, and picture-window doors that lead to private balconies. Bathrooms are small with shower units.

The Marlin Cottage, although much altered, was one of Hemingway's retreats in the 1930s. He used it as a main setting in *Islands in the Stream.* It has three bedrooms, three bathrooms, a large living room, and two porches. In honor of his memory, the hotel sponsors the Hemingway Billfish Tournament every March.

King's Hwy. (P.O. Box 601), Alice Town, Bimini, The Bahamas. © **242/347-3166.** Fax 242/347-3293. 12 units. $90 double; $190 suite; $285 Marlin Cottage. AE, MC, V. **Amenities:** Dining room, bar; 2 pools; babysitting; marina. *In room:* A/C, TV, no phone.

Compleat Angler Hotel Right on the main street, and affiliated with the Bimini Blue Water Resort, this small timeworn hotel was built in the 1930s, when big-game fishing was at its peak. The building is designed like an old country house, with Bahamian timber. The wood on the face of the building is from rum barrels used during the Prohibition era. Don't expect anything too fancy, but the Compleat Angler is loaded with island atmosphere. Ernest Hemingway made the hotel his headquarters on and off from 1935 to 1937 while he was stalking marlin, and the room in which he stayed is still available to guests. He penned parts of *To Have and Have Not* here. The small to midsize rooms are tidily maintained and comfortable, with cramped bathrooms containing shower stalls. The best units are those in the front opening onto the encircling veranda, overlooking the courtyard bar and the street. You can swim, dine, shop, or fish right at your doorstep, and book fishing charters at the hotel. *Note:* Because of the famous, noisy bar on the premises (see "Bimini After Dark," below), this hotel is suitable only for night owls.

King's Hwy., P.O. Box 601, Alice Town, Bimini, The Bahamas. © **242/347-3122.** Fax 242/347-3293. 12 units. $68–$83 double. AE, MC, V. **Amenities:** 3 bars; pool. *In room:* A/C, no phone.

Sea Crest Hotel & Marina Built in 1981 and upgraded every year since, this hotel lies right on the main highway and was the first place to give the Bimini Big Game Fishing Club & Hotel some real competition. It's still not as good as that traditional leader, but the price is right. Rooms in this three-story hotel, which looks like a motel, are at their best on the third floor, because they have better ocean or bay views. Rooms don't have phones, and many are small, with rather cramped bathrooms, each with a shower stall, but they're comfortably furnished in a simple, traditional way. Accommodations open onto small balconies.

Since the location is right in the heart of Alice Town, you can generally walk where you want to go. The Sea Crest is a family favorite, and children under 12 stay free. There's an on-site restaurant, Captain Bob's, which is independently operated and serves good seafood. The hotel is also a favorite of the boating crowd, because it offers a small 18-berth marina.

King's Hwy. (P.O. Box 654), Alice Town, Bimini, The Bahamas. ✆ **242/347-3071.** Fax 242/347-3495. www.seacreastbimini.com 12 units. $95.40 double. MC, V. **Amenities:** Restaurant, bar; marina. *In room:* A/C, TV, no phone.

WHERE TO DINE

Anchorage Dining Room SEAFOOD/BAHAMIAN/AMERICAN This dining room overlooks the harbor of Alice Town; you can see the ocean through picture windows. The modern, paneled room is filled with captain's chairs and Formica tables. You might begin your dinner with conch chowder, then follow with one of the tempting seafood dishes, including spiny broiled lobster or perhaps a chewy cracked conch. They also do a good fried Bahamian chicken and a tender New York sirloin. The cooking is straightforward and reliable, never pretending to be more than it is.

In the Blue Hole Water Resort, King's Hwy., Alice Town. ✆ **242/347-3166.** Main courses $13–$27. AE, MC, V. Daily 6–10pm.

Big Game Sports Bar SEAFOOD This sports bar, always packed with serious fishermen from South Florida, is upstairs overlooking the marina. It offers standard fare, but the food is as reliable as the view. Menu items are displayed near the cash register. During lunch, the popular bar serves conch fritters, conch salad, conch chowder, and cracked conch, which is breaded like veal cutlet. But conch pizza is the specialty and is well worth the visit here. You can also order grouper fingers, barbecued back ribs, hamburgers, sandwiches, or a daily special.

In the Bimini Big Game Fishing Club & Hotel, King's Hwy., Alice Town. ✆ **242/347-3391.** Main courses $7–$14. AE, MC, V. Tues–Sun noon–10pm.

Gulfstream Restaurant ★ CARIBBEAN FUSION This restaurant, the most upscale on the island, offers innovative cookery—probably the finest ever to be offered in Bimini, and it's now under committed new management. Well-known chef and food guru Peter Birkwieser has taken over recently and is a master of the artistic merging of local flavors and ingredients; he shows both California and Asian influences. The overall result is a kind of West Indian fusion cuisine. Fresh fish, as always, is the high point of the menu. You can enjoy freshly caught kingfish, grilled to perfection; Bahamian grouper; or freshly grilled lobster, along with choice cuts of meats, including steaks, roast prime rib, and lamb chops shipped in from Miami.

In the Bimini Big Game Resort & Marina, King's Hwy., Alice Town. ✆ **242/347-3391.** Reservations recommended for dinner. Main courses $15–$30. AE, MC, V. Wed–Mon 7:30–11am and 7–10pm. Closed Jan to mid-Feb.

Red Lion Pub BAHAMIAN This centrally located restaurant is far larger than its simple facade would indicate. In a relaxed, friendly atmosphere, it's one of the best places on the island to retreat to after a day of fishing and sailing. It's one of the few nonsmoking restaurants in the Out Islands. The dining room is in a large extension of the original pub and overlooks the marina in back. The well-prepared meals are local home-cooking: the local fish of the day, cracked conch, barbecued ribs, baked grouper in foil, followed by either Key lime pie or banana cream pie. The price of the main course practically gets you a dinner unto itself.

King's Hwy., Alice Town. ✆ **242/347-3259.** Main courses $13–$27. No credit cards. Tues–Sun 6–10pm; pub Tues–Sun until 10:30pm.

WATERSPORTS & OTHER OUTDOOR ACTIVITIES

BEACHES

The beaches on Bimini are all clearly marked and signposted from the highways.

The beach that's closest to Alice Town is **Radio Beach,** the only one on Bimini with toilets, vendors, and snack bars. It's set adjacent to the piers and wharves of Alice Town, and consequently, it's the most popular and crowded beach on the island.

About 3km (2 miles) north of Alice Town, facing west, is **Spook Hill Beach.** Both it and its cousin, **Bimini Bay Beach,** about 4km (2½ miles) north of Alice Town, offer fewer crowds, good snorkeling, and lots of sunshine. Both are sandy-bottomed and comfortable on your feet. **Bimini Bay Beach,** wider than any other on the island, is the favorite of many local residents.

On South Bimini, the two favorites are the west-facing **Bimini Sands Beach,** a sandy-bottomed stretch that's immediately south of the channel that separates North from South Bimini; and the **Bimini Reef Club Beach,** south of the airport, where offshore snorkeling is worthwhile, thanks to very clear waters.

FISHING

Ernest Hemingway made fishing here famous. But Zane Grey came this way, too, as did Howard Hughes. Richard Nixon used to fish here aboard the posh cruiser of his friend Bebe Rebozo. In the trail of Hemingway, fishermen still flock to cast lines in the Gulf Stream and the Bahama Banks. The annual **Bacardi Rum Billfish Tournament** and the **Hemingway Billfish Tournament** bring world anglers to Bimini in March.

Of course, everyone's still after the big one, and a lot of world records have been set in this area for marlin, sailfish, swordfish, wahoo, grouper, and tuna. But these fish are becoming evasive and their dwindling numbers are edging them close to extinction. Fishing folk can spin cast for panfish and boat snapper, yellowtail, and kingfish. Many experts consider stalking bonefish, long a pursuit of baseball great Ted Williams, to be the toughest challenge in the sport.

Five charter boats are available in Bimini for big-game and little-game fishing, with some center-console boats rented for both bottom and reef angling. At least eight bonefishing guides are available, and experienced anglers who have made repeated visits to Bimini know the particular skills of each of these men who will take you for a half or full day of "fishing in the flats." Most skiffs hold two anglers, and part of the fun in hiring a local guide is to hear his fish tales and other island lore. If a guide tells you that 16-pound bonefish have turned up, he may not be exaggerating—catches that large have really been documented.

Reef and bottom-fishing on Bimini are easier than bonefishing and can be more productive. There are numerous species of snapper and grouper to be found, as well as amberjack. This is the simplest and least expensive boat fishing, because you need only a local guide, a little boat, tackle, and a lot of bait. Sometimes you can negotiate to go out bottom-fishing with a Bahamian, but chances are he'll ask you to pay for the boat fuel for his trouble. That night, back at your Bimini inn, the cook will serve you the red snapper or grouper you caught that day.

Most hotel owners will tell you to bring your own fishing gear to Bimini. A couple of small shops sell some items, but you'd better bring major equipment with you if you're really serious. Bait, of course, can be purchased locally.

At the **Bimini Big Game Fishing Club & Hotel,** King's Highway, Alice Town (© **242/347-3391**), you can charter a 12m (41-ft.) Hatteras at $700 to $800 for a full day of fishing, or $400 to $600 for a half day. A Bertram, either 8.5 or 9.5m (28 or 31 ft.), will also cost $800 to $900 for a full day or $400 to $500 for a half day. Although this outfitter is your best bet, you can also pick up a list of locals whose boats are available for charter at **Bimini Blue Water Marina,** King's Highway, Alice Town (© **242/347-3166**). The average rate is around $400 to $600 per half day or $650 to $1,000 for a full day.

SCUBA DIVING & SNORKELING

There are black coral gardens and reefs to explore, plus wrecks and blue holes, plus a mysterious stone formation on the bottom of the sea that some people claim is part of the lost continent of **Atlantis** (it's 500 yardsd offshore at Bimini Bay under about 6m/20 ft. of water). Bimini waters are known for a breathtaking drop-off at the rim of the continental shelf, a cliff extending 600m (2,000 ft.) down, a veritable underwater mountain.

The finest and most experienced outfitter is **Bimini Undersea,** King's Highway, Alice Town (© **242/347-3089;** www.biminiundersea.com).

The people to see here are Bill and Nowdla Keefe. Half-day snorkeling trips cost $29. Scuba rates are $49 for a one-tank dive, $89 for a two-tank dive, and $119 for a three-tank dive. Night dives Tuesday and Friday go for $49. All-inclusive dive packages are also available. For further information or reservations, the Keefes can be reached at © **800/348-4644** or 305/653-5572. You can also swim with dolphins in the wild two or three times a week, depending on demand. Most excursions take from 3 to 4 hours and cost $109 for adults or $69 for children 11 and under (free for children 7 and under).

TENNIS

You'll find hard-surface courts at the **Bimini Big Game Fishing Club & Hotel** (© **242/347-3391**), King's Highway, which are complimentary and reserved for hotel guests and members. The courts are lit for night play, and you can purchase balls at the club. There are no public tennis courts.

TRACING THE FOOTSTEPS OF PONCE DE LEON & PAPA

At the southern tip of North Bimini, ramshackle **Alice Town** is all that many visitors ever see of the islands, since the major hotels are found here. You can see

---

Finds Ruins of the Roaring '20s

A major attraction for both snorkelers and divers, not to mention rainbow-hued fish, is the ***Sapona,*** lying hard aground in 4.5m (15 ft.) of water between South Bimini and Cat Cay ever since it was blown here by a hurricane in 1929. In the heyday of the Roaring Twenties, the ship, which was built by Henry Ford, served as a private club and speakeasy. You'll have to take a boat to reach the wreck site. Spearfishermen are attracted to the ruins, looking for the giant grouper, and dive operators on Bimini include the site in their repertoire. It's shallow enough that even snorkelers can see it.

Fun Fact Myths of Bimini

Bimini has long been shrouded in myths, none more far-fetched than the one claiming that the lost continent of **Atlantis** lies off the shores of North Bimini. This legend grew because of the weirdly shaped rock formations that lie submerged in about 9m (30 ft.) of water near the shoreline. Pilots flying over North Bimini have reported what they envision as a "lost highway" under the sea. This myth continues, and many scuba divers are attracted to North Bimini to explore these rocks.

Ponce de León came to South Bimini looking for that legendary **Fountain of Youth.** He never found it, but people still come to South Bimini in search of it. Near the end of the 19th century, a religious sect reportedly came here to "take the waters." Supposedly, there was a bubbling fountain, or at least a spring, in those days. If you arrive on South Bimini and seem interested enough, a local guide (for a fee) will be only too happy to show you "the exact spot" where the Fountain of Youth once bubbled.

the whole town in an hour or two. The **Bimini Big Game Fishing Club & Hotel,** King's Highway, has some of the best duty-free liquor buys in town. If you're a souvenir collector, ask at the front office for T-shirts, sunglasses, coffee mugs, and Big Game Club hats.

If you're on the trail of Papa Hemingway, you'll want to visit **The Compleat Angler,** King's Highway in Alice Town (✆ **242/347-3122**), where there is a museum of Hemingway memorabilia. The collection of prints and writings describes the times he spent in Bimini, mainly from 1935 to 1937. The prints are posted in the sitting room downstairs, and much of this memorabilia makes interesting browsing. There are a number of books by Hemingway in the library collection.

As you're exploring the island, you may want to stop off at the **Bimini Straw Market,** strike up a conversation with some islanders, and perhaps pick up a souvenir.

The **Queen's Highway** runs up the western side of North Bimini, and as you head north along it, you'll find it lined with beautiful beachfront. **King's Highway** runs through the town and continues north. It's lined with houses painted gold, lime, buttercup yellow, and pink that gleam in the bright sunshine.

At some point, you may notice the ruins of Bimini's first hotel, the **Bimini Bay Rod and Gun Club,** sitting unfinished on its own beach. Built in the early 1920s, it did a flourishing business until a hurricane wiped it out later in that decade. It was never rebuilt, though developers once made a never-finished attempt.

If you want to visit **South Bimini,** you can rent a taxi to see the island's limited attractions for about $17, which, regrettably, at least to our knowledge, does not include Ponce de León's legendary Fountain of Youth, as once rumored. There's not a lot to see, but you are likely to hear some tall tales worth the cab fare. You can also stop off at some lovely, uncrowded beaches.

BIMINI AFTER DARK

You can dance to a Goombay beat or try to find some disco music. Most people have a leisurely dinner, drink a lot in one of the local watering holes, and go back to their hotel rooms by midnight so they can get up early to continue

Moments A Drink at the End of the World

Everybody eventually makes his or her way to the **End of the World Bar** (no phone) on King's Highway in Alice Town. When you get here, you may think you're in the wrong place—it's just a waterfront shack with sawdust or sand on the floor and graffiti everywhere. It was the late New York congressman Adam Clayton Powell who put this bar on the map in the 1960s. Between stints in Washington battling Congress and preaching at the Abyssinian Baptist Church in Harlem, the controversial congressman could be found sitting at a table here. While the bar doesn't attract the media attention it did in Powell's heyday, it's still a strong local favorite. Open daily from 9am to 3am.

pursuing the elusive "big one" the next morning. Every bar in Alice Town is likely to claim that it was Hemingway's favorite. He did hit quite a few of them, in fact. There's rarely a cover charge anywhere unless some special entertainment is being offered.

Beginning at midmorning and lasting until midnight at least, the bars at the **Bimini Big Game Fishing Club & Hotel,** King's Highway, Alice Town (✆ **242/347-3391**), are the place to hang out. Tall fish tales of the big one that got away fill the air. The **Big Game Sports Bar** (see "Where to Dine," above) starts serving its famed conch pizza at noon. No fewer than four TV sets are positioned for your favorite sports program, or you may want to enjoy a hand of cards. It's the best room in which to entertain yourself during those lazy days in Bimini. The poolside **Barefoot Bar,** open from midmorning to late afternoon, serves favorite island drinks and ice-cold beer. Off the main dining room of the Gulfstream Restaurant is the **Gulfstream Bar,** featuring Ratti, the island's best-known calypsonian, singing the songs of the island and strumming them on his guitar. Naturally, since Bacardi owns the place, all the rum punches are made with Bacardi rums.

Constructed of Prohibition-era rum kegs, the bar at **The Compleat Angler Hotel,** King's Highway, Alice Town (✆ **242/347-3122**), hosts an eclectic clientele who come to dance to the nightly calypso band and drink Goombay Smashes. The bartender makes the best planter's punch in The Bahamas, challenging anyone to make it better. The place, as mentioned, is filled with Hemingway memorabilia, and it's open daily from 11am "until . . ."

2 The Berry Islands ★

A dangling chain of cays and islets on the eastern edge of the Great Bahama Bank, the unspoiled and serene Berry Islands begin 56km (35 miles) northwest of New Providence (Nassau), 242km (150 miles) east of Miami. This 30-island archipelago is known to sailors, fishermen, yachtspeople, Jack Nicklaus, and a Rockefeller or two, as well as to the beachcombers who love its pristine sands.

As a center of fishing, the Berry Islands are second only to Bimini. At the tip of the Tongue of the Ocean, a.k.a. TOTO, world-record-setting big-game fish are found, along with endless flats (the shallow bodies of water near the shore where bonefish congregate). In the "Berries," you can find your own tropical paradise islet, and enjoy—sans wardrobe—totally isolated white-sand beaches and palm-fringed shores. Some of the best shell collecting in The Bahamas is found on the beaches of the Berry Islands and in their shallow-water flats.

The main islands are, beginning in the north, Great Stirrup Cay, Cistern Cay, Great Harbour Cay, Anderson Cay, Haines Cay, Hoffmans Cay, Bond's Cay, Sandy Cay, Whale Cay, and Chub Cay. One of the very small cays, lying north of Frazer's Hog Cay and Whale Cay, has, in our opinion, the most unappetizing name in the Bahamian archipelago: Cockroach Cay.

The largest island within the Berry Islands is **Great Harbour Cay,** which sprawls over 3,800 acres of sand, rock, and scrub. Development here received a great deal of publicity when Douglas Fairbanks Jr., was connected with its investors. It became a multimillion-dollar resort for jet-setters who occupied waterfront town houses and villas overlooking the golf course or marina. There are 12km (7½ miles) of almost-solitary beachfront. Once Cary Grant, Brigitte Bardot, and other stars romped on this beach.

Bond's Cay, a bird sanctuary in the south, and tiny Frazer's Hog Cay (stock is still raised here) are both privately owned. An English company used to operate a coconut and sisal plantation on Whale Cay, also near the southern tip. Sponge fishermen and their families inhabit some of the islands.

BERRY ISLANDS ESSENTIALS

GETTING THERE Great Harbour Cay is an official point of entry for The Bahamas if you're flying from a foreign territory such as the United States.

You can get here only via charter flights from South Florida, making these some of the most inconvenient islands to reach in all The Bahamas. **Tropical Diversions** (© **954/921-9084**) flies from Fort Lauderdale to Great Harbour Cay, usually in a five-passenger, twin-engine Piper Seneca; and **Island Express** (© **954/359-0380**) also operates charters from Fort Lauderdale, winging in to Chub Cay Airport.

If you're contemplating the **mail-boat** sea-voyage route, the **MV *Captain Gurthdean*** leaves Potter's Cay Dock in Nassau once a week on Friday at 7pm, heading for the Berry Islands. Inquire at the **Potter's Cay Dock** for an up-to-the-minute report (contact the dockmaster at © **242/393-1064**).

FAST FACTS The **Great Harbour Cay Medical Clinic** is at Bullock's Harbour on Great Harbour Cay (© **242/367-8400**). The **police station** is also at Bullock's Harbour (© **242/367-8344**).

GREAT HARBOUR CAY

An estimated 700 residents live on Great Harbour Cay, making it the most populated island of the Berry chain. Its main settlement is **Bullock's Harbour,** which might be called the "capital of the Berry Islands." The cay is about 2.5km (1½ miles) wide and some 13km (8 miles) long. There isn't much in town: a grocery store and some restaurants. Most visitors arrive to stay at the **Great Harbour Cay Yacht Club & Marina** (see below), outside of town.

Great Harbour Cay lies between Grand Bahama Island and New Providence (Nassau). It's 97km (60 miles) northwest of Nassau and 242km (150 miles) east of Miami, about an hour away from Miami by plane or half a day by powerboat. Unlike most islands in The Bahamas, the island isn't flat but contains rolling hills.

Deep-sea fishing possibilities abound here, including billfish, dolphinfish, king mackerel, and wahoo. Light-tackle bottom-fishing is also good. You can net yellowtail, snapper, barracuda, triggerfish, and plenty of grouper. Bonefishing here is among the best in the world. The Great Harbour Cay marina is an excellent facility, with some 80 slips and all the amenities. Some of Florida's fanciest yachts pull in here.

When you tire of fishing, there are 13km (8 miles) of gorgeous white-sand beaches, a nine-hole golf course designed by Joe Lee, and four clay tennis courts.

ACCOMMODATIONS & DINING

Great Harbour Cay Yacht Club & Beach Villas ★ The two-level waterfront town houses here overlook the marina (the staff will help you arrange fishing excursions). Each has its own private dock, topped off with a garage and patio. Other units are on the beach. Although privately owned, these accommodations are rented on a daily or weekly basis by the resort. Each unit is furnished individually by the owner. The town houses have a light, airy feeling, with some 149 square m (1,600 sq. ft.) of living space. Each has two bedrooms and two and a half bathrooms with shower-tub combinations, suitable for up to six people. All have fully equipped kitchens, and some accommodations have TV. Beach villas, covered in cedar shakes, have tile floors and a Mediterranean-type decor. Units range from studio apartments (the cheapest rentals) to two-bedroom units, and daily maid service is included.

Dining facilities include the Wharf, serving breakfast and lunch, and the Tamboo Club, at the west end of the marina, open Wednesday through Saturday for drinks and dinner only.

Great Harbour Cay, Berry Islands, The Bahamas (mailing address 3512 N. Ocean Dr., Hollywood, FL 33019). ✆ **242/367-8854.** Fax 242/367-8076. www.tropicaldiversions.com. 18 units. $90–$275 double; $425–$600 beach house or villa suitable for 5–6 guests. AE, MC, V. **Amenities:** 2 restaurants, bar; dock; snorkeling; fishing; laundry; bikes for guests; 9-hole golf course. *In room:* A/C, no phone.

CHUB CAY

Named after a species of fish that thrives in nearby waters, Chub Cay is well known to sportfishing enthusiasts. A self-contained hideaway with a devoted clientele, it's the southernmost of the Berry Islands, separating the mainland of South Florida from the commercial frenzy of Nassau.

Chub Cay's development began in the late 1950s as the strictly private (and rather spartan) enclave of a group of Texas-based anglers and investors. It was originally uninhabited, but over the years a staff was imported, dormitory-style housing was built, and the island's most famous man-made feature (its state-of-the-art, 90-slip marina) was constructed in the 979-acre island's sheltered lagoon.

After recovering from severe damage inflicted in 1992 by Hurricane Andrew, Chub Cay is today a tranquil, scrub-covered sand spit with awesome amounts of marine hardware, a dozen posh private homes, the marina, and a complex of buildings devoted to the **Chub Cay Club** (see below). Today, membership in the club begins at around $2,000 a year and grants reduced rates for marina slip rental, boat repairs, and hotel-room and villa rental. Nonmembers, however, are welcome to use the facilities, and rent rooms at the rates listed below.

There are a liquor store and a yachties' commissary on the island, an outlet for the sale of marine supplies, and a concrete runway for landing anything up to and including a 737. Most visitors reach Chub Cay by private yacht from the Florida mainland, but if you prefer to charter your fishing craft on Chub Cay, you'll find a mini-armada of suitable craft at your disposal. **Island Express Airlines** (✆ **954/359-0380**) flies charter flights to Chub Cay from Fort Lauderdale. Charter flights can be arranged with the help of the Chub Cay Club's desk staff. If you opt to fly here, travel light; there's a baggage allowance of no more than 50 pounds per passenger.

The water temperature around Chub Cay averages a warm 80°F to 85°F year-round, even at relatively deep depths. There's only a small tidal change, and under normal conditions, there is no swell or noticeable current in offshore waters. The waters are incredibly clear, making for great snorkeling.

ACCOMMODATIONS & DINING

Chub Cay Club ★ Breezy and comfortable, these air-conditioned accommodations are the only available option on all of Chub Cay. The place prides itself on its marina, freshwater swimming pools, and many nearby sandy beaches. Throughout the resort, there's a nautical, laid-back kind of feeling and a clubby atmosphere. Don't expect inspired architecture. None of the rooms has a phone, although a phone is available at the reception desk. The decor consists of modern wicker with firm beds, plus small, well-organized bathrooms with shower-tub combinations. The remote feeling here is a welcome relief to many guests.

There's a restaurant (the Harbour House), with its own bar, as well as the Cay Bar set beside the pool, and the Hilltop Bar on the island's highest elevation. The latter offers a TV for sports broadcasts, pool tables, and occasional live music.

Chub Cay, Berry Islands, The Bahamas. (Or write to Chub Cay Club, P.O. Box 661067, Miami Springs, FL 33266.) ✆ **800/662-8555** or 242/325-1490. Fax 242/322-5199. www.chubcay.com. 44 units. $135–$170 double; $400 2-bedroom villa with kitchen, $500 3-bedroom villa with kitchen, $600 4-bedroom villa with kitchen. Discounts available for stays of a week or more. AE, MC, V. **Amenities:** Restaurant, 3 bars; laundry; babysitting; pool; exercise room; 2 tennis courts. *In room:* A/C, TV, hair dryer, no phone.

3 Andros ★★

The largest island in The Bahamas, Andros is one of the biggest unexplored tracts of land in the Western Hemisphere— and an excellent budget destination. Mostly flat, its 5,957 square km (2,300 sq. miles) are riddled with lakes and creeks, and most of the local residents, who still indulge in fire dances and go on wild boar hunts on occasion, live along the shore.

The most mysterious island in The Bahamas, Andros is 161km (100 miles) long and 64km (40 miles) wide. Its interior consists of a dense, tropical forest, really rugged bush, and mangrove country. The marshy and relatively uninhabited west coast is called the "Mud," and the east coast is paralleled for 193km (120 miles) by the second-largest underwater barrier reef in the world. The reef drops to more than 1.5km (1 mile) into the Tongue of the Ocean, or TOTO. On the eastern shore, this "tongue" is 229km (142 miles) long and 1,000 fathoms (1.136 miles or .3788 leagues) deep.

Lying 274km (170 miles) southeast of Miami and 48km (30 miles) west of Nassau, Andros is actually three major land areas: North Andros, Middle Andros, and South Andros. In spite of its size, Andros is very thinly populated (its residents number only around 5,000), although the tourist population swells it a bit. The temperature range here averages from 72°F to 85°F.

You won't find the western side of Andros written about much in yachting guides, because tricky shoals render it almost unapproachable by boat. The east coast, however, has kilometers of unspoiled beaches and is studded with little villages. Hotels that range from simple guest cottages to dive resorts to fishing camps have been built here. "Creeks" (we'd call them rivers) intersect the island at its midpoint. Also called "bights," they range in width from 8 to 40km (5–25 miles), and they are dotted with tiny cays and islets.

The fishing at Andros is famous, establishing records for blue marlin caught offshore. Divers and snorkelers find that the coral reefs are among the most beautiful in the world, and everyone loves the pristine beaches.

A word of warning: Be sure to bring along plenty of mosquito repellent.

ESSENTIALS

GETTING THERE Reaching Andros is not that difficult. **Bahamasair** (✆ **800/222-4262** in the U.S.) has twice-daily 15-minute flights from Nassau to the airport at Andros Town in Central Andros (✆ **242/368-2030**). There are also airports at San Andros in the north (✆ **242/329-4224**); at Mangrove Cay (✆ **242/369-0083**), and at Congo Town in South Andros (✆ **242/369-2640**). Small carriers winging in to Andros include **Lynx Air International** (✆ **888/596-9247**), coming from Fort Lauderdale chartering flight to Congo Town 7 days a week.

Make sure you know where you're going in Andros. For example, if you land at Congo Town on South Andros and you've booked a hotel in Nicholl's Town, you'll find connections nearly impossible at times (involving both ferryboats and a rough haul across a bad highway).

Andros's few available taxis know when the planes from Nassau are going to land, and they drive out to the airports, hoping to drum up some business. Taxis are most often shared. A typical fare from Andros Town Airport to Small Hope Bay Lodge is about $25.

Many locals, along with a few adventurous visitors, use the **mail boats** to get to Andros; the trip takes 5 to 7 hours across some beautiful waters. North Andros is serviced by the **MV *Lisa J. II,*** a mail boat that departs Potter's Cay Dock in Nassau heading for Morgan's Bluff, Mastic Point, and Nicholl's Town. It departs Nassau on Wednesday, returning to Nassau on Tuesday. The **MV *Moxey*** departs Nassau on Monday, calling at Long Bay Cays, Kemps Bay, and the Bluff on South Andros. It heads back to Nassau on Wednesday. For details about sailing and costs, contact the dockmaster at **Potter's Cay Dock** in Nassau (✆ **242/393-1064**).

ORIENTATION Chances are your hotel will be in **North Andros,** in either Andros Town or Nicholl's Town. North Andros is the most developed of the three major Andros islands. **Nicholl's Town** is a colorful old settlement with some 600 people and several places serving local foods. Most visitors come to Nicholl's Town to buy supplies at a shopping complex. Directly to the south is **Mastic Point,** which was founded in 1781. If you ask around, you'll be shown to a couple of concrete-sided dives that offer spareribs and Goombay music. To the north of Nicholl's Town is **Morgan's Bluff,** namesake of Sir Henry Morgan, a pirate later knighted by the British monarch. **Andros Town,** with its abandoned docks, is another village, about 47km (29 miles) south of Nicholl's Town. Most visitors come to Andros Town to stay at the **Small Hope Bay Lodge** (see below) or to avail themselves of its facilities. The biggest retail industry, Androsia batik, is in the area, too. The scuba diving—minutes away on the barrier reef—is what lures much of the world to this tiny place; others come here just for the shelling. On the opposite side of the water is **Coakley Town.** If you're driving, before you get to Andros Town, you may want to stop and spend some restful hours on the beach at **Staniard Creek,** another old settlement on Andros that feels lifted from the South Seas.

Moving south to the second major landmass, **Central Andros** is smaller than either North or South Andros. The least developed of the three, the island is

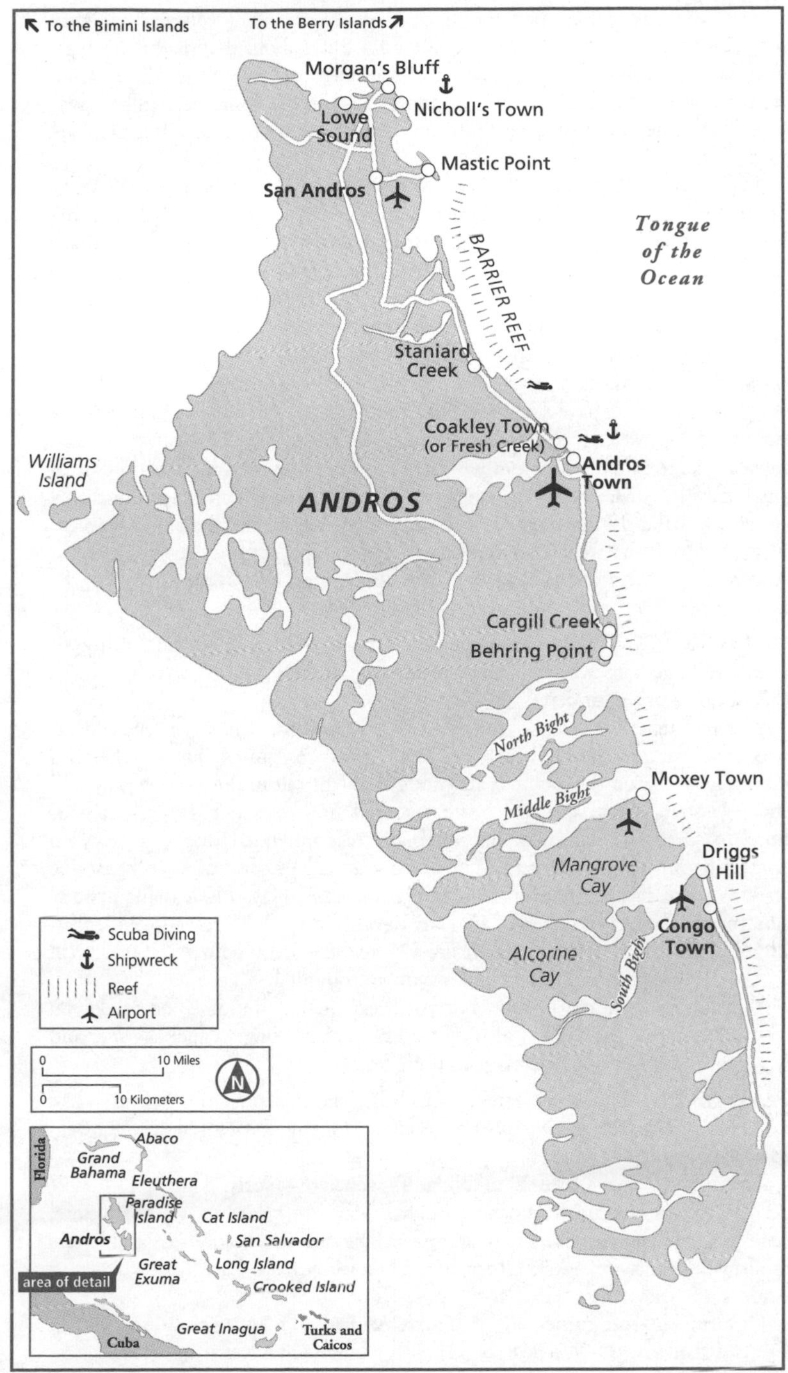
To the Bimini Islands
To the Berry Islands
Morgan's Bluff
Nicholl's Town
Lowe Sound
Mastic Point
San Andros
Tongue of the Ocean
BARRIER REEF
Staniard Creek
Coakley Town (or Fresh Creek)
Andros Town
Williams Island
ANDROS
Cargill Creek
Behring Point
North Bight
Moxey Town
Middle Bight
Mangrove Cay
Driggs Hill
Congo Town
Alcorine Cay
South Bight
Scuba Diving
Shipwreck
Reef
Airport
0
10 Miles
0
10 Kilometers
N
Florida
Abaco
Grand Bahama
Eleuthera
Paradise Island
Andros
Cat Island
San Salvador
Great Exuma
Long Island
area of detail
Crooked Island
Great Inagua
Turks and Caicos
Cuba

studded with hundreds upon hundreds of palm trees. The Queen's Highway runs along the eastern coastline, but the only thing about this road that's regal is its name. In some 7km (4½ miles) you can practically travel the whole island. It's truly sleepy, and for that very reason, many people come here to get away from it all. They don't find much in the way of accommodations, but there are some.

The third and last major land area, **South Andros** is the home of the wonderfully named **Congo Town,** where life proceeds at a snail's pace. The Queen's Highway, lined in part with pink-and-white conch shells, runs for about 40km (25 miles) or so. The island, as yet undiscovered, has some of the best beaches in The Bahamas, and you can enjoy them almost by yourself.

Another tiny island, undeveloped **Mangrove Cay** is an escapist's dream, attracting naturalists and anglers, as well as a few divers. It's separated from the northern and southern sections of Andros by bights. The settlements here only got electricity and a paved road in 1989. The best place for snorkeling and diving on Mangrove Cay is **Victoria Point Blue Hole** (any local can point you there if you're interested). Another village (don't blink as you pass through or you'll miss it) is **Moxey Town,** where you are likely to see fishermen unloading conch from the fishing boats. Ferries, operated free by the Bahamian government, ply back and forth over the waters separating Mangrove Cay from South Andros. At the end of the road in North Andros, private arrangements can be made to have a boat take you over to Mangrove Cay.

GETTING AROUND Transportation can be a big problem on Andros. If you have to go somewhere, it's best to use one of the local taxi drivers, though this can be a pricey undertaking.

The few rental cars available are in North Andros. These are few and far between, owing to the high costs of shipping cars to Andros. The weather also takes a great toll on the cars that are brought in (the salt in the air erodes metal), so no U.S. car-rental agencies are represented. Your best bet is to ask at your hotel to see what's available. It's not really recommended that you drive on Andros because roads are mainly unpaved and in bad condition, and gasoline stations are scarce. Outlets for car rentals come and go faster here than anybody can count. Currently, **AMKLCO Car Rental** at Fresh Creek (**© 242/368-2056**) rents a few cars, costing from $75 to $85 daily, with a $250 deposit required. Mileage is unlimited "unless you go too much."

You may want to rent a bike, but you'll experience the same bad roads you would in a rental car. Guests of the Small Hope Bay Lodge, Chickcharnie, and Mangrove Cay Inn can rent bikes at these hotels.

FAST FACTS Banks are rare on Andros. There is one, the **Scotia Bank** (**© 242/329-2700**), in Nicollstown, open Monday through Friday 9:30am to 3pm.

The island's post office is in Nicholl's Town on North Andros (**© 242/329-2034**). Hours are Monday through Friday from 9am to 4:30pm. Hotel desks will also sell you Bahamian stamps. Make sure you mark cards and letters as airmail; otherwise, you'll return home before they do. Each little village on Andros has a store that serves as the post office.

Government-run clinics are at **North Andros** (**© 242/329-2055**) and at **Central Andros** (**© 242/368-2038**). Bring along whatever drugs (legal ones) or medicines you'll need while visiting Andros, because local supplies are very limited.

Call the **police** on **North Andros** at ✆ **919;** on **Central Andros** at ✆ **242/368-2626;** and on **South Andros** at ✆ **242/369-0083.**

WHERE TO STAY

At the hotels listed below, phone service is available only at the front desks.

IN STANDARD CREEK

Kamalame Cay ★★★ In 1995, a group of international investors created one of the most exclusive resorts in the Out Islands from the scrub-covered landscape of a private cay off the east coast of Andros Island. Since then, it has discreetly and quietly attracted a clientele of banking moguls and financial wizards from Europe and North America, all of whom come for the superb service, escapist charm, 5km (3 miles) of white-sand beaches, and a series of waterborne adventures that are among the best of their kind in The Bahamas. A staff of up to 50, some of whom were imported from other parts of The Bahamas, includes six full-time gardeners, an army of chambermaids and cooks, and a sporting-adventure staff that's ready, willing, and able to haul groups of urban refugees out for scuba, windsurfing, snorkeling, deep-sea, and bonefishing excursions above one of the largest barrier reefs in the world.

Accommodations include a few smaller rooms, tasteful and very comfortable, located next to the marina. More opulent are the cottages and suites, all of which lie adjacent to the beach; these are mainly crafted from local coral stone, cedar shingles, tropical-wood timbers, tile, and in some cases thatch. Each is outfitted in a breezy but stylish tropical motif that evokes a decorator's journal. Food is superb, focusing on fresh fish, lobster, local soups, homemade breads, and surprisingly good wines.

Staniard Creek, Andros, The Bahamas. ✆ **242/368-6281.** Fax 242/368-6279. www.kamalame.com. $370 per person double; $550–$1,040 per person cottage or suite for 2; $675 per person 2-bedroom villa for 4; $4,150 per day 4-bedroom villa for up to 8. Rates all-inclusive, with transfers to and from the nearest airport, Andros Town, a 30-min. car and boat ride from Kamalame Cay. Discounts of up to 20% June–Oct. MC, V. **Amenities:** Restaurant, bar; private 5km (3-mile) long beach; pool; tennis court; 8-slip marina; bonefishing and deep-sea excursions with guides; scuba and snorkeling facilities; seasonal wing-shooting for wild quail and mallards; guided tours of Andros Island's "mainland"; laundry; limited room service; babysitting; concierge. *In room:* A/C, minibar, safe, no phone.

IN ANDROS TOWN

Lighthouse Yacht Club & Marina This complex lies at the mouth of Fresh Creek and features an 18-slip marina. A favorite of the yachting crowd, who needed such a place in Andros, the hotel rents comfortably furnished villas, each with a certain flair enhanced by Caribbean fabrics and ceiling fans. Accommodations open onto private patios and come with well-maintained private bathrooms with shower units. Scuba divers, snorkelers, and fishermen make ample use of the beach and the offshore waters, because the hotel lies near one of the world's largest barrier reefs and the deep Tongue of the Ocean.

The hotel has a good restaurant serving Bahamian and American dishes. Fishing charters are readily available, and scuba diving and snorkeling can easily be arranged through the hotel. The package rates offered by the hotel, in addition to room and meals, include airport pickup.

Andros Town, Andros, The Bahamas. ✆ **242/368-2308.** Fax 242/368-2300. www.androslighthouse.com. 20 units. $120–$140 double; $140 villa. MAP (breakfast and dinner) $40 extra per person. Ask about dive packages. AE, DC, DISC, MC, V. **Amenities:** Restaurant, bar; limited room service; laundry; babysitting; marina; pool; 2 clay tennis courts. *In room:* A/C, TV, refrigerator, hair dryer, safe.

IN BEHRING POINT

Tranquility Hill At the eastern entrance to north Bight, this is a fisherman's haven, lying just a short drive from Middle and South Bights. Newly constructed, the rustic inn lies near kilometers and kilometers of virgin flats teaming with trophy-size bonefish. Numerous creeks and lakes also are found in the area where record catches have been made of gray snapper, tarpon, and jacks. There are also three "Sunken Rocks," with large colonies of barracuda, Spanish mackerel, and mutton snapper. Nearby is the third largest reef in the world, with a sea of dolphins, kingfish, wahoo, marlin, and tuna. Bedrooms are spacious and well-furnished with comfortable beds and bathrooms with shower units. Units are equipped with double or king-size beds. Meals are prepared Bahamian-style, and guess what's on the menu? Enough fish and seafood to delight, although the cook will also prepare special requests. Meals are served family-style.

Behring Point, Andros, The Bahamas. ✆ or fax **242/368-4132.** www.bahamas-mon.com/hotels/tranquil/. 11 units. Winter $378 double; off-season $345 double. Rates include meals. MC, V. **Amenities:** Dining room, bar; laundry. *In room:* A/C, TV.

IN CARGILL CREEK

Andros Island Bonefishing Club ★ If Hemingway were around today and wanted to go bonefishing, you'd invite him here. This rustic lodge lies at the confluence of Cargill Creek, the Atlantic Ocean, and the eastern end of North Bight. It fronts a small protected creek, a short distance from a wadeable flat, and fishing boats can dock directly in front of the lodge. Constructed in 1988, this is a modern but rather bare-bones facility that draws more repeat guests than any other hostelry in The Bahamas. More than two dozen fishermen can stay here at any time in accommodations with queen-size beds, ample dresser and closet space, bathrooms equipped with shower-tub combinations, and ceiling fans. Several rooms also have satellite TV, and some units also contain a refrigerator. The club is the domain of Captain Rupert Leadon, who knows more fishing stories than anybody else in Andros.

Food is hearty and plentiful, with an emphasis on fresh seafood, including Bahamian lobster and conch. Service is family-style.

Cargill Creek, Andros Island, The Bahamas. ✆ **242/368-5167.** Fax 242/368-5235. www.androsbonefishing.com. 12 units. $955 per person 3 nights, $1,715 per person 5 nights, $2,475 per person 7 nights. Rates include all meals, all-day fishing with boat and guide. Room only $165 per person. MC, V. **Amenities:** Dining room, honor bar; laundry. *In room:* A/C, no phone.

IN FRESH CREEK

Small Hope Bay Lodge ★★ This is the premier diving and fishing resort of Andros, and one of the best in the entire Bahamas, with a white sandy beach right at its doorstep. It's an intimate and cozy beachside cottage colony, where tall coconut palms line a lovely beach and a laid-back atmosphere always prevails. And, because this place is all-inclusive, the price you pay includes all accommodations, meals, drinks, taxes, service charges, airport taxi transfers, even the use of kayaks, windsurfers, and other boats.

Its name comes from a prediction (so far, accurate) from pirate Henry Morgan, who claimed there was "small hope" of anyone finding the treasure he'd buried on Andros. There is a spacious living and dining room where guests congregate for conversations and meals. Andros Town Airport is a 10-minute taxi ride from the lodge. Spacious cabins, cooled by ceiling fans, are made of coral rock and Andros pine and are decorated with Androsia batik fabrics. Honeymooners like to order breakfast served on their water bed.

For groups of three or more, the resort has a limited number of family cottages, featuring two separate rooms connected by a single bathroom. Single travelers have a choice of staying in a family cottage with private accommodations (which is the same as per-person double occupancy) or staying in a regular cottage with private bathroom, which is $45 extra per person nightly. All bathrooms are neatly kept and contain bathrooms.

The bar is an old boat, dubbed the *Panacea.* The food is wholesome, plentiful, and good—conch chowder, lobster, and hot johnnycake. The chef will even cook your catch for you or make up a picnic lunch. Lunch is a buffet; dinner, a choice of seafood and meat every night. Children under 12 dine in the game room. Drinks are offered on a rambling patio built out over the sea. Nightlife is spontaneous—with dancing in the lounge or on the patio, and water slides. Definitely do not wear a tie at dinner. Diving is the lodge's specialty. The owners have been diving for more than 3 decades, and their well-respected dive shop has sufficient equipment, boats, and flexibility to give guests any diving experience they want, including a resort course for beginners. If you'd rather fish, the lodge can hook you up with an expert guide, especially for bonefishing.

Fresh Creek, Andros, The Bahamas (P.O. Box 21667, Fort Lauderdale, FL 33335). ✆ **800/223-6961** in the U.S. and Canada, or 242/368-2013. Fax 242/368-2015. 20 units. www.smallhope.com. Year-round $350–$700 double. Rates all-inclusive. Ask about dive packages. AE, MC, V. **Amenities:** Dining room; babysitting; exercise room; Jacuzzi; hot tub; massage; bikes for guests; library; laundry. *In room:* Ceiling fan, no phone.

IN NICHOLL'S TOWN

Green Windows Inn Kenny Robinson and her husband, Patrick, run this small, laid-back hotel set in a landscape of fruit trees and palms, where guests like to take their after-meal walks. The small rooms are on the second floor of the two-story inn, over the restaurant and bar. A recent improvement at the inn is the installation of tiny private bathrooms with shower-tub combinations in every bedroom along with both ceiling fans and air-conditioning. The restaurant caters only to hotel guests, with mainly seafood and local food cooked to order. The beach is a 10-minute walk from the inn, and the Robinsons can arrange bonefishing and snorkeling trips.

Rawfon St. (P.O. Box 23076), Nicholl's Town, Andros, The Bahamas. ✆ **242/329-2194.** Fax 242/329-2016. 10 units. $90 double. AE, MC, V. **Amenities:** Restaurant, bar; laundry; babysitting; on-site small grocery store and car rental agency. *In room:* A/C, TV.

ON MANGROVE CAY

Mangrove Cay Inn This pleasant, well-managed inn belongs to a native son, Elliott Greene, who returned with his wife Pat after years of cold-weather life in Syracuse, New York, to establish this breezy motel a short walk from the center of Grants, the third-largest village on Mangrove Cay (Moxey Town and Burnt Rock, though tiny, are still larger). Positioned amid scrubland, in the geographic center of the 14km- (9-mile-) long island, the hotel was built in the early 1990s, 2 years after the inn was established as an easygoing and affable restaurant.

Separated from Grant's Beach by a brackish lake, with a mysterious blue hole positioned beside the path connecting the hotel to the beach, the accommodations have cozy but completely unpretentious furnishings. Each unit contains a small bathroom with a shower-tub combination. How do guests spend their time here? Veranda-sitting on a porch that runs the length of the building and overlooks the water; riding on any of the bicycles that the hotel rents for a fee of around $10 a day; snorkeling with the hotel's equipment on the outlying reef (waters offshore are particularly rich in natural sponges and spiny Caribbean lobster); hiking; hill climbing; and looking for chickcharnies (mythical red-eyed, three-toed, bird-like creatures). And if you're interested in fishing excursions, the Greenes can hire a local fishing guide for a full-day outing (about $300 a day for up to four).

The wing that contains the bedrooms is attached to a restaurant that serves a combination of Bahamian and American food with specialties of cracked conch, grilled grouper and snapper, burgers, and steaks.

c/o General Post Office, Grants, Mangrove Cay, Middle Andros, The Bahamas. © **242/369-0069.** Fax 242/369-0014. www.mangrovecay.com. 12 units. $105 double; $300 cottage. No credit cards. **Amenities:** Restaurant, lounge; laundry; bike rental. *In room:* A/C, no phone.

SOUTH ANDROS

Ritz Beach Resort ★ Lodging at this laid-back place, 3km (2 miles) from the Congo Town airport, is a lot like staying at a beachside ranch. The accommodations are set on 8km (5 miles) of beachfront on an island that contains 10,000 palm trees. The hotel is casual—a place to get away from urban life and rest your jangled nerves on a white-sand beach. Guests are treated like members of the family.

The rooms are large and comfortable, with well-laid-out bathrooms with adequate shelf space and shower stalls. This resort has some of the fanciest decorations in Andros, and some of the most special amenities, including lanai-style rooms and four-poster beds with mosquito netting—all in all, a relaxed, tropical ambience.

Scattered over the palm-studded property are hammocks and a freshwater swimming pool. The dining room features Bahamian seafood, and outdoor steak barbecues and seafood buffets are sometimes held. South Bight marina is 2.5km (1½ miles) away, serving as a yacht anchorage for anyone who arrives by boat. The hotel will rent you a car or bike.

Driggs Hill, P.O. Box 800, South Andros, The Bahamas. © **800/742-4276** or 242/369-2661. Fax 242/369-2711. 20 units. Winter $110 double; off-season $100 double. MAP (breakfast and dinner) $40 per person extra. AE, MC, V. **Amenities:** Restaurant, 2 bars; limited room service; laundry; nature walks. *In room:* A/C, TV, minibar.

WHERE TO DINE

Andros follows the rest of The Bahamas in its cuisine. Conch, in all its many variations, is the staple of most diets, along with heaping portions of peas 'n' rice and johnnycake, and pig or chicken souse.

The best places to dine are at the major hotels, including those previously recommended: the **Chickcharnie Hotel,** Fresh Creek, near Andros Town (© **242/368-2025**); and if you're in South Andros, **Ritz Beach Resort,** outside Congo Town (© **242/369-2661**). Most guests book into these hotels on the Modified American Plan, which takes care of breakfast and dinner but frees them to shop around for lunch. At any of these hotels, a dinner will run around $25 to $40 per person.

If you're touring the island during the day, you'll find some local spots that serve food. If business has been slow at some of these little places, however, you might find nothing on the stove. You take your chances. On Mangrove Cay, try **Dianne Cash's Ultimate Delight,** Main Road (© **242/369-0430**), where you can sample Dianne's version of baked crab backs served with peas and rice. Don't plan on dropping by this place without some kind of advance notification.

BEACHES, WATERSPORTS & OTHER OUTDOOR PURSUITS

Golf and tennis fans should go elsewhere, but if you want some of the best bonefishing and scuba diving in The Bahamas, head to Andros.

HITTING THE BEACH

The eastern shore of Andros, stretching for some 161km (100 miles), is an almost uninterrupted palm grove opening onto beaches of white or beige sand. There are several dozen access points that lead to the beach along the eastern shore. The roads are unmarked but clearly visible. The clear, warm waters offshore are great for snorkeling.

FISHING

Andros ★★★ is called the "Bonefish Capital of the World." The actual capital is Lowe Sound Settlement, a tiny hamlet with only one road, 6.5km (4 miles) north of Nicholl's Town. Anglers come here to hire bonefish guides. **Cargill Creek** is one of the best places for bonefishing on the island; nearby, anglers explore the flats in and around the bights of Andros (some excellent flats, where you can wade in your boots, lie only 68–113m/75–125 yd. offshore).

Whether you're staying in North, Central, or South Andros, someone at your hotel can arrange a fishing expedition, since there are many local guides and charter companies. In particular, the **Small Hope Bay Lodge,** in Andros Town on North Andros (✆ **242/368-2013**), is known for arranging fishing expeditions for both guests and nonguests; a guide will take you out for superb bonefishing. They also offer fly, reef, and deep-sea fishing, and provide tackle and bait.

SCUBA DIVING & SNORKELING

Divers from all over the world come to explore the **Andros barrier reef** ★★★, which runs parallel to the eastern shore of the island. It's one of the largest reefs in the world, but unlike Australia's Great Barrier Reef, which is kilometers off the coast, the barrier reef of Andros is easily accessible, beginning a few hundred yards offshore.

One side of the reef is a peaceful haven for snorkelers and novice scuba divers, who report that the fish are tame (often a grouper will eat from your hand, but don't try it with a moray eel). The water here is from 2.5 to 4.5m (9–15 ft.) deep.

On the other side of the reef it's a different story. The water plunges to a depth of 1.5km (1 mile) into the awesome **TOTO (Tongue of the Ocean)** ★★★. One diver reported that, as an adventure, diving in the ocean's "tongue" was tantamount to a flight to the moon.

Myriad, multicolored marine life thrives on the reef, and it attracts nature lovers from all over the world. The weirdly shaped coral formations alone are worth the trip. This is a living, breathing garden of the sea, and its caves feel like cathedrals.

For many years the U.S. Navy has conducted research at a station on the edge of TOTO. The research center is at Andros Town. It is devoted to oceanographic, underwater weapons, and anti-submarine research. Called **AUTEC (Atlantic Undersea Testing and Evaluation Centre),** this is a joint U.S. and British undertaking.

Among other claims to fame, Andros is known for its **"blue holes,"** which rise from the brine. Essentially, these are narrow, circular pits that plunge as much as 60m (200 ft.) straight down through rock and coral into murky, difficult-to-explore depths. Most of them begin under the level of the sea, although others

Fun Fact The Bahamian Loch Ness Monster

When the Atlantic Undersea Testing and Evaluation Centre (AUTEC) first opened, Androsians predicted that the naval researchers would turn up **"Lusca."** Like the Loch Ness monster, Lusca reportedly had been sighted by dozens of locals. The sea serpent was accused of sucking both sailors and their vessels into the dangerous blue holes around the island's coastline. No one has captured Lusca yet.

appear unexpectedly—and dangerously—in the center of the island, usually with warning signs placed around the perimeter. Scattered at various points along the coast, they can be reached either in rented boats or as part of a guided trip. The most celebrated blue hole is Uncle Charlie Blue Hole, mysterious and fathomless, and once publicized by Jacques Cousteau. The other blue holes are almost as incredible.

One of these blue holes, called **Benjamin's Blue Hole** ★, is named after its discoverer, George Benjamin. In 1967, he found stalactites and stalagmites 360m (1,200 ft.) below sea level. What was remarkable about this discovery is that stalactites and stalagmites are not created underwater. This has led to much speculation that The Bahamas are actually mountaintops, all that remains of a mysterious continent that sank beneath the sea (perhaps Atlantis?). Although Cousteau made a film—making the Blue Holes of Andros internationally famous—most of the blue holes, like most of the surface of the island itself, remain unexplored. Tour boats leaving from Small Hope Bay Lodge will take you to these holes.

As for snorkeling, you might head a few kilometers north of Nicholl's Town, where you'll find a crescent-shaped strip of white-sand beach, along with a headland, **Morgan's Bluff,** honoring the notorious old pirate himself. If you're not a diver, and can't go out to the Andros Barrier Reef off the shorefront at Fresh Creek and Andros Town, you can do the second-best thing and snorkel near a series of reefs known as "The Three Sisters." Sometimes, if the waters haven't turned suddenly murky, you can see about 3.5m (12 ft.) down—all the way to the sandy bottom. The schools of elkhorn coral are especially dramatic here.

Since **Mangrove Cay** is very underdeveloped, rely on the snorkeling advice and gear rentals you'll get from the dive shop at the **Seascape Inn** (✆ **242/369-0342**). A two-tank dive costs $65 for guests of the hotel, or $75 for nonguests. Night dives are also possible ($50 for guests only of the Seascape).

Small Hope Bay Lodge, Fresh Creek, Andros Town, Central Andros (✆ **800/223-6961** in the U.S. and Canada, or 242/368-2013; www.smallhope.com), lies a short distance from the barrier reef, with its still-unexplored caves and ledges. A staff of trained dive instructors at the lodge caters to beginners and experienced divers alike. Snorkeling expeditions can be arranged, as well as scuba outings (visibility underwater exceeds 100 ft. on most days, with water temperatures ranging from 72°F–84°F). You can also rent gear here. To stay at the hotel here for 7 nights and 6 days, all-inclusive (meals, tips, taxes, airport transfers, and three dives a day), costs adults $1,585 or ages 12 to 17 $1,330. All guests are allowed access to the beachside hot-tub whirlpool, as well as to all facilities, such as free use of sailboats, windsurfers, and bicycles.

EXPLORING THE ISLAND

Andros is largely unexplored, and with good reason—getting around takes some doing. With the exception of the main arteries, the few roads that exist are badly maintained and full of potholes. Sometimes you're a long way between villages or settlements, and if your car breaks down, all you can do is wait and hope that someone comes along to give you a ride to the next place, where you'll hope to find a skilled mechanic. If you're striking out on your own, make sure you have a full tank, because service stations are few and far between.

Not all of Andros can be explored by car, although there is a dream that as Andros develops, it will be linked by a road and causeways stretching some 161km (100 miles) or more. Most of the driving and exploring is confined to North Andros, and there, only along the eastern sector, going by Nicholl's Town, Morgan's Bluff, and San Andros.

If you're driving on Central or South Andros, you must stay on the rough **Queen's Highway.** The road in the south is paved and better than the one in Central Andros, which should be traveled only in an emergency or by a local.

Near Small Hope Bay at Andros Town, you can visit the workshop where **Androsia batik** is made (the same Androsia batik sold in the shops of Nassau and other towns). Androsia's artisans create their designs using hot wax on fine cotton and silk fabrics. The fabrics are then made into island-style wear, including blouses, skirts, caftans, shirts, and accessories. All hand-painted and hand-signed, the resort wear comes in dazzling red, blue, purple, green, and earth tones. You can visit the factory in Andros Town (✆ **242/368-2080**) Monday through Friday from 8am to 4pm.

Morgan's Bluff, at the tip of North Andros, lures men and women hoping to strike it rich. The pirate Sir Henry Morgan is supposed to have buried a vast treasure here, but it has eluded discovery to this day, although many have searched for it.

Bird-watchers are attracted to Andros for its varied **bird population.** In the dense forests, in trees such as lignum vitae, mahogany, Madeira, "horseflesh," and pine, lives a huge feathered population: many parrots, doves, and marsh hens. Ever hear a whistling duck?

Botanists are lured here by the **wildflowers** of Andros. It is said that some 40 to 50 species of wild orchids thrive here, some found nowhere else. New discoveries are always being made, as more and more botanists study the rich vegetation of Andros.

Moments What Would Tennessee Have Thought?

One custom in Andros is reminiscent of the Tennessee Williams drama *Suddenly, Last Summer:* catching **land crabs,** which leave their burrows and march relentlessly to the sea to lay their eggs. The annual ritual occurs between May and September. However, many of the hapless crabs will never have offspring; both visitors and Androsians walk along the beach with baskets and catch the crustaceans before they reach the sea. Later, they clean them, stuff them, and bake them for dinner.

Red Bay Village is the type of discovery that continues to make Andros seem mysterious. An ancient tribe, headed by a chief and religiously following old rituals, was found living here as recently as a quarter of a century ago. The passage of time has made little difference to these people. Now the world comes to their door, and changes are inevitable; although the people still follow their ancient customs. The village, it is believed, was settled sometime in the 1840s by Seminoles and blacks fleeing slavery in Florida. The village is located off the northwestern coast of Andros. A causeway now connects the village to the mainland, and tourists can visit. You can reach Red Bay Village by road from Nicholl's Town and San Andros. You should be polite and ask permission before indiscriminately photographing these people.

7

The Abaco Islands

Called the "top of The Bahamas," the Abaco Islands compose the northernmost portion of the nation. This boomerang-shaped mini-archipelago is 209km (130 miles) long and consists of both Great Abaco and Little Abaco, as well as a sprinkling of cays. The islands are about 322km (200 miles) east of Miami and 121km (75 miles) north of Nassau.

People come here mainly to explore the outdoors, and the **sailing** ★★ and **fishing** ★★ are spectacular. The diving is excellent, too, and there are many lovely, uncrowded beaches. The Abacos are definitely a world apart from the glitzy pleasures of Freeport/Lucaya, Nassau, or Paradise Island.

Many residents of the Abacos descend from Loyalists who left New England after the American Revolution. Against a backdrop of sugar-white beaches and turquoise water, their pastel-colored clapboard houses and white-picket fences retain the Cape Cod architectural style of the first settlements on Abacos. One brightly painted sign in Hope Town says it all: SLOW DOWN. YOU'RE IN HOPE TOWN. The same could be said for all the Abacos.

The weather is about 10°F warmer here than in southern Florida, but if you visit in January or February, remember that you're not guaranteed beach weather every day (remember, Miami and Fort Lauderdale, even Key West, can get chilly at times). When winter squalls hit, temperatures can drop to the high 40s in severe cases. Spring in the Abacos, however, is one of the most glorious and balmy seasons in all the islands. In summer, it gets very hot around noon, but if you act as the islanders do and find a shady spot to escape the broiling sun, the trade winds will cool you off.

Some yachters call the Abacos the world's most beautiful cruising grounds. Excellent marine facilities, with guides, charter parties, and boat rentals, are available here; in fact, Marsh Harbour is the bareboat-charter center of the northern Bahamas. There you can rent a small boat, pack a picnic, and head for one of many uninhabited cays just big enough for two.

Anglers from all over the world come to test their skill against blue marlin, kingfish, dolphinfish, yellowfin tuna, sailfish, wahoo, amberjack, and grouper. Like fishing tournaments? They abound at Walker's Cay.

Finally, scuba divers can plumb the depths and discover caverns, inland "blue holes," coral reefs, and gardens, along with marine preserves and wrecks. Some scuba centers even feature night dives.

ABACOS ESSENTIALS

GETTING THERE

BY PLANE Three airports are found in the Abacos: **Marsh Harbour** (the major one, on Great Abaco Island), **Treasure Cay,** and **Walker's Cay.** The official points of entry are Marsh Harbour, Treasure Cay, Walker's Cay, and Green

Turtle Cay (New Plymouth). Green Turtle Cay doesn't have an airstrip, but many members of the yachting crowd clear Customs and Immigration there.

Many visitors arrive from Nassau or Miami on **Bahamasair** (✆ **800/222-4262** or 242/367-2095). Flight schedules change frequently in The Bahamas, but you can usually get two to three daily flights out of Nassau, going first to Marsh Harbour, then on to Treasure Cay. If you're in West Palm Beach, you can often take a direct morning flight to Marsh Harbour and Treasure Cay.

Other connections include **American Eagle** (✆ **800/433-7300** or 242/367-2231), with two daily flights from Miami to Marsh Harbour; **Air Sunshine** (✆ **242/367-2800** in Marsh Harbour, or 242/365-8900 in Treasure Cay), flying from Fort Lauderdale to both airports; and **Continental Connection** (✆ **800/231-0856** or 242/367-3415 in Marsh Harbour, 242/365-8615 in Treasure Cay), which flies to Marsh Harbour and Treasure Cay from several Florida locales. Smaller carriers include **U.S. Airways Express** (✆ **800/622-1015**), winging into both airports from Palm Beach and Orlando, and **Twin Air** (✆ **954/359-8266**), flying from Fort Lauderdale to both Treasure Cay and Marsh Harbour.

BY BOAT The mail boat **MV** ***Captain Gurthdean*** sails on Tuesday from Nassau to Hope Town, Marsh Harbour, Turtle Cay, and Green Turtle Cay. It returns to Nassau on Friday. Trip time is 12 hours. **MV** ***Champion II*** leaves Nassau on Tuesday, arriving Wednesday at Sandy Point, Moore's Island, and Bullock Harbour, returning to Nassau on Thursday. For details on sailings (subject to change) and costs, contact the dockmaster at **Potter's Cay Dock** in Nassau (✆ **242/393-1064**).

GETTING AROUND

BY TAXI Unmetered taxis, which you often have to share with other passengers, meet all arriving flights. They will take you to your hotel if it's on the Abaco "mainland"; otherwise, they will deposit you at a dock where you can hop aboard a water-taxi to one of the neighboring offshore islands, such as Green Turtle Cay or Elbow Cay. Most visitors use a combination taxi and water-taxi ride to reach the most popular hotels. From Marsh Harbour Airport to Hope Town on Elbow Cay, the cost is about $12 for the transfer. From the Treasure Cay Airport to Green Turtle Cay, the charge is about $15. Elbow Cay costs about $11 for the transfer.

It's also possible to make arrangements for a taxi tour of Great or Little Abaco. These, however, are expensive, and you don't really see much.

BY FERRY Mostly, you'll get around with **Albury's Ferry Service** (✆ **242/367-3147**), which provides several ferry connections between Marsh Harbour and both Elbow Cay (Hope Town) and Man-O-War Cay, a 20-minute trip to either destination. The one-way fare is $8 adults, $4 children. (There are also ferries to Guana Cay.) The ferry docks are not far from the Marsh Harbour Airport; it's about a 10-minute, $12 cab ride for two passengers (plus $3 for each additional passenger).

For car-ferry service to Green Turtle Cay, see the section, "Green Turtle Cay (New Plymouth)," later in this chapter. There are ferries from Great Abaco Island to Green Turtle Cay, but those docks are a 35-minute $65 cab ride for up to four passengers from the Marsh Harbour Airport. It's better to fly to Treasure Cay rather than Marsh Harbour to do this, and then take a taxi to the ferry docks.

0
15 Miles
0
15 Kilometers
N
WALKER'S CAY
GRAND CAY
STRANGER'S CAY
Carter's Cay
Little Abaco Island
SPANISH CAY
PENSACOLA CAYS
LITTLE CAVE CAY
CROSS CAYS
Cooper's Town
GREEN TURTLE CAY
New Plymouth
Treasure Cay Airport
TREASURE CAY
GREAT GUANA CAY
MAN O' WAR CAY
Marsh Harbour
Tahiti Beach
Hope Town
THE MARIS
Marsh Harbour Airport
Elbow Cay
MOORE'S ISLAND
Great Abaco Island
Pelican Cays Land & Sea Park
Pelican Harbour
Little Harbour
Casaurina Point
Cherokee
Eight Mile Bay
GORDA CAY
Crossing Rocks
Sandy Point
Cross Harbour
Bahamas National Trust Sanctuary
Hole-in-the-Wall
Florida
Abaco
Grand Bahama
area of detail
Eleuthera
Paradise Island
Andros
Cat Island
San Salvador
Great Exuma
Long Island
Crooked Island
Great Inagua
Turks and Caicos
Cuba
Airport
Scuba Diving
Shipwreck

1 Marsh Harbour (Great Abaco Island)

The largest town in the Abacos, and the third largest in The Bahamas, Marsh Harbour lies on Great Abaco Island and is the major gateway to this island group.

Marsh Harbour is also a shipbuilding center, but tourism accounts for most of its revenues: There are a number of good inns here. Although the town doesn't have the quaint New England charm of either New Plymouth or Hope Town, it does have a shopping center and various other facilities not found in many Out Island settlements. There are good water-taxi connections, too, making this a popular place from which to explore offshore cays including Man-O-War and Elbow Cays. Several hotels will also rent you a bike if you want to pedal around town.

ESSENTIALS

GETTING THERE See "Abacos Essentials: Getting There," above . Marsh Harbour is the most easily accessible point in the Abacos from the U.S. mainland, with daily flights from Florida.

GETTING AROUND You won't need a car to get around the town itself, but if you want to explore the rest of the island on your own, you can rent a car, usually for $70 a day or $350 per week (be prepared for bad roads, though). In Marsh Harbour, call **A&P Rentals** at © **242/367-2655** to see if any vehicles are available.

Rental Wheels of Abaco at Marsh Harbour (© **242/367-4643**) will rent bikes at $8 a day or $35 a week, and also mopeds at $25 to $35 per day or $150 to $185 a week.

VISITOR INFORMATION The **Abaco Tourist Office** is at Queen Elizabeth Drive in the commercial heart of town (© **242/367-3067**). It's open Monday to Friday from 9am to 5:30pm.

FAST FACTS There's a **Barclays Bank** on Don MacKay Boulevard (© **242/367-2152**), plus several other banks and a **post office** (© **242/367-2571**).

For medication, go to the **Chemist Shop Pharmacy,** Don MacKay Boulevard (© **242/367-3106**), open Monday through Saturday 8:30am to 5:30pm. The best medical clinic in the Abacos is at the **Government Clinic,** Queen Elizabeth Road (© **242/367-2510**); hours are Monday through Friday from 9am to 5pm.

Dial © **242/367-2560** if you need the **police.**

SPECIAL EVENTS In July, Marsh Harbour hosts **Regatta Week,** the premier yachting event in the Abacos, attracting sailboats and their crews from around the world. It's held sometime between the U.S. and Bahamian Independence Days (July 4th and July 10). Many of the yachters participating in this event stay at the Green Turtle Club (p. 227). For registration forms and more information, write to **Regatta Time in Abaco,** P.O. Box AB20551, Marsh Harbour, Abaco.

WHERE TO STAY

Abaco Beach Resort & Boat Harbour ★ This beachfront resort—the biggest and best in Marsh Harbour—is a good choice, especially if you're serious about diving or fishing. Extending over a sprawling acreage at the edge of town and fronting a small but lovely beach, it's a business with several different faces: the hotel, with handsomely furnished rooms that overlook the Sea of Abaco; the well-managed restaurant and bar; the Boat Harbour Marina, which has slips for 180 boats and full docking facilities; and a full-fledged dive shop.

Angler's Restaurant is one of Marsh Harbour's best (see separate recommendation under "Where to Dine," below). There's a swim-up bar and a beachfront bar serving light snacks and grog. To reach the resort from Marsh Harbour Airport, take a taxi ($14, but be sure to agree on the price first with the driver; 6.5km/4miles).

P.O. Box 20511, Marsh Harbour, Abaco, The Bahamas. ✆ **800/468-4799** in the U.S., or 242/367-2158. Fax 242/367-4154. www.abacobeachresort.net/. 82 units. $195–$275 double; $375 1-bedroom suite; $550 cottage for up to 4. AP (all meals) $45 extra per adult. AE, DISC, MC, V. **Amenities:** Restaurant, 2 bars; limited room service; babysitting; 2 pools; 150-slip marina; 2 tennis courts; fitness center; sauna; massage; laundry; fishing charters; full dive shop with dive master who arranges outings all over the Abacos; boat rentals. *In room:* A/C, TV, minibar, hair dryer, safe.

Conch Inn Resort & Marina Set at the southeastern edge of the harbor, this is a casual, one-story hotel leased on a long-term basis by one of the world's largest yacht-chartering companies, The Moorings. A number of small sandy beaches are within walking distance. Its motel-style, midsize bedrooms are small, each with two double beds (rollaways are available for extra occupants). Bathrooms are small but neatly kept with shower-tub combinations. All units overlook the yachts bobbing in the nearby marina.

On the premises are an open-air swimming pool, fringed with palm trees, and a nearby branch of the Dive Abaco scuba facility. The on-site restaurant and bar (Bistro Mezzamare), under independent management, is recommended in "Where to Dine," below.

E. Bay St. (P.O. Box AB20469), Marsh Harbour, Abaco, The Bahamas. ✆ **242/367-4000.** Fax 242/367-4004. www.conchinn.com. 9 units. $120 double. Extra person $20. MC, V. **Amenities:** Restaurant, bar; pool; dive shop; laundry. *In room:* A/C, TV, refrigerator.

Lofty Fig Villas This family-owned bungalow colony across from the Conch Inn overlooks the harbor. It doesn't have the services of a full-fledged resort, but it's good for families and self-sufficient types. Built in 1970, it stands in a tropical landscape with a freshwater pool and a gazebo where you can barbecue. Rooms have one queen-size bed and a queen-size hide-a-bed sofa, a fully tiled bathroom with shower, a dining area, a kitchen, and a private screened-in porch. Maid service is provided Monday through Saturday.

You're about a 10-minute walk from a supermarket and shops, and restaurants and bars lie just across the street. Marinas, a dive shop, and boat rentals are also close at hand. From the Lofty Fig, you have to walk, bike, or drive 1.5km (1 mile) east to a point near the Marsh Harbour ferryboat docks for access to a sandy beach and a snorkeling site (many visitors opt to go to Guana Cay for their day at the beach, via ferryboat).

P.O. Box AB20437, Marsh Harbour, Abaco, The Bahamas. ✆ and fax **242/367-2681.** 6 villas. Dec 15–Sept 15 $135 daily for 2, $877 weekly for 2, extra person $25; Sept 16–Dec 14 $105 daily for 2, $630 weekly for 2, extra person $15. MC, V. *In room:* A/C, kitchen, no phone.

NEARBY CHOICES

Nettie's Different of Abaco ★ *Finds* Set within the hamlet of Casuarina Point, 29km (18 miles) south of Marsh Harbour, this is a small family-managed bonefishing club surrounded by a wide deck and a garden. It's an ecologically conscious place, built at the edge of a saltwater marsh favored by a variety of birds, wild hogs, and iguana—a good choice for bird-watchers and superb for bonefishing enthusiasts. It's not luxurious, though, and it won't be to everyone's liking; come if you like a peaceful place near good snorkeling and virgin beaches. The hotel is closely associated with several bonefishing guides in the area, any of whom can arrange full-day excursions for around $350 per couple. (Not all equipment is included in this fee; check when booking, before paying.)

Each of the small to midsize bedrooms has a screened-in porch, a ceiling fan, and simple furnishings, but only eight are air-conditioned. During your stay, you'll be in the midst of a closely knit, isolated community that's firmly committed to preserving the local environment and heritage. Nettie has created a living museum that takes you back through 100 years of the island's history.

There's a bar and restaurant where the staff serves a selection of simple Bahamian fare to guests and nonguests. The food is quite good.

Casuarina Point (P.O. Box AB20092), Abaco, The Bahamas. ✆ **242/366-2150.** Fax 242/327-8152. www.differentofabaco.com 20 units. $1,400–$1,536 double for 4 nights/3 days including bonefishing, $700–$1,095 double for 4 days/3 days nonfishing. Rates include all meals. AE, MC, V. **Amenities:** Restaurant, bar; lap pool; Jacuzzi; boating; fishing; coin laundry; bikes for guests. *In room:* A/C, hair dryer, no phone.

Sunset Point Resort ★ *Finds* One of the newest resorts in the Abacos is this complex overlooking Bustick Bay, a 10-minute drive south of the airport. On the east coast of Abaco (called by locals for some strange reason "the south side"), the resort attracts those who want to go bonefishing in the "Marls" (local name for Bustick Bay). Bedrooms are freshly decorated and generous in size, each with a view of the water, which is best seen from one of the private balconies. You have a choice of two queen-size beds or a king-size bed if you're feeling romantic. On-site is the Lazy Parrot Restaurant, serving a Bahamian and Continental cuisine. Kayaks are available to explore local creeks and shallows, and bonefishing can be arranged, too.

Marsh Harbour (P.O. Box AB20030), Abaco, The Bahamas. ✆ **242/367-5333.** Fax 242/367-5332. 8 units. Winter $130–$140 double; off-season $120–$130 double. MC, V. **Amenities:** Restaurant, bar; kayaks; bonefishing. *In room:* A/C, TV, no phone.

WHERE TO DINE

If you'd like to go really casual, try **Island Bakery,** Don McKay Boulevard (✆ **242/367-2129**), which has the best Bahamian bread and cinnamon rolls on the island, often emerging fresh from the oven. You might even pick up the makings for a picnic.

The best pizzas are sold at **Sapodilly's Bar & Grill,** Queen Elizabeth Drive (✆ **242/367-3498**); see below.

Angler's Restaurant ★ BAHAMIAN/INTERNATIONAL At the Boat Harbour, overlooking the Sea of Abaco, this is the main restaurant of the town's major resort. With a nautical theme and Bahamian decor, it showcases the cuisine of Austrian-born chef Dietmar Uiberreiter. Within a few steps of your seat, dock pilings rise from the water, yachts and fishing boats come and go, and the place is open and airy. The menu changes daily, but fresh seafood, which the chef prepares with finesse, is always featured, along with a well-chosen selection of meat and poultry dishes. Begin with spicy lobster bisque, or perhaps a timbale of grilled vegetables or crab Rangoon, served on bean-sprout slaw with a pineapple-coconut sauce. Main dishes often dance with flavor, notably the lobster stir in a mango chili sauce and the guava-glazed charred lamb chops; freshly caught red snapper is seasoned with just the right infusion of fresh basil.

In the Abaco Beach Resort & Boat Harbour, Marsh Harbour. ✆ **242/367-2158.** Reservations recommended for dinner. Main courses $14.50–$28.50. AE, MC, V. Daily 7:30–2:30pm and 6–10pm.

Bistro Mezzamare ★ BAHAMIAN/ITALIAN Only the Angler's Restaurant (see above) is more sophisticated and international than this winning choice. Set adjacent to the Conch Inn and the upscale marina facilities of The Moorings, it attracts a lot of yachties and visiting professional athletes. The menu includes shrimp and crabmeat salad, lobster salad, seafood platters, at least four preparations of grouper and snapper, and just about everything a chef could conceivably concoct from a conch. The regulars don't even have to consult the menu; they just ask, "What's good?" on any given night. Many diners gravitate to the succulent pasta dishes, such as penne mirella (with shiitake mushrooms). If you're frittering away a few hours, drop in for a "Horny Conch," a rum-based drink with secret ingredients. The bar, set beneath an octagon gazebo near the piers, is a fine place to meet people.

At the Conch Inn (The Moorings), Bay St. ✆ **242/367-4444.** Lunch salads, sandwiches, and platters $7–$13; dinner main courses $16–$21. MC, V. Wed–Mon 8am–9:30pm.

Flippers Restaurant BAHAMIAN/AMERICAN This is a straightforward and uncomplicated diner-style restaurant, without the flair and pizzazz of Sapodilly's, Mangoes, or Wally's. It was established in the town's biggest shopping center in the late 1990s, with a well-scrubbed, no-nonsense decor that includes ceramic-tile floors, plastic-laminate bar tops, and half paneling. Menu items include burgers, sandwiches, and platters of grouper, shrimp, steak, chicken, and lobster.

Memorial Plaza. ✆ **242/367-4657.** Reservations not accepted. Lunch main courses $5–$12; dinner main courses $17–$28. AE, MC, V. Mon 8am–3pm; Tues–Sat 8am–9:30pm; Sun noon–3pm.

The Jib Room BAHAMIAN/AMERICAN This funky restaurant/bar is a hangout for local residents and boat owners who savor its welcoming spirit. If you want the house-special cocktail, a Bilge Burner, get ready for a head-spinning combination of apricot brandy, rum, coconut juice, and vodka. Sunday night brings Jib's steak barbecue, when as many as 300 steaks are served. The only other dinner option is Wednesday, when grilled baby back ribs might be the featured dish of the day. Other choices include a seafood platter, New York strip steak, and broiled lobster—and yes, you've had it all before in better versions, but dishes are well-prepared. Go for the convivial atmosphere rather than the food.

Marsh Harbour Marina, Pelican Shores. ✆ **242/367-2700.** Lunch platters $5–$12; fixed-price dinners $18–$22. MC, V. Thurs–Sat 11:30am–2:30pm; dinner Wed and Sat 7–11pm.

Mangoes Restaurant ★ BAHAMIAN/AMERICAN Set near the harbor front, in one of the town's most distinctive buildings, Mangoes is the best, and certainly the most popular, restaurant on the island, attracting both yachties and locals. It boasts a cedar-topped bar and a cathedral ceiling that soars above a deck jutting out over the water. Somehow the chefs seem to try a little harder here, offering a typical menu adding a hint of island spirit. Our faithful friend, grilled grouper, is dressed up a bit with mango and tomatoes, and cracked conch make an appearance as well. Your best bet, as in nearly all Bahamian restaurants, is probably the fresh catch of the day and Mangoes is no exception. At lunch you can sample their locally famous "conch burger."

Front St. ✆ **242/367-2366.** Reservations recommended. Lunch $10.50–$16.50; main courses $13.50–$27.50. AE, MC, V. Daily 7am–3pm and 6:30–9pm; bar daily 11:30am–midnight.

Mother Merle's Fishnet ★ *Finds* BAHAMIAN Many of the meals eaten aboard the yachts and sailing craft in the nearby harbor are prepared here. There's no dining room on the premises, so don't expect a place to sit and linger, although the well-prepared food, if you don't mind hauling it off to another venue, makes the limitations most palatable. The setting is a cement house on the town's main street. Inside, you'll find the gentle but aging matriarch Merle Williams, who is assisted by her able-bodied daughters, Angela and Shirley. As Mother Merle tells it, all Bahamian women are good cooks, a bit of an exaggeration, but you'll believe her words when you taste her family's three different preparations of chicken, all prepared by secret family recipes. Locals swear that Mother Merle makes the best cracked conch in the Abacos, and she's also known for her different preparations of grouper.

Dundas Town. ✆ **242/367-2770.** Takeout service only. Main courses $11–$17. No credit cards. Mon–Sat 6:30–10:30pm.

Sapodilly's Bar & Grill BAHAMIAN One of Marsh Harbour's newest restaurants occupies an open-air pavilion across the road from the harbor front, in an area of town known as "the tourist strip." Even if you eventually head into the high-raftered interior dining room, take time out for a drink or two on the covered open-air deck, surrounded by vibrant Junkanoo colors and a crowd of local hipsters, yacht owners, marina workers, and businessmen visiting from other parts of The Bahamas. Lunch might consist of grilled fish sandwiches, burgers, salads, and quiche. Dinners are more elaborate, with 12-ounce New York strip steak, a flavor-filled shrimp kebabs in teriyaki sauce, and zesty curried filets of grouper. There's live music every Friday and Saturday from 8 to 11pm.

E. Bay St. ✆ **242/367-3498.** Reservations recommended. Lunch platters and sandwiches $5–$12; dinner main courses $17–$26. AE, MC, V. Tues–Sun 11:30am–3pm, daily 6–9pm; bar daily 11am–midnight.

Wally's ★ BAHAMIAN/INTERNATIONAL This eatery occupies a tidy pink colonial villa on a lawn dotted with hibiscus, across the street from the water. There are an outdoor terrace, a boutique, and an indoor bar and dining area filled with Haitian paintings. The special drink of the house is a Wally's Special, containing four kinds of rum and a medley of fruit juices. The chef prepares the best Bahamian cracked conch at Marsh Harbour, as well as tender filet mignon, lamb chops, tarragon chicken, and an excellent version of smothered grouper. Main dishes come with a generous house salad and vegetables. The place really shines at lunchtime, when things can get very busy as hungry diners devour dolphinfish burgers, several kinds of chicken platters, and some well-stuffed sandwiches. Part of the style here comes courtesy of sisters Barbara and Maureen Smith, who head to Paris every fall and bring their culinary discoveries back to their enterprise in Marsh Harbour.

E. Bay St. ✆ **242/367-2074.** Reservations recommended for dinner. Lunch sandwiches and platters $9.50–$12; dinner main courses $19.75–$28.50. AE, DISC, MC, V. Mon–Sat 11:30am–3pm; Fri–Sat 6–9pm (except Mar–July, when it's open Tues–Sat 6–9pm). Closed 6 weeks Sept–Oct.

WATERSPORTS & OTHER OUTDOOR PURSUITS

All the innkeepers at Marsh Harbour can help fix you up with the right people or equipment for whatever sport you want to pursue, whether you just want to rent snorkel gear or you're looking for a full-day's fishing charter. For variety, you can also take the ferry over to Hope Town and check out the facilities and outfitters there.

BOAT CHARTERS

Ask about the depth of the harbor before you rent, or even more importantly, before you attempt to navigate your way in or out of Marsh Harbour, since Hurricane Floyd changed the configuration of the channel. Yachts with deep drafts have reported trouble getting in and out of the port recently.

If you'd like to try bareboating in The Bahamas—seagoing without captain or crew—**Abaco Bahamas Charters,** 505 Beachland Blvd. (© **800/626-5690;** fax 242/366-0151), can set you up; weekly charters of a 13m (44-ft.) boat begin at $2,500, with a $1,500 deposit required. Only experienced sailors can rent.

The Moorings (© **800/535-7289** or 242/367-4000) is one of the leading charter sailboat outfitters in the world. It operates from an eagle's nest perch behind the Conch Inn Resort and Marina, overlooking a labyrinth of piers and wharves—at least 75 berths, with more on the way—where hundreds of upscale watercraft are tied up (many of them are for rent). With one of its vessels, you can enjoy short sails between the islands, stopping at white sandy beaches and snug anchorages. Yacht rentals generally range from $405 to $1,255 a day, with a skipper costing another $144 per day, and an onboard cook (if you want one) priced at an additional $124 per day.

For the more casual boater, **Sea Horse Boat Rentals,** at the Abaco Beach Resort (© **242/367-2513**), offers some of the best rentals. A 5.5m (18-ft.) Boston Whaler rents for $150 per day, and you can also book a 6.5m (22-ft.) Privateer for $170 per day. Other vessels are also for rent, and all boats are equipped with a Bimini top, coolers, a compass, and a swimming platform, along with life jackets, a paddle, docking lines, and other equipment. Open daily from 8am to 5pm.

SNORKELING & SCUBA DIVING

Sea Horse Boat Rentals at the Abaco Beach Resort/Boat Harbour Marina (© **242/367-2513**) also rents snorkel gear. One of the best places to snorkel, with a colorful reef, moray eels, and a plethora of beautiful rainbow-hued fish, is **Mermaid Beach.**

Scuba divers might try to check out the nearby **Pelican Cays Land and Sea Park** ★ nearby. There are no organized excursions, but Dive Abaco (see below) is the best source of information and might arrange a trip there. You can also drive down to the park by following the road immediately south of Marsh Harbour and then turning east at the sign leading toward the park. There are several areas here with small beaches suitable for swimming. The easiest jumping-off point is at Pelican Harbour.

Dive Abaco, Marsh Harbour (© **800/247-5338** in the U.S., or 242/367-2787), can provide services as simple as renting snorkel gear or as in-depth as offering full dive trips to tunnels and caverns in the world's third-longest barrier reef. There are resort courses for uncertified novice divers; these are all-inclusive for $140. Two-tank dives, including tanks and weights for certified divers, are $75. Trips depart daily at 9:30am, and afternoon trips are dictated by demand. Shop hours are daily from 8:30am to 5pm; ask for owner-operator Keith Rogers.

SHOPPING

Solomon's Mines, Queen Elizabeth Drive, at the entrance to the Abaco Beach Resort (© **242/367-3191**), is a gem of a store that serves as a fine-gifts shop and a not-so-run-of-the-mill souvenir outlet. Its merchandise includes fine china and crystal from Waterford and Lenox, fine watches, perfumes, plus locally designed gold and silver Bahamian jewelry. There are souvenirs galore, as well as a boutique that features bathing suits and evening wear for women, and sportswear for men. Another possibility, **Cultural Illusions,** Memorial Plaza (© **242/367-4648**), carries a collection of Androsia batik clothing, along with some local crafts. For that souvenir item, there is **Iggy Biggy,** Queen's Highway (✆ **242/367-3596**).

2 Elbow Cay (Hope Town) ★

Elbow Cay is noted for its spectacular white-sand beaches. One of The Bahamas's best, **Tahiti Beach** ★★ lies in splendid isolation at the far end of Elbow Cay island, with sparkling waters and powdery white sands. Access is possible only on foot, by riding a rented bicycle across sand and gravel paths from Hope Town, or by private boat.

The cay's largest settlement is **Hope Town,** a little village with a candy-striped, 36m (120-ft.) lighthouse, the most photographed attraction in the Out Islands. (You can climb to the top of the lighthouse for a sweeping view of the surrounding land and water.) Hope Town seems frozen in time. Like other offshore cays of the Abacos, it was settled by Loyalists who left the new United States and came to The Bahamas to remain subjects of the British Crown. Its clapboard, saltbox cottages are weathered to a silver gray or painted in pastel colors, with white-picket fences setting them off. The buildings may remind you of New England, but this palm-fringed island has a definite South Seas flavor.

The island is almost free of cars. In exploring Hope Town, you can take one of two roads: "Up Along" or "Down Along," which runs along the water.

ESSENTIALS

GETTING THERE You can reach Elbow Cay in about 40 minutes, via regularly scheduled ferry service from Marsh Harbour on Great Abaco. A one-way fare is $8, round-trip is $12, and service is three times daily. Call **Albury's Ferry Service** at ✆ **242/365-6010** for more information.

FAST FACTS Visitors and residents must go to Marsh Harbour for medical attention. There is a local **post office** (✆ **242/366-0098**) at the head of the upper public dock, but expect mail sent from here to take a long time. Hours are Monday through Friday from 9am to noon and from 1 to 5pm.

WHERE TO STAY

Abaco Inn ★ A sophisticated little hideaway, set about 3km (2 miles) south of Hope Town, the Abaco Inn faces a lovely sandy beach on White Sound. It was radically overhauled and improved after the devastation of the 1990s hurricanes. It is more of a resort than its main rivals, Hope Town Hideaways and Club Soleil Resort and Marina. An informal barefoot elegance and a welcoming spirit prevail. The resort nestles on the narrowest section of Elbow Cay, between the crashing surf of the jagged eastern coast and the sheltered waters of White Sound and the Sea of Abaco to the west. From the cedar-capped gazebo, you can gaze out over the rocky tidal flats of the Atlantic. Excellent snorkeling is close at hand.

The midsize accommodations are arranged in a crescent facing the beach. They're set amid palms and sea grapes, and each has its own hammock placed conveniently nearby for quiet afternoons of reading or sleeping. Your room will have a ceiling fan, a bathroom with a shower-tub combination, and a comfortable decor of white tile floors, sliding glass doors, and conservative furniture.

A modern, rambling clubhouse with a fireplace serves as both the social center and the most appealing restaurant/bar on the island (see "Where to Dine," below).

White Sound, Hope Town, Elbow Cay, Abaco, The Bahamas. ✆ **800/468-8799** in the U.S., or 242/366-0133. Fax 242/366-0113. www.abacoinn.com. 22 units. $140–$165 double; $215 villa for 2. Extra person $25. AE, DISC, MC, V. **Amenities:** Restaurant, bar; pool; live entertainment; babysitting; coin laundry; bikes; airport shuttle; boating and fishing arranged. *In room:* A/C, hair dryer, no phone.

Club Soleil Resort Abaco Inn may have better accommodations, but nothing surpasses the tranquillity of this inn. Because of its isolated position near the lighthouse on the western edge of Hope Town's harbor, the only way to get to this Spanish-style resort is by boat. Once there, you're just a short walk from some lovely sandy beaches. If you bring your own boat, you can moor it at this hotel's marina, but if you just happen to have left your boat at home, call the owners. They will quickly arrange a free waterborne transfer from any nearby coastline you designate. Midsize rooms with shower units are contained in a two-story, Mediterranean-inspired annex, and they overlook a swimming pool and the boats that moor in the harbor. Each room contains two double beds and a clean and tasteful decor. Significant renovations and improvements have been made to this place since the hurricane damage of 1999. The restaurant is covered separately under "Where to Dine," below.

Western Harbourfront, Hope Town, Elbow Cay, The Bahamas. ✆ **242/366-0003.** Fax 242/366-0254. www.clubsoleil.com. 7 units. $130 per night double; $1,000 per week 2-bedroom apt with kitchen. AE, MC, V. Closed Sept. **Amenities:** Restaurant, bar; pool; laundry; dock. *In room:* A/C, TV, coffeemaker, hair dryer, minibar, laundry, no phone.

Hope Town Hideaways ★ These complete island homes let guests live like locals, or at least like second-home owners. These gingerbread-trimmed villas, across the harbor from where ferryboats arrive from the Great Abaco "mainland," within the shadow of the town's red-and-white striped lighthouse, are part of a larger complex of privately owned homes, surrounded by grounds that are dotted with bougainvillea, mangoes, and citrus trees. The spacious villas sleep one or two couples (the limit is six guests per villa). Each has a big kitchen, a dining room, a living area with two single daybeds, and two bedrooms with queen-size beds and separate entrances. Each bedroom includes custom built-in beds, dressers, makeup vanities, reading lamps, a private bathroom with a shower-tub combination for each bedroom, and direct access to a private deck. Owners Chris and Peggy Thompson oversee housekeeping services and arrange rental boats, guided fishing trips, picnics, island-hopping excursions, and scuba or snorkeling trips.

When you first arrive, you'll have to call the hotel, which will send an employee for you in a putt-putt motorboat. (There's no access to this place by road from the center of Hope Town.) After that, you'll be assigned any of four putt-putt motorboats (included in the cost of your villa rental) as a means of getting from your rented home to anywhere else in Hope Town. Within about 24 hours, you'll become adept at lashing your boat to the piers, wharves, and pilings of Hope Town, and you'll even be able to navigate your way around the harbor at night.

Hope Town, Elbow Cay, Abaco, The Bahamas. ✆ **242/366-0224.** Fax 242/366-0434. www.hopetown.com. 4 units. Winter $240 double, $350 triple or quad; off-season $190 double, $250 triple or quad. Rates include use of motorboat during your stay. DISC, MC, V. **Amenities:** Pool. *In room:* A/C, TV, kitchenette.

Sea Spray Resort and Villas ★ On 6 acres of landscaped grounds, 5.5km (3½ miles) south of Hope Town and near the southernmost tip of Elbow Cay, these beachfront villas are owned and operated by Ruth Albury, who runs them in a welcoming, personal way. In the aftermath of 1999's Hurricane Floyd, two of the original six units were literally blown away, but the remaining four were renovated and brought back into proper working order. They have full kitchens and decks that overlook the water. Villas are spacious and comfortably furnished, each with a small bathroom containing a shower-tub combination. In 2000, the original pier and marina facilities were repaired, and many more slips and luxuries were added. The Alburys and their hardworking staff are happy to share their vast experience of what to see and do on Elbow Cay and in the Abaco area: You can bike, sail, go deep-sea fishing, snorkel, go bonefishing, or explore nearby deserted islands.

Sea Spray also operates a restaurant serving well-prepared food at all three meals while diners enjoy a view of the crashing surf and a weathered gazebo. Nonguests are welcome, too; if you phone in advance for a reservation, management will send a van to collect you from Hope Town.

White Sound, Elbow Cay, Abaco, The Bahamas. ✆ **242/366-0065.** Fax 242/366-0383. www.seasprayresort.com. 5 units. $180 per night or $950 per week 1-bedroom apt, $305 per night or $1,950 per week 2-bedroom apt. MC, V. **Amenities:** Restaurant, bar; limited room service; laundry; unlimited use of Sunfish; barbecue pit; free boat dockage (up to 7m/23 ft.); pool; bikes and snorkel gear for rent. *In room:* A/C, kitchenette, no phone.

Turtle Hill Vacation Villas ★ On the outskirts of Hope Town, a trio of luxury villas lie just steps from a vast secluded beach where sea turtles return to nest. Fruit trees and other tropical foliage make this a secluded getaway. Each house sleeps six persons comfortably in two large bedrooms, with a queen-size sleeper sofa in the living room, plus a full bathroom, well-equipped kitchen, a spacious living and dining area, and both central air-conditioning and ceiling fans. Linen is provided, and there is a Caribbean-style cabana bar serving drinks and finger foods daily.

Between Abaco Sea and Hope Town, Hope Town, Abaco, The Bahamas. ✆ **800/339-2124** in the U.S., or 242/366-0557. Fax 242/366-0557. www.turtlehill.com. 3 units. Winter $1,850–$2,050 per week; off-season $1,300–$1,500 per week. AE, MC, V. **Amenities:** Freshwater pool and barbecue grills. *In room:* A/C, kitchen, hair dryer, no phone.

WHERE TO DINE

Abaco Inn ★ BAHAMIAN/AMERICAN Flavor-filled food is served in a breezy, almost elegant waterfront setting. The chef prepares lunch dishes such as conch chowder, pasta primavera, and salads with delectable homemade dressings laced with tarragon and other herbs. The dinner menu changes frequently but usually features seafood, vegetarian, and meat dishes, each expertly seasoned and well-prepared. Typical meals are likely to begin with seafood bisque or vichyssoise, followed by coconut grouper (a house specialty), spinach fettuccine Alfredo, roasted lamb with herbs and mint sauce, or, our favorite, broiled red snapper with a light salsa. The Key lime, crème brûlée, coconut and chocolate silk pies are delectable. The inn will send a minivan to pick you up from other parts of the island if you phone in advance.

About 3km (2 miles) south of Hope Town. ✆ **242/366-0133.** Reservations required for dinner. Lunch sandwiches, salads, and platters $8–$14; dinner main courses $18–$32. DISC, MC, V. Daily 8–10:30am, noon–3pm, and 6:30–9pm.

Club Soleil Resort BAHAMIAN/SEAFOOD This pleasant restaurant lies within a sunny Spanish-inspired building on the western side of Hope Town's harbor. To reach it from other points along Hope Town's harbor front, you'll either have to borrow or rent a motorboat, or phone the owners in advance to send a boat to meet you. Your choice of table is either inside the dining room or on a covered waterfront terrace. Lunch might include conch burgers, cheeseburgers, and an array of such salads as niçoise and lobster.

The dinner menu usually features snapper, golden-fried grouper, or kingfish, cooked just right and with butter and garlic sauce. The broiled seafood platter served with lemon and garlic is another good choice. For those who don't want fish, either the rack of lamb Provençale or one of the excellent steaks should do the trick. The fixed-price Sunday brunch is always popular.

Western Harbourfront, Hope Town. ✆ **242/366-0003.** Reservations recommended for dinner. Dinner main courses $16–$28. Tues–Sun 8am–10pm and 6–9pm.

Harbour's Edge ★ BAHAMIAN Hope Town's best and most popular restaurant is set on piers above the water in a clapboard house. It's the island's lighthearted social center. The bar here has an adjacent waterside deck where you can moor if you arrive by boat, as many visitors do. Here and in the dining room as well, the crackle of VHF radio is always audible—boat owners and local residents often reserve tables on shortwave radio, channel 16.

Lunch includes such typical yet flavor-filled dishes as conch fritters, conch chowder, hamburgers, sandwiches, and conch platters. In the evening, dinners are also well-prepared—generous portions of chicken in white wine with potatoes, Greek or Caesar salad, pan-fried pork chops, chargrilled grouper, New York strip steak, fish in coconut milk, and more.

Hope Town, next to the post office. ✆ **242/366-0087.** Reservations not accepted. Lunch main courses $7–$11; dinner main courses $15–$23. MC, V. Wed–Mon 11:30am–3pm and 6–9pm; bar Wed–Mon 10am–midnight. Closed mid-Sept to mid-Oct.

Hope Town Harbour Lodge ★ BAHAMIAN In one of the first lodges or inns ever built in Hope Town, this restaurant is still winning new friends, even those hard to please. At night, loving couples opt for a table on the cozy terrace with views of the harbor and the lights from the yachts. Menu items always taste better when preceded by one of those rum punches in the Wrecker's Bar overlooking the water. The menu is hardly inventive, but it's good, featuring the usual array of chicken, steaks, and pork chops. Occasionally, a fisherman will bring in a big marlin that can be grilled to perfection. Bahamian lobster appears delightfully in a creamy fettuccine and the local grouper is fashioned into spring rolls, Chinese-style, and served with a mustard-laced chutney sauce. In the main dining area are found picture windows, rattan chairs, and nautical prints. During lunch, diners gravitate to the Reef Bar and Grill fronting the water.

Don't overlook the lodge as a possibility for rooms. It rents 19 comfortably furnished and air-conditioned doubles, with prices going from $130 to $170 all year. Accommodations lie on any of three floors, each with a patio or balcony, sliding glass doors, a small bathroom with shower stall, and wicker furnishings.

Hope Town. ✆ **242/366-0095.** Reservations recommended for dinner. Lunch main courses $8–$15; dinner main courses $15–$35. MC, V. Daily 11:30am–2:30pm; Tues–Sun 6:30–9pm.

Rudy's Place ★ *Finds* BAHAMIAN/AMERICAN Because of its isolated position, in a wooden house in a valley in the center of the island, this restaurant provides free transportation before and after dinner. It's owned by Rudy Moree, who prepares recipes handed down from his Bahamian grandmother. These, adapted to the tastes of his international clientele, might include crayfish tails baked with Parmesan and butter, a delectable broiled shrimp in a white wine and garlic sauce, or even a passable roasted duck in an orange sauce.

Center Line Rd. ✆ **242/366-0062.** Reservations recommended. Fixed-price dinners $20–$30. MC, V. Mon–Sat 6:30–8:30pm (last order). Closed Sept–Oct.

Finds Exploring the Abacos by Boat

The ideal way to explore the Abacos is by boat. **Island Marine,** Parrot Cay in Hope Town (© **242/366-0282;** fax 242/366-0281), will set you up. In one of its rental boats, you can cruise to the boat-building settlement of Man-O-War Cay, to artist Pete Johnson's bronze foundry-gallery in Little Harbour (see section 1, "Marsh Harbour (Great Abaco Island)," later in this chapter), and to many uninhabited cays and deserted beaches where you can go shelling, exploring, and picnicking in peace.

Small-boat rentals range from a 5m (17-ft.) Boston Whaler to 7m (23-ft.) Man-O-War boats, or even 6.5m (22-ft.) Aquasports. Prices run from $90 to $135 per day or $500 to $800 per week.

SCUBA DIVING & OTHER WATERY ADVENTURES

Set about 20 steps south of Hope Town's post office, **Froggie's Out Island Adventure,** Harbour Road (© **242/366-0024**), is the largest dive outfitter in the Abacos, with three boats (ranging from 11–17m/35–55 ft. in length) that owner Tito Baldwin ("Froggie") uses to haul divers out to fabulous local dive sites. Beginners pay $110 for a half day, $130 for a full day, with a lesson included. Experienced divers with their own gear are charged $80 for a half-day excursion, $90 for a full-day excursion.

The company also organizes tours, from snorkel cruises to dolphin-watching trips. A full-day cruise out to Great Guana Cay costs $50 per person. An equivalent tour to Little Harbour, near the southernmost point of the Abacos, including visits to selected restaurants, bars, and an art gallery, also costs $50 per person. Froggie's Sunset Cruise, departing an hour before sunset and returning an hour after it's dark, costs $30 per person.

SHOPPING

Of course, no one comes to Hope Town just to shop, but once you're here, you might want to pick up a souvenir. At **Kemp's Straw Market,** Hope Town, you can find some gift items made by local artisans.

The **Ebb Tide Gift Shop** (© **242/366-0088**), the best-stocked gift shop in town, lies in a white clapboard house with yellow trim 1 block from the harbor. Inside, you'll find many treasures, including Androsia batiks made on Andros, costume jewelry, T-shirts, original watercolors, and fabrics sold by the yard.

3 Man-O-War Cay

Visiting here is like going back in time. The island has some lovely beaches, and many visitors come here to enjoy them—but it's best to leave your more daring swimwear at home. The people who call this island home are deeply religious and conservative. There is no crime—unless you bring it with you. No alcoholic beverages are sold on the island, although you can bring your own supply.

Like New Plymouth, Man-O-War is a Loyalist village, with similarities to a traditional New England town. The pastel clapboard houses, built by ships' carpenters and trimmed in gingerbread, are set off by freshly painted white-picket fences intertwined with bougainvillea.

The people here are basically shy, but they do welcome outsiders to their remote, isolated island. They are proud of their heritage, which includes a proud boat-building tradition, and many, especially the old-timers, have known plenty of hard times. Many of them are related to the "conchs" of Key West and, like them, are a tough, insular people who have exhibited a proud independence for many years.

Tourism has only just begun to infiltrate Man-O-War Cay. Because of the relative lack of hotels and restaurants, many visitors come over just for the day, often in groups from Marsh Harbour. If you do stay for a while, stop by the Man-O-War Marina to arrange your boat rentals and watersports; there's also a dive shop there.

GETTING THERE & GETTING AROUND

To reach Man-O-War Cay, you must cross the water from Marsh Harbour. **Albury's Ferry Service** (✆ **242/367-3147** in Marsh Harbour or **242/365-6010** in Man-O-War) leaves from a dock near the Abaco Beach Resort. The round-trip fare is $12 for adults and $6 for children ages 6 to 12. The ride takes about 35 minutes.

Except for a few service vehicles, Man-O-War Cay has almost no cars. If you want to explore farther than your own two feet will carry you, ask around and see if one of the locals will rent you a golf cart.

WHERE TO STAY

Schooner's Landing Set in isolation on Man-O-War Cay's northeastern edge, this four-unit apartment complex is the only officially designated place to stay on the island. A seawall separates its lawns and hibiscus shrubs from the crashing surf, so swimmers and snorkelers meander a short distance down to the sands of a nearby beach. Each two-story unit contains a kitchen, ceiling fans, two private bathrooms, a TV that receives from an adjacent VCR only (you can rent videos at the hotel), and a summery decor of wicker and rattan furniture. Each comes with a small, tidily kept bathroom with a shower-tub combination. There's no bar or restaurant, but either of two grocery stores on the island will deliver; most visitors opt to cook in, anyway.

Man-O-War Cay, Abaco, The Bahamas. ✆ **242/365-6072.** Fax 242/365-6285. www.schoonerslanding.com. $250 daily or $1,750 weekly. 3-day minimum stay required. AE, MC, V. **Amenities:** Private dock; barbecue grill; pool, laundry. *In room:* A/C, TV, VCR, no phone.

WHERE TO DINE

Man-O-War Marina Pavilion AMERICAN/BAHAMIAN The sides of this wooden pavilion are open to the breezes and a view of the boats bobbing at the nearby harbor. A crowd of loyal boat owners and local residents is always here, enjoying the simple but savory cuisine of Marjorie Eldon. Monday to Thursday, the focus is on such time-favored staples as roasted chicken fingers, grilled fish, burgers, fried conch with peas 'n' rice, and steaks. On Friday and Saturday nights, however, many locals arrive for grilled lamb, fish, steaks, or chicken, and the place is practically transformed into a neighborhood block party. Though liquor isn't served, you can BYOB.

Harbour's Edge, Man-O-War Cay. ✆ **242/365-6185.** Lunch main courses $7–$11; dinner main courses $10.50–$24. No credit cards. Mon–Sat 10:30am–2pm and 5:30–8:30pm. Closed Aug 15–Sept 30.

SHOPPING

Joe's Studio (✆ **242/365-6082**), on the harbor front, sells island-related odds and ends, like models of local sailing dinghies crafted from mahogany and mounted in half profile on a board. They're a great souvenir of your visit. Other items include original watercolors, handcrafted woodwork from native woods, and nautical souvenirs and gifts. Hours are Monday through Saturday from 10am to 4pm.

The most unusual store and studio on the island, **Albury's Sail Shop** (© **242/365-6014**) occupies a house at the eastern end, overlooking the water. The floor space is devoted to the manufacture and display of an inventory of brightly colored canvas garments and accessories. The 8-ounce cotton duck fabric once served as sailcloth for the community's boats. When synthetic sails came into vogue, four generations of Albury women put the cloth and their talents to use. Don't stop without chatting with the Albury women. Hours are Monday through Saturday from 7am to 5pm.

4 Great Guana Cay ★

Longest of the Abaco cays, Great Guana, on the east side of the chain, stretches 11km (7 miles) from tip to tip and lies between Green Turtle Cay and Man-O-War Cay. The beachfront running the length of the cay is spectacular, one of the loveliest in The Bahamas. The reef fishing is superb, and bonefish are plentiful in the shallow bays.

The settlement stretches along the beach at the head of the palm-fringed Kidd's Cove, named after the pirate, and the ruins of an old sisal mill near the western end of the island make for an interesting detour. The island has about 150 residents, most of them descendants of Loyalists who left Virginia and the Carolinas to settle in this remote place, often called the "last spot of land before Africa."

As in similar settlements in New Plymouth and Man-O-War Cay, houses here resemble those of old New England. Over the years the traditional pursuits of the islanders have been boat-building, carpentry, farming, and fishing. It won't take you long to explore the village because it has only two small stores, a one-room schoolhouse, and an Anglican church—that's about it.

GETTING THERE & GETTING AROUND

Albury's Ferry Service, Marsh Harbour (© **242/365-6010**), runs a twice-daily service to Great Guana Cay. A round-trip ticket costs $12 for adults, $6 for children.

Instead of driving around the island, most people get around in small boats. On the cay, boats are available to charter for a half-day or a full day (or a month, for that matter). For example, a 7m (23-ft.) sailboat, fully equipped for living and cruising, is available for charter, and deep-sea fishing trips can be arranged.

WHERE TO STAY

Dolphin Beach Resort ★ Set directly astride one of the best beaches in The Bahamas, a 15-minute walk north of Guana Cay's largest settlement (Guana Village), with miles of powder-soft sand in front of you, this resort offers informal but very comfortable lodgings. Four of the units are in the main house and have queen-size beds and ceiling fans, small refrigerators, and microwaves; three of them have private screened-in decks with teakwood furniture. The oceanfront cottages (nine in all) also have queen-size beds, ceiling fans, air-conditioning, and full-size kitchenettes with stoves. Cottages can accommodate between two and four guests, depending on their size. The showers are placed outside but secluded and screened off by island flora. The place is private, intimate, and laid-back.

There's a restaurant on the premises, The Landing, with a "conch crawl," a Bahamian take on a lobster tank. Nippers, a beachfront bar and grill, is within a 5-minute walk.

Great Guana Cay, Abaco, The Bahamas. (Write to Dolphin Beach Resort, 69 AB, P.O. Box 59-2548, Miami, FL 33159.) ✆ **800/222-2646** or 242/365-5137. www.dolphinbeachresort.com. 10 units. $120–$155 double; $170–$240 cottage. AE, MC, V. **Amenities:** Restaurant, beachfront bar/grill; limited room service; laundry; babysitting; pool; bikes; kayaks; snorkeling. *In room:* A/C, TV, hair dryer, coffeemaker, kitchenette, no phone.

WHERE TO DINE

For fun on the beach, head for **Nipper's Beach Bar & Grill** (✆ **242/365-5143**), a dive where visitors hang out with the locals. Right on the sands, you sit in split-level gazebos and take in the surf, the most stunning seascape in the Abacos, with a snorkeling reef just 12 yards offshore. Burgers and well-stuffed sandwiches satisfy your hunger at lunch. But the best times to go are on a Wednesday, for one of the bonfires and fireworks displays, or on a Sunday afternoon, for a pig roast. One guest is said to have consumed five "Nipper Trippers"—and lived to tell about it. This is the bartender's specialty, a mix of five different rums along with tropical juices. It's lethal.

5 Treasure Cay ★

Treasure Cay now contains one of the most popular and elaborate resorts in the Out Islands. On the east coast of Great Abaco, it boasts not only 5.5km (3½ miles) of spectacular sandy beach, widely recognized as one of the top-10 beaches in the world, but also one of the finest marinas in the Commonwealth, with complete docking and charter facilities.

Before the tourist complex opened, the cay was virtually unsettled. As a result, the resort has become the "city," providing its visitors, who number in the thousands, with everything they need, including medical supplies, grocery-store items (liquor, naturally), and even bank services. But don't count on these services when you need them. There are no ATMs on the island, and the bank is only open Tuesday and Thursday (and Thurs is payday on island, so it's impossibly overcrowded). Medical supplies, even solutions for contact lenses, aren't available weekends. The real-estate office peddles condos, and the builders predict that they will one day reach a capacity of 5,000 guests. They hope that many visitors will like Treasure Cay so much that they'll buy into it.

See "Getting There" under "Abacos Essentials," at the beginning of this chapter, for details on flying to Treasure Cay. Some direct service is available to the island from Florida. You could also fly into Marsh Harbour (see section 1, "Marsh Harbour (Great Abaco Island)," earlier in this chapter) and take a 32km (20-mile) taxi ride north along the paved but bumpy Sherben A. Boothe Highway.

Treasure Cay also hosts one of the most popular fishing tournaments in The Bahamas: the **Treasure Cay Billfish Championship** in May.

WHERE TO STAY

Banyan Beach Club Resort ★ Although it doesn't have the scale or amenities of the much larger Treasure Cay Resort, about 1km (½ mile) away, this well-maintained compound of apartments, each with a kitchenette, has a slightly lower price tag and an idyllic location on the sands of a stunning beach. It was built in the 1970s, but because of a radical renovation that was completed in the 1990s, it looks much newer. The apartments are simple, streamlined, and modern, with small bathrooms equipped with shower-tub combinations. Those with water views are larger and a bit more expensive. This is a good place for a quiet vacation of swimming, reading, and relaxing. The new Tiki Bar is the setting for weekly cocktail parties.

P.O. Box AB 22158, Treasure Cay, Abaco, The Bahamas. © **888/625-3060** or 242/365-8111. Fax 242/365-8112. www.banyanbeach.com. 22 units. $175–$200 1-bedroom suite, $200–$275 2-bedroom suite, $300 3-bedroom suite. MC, V. Closed Sept–Oct. **Amenities:** Bar; wading pool; golf carts for rent; snorkeling. *In room:* A/C, TV, kitchenette.

Treasure Cay Hotel Resort & Marina ★ One of the biggest of the Out Island resorts, this property attracts boaters, golfers, fishers, and divers, as well as yachties and escapists seeking a remote, yet rather -luxurious, retreat. The foundation for this resort was laid in 1962, when a group of international investors recognized the potential of the property. The vast majority of the peninsula, as well as the marina facility, all of the villas, 80 privately owned condominiums, the tennis courts, and several blocks of other housing, remains under the ownership of the original investors. Guests sometimes rent electric golf carts (around $35 a day) or bicycles to explore the far-flung palm and casuarina groves of the sprawling compound.

Guests of the resort appreciate the *House and Garden* look of the architecture, the tropical plantings, the spectacular beachfront, an excellent golf course, and the marina facilities. Simply furnished in conservatively modern tropical motifs, most accommodations overlook the dozens of sailing craft moored in the marina. The recently renovated villas are very attractive, with full kitchens, two bedrooms, and washer/dryers, plus a midsize bathroom with a shower-tub combination.

The restaurant, the Spinnaker, serves mediocre fare, and two bars dispense tropical drinks.

Treasure Cay, Abaco, The Bahamas. (For reservations, contact Treasure Cay Services, Inc., 2301 S. Federal Hwy., Fort Lauderdale, FL 33316; © **954/525-7711.**) © **800/327-1584** or 242/365-8535. Fax 242/365-8362. www.treasurecay.com. 95 units. Winter $250 double, $395 villa for up to 4; off-season $180 double, $325 villa for up to 4. MAP (breakfast and dinner) $50 extra per person. AE, DISC, MC, V. **Amenities:** Restaurant, 2 bars; pool; babysitting; 18-hole golf course; 6 tennis courts; boat rentals; fishing guides; snorkeling; 150-slip marina; scuba charters; golf-cart rentals; watersports. *In room:* A/C, TV, hair dryer, kitchenette.

WHERE TO DINE

We prefer to skip resort dining and head for one of the local joints patronized by islanders. There are several little dives and bars here; our favorite is a place called **"Island Boil"** (© **242/365-8849**), a yellow wooden shack near the Treasure Cay ferry. It serves cheap and filling Bahamian dishes, including fried fish for breakfast. Cracked lobster is another house specialty, and you can also order such regional fare as "stew fish," chicken souse, and sheep tongue souse. Full dinners cost from $9 to $14. On site is **Disco 404,** where you can dance the night away on Friday and Saturday after 10pm.

WATERSPORTS & OTHER OUTDOOR PURSUITS

Treasure Cay Golf Club (© **242/365-8535**), designed by Dick Wilson, offers 6,985 yards of fairways, though it's hardly the best course this famed golf architect ever designed. Greens fees are $75 for 18 holes. This is the only golf course in the Abacos, and it lies 1km (½ mile) from the center of the resort.

Treasure Cay Marina (© **242/365-8250**) offers full-service facilities for a variety of watersports. Fishing boats with experienced skippers will guide anglers to tuna, marlin, wahoo, dolphinfish, barracuda, grouper, yellowtail, and snapper. Treasure Cay's own bonefish flats are just a short cruise from the marina. A full day of bonefishing costs $325. A sportfishing boat goes for $375 for a half day, $500 for a full day. In addition, you can arrange to rent a sailboat, a Hobie Cat, windsurfing boards, and snorkeling gear. The marina has showers, fish-cleaning facilities, 24-hour weekday laundry service, and water and electricity hookups.

Deep-sea fishing is arranged through the reception desk of the **Treasure Cay Resort and Marina** (**© 242/365-8535**), which will also arrange for you to hire a bonefishing guide. The same resort has six of the best tennis courts in the Abacos, four of which are lit for night games. Fees are $14 hourly for the hard courts or $16 hourly for the clay courts.

The best diving is provided by **Divers Down** (**© 242/365-8465**), which rents equipment and takes scuba divers to some of the best sites in the Abacos where the marine life down below is spectacular in all its rainbow-hued glory. Whale Cay and No Name Cay are some of the best sites for viewing Bahamian marine life. Divers are also taken to the site of the 1865 wreck of *San Jacinto,* a steamship freighter that went down. If you're not a serious diver but want a close encounter with the water, call **C & C Boat Rentals** (**© 242/365-8585**) which can take you on $65 snorkeling and island-exploring trips that feature a cookout on the beach.

6 Green Turtle Cay (New Plymouth) ★★

Five kilometers (3 miles) off the east coast of Great Abaco, Green Turtle Cay is the jewel of the archipelago, a little island with an uneven coastline, deep bays, sounds, and good beaches, one of the best stretching for 1080m (3,600 ft.). Here you can roam through green forests, gentle hills, and secluded inlets. The island is 5.5km (3½ miles) long and 1km (½ mile) across, lying some 274km (170 miles) due east of Palm Beach, Florida.

Water depths seldom exceed 4.5 to 6m (15–20 ft.) inside the string of cays that trace the outer edge of the Bahama Bank. Coral gardens teem with colorful sea life, making for fabulous snorkeling. Shelling on the lovely beaches and offshore sandbars is among the finest in The Bahamas. If you have a boat, you can explore such deserted islands as Fiddle Cay to the north and No Name Cay and Pelican Cay to the south of Green Turtle Cay.

New Plymouth, at the southern tip of the cay, is an 18th-century settlement that has the flavor of an old New England sailing port. Much of the original masonry was made from lime that was produced when conch shells were broken up, burned, and sifted for cement (records say that the alkali content was so high that it would burn the hands of the masons who used it). Clapboard houses with gingerbread trim line the narrow streets of the little town, which once had a population of 1,800 people, now shrunk to 400. Green Turtle Cay became known for the skill of its shipbuilders, although the industry, like many others in the area, failed after slaves were totally emancipated in The Bahamas in 1838.

Parliament is the village's main street, and you can walk its length in just 10 minutes, acknowledged only by a few clucking hens. Many of the houses have front porches, occupied in the evening by locals enjoying the breezes.

ESSENTIALS

GETTING THERE Fly to **Treasure Cay Airport,** where a taxi will take you to the ferry dock for departures to Green Turtle Cay (New Plymouth). At the dock, you may have to wait a while for the ferry. It's about a 15- to 20-minute ride to Green Turtle Cay from the dock. The ferry will take you directly to the

Green Turtle Club, if you're staying there, or to New Plymouth. This land-and-sea transfer costs $16 per person round-trip.

FAST FACTS **Barclay's Bank PLC** operates a branch (✆ **242/365-4144**) open only from 10am to 1pm on Tuesday and Thursday.

If you need medical attention on **Green Turtle Cay,** there is a government clinic (✆ **242/365-4028**) run by a nurse.

You enter Green Turtle Cay's **post office** (✆ **242/365-4242**) through a pink door. It has a public telephone. Hours are Monday through Friday from 9am to 5pm.

As for safety, there's no crime in New Plymouth, unless you import it yourself. There is a little jail made of stone, which makes visitors chuckle. No one can remember when, if ever, it held a prisoner.

SPECIAL EVENTS One event that draws visitors in droves is the **Green Turtle Club Fishing Tournament,** held in May. In 1984, the winner hooked a 500-pound blue marlin that was so heavy that the competing participants from other boats generously came aboard the winning craft to bring the fish in. For more information, contact one of the Bahamian Tourist Offices or the **Green Turtle Club Hotel** (✆ **242/365-4271**), which is more or less the official headquarters, when the tournament is held.

WHERE TO STAY

Bluff House Club Beach Hotel ★ One of the most famous and legendary hotels in the Out Islands, Bluff House originated in the 1950s when it was the private home of C. Pearce Cody III and his wife, Kitty. When friends of their friends asked if they could pay for a few days' stay, the Codys reinvented their home as the first hotel in the Out Islands. It's welcomed some extremely famous guests in the intervening years, including a well-heeled "same time next year" group. Bluff House occupies one of the most desirable pieces of real estate in The Bahamas, 10 acres on the highest point in the Abacos with panoramic views; it fronts the Sea of Abaco on one side and the sheltered harbor of White Sound on the other. A romantic spot, it has a lovely nautical charm with British colonial overtones. Against a backdrop of palm, oak, and pine-forested jogging trails, it lies within a 5-minute boat ride from the village of New Plymouth. (The hotel's boat hauls guests to town 3 mornings a week for sightseeing and shopping, and also for a Sat-night dance.)

The hotel offers villas and hotel rooms in a variety of configurations and sizes, either set beside the beach or cantilevered into the steep hillside facing the sheltered harbor; all have lovely views and some have kitchens. The best accommodations are the spacious colonial-style suites, with cathedral ceilings and balconies that overlook the Sea of Abaco. Inside, decor includes floral bed covers and tropical furniture. Each room comes with a small tidy bathroom containing a shower unit.

Breakfast and dinner (including complimentary wine) are served in the main Club House, where drinks and fresh hors d'oeuvres are offered before a candlelit dinner that features local conch, grouper, snapper, and lobster, as well as roast duck a l'orange. (See "Where to Dine," below.) The bar/lounge in the hotel's main building is one of our favorite rooms in The Bahamas, with sweeping vistas out across Green Turtle Cay; the blue-and-white, cypress-paneled interior is cozy and comfortable, with simple good taste. Peace and prosperity prevail among nautical memorabilia and a flickering fire within an iron stove as slow-whirling tropical fans, wicker furnishings, and polished wooden floors create an upscale and highly appealing ambience. The daytime bar and grill, the Bluff House Mama, specializes in light meals. Most Thursdays, dinner is served as part of an elaborate beachfront barbecue that's accompanied by music from a live local band.

Green Turtle Cay, Abaco, The Bahamas. © **242/365-4247.** Fax 242/365-4248. www.bluffhouse.com. 31 units. $120–$250 double; $225–$340 1-bedroom villa, $340–$410 2-bedroom villa, $415–$565 3-bedroom villa. MAP (breakfast and dinner) $36 extra per person. AE, DISC, MC, V. **Amenities:** 2 restaurants, 2 bars; 45-slip marina with boats for rent; pool; tennis court; free use of rackets, balls, and snorkeling equipment; arrangements for reef fishing, deep-sea fishing, and bonefishing; babysitting; laundry. *In room:* A/C, hair dryer, no phone.

Coco Bay Cottages On the north end of Green Turtle Cay, at a point where 150m (500 ft.) of land separate the Atlantic from the Sea of Abaco, this cottage complex opens onto a beach on the Atlantic side of the island and another sandy beach on the more tranquil bay. It is ideal for those who'd like to anchor in for a while (literally—lots of folks arrive by private boat, which you can moor here free, or otherwise you come directly by water taxi from the airport dock). It enjoys a 70% repeat clientele. Furnished in a refreshing style of Caribbean furnishings and pastel colors, the oceanfront property occupies 5 acres, dotted with some 50 tropical fruit trees. Each of the cottages has two bedrooms, a living room, a dining room, and a fully equipped kitchen with microwave, plus a small bathroom with a shower unit. Rebuilt in 1988 and renovated in 1996, the spacious cottages have improved over the years. Linens and kitchen utensils are provided (there are three shops in New Plymouth where you can stock up), and ceiling fans and trade winds cool the rooms.

P.O. Box AB22795, Green Turtle Cay, Abaco, The Bahamas. © **800/752 0166** or 242/365-5464. Fax 242/365-5465. www.cocabaycottages.com. 4 cottages. $185–$250 per day or $1,100–$1,800 per week. MC, V. *In room:* Kitchen, no phone.

Deck House These cottages lie on the leeward side of the island at the entrance to White Sound. Rented weekly as a complex, it can house up to six people. It consists of two bedrooms and two bathrooms, each with a shower stall, plus a small guesthouse for two with bathroom—in other words, it houses three couples "with privacy." There is a living room, plus a kitchen, and linens and all utensils are provided. Out back is a sun deck. Owner Dorothy Lang prefers bookings from Saturday noon to the following Saturday noon, and only one group at a time can rent the site. Incidentally, a maid comes in Saturday to put things in order.

White Sound, Green Turtle Cay, Abaco, The Bahamas. © **513/821-9471** in Cincinnati, OH (for information, write to Dorothy Lang, 535 Hickory Hill Lane, Cincinnati, OH 45215). 2 units. $850 per week for 4; $1,100 per week for 6. No credit cards. **Amenities:** Free use of boat and Sunfish. *In room:* No phone.

Green Turtle Club ★★ An outstanding choice for laid-back luxury, a bit more elegant than Bluff House, this resort attracts honeymooners and snorkelers. But it is a superb choice if you're a serious angler, boater, or diver, because there's an excellent full-service marina and dive shop on the premises. Although it sustained heavy damage during the 1999 hurricanes, the Green Turtle Club immediately undertook major renovations and repair work, and it emerged into the new millennium in tip-top shape. It is spread across 80 acres of low-lying scrubland. The waters around the resort are shallow enough that from a position on shore, you can spot schools of fish and sometimes even a green turtle paddling along above the sandbanks. Today the inn's ambience is very much that of a clubhouse, lodge, and country club; the courteous staff offers assistance yet doesn't intrude on anyone's peace and privacy.

The Green Turtle Yacht Club, host of the prestigious Bahama Cup Around the Island Race, has its base here. It's associated with the Birdham Yacht Club, one of the oldest in England, and with the Palm Beach Yacht Club. Members have their own villas right on the water, often with private docks, although temporary guests will be lodged in spacious bungalows (usually two accommodations to a building) set within a gently sloping, carefully landscaped garden. Rooms are among the most upscale and luxurious in the Out Islands. Think England in the tropics, for the bedrooms boast Sheraton-style mahogany furniture, four-poster beds, French-inspired draperies, oak floors, terra-cotta-tiled patios, and wicker or rattan furniture. Each comes with an immaculate midsize bathroom with almost all containing shower-tub combinations and generous shelf space.

The flag-festooned bar is the social center of the resort, where there's occasionally live music. There's an unmistakable British note to evenings here, beginning with pre-dinner cocktails beside a roaring fire in the bar's iron stove (in chilly weather only, of course), before everyone adjourns to the pine-paneled dining room for well-prepared dinners. Breakfast and lunch are usually served on a veranda.

Green Turtle Cay, Abaco, The Bahamas. ✆ **242/365-4271.** Fax 242/365-4272. www.greenturtleclub.com. 34 units. $190–$210 double; $260–$270 suite; $325–$455 villa for up to 4. Prices higher at Christmas. Children under 12 stay free in parents' room. Extra person $20. MAP (breakfast and dinner) $41 extra per adult. AE, DISC, MC, V. Most guests arrive at Treasure Cay Airport, then take a taxi (there are usually plenty there) to the ferry dock, where a water taxi will take you to the club for a fee of about $8 each way. **Amenities:** Restaurant, 2 bars; pool; watersports; marina; boat rental; bike rental; dive shop; laundry. *In room:* A/C, VCR, refrigerator, no phone.

New Plymouth Inn ★ This two-story inn, a mix of New England and Bahamian styles, stands next door to the former home of Neville Chamberlain, the prime minister of Great Britain on the eve of World War II. It's more like a guesthouse or a big B&B than either the Green Turtle Club or Bluff House. In the heart of New Plymouth Village, the inn has colonial charm, a Loyalist history, cloistered gardens, and a patio pool. It was one of the few buildings in town to survive the 1932 hurricane. The inn is run by Wally Davies, an expert diver and swimmer, who has turned New Plymouth Inn into a charming oasis, refurbishing the 120-year-old building with taste and care.

The inn has wide, open verandas, intricate cutout wooden trim, and an indoor A-frame dining room. The comfortable hammock on the front porch is constantly fought over. The light and airy rooms are kept spotlessly clean; some units are air-conditioned, and each comes with a bathroom containing a shower unit. Many of the same guests have come back every year since the inn opened in 1974.

Out on the veranda, you can smell night-blooming jasmine mixing with fresh-baked island bread. Dinners of fresh native lobster, snapper, conch, and vintage wines are served by candlelight. Roasts, steaks, chops, and imported beer in frosty steins are also part of the menu. The bar and lounge are the social center. Sunday brunch is the most popular on the island.

New Plymouth, Green Turtle Cay, Abaco, The Bahamas. ✆ **242/365-4161.** Fax 242/365-4138. 9 units. $140 double. Rates include breakfast and dinner. MC, V. Closed Sept–Oct. **Amenities:** Restaurant; pool; fishing; snorkeling. *In room:* A/C, no phone.

WHERE TO DINE

The previously recommended hotels have the best food on the island, but consider one of the local spots as well.

The Club House Restaurant ★ INTERNATIONAL You can drop in here at midday for a burger, sandwich, or salad, but a note of elegance emerges at dinner, which is always kicked off at the cocktail hour in what we think is the most beautiful and appealing bar in the Bahamian Out Islands. Lined with limed cypress, trimmed in cerulean blue, and beautifully proportioned, it includes sweeping views out over two shorefronts from the highest point in the Abacos. Dinner is served within a Queen Anne–style dining room. It's always a set menu, with items that change every night, but the cuisine is invariably excellent. You might start with something like Waldorf salad or smoked salmon, followed by grilled and mango-flavored chicken breast or lobster tail that's simply broiled with lemon and butter. Triple chocolate cheesecake or Key lime pie makes a soothing dessert.

At the Bluff House Club Beach Hotel, Green Turtle Cay. ✆ **242/365-4247.** Reservations required. Lunch platters $6–$12; fixed-price dinners $33 per person. AE, DISC, MC, V. Daily 11:30am–2pm and daily at 7:30pm, with hors d'oeuvre service (included in the price) beginning at 6:30pm.

Laura's Kitchen BAHAMIAN/AMERICAN On the main street of town, across from the Albert Lowe Museum, this family-owned spot occupies a well-converted white Bahamian cottage. Laura Sawyer serves up lunch and dinner in a simple, homey decor. The menu changes nightly, depending on what's at the market, but she always serves the old reliables her family has eaten for generations: fried grouper, fried chicken, and a tasty cracked conch.

King St. ✆ **242/365-4287.** Reservations recommended for dinner. Lunch $5–$8.50; dinner $14–$18. MC, V. Daily 11am–3pm and 6–9pm. Closed Sept and Thanksgiving.

Plymouth Rock Liquors & Café BAHAMIAN/AMERICAN This place has the best selection of wines and liquors for sale in New Plymouth, including at least 60 kinds of rum, plus Cuban cigars. Part of its space is set aside for a pleasant and attractive luncheonette run by hardworking co-owners Kathleen and David Bethell. They serve up tasty sandwiches, split pea soup, beef souse, and cracked conch with cucumber slices and potato salad. There's also an art gallery on the premises, featuring works by about 50 artists, many of whom specialize in local themes.

Parliament St., Green Turtle Cay. ✆ **242/365-4234.** Sandwiches and platters $2.75–$7.50. DISC, MC, V. Cafe Mon–Sat 9am–5pm; liquor store Mon–Thurs 9am–6pm, Fri–Sat 9am–9pm.

Rooster's Rest Pub & Restaurant BAHAMIAN Just beyond the edge of town, Rooster's, the local dive, serves good Bahamian food, including lobster, conch, and your best bet, fresh fish. It's casual through and through, the way The Bahamas used to be; nouvelle cuisine hasn't washed up on these shores yet. All main courses in the evening are served with peas 'n' rice, coleslaw, and potato salad. The cook also prepares some tasty ribs. Live music is offered at least 2 nights a week.

Gilliam's Bay Rd. ✆ **242/365-4066.** Reservations recommended for dinner. Lunch burgers and snacks $5–$9; main courses $10–$18. MC, V. Mon–Sat 11:30am–9:30pm.

The Wrecking Tree Bar & Restaurant BAHAMIAN This funky wooden place is recognized by its coral and terra-cotta colors, and by the much-mangled casuarinas tree that grows next to its foundation. The hearty menu is as simple as can be, featuring mostly peas 'n' rice, conch, grouper fingers, chicken souse, and burgers. Come here for a simple lunch, a midday beer, and a view over the boats in the nearby harbor.

The Harbourfront. No phone. Main courses $6–$10. No credit cards. Daily 11am–3pm.

WATERSPORTS & OTHER OUTDOOR PURSUITS

If you want to go deep-sea fishing, the people to see are the Sawyer family, father and son. Referrals are usually made through the **Green Turtle Club** (© **242/365-4271**), or you can call directly at © **242/365-4173.** A half-day of fishing costs $240; a full day is $340. These costs can be divided among four people. If you want to go bonefishing, the charge is $140 per half day or $240 for a full day.

You can make scuba-diving arrangements with **Green Turtle Club Divers** (© **242/365-4271**), which has a full-service dive shop right at the hotel. Both divers and snorkelers get a 15% discount if they are registered at the hotel. **Brendal's Dive Shop** (© **242/365-4411;** www.brendal.com) also has a good reputation, and they can organize memorable outings. Both places will rent you snorkel gear.

Call **Lincoln Jones** at © **242/365-4223,** and he'll arrange a snorkeling adventure for you—probably on some deserted beach that only he knows about. Prices are to be negotiated, of course, but a lunch of fresh conch or lobster is a fine addition to any day.

You can usually rent a boat through **Donny's Boat Rentals** at © **242/365-4119.** You'll find everything for rent from 4m (14-ft.) Whalers to 7.5m (25-ft.) Makos. The Bluff House and the Green Turtle Club both have full-service marinas.

There's a tennis court at **Bluff House** (© **242/365-4247**), where everyone plays free.

EXPLORING THE ISLAND: A JOURNEY TO THE 18TH CENTURY

New Plymouth celebrated its bicentennial in 1984 by establishing a memorial that honors American Loyalists and also some of their notable descendants,

---

Finds Miss Emily's Blue Bee Bar

Our favorite bar in the Out Islands is **Miss Emily's Blue Bee Bar,** on Victoria Street in New Plymouth (© **242/365-4181**). This simple bar is likely to be the scene of the liveliest party in the Out Islands at any time of day; even normally buttoned-up types find themselves flirting or dancing before long. You never know what will be going on here. Until rising waters from the 1999 hurricanes washed some of them away, most of its walls were covered with the business cards of past guests and celebrities. Only some now remain, but stop by and see how many replacements have been plastered up. The Goombay Smash, the specialty here, has been called "Abaco's answer to atomic fission." Its recipe includes secret proportions of coconut rum, "dirty" rum, apricot brandy, and pineapple juice. Miss Emily (Mrs. Emily Cooper) was a legend in these parts. She's gone now, but her memory lives on: Her daughter, Violet Smith, knows her secret recipe for The Goombay Smash, as well as a potent version of a rum punch. Tips at the bar go to St. Peter's Anglican Church. No food is ever served here, but the bar is open Monday to Saturday from 11am until late.

---

including Albert Lowe, a pioneer boat-builder and historian. The garden, complete with busts of notable islanders, is designed in the pattern of the Union Jack and lies across from the New Plymouth Inn.

There isn't much shopping, but consider a visit to the Ocean Blue Gallery, adjoining the **Plymouth Rock Café** on Parliament Street (© **242/365-4234**). This two-room outlet has one of the best collections of local artwork in the Abacos: some sculptures, some paintings, but all originals.

Albert Lowe Museum ★★ More than anything else we've seen in The Bahamas, this museum gives a view of the rawboned and sometimes-difficult history of the Out Islands. You could easily spend a couple of hours reading the fine print of the dozens of photographs that show the hardship and the valor of citizens who changed industries as often as the economic circumstances of their era dictated.

There's a garden in the back of the beautifully restored Loyalist home; the caretaker will give you a guided tour of the stone kitchen, which occupants of the house used as a shelter when a hurricane devastated much of New Plymouth in 1932. Inside the house, a narrow stairway leads to three bedrooms that reveal the simplicity of 18th-century life on Green Turtle Cay. Amid antique settees, irreplaceable photographs, and island artifacts, you'll see a number of handsome ship models, the work of Albert Lowe, for whom the museum was named.

The paintings of Alton Lowe, son of the former boat-builder and founder of the museum, are also on display. Cherub-faced and red-haired, Alton has for some time been one of the best-known painters in The Bahamas. His works hang in collections all over the world; some appears on Bahamian postage stamps, blowups of which are displayed here. Your tour guide might open the basement of the house, as well, where you'll find some of Alton's paintings for sale alongside work by other local artists.

Parliament St. © **242/365-4094.** Admission $3 adults, $2 students. Mon–Sat 9am–noon and 1–4pm.

NEW PLYMOUTH AFTER DARK

Ask at your hotel if the local junkanoo band, the ***Gully Roosters,*** are playing their reggae- and calypso-inspired sounds. They're the best in the Abacos and often appear at various spots on island. Also make sure to visit **Miss Emily's Blue Bee Bar** (described above). You might catch a live band and you'll certainly enjoy a wonderful setting for a drink in the bars at the **Bluff House** and the **Green Turtle Club** (see "Where to Stay," above). **Rooster's Rest Pub and Restaurant** (see "Where to Dine," above) is yet another option.

7 Spanish Cay

Set 19km (12 miles) northwest of Green Turtle Cay, this island was named after a pair of Spanish galleons that sank offshore during the 17th century. Originally owned by Queen Elizabeth II, the island was purchased in the 1960s by Texas-based investor (and former owner of the Dallas Cowboys) Clint Murchinson. After his death in the early 1980s, two successive Florida conglomerates poured time, money, and landscaping efforts into developing the island as a site for upscale private homes. Today, guests of the inn (see below) and local residents putter along the island's paved roads in electric-powered golf carts.

Most visitors arrive by private boat or chartered aircraft from Fort Lauderdale. You can also fly to Treasure Cay on **Bahamasair** (© **800/222-4262** or 242/367-2095), then have the inn arrange water transportation.

WHERE TO STAY & DINE

The Spanish Cay Resort & Marina ★ Recent renovations and improved transportation have made this property better and more accessible. Bedrooms have been improved and completely refurbished to accommodate more than two guests per room. All the suites are roomy and spacious, with a double bed, a foldout sofa bed, and a small refrigerator, plus a tidy bathroom with a shower stall. The apartments, of course, are even more spacious, with both king-size beds and twins in their two bedrooms, plus a full kitchen, living room, dining room, and deck overlooking the marina. A one-bedroom apartment can sleep up to four people; a two-bedroom accommodates six.

Two on-site restaurants serve conch, chicken, fish, steak, and occasionally lobster. Dinners are reasonably priced, always including some kind of fresh fish.

Cooper's Town, Abaco, The Bahamas. © **888/722-6474** or 242/365-0083. Fax 242/365-0453. www.spanishcay.com. 22 units. Winter $225–$265 double, $425 2-bedroom condo; off-season $165–$195 double, $350 2-bedroom condo. MC, V. **Amenities:** 2 restaurants, bar; 4 tennis courts; boat rental; deep-sea fishing; snorkeling. *In room:* A/C, TV, refrigerator, no phone.

8 Walker's Cay

Lying at the edge of the Bahama Bank, this is the northernmost, the outermost, and one of the smallest islands in the Abaco chain. The cay produces its own fresh water and electricity. Coral reefs surround this island, dropping off to depths of some 300m (1,000 ft.). It's known around the world as one of the best deep-sea fishing resorts.

Ponce de León reportedly stopped here in 1513 in search of fresh water—just 6 days before he "discovered" Florida. From the 17th century, this was a place known to pirates, who stored their booty here. It became a bastion for blockade-runners during the American Civil War, and later it was a hide-out for rumrunners in the days of U.S. Prohibition.

To get here, prospective guests should call the Walker's Cay Hotel and Marina at © **800/WALKERS** and make arrangements for a flight from Fort Lauderdale.

WHERE TO STAY & DINE

Walker's Cay Hotel & Marina ★ Established in the 1930s and a legend among sports fishermen ever since, this resort occupies all 100 acres of a private island that contains the largest and most elaborate full-service marina in The Abacos. Each year, it runs at least two of the country's biggest deep-sea fishing tournaments. Come here for the fishing, for the marina and its charter boats, and for the way that sports permeate the air, but not necessarily for the luxury of the accommodations. These are rather-standard motel-style units, which benefited in 1999 from a complete renovation. Each accommodation contains a small bathroom with a shower stall. Meals are generally adequate, served in the Lobster Trap and Conch Pearl restaurants; both have bars and offer American/Bahamian fare, chiefly steak and fresh fish.

Walker's Cay, Abaco, The Bahamas. (Address mail to 700 SW 34th St., Fort Lauderdale, FL 33315.) © **800/WALKERS** in the U.S. and Canada, 954/359-1400 in Fort Lauderdale, 242/353-1252 in the Abacos. Fax 954/359-1414. Mar 1–Sept 3 $150–$160 double, $325–$375 2-bedroom villa without kitchen; Sept 4–Feb 28 $110–$120 double, $300–$325 2-bedroom villa without kitchen. MAP supplement $37.50 per person per day. AE, DISC, MC, V. **Amenities:** 2 restaurants, 2 bars; 2 tennis courts; laundry; babysitting; watersports; freshwater and saltwater swimming; gift shop. *In room:* A/C, hair dryer, no phone.

8

Eleuthera

A sort of Bahamian Plymouth Rock, Eleuthera Island was the first permanent settlement in The Bahamas, founded in 1648. A search for religious freedom drew the Eleutherian Adventurers from Bermuda here, to the "birthplace of The Bahamas." The long narrow island they discovered and colonized still bears the name "Eleuthera"—Greek for freedom. The locals call it "Cigatoo."

These adventurers found an island of white- and pink-sand beaches framed by casuarina trees, high, rolling green hills, sea-to-sea views, dramatic cliffs, and sheltered coves, and they're still here, unspoiled, waiting for you to discover today. More than 161km (100 miles) long but merely 3km (2 miles) wide (guaranteeing that you're never far from the beach), Eleuthera is about 113km (70 miles) east of Nassau (a 30-min. flight). The population of 10,000 is largely made up of farmers, shopkeepers, and fishermen who live in old villages of pastel-washed cottages. The resorts here are built around excellent harbors, and roads run along the coastline, though some of them are inadequately paved.

Eleuthera and its satellite islands, **Spanish Wells** and **Harbour Island,** offer superb snorkeling and diving amid coral gardens, reefs, drop-offs, and wrecks. Anglers come to Eleuthera for bottom, bone- and deep-sea fishing, testing their skill against the dolphinfish, the wahoo, the blue and the white marlin, the Allison tuna, and the amberjack. Charter boats are available at Powell Point, Rock Sound, Spanish Wells, and Harbour Island. You can also rent Sunfish, sailboats, and Boston Whalers for reef fishing.

Eleuthera rivals the Abacos in terms of popularity among foreign visitors, although boaters are more drawn to the Abacos and the Exumas. Along with the Abacos, Eleuthera has the largest concentration of resort hotels outside of the major developments of Nassau/Paradise Island and Freeport/ Lucaya.

In many ways, we love gorgeous **Harbour Island,** with its charming Dunmore Town, even more than New Plymouth or Hope Town in the Abacos; it's almost a Cape Cod in the tropics. Of the 10 destinations recommended in this chapter, Harbour Island gets our vote as the number-one choice.

Spanish Wells is another small island just off the north end of Eleuthera. Spanish galleons put sailors ashore to fill the ships' casks with fresh water after long sea voyages—hence the present-day name of the island.

ELEUTHERA ESSENTIALS

GETTING THERE

BY PLANE Eleuthera has three main airports. **North Eleuthera Airport** (**© 242/335-1242**), obviously, serves the north along with the two major offshore cays, Harbour Island and Spanish Wells. **Governor's Harbour Airport** (**© 242/332-2321**) serves the center of the island, and **Rock Sound International Airport** (**© 242/334-2171**) handles traffic to South Eleuthera. Make sure, when making your reservations, that your flight will arrive at the appropriate airport; one visitor flew into Rock Sound Airport, only to face a $100 taxi ride and a water-taxi trip before reaching his final destination of Harbour Island in the north.

Bahamasair (✆ **800/222-4262**) offers daily flights between Nassau and the three airports, North Eleuthera, Governor's Harbour, and Rock Sound.

In addition, several commuter airlines, with regularly scheduled service, fly from the Florida mainland with either nonstop or one-stop service. Many private flights use the North Eleuthera Airport, with its 1,350m (4,500-ft.) paved runway. It is an official Bahamian port of entry, and a Customs and Immigration official is on hand.

USAir Express (✆ **800/428-4322**) operates what might be the most popular way of reaching two of Eleuthera's airports directly from the mainland of Florida. Flights depart once a day from Miami flying nonstop to North Eleuthera, then continue on, after briefly unloading passengers and baggage, to Governor's Harbour.

American Eagle (✆ **800/433-7300**) offers daily flights from Miami to Governor's Harbour. Usually there is only one flight a day, but if demand merits it, there can be two flights on Friday and three on Saturday and Sunday, since most visitors fly over for the weekend.

Small carriers include **Twin Air** (✆ **954/359-8266**), flying from Fort Lauderdale three times a week to Rock Sound and Governor's Harbour and four times a week to North Eleuthera.

BY FERRY A new interisland link, **Bahamas Fast Ferries** (✆ **242/323-2166**), originates in Potter's Cay, beneath the Paradise Island Bridge, and fans out at regular intervals to Harbour Island, North Eleuthera, and Governor's Harbour. Round-trip fares are $100 for adults, $60 for children under 12.

BY MAIL BOAT Several mail boats visit Eleuthera from Nassau, leaving from Potter's Cay Dock. Weather conditions often cause their schedules to change. For details about sailings, consult the dockmaster at **Potter's Cay Dock** in Nassau (✆ **242/393-1064**).

MV *Current Pride* goes from Nassau to Current Island, serving lower and upper Bogue. It departs Nassau at 7am Thursday and returns on Tuesday.

The ***Bahamas Daybreak III*** departs on Monday for South Eleuthera, stops at Rock Sound, and returns to Nassau on Tuesday. It then leaves from Nassau on Thursday for The Bluff and Harbour Island, with a Sunday return scheduled. The ***Eleuthera Express*** sails from Nassau to Spanish Wells and Governor's Harbour on Monday and Thursday, and returns to Nassau on Sunday and Tuesday.

GETTING AROUND

It's virtually impossible to get lost on Eleuthera—there's only one road that meanders along the entire length of its snake-shaped form, and you'll stray from it only very rarely. Because it's so easy to tour the island, most visitors rent a car at least for 1 day (prices are usually around $80 a day). This can be arranged simply by asking your hotel or any of the taxi drivers lined up either outside the North Eleuthera Airport or at the ferryboat docks heading to Harbour Island.

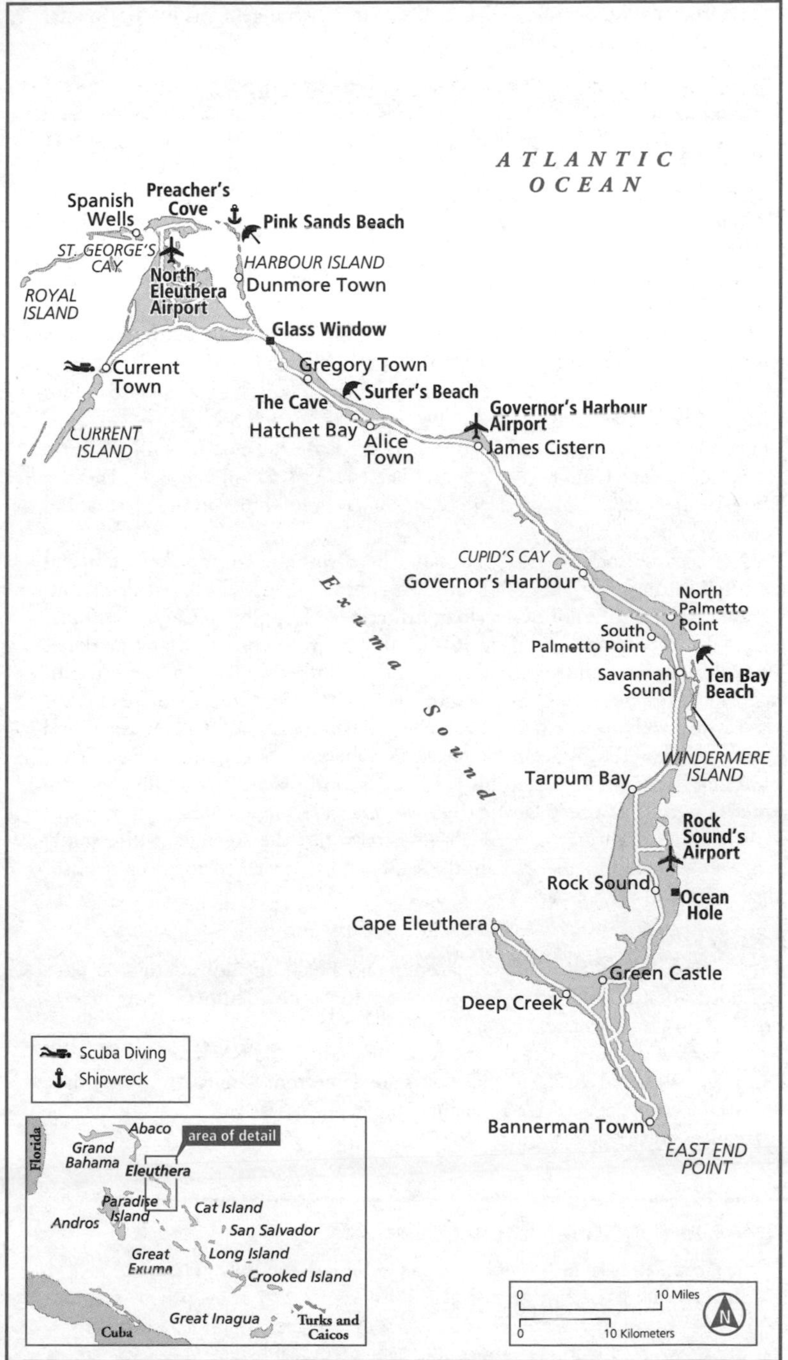
ATLANTIC OCEAN
Spanish Wells
Preacher's Cove
Pink Sands Beach
ST. GEORGE'S CAY
HARBOUR ISLAND
North Eleuthera Airport
Dunmore Town
ROYAL ISLAND
Glass Window
Current Town
Gregory Town
Surfer's Beach
The Cave
Governor's Harbour Airport
Hatchet Bay
Alice Town
James Cistern
CURRENT ISLAND
CUPID'S CAY
Governor's Harbour
Exuma Sound
North Palmetto Point
South Palmetto Point
Savannah Sound
Ten Bay Beach
WINDERMERE ISLAND
Tarpum Bay
Rock Sound's Airport
Rock Sound
Ocean Hole
Cape Eleuthera
Green Castle
Deep Creek
Scuba Diving
Shipwreck
Bannerman Town
EAST END POINT
Florida
Abaco
area of detail
Grand Bahama
Eleuthera
Paradise Island
Cat Island
Andros
San Salvador
Great Exuma
Long Island
Crooked Island
Great Inagua
Turks and Caicos
Cuba
0
10 Miles
0
10 Kilometers
N

The front desk of any hotel will help you make arrangements for a car rental if you don't choose to go with Fine Threads.

1 Rock Sound

Located in South Eleuthera, Rock Sound is a small shady village, the island's main town and once its most exclusive enclave. The closing of two old-time landmark resorts, the Cotton Bay Club and the Windermere Club, has at least for now halted the flow of famous visitors, who once included everybody from the late Princess Diana to a parade of CEOs. No reopenings are yet in sight, but at least that means that you can have many of South Eleuthera's best beaches practically to yourself.

Rock Sound opens onto Exuma Sound and is located to the south of Tarpum Bay. The town is at least 2 centuries old, and it has many old-fashioned homes with picket fences out front. Once notorious for wreckers who lured ships ashore with false beacons, it used to be known as "Wreck Sound."

The main reason to come here is to play the **Robert Trent Jones, Jr. Course** at the Cotton Bay Club on Rock Sound (© **242/334-6156**), a par-72, 18-hole, 7,068-yard course. Greens fees are $100 for 18 holes, but you must call ahead to reserve a tee time.

After leaving Rock Sound, head south, bypassing the Cotton Bay Club, and continue through the villages of Green Castle and Deep Creek. At this point, you take a sharp turn northwest along the only road leading to **Cape Eleuthera.** Locals call this "Cape Eleuthera Road," though you won't find any markings other than a sign pointing the way. If you continue to follow this road northwest, you'll reach the end of the island chain, jutting out into Exuma Sound.

Now relatively deserted, Cape Eleuthera was once home to a chic resort and yacht club that drew some of the movers and shakers from America's East Coast, including Richard Nixon and his pal Bebe Rebozo; some of the top golfers in America played its Bruce Devlin–Bob van Haage 18-hole course, which winds its way along the water. They're all gone now, but the splendid **white sandy beaches**—three of them—remain the same, and locals claim the deep-sea fishing is as fine as it ever was.

ESSENTIALS

Rock Sound itself boasts a shopping center and a bank in addition to its airport, but not a lot else. Many residents who live in South Eleuthera come here to stock up on groceries and supplies.

A doctor and four resident nurses form the staff of the **Rock Sound Medical Clinic** (© **242/334-2226**). Office hours are daily from 9am to 1pm; after that, the doctor is always available to handle emergency cases.

If you need the police, call © **242/334-2244.**

Fun Fact A "Hole" in the Ocean

The **Ocean Hole,** which is about 2km (1¼ miles) east of the heart of rock sound, is said to be bottomless. This saltwater lake that eventually meets the sea is one of the most attractive spots on Eleuthera. You can walk right down to the edge of the water. Many tropical fish can be seen here; they seem to like to be photographed—but only if you feed them first.

WHERE TO STAY & DINE

Sammy's Place BAHAMIAN Hot gossip and cheap, juicy burgers make Sammy's the most popular hangout in Rock Sound—come here for a slice of local life. Sammy's is on the northeastern approach to the settlement, in a neighborhood that even the owner refers to as "the back side of town." Sammy Culmer (who's assisted by Margarita, his daughter) will serve you drinks (including Bahama Mamas and rum punches), conch fritters, Creole-style grouper, breaded scallops, pork chops, and lobster. If you drop in before 11am, you might be tempted by a selection of egg dishes or omelets.

This is primarily a restaurant and bar, but Sammy does rent four rooms with air-conditioning and satellite TV, plus two efficiency cottages containing two bedrooms with a kitchen. These accommodations can be yours for $76 per night, double occupancy.

Albury's Lane, Rock Sound. ✆ **242/334-2121.** Reservations recommended only for special meal requests. Bahamian breakfasts $7; lunch $3–$12; main courses $8–$15. No credit cards. Daily 7:30am–10pm.

2 Tarpum Bay

If you're looking for an affordable vacation on high-priced Eleuthera, head here. This charming waterfront village, some 15km (9 miles) north of Rock Sound, is good for fishing and has a number of simple, inexpensive guesthouses. This tiny settlement with its many pastel-washed, gingerbread-trimmed houses is a favorite of artists, who have established a small colony here with galleries and studios.

Gaulding's Cay, north of town, has a lovely beach with exceptional snorkeling.

WHERE TO STAY & DINE

Cartwright's Ocean Front Cottages Cartwright's is a cluster of simple cottages right by the sea, with fishing, snorkeling, and swimming at your door. This is one of the few places where you can sit on your patio and watch the sunset. The small cottages, most recently renovated in 1996, are fully furnished, with utensils, stove, refrigerator, pots and pans, and maid service provided. Each unit comes with a small bathroom containing a shower stall. You'll be within walking distance of local stores and restaurants.

Bay St., Tarpum Bay, Eleuthera, The Bahamas. ✆ **242/334-4215.** cartwrights@hotmail.com. 3 units. $90 1-bedroom cottage, $130 2-bedroom cottage, $150 3-bedroom cottage. No credit cards. **Amenities:** Laundry; babysitting. *In room:* A/C, TV, no phone.

Hilton's Haven Motel and Restaurant Across the road from the beach and a short drive from the Rock Sound airport, this Bahamian two-story structure with covered verandas is modest and completely unpretentious, with decent prices. Comfortably furnished apartments, each with a private sun patio and bathroom with shower stalls, come with either air-conditioning or ceiling fans. What makes this place special is Mary Hilton herself, everybody's "Bahama Mama." In fact, as a professional nurse, she has delivered some 2,000 of Eleuthera's finest citizens. She started Hilton's Haven to provide retirement income for herself. "Hilton is my God-given name," she says. "I never met Conrad."

The main tavern-style dining room, with a library in the corner, provides well-cooked food daily; the emphasis is on freshly caught fish. You can order grouper cutlets with peas 'n' rice, steamed conch, and the occasional lobster.

Tarpum Bay, Eleuthera, The Bahamas. ✆ **242/334-4231.** Fax 242/331-4020. hilhaven@batelnet.bs. 11 units. $80 double; $125 apt for 4. MAP (breakfast and dinner) $11 extra per person. No credit cards. **Amenities:** Restaurant, bar. *In room:* A/C, TV, no phone.

3 Windermere Island

Windermere is a very tiny island, connected by ferry to "mainland" Eleuthera. It is midway between the settlements of Governor's Harbour and Rock Sound.

This island couldn't be more discreet. "We like to keep it quiet around here," one of the staff at the presently closed Windermere Island Club once told us. Regrettably, that wasn't always possible for this once-deluxe and snobbish citadel. When Prince Charles first took a pregnant Princess Diana here in the 1980s, she was photographed by paparazzi in her swimsuit. Much to the horror of the club, the picture gained worldwide notoriety.

Even without its posh hotel, Windermere Island is worth a day trip. **Savannah Sound,** with its sandy sheltered beaches and outstanding snorkeling, is particularly appealing (bring your own gear). There are also excellent beaches for shelling and picnicking, and there is good bonefishing, with some catches more than 10 pounds.

West Beach, a good place for sunning and swimming (great for children), is about a 10-minute walk from the shut-down Windermere Club. The beach is on Savannah Sound, the body of calm, protected water separating Windermere from the main island of Eleuthera.

Visitors can enjoy a number of activities, from bonefishing to windsurfing. The dockmaster at West Beach is well-qualified to guide and advise about bonefishing, or perhaps you'd like to go deep-sea fishing for white marlin, dolphinfish, grouper, wahoo, Allison tuna, and amberjack. Since there is no permanent outfitter, you have to ask around locally about who can take you out.

4 Palmetto Point

On the east side of Queen's Highway, south of Governor's Harbour, North Palmetto Point is a little village where visitors rarely venture (although you can get a meal there). This laid-back town will suit you if you want peace and quiet off the beaten track.

Ten Bay Beach ★★ is one of the best beaches in The Bahamas, with its sparkling turquoise water and wide expanse of soft white sand. The beach lies a 10-minute drive south of Palmetto Point and just north of Savannah Sound. There are no facilities, only idyllic isolation.

WHERE TO STAY

Palmetto Shores Vacation Villas This is a good choice if you want your own apartment and value independence and privacy over hotel services. Asa Bethel rents villas suitable for two to four guests. Units are built in a plain Bahamian-style, with living rooms, kitchens, small bathrooms with shower-tub combinations, and wraparound balconies that open directly onto your own private beach. Furnishings are simple but reasonably comfortable, VCRs are included, and the villas lie within walking distance of local shops and tennis courts.

P.O. Box EL25131, Governor's Harbour, Eleuthera, The Bahamas. ✆ **888/688-4752** or 242/332-1305. Fax 242/332-1305. www.ivacation.com/p6835.htm. 12 units. Winter $100–$120 1-, 2-, and 3-bedroom villa for 2; off-season $90–$110 1-, 2-, and 3-bedroom villa for 2. Year-round $180 2-bedroom villa for 4. Extra person $20–$30 summer, $30 winter. MC, V. **Amenities:** Deep-sea fishing; free Sunflower sailboats; snorkeling; car rentals. *In room:* A/C, TV, VCR, kitchen.

Unique Village Located on a steep rise above the Atlantic coast of Eleuthera, this hotel is the creative statement of a Palmetto Point businessman who also owns the local hardware store (Unique Hardware). Built in 1992, the hotel offers accommodations in several configurations (everything from conventional single or double rooms to a one-bedroom apartment with a kitchenette to two-bedroom villas with full kitchens). Each comes with a small bathroom with a shower-tub combination. A flight of wooden steps will bring you to the beach, where a reef breaks up the Atlantic surf and creates calm waters on this sandy cove. There's a bar and restaurant, also called Unique Village, on-site (see "Where to Dine," below), but few other luxuries. Although there is no sailing, scuba, or tennis on-site, the staff can direct you to other facilities that lie within a reasonable drive (you'll probably want a car here).

N. Palmetto Point, The Bahamas (send mail to P.O. Box EL25187, Governor's Harbour, Eleuthera, The Bahamas). ✆ **800/688-4752** or 242/332-1830. Fax 242/332-1838. www.bahamasvg.com. 14 units. Winter $120–$140 double, $160 1-bedroom apt for 2, $190 2-bedroom apt for up to 4; off-season $90–$110 double, $130 1-bedroom apt for 2, $160 2-bedroom apt for up to 4. Extra person $25. MAP (breakfast and dinner) $35 per person per day. MC, V. **Amenities:** Restaurant, bar. *In room:* A/C, TV.

WHERE TO DINE

Mate & Jenny's Pizza Restaurant & Bar BAHAMIAN/AMERICAN This popular restaurant, known for its conch pizza, has a jukebox and a pool table. It's the most popular local joint, completely modest and unassuming. In addition to pizza, the Bethel family will prepare pan-fried grouper, cracked conch, or light meals, including snacks and sandwiches. Lots of folks come here just to drink. Try their Goombay Smash, Rumrunner, or piña colada, or just a Bahamian Kalik beer.

S. Palmetto Point, right off Queen's Hwy. ✆ **242/332-1504.** Pizza $7–$24; main courses $12–$20. No credit cards. Wed–Sat and Mon 11am–3pm and 6–10pm.

Muriel's Home Made Bread and Restaurant ★ *Finds* BAHAMIAN Muriel Cooper's operation runs a bakery and a takeout food emporium. Her rich and moist pineapple and coconut cakes are some of the best you'll find in the Out Islands. A limited menu of true local cooking includes full dinners, such as chicken with chips, cracked conch, conch chowder, and conch fritters. If you want a more elaborate meal, you'll have to stop by in the morning to place your order. This is an ideal arrangement if you're staying in a cottage or villa nearby.

N. Palmetto Point. ✆ **242/332-1583.** Main courses $7–$10. No credit cards. Mon–Sat 10am–6pm.

Unique Village Restaurant & Lounge BAHAMIAN/AMERICAN This is the best place for food in the area, offering the widest selection. You can drop in for a Bahamian breakfast of boiled or stewed fish served with johnnycakes, or steamed corned beef and grits ("regular" breakfasts, including hearty omelets, are also available). Lunch offerings include zesty conch chowder and an array of salads. Burgers are served, along with what the kitchen calls "Bahamian belly pleasers," including the steamed catch of the day. At night the choices grow, and you'll find the best New York sirloin available in mid-Eleuthera, ranging in size from 8 to 16 ounces. Cracked conch fried in a light beer batter is one of the better renderings of this dish on the island.

In the Unique Village, N. Palmetto Point. ✆ **242/332-1830.** Main courses $13.95–$32. MC, V. Daily 7:30–11:30am, noon–5pm, and 6–9:30pm.

5 Governor's Harbour

At some 300 years old, Governor's Harbour is the island's oldest settlement, reportedly the landing place of the Eleutherian Adventurers. The largest town on Eleuthera after Rock Sound, it lies midway along the 161km- (100-mile-) long island; its airport is likely to be your gateway to the island.

The town today has a population of about 1,500, with some bloodlines going back to the original settlers, the Eleutherian Adventurers, and to the Loyalists who followed some 135 years later. Many old homes line the streets amid the bougainvillea and casuarina trees. **Brenda's Boutique,** Haynes Avenue (✆ **242/332-2089**), is a two-room store occupying a clapboard-sided building a few steps away from the only traffic light in Eleuthera. Inside is a large selection of T-shirts, sundresses, bathing suits, and Bahamian souvenirs like conch jewelry. Hours are Monday to Saturday 9am to 5:30pm.

ESSENTIALS

GETTING THERE See "Eleuthera Essentials: Getting There," at the beginning of this chapter, for details. The town airport is one of the island's major gateways, with daily flights arriving from Nassau and Florida.

VISITOR INFORMATION The **Eleuthera Tourist Office** is on Queens Highway (✆ **242/332-2142**); it's generally open Monday to Friday 9am to 5pm.

FAST FACTS If you're staying outside the town in a cottage or an apartment, you may find services and supplies in Governor's Harbour or at nearby Palmetto Point.

Governor's Harbour has a branch of **Barclays Bank International** on Queen's Highway (✆ **242/332-2300**).

Also on Queen's Highway is the **Governor Harbour's Medical Clinic** (✆ **242/332-2001**), open Monday through Friday from 9am to 5:30pm. The clinic is also the site of a dentist's office. The dentist is here from 9:30am until 3pm, Monday through Wednesday and Friday only. Call for an appointment before going here.

If you need the police, call ✆ **242/332-2111.**

There's a **post office** on Haynes Avenue (✆ **242/332-2060**).

WHERE TO STAY

Buccaneer Club This three-story farmhouse, built more than a century ago, offers views over the harbor. Today, it sports yellow-painted plank siding, white trim, and an old-fashioned design. The beach lies within a 10-minute stroll. Bedrooms are comfortable, unpretentious, well-maintained, clean, and outfitted with simple but colorful furniture, plus a small bathroom with a shower-tub combination Your host and hostess are Michelle and Dwight Johnson, an Indian/Bahamian entrepreneurial team who foster a calm, quiet atmosphere.

Lunch and dinner are served daily in an airy, newly built annex with island murals. Specialties include Bahamian and American standbys: steaks, burgers, club sandwiches, cracked conch, grilled grouper with lemon butter sauce, and chili.

Haynes Dr. at Buccaneer Dr. (P.O. Box 86), Governor's Harbour, Eleuthera, The Bahamas. ✆ **242/332-2000.** Fax 242/332-2888. 5 units. Mid-Dec to mid-Apr $105 double; mid-Apr to mid-Dec $94 double. DISC, MC, V. **Amenities:** Restaurant, bar; pool; laundry; babysitting; gift shop. *In room:* A/C, TV, no phone.

Duck Inn and Orchid Gardens ★ *Finds* The accommodations you'll rent here are larger, plusher, more historic, and more charming than what you'd expect in a conventional hotel. All come with kitchenettes. The complex consists of three clapboard-sided houses, each built between 80 and 175 years ago, and each almost adjacent to another, midway up a hillside overlooking the sea. Nassau-born John (J.J.) Duckworth and his Michigan-born wife, Katie, along with their son John Lucas, are your hosts. Much of their time is spent nurturing a sprawling collection of beautiful orchids being cultivated for export to Europe and the U.S. The collection of orchids, some 4,000 strong, is one of the largest in North America.

Queen's Hwy., Governor's Harbour, Eleuthera, The Bahamas. © **242/332-2608.** www.theduckinn.com. 3 units. $110 studio for 2; $220 4-bedroom cottage for up to 8. MC, V. *In room:* A/C, TV, kitchenette, no phone.

Laughing Bird Apartments These simple apartments lie near the edge of town on a beach in the center of Eleuthera and are a good bet if you want to settle in for a week or so. Efficiencies come with a living/dining/sleeping area, with a separate kitchen and a separate bathroom with shower stall. Apartments front the beach on an acre of landscaped property. The units are bright, clean, and airy.

Haynes Ave. and Birdie St. (P.O. Box EL25076), Governor's Harbour, Eleuthera, The Bahamas. © **800/688-4752** or 242/332-2012. Fax 242/332-2358. www.vrbo.com. 4 units. $95–$105 double; $115–$120 triple; $125–$130 quad. DISC, MC, V. **Amenities:** Bike rentals; garden; tables and chairs for outdoor eating; garden barbecue; arrangements made for water-skiing, surfing, fishing, sailing, tennis, golf, and snorkeling. *In room:* A/C, TV, no phone.

WHERE TO DINE

Pammy's BAHAMIAN Tile-floored and Formica-clad, this is just a little cubbyhole with a few tables. Lunchtime brings sandwiches, and dinner features platters of cracked conch, pork chops, and either broiled or fried grouper. Don't expect anything fancy, 'cause this definitely ain't it. It's a true local joint serving up generous portions of flavor-filled food.

Queen's Hwy. at Gospel Chapel Rd. © **242/332-2843.** Reservations not accepted. Breakfast platters $2–$6; lunch platters $3–$9; dinner main courses $11–$20. No credit cards. Mon–Sat 8am–9pm.

HITTING THE BEACH

Near the center of town are two sandy beaches known locally as the **Buccaneer Public Beaches;** they're adjacent to the Buccaneer Club, on the sheltered western edge of the island, facing Exuma Sound. Snorkeling is good here—it's best at the point where the pale turquoise waters near the coast deepen to a dark blue. Underwater rocks shelter lots of marine flora and fauna. The waves at these beaches are relatively calm.

On Eleuthera's Atlantic (eastern) side, about 1km (½ mile) from Governor's Harbour, is a much longer stretch of mostly pale pink sand, similar to what you'll find in Harbour Island. Known locally as the **Club Med Public Beach,** it's good for bodysurfing and, on days when storms are surging in the Atlantic, even conventional surfing.

Don't expect any touristy kiosks selling drinks, snacks, or souvenirs at any of these beaches, because everything is very pristine and undeveloped.

GOVERNOR'S HARBOUR AFTER DARK

Ronnie's Smoke Shop & Sports Bar, Cupid's Cay (© **242/332-2307**), is the most happening nightspot in central Eleuthera, drawing folks from miles in either direction. It's adjacent to the cargo depot of Cupid's Cay, in a connected cluster of simple buildings painted in combinations of black with vivid Junkanoo colors. Most folks come here just to drink Kalik beer and talk at either of the two bars. But if you want to dance, there's an all-black room just for disco music on Friday and Saturday nights. There's also the only walk-in cigar humidor on Eleuthera. If you get hungry, order up a plate of barbecue, a pizza, chicken wings, or popcorn. The place is open daily from 10am until at least 2am, and sometimes 5am, depending on business.

6 Hatchet Bay

Forty kilometers (25 miles) north of Governor's Harbour, Hatchet Bay was once known for a sprawling British-owned plantation that had 500 head of dairy cattle and thousands of chickens. Today, that plantation is gone, and this is now one of the sleepiest villages on Eleuthera, as you can see if you veer off Queen's Highway onto one of the town's ghostly main streets, Lazy Shore Road or Ocean Drive.

WHERE TO STAY & DINE

Rainbow Inn ★ Three kilometers (2 miles) south of Alice Town, and near a sandy beach, the Rainbow Inn is a venerable survivor in an area where many competitors have failed. Quirky and appealing to guests who return for quiet getaways again and again, it's an isolated collection of seven cedar-sided octagonal bungalows. The accommodations are simple but comfortable, spacious, and tidy; each has a kitchenette, lots of exposed wood, a ceiling fan, a small bathroom with a shower unit, and a porch. There's a sandy beach a few steps away.

One of the most appealing things about the place is its bar and restaurant, a destination for residents far up and down the length of Eleuthera. It's an octagon with a high-beamed ceiling and a thick-topped woodsy-looking bar where guests down daiquiris and piña coladas amid nautical trappings. It has live Bahamian music twice a week and one of the most extensive menus on Eleuthera. The owners take pride in the fact that the menu hasn't changed much in 20 years, a fact that suits its loyal fans just fine. Local Bahamian food includes fish, conch chowder, fried conch, fresh fish, and Bahamian lobster. International dishes feature French onion soup, escargots, and steaks, followed by Key lime pie for dessert. Table no. 2, crafted from a triangular teakwood prow of a motor yacht that was wrecked off the coast of Eleuthera in the 1970s, is a perpetual favorite.

P.O. Box EL25053, Governor's Harbour, Eleuthera, The Bahamas. ✆ **800/688-0047** in the U.S., or 242/335-0294. Fax 242/335-0294. www.rainbowinn.com. 5 units. $120–$150 studio; $200–$220 2- or 3-bedroom villa. MAP (breakfast and dinner) $40 extra per person. MC, V. Closed Sept 7–Nov 15. **Amenities:** Restaurant, bar; pool; tennis court (free tennis balls and rackets provided); snorkeling gear; bikes; car rental. *In room:* A/C.

7 Gregory Town

Gregory Town stands in the center of Eleuthera against a backdrop of hills, which break the usual flat monotony of the landscape. A village of clapboard cottages, it was once famed for growing pineapples. Though the industry isn't as strong as it was in the past, the locals make a good pineapple rum out of the fruit, and you can visit the Gregory Town Plantation and Distillery, where it's produced. You're allowed to sample it, and we can almost guarantee you'll want to take a bottle home with you.

WHERE TO STAY

The Cove Eleuthera On a private sandy cove 2.5km (1½ miles) northwest of Gregory Town and 5km (3 miles) southeast of the Glass Window, this year-round resort is set on 28 acres partially planted with pineapples; it consists of a main clubhouse and seven tropical-style buildings, each containing four units, nestled on the oceanside. The resort was devastated during the hurricanes of 1999, and a radical rebuilding program was needed. By late 2000, rooms were back in shape. Each one has tile floors and a porch, with no TVs or phones to

Finds For a Drop-Dead Pineapple Tart

Follow the smell of fresh-baked goods to **Thompson's Bakery,** Johnson Street (✆ **242/335-5053**), which is open Monday to Saturday 8:30am to 6pm. Run by two local sisters, Monica and Daisy Thompson, this simple bakery occupies a wooden lime-green building near the highest point in town. Although it churns out lots of bread, including raisin, whole-wheat, and coconut bread, every day, its fresh pineapple tarts, priced at $1 each, are among the best we've ever tasted. You might also find fresh-baked doughnuts and cinnamon rolls.

distract you. All accommodations are equipped with a small bathroom with shower stalls.

The restaurant (see below) serves three meals a day, and the lounge and the Pineapple Patio, poolside, are open daily for drinks and informal meals. Kayaks, bicycles, two tennis courts, and a small freshwater pool compete with hammocks for your time. There's fabulous snorkeling right off the sands here, with colorful fish darting in and out of the offshore reefs.

Queen's Hwy. (P.O. Box GT1548), Gregory Town, Eleuthera, The Bahamas. ✆ **800/552-5960** in the U.S. and Canada, or 242/335-5142. Fax 242/335-5338. www.thecoveeleuthera.com. 26 units. Winter $130–$145 double, $149 triple; off-season $110–$130 double, $120–$140 triple. 1 child under 12 stays free in parents' room. MAP (breakfast and dinner) $33 extra per person. AE, MC, V. **Amenities:** Restaurant, bar; tennis courts; pool; kayaks; bikes; snorkeling. *In room:* A/C, hair dryer, no phone.

WHERE TO DINE

Cambridge Villas BAHAMIAN This is one of the few choices in town, occupying a large cement-sided room on the ground floor of a battered hotel (the accommodations aren't as appealing as the restaurant). Harcourt and Sylvia Cambridge, the owners, serve conch burgers, conch chowder, and sandwiches, usually prepared by Sylvia herself. It's just a simple spot, where you might be entertained by the continually running soap operas broadcast from a TV over the bar.

Main St. No phone. Reservations not accepted. Sandwiches and platters $4–$10. MC, V. Daily 7:30am–9pm.

The Cove BAHAMIAN/CONTINENTAL In the previously recommended hotel 2.5km (1½ miles) north of Gregory Town, this spacious dining room is your best bet in the area. It's nothing fancy but good homemade local fare. The restaurant is decorated in a light, tropical style. Lunch begins with the inevitable conch chowder; we recommend you follow it with a conch burger, a generous patty of ground conch blended with green pepper, onion, and spices. Conch also appears several times in the evening, including the best cracked conch in town, which has been tenderized and dipped in a special batter and fried to a golden perfection. The kitchen serves the best fried chicken in the area. People travel from miles around to attend the Saturday-night $28 buffet—the smoked dolphinfish dip is reason enough to stop in. They also offer a vegetarian buffet for $17.25.

Queen's Hwy. ✆ **242/335-5142.** Breakfast $5–$10; lunch $6–$12; main courses $10–$32. AE, MC, V. Daily 8–10:30am, noon–2:30pm, and 6:30–8:30pm.

Cush's Place BAHAMIAN Macushla Scavella (Cush, for short) is the owner of this big yellow stucco-sided building set about 1km (½ mile) south of Gregory Town. Inside the somewhat sterile-looking interior, you'll find a jukebox, a pool table, and a bartender named Walter. Generous portions of Bahamian food are (slowly) served throughout the day and evening. Pork chops and chicken a la Cush (fried chicken) are ongoing staples, along with sandwiches, lobster tail, and steamed conch with black-eyed peas and corn on the cob. Come here to hang out with the locals, perhaps over drinks and a platter of food.

Queen's Hwy. ✆ **242/335-5301.** Sandwiches $2.75–$4; lunch and dinner main courses $12–$18. No credit cards. Daily 10am–midnight.

EXPLORING THE AREA: THE GLASS WINDOW & BEYOND

On Queen's Highway in the heart of town, behind a colorful facade, is the **Island Made Gift Shop** (✆ **242/335-5369**), with an outstanding inventory that owes its quality to the artistic eye and good taste of owner Pamela Thompson. Look for one-of-a-kind paintings on driftwood or crafted on the soles of discarded shoes, handmade quilts from Androsian fabrics, Abaco ceramics, and jewelry made from pieces of glass found on the beach. There are extraordinary woven baskets from the descendants of Seminole Indians and escaped slaves living in remote districts of Andros Island. Especially charming are bowls crafted from half-sections of conch shells.

Dedicated surfers have come here from as far away as California and Australia to test their skills at **Surfer's Beach,** a couple of kilometers south of town on the Atlantic side. The waves are at their highest in winter and spring; even if you're not brave enough to get out there, it's fun to watch.

South of town on the way to Hatchet Bay are several caverns worth visiting, the largest of which is called simply **the Cave.** It has a big fig tree out front, which the people of Gregory Town claim was planted long ago by area pirates who wanted to conceal the cave because they had hidden treasure in it.

Local guides (you have to ask around in Gregory Town or Hatchet Bay) will take you into the interior of the cave, where the resident bats are harmless (even though they must resent the intrusion of tourists with flashlights). At one point the drop is so steep—about 3.5m (12 ft.)—that you have to use a ladder to climb down. Eventually, you reach a cavern studded with stalactites and stalagmites. At this point, a maze of passageways leads off through the rocky underground recesses. The cave comes to an abrupt end at the edge of a cliff, where the thundering sea is some 27m (90 ft.) below.

After leaving Gregory Town and driving north, you come to the famed **Glass Window,** Eleuthera's chief sight and narrowest point. Once a natural rock arch bridged the land, but it's gone now, replaced by an artificially constructed bridge. As you drive across it, you can see the contrast between the deep blue ocean and the emerald green shoal waters of the sound. The rocks rise to a height of 21m (70 ft.). Often, as ships in the Atlantic are being tossed about, the crew looks across the narrow point to see a ship resting quietly on the other side. Hence the name Glass Window. Winslow Homer was so captivated by this spot that he once captured it on canvas.

GREGORY TOWN AFTER DARK

The place to be in Gregory Town, especially on a Saturday night, is **Elvina** on Main Street (✆ **242/335-5032**). Owners Ed and Elvina Watkins make you feel right at home and practically greet you at the door with a cold beer. Surfers and locals alike flock here to chow down on burgers, Bahamian dishes, and Cajun grub, served daily from 10am to "whenever we close." Elvina's husband, "Chicken Ed," is from Louisiana, makes great jambalaya.

8 The Current

The inhabitants of the Current, a settlement in North Eleuthera, are believed to have descended from a tribe of Native Americans. A narrow strait separates the village from Current Island, where most of the locals make their living from the sea or from plaiting straw goods.

This is a small community where the people often welcome visitors. There are no crowds and no artificial attractions. Everything focuses on the sea, a source of pleasure for the visiting tourists, but a way to sustain life for the local people.

From the Current, you can explore some interesting sights in North Eleuthera, including **Preacher's Cave,** where the Eleutherian Adventurers found shelter in the mid–17th century when they were shipwrecked with no provisions. (Note that your taxi driver may balk at being asked to drive there; the road is hard on his expensive tires.) If you do reach it, you'll find a cave that seems like an amphitheater. The very devout Eleutherian Adventurers held religious services inside the cave, which is pierced by holes in the roof, allowing light to intrude. The cave is not far from the airport, in a northeasterly direction. Another sight is **Boiling Hole,** which is in a shallow bank that seems to boil at changing tides.

WHERE TO STAY

Sandcastle Apartments For escapists seeking a location far removed from the usual tourist circuit, this utterly plain but airy accommodation is a good bet. The on-site kitchen, the easy access to a simple grocery store within a 5-minute walk, and the self-contained nature of this extremely modest accommodation often appeal to families. There is a double bed in the bedroom, a queen-size pullout bed in the living room, and a view over shallow offshore waters, where children can wade safely for a surprisingly long distance offshore. The accommodation comes with a small bathroom with a shower stall. The unit lies just across the road from the sea, and if you want to explore, bicycles are available.

The Current, Eleuthera, The Bahamas. ✆ **242/335-3244.** Fax 242/393-0440. 1 unit. $75–$90 double. Extra person $10. No credit cards. *In room:* A/C.

9 Harbour Island ★★★

One of the oldest settlements in The Bahamas, founded before the United States was a nation, Harbour Island lies off the northern end of Eleuthera, some 322km (200 miles) from Miami. It is 5km (3 miles) long and 1km (½ mile) wide.

Affectionately called "Briland," Harbour Island is studded with good resorts. The spectacular **Pink Sands Beach** ★★★ runs the whole length of the island on its eastern side. The famous beach is protected from the ocean breakers by an outlying coral reef, which makes for some of the safest swimming in The Bahamas. Except for unseasonably cold days, you can swim and enjoy watersports year-round. The climate averages 72°F in winter, 77°F in spring and fall, and 82°F in summer. Occasionally, evenings are cool, with a low of about 65°F from November to February.

ESSENTIALS

GETTING THERE To reach Harbour Island, take a flight to the **North Eleuthera airstrip,** which is only a 1½-hour flight from Fort Lauderdale or Miami and a 30-minute flight from Nassau (see "Eleuthera Essentials: Getting There," at the beginning of this chapter, for details on which airlines provide service). From there, it's a 1.5km (1-mile) taxi ride to the ferry dock. The taxi costs about $4 per person if you share the expense with other passengers. From the dock, you'll take a 3km (2-mile) motorboat ride to Harbour Island. There's usually no waiting, because a flotilla of high-powered motorboats makes the crossing whenever at least two customers show up, at a cost of around $5 per person. (If you're traveling alone and are willing to pay the $8 one-way fare, the boat will depart immediately, without waiting for a second passenger.)

GETTING AROUND Once they reach Harbour Island, most people don't need transportation. They walk to where they're going, rent a bicycle (check your equipment carefully before you rent it, since some bicycles rented to tourists on Harbour Island are way past their prime), or putt-putt around the island on an electric golf cart. Most hotels offer these for rent, or at least will arrange for a cart or bicycle; usually, they'll be delivered directly to your hotel.

If you want to go some distance on the island, call **Big M Taxi Service** at **© 242/333-2043.**

Michael's Cycles on Colebrook Street (**© 242/333-2384**) is the best place to go if you want some mobility other than your own two feet. The shop is open daily from 8am to 7pm. Bikes rent for $10 per day, and you can also rent two-seater motorbikes for $30 a day, or even a two-seater golf cart for between $40 and $48 per day, depending on the model.

VISITOR INFORMATION The **Harbour Island Tourist Office** is on Bay Street (**© 242/333-2621**); it's generally open Monday to Friday 9am to 5pm.

FAST FACTS **The Royal Bank of Canada** is just up the hill from the city dock (**© 242/333-2250**).

The Harbour Island Health Centre, South Street, Dunmore Town (**© 242/333-2227**), handles routine medical problems. Hours are Monday through Friday from 9am to 5pm. The on-call doctor can be reached at **© 242/333-2822.** **Harbour Pharmacy Health Care and Prescription Service** can be found on the waterfront near the corner of King Street (**© 242/333-2514**). It sells health-and-beauty aids, fills prescriptions, and offers over-the-counter drugs Monday to Saturday 8am to 9pm.

The police can be reached at either **© 919** or **© 242/333-2111.**

WHERE TO STAY

VERY EXPENSIVE

Dunmore Beach Club ★★★ This formal and very exclusive colony of cottages is the quintessentially elegant hideaway, with 8 acres of well-manicured grounds along the island's legendary 5km (3-mile) pink-sand beach. It's not as elaborate or sleek as its nearest rival, Pink Sands, but it's cozier and, in a way, more posh. Renovations in 1999 brought it up to the standards of the very best accommodations in Harbour Island; huge showers and whirlpool tubs are all-new and the air-conditioning system is state-of-the-art. The Bahamian-style bungalows attractively combine traditional furnishings and tropical accessories, with no phones or TVs to distract you. Overall, the feeling is dignified, comfortable, and very pleasant.

Breakfast is offered on a garden terrace under pine trees with a view of the beach. Dinner is served, at one sitting, at 8pm; men must wear jackets (ties are optional). Superb Bahamian and international cuisine is served formally in a dining room with a beamed ceiling, louvered doors, Villeroy & Bosch china, and windows with views over the blue Atlantic. A clubhouse is the focal point for socializing; a living room with a library and fireplace provides additional cozy nooks, as does an oceanview bar.

Colebrook Lane (P.O. Box EL27122), Harbour Island, The Bahamas. ✆ **877/891-3100** or 242/333-2200. Fax 242/333-2429. www.dunmorebeach.com. 14 units. Nov–Apr $445–$480 double, $520 suite; off-season $390–$415 double, $440 suite. Winter rates include all meals; off-season rates include MAP (breakfast and dinner). MC, V. Closed Sept–Oct. **Amenities:** Restaurant, bar/lounge; laundry; babysitting; bike rental; tennis court. *In room:* A/C, hair dryer, safe, no phone.

Pink Sands ★★★ This is a posh and sophisticated hideaway, just the place to sneak away to with that special (wealthy) someone, adjacent to a 5km (3-mile) stretch of pink sand beach, sheltered by a barrier reef. Yes, that was Julia Roberts in a bikini we spotted leaving the cottage next door. It's an elegant, relaxed retreat on a 28-acre beachfront estate; it feels a bit like a pricey private club, but it's less snobbish and a lot more hip than the Dunmore Beach Club. Its owner is Chris Blackwell, the founder of Island Records, who is increasingly known as a hotel entrepreneur and who spared no expense here. The resort's outrageous clubhouse is the most beautifully and imaginatively decorated room in the Out Islands.

The airy, spacious bedrooms have either an ocean or a garden view. Smaller units contain art-deco touches straight out of Miami's South Beach; larger, more expensive units have Indonesian (especially Balinese) furnishings and art, and huge decks. All rooms have kitchenettes or kitchens, central air-conditioning, pressurized water systems, walk-in closets, satellite TVs, CD players and a CD selection, wet bars, private patios with teak furnishings, and beautifully tiled bathrooms with tubs and showers. The interior design features marble floors with area rugs, oversize Adirondack furnishings, local artwork, and batik fabrics. The rooms have dataports, and fax machines and cellular phones can be supplied if you need them.

Hotel guests get some of the best meals on the island, an ABC fusion of Asian, Bahamian, and Caribbean cuisine. Dinner is a four-course nightly affair, included in the MAP price for guests and priced at $70 per person, without drinks, for nonguests who phone ahead for reservations. Lunches are much less formal, served in the Blue Bar, a postmodern pavilion beside the beach.

Chapel St., Harbour Island, The Bahamas. ✆ **800/OUTPOST** or 242/333-2030. Fax 242/333-2060. www.islandoutpost.com/PinkSands/. 25 units. Winter $655–$765 1-bedroom cottage, $1,150–$2,100 2-bedroom cottage; off-season $500–$600 1-bedroom cottage, $925–$1,300 2-bedroom cottage. Rates include MAP (breakfast and dinner). AE, MC, V. **Amenities:** Restaurant, bar; freshwater pool; 3 tennis courts; personal laundry services; gym; clubhouse; beach palapa/tiki bar; gift shop. *In room:* A/C, TV, VCR, coffeemaker, hair dryer, safe.

Romora Bay Club ★ This is one of the quirkiest, most cosmopolitan hotels on Harbour Island. It's more akin to the whimsy and music-industry celebrity chic of Pink Sands than anything else, but here the price tag's lower, there's a stronger French flavor, and the design isn't as self-conscious. It was originally developed as a private club for reclusive millionaires. Later, Lionel Rotcage, the French-born son of Paris's leading nightlife impresario (Régine), rebuilt all rooms with the flair of Morocco, central Africa, or Italy—and sometimes all three, always with lots of postmodern whimsy, unusual tile work, and bold colors. The guests tend to range in age from 25 to 50 and tend to view it as a private club, where hanging out with a chic international crowd is part of the entertainment. The social center is a dramatic living room with oversize art (one piece is a Picasso). Thanks to a cooperative arrangement with a local dive outfit, the place is a favorite spot for divers (see "Beaches & Watersports," later in this chapter). Bungalows and villas are spacious and newly refurbished, with bright Caribbean colors, and comfortable king-size or twin beds. Most of the units come with a large bathroom with tub or shower combos. Check into numbers 7, 8, or 9 for the most panoramic views.

Lunches in the hotel's Restaurant Ludo (see "Where to Dine," below) tend to be buffet-style, featuring light-textured but elegant salads and warm-weather foods. Dinners are more formal, prepared by a young highly skilled chef, Thomas Chiarell whose culinary expertise is sure to prove worthy of all your dining needs. All flights are met at the airport by taxis for the 1.5km (1-mile) drive to the ferry dock, and there's a 3km (2-mile) ferry ride direct to the club's private dock.

Colebrook St., Harbour Island, The Bahamas. ✆ **800/688-0425** in the U.S., or 242/333-2325. Fax 242/333-2500. www.romorabay.com. 22 units. Winter $300–$400 double, $540–$580 suite; off-season $220–$320 double, $440–$480 suite. Rates include breakfast and lunch. AE, MC, V. **Amenities:** Restaurant, bar; pool; tennis courts; Sunfish rentals; deep-sea fishing; garden; access to sandy beach. *In room:* A/C, TV, hair dryer.

EXPENSIVE

Coral Sands ★★ The hotel, whose exterior is painted a soft coral pink, stands on 9 hilly acres overlooking the beach and within walking distance of the center of Dunmore Town. Coral Sands is a longtime favorite that does a big business with happy repeat visitors. Originally built with an airy design that featured big-windowed loggias and arcades, it opens directly onto the 5km (3-mile) pink-coral-sand beach for which the town is famous. Casual elegance, with ample doses of personal charm and friendliness, permeates every aspect of this hotel. Recent renovations and improvements have revitalized the property and freshened up the decor. Many rooms have private verandas or terraces, all are eminently comfortable, and all allow you to fall asleep to the soothing sounds of waves breaking on the shore. The owners are Latex Foam Products (LIS, Inc.) of Ansonia, Connecticut, so all beds have the antibacterial, dust-mite-resistant latex mattresses produced by this company. Bathrooms are midsize and well-kept, mostly with shower and tub combos.

The hotel's restaurant, The Poseidon, offers the finest cuisine on Harbour Island (see "Where to Dine," below). Simpler, less elaborate food is also offered at the beachfront Commander's Beach Bar & Restaurant, which is dramatically cantilevered high above the pale pink sands.

Chapel St., Harbour Island, The Bahamas. ✆ **800/468-2799** in the U.S. and Canada, or 242/333-2350. Fax 242/333-2368. www.coralsands.com. 39 units. Winter $215–$330 double, $345–$450 1-bedroom suite, $450–$695 2-bedroom suite; off-season $205–$265 double, $260–$325 1-bedroom suite, $325–$475 2-bedroom suite. MAP (breakfast and dinner) $25 extra per person. AE, MC, V. **Amenities:** Restaurant, beach bar and restaurant; free-form swimming pool; tennis court; boogie boards; snorkeling equipment; cabanas; sailboat rental. *In room:* A/C, hair dryer, safe, coffeemaker, kitchens (some units).

Runaway Hill Club Small and intimate, this conservative, comfortable hotel overlooks acres of pink sandy beachfront. It has a huge lawn and is separated from Colebrook Street by a wall. The building's original English colonial dormers are still prominent, as are many of its original features. In winter, a crackling fire is sometimes built in the hearth near the entrance. The social center is a cheerfully decorated lounge/dining room/bar/reception area painted in joyful island colors with a sense of Bahamian whimsy. Each of the bedrooms is different, giving the impression that you are lodging in a private home—as indeed this used to be. Only two of the rooms at this place are in the original house, and these are accessible via the building's original 18th-century staircase. The others are within comfortable annexes built during the '70s and '80s. Bathrooms are small but well-maintained, and seven contain tub-and-shower combos, the rest showers.

Dinners are served on the breeze-filled rear porch overlooking the swimming pool, and nonguests are welcome (see "Where to Dine," below).

Colebrook St. (P.O. Box EL27031), Harbour Island, The Bahamas. ✆ **800/728-9803** in the U.S., or 242/333-2150. Fax 242/333-2420. www.runawayhill.com. 10 units. Winter $250–$260 double; off-season $230–$245 double. MAP (breakfast and dinner) $60 extra per person. AE, MC, V. Closed Sept 5–Nov 15. No children under 18 accepted. **Amenities:** Restaurant, bar; pool; bike rental; fishing trips; watersports; laundry. *In room:* A/C, safe, no phone.

MODERATE

The Landing ★★ This intimate inn is understated, tasteful, and lovely. Virtually destroyed by a hurricane in 1999, it was well-restored by its owners, Tracy and Brenda Barry, the latter a former Miss Bahamas. The first doctor on Harbour Island built the house in the 1850s as his private residence. It's set within a pair of stone and clapboard-sided buildings constructed in 1800 and 1820, respectively, very close to the piers where ferryboats arrive from Eleuthera. A veranda looks out over the harbor. Accommodations are breezy, airy, and high-ceilinged, and they open onto wraparound verandas, which seem to expand the living space within. Expect bold, cheerful island colors, and design touches that evoke the seafaring days of old Harbour Island. The bathrooms are large and tiled, with tubs and showers.

Bay St. (P.O. Box 190), Harbour Island, The Bahamas. ✆ **242/333-2707.** Fax 242/333-2650. www.harbourislandlanding.com. 7 units. Mid-Dec to mid-Apr $205–$295 double. Rates 10% lower off-season. Rates include breakfast. MC, V. **Amenities:** Restaurant, bar; laundry; kayak rental; library. *In room:* A/C, no phone.

INEXPENSIVE

Bahama House Inn ★ *Finds* This is the only true B&B, with the owners living on-site, on Harbour Island. The setting is a pink-sided clapboard house that was built between 1798 and 1800 by the island's first justice of the peace, Dr. Johnson. In 1999, Denver-born owners John and Joni Hersh bought a 1950s-era house next door for future expansions. Midsize rooms are artfully old-fashioned, low-key, and comfortable, and they are usually accessible via gracious verandas that wrap around the upper and lower floors. Bathrooms are tiled, beautifully maintained, and come with shower stalls. Everything shows a personal touch here, including the beautiful gardens. The beach is a 5-minute walk away, and the house's living room has satellite TV.

At the corner of Dunmore and Hill sts., Harbour Island, The Bahamas. ✆ **242/333-2201.** Fax 242/333-2850. www.bahamahouseinn.com. 7 units. Winter $135–$155 double; off-season $105–$130 double. Rates include breakfast. MC, V. Closed Sept–Oct. *In room:* A/C, ceiling fan, kitchenette (1 unit), no phone.

Tingum Village This is a simple, no-frills choice, but it does the trick at bargain prices and draws a loyal repeat business. It lies just off the main street, a 3-minute walk to the beach. Set in a steamy tropical garden, Tingum Village offers basic accommodations in small cement-sided bungalows. Each of the rooms has air-conditioning, ceiling fans, and a patio with plastic furniture, plus a small bathroom with a shower stall. Rooms aren't the most comfortable, and you'll really wish they'd improve the wattage in the reading lamps, and that the ceiling fans wouldn't squeak. But it has its charming moments as well. The cottage is meant for six to eight people, though it can hold up to 10 (but that would be very cramped).

The hotel's restaurant, Ma Ruby's, overlooks the garden and offers standard Bahamian and American food (see "Where to Dine," below).

P.O. Box 61, Colebrook St., Harbour Island, Eleuthera, The Bahamas. ✆ **242/333-2161.** Fax 242/333-2161. 19 units. Winter $105–$135 double, $95–$145 triple, $250 cottage; off-season $85–$125 double, $95 triple, $200 cottage. MC, V. **Amenities:** Restaurant, bar; some room service; laundry; babysitting. *In room:* A/C, no phone.

WHERE TO DINE

If you don't want to dress up for lunch, you can head for **Seaview Takeaway** (✆ **242/333-2542**), at the foot of the ferry dock. Here you can feast on all that good stuff: pig's feet, sheep-tongue souse, and most definitely cracked conch. Everything tastes better with fungi or rice 'n' peas. Daily specials range from $3 to $8, and service is Monday to Saturday 9am to 5pm.

EXPENSIVE

The Landing ★ INTERNATIONAL This restaurant occupies the ground floor and most of the garden of the previously recommended hotel, a stately looking antique building that's just to the right of the dock as your ferryboat pulls into Harbour Island. Designed and built with a combination of thick stone walls and clapboards in 1800, with an annex that's only 20 years younger, it's the domain of Brenda Barry and her daughter and son-in-law Tracy and Toby Tyler. Their cuisine derives from the talent of Aussie-born Jennifer Learmonth, who blends her natural talents with international training.

The menu changes with the availability of fresh ingredients but might include conch and sweet-corn chowder, or capellini with lobster, braised romaine, chili, and lime juice. Other pleasing choices include linguine with pesto and mozzarella, fried squid with aïoli, and Angus tenderloin with green peppercorns.

Bay St. ✆ **242/333-2707.** Reservations recommended. Lunch main courses $12–$22; dinner main courses $18–$38. MC, V. Sun 9am–2pm; Thurs–Tues 6–10pm.

The Poseidon ★ INTERNATIONAL This is one of the finest restaurants in The Bahamas, thanks to executive chef Susan Neff, a passionate devotee of her craft, who has a high-energy, highly humorous approach to cuisine and life. She's usually on hand to greet diners before or after their meal. Start off with the house drink (a version of Pimm's Cup called Commander's Choice) at the bar, and then you'll be seated on a terrace overlooking the sea. Signature dishes include Poseidon lobster, served with a sauce made from Italian asiago cheese and sauvignon blanc. White conch chowder is as superb as it is unusual, based as it is on New England–style clam chowder but not seen as often as you'd think.

Finds **Ma Ruby's Conch Burger**

If you'd like to sample some real local fare, head to **Ma Ruby's** on Colebrook Street (✆ **242/333-2161**). Some islanders claim you will get the best meal in Eleuthera if Ma Ruby (the cook and owner) is personally in the kitchen. Her conch burger is certainly worthy of an award. She's been stewing chicken, baking grouper, and serving hearty meals in a trellised courtyard for a long while, and she's got a lot of devoted fans. The place is well-known for its cheeseburgers, which the manager says were ranked as one of the 10 best in the world by "Mr. Cheeseburger in Paradise" himself, Jimmy Buffett. The prices range from $6 to $18 for the a la carte menu; a four-course fixed-price Bahamian dinner costs $18 to $35. The restaurant is open daily 8am to midnight.

Yellowfin tuna in an Asian marinade carries the aromas of ginger, soy, Eleutherian honey, fresh tangerines, and sesame seed. Dessert might be an amaretto chocolate mousse. Many of the herbs used to flavor Ms. Neff's dishes are grown a few steps from the kitchen.

In the Coral Sands hotel, Chapel St. ✆ **242/333-2350.** Reservations recommended. Main courses $18–$30. AE, MC, V. Daily 7–9pm.

Restaurant Ludo FRENCH/INTERNATIONAL The French-inspired meals at the Dunmore Beach Club are traditional, impeccably orchestrated affairs, but the Romora Bay Club's restaurant, its leading competitor, is all sleek French chic. The trendiness doesn't detract from what might be a charming meal—it just means that you should be prepared for the unpredictable. You'll dine on a covered terrace. The menu changes according to the season and the chef's inspiration, but it might include a tartine of potatoes with foie gras, grouper or red snapper cooked in a salt crust (the flavor is flaky and delicious), and mahimahi with a lemon and ginger sauce. Dessert might consist of a slice of chocolate cake, with the moist chocolate artfully arranged to seem half-melted.

In the Romora Bay Club, Colebrook St. ✆ **242/333-2325.** Reservations recommended. Fixed-price 4-course menu $65. AE, MC, V. Daily 7:30–9pm.

Runaway Hill Club ★ BAHAMIAN/AMERICAN/INTERNATIONAL The dining room here enjoys a sweeping view over the beachfront. Inside, the decor is brightly painted in strong, whimsical colors, with wicker and rattan furniture and a fine collection of watercolors the owner has spent years collecting. The kitchen is known for such well-prepared dishes as rack of veal with a sherry-flavored caper sauce and noodles, conch marinara, crabmeat soup with scotch, spicy lobster bisque, beef tenderloin, and many versions of local fish.

Colebrook St. ✆ **242/333-2150.** Reservations required. Fixed-price dinner from $60. AE, MC, V. Mon–Sat dinner at 8pm. Closed Sept 5–Nov 15.

MODERATE

The Harbour Lounge INTERNATIONAL This old clapboard-sided building is the first place you're likely to see as you step off the ferryboat arriving from the "mainland" of Eleuthera. Built in the early 1800s, it's one of the most satisfying and authentic choices on the island. Sometimes dining here is like attending an island dinner party. These might be followed with such menu items as marinated blackened grouper, soft-shell or stone crabs, lobster tail, different preparations of conch, and a combination of feta cheese and shrimp marinara. Overall, it's a charming place, and the veranda will give you a front-row seat for all the goings-on of Harbour Island.

Bay St. ✆ **242/333-2031.** Reservations recommended for dinner. Lunch salads, sandwiches, platters $9–$13.50; dinner main courses $18–$35. MC, V. Tues–Sun noon–2:30pm and 6–9:30pm.

INEXPENSIVE

Angela's Starfish Restaurant BAHAMIAN/AMERICAN This is the local joint where many of the islanders go themselves, and it serves the most authentic Eleutherian cuisine. Residents as well as visitors plan their Sunday around an evening meal here, although it's equally crowded on other nights. Run by Bahamians Angela and Vincent Johnson, the house sits on a hill above the channel in a residential section somewhat removed from the center of town. Angela can often be seen in the kitchen baking. Cracked conch and an array of seafood are specialties, and chicken potpie and pork chops are also favorites. You can dine on the palm-dotted lawn with its simple tables and folding chairs, although for chilly weather there's an unpretentious dining room inside near the cramped kitchen. It can get quite festive at night, after the candles are lit and the crowd becomes jovial.

Dunmore and Grant sts. ✆ **242/333-2253.** Reservations required. Breakfast $4–$7; lunch $3–$10; main courses $13–$25. No credit cards. Daily 8am–8:30pm.

Avery's Restaurant & Grill BAHAMIAN From the moment you enter, you'll get the immediate sense that this is a simple, friendly, family-run restaurant. It occupies a tiny wooden house, painted in pastel tones of purple, green, and pink, near Tingum Village. Inside, you'll find a clean, white-tiled room with no more than four tables, and a deck with three more. Gaylean Cleare and her daughter, Avery, are the owners. Their breakfasts provide nourishment to city employees around town. The rest of the day, sandwiches and platters of seafood and steaks emerge steaming from the kitchens in an unending stream.

Colebrook St. ✆ **242/333-3126.** Reservations not accepted. Breakfast and lunch platters $3–$10; dinner main courses $10–$28. MC, V. Daily 6:30am–10pm.

BEACHES & WATERSPORTS

Pink Sands Beach is our favorite beach in all The Bahamas; its sands stretch for 5 uninterrupted kilometers (3 miles). Although the beach is set against a backdrop of low-rise hotels and villas, it still feels tranquil and pristine. The sun is best in the morning (afternoons start to become shadowy), and waves are generally gentle, owing to an offshore reef that breaks the waves coming in from the Atlantic. There are many good places for snorkeling, and this also is the best place on the island for a long, leisurely morning stroll.

Big Red Rentals (✆ **242/333-2045**) rents boats and snorkel gear, and offers various snorkel cruises and other outings.

The **diving** in this part of The Bahamas is among the most diverse in the region. The most spectacular dive site, judged among the 10 top dives in the world, is the **Current Cut Dive** ★★★. One of the fastest (9 knots) drift dives in the world, it involves descending into the fast-moving current racing between the rock walls that define the underwater chasm between Eleuthera and Current Island. Swept up in the currents with schools of stingrays, mako sharks, and reef fish, divers are propelled along 1km (½ mile) of underwater distance in less than 10 minutes. The dive may be one of the highlights of your whole life.

Valentine's Dive Center, Harbourfront (✆ **242/333-2080** or 242/333-2142), maintains a full range of dive activities. The dive center is in a wooden building near the entrance to Valentine's Marina. Lessons in snorkeling and scuba diving for beginners are given daily at 10am. Snorkeling from a boat costs $35 for a half-day tour. A full certification course for scuba is taught for $650. Single-tank dives, daily at 9:30am and 1:30pm, cost $45; two-tank dives go for $65; and night dives (four divers minimum) are $60 per person.

SHOPPING

Miss Mae's Tea Room and Fine Things, Dunmore Street (✆ **242/333-2002**), lives up to its billing. It's one of the island's finest boutiques, with not only standard T-shirts and bathing suits, but also antique furniture, jewelry, books, and even cups and dishes.

Works by local artists are for sale at the **Sugar Mill** (✆ **242/333-2173**), which also sells Bahamian coin jewelry and shell objects gathered in Eleuthera.

Briland's Ambrosia (✆ **242/333-2342**) sells the best selection of bathing suits, with bright batik fabrics printed on the island of North Andros.

Finally, check out **Princess Street Gallery** (© **242/333-2788**), where Charles Carey has restored an ancestral home and uses it as a showcase to display works by local artists.

HARBOUR ISLAND AFTER DARK

Unpretentious **Gusty's,** Coconut Grove Avenue (© **242/333-2165**), boasts sweeping sea and sunset views. Inside, you'll find a sand-covered floor, while the outdoor veranda is sometimes the scene of fashion shows of local dressmakers. Live music by a DJ is featured every night.

Seagrapes, Colebrook Street (no phone), is another favorite place of the locals, where you can boogie down to the sounds of disco or catch a live band. Expect to be jostled and crowded on a Saturday night, because everyone on the island comes here for a wild Bahamian hoedown.

Vic-Hum Club, Barracks Street (© **242/333-2161**), established in 1955, is the quintessential Harbour Island dive. Walls have been layered with the covers of hundreds of record albums and sports posters that music-industry and basketball buffs find fascinating. The Vic-Hum is open 24 hours a day, catering to breakfasting construction workers in the morning, and locals meeting friends for a beer all afternoon. Some of them play basketball on an indoor court that's transformed later in the evening into a dance floor (disco music begins at 10pm every Fri and Sat).

10 Spanish Wells

Called a "quiet corner of The Bahamas," Spanish Wells is a colorful cluster of houses on St. George's Cay, 1km (½ mile) off the coast of northwest Eleuthera. It is characterized by its sparkling bays and white beaches, sleepy lagoons, excellent diving, and fine fishing colony.

You can walk or bicycle through the village, looking at the houses, some more than 200 years old, which have New England saltbox styling but bright tropical coloring. You can see handmade quilts in many colors, following patterns handed down from generations of English ancestors. Homeowners display these quilts on their front porches or out their windows, and they are for sale. No one locks doors here or removes ignition keys from cars.

GETTING THERE

To reach the island, you can fly to the **airstrip on North Eleuthera,** from which taxis will deliver you to the ferry dock. Regardless of the time of day you arrive, a ferryboat will be either waiting for passengers or about to arrive with a load of them.

A boat runs between Gene's Bay in North Eleuthera to the main pier at Spanish Wells. The ferries depart whenever passengers show up, and the cost is $10 per person round-trip.

WHERE TO STAY

The Adventurer's Resort Since the 1999 hurricane demolished all the competition, this has emerged as the most appealing, most solid-looking, and most recommendable hotel in Spanish Wells. It occupies a two-story, pale lavender-colored building in a well-tended garden about .5km (¼ mile) west of the town center. There's no restaurant or bar on-site, but the staff member will direct you to nearby eateries and to the beach, which lies about 1km (½ mile) away. The small bedrooms have simple, durable furniture with tropical upholstery; six of the units are apartments with kitchenettes. Each comes with a shower-tub combination. Maid service is provided when you rent the regular double room, but not the apartments.

Harbourfront (P.O. Box EI 27498), Spanish Wells, The Bahamas. ✆ **242/333-4883.** Fax 242/333-5073. www.bahamasvg.com. 18 units. $75 double; $110 1-bedroom apt with kitchenette, $165 2-bedroom apt with kitchenette. AE, MC, V. **Amenities:** Laundry. *In room:* A/C, TV, no phone.

WHERE TO DINE

Jack's Outback BAHAMIAN Decent, unpretentious, and well-scrubbed, this little place stands along the waterfront in the heart of town. There's a hint of funkiness here, in its luncheonette-style combination of wood, plastic, and Formica, and its color scheme of pink and blue. Known for its home-cooking, it offers the usual array of sandwiches and cheeseburgers, as well as Bahamian foods like cracked conch, conch burgers, and conch chowder. There are also steaks, barbecued ribs, and cheesy shrimp poppers. The interior is air-conditioned, with views of the sea.

Harbourfront, Spanish Wells, The Bahamas. ✆ **242/333-4219.** Sandwiches $2.50–$10; main courses $12–$26. MC, V. Daily 8:30am–1am.

9

The Exuma Islands

The Exumas are some of the prettiest islands in The Bahamas. Shades of jade, aquamarine, and amethyst in deeper waters turn to transparent opal near sandy shores: The water and the land appear almost inseparable. Sailors and their crews like to stake out their own private beaches and tropical hideaways, and several vacation retreats have been built by wealthy Europeans, Canadians, and Americans.

A spiny, sandy chain of islands, the Exumas, which begin just 56km (35 miles) southeast of Nassau, stretch more than 161km (100 miles) from Beacon Cay in the north to Hog Cay and Sandy Cay in the south. These islands have not been developed like the Abacos and Eleuthera, so they are relatively inexpensive. But they still have much to offer, with crystal-clear waters on the west around the Great Bahama Bank and the 1,500m- (5,000-ft.) deep Exuma Sound on the east, uninhabited cays ideal for picnics, rolling hills, ruins of once-great plantations, and coral formations of great beauty. Although they're crossed by the Tropic of Cancer, the islands have average temperatures ranging from the mid-70s to the mid-80s.

Most of our resort recommendations are in and around George Town, the pretty, pink capital of the Exumas, on Great Exuma. A community of some 900 residents, it was once considered a possible site for the capital of The Bahamas because of its excellent **Elizabeth Harbour** (see "Exploring Georgetown," below).

Nearly all the other cays are uninhabited or sparsely populated. Over the years, remote accommodations have come and gone on these islands. Today, the only resort hotels, which attract mostly the yachting set, are found at Staniel Cay and Sampson Cay.

The cruising grounds around the Exumas, which are scattered over an ocean area of 233 square km (90 sq. miles), are among the finest to be found in the western hemisphere, if not in the world, for both sail- and powerboats. The **sailing** rivals both those of the Grenadines in the Caribbean and the Abacos in The Bahamas. Which one yachters prefer depends on personal taste; each is paradise, if you're a boater. If you don't come in your own craft, you can rent one here, from a simple little Daysailer to a fishing runabout, with or without a guide. The annual regatta in April in Elizabeth Harbour has attracted such notables as Prince Philip and the ex-king of Greece, Constantine. The Exumas are often referred to by yachting people as "where you go when you die if you've been good."

Snorkeling and scuba-diving opportunities draw aficionados from around the world to the **Exuma Cays National Land and Sea Park** ★★★, a vast underwater preserve, and to the exotic limestone and coral reefs, blue holes, drop-offs, caves, and night dives. Dive centers in George Town and Staniel Cay provide air fills and diving equipment.

Fishing is superb here, and the "flats" on the west side of Great Exuma are famous for bonefishing. You can find (if you're lucky) blue marlin on both sides of Exuma Sound, as well as sailfish, wahoo, and white marlin, plus numerous others.

The Exumas are among the friendliest islands in The Bahamas; the people are warmhearted and not (yet) spoiled by tourism. They seem genuinely delighted to receive and welcome visitors to their shores. They grow a lot of their own food, including cassava, onions, cabbages, and pigeon peas, on the acres their ancestors worked as slaves. Many fruits grow on the cays, including guavas, mangoes, and avocados. You can watch these fruits being loaded at Government Wharf in George Town for shipment to Nassau. The sponge industry is being revived locally; this product of the sea is found in shallow waters and creeks to the south side of the Exumas.

EXUMAS ESSENTIALS

GETTING THERE

BY PLANE The Exumas' major commercial airport—the **Exuma International Airport**—is 16km (10 miles) from George Town, the capital. The most popular way to visit the Exumas is to fly there aboard **Bahamasair** (**© 800/222-4262**), which has daily service from Nassau to George Town. A flight usually leaves Nassau in the morning sometime between 6:15 and 6:45am, depending on the day. There are also midafternoon flights on Monday, Friday, and Saturday. Be sure and call ahead because flight schedules are subject to change.

American Eagle (**© 800/433-7300**) serves Exuma from Miami daily.

Other minor carriers servicing the archipelago include **Lynx Air International** (**© 888/596-9247**), with air links from Fort Lauderdale. **Air Sunshine** (**© 800/327-8900** or 954/434-8900) flies from Fort Lauderdale, but only on Sunday and Thursday. Returns are possible aboard this airline on Monday and Friday.

For flights to the private airstrip at Staniel Cay, refer to section 3 of this chapter.

BY MAIL BOAT Several mail boats leave from Potter's Cay Dock in Nassau, stopping at various points along the Exumas.

The **MV *Grand Master*** goes from Nassau to George Town. Departures are on Tuesday at 2pm with a return to Nassau on Friday morning.

Since hours and sailing schedules are subject to change because of weather conditions, it's best to check with the dockmaster at **Potter's Cay Dock** in Nassau (**© 242/393-1064**).

Finds Saddle Cay: The Perfect Beach

For years boaters have known of a special beach, **Saddle Cay,** whose horseshoe-shaped curve lies near the northern tip of the small archipelago. The only way to reach it is by private boat; there are no organized excursions or tours (the Exumas are much too laid-back for that). However, if you own a boat, head for Saddle Cay, and you won't be disappointed when you see this totally unspoiled beach of white sands and tranquil waters. The cay is perfect for beachcombers, bird-watchers, and snorkelers—but don't expect facilities.

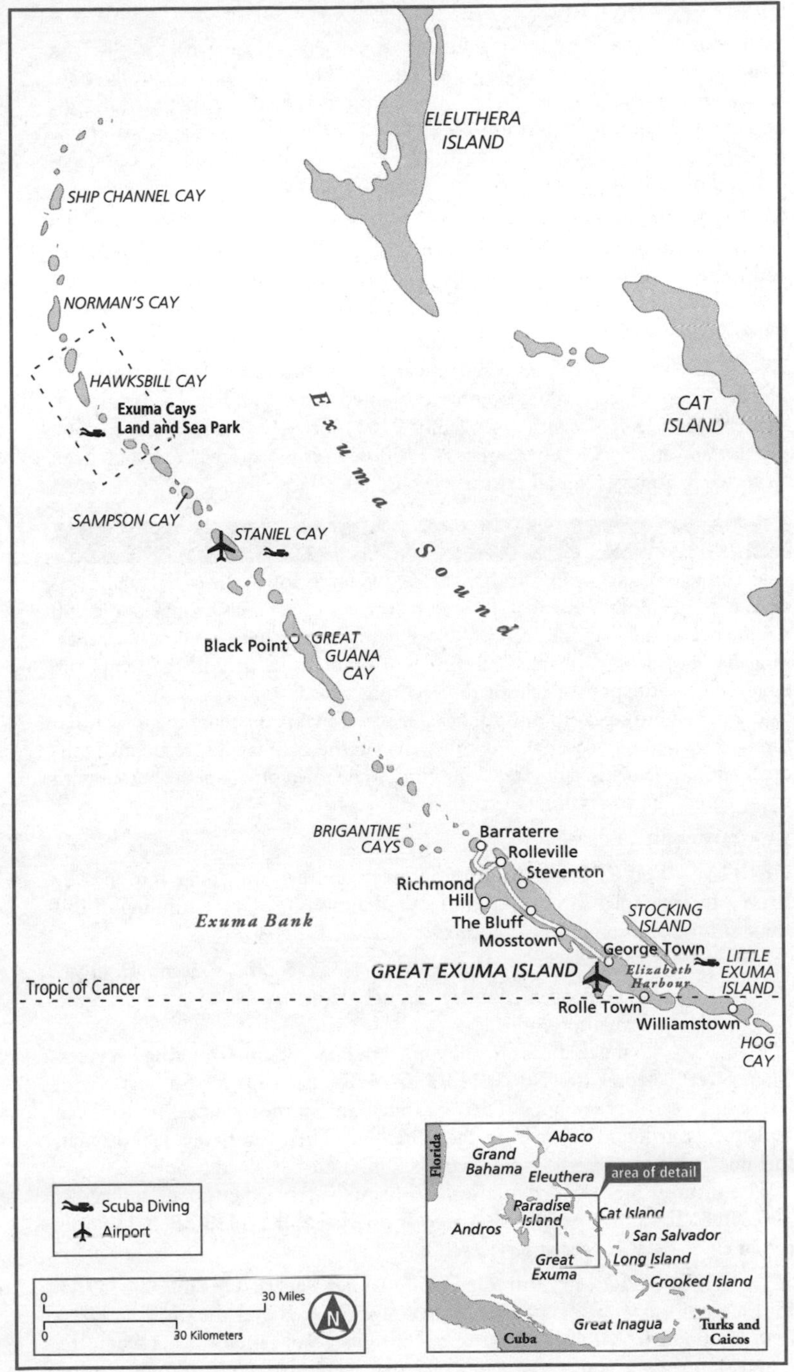
ELEUTHERA ISLAND
SHIP CHANNEL CAY
NORMAN'S CAY
HAWKSBILL CAY
Exuma Cays Land and Sea Park
SAMPSON CAY
STANIEL CAY
Exuma Sound
CAT ISLAND
Black Point
GREAT GUANA CAY
BRIGANTINE CAYS
Barraterre
Rolleville
Steventon
Richmond Hill
The Bluff
Mosstown
Exuma Bank
STOCKING ISLAND
George Town
GREAT EXUMA ISLAND
Elizabeth Harbour
LITTLE EXUMA ISLAND
Tropic of Cancer
Rolle Town
Williamstown
HOG CAY
Scuba Diving
Airport
0
30 Miles
0
30 Kilometers
N
Florida
Abaco
Grand Bahama
Eleuthera
area of detail
Paradise Island
Cat Island
Andros
San Salvador
Great Exuma
Long Island
Crooked Island
Great Inagua
Turks and Caicos
Cuba

GETTING AROUND

After your arrival at the airport in George Town, chances are you'll meet Kermit Rolle. Kermit, who runs things up in Rolleville, knows as much about the Exumas as anyone else (maybe more). You can stop in at **Kermit's Airport Lounge,** Exuma International Airport (✆ **242/345-0002**), which is just across from the airport terminal building. If you're lucky, Kermit will be free, and you can negotiate a deal with him to take you in his car for a tour.

BY TAXI If your hotel is in George Town, it will cost about $24 to get here in a taxi from the airport. Rides often are shared. The island has only a few taxis, and most of them wait at the airport. Hotels can usually get you a taxi if you need to go somewhere and don't have a car. For a taxi, call **Leslie Dames** at ✆ **242/357-0015.**

BY CAR It's also possible to rent a car during your stay, though the major North American companies aren't represented here. Try **Exuma Transport,** Main Street, George Town (✆ **242/336-2101**). They have cars to rent for $60 per day and up, or $300 per week. A $200 deposit is required. Your hotel can also usually arrange a rental car for you through a local firm.

1 George Town

The Tropic of Cancer runs directly through George Town, the capital and principal settlement of the Exumas, located on the island of Great Exuma. Some 900 people live in this tranquil seaport village, which opens onto a 24km (15-mile)-long harbor. George Town, partly in the tropics and partly in the temperate zone, is a favorite port of call for the yachting crowd.

If you need to stock up on supplies, George Town is the place to go, as it has more stores and services than any other spot in the Exumas. There are dive centers, marinas, markets, a doctor, and a clinic. The town often doesn't bother with street names, but everything's easy to find.

ESSENTIALS

GETTING THERE Flights from Nassau and Miami come into nearby Exuma International Airport, 16km (10 miles) away. See the beginning of this chapter for details on airlines and taxis.

FAST FACTS A branch of the **Bank of Nova Scotia,** Queen's Highway (✆ **242/336-2651**), is open Monday through Thursday from 9:30am to 3pm, on Friday from 9:30am to 5pm.

If you come to the Exumas aboard your own boat, **Exuma Docking Services,** Main Street, George Town (✆ **242/336-2578**), has slips for 52 boats, with water and electricity hookups. There's a restaurant on the premises, and you can replenish your liquor stock from the store here. They also have a laundromat, fuel dock, fuel pumps, and a store with supplies for boats and people.

The government-operated **medical clinic** can be reached by phone at ✆ **242/336-2088.** To call the **police** in George Town, dial ✆ **242/336-2666,** but only for an emergency or special services.

SPECIAL EVENTS In April, the **Family Island Regatta** (✆ **800/32-SPORT** for more information) draws a yachting crowd from all over the world to Elizabeth Harbour. It's a rollicking week of fun, song, and serious racing when the island sloops go all out to win. It's said that some determined skippers bring along extra crewmen to serve as live ballast on windward tacks, then drop them

Tips Big-Boom Tourism on the Horizon

After a sleep of centuries, Great Exuma is heading for major development at last. One of the largest resort developments in the history of the Out Islands has been announced, with the development of a 235-room **Four Seasons Resort** set on 470 acres at Emerald Bay. Its opening may occur as soon as late 2003. This Four Seasons will become the only five-star resort in The Bahamas, with a fully functional spa, European-style casino with entertainment, and tennis and health clubs among other deluxe features. Rooms will supposedly be among the most spacious and luxurious in the entire archipelago nation, and each will have an ocean view. The first-class array of dining facilities, as well, will be unlike any ever seen in the Out Islands. The entire resort will overlook a 1.5km- (1-mile-) long stretch of sandy beach and, as a special feature, will feature an 18-hole golf course being designed by Australian Greg Norman. By the time you arrive in The Exumas, the 6,873-yard golf course may already be operational; Norman is telling the press this course will be "one of the finest oceanfront courses in the world" when it opens. For the latest news, check the Web at www.fourseasons.com or call ✆ **800/819-5053** from the U.S. or Canada.

over the side to lighten the ship for the downwind run to the finish. The event, a tradition since 1954, comes at the end of the crawfish season.

WHERE TO STAY

EXPENSIVE

Hotel Higgins Landing ★★ The beach at this resort is spectacular, the stuff of tropical fantasies. The only hotel on undeveloped Stocking Island, this is one of the first eco-resorts in The Bahamas, and it has taken great care to preserve the natural beauty of its surroundings on this gorgeous island. This solar-powered hideaway is one of the self-billed great escapes of The Bahamas. It's bordered by Elizabeth Harbour and the Atlantic on one side, and the crystal blue waters of Turtle Lagoon, with the colorful reefs, on the other.

Cottages are exquisitely decorated with antiques, mirrors, and the Higgins family heirlooms. Accommodations are furnished with queen-size beds, and each unit is given an island accent with cool tile floors and ceiling fans, plus a well-maintained private bath with shower stalls. The landscaped grounds are as colorful as your imagination, attracting many types of wildlife, ranging from herons and hummingbirds to green sea turtles. The island is reached by hotel ferry service from George Town.

Rates include a full breakfast and a candlelit first-rate dinner (nonguests are welcome, too, with advance reservations). The open-air bar overlooks the water. Stocking Island, (P.O. Box EX29146), George Town, Exuma, The Bahamas. ✆ **888/688-4752** in the U.S., or ✆ and fax 242/336-2460. www.higginslanding.com. 5 units. $390 double; $570 triple; $700 quad. MAP (breakfast and dinner) included. AP (also with lunch) $20 extra. Minimum stay of 4 nights required; 50% deposit required to secure reservation. MC, V. No children under 18. Closed Dec 15–Apr 15. **Amenities:** Restaurant, bar; library; watersports; rowboats. *In room:* Ceiling fan, no phone.

Peace & Plenty Bonefish Lodge ★ Kilometers south of George Town, this is one of three Peace & Plenty properties in the Exumas—and the poshest of them all. It caters almost exclusively to fishermen and their companions. In a

Finds Life on a Houseboat

The most offbeat way to live in the Exumas is on a brightly decorated floating houseboat. Each boat is like a hotel suite that can be used to explore Elizabeth Harbour and the coast of the Exumas. In between moving your houseboat from anchorage to anchorage, you can go fishing, snorkeling, scuba diving, or just beachcombing; brand new in 1999, each houseboat is fully equipped, sleeping 6 to 8, with air-conditioning, hot and cold running water, a marine radio, an inflatable dinghy, a fully equipped galley, all linens, purified water, and a propane barbecue grill. Boats range from a one-bedroom 11m (35-ft.) to a two-bedroom 13m (43-ft.). It doesn't take a special license or even much experience to operate one of these boats. For reservations, write to **Bahamas Houseboats,** P.O. Box EX 29031, Government Dock, George Town, Exuma, The Bahamas (© **242/336-BOAT;** fax 242/336-2629; www.bahamahouseboats.com/accommodations.htm). Daily rentals (3-day minimum) range from $275 to $350, with a security deposit of $500 required. Rentals can be paid by MasterCard or Visa.

setting of young palms, the two-story inn is built of concrete and stone and lies on a peninsula enveloped by crystal-clear waters and sandy flats. This is the most elegant bonefishing inn in The Bahamas—you can fish all day and come back to be pampered in luxury.

The lobby is inviting, with tile floors and rattan pieces. From many of the midsize rooms opening onto the wraparound balcony, you'll have a great view of the turquoise waters, or perhaps you'd rather doze in a hammock. Accommodations are furnished in bright floral spreads and prints, with air-conditioning and ceiling fans, along with spacious, immaculate bathrooms and shower-tub combinations. You don't have to be an angler to stay here—but it helps. If you don't fish, you may be left out of the conversation at night.

The food served in the clubby dining room is excellent, with a well-trained chef who not only knows how to grill your steak to perfection, but can whip up a vegetarian platter, too. Of course, the finest way to dine here is on fish caught that day by the chef or one of the guests. After cleaning the fish, he tosses scraps to the resident sharks in the adjoining waters. This is the chief evening entertainment, although there are an honor bar and a lobby lounge upstairs with TV and VCR.

Queens Hwy. (P.O. Box EX29173), George Town. © **242/345-5555.** Fax 242/345-5556. www.peaceandplenty.com. 8 units. $998 per person 3 nights, 2 days; $1,317 per person 4 nights, 3 days. Rates are all-inclusive. MC, V. **Amenities:** Restaurant, bar; free shuttle to Stocking Island, van to George Town; snorkeling; bonefishing; bikes; laundry. *In room:* A/C, no phone.

MODERATE

Club Peace & Plenty This attractive, historic waterside inn, though not as luxurious as the Coconut Cove Hotel (see below), is a classic island hotel in the heart of George Town. Once a sponge warehouse and later the home of a prominent family, it was converted into a hotel in the late 1940s, making it the oldest in the Exumas. The two-story pink and white hotel has dormers and balconies opening onto a water view. The grounds are planted with palms, crotons, and bougainvillea. Peace & Plenty fronts Elizabeth Harbour, which makes it a favorite of the yachting set, including former visitor Prince Philip.

The midsize units are all tastefully furnished, although there is still a lingering 1950s vibe. A recent refurbishment has freshened things up a bit, though, with bright print spreads and draperies, and furnishings in white wicker or rattan. All rooms have queen, double, or twin beds, and a tiled bathroom with shower-tub combinations. Many also contain balconies opening onto harbor views; oceanfront rooms are the most desirable.

You can dine either indoors or outside, with calypso music on the terrace (see "Where to Dine," below). There are also two cocktail lounges, one of which was converted from an old slave kitchen and is now filled with nautical gear, including lanterns, rudders, and anchors. The hotel faces Stocking Island and maintains a private beach club there, offering food and bar service, as well as kilometers of sandy dunes. A boat, free for hotel guests ($8 round-trip for nonguests), makes the run.

Queen's Hwy. (P.O. Box EX29055), George Town, Great Exuma, The Bahamas. ✆ **800/525-2210** in the U.S. and Canada, or 242/336-2551. Fax 242/336-2550. www.peaceandplenty.com. 34 units. Winter $150–$165 double; off-season $120–$130 double. MAP (breakfast and dinner) $40 per person per day. Ask about bonefishing packages. AE, MC, V. **Amenities:** On-site restaurant, 2 bars, offshore beach club with food and drink; free boat; pool. *In room:* A/C, TV, hair dryer, safe, no phone.

Latitude Exuma Resort ★ *Kids* Just a short walk from a white sandy beach, this is an eco-oriented resort, renting four cottages by the week only. It lies on a private island about 3,000 yards from the mainland of Great Exuma. The complex consists of a series of attractive West Indian cottages—of one, two, or three bedrooms each—on the waterfront with views of Elizabeth Harbour and Stocking Island; there were four such cottages at press time, but additional units were said to be on the horizon, and may have opened by the time you read this.

The pastel colors and matching roof lines recreate the harmony of a Bahamian village; wood interiors feature cathedral-high ceilings and large windows, and several include intimate lofts which make those cottages ideal for families—especially since they're equipped with kitchens, rocking chairs, and large verandas fronting the water. (As a bonus, there's no charge for up to 2 children under age the age of 16 per room.) The comfortable furnishings—including private bathrooms with oversize showers—really make the place truly appealing. Daily maid service is even possible, though it does involve a surcharge; otherwise, your cottage is cleaned once weekly. There is ferry service to the mainland, too, landing in the capital of George Town.

Rolle Cay, Elizabeth Harbour, George Town, Great Exuma, The Bahamas. ✆ **242/336-2763** or 954/632-7057. Fax 242/336-3033. http://latitudeexuma.com/invest.htm. 4 cottages. Winter $1,500 per week; call for summer rates. MC, V. **Amenities:** Cabana-style outdoor restaurant; pool; watersports; bonefishing. *In room:* A/C, wet bar, refrigerator, kitchen, no phone.

The Palms at Three Sisters In 1994, this low-key resort opened on an isolated spot 11km (7 miles) from its nearest neighbor, on a 360m (1,200-ft.) stretch of lovely white sand. Rooms lie within a two-story, motel-like building and have English colonial details and simple, summery furniture. It's a great place for privacy and seclusion. The resort, incidentally, is named after a trio of rocks (the Three Sisters) with a composition that differs radically from the coral formations throughout the rest of the Exumas. They jut about 4.5m (15 ft.) above sea level just offshore from the beach. Bedrooms are comfortable, containing small bathrooms with shower units.

Meals and drinks are served in a low-slung annex, with views stretching out over the Atlantic (see "Where to Dine," below). Live music is presented every Saturday on a flowering patio.

Queen's Hwy., Bahama Sound Beach (P.O. Box EX29215; 15km/9 miles northwest of George Town), George Town, Great Exuma, The Bahamas. © **888/688-4752** or 242/358-4040. Fax 242/358-4043. seaoats@batelnet.bs. 14 units. Winter $110 double, $130 triple, $125 cottage; off-season $95 double, $105 triple, $100 cottage. Extra person $20. MC, V. **Amenities:** Restaurant; snorkeling; tennis court (lit for night play); swimming pool; bikes; boat outings nearby to a sandy cay offshore for picnics. *In room:* A/C, TV, no phone.

Peace & Plenty Beach Inn *Kids* This tranquil inn is a world-class bonefishing resort, opening onto 90m (300 ft.) of white-sand beach. Its sibling, the Peace & Plenty Bonefish Lodge, is more posh, but the price tag here compensates. This is also a favorite resort for snorkelers, offering a special Jean-Michel Cousteau snorkeling program. The inn contains first-class, well-furnished double rooms, plus small bathrooms with shower-tub combinations. The bedrooms have Italian tile floors, as well as balconies overlooking Bonefish Bay and Elizabeth Harbour. For some action, and additional activities and facilities, you can go over to the Club Peace & Plenty (there are shuttles between all the Peace & Plenty properties).

An adjacent structure housing the attractive bar and restaurant was designed to reflect the colonial flavor of George Town. Very good meals are served here.

Harbourfront (P.O. Box EX29055), George Town, Great Exuma, The Bahamas. © **800/525-2210** in the U.S. and Canada, or 242/336-2250. Fax 242/336-2253. www.peaceandplenty.com. 16 units. Winter $160–$185 double; off-season $140–$150 double. Up to 2 children under 12 stay free in parents' room. AE, MC, V. **Amenities:** Restaurant, bar; shuttle bus to George Town; ferry to Stocking Island; freshwater pool; boat rentals; scuba diving, snorkeling, and fishing excursions arranged. *In room:* A/C, TV, no phone.

Regatta Point ★ This inn lies on a small cay just across the causeway from George Town, opening onto a small sandy beach. The cay used to be known as Kidd Cay, named after the notorious pirate. Overlooking Elizabeth Harbour, the present complex consists of six efficiency apartments, which are not air-conditioned, although the cross ventilation is good. Ceiling fans help, too. Each of the pleasantly furnished, summery units has its own kitchen and maid service, plus a small bathroom containing shower-tub combinations. This is a good choice for families. Those who don't wish to cook can have dinner at one of the previously mentioned hotels in town, or at a local restaurant. Nearby grocery stores are fairly well-stocked if you feel like cooking. Sunfish and bicycles are available at no extra charge. This colony hums in April during the Family Island Regatta.

Regatta Point, Kidd Cove (P.O. Box 6), George Town, Great Exuma, The Bahamas. © **800/688-0309.** Fax 242/336-2046. www.regattapointbahamas.com. 6 units. Winter $158–$172 double, $228 2-bedroom apt for up to 4; off-season $126–$144 double, $182 2-bedroom apt for up to 4. Extra person $15. No credit cards. *In room:* Kitchen, no phone.

INEXPENSIVE

Two Turtles Inn Set opposite the village green, midway between the harbor front and a saltwater estuary known as Victoria Pond, this two-story hotel is as popular for its bar and restaurant as for its plain accommodations. Originally built of stone and stained planking in the early 1960s, it's arranged around a courtyard. Each room has a ceiling fan, plus a somewhat cramped bathroom with a shower stall. For hitting the beach or enjoying watersports, head to Peace & Plenty, a short walk away, where both guests and nonguests can rent equipment. Tennis, sailing, boating, snorkeling, and scuba diving can be arranged through other nearby hotels.

Finds Fresh, Sexy Conch

The best conch salad is found at **Big D's Conch Spot No. 2,** Government Dock (no phone). "Fresh, sexy conch," as it's called here, is served daily. They'll make it right in front of you, so you know what's going into your salad. For some reason, they're open only on Monday, Wednesday, and Friday.

Main St. (P.O. Box EX29251), George Town, Great Exuma, The Bahamas. ✆ **242/336-2545.** Fax 242/336-2528. 12 units. Winter $118 double; off-season $106 double. Children under 12 stay free in parents' room. MC, V. **Amenities:** Restaurant, bar. *In room:* A/C, TV.

WHERE TO DINE

With a few exceptions, the best places to take meals in George Town are in the main hotels reviewed above.

There are several casual joints in George Town where you can grab a quick meal. **Towne Cafe,** Marshall Complex (✆ **242/336-2194**), serves one of the best breakfasts in George Town. It's really the town bakery. Drop in any day but Sunday for a lunch of local Exumian specialties such as stewed grouper or chicken souse or a sandwich.

A former school bus was recycled and turned into **Jean's Dog House,** along Queen's Highway in George Town. Here you'll find the island's best lobster burger in a cramped but spotless kitchen on wheels. Instead of eating in the hotel dining room, we like to go here for breakfast and order the "MacJean," a robust sandwich with sausage or bacon, plus cheese, on freshly baked bread. Of course, she's also noted for her "dogs," or frankfurters. The owner is a well-loved personality known only as Jean. Visit her only from 7am to 3pm, and don't bother bringing your credit card.

MODERATE

Club Peace & Plenty Restaurant CONTINENTAL/BAHAMIAN/AMERICAN Go here for the finest island dining, with plentiful, good home-cooking that leaves everyone satisfied. You might begin with conch salad or one of the salads made with hearts of palm or artichoke hearts, then follow with local lobster. Bahamian steamed grouper regularly appears on the menu (of course), simmered with onions, sweet pepper, tomatoes, and thyme. But you can also order such special dishes as an herb-flavored Cornish game hen that is juicy and perfectly roasted and flavored. Lunch options include homemade soups, conch burgers, a chef's salad, or deep-fried grouper. Breakfast offerings range from traditional French toast or scrambled eggs and sausage to the truly Bahamian boiled fish and grits.

You sit under ceiling fans, looking out over the harbor. Windows on three sides and candlelight make it particularly nice in the evening. And who knows who will be at the next table? A celeb or two, or a crowd of yachters providing conversation and amusement.

In the Club Peace & Plenty, Queen's Hwy. ✆ **242/336-2551.** Reservations required for dinner. Breakfast $7.50; lunch $7; main courses $18–$26. AE, DC, DISC, MC, V. Daily 7:30am–10pm.

The Palm INTERNATIONAL Set beside a sandy, isolated beach, 15km (9 miles) northwest of the Exuma capital, this airy, oceanfront restaurant is associated with one of the island's best resorts. Breakfasts are hearty steak-and-egg fare, although you can also get Bahamian coconut pancakes. Lunches include lobster salads, conch chowder, grouper fingers, burgers, and sandwiches. Dinners are more formal. Although the food is familiar, it's well-prepared. Flame-broiled grouper might be your best and freshest choice.

At the Palms at Three Sisters hotel, Queen's Hwy., Bahama Sound Beach (15km/9 miles northwest of George Town). ✆ **242/358-4040.** Breakfast $5–$10; lunch platters and sandwiches $5.95–$12; dinner main courses $16–$28; sunset specials $14.50–$20. MC, V. Daily 7am–10pm.

Sam's Place BAHAMIAN/INTERNATIONAL If Bogie were alive today, he'd surely head for this laid-back second-floor restaurant and bar overlooking the harbor in George Town. Sam Gray, the owner, offers breakfasts to catch the early boating crowd. Lunches could include everything from freshly made fish chowder to spaghetti with meat sauce. You'll also be able to order an array of sandwiches throughout the day. The dinner menu changes daily, but you're likely to find such well-prepared main courses as Exuma lobster tail, roast lamb, and Bahamian pan-fried grouper. Of course, you can always get native conch chowder. At dinner, the talk here is of one of everybody's dreams—owning a private utopia, one of those uninhabited cays still remaining in the Exuma chain.

Main St. ✆ **242/336-2579.** Breakfast and lunch $5.50–$8.50; dinner main courses $14–$24. MC, V. Daily 7:30am–9:30pm.

INEXPENSIVE

Eddie's Edgewater BAHAMIAN This dive serves traditional Bahamian food in an unpretentious and unfussy atmosphere. It opened as a one-room bar during World War II, serving U.S. sailors stationed at a long-departed Navy base here. The original bar still stands, its high-beamed ceilings and flags still advertising Ole Nassau rum. The wooden front porch overlooks Lake Victoria, a saltwater estuary in the center of George Town. Among the good choices here are conch chowder, okra soup, and grouper. On Monday nights, a local band stages "Rake 'n' Scrape" from 7:30 to 11pm. What's that? Well, one musician strums a washtub bass while another scrapes a screwdriver across the teeth of a saw, all to the sound of maracas, tambourines, bongos, and even cowbells. Needless to say, this place is very casual, and it doesn't close down until the last person staggers out—which is sometimes as late as 2am.

Charlotte St., George Town. ✆ **242/336-2050.** Main courses $6–$14. MC, V. Mon–Sat 7am–midnight.

Kermit's Airport Lounge BAHAMIAN Owned by one of the island's most entrepreneurial taxi drivers, Kermit Rolle, this simple but appealing place lies across the road from the entrance to the airport. It's the semiofficial waiting room for most of the island's flights, and it might make your wait more convenient and fun. The cook will fry you some fish, and there's always beans and rice around. Johnnycake and sandwiches are also available, along with burgers and an array of tropical drinks. Until an airplane flies you to a better restaurant, this place might come in handy.

Exuma International Airport. ✆ **242/345-0002.** Beer $3.50; cheeseburgers $5–$7; platters from $7. No credit cards. Daily 6:30am–5:30pm.

BEACHES, WATERSPORTS & OTHER OUTDOOR PURSUITS

STOCKING ISLAND ★

Stocking Island, which lies in Elizabeth Harbour, faces the town across the bay, less than 1.5km (1 mile) away. This long, thin barrier island has some of the most gorgeous white-sand beaches in The Bahamas. Snorkelers and scuba divers come here to explore the blue holes, and it is also ringed with undersea caves and coral gardens. Boat trips leave daily from Elizabeth Harbour heading for Stocking Island at 10am and 1pm. The cost is $9 per person one-way. However, guests of Club Peace & Plenty ride free.

If you'd like to go shelling, walk the beach that runs along the Atlantic side of Stocking Island.

The island has a beach club run by **Club Peace & Plenty** (✆ **242/336-2551**). (Stocking Island used to be a private enclave for guests at Club Peace & Plenty, but now all visitors use it.) Here you can rent kayaks for only $25 per day or Sunfish for $35 a day; snorkel gear goes for $10 a day. Visibility is great in these waters, and there are many kinds of colorful fish to see.

BOATING, SEA KAYAKING & SAILING

Landlocked **Lake Victoria** covers about 2 acres in the heart of George Town. It has a narrow exit to the harbor and functions as a diving-and-boating headquarters.

Exuma Dive Centre (✆ **242/336-2390**) rents motorboats for $45 per half day or $80 per full day.

On Stocking Island, visit the kiosk operated by Peace & Plenty Beach Club for rental information.

If you come to the Exumas aboard your own boat, **Exuma Docking Services,** Main Street, George Town (✆ **242/336-2578**), has slips for 52 boats, with water and electricity hookups. You can stock up on supplies here, get fuel, and do laundry.

FISHING

Many visitors come to the Exumas just to go bonefishing. Arrangements for outings can be made at **Club Peace & Plenty,** Queen's Highway (✆ **242/345-5555**), the central office for the Peace & Plenty properties. The Exumas offer kilometers of wadeable flats (shallow bodies of water), and trained guides accompany you. Fly-fishing instruction and equipment are also offered.

SNORKELING

The best snorkeling within easy reach of George Town is on Stocking Island (see above).

You can also rent snorkeling equipment for $8 a day at **Minns Water Sports** in George Town (✆ **242/336-3483**).

SCUBA DIVING

Divers should head for the **Exuma Dive Center** in George Town (✆ **800/874-7213** or 242/336-2390), which features dives to "walls," coral heads, and blue holes. They also offer resort courses. Most reefs lie only 20 minutes by boat from the outfitter's dive shop. Dives start at $65, with basic scuba instruction costing $405. The center can also arrange dive and hotel packages for you if you call.

Mystery Cave is a famous dive site, tunneling for more than 120m (400 ft.) under the island.

EXPLORING GEORGE TOWN

There isn't much to see here in the way of architecture except the confectionery pink and white **Government Building,** which was "inspired" by the Government House architecture in Nassau. Under an old ficus tree in the center of town, there's a **straw market** where you can talk to the friendly Exumian women and perhaps purchase some of their handcrafts.

George Town has a colorful history, despite the fact that it appears so sleepy today. (There's so little traffic, there is no need for a traffic light.) Pirates used its deep-water harbor in the 17th century, and those called the "plantation aristocracy," mainly from Virginia and the Carolinas, settled here in the 18th century. In the next 100 years, **Elizabeth Harbour,** the focal point of the town, became a refitting base for British man-of-war vessels, and the U.S. Navy used the port again during World War II.

There's not too much shopping, but there are a few places where you can purchase souvenirs and gifts. **Exuma Liquor and Gifts,** Queen's Highway (**© 242/336-2101**), is the place to stock up on liquor, wine, and beer. The **Peace & Plenty Boutique,** Queen's Highway (**© 242/336-2761**), stands next to the Sandpiper and across the street from the previously recommended Club Peace & Plenty, which owns it. Its main draw is a selection of Androsia batiks for women, and Androsia cloth is sold by the yard. You can also find such practical items as film and suntan oil. They also have a large selection of men and women's sportswear.

The Sandpiper, Queen's Highway (**© 242/336-2084**), stands across from Club Peace & Plenty. Its highlights are the original serigraphs by Diane Minns, but it also offers a good selection of Bahamian arts and crafts, along with such items as Bahamian straw baskets (or other handcrafted works), sponges, ceramics, watches, and postcards. Diane designs and silk-screens T-shirts here in the shop, and she welcomes anyone to watch her at work.

One of the offshore sights in Elizabeth Harbour is **Crab Cay,** which can be reached by boat. This is believed to have been a rest camp for British seamen in the 18th century.

GEORGE TOWN AFTER DARK

The best place to head for some after-dark diversion is **Club Peace & Plenty** (see above). Although summer nights are slow here, there's usually something happening in winter, ranging from weekly poolside bashes to live bands that keep both locals and visitors jumping up on the dance floor. You might also check out the action at the previously recommended **Two Turtles Inn.** If it's a Monday night, head over to **Eddie's Edgewater** (see above) for a Rake 'n' Scrape evening, featuring cowbells, goatskin drums, and other unusual musical instruments.

EXPLORING FARTHER AFIELD

Queen's Highway, which is still referred to as the "slave route," runs the length of Great Exuma, and you can travel it in either a taxi or a rented car to take in the sights in and around George Town.

Forty-five kilometers (28 miles) north of George Town, **Rolleville,** named after Lord Rolle, is still inhabited by descendants of his freed slaves. It is claimed that his will left them the land. This land is not sold but is passed along from one generation to the next.

As you travel along the highway, you'll see ruins of plantations. This land is called **"generation estates,"** and the major ones are **Steventon, Mount Thompson,** and **Ramsey.** You pass such settlements as Mosstown (which has working farms), Ramsey, the Forest, Farmer's Hill, and Roker's Point. Steventon is the last settlement before you reach Rolleville, which is the largest of the plantation estates. There are several **beautiful beaches** along the way, especially the one at **Tarr Bay** and **Jimmie Hill.**

Some visitors may also want to head south of George Town, passing Flamingo Bay and Pirate's Point. In the 18th century Captain Kidd is said to have anchored at **Kidd Cay.** You, however, can stay at the previously recommended Regatta Point.

Flamingo Bay, the site of a hotel and villa development, begins just 1km (½ mile) from George Town. It's a favorite rendezvous of the yachting set and bonefishers.

WHERE TO DINE

Iva Bowe's Central Highway Inn Restaurant & Bar BAHAMIAN This roadside tavern, operated by Mrs. Lorraine Bowe-Lloyd, specializes in very tender cracked conch. The conch is marinated in lime, pounded to make it tender, and then fried with her own special seasonings. It's the best in the Exumas. You might also try her lobster linguini or shrimp scampi. This is good Bahamian cookery.

Queen's Hwy. (.5km/¼ mile from the entrance to the International Airport and about 9.5km/6½ miles northwest of George Town). ✆ **242/345-7014.** Lunch $5–$10; main courses $10–$20. No credit cards. Mon–Sat 10am–10pm.

Kermit's Hilltop Tavern BAHAMIAN Originally built in the 1950s by members of the Rolle family, this stone-sided restaurant sits atop the highest point in Rolleville (32km/20 miles north of Georgetown), with a view over the rest of the town. Today, it's open as a tavern and general meeting place for almost everyone in town, as well as for those passing through. Lunch and drinks are served continuously throughout the day and early evening, but more formal meals of chicken, fish, or lobster should be arranged by phone in advance. Try Kermit's curried mutton, steamed conch, or pan-fried grouper. This is one of the most authentic places for true Bahamian cuisine. "They cook the way my mama used to," one diner told us, "and that's why we come here." Call it Bahamian soul food. (Some of the produce comes fresh from Kermit's farm.)

Rolleville. ✆ **242/345-6006.** Reservations required for dinner. Lunch platters $7–$10; 3-course dinners $11–$20. No credit cards. Lunch and snacks daily 9am–closing (time varies); dinner by prior arrangement only.

2 Little Exuma ★

This is a faraway retreat, the southernmost of the Exuma Cays. It has a subtropical climate, despite that it's in the tropics, and lovely white-sand beaches. The waters are so crystal-clear in some places that you can spot the colorful tropical fish more than 18m (60 ft.) down. The island, about 31 square km (12 sq. miles) in area, is connected to Great Exuma by a 200-yard-long bridge. It's about a 16km (10-mile) trip from the George Town airport.

Less than a kilometer offshore is **Pigeon Cay,** which is uninhabited. Visitors often come here for the day and are later picked up by a boat that takes them back to Little Exuma. You can go snorkeling and visit the remains of a 200-year-old wreck, right offshore in about 2m (6 ft.) of water.

On one of the highest hills of Little Exuma are the remains of an old pirate fort. Several cannons are located nearby, but documentation is lacking as to when it was built or by whom. (Pirates didn't leave too much data lying around.)

Coming from Great Exuma, the first community you reach on Little Exuma is called **Ferry,** so named because the two islands were linked by a ferry service before the bridge was built. See if you can visit the private chapel of an Irish family, the Fitzgeralds, erected generations ago.

Fun Fact A Romantic Legend

On the road to Little Exuma, you come to the hamlet of **Rolle Town,** which is another of the generation estates that was once, like Rolleville in the north, owned by Lord Rolle and is populated today with the descendants of his former slaves. This sleepy town has some 100-year-old houses.

In an abandoned field, where goats frolic, you can visit the Rolle Town Tombs, burial ground of the McKay family. Capt. Alexander McKay, a Scot, came to Great Exuma in 1789 after he was granted 400 acres for a plantation. His wife joined him in 1791, and soon after, they had a child. However, tragedy struck in 1792 when Anne McKay, who was only 26, died along with her child. Perhaps grief stricken, her husband died the following year. Their story is one of the romantic legends of the island.

The village claims a famous daughter, Esther Rolle, the actress. Her parents were born here, but they came to the United States before she was born.

Along the way, you can take in **Pretty Molly Bay,** site of the now-shuttered Sand Dollar Beach Club. Pretty Molly was a slave who committed suicide by walking into the water one night. The natives claim that her ghost can still be seen stalking the beach every night.

Many visitors come to Little Exuma to visit the **Hermitage,** a plantation constructed by Loyalist settlers. It is the last surviving example of the many that once stood in the Exumas. It was originally built by the Kendall family, who came to Little Exuma in 1784. They established their plantation at **Williamstown** and, with their slaves, set about growing cotton. But they encountered so many difficulties having the cotton shipped to Nassau that in 1806 they advertised the plantation for sale. The ad promised "970 acres more or less," along with "160 hands" (referring to the slaves). Chances are you'll be approached by a local guide who, for a fee, will show you around. Also ask to be shown several old tombs in the area.

Also at Williamstown (look for the seaside marker), you can visit the remains of the **Great Salt Pond.**

If you really have to see everything, maybe you can get a local to take you over to **Hog Cay,** the end of the line for the Exumas. This is really just a spit of land, and there are no glorious beaches here. It's visited mainly by those who like to add obscure islets at the very end of the road to their list of explorations. Hog Cay is privately owned, and it is farmed. The owner seems friendly to visitors. His house lies in the center of the island.

3 Staniel Cay ★

Staniel Cay lies 129km (80 miles) southeast of Nassau at the southern end of the little Pipe Creek archipelago, which is part of the Exuma Cays. It's an 13km (8-mile) chain of mostly uninhabited islets, sandy beaches, coral reefs, and bonefish flats. There are many places for snug anchorages, making this a favorite yachting stopover in the mid-Exumas. Staniel Cay, known for years as "Stanyard," has no golf course or tennis courts, but it's the perfect island for "the great escape."

An annual bonefishing festival is sponsored here on August 5, during the celebration of Bahamian Independence Day. **The Happy People Marina** (✆ **242/355-2008**) arranges sportfishing trips with local guides, as well as snorkeling trips.

About 100 Bahamians live here, and there's a **straw market** where you can buy crafts, hats, and handbags.

Visitors to this island arrive by private boat or a chartered flight. To arrange a possible flight, contact **Executive Air Travel** and speak to Capt. Dennis Rotolo (✆ **954/224-6022**) in Fort Lauderdale.

WHERE TO STAY & DINE

Happy People Marina Exumas native Kenneth Rolle operates this marina. His mother was the regionally famous Ma Blanche, who had a mail boat named for her. Guests who check in here are interested mainly in boating, as this place is just a decent motel to spend the night. Rooms are small and utterly basic, adjoined by a little bathroom with a shower stall. There are a meager private beach and dockage facilities, but there's no service or fuel for the majority of the island's visiting yachts. The prevailing atmosphere is casual, and all of the rooms face the waterfront. A recently added apartment features a full kitchen, two bedrooms, two bathrooms, and a living room.

Meals and drinks are served in a separate building closer to the center of town, within a minute of the marina. Known as the Royal Entertainer Lounge, it sometimes welcomes local bands and serves meals.

Staniel Cay, the Exumas, The Bahamas. ✆ **242/355-2008.** 9 units. $90 double; $200 apt. No credit cards. **Amenities:** Restaurant, bar; laundry. *In room:* A/C, no phone.

Staniel Cay Yacht Club Staniel Cay is a great getaway, and the Staniel Cay Yacht Club is the place to get away to. Although once famous in yachting circles, drawing celebrities like Malcolm Forbes, it fell off for several years before bouncing back. Now it once again welcomes the yachting world to its location near a white sandy beach. Guest cottages, each with a small shower unit, have been completely remodeled and refurbished and are quite charming. Each cottage is painted a different color and has different decorative features. The cottages also have west-facing balconies, which make for unimpeded views of the sun setting over the water. This is one of the few guarantees each day on Staniel Cay. Since the island is only a kilometer wide, you can easily walk to the local village, which has a grocery store, straw market, church, and post office.

An on-site clubhouse offers American/Bahamian cuisine for breakfast, lunch, and dinner, with a menu featuring steaks and seafood, nothing too foreign or experimental. The club can rent you boats for activities, from a 4m (13-ft.) Boston Whaler including fuel for $85, to something smaller, plus scuba and snorkeling gear.

Staniel Cay, the Exumas, The Bahamas. (For information, write 2233 S. Andrews Ave., Fort Lauderdale, FL 33316.) ✆ **954/467-8920** in the U.S., or 242/355-2024. Fax 242/355-2044. www.stanielcay.com. 6 units. Winter $125 double; off-season $95 double. Extra person $25–$35. MC, V. **Amenities:** Restaurant, bar; laundry; gift shop. *In room:* A/C, no phone.

Norman's Cay

Throughout the Exumas, you'll see islands with NO TRESPASSING signs posted. In the early 1980s, on Norman's Cay, they meant it seriously: You could have been killed if you had gone ashore.

Once upon a time, you might have run into Ted Kennedy, Walter Cronkite, or William F. Buckley, Jr. enjoying the island's pleasures. The remote outpost enjoyed great popularity with the Harvard/Boston clique. During the 1980s, however, all this changed when German-Colombian Carlos Lehder Rivas purchased most of the island. Experts say it soon became the major distribution point for drug export to the United States. Millions of dollars worth of cocaine was flown from Colombia to Norman's Cay before being smuggled onward to the United States.

Eventually, the U.S. applied strong pressure on the Bahamian government to clean up the island. Lehder fled for Colombia, where he was captured and extradited to the United States. He is now in prison. Norman's Cay may one day realize its tourist potential again, but for now it remains relatively quiet, visited only by a stray yachting parties and occasional cruise vessels.

4 Sampson Cay

Tiny Sampson Cay, directly northwest of Staniel Cay and just to the southeast of the Exuma Cays National Land and Sea Park, has a certain charm. It has a full-service marina, as well as a small dive operation. Other than Staniel Cay, Sampson Cay has the only marina in the Central Exumas. To fly here, you'll need to go to Staniel Cay first. However, most visitors arrive in their own boats. Local guides take out sportfishers for the day. Sampson Cay lies 67 nautical miles southeast of Nassau and is one of the safest anchorages in the Exumas and a natural "hurricane hole." The cay lies near the end of Pipe Creek, which has been called a "tropical Shangri-La."

WHERE TO STAY & DINE

Sampson's Cay Colony ★ This is a rather remote outpost, and none too fancy, either. Each of the 10 units here has a tiny kitchenette (with hot plate, sink, and refrigerator, but no oven). The medium-size bedrooms here were totally renovated in 2001, and are of a typical motel standard, each with a private shower bath. Community life here revolves around the grocery store and commissary, the fuel and dockage facilities of the marina, and a bar and restaurant favored by visiting yachters. The nautically decorated clubhouse serves drinks and sandwiches any time of day to anyone who shows up, but reservations are required before 4pm for the single-seating dinner, which is served nightly at 7:30pm.

Sampson Cay, the Exumas, The Bahamas. ✆ **242/355-2034.** Fax 242/355-2034. 10 units. $350–$500 double. MC, V. **Amenities:** Restaurant, bar; sports equipment. *In room:* A/C, no phone.

10

The Southern Bahamas

This cluster of islands on the southern fringe of The Bahamas is one of the last frontier outposts that can be reached relatively quickly from the U.S. mainland. Their remoteness is one of the most compelling reasons to visit them—that, and a chance to see life in The Bahamas the way it used to be. Some of the islands are proud to proclaim that "we are as we were when Columbus first landed here," an exaggeration that nonetheless contains a kernel of the truth.

The Southern Bahamas have a colorful history. In the 18th century, Loyalists from the Carolinas and Virginia came here with slave labor and settled many of the islands. For about 20 years they had thriving cotton plantations until a blight struck, killing crops and destroying the industry. In 1834, the United Kingdom Emancipation Act freed slaves throughout the British Empire. When the Loyalists moved on to more fertile ground, they often left behind the emancipated blacks, who then had to eke out a living as best they could.

With some notable exceptions, such as Long Island, tourism developers have stayed clear of these islands, although they have enormous potential, as most of them have excellent beaches, good fishing, and fine dive sites.

If you consider visiting any of these islands, be forewarned that transportation is inconvenient, and except for two or three resorts, accommodations are limited. For these and other reasons, the boating and yachting crowd composes the majority of visitors.

Many changes are in the wind for the Southern Bahamas. Right now, however, there's almost no traffic, no banks, no lawyers. There are, however, mosquitoes. You may want to plan ahead and bring a good insect repellent and a long-sleeved shirt for protection.

1 Cat Island ★

Untainted by tourism, lovely Cat Island is the sixth-largest island in The Bahamas. The fishhook-shaped island—some 77km (48 miles) long and 1 to 6.5km (4 miles) wide—lies about 209km (130 miles) southeast of Nassau and 523km (325 miles) southeast of Miami. (Don't confuse Cat Island with Cat Cay, a smallish, private island near Bimini.)

Cat Island, named after the pirate Arthur Catt (and not wild packs of marauding cats), is located near the Tropic of Cancer, between Eleuthera and Long Island. It has one of the best climates in The Bahamas, with temperatures in the high 60s during the short winters, rising to the mid-80s in summer, with trade winds making the place even more comfortable. It is home to some 2,000 residents, some of the friendliest in The Bahamas.

With its pristine virgin **beaches,** the island is one of the most beautiful in The Bahamas and is so little visited that it remains relatively inexpensive and undiscovered.

Many local historians claim that Cat Island residents were the first to see Columbus. The great explorer himself was believed by some to have been welcomed here by the peaceful Arawaks. Regardless of whether Columbus stopped here, the island has a rich history of adventurers, slaves, buccaneers, farmers, and visionaries of many nationalities. Cat Island remains mysterious to some even now. It's known as a stronghold of such strange practices as obeah (West Indian witchcraft) and of miraculously healing bush medicines.

A straight asphalt road (in terrible shape) leads from the north to the south of the island. Along the way you can select your own beach—and chances are you'll have complete privacy. These beaches offer an array of watersports, and visitors can go swimming or snorkeling at several places. **Fernandez Bay** is a picture-postcard, white-sand beach set against a turquoise blue sea and lined with casuarina trees. The island's north side is wild, untamed shoreline. Boating and diving are among the main reasons to go to Cat Island, and diving lessons are available for novices.

Arthur's Town, in the north, is the major town and the boyhood home of actor Sidney Poitier. (He has many relatives still living on the island, including one or two amazing look-alikes we recently spotted.) Poitier shared memories of his childhood home in his book *This Life.*

ESSENTIALS

GETTING THERE A commercial flight on **Bahamasair** (✆ **800/222-4262** in the U.S.) leaves Nassau for Arthur's Town on Tuesday, Friday, and Sunday at 10:30am. There is also an airport near the **Bight,** the most scenic village on the island. Other minor carriers serving the island include **Air Sunshine** (✆ **800/327-8900**), flying to New Bight from Fort Lauderdale, and **Lynx Air International Launches** (✆ **888/596-9247**), which has service between Fort Lauderdale and Cat Island three times a week.

Cat Island is also serviced by **mail boat.** The **MV *North Cat Island Special*** (✆ **242/393-1064**) departs Potter's Cay Dock in Nassau weekly, heading for Bennett's Harbour and Arthur's Town. It leaves on Thursday at 6pm and returns to Nassau on Sunday. Another vessel, **MV *Sea Hauler*** (✆ **242/393-1064**), departs Potter's Cay in Nassau on Tuesday at 3pm, going to Old and New Bight, and returns on Monday.

GETTING AROUND No taxi service is available on Cat Island. Hotel owners, if notified of your arrival time, will have someone drive to the airport to pick you up. You can, however, rent a car from **Russell Brothers,** Bridge Inn, New Bight (✆ **242/342-3014**), to go exploring on your own. Prices begin at $80 daily, with unlimited mileage. A special rate of $70 daily is offered to guests of Bridge Inn. Hours are Monday through Saturday from 8am to 6pm.

FAST FACTS There are three medical clinics, each of which is among the simplest in The Bahamas. They are found in the settlements of Arthur's Town, Old Bight, and Smiths Bay, and they're not always open. In case of an emergency, notify your hotel staff immediately. Someone will try to get in touch with a medical person. Serious cases are flown to Nassau. If you're not in good health and might require medical assistance on vacation, Cat Island is not the island to choose. There is no central number to call for help.

SPECIAL EVENTS The island's annual **Three-Day Regatta** takes place every summer, usually at the end of July. It attracts the largest collection of visitors to Cat Island; the inns prove inadequate to receive them. Call your local Bahamas Tourist Office (see chapter 2) for more information.

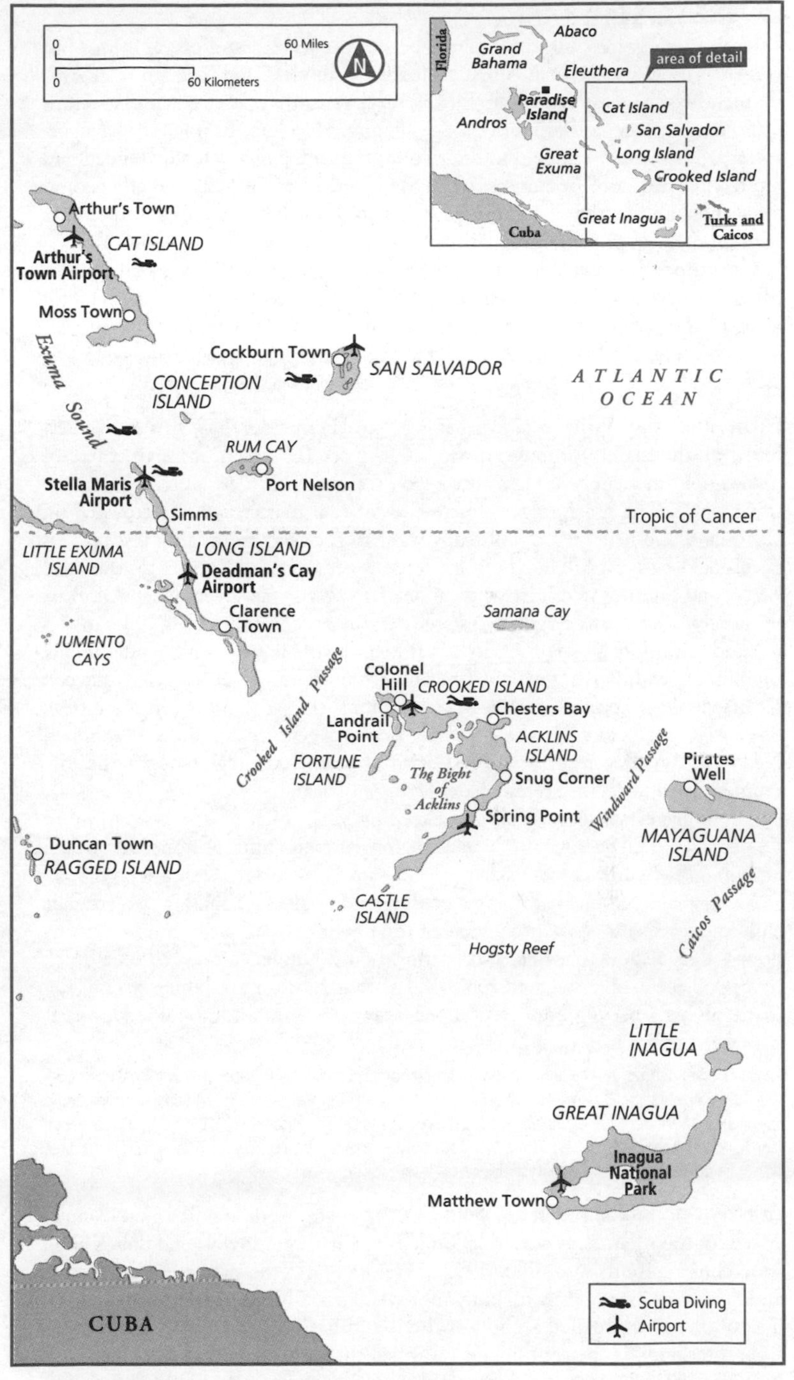
0
60 Miles
0
60 Kilometers
N
Florida
Grand Bahama
Abaco
Eleuthera
area of detail
Paradise Island
Andros
Cat Island
San Salvador
Great Exuma
Long Island
Crooked Island
Great Inagua
Cuba
Turks and Caicos
Arthur's Town
CAT ISLAND
Arthur's Town Airport
Moss Town
Exuma Sound
Cockburn Town
SAN SALVADOR
CONCEPTION ISLAND
ATLANTIC OCEAN
RUM CAY
Stella Maris Airport
Port Nelson
Simms
Tropic of Cancer
LITTLE EXUMA ISLAND
LONG ISLAND
Deadman's Cay Airport
Clarence Town
Samana Cay
JUMENTO CAYS
Crooked Island Passage
Colonel Hill
CROOKED ISLAND
Chesters Bay
Landrail Point
ACKLINS ISLAND
Windward Passage
Pirates Well
FORTUNE ISLAND
The Bight of Acklins
Snug Corner
Spring Point
MAYAGUANA ISLAND
Duncan Town
RAGGED ISLAND
CASTLE ISLAND
Caicos Passage
Hogsty Reef
LITTLE INAGUA
GREAT INAGUA
Inagua National Park
Matthew Town
CUBA
Scuba Diving
Airport

WHERE TO STAY & DINE

Bridge Inn Lying 300 yards from a beach, the relaxed and casual Bridge Inn is owned by Cat Islander Allan Russell, who is ably assisted by a group of family members. The inn offers babysitting services so that parents can play tennis or go diving, sailboarding, snorkeling, jogging, bicycling, fishing, or just sightseeing with the knowledge that their youngsters are being carefully tended and are having fun, too. Bedrooms are modest and small, motel-style affairs, and each unit can house three to four guests. Each of the high-ceilinged units comes with a private bath containing a shower stall.

On the premises you'll find a full bar and a restaurant that serves a rather simple Bahamian and international cuisine. Local jam sessions ("Rake 'n' Scrape") are easily arranged for your entertainment, usually on Friday night.

New Bight, Cat Island, The Bahamas. ✆ 242/342-3013. Fax 242/342-3041. www.bridgeinn.net. 12 units. $100 double; $110 triple. MC, V. **Amenities:** Restaurant, bar; laundry; babysitting. *In room:* A/C, TV.

Fernandez Bay Village ★ Opening onto Fernandez Bay, this is the best resort on the island. Although rustic, it has a certain charm, mainly because of its position on a curvy white sandy beach set against casuarinas blowing in the trade winds. The beach, or anywhere else for that matter, is never crowded on Cat Island. Go here only if you really want to get away from it all; this place is far too laid-back for full hotel service. Things get done, but it takes time around here—and no one's in a hurry. Fernandez Bay Village has been in the Armbrister family since it was originally established on a plantation in 1870. Its rusticity and seclusion are part of its charm, and yet, if you wish, you can get acquainted with other guests with similar interests (or even watch videos). Yachtspeople, who moor in the water offshore (there are no marina facilities), often visit the resort to take advantage of the general store's fresh supplies. Nearby Smith's Bay is one of the best storm shelters in the region—even the government mail boats take refuge here during hurricanes.

The "village" consists of full housekeeping villas, each of which sleeps up to six people, as well as three double-occupancy cottages, built of stone, driftwood, and glass. Each unit comes with a private garden bathroom with a shower stall.

Meals are served in a clubhouse decorated with antiques and Haitian art. The clubhouse, which opens onto a view of the beach and sea, also features a sitting library area, a stone fireplace, and overhead fans. Dinners are served on a beach terrace adjacent to a thatched-roof tiki bar that runs on the honor system. On many nights a blazing bonfire near the water becomes a focal point for guests who want to listen to island music.

1.5km (1 mile) north of New Bight, Cat Island, The Bahamas. ✆ **800/940-1905** or 242/342-3043, or 954/474-4821 in Plantation, FL. Fax 242/342-3051, or 954/474-4864 in Plantation, FL. 14 units. www.fernandezbayvillage.com. Winter $280–$345 villa for 4, $190 cottage for 2; off-season $255–$295 villa for 2, $170 cottage for 2. Half-board $45 per person. AE, MC, V. **Amenities:** Restaurant, bar; kayaks; bikes; snorkeling; waterskiing; fly-fishing; car rentals; laundry; babysitting. *In room:* Kitchen, no phone.

Greenwood Beach Resort & Dive Center The location on a 13km (8-mile) stretch of the Atlantic, bordered by pink sands, is always idyllic, and there's good snorkeling right offshore. Since 1992, a German family has run this beach resort and dive center, constantly making improvements. This group of modern buildings on the most isolated section of the island has a private sandy beach and a freshwater pool. It's better run and equipped than the Bridge Inn, and it attracts mostly divers. The small oceanview double rooms are all equipped with full bathrooms and showers and their own terraces. There is an all-purpose bar and a dining room.

The hotel's dive center is the best on the island. The inn has a 12m (40-ft.) motorboat for diving excursions, and its Cat Island Dive Center has complete equipment for 20 divers at a time. A two-tank dive is $75, and equipment is $5 to $10 extra depending on your needs. The resort also has two fishing boats available for both bonefishing ($150 for a half-day, $200 for a full day) and deep-sea fishing ($200 for a half-day, $300 for a full day). The staff greets each arriving Bahamasair flight.

Port Howe, Cat Island, The Bahamas. ✆ **877/228-7475** in the U.S., or 242/342-3053. Fax 242/342-3053. www.greenwoodbeachresort.net. 20 units. Nov–Apr $99 double; May–Oct $90 double. Free meals for children under 7. AE, MC, V. **Amenities:** Dining room, bar; pool; dive center; fishing boats; babysitting; laundry; bike rental. *In room:* Ceiling fan, no phone.

Hawk's Nest Resort & Marina This remote getaway and marina lies on the southwestern side of Cat Island, fronting a long, sandy beach and containing its own runway for charter flights and private planes, plus an eight-slip marina attracting the yachting crowd. This intimate resort is set near the village of Devil's Point, lying some 16km (10 miles) west of Columbus Point close to the ruins of the once-flourishing but now-abandoned Richman Hill and Newfield Plantation. Bedrooms, with either two queen-size beds or a king-size bed, are well-furnished and brightly decorated, each with a shower unit. Each room features a patio for those late-afternoon toddies overlooking the sunset. If you bring the family, you may want to look at the two-bedroom house on the beach, separate from the other structures. The clubhouse, the rooms, and the main house are spacious and inviting.

They serve full breakfasts (cooked to order), sandwiches for lunch, and a buffet-style dinner, with the unannounced fare changing nightly. The club can rent out snorkeling equipment for as little as $10 per day, or you can go scuba diving for $55 for a one-tank dive. A 7m (24-ft.) hydrosport boat is also made available to guests for a charge of $475 for a half day or $675 for a full day.

Devil's Point, Cat Island, The Bahamas. ✆ **800/688-4752** or 242/342-7050. Fax 242/342-7051. www.hawks-nest.com. 10 units, 1 2-bedroom house. $135–$220 per day double. MAP (breakfast and dinner) $50 extra per person. MC, V. **Amenities:** Restaurant; pool; 2 tennis courts; laundry; dive shop; snorkel gear; bike and kayak rental. *In room:* A/C, TV, coffeemaker, hair dryer.

Pigeon Cay Beach Club This B&B lies at the north end of the island, about a 15-minute ride from the airport and fronting a tranquil bay. The main building consists of a trio of separate but attached units, a small store, and the check-in office. Each accommodation comes with a fully equipped kitchen. In addition, there are some light and airy cottages, ranging from one bedroom to three bedrooms. Cottages are built of stucco and coral stone with beamed ceilings, along with Mexican tile floors. Each unit comes with a shower stall.

North End, Cat Island, The Bahamas. ✆ and fax **242/354-5084.** www.pigeoncaybahamas.com. 7 units. $160 1-bedroom unit, $225 2-bedroom unit, $375 3-bedroom unit. AE, MC, V. **Amenities:** Laundry. *In room:* Kitchen, ceiling fan, no phone.

EXPLORING THE ISLAND: PLANTATIONS, PEAKS & A HERMITAGE

There's an interesting Arawak cave at Columbus Point on the southern tip of the island. In addition, you can see the ruins of many once-flourishing plantations. Some old stone mounds are nearly 200 years old. Early planters, many of them Loyalists, marked their plantation boundaries with these mounds. These include the Deveaux Mansion, built by Col. Andrew Deveaux of the fledgling U.S. Navy, who recaptured Nassau from the Spanish in 1783. The plantation's heyday was during the island's short-lived cotton boom. Yet another mansion, Armbrister Plantation, lies in ruins near Port Howe.

You can hike along the natural paths through native villages and past exotic plants. Finally, you reach the peak of Mount Alvernia, the highest point in The Bahamas, at 62m (206 ft.) above sea level, where you will be rewarded with a spectacular view. The mount is capped by the **Hermitage,** a religious retreat built entirely by hand by the late Father Jerome, the former "father confessor" of the island, who was once a mule skinner in Canada. Curiously, the building was scaled to fit his short stature (he was a very, very short man). Formerly an Anglican, this Roman Catholic hermit priest became a legend on Cat Island. He died in 1956 at the age of 80, but his memory is kept very much alive here.

The **dive center at the Greenwood Beach Resort** (© **242/342-3053**) will take you out on diving or snorkeling excursions, or will rent you snorkel gear and other water toys.

2 San Salvador ★

This may be where the New World began. For some years it has been believed that Christopher Columbus made his first footprints in the western hemisphere here, although some scholars strongly dispute this. The easternmost island in the Bahamian archipelago, San Salvador lies 322km (200 miles) southeast of Nassau. It is some 163 square km (63 sq. miles) in area, much of which is occupied by water. There are 28 landlocked lakes on the island, the largest of which is 19km (12 miles) long and serves as the principal route of transportation for most of the island's population of 1,200. A badly maintained 64km (40-mile) road circles the perimeter of San Salvador.

The tiny island keeps a lonely vigil in the Atlantic. **The Dixon Hill Lighthouse** at South West Point, about 50m (165 ft.) tall, can be seen from 145km (90 miles) away. The light is a hand-operated beacon fueled by kerosene. Built in the 1850s, it is the last lighthouse of its type in The Bahamas. The highest point on the island is **Mount Kerr** at 41m (138 ft.).

Except for the odd historian or two, very few people ever used to visit San Salvador. Then **Club Med-Columbus Isle** opened, and the joint's been jumping ever since—at least at the Club Med property. Away from here, San Salvador is as sleepy as it ever was, although it's been known for years as one of the best dive sites in The Bahamas. The snorkeling, fishing, and lovely white-sand beaches are equally good.

ESSENTIALS

GETTING THERE Club Med (see below) solves transportation problems for its guests by flying them in on weekly charter planes from Miami or Eleuthera. Otherwise, **Riding Rock Inn** (see below) has charter flights every Saturday from Fort Lauderdale. You can also rely on public transportation by land or sea, but if you do, you'll have to wait a long time before getting off the island.

Bahamasair (© **800/222-4262**) has lots of flights to the island because of the Club Med. Departure times from Nassau are constantly changing, so check with the airline for a schedule.

From Nassau, the mail boat **M/VT *Lady Francis*** leaves Tuesday heading for San Salvador and Rum Cay. The trip takes 18 hours under uncomfortable conditions. For details about sailing, contact the dockmaster at **Potter's Cay Dock** in Nassau (✆ **242/393-1064**).

GETTING AROUND Taxis meet arriving planes and will take you to **Riding Rock Inn** (see below), where you can rent a car from $85 a day to explore the island on your own. You can also rent bicycles here at $10 a day. The latter are the most popular means of transport for visitors.

FAST FACTS **The San Salvador Medical Clinic** (✆ **242/331-2105**) serves the island's residents, but serious cases are flown to Nassau. The clinic is open Monday through Friday from 9am to 5pm, and only emergencies are handled on Saturday and Sunday.

To call the police, dial ✆ **919.** (Phones are rare on the island, but the front desk at Riding Rock Inn will place calls for you.)

WHERE TO STAY & DINE

Club Med-Columbus Isle ★★ This is one of the most ecologically conscious, and one of the most luxurious, Club Meds in the western hemisphere. Set at the edge of one of the most pristine beaches in the archipelago (3km/2 miles of white sand), about 3km (2 miles) north of Cockburn Town, the resort is the splashiest place in the entire Southern Bahamas. Its promoters estimate that more than 30% of the island's population works within the club.

Most of the prefabricated buildings were barged to the site in 1991. The resort is built around a large free-form swimming pool. The public rooms are some of the most lavish and cosmopolitan in the country, with art and art objects imported from Asia, Africa, the Americas, and Europe, and assembled by a battalion of designers. Bedrooms each contain a private balcony or patio, furniture that was custom-made in Thailand or the Philippines, sliding glass doors, and feathered wall hangings crafted in the Brazilian rain forest by members of the Xingu tribe. Rooms are large (among the most spacious in the entire chain). Most have twin beds, but you might be able to snag one of the units with a double or a king-size bed if you're lucky. Each comes with a midsize bathroom with shower stall. Dozens of multilingual GOs (guest relations organizers, or *gentiles organizateurs*) are on hand to help initiate newcomers into the resort's many diversions. Unlike many other Club Meds, this one does not encourage children and deliberately offers no particular facilities for their entertainment.

The main dining room, where meals are an ongoing series of buffets, lies in the resort's center. Two specialty restaurants offer Italian and grilled food, respectively. Nonfat, low-calorie, and vegetarian dishes are also featured. Nightly entertainment is presented in a covered, open-air theater and dance floor behind one of the bars.

3km (2 miles) north of Cockburn Town, San Salvador, The Bahamas. ✆ **800/CLUB-MED** or 242/331-2000. Fax 242/331-2458. www.clubmed.com. 270 units. Winter $1,379–$2,079 per person double; off-season $1,134–$1,379 per person double. No discounts for children. Weekly rates include all meals, drinks during meals, and most sports activities. AE, MC, V. Children under 12 not recommended. **Amenities:** 3 restaurants, bar lounge; 10 tennis courts (3 lit for night play); pool; fitness center; largest scuba facility in the Club Med chain; windsurfing, kayaking and kayak-scuba diving; mini-armada of Hobie Cats and other sailing craft. *In room:* A/C, TV, refrigerator, hair dryer, safe.

Riding Rock Inn Resort & Marina San Salvador's second resort is the motel-style Riding Rock Inn, catering largely to divers. Its simple ambience is a far cry from the extravagant Club Med. Each accommodation faces either a pool or the open sea. The most recent improvement to the inn is an 18-room oceanfront building, where the bedrooms are decorated in a tropical decor, with two

Fun Fact The Columbus Question

In 1492, a small group of peaceful Lucayan natives (Arawaks) were going about their business on a little island they called Guanahani, where they and their forebears had lived for at least 500 years. Little did they know how profoundly their lives would change when they greeted the arrival of three small strange-looking ships bearing Columbus and his crew of pale, bearded, oddly costumed men. It is said that when he came ashore, Columbus knelt and prayed—and claimed the land for Spain.

Unfortunately, the event was not so propitious for the reportedly handsome natives. Columbus later wrote to Queen Isabella that they would make ideal captives—perfect servants, in other words. It wasn't long before the Spanish conquistadors cleared the island, as well as most of The Bahamas, of Lucayans, sending them into slavery and early death in the mines of Hispaniola (Haiti) in order to feed the Spanish lust for gold from the New World.

But is the island now known as San Salvador the actual site of Columbus's landing? Columbus placed no lasting marker on the sandy, sun-drenched island of his landfall, and the result has been much study and discussion during the past century or so as to just where he actually landed.

In the 17th century, an English pirate captain, George Watling, took over the island and built a mansion to serve as his safe haven. The island was listed on maps for about 250 years as Watling's (or Watling) Island.

In 1926 the Bahamian legislature formally changed the name of the island to San Salvador, feeling that enough evidence had been

double beds, satellite TV, a refrigerator, a telephone, ceiling fans, and air-conditioning. Each unit is equipped with a midsize bathroom with a shower-tub combination.

The resort specializes in weeklong packages that include three dives a day, all meals, and accommodations. Packages begin and end on Saturday and, if a client pays a $300 supplement, can include specially chartered round-trip air transportation from Fort Lauderdale. Although most of the guests are already experienced and certified divers, beginners can arrange a $105 resort course for the first day of their visit and afterward participate in most of the community's daily dives. Full PADI certification can also be arranged for another supplement of $400.

An island tour is included in the rates, but after that, most folks rent a bike or scooter from the hotel. On the premises are a restaurant serving routine Bahamian specialties and a bar with a seating area that juts above the water on a pier.

Cockburn Town, San Salvador, The Bahamas. ✆ **800/272-1492** in the U.S., or 954/359-8353 in Florida. Fax 242/331-2020. www.ridingrock.com. 42 units. $137–$170 double; $160–$190 triple; $194 quad. Dive packages available. MC, V. **Amenities:** Restaurant, bar; pool; dive shop; tennis court. *In room:* A/C, TV, hair dryer.

brought forth to support the belief that this was the site of Columbus's landing. Then in 1983, artifacts of European origin (beads, buckles, and metal spikes) were found here together with a shard of Spanish pottery, and Arawak pottery and beads. It is unlikely that the actual date of these artifacts can be pinned down, although they are probably from about 1490 to 1560. However, the beads and buckles fit the description of goods recorded in Columbus's log.

National Geographic published a meticulously researched article in 1986 written by its senior associate editor, Joseph Judge, with a companion piece by the former chief of the magazine's foreign editorial staff, Luis Marden, setting forth the belief that Samana Cay, some 105km (65 miles) to the southeast of the present San Salvador, was Guanahani, the island Columbus named San Salvador when he first landed in the New World. The question may never be absolutely resolved, but there will doubtless be years and years of controversy about it. Nevertheless, history buffs still flock here every year hoping to follow in the footsteps of Columbus.

Whether or not it was actually on this island, Columbus and his men did hit land at around 2am on the moonlit night of October 12, 1492. The native population, probably awakened from a sound sleep, called these strange creatures "men from Heaven." Perhaps "men from Hell" would have been a better description. The Spanish discovery of this island and others led to a holocaust, as the Spanish wiped out the native populations.

BEACHES, WATERSPORTS & OTHER OUTDOOR PURSUITS

The beaches of San Salvador, kilometers and kilometers of sandy shores with rarely another person in sight, are ideal for shelling, swimming, or snorkeling. Try **Bamboo Point, Fernandez Bay, Long Bay,** or **Sandy Point.**

Associated with the Riding Rock Inn (see above), **Guanahani Dive Ltd.** (**© 242/331-2631**) offers dive packages, as well as snorkeling, fishing, and boating trips. Year-round divers can book a getaway package for 5 days and 4 nights that costs from $654 to $710 per diver, including meals, transportation, diving, rental gear, and a charter flight. Prices are based on double occupancy.

Riding Rock Inn also has a tennis court where guests can play for free.

Bonefishers are attracted to **Pigeon Creek,** and some record catches have been chalked up here.

EXPLORING THE ISLAND: COMMEMORATING COLUMBUS

Among the settlements on San Salvador are Sugar Loaf, Pigeon Creek, Old Place, Holiday Track, and Fortune Hill. United Estates, which has the largest population, is a village in the northwest corner near the Dixon Hill Lighthouse. The U.S. Coast Guard has a station at the northern tip of the island.

Except for the party people at Club Med, San Salvador is mainly visited by the boating set, who can live aboard their craft. If you're exploring for the day, you'll find one or two local cafes that serve seafood.

The attractions listed below charge no admission and may be viewed at any time. If a preponderance of monuments is anything to go by, this would have to be the San Salvador Columbus visited and named.

The Chicago Herald installed the **Chicago Herald Monument** on Crab Cay to the explorer in 1892, but it is highly unlikely—in fact, almost impossible—that any landing was made at this site. It opens onto reefs along the eastern shore, surely a dangerous place for a landing.

At Long Bay, the **Olympic Games Memorial** to Columbus, located 5km (3 miles) south of Cockburn Town, was erected in 1968 to commemorate the games in Mexico. Runners carrying an Olympic torch circled the island before coming to rest at the monument and lighting the torch there. The torch was then taken to Mexico on a warship for the games. Another marker is underwater, supposedly where Columbus dropped anchor on his *Santa Maria.*

Just north of the Olympic Games Memorial stands the **Columbus Monument.** On December 25, 1956, Ruth Durlacher Wolper Malvin—a leading U.S. expert on Columbus research—established a simple monument commemorating the explorer's landfall in the New World. Unlike the spot marked by the *Chicago Herald* monument, this is actually supposed to be the place where Columbus and his men landed.

At French Bay, **Watling's Castle,** also known as Sandy Point Estate, has substantial ruins that are about 26m (85 ft.) above sea level. The area is located some 4km (2½ miles) from the "Great Lake," on the southwestern tip of the island. Local "experts" will tell you all about the castle and its history. The only problem is each "expert" we've listened to (three in all, at different times) has told a different story about the place. Ask around and perhaps you'll get yet another version; they're entertaining, at least. One of the most common legends involves a famous pirate who made his living either by salvaging the wreckage from foundered ships or by attacking ships for their spoils.

Once plantations—all doomed to failure—were scattered about the island. The most impressive ruins of this former life are **Farquharson's Plantation,** west of Queen's Highway, near South Victoria Hill. In the early part of the 19th century, some Loyalist families moved from the newly established United States to this island, hoping to get rich from farmland tended by slave labor. That plan collapsed when the United Kingdom Emancipation Act freed the slaves in 1834. The plantation owners moved on, but the former slaves stayed behind.

A relic of those times, Farquharson's Plantation is the best-known ruin on the island. People locally call it "Blackbeard's Castle," but it's a remnant of slavery, not piracy. You can see the foundation of a great house, a kitchen, and what is believed to have been a jail.

COCKBURN TOWN

San Salvador's capital, Cockburn (pronounced "Coburn") Town, is a harbor village that takes its name from George Cockburn, who is said to have been the first royal governor of The Bahamas to visit this remote island. That was back in 1823.

Look for the town's landmark: a giant almond tree. Major events in San Salvador, like the Columbus Day parade held every October 12, generally take place here.

Holy Saviour Roman Catholic Church The very first Christian worship service in the New World was Catholic. It thus seems fitting that the Roman Catholic Diocese of The Bahamas in 1992, on the eve of the 500th anniversary of the Columbus landfall, dedicated a new church on San Salvador.

Cockburn Town. Free admission. Services Sun at 10am.

New World Museum This museum, located 5.5km (3½ miles) north of Riding Rock Inn, has relics dating from Indian times, but you'll have to ask until you find someone with a key if you want to go inside. The museum lies just past Bonefish Bay in the little village of North Victoria Hill. Part of a large estate, called Polaris-by-the-Sea, it's owned by Ruth Durlacher Wolper Malvin.

North Victoria Hill. No phone. Free admission. Open anytime during the day.

DISCOVERING RUM CAY & CONCEPTION ISLAND

"Where on earth is Rum Cay?" you ask. Even many Bahamians have never heard of it. Located midway between San Salvador and Long Island, this is another cay, like Fortune Island (see "The Ghost Island of Fortune" below), that time forgot.

That wasn't always the case, though. The very name conjures up images of swashbucklers and rumrunners. Doubtless, it was at least a port of call for those dubious seafarers, as it was for ships, as well, to take on supplies of salt, fresh water, and food before crossing the Atlantic or going south to Latin America. The cay's name is supposed to have derived from a rum-laden sailing ship that wrecked upon its shores.

With the demise of the Rum Cay Club, tourist traffic to the island came to a halt except for the odd yachting party or two. But with the increased interest in tourism that followed the 1992 Columbus celebrations, the area is gaining renewed interest. At present, you can arrange for boaters on San Salvador to take you to see these islands, which remain frozen in time.

3 Long Island

The Tropic of Cancer runs through this long, thin sliver of land, located 242km (150 miles) southeast of Nassau. The island stretches north to south for some 97km (60 miles). It's 2.5km (1½ miles) wide on average, and only 5km (3 miles) wide at its broadest point.

Long Island is characterized by high cliffs in the north, wide and shallow sand beaches, historic plantation ruins, native caves, and Spanish churches. It is also the site of the saltworks of the **Diamond Crystal Company.** The island's present population numbers some 3,500 people.

The famed **diving sites** ★ are offshore, such as the Arawak "green" hole, a "bottomless" blue hole of stunning magnitude. The best beach bets include Deal's Beach, Cape Santa Maria Beach, Salt Pond Beach, Turtle Cove Beach, and the South End beaches, the latter offering kilometers of waterfront with powdery white or pink sands.

Most historians agree that Long Island, which has only recently emerged as a minor tourist resort, was the third island Columbus sailed to during his first voyage of discovery.

ESSENTIALS

GETTING THERE There are two airstrips here, connected by a bad road. The **Stella Maris strip** is in the north, and the other, called **Deadman's Cay,** is in the south, north of Clarence Town (it's highly unlikely that you'll land here, and this one is a very expensive cab ride from most of the island's accommodations). **Bahamasair** (✆ **800/222-4262** in the U.S.) flies direct and daily from Fort Lauderdale, landing at the Stella Maris airport, which is near most of the hotels.

From Nassau, a mail boat sails weekly to Clarence Town on the southern end of Long Island. Departures are on Tuesday, and the trip takes a grueling 18 hours. For information contact the dockmaster at **Potter's Cay Dock,** Nassau (✆ **242/393-1064**).

GETTING AROUND The **Stella Maris Resort Club** (✆ **242/338-2051**) can make arrangements to have you picked up at the airport upon arrival and can also arrange for a rental car. Otherwise, you can contact **Taylor's Rentals** (✆ **242/338-7002**). This outfitter also rents scooters for $46 per day.

FAST FACTS The **police** can be reached by calling ✆ **242/337-0999** or 242/337-0444.

The **Bank of Nova Scotia** (✆ **242/338-2002**) operates a small currency-exchange facility at the Stella Maris Resort. Hours are only on Tuesday and Thursday from 9:30am to 2pm, and Friday from 9:30am to 5pm.

SPECIAL EVENTS In June, Long Island sailors participate in the big event of the year, the 4-day **Long Island Regatta.** They've been gathering since 1967 at Salt Pond for this annual event. In addition to the highly competitive sailboat races, Long Island takes on a festive air with calypso music and reggae and lots of drinking and partying. Many expatriate Long Islanders come home at this time, usually from Nassau, New York, or Miami, to enjoy not only the regatta but Rake 'n' Scrape music. Call your local Bahamas Tourist Office (see chapter 2) for more information.

WHERE TO STAY

Cape Santa Maria Beach Resort ★ This cozy nest has become the most luxurious resort on the island, taking over the position long held by the Stella Maris Resort Club. Cottages with two rooms are centered around a clubhouse, and the entire complex opens onto a stunning 6.5km (4-mile) strip of white sand. All units are only 18m (60 ft.) from the beach, which offers great snorkeling. Although the accommodations don't have phones or TVs, each room is air-conditioned and also has ceiling fans, plus a small bathroom with a shower-tub combination. Bedrooms have a light, tropical, and airy feeling, with marble floors and tasteful rattan furniture. There's also a screened-in porch with ceiling fans so you can enjoy the outdoors without the mosquitoes, the curse of the Southern Bahamas.

The place is ideal for families, and several accommodations are configured so that children will have a separate room.

The hotel's 65-seat restaurant is also good, serving a tasty Bahamian, North American, and seafood cuisine.

Cape Santa Maria, off Queen's Hwy., Long Island, The Bahamas. ✆ **800/663-7090** or 242/338-5273. Fax 242/338-6013. www.capesantamaria.com. 20 units. Winter $570 double for 1 night, $1,156 for 4 nights, $2,016 for 7 nights; off-season $390 double for 1 night, $876 for 4 nights, $1,526 for 7 nights. Extra person $56. All meals $75 extra per person. AE, MC, V. **Amenities:** Restaurant; health club; watersports; bike rental; car rental; snorkeling gear; scuba diving; sailboats. *In room:* A/C, coffeemaker, hair dryer, no phone.

Lochabar Beach Lodge One of the most remote retreats in this guide, this lodge offers escapist studios for those fleeing from the civilized world. You step from your studio to a pristine beach of white sand 23m (75 ft.) away, surrounding a "blue hole" in a natural cove. The only acceptable lodgings in the southern part of Long Island, these guest studios measure 56 or 111 square m (600 or 1,200 sq. ft.) each. In lieu of ceiling fans, the studios were built to take advantage of the trade winds. Guests keep their Bahama shutters and double screen doors open to capture those breezes. Each studio comes with a small bathroom containing a shower stall. Studios have kitchenettes, and a member of the staff will drive you to a nearby store to stock up on provisions.

Big Blue Hole, 1.5km (1 mile) south of Clarence Town, Long Island, The Bahamas. ✆ and fax **242/337-3123.** lochabar@hotmail.com. 3 units. $115–$150 double. Extra person $20. MC, V. **Amenities:** Snorkeling; bonefishing excursions; car rentals. *In room:* A/C, kitchenette, ceiling fan.

Stella Maris Resort Club ★ Situated on a ridge overlooking the Atlantic, the Stella Maris Resort Club stands in a palm grove on the grounds of the old Adderley's Plantation. Although you can swim here, the beach isn't the best, so the hotel maintains a cabana at Cape Santa Maria, a gorgeous white sandy beach directly north, and offers shuttle service for its guests.

Accommodations vary widely—rooms, studios, apartments, and cottages with one to four bedrooms. Each accommodation has its own walk-in closet and fully equipped bathroom. Some are directly on the water. All of the buildings, including the cottages and bungalows, are set around a central clubhouse and a trio of pools. The resort makes a great honeymoon destination; everything is relaxed and informal.

The inn serves a good Bahamian cuisine, as well as continental specialties. There are rum-punch parties, cave parties, barbecue dinners, Saturday dinners, and dancing. Numerous watersports include complete diving facilities. Divers and snorkelers can choose from coral head, reef, and drop-off diving along the protected west coast of the island, at the north, and all along the east coast, around Conception Island and Rum Cay. Water-skiing and bottom and reef fishing are also offered; there are three good bonefishing bays close by. Some 3.5m (12-ft.) Scorpion and Sunfish sailboats are free to hotel guests.

Ocean View Dr. (P.O. Box LI30105), Long Island, The Bahamas. ✆ **800/426-0466** or 242/338-2051, or 954/359-8236 for the Ft. Lauderdale booking office. Fax 242/338-2052. www.stellamarisresort.com. 45 units. Winter $160 double, $180 1-bedroom cottage, $290–$580 bungalow or villa; off-season $120 double, $145 1-bedroom cottage, $240–$495 bungalow or villa. AE, MC, V. **Amenities:** Restaurant, bar; 3 pools; watersports; boats. *In room:* A/C, hair dryer, fridge, private pool (some units), no phone.

WHERE TO DINE

All the inns above serve food, but you should call for a reservation. In addition, you can try some local joints. Try **Kooters,** Queen's Highway, Mangrove Bush

---

Finds **The Old Hamlet of Simms**

At a point 13km (8 miles) south of Stella Maris, you come to the hamlet of Simms, oldest on the island. Here the inhabitants of the little pastel-colored shacks live pretty much as they did a half-century ago.

If you're here for lunch, try one of the roadside eateries serving conch salad. Our favorites are **Jeraldine's Jerk Pit** (no phone) along Queen's Highway. You can order even more substantial food, especially grouper fingers and fresh crayfish, at **Mario's Blue Chip,** Queen's Highway (✆ **242/338-8964**). Leave your credit cards at home, of course, and don't anticipate regular opening hours.

(© **242/337-0340**), which couldn't be more casual or laid-back, but is known for serving the best conch burger on Long Island. You can also drop in for sandwiches, and the cook does a mean batch of home fries. They also do daily specials such as fresh grilled fish or barbecue baby back ribs.

Another joint worth checking out is **The Forest,** Queen's Highway, Miley's (© **242/337-3287**), lying south of Clarence Town. Its cracked conch is the island's finest, and you can also order the standard grouper fingers or even barbecued chicken. Spicy wings and potato skins are also served. The bar is made of seashells. On Friday nights, a live band plays for dancing, and The Forest becomes an island hot spot.

EXPLORING THE ISLAND

There isn't much shopping, but you can visit **Wild Tamarind,** lying 1km (½ mile) east of Queen's Highway at the hamlet of Petty's (© **242/337-0262**). Here Denis Knight makes the best ceramics on the island. You might want to carry off one of his ceramic sculptures or at least a bowl or vase.

Most of the islanders live at the unattractively named **Deadman's Cay.** Other settlements have equally colorful names: Roses, Newfound Harbour, Burnt Ground, Indian Head Point, and, at the northern tip of the island, Cape Santa Maria, generally believed to be the place where Columbus landed and from where he looked on the Exumas (islands that he did not visit). Our favorite name, however, is Hard Bargain. No one seems to know how this hamlet got its name. **Hard Bargain,** now a shrimp-breeding farm, lies 16km (10 miles) south of Clarence Town.

Try to visit **Clarence Town** ★, located 16km (10 miles) south of Deadman's Cay, along the eastern coastline. It was here that the stubby little priest, Father Jerome, who became known as the "father confessor" of the islands, built two churches before his death in 1956—**St. Paul's,** an Anglican house of worship, and **St. Peter's,** a Roman Catholic church. The "hermit" of Cat Island (you can visit his Hermitage there) was interested in Gothic architecture. He must also have been somewhat ecumenical, because he started his ministry as an Anglican but embraced Roman Catholicism along the way.

Many of the ruins recall the days when local plantation owners figured their wealth in black slaves and white cotton. The remains of **Dunmore's Plantation** at Deadman's Cay stand on a hill with the sea on three sides. There are six gateposts (four outer and two inner), as well as a house with two fireplaces and wall drawings of ships. At the base of the ruins is evidence that a mill wheel was once used. It was part of the estate of Lord Dunmore, for whom Dunmore Town on Harbour Island was named.

In the village of Grays stand the ruins of **Gray's Plantation,** where you'll see the remnants of at least three houses, one with two chimneys. One is very large, and another seems to have been a one-story structure with a cellar.

Adderley's Plantation, off Cape Santa Maria, originally occupied all the land now known as Stella Maris. The ruins of this cotton plantation's buildings consist of three structures that are partially intact but roofless.

Two underground sites that can be visited on Deadman's Cay are **Dunmore's Caves** and **Deadman's Cay Cave.** You'll need to hire a local guide to explore these. Dunmore's Caves are believed to have been inhabited by Lucayans and later to have served as a hideaway for buccaneers. The cave at Deadman's Cay, one of two that lead to the ocean, has never been fully explored. There are two native drawings on the cavern wall.

A lot of savvy anglers come here to fish instead of the more famous places, such as Andros. The secret of the good fishing found here is the presence of a major current stream, called the **North Equatorial Current,** which originates in the Canary Islands. This stream washes the shores of Long Island. In its wake the current transports huge schools of blue marlin, white marlin, sailfish, rainbow runners, yellowfin tuna, blackfin tuna, wahoo, and dolphinfish. Wahoo is best hunted from September through November. Catches weigh from 10 to 90 pounds, and some yellowfin have weighed up to 150 pounds. The small blackfin tuna (July–Dec) weigh from 10 to 30 pounds. In addition, there are kilometers and kilometers of reef fishing, with hundreds of species, including snapper or grouper that have been known to weigh 100 pounds. A jewfish caught here weighed 500 pounds. Inshore fishing for bonefish is also possible. These fish can be caught from an anchored boat, from the beach, or while wading in foot-deep water.

Although there are no watersports outfitters on Long Island, the two major resorts, the **Stella Maris Resort Club** and the **Cape Santa Maria Beach Resort** (see above) fill the void and offer more watersports than you can do in a week. Both offer bonefishing at a rate of $250 per day for up to two people; reef fishing is from $600 per day for up to six people; deep-sea fishing is $800 per day for up to six people. **Snorkeling** ★ off the beach is complimentary at both resorts. However, boat excursions can be as little as $10 per hour at Cape Santa Maria; on Wednesday and Saturday, these excursions are complimentary at the Stella Maris. Both resorts offer scuba diving ranging from $45 to $75 per person per day, with equipment rentals ranging from $17.50 to $25. Both also offer Hobie Cats, boogie boards, Windsurfers, and bicycles; the Stella Maris offers water-skiing for about $40 per person.

4 Acklins Island & Crooked Island

These little tropical islands, approximately 386km (240 miles) southeast of Nassau, make up an undiscovered Bahamian frontier outpost. Columbus came this way looking for gold. Much later, Acklins Island, Crooked Island, and their surrounding cays became hide-outs for pirates who attacked vessels in the Crooked Island Passage (the narrow waterway Columbus sailed), which separates the two islands. Today a well-known landmark, the **Crooked Island Passage Light,** built in 1876, guides ships to a safe voyage through the slot. Also known as the Bird Rock Lighthouse, it is a popular nesting spot for ospreys, and the light still lures pilots and sailors to the **Pittstown Point Landing Resort.** A barrier reef begins near the lighthouse, stretching down off Acklins Island for about 40km (25 miles) to the southeast.

Although Acklins Island and Crooked Island are separate, they are usually mentioned as a unit because of their proximity to one another. Together, the two islands form the shape of a boomerang. Crooked Island, the northern one, is 181 square km (70 sq. miles) in area, whereas Acklins Island, to the south, occupies 311 square km (120 sq. miles). Both islands, which have good white-sand beaches and offer fishing and scuba diving, are inhabited mainly by fishermen and farmers.

In his controversial article in *National Geographic* in 1986, Joseph Judge identified Crooked Island as the site of Columbus's second island landing, the one he named Santa Maria de la Concepcion.

It is estimated that by the end of the 18th century, there were more than three dozen working plantations on these islands, begun by Loyalists fleeing mainland

North America in the wake of the Revolutionary War. At the peak plantation period, there could have been as many as 1,200 slaves laboring in the 3,000 "doomed" acres of cotton fields (which were later wiped out by a blight). The people who remained on the island survived not only by fishing and farming, but also, beginning in the mid–18th century, by stripping the Croton cascarilla shrub of its bark to produce the flavoring for Campari liquor.

ESSENTIALS

GETTING THERE There's an airport at Colonel Hill on Crooked Island and another airstrip at **Spring Point,** Acklins Island.

Bahamasair (✆ **800/222-4262** in the U.S.) has two flights a week from Nassau, on Wednesday and Saturday, to Crooked Island and Acklins Island, with returns to Nassau scheduled on the same day.

There is also mail-boat service, with the **MV *United Star*,** leaving Potter's Cay Dock in Nassau and heading for Acklins Island, Crooked Island, Fortune Island (Long Cay), and Mayaguana Island each week. Check the schedule and costs with the dockmaster at **Potter's Cay Dock** in Nassau (✆ **242/393-1064**).

A government-owned **ferry** service connects the two islands; it operates daily from 9am to 4pm. It links Lovely Bay on Acklins Island with Browns on Crooked Island. The one-way fare is $4.

Once you arrive at Crooked Island, a **taxi** service is available, but because of the lack of telephones, it's wise to advise your hotel of your arrival—they'll probably send a van to meet you.

FAST FACTS There are two government-operated clinics. Phones are scarce on the islands, but your hotel desk can reach one of these clinics by going through the operator. The clinic on Acklins Island is at **Spring Point and Chesters Bay,** and the one on Crooked Island is at **Landrail Point.**

The **police** station on Crooked Island can be reached by dialing ✆ **242/344-2599.**

WHERE TO STAY & DINE

Pittstown Point Landing Located on a beach at the extreme northwestern tip of Crooked Island, this hotel is so isolated you'll forget all about the world outside. For most of the early years of its life, it was a well-guarded secret shared mostly by the owners of private planes who flew in from the mainland of Florida for off-the-record weekends. Even today, about 80% of the clients arrive by one- or two-engine aircraft that they fly themselves as part of island-hopping jaunts around The Bahamas. The island maintains its own 690m (2,300-ft.), hard-surface landing strip, which is completely independent from the one used for the flights from Nassau on Bahamasair.

In 1994, a group of investors upgraded the place, taking great care not to alter its funky appeal. Surrounded by scrub-covered landscape at the edge of a turquoise sea, it lies 4km (2½ miles) north of the hamlet of Landrail Point (pop. 60) on a sandy peninsula. Within easy access are some of the weirdest historic sites in The Bahamas, including the sun-baked ruins of a salt farm (Marine Farms Fortress) that was sacked by American-based pirates in 1812.

Spartan accommodations with shower-tub combination bathrooms lie within three low-slung, cement-sided buildings. They lie directly on the beach, usually with screened-in porches facing the sea. Because of the constant trade winds blowing in, not all bedrooms have air-conditioning, but do contain large paddle-shaped ceiling fans. The entire resort shares only one telephone/fax, which is reserved for emergency calls.

Finds The Ghost Island of Fortune

Lying off the coast of Crooked Island, **Fortune Island** is truly a place that time forgot. Your hotel can put you in touch with a boater on Crooked Island who will take you here. Experts believe, based on research done for *National Geographic,* that Fortune Island (sometimes confusingly called Long Cay) is the one Columbus chose to name Isabella, in honor of the queen who funded his expedition. Its only real settlement is Albert Town, which is classified as a ghost town, but officially isn't—some hardy souls still live here. Fortune Hill, visible from 19km (12 miles) away at sea, is the local landmark. Hundreds of Bahamians came here in the 2 decades before World War I and would wait to be picked up by oceangoing freighters, which would take them to seek their fortunes as laborers in Central America—hence, the name Fortune Hill.

Meals are served in a stone-sided building that was originally erected late in the 1600s as a barracks for the British West Indies Naval Squadron and later was the region's post office. The restaurant serves seafood and North American and Bahamian specialties. Guests always take the meal plan, but they're joined by a scattering of yacht owners or aviators who drop in spontaneously for drinks and dinner.

Landrail Point, Crooked Island, The Bahamas. (For reservations and information, contact Pittstown Point Landing, 238A Airport Rd., Statesville, NC 28677.) ✆ **800/PLACE-2-B** or 242/344-2507. www.pittstownpointlandings.com. 12 units. $150–$180 double. $60 AP (all meals) extra. AE, MC, V. **Amenities:** Restaurant, bar; laundry. *In room:* A/C (8 units), ceiling fan, no phone.

UNCOVERING A PIRATE HIDE-OUT

Crooked Island opens onto the **Windward Passage,** the dividing point between the Caribbean Sea and The Bahamas. Whatever else he may have named it, it is said that when Columbus landed at what is now Pittstown Point, he called it Fragrant Island because of the aroma of its many herbs. One scent was cascarilla bark, used to flavor Campari liquor as well as the native Cascarilla Liqueur, which is exported. For the best view of the island, go to **Colonel Hill** ★—unless you arrived at the Crooked Island Airport (also known as the Colonel Hill Airport), which has the same vantage.

Guarding the north end of this island is the **Marine Farms Fortress,** an abandoned British fortification that saw action in the War of 1812. It looks out over Crooked Island Passage and can be visited (ask your hotel to make arrangements for you).

Hope Great House is also on the island, with orchards and gardens that date from the time of George V of England.

Other sights include **French Wells Bay,** a swampy delta leading to an extensive mangrove swamp rich in bird life, and the **Bird Rock Lighthouse,** built a century ago.

At the southern end of Acklins Island lies **Castle Island,** a low and sandy bit of land where an 1867 lighthouse stands. Pirates used it as a hide-out, sailing forth to attack ships in the nearby passage.

Acklins Island has many interestingly named villages—Rocky Point, Binnacle Hill, Salina Point, Delectable Bay, Golden Grove, Goodwill, Hard Hill, Snug Corner, and Lovely Bay. Some Crooked Island sites have more ominous names, such as Gun Point and Cripple Hill.

5 Mayaguana Island

Sleepy Mayaguana seems to float adrift in the tropical sun at the remote extremities of the southeastern edge of The Bahamas. It occupies 285 square km (110 sq. miles) and has a population of about 300. It's a long, long way from the development of Nassau and Paradise Island.

Standing in the Windward Passage, Mayaguana is just northwest of the Turks and Caicos Islands. It's separated from the British Crown Colony by the Caicos Passage. Around the time of the American Civil War, inhabitants of Turks Island began to settle in Mayaguana, which before then had dozed undisturbed for centuries.

Acklins Island and Crooked Island lie across the Mayaguana Passage. Mayaguana is only 9.5km (6 miles) across at its widest point, and about 39km (24 miles) long. Its beaches are enticing, but you'll rarely see a tourist on them, other than the occasional German. A few developers have flown in to check out the island, but to date no new development has occurred.

GETTING THERE

Bahamasair (© **800/222-4262** in the U.S.) flies in here to a little airstrip. Flights arrive from Nassau Monday, Wednesday and Friday at 10:30am, 9:15am, and 10am, respectively.

From Nassau, a **mail boat,** going also to Crooked Island, Acklins Island, and Fortune Island (Long Cay), makes a stop at Mayaguana. For information, check with the dockmaster at **Potter's Cay Dock** in Nassau (© **242/393-1064**).

WHERE TO STAY & DINE

Few other outposts in The Bahamas are as remote as Mayaguana, which is the main reason why many visitors come—to get away from everything. Many visitors arrive by boat and just ask around for availability at one of the ultra-simple lodgings here. Some locals are willing to house you in one of their spare bedrooms for a rate that can be negotiated up or down to almost anything.

The most "substantial" place to stay, if one can call it that, is **Reggie's Guest House & Lounge,** Mayaguana, The Bahamas (© **242/339-3065** or 609/859-8582 in the U.S.; powel@bellatlantic.net). It is the picture of barebones simplicity. A room rents for $65 per person for two, with $15 charged per each additional person. You can order breakfast or lunch for $6 each, with dinners costing $10; the cook will even prepare your day's catch if you wish. Fishing excursions can also be arranged for $125 per day for two, and snorkeling trips cost $100 per day for two, with each extra person in the party costing $10 to $15. Remember, however, that you must bring your own equipment—they don't supply it here.

EXPLORING THE ISLAND

Abraham's Bay is the main town on the south coast, with an excellent harbor. The other little settlement on Mayaguana is **Betsy Bay,** secluded and lost in time. Wild corn and saucy hummingbirds share this spot along with some little sun-worn cottages basking in the hot sun. At **Pirate's Well,** goats are now the chief residents, although buccaneers used to roam past here. Locals still dream of finding buried treasure.

The best views of the Mayaguana Passage can be had from both Betsy Bay and Pirate's Well.

Fishing is good on the island. Locals will often take you out on one of their boats, but you've got to ask around. In summer and early autumn, temperatures can soar beyond 100°F. Winters, however, are ideal, and it never gets cold here as it can in the North Bahamas.

Mayaguana might be called The Bahamas's "great outback" or "wild west." It's a rugged and salty environment, with no organized activities of any kind. Sailing, deep-sea fishing, scuba diving, snorkeling, swimming, and walking are the main pastimes. If you need rental gear or want to hire a guide for an organized outing, your best bet is to inquire at your hotel; they can usually hook you up with the right person. The island is still too laid-back to have many organized outfitters.

6 Great Inagua ★

The most southerly and the third-largest island of The Bahamas, flat Great Inagua, some 64km (40 miles) long and 32km (20 miles) wide, is home to 1,200 people. It lies 527km (325 miles) southeast of Nassau.

This is the site not only of the **Morton Salt Crystal Factory,** here since 1800, but also of one of the largest nesting grounds for **flamingos** in the western hemisphere. The National Trust of The Bahamas protects the area around Lake Windsor, where the birds breed and the population is said to number 50,000. Flamingos used to inhabit all of The Bahamas, but the bird is nearly extinct in many places. The reserve can be visited only with a guide. Besides the pink flamingo, you can see roseate spoonbills and other bird life here.

Green turtles are raised here, too, at **Union Creek Reserve.** Tours here are not well-organized; it's all very informal. You can ask your inn to arrange a tour for you, or call **Larry Ingraham's Great Inagua Tours** at **© 242/339-1862** to ask if he'll set up something for you. They are then released into the ocean to make their way as best they can; they, too, are an endangered species. The vast windward island, almost within sight of Cuba, is also inhabited by wild hogs, horses, and donkeys.

The settlement of **Matthew Town** is the chief hamlet of the island, but it's not of any great sightseeing interest. Other sites have interesting names, such as Doghead Point, Lantern Head, Conch Shell Point, Mutton Fish Point, and Devil's Point (which makes one wonder what happened there to give rise to the name). There's an 1870 lighthouse at Matthew Town.

Little Inagua, 8km (5 miles) to the north, has no population and is just a speck of land off the northeast coast of Great Inagua, about 78 square km (30 sq. miles) in area. It has much bird life, though, including West Indian tree ducks. There are also wild goats and donkeys.

ESSENTIALS

GETTING THERE **Bahamasair** (**© 800/222-4262** in the U.S.) flies to Matthew Town Airport from Nassau on Monday, Wednesday, and Friday at 10:30am, 9:15am, and 10am, respectively.

You can also go by **mail boat,** which makes weekly trips from Nassau to Matthew Town (schedule varies). The boat leaves Nassau on Tuesday and comes back on Sunday. Call the **Potter's Cay Dockmaster** (**© 242/393-1064**) in Nassau for details.

GETTING AROUND **Taxis** (**© 242/339-1284**) meet incoming flights from Nassau.

If you need a car, check with one of the guesthouses, but don't expect the vehicles to be well-maintained. One of the best ways to explore the island is by bike: Call **Pour More Bar** at **© 242/339-1659.** The cost is $1 per hour.

FAST FACTS The **Inagua Hospital** can be called at ✆ **242/339-1249.** The **police** can be reached at ✆ **242/339-1263.**

WHERE TO STAY

The choices aren't great on this island, but most visitors are willing to forgo comfort to see the spectacular flamingos.

Morton Main House The Main House is owned by Morton Bahamas Ltd., the salt people, whose employees often fill up all the rooms. Only six bedrooms are rented, and the furnishings are extremely modest, though everything is clean. Each unit comes with a small bathroom containing a shower-tub combination. Life here is casual and completely informal. You can order breakfast or lunch here—no dinner. It unfortunately sits near a noisy power plant.

Matthew Town, Inagua, The Bahamas. ✆ **242/339-1267.** Fax 242/339-1265. 6 units. $63.60 double. No credit cards. *In room:* A/C, TV, no phone.

Walkine's Guest House Set 1km (½ mile) south of Matthew Town, this simple guesthouse has a blue exterior and rosy, shell-pink bedrooms. Your hosts are Eleanor and Kirk Walkine, who built their place in 1984 across the road from the beach. Rooms are very modest but spacious, with only racks to hang your clothes in lieu of a closet. Bathrooms are large, each containing a shower-tub combination.

Gregory St., Matthew Town, Inagua, The Bahamas. ✆ **242/339-1612.** 5 units, 3 with private bathroom. $84.80 double. No credit cards. *In room:* A/C, TV, no phone.

WHERE TO DINE

Cozy Corner BAHAMIAN/AMERICAN The most consistently reliable restaurant outside any of the guesthouses is this lime-green, stone-built house 2 blocks from the sea. Your hosts, Rosemary Ingraham and her daughter, Veronica, maintain a friendly bar, where beer, rum punch, and gossip seem to be the staples of the town. Menu items include a simple roster of mostly fried foods that are almost always accompanied by french fries. Dishes include fried conch, fried chicken, burgers and "whopper burgers," and whatever kind of fried seafood is available from local fishermen on the day of your visit.

William St., Matthew Town. ✆ **242/339-1440.** Breakfast $5; lunch $6; dinner $7–$10. No credit cards. Daily 9:30am–10:30pm (closing time could vary).

EXPLORING THE ISLAND: PINK FLAMINGOS & MORE

Inagua, the southernmost island of The Bahamas, and third-largest in the chain, lies just off the eastern tip of Cuba. Partially because of its isolation, it's home to some of the best-stocked bird colonies in the western hemisphere. In fact, the island's vast number of **pink flamingos** ★★★ outnumbers its human population of 1,200. They're so plentiful on Inagua that some of them even roost on the runway of the island's airport, as well as at thousands of other locations throughout the flat, heat-blasted landscape. When seen in a huge flock, they present a surreal vision.

Dedicated bird-watchers who are willing to forgo comforts usually trek inland to the edges of the many brackish lakes in the island's center. About half the island is devoted to a national park; the island's most viable industry involves distilling salt from the local salt flats.

To visit **Inagua National Park** ★★ to see the birds is reason enough to come here in the first place. Anyone going into the park must be accompanied by a warden, and reservations and a day pass costing $25 for adults and $10 for students must be obtained in advance, either through The Bahamas National Trust in Nassau (✆ **242/393-1317** for information or reservations), or else by contacting one of the local wardens on Inagua, either Randolph Burrows or Henry Nixon at ✆ **242/339-1616.** In addition to the park fee, it is expected that you'll offer the wardens a large tip. Figure on about $50 a day, the usual payment. The best time to see our feathered friends is from November until June.

One of the best panoramas on the island is **Southwest Point,** lying 2km (1¼ miles) south of the "capital." From here you can see Cuba on a clear day, because it lies just 81km (50 miles) to the west. There's a lighthouse here dating from 1870. From it, you can wave at Castro. The reefs off this point are treacherous, as many a captain learned when his ship was wrecked here. The lighthouse is one of the last quartet of hand-operated kerosene lighthouses left in The Bahamas.

Seawater is pumped into the interior of the island and held in dikes. The island's salt ponds, about 80 of them, cover some 12,000 acres. As the water evaporates, it turns into heavy brine. Continuously, the salt solidifies at night and melts during the heat of the day, and a crystallized bed forms at the bottom of the pond. In the final stage, any remaining water is drained, and the salt is bulldozed into bleached white mountains and shipped around the world for processing. As the water evaporates in the salt ponds, brine shrimp concentrate and provide great meals for the flamingos. If you'd like to marvel at salt, you can call **Morton Salt Company** (✆ **242/339-1300**) and ask if a tour would be possible. They produce more than 1 million tons of salt a year.

You can also visit the **Erickson Museum & Library,** Gregory Street, at the northern edge of Matthew Town (✆ **242/339-1863**). Exhibits detail the history of the island and Morton Salt. The museum is named for the Erickson family, who came here in 1934 to run the salt company. Hours are Monday to Friday 9am to 1pm and 3 to 6pm.

Index

See also Accommodations and Restaurant indexes, below.

General Index

Accommodations

Restaurants

Frommer's® Complete Travel Guides

Alaska
Alaska Cruises & Ports of Call
Amsterdam
Argentina & Chile
Arizona
Atlanta
Australia
Austria
Bahamas
Barcelona, Madrid & Seville
Beijing
Belgium, Holland & Luxembourg
Bermuda
Boston
Brazil
British Columbia & the Canadian Rockies
Budapest & the Best of Hungary
California
Canada
Cancún, Cozumel & the Yucatán
Cape Cod, Nantucket & Martha's Vineyard
Caribbean
Caribbean Cruises & Ports of Call
Caribbean Ports of Call
Carolinas & Georgia
Chicago
China
Colorado
Costa Rica
Denmark
Denver, Boulder & Colorado Springs
England
Europe
European Cruises & Ports of Call
Florida
France
Germany
Great Britain
Greece
Greek Islands
Hawaii
Hong Kong
Honolulu, Waikiki & Oahu
Ireland
Israel
Italy
Jamaica
Japan
Las Vegas
London
Los Angeles
Maryland & Delaware
Maui
Mexico
Montana & Wyoming
Montréal & Québec City
Munich & the Bavarian Alps
Nashville & Memphis
Nepal
New England
New Mexico
New Orleans
New York City
New Zealand
Northern Italy
Nova Scotia, New Brunswick & Prince Edward Island
Oregon
Paris
Philadelphia & the Amish Country
Portugal
Prague & the Best of the Czech Republic
Provence & the Riviera
Puerto Rico
Rome
San Antonio & Austin
San Diego
San Francisco
Santa Fe, Taos & Albuquerque
Scandinavia
Scotland
Seattle & Portland
Shanghai
Singapore & Malaysia
South Africa
South America
South Florida
South Pacific
Southeast Asia
Spain
Sweden
Switzerland
Texas
Thailand
Tokyo
Toronto
Tuscany & Umbria
USA
Utah
Vancouver & Victoria
Vermont, New Hampshire & Maine
Vienna & the Danube Valley
Virgin Islands
Virginia
Walt Disney World® & Orlando
Washington, D.C.
Washington State

Frommer's® Dollar-a-Day Guides

Australia from $50 a Day
California from $70 a Day
Caribbean from $70 a Day
England from $75 a Day
Europe from $70 a Day
Florida from $70 a Day
Hawaii from $80 a Day
Ireland from $60 a Day
Italy from $70 a Day
London from $85 a Day
New York from $90 a Day
Paris from $80 a Day
San Francisco from $70 a Day
Washington, D.C. from $80 a Day

Frommer's® Portable Guides

Acapulco, Ixtapa & Zihuatanejo
Amsterdam
Aruba
Australia's Great Barrier Reef
Bahamas
Berlin
Big Island of Hawaii
Boston
California Wine Country
Cancún
Charleston & Savannah
Chicago
Disneyland®
Dublin
Florence
Frankfurt
Hong Kong
Houston
Las Vegas
London
Los Angeles
Los Cabos & Baja
Maine Coast
Maui
Miami
New Orleans
New York City
Paris
Phoenix & Scottsdale
Portland
Puerto Rico
Puerto Vallarta, Manzanillo & Guadalajara
Rio de Janeiro
San Diego
San Francisco
Seattle
Sydney
Tampa & St. Petersburg
Vancouver
Venice
Virgin Islands
Washington, D.C.

Frommer's® National Park Guides

Banff & Jasper
Family Vacations in the National Parks
Grand Canyon
National Parks of the American West
Rocky Mountain
Yellowstone & Grand Teton
Yosemite & Sequoia/ Kings Canyon
Zion & Bryce Canyon

Frommer's® Memorable Walks

Chicago
London
New York
Paris
San Francisco
Washington, D.C.

Frommer's® Great Outdoor Guides

Arizona & New Mexico
New England
Northern California
Southern New England
Vermont & New Hampshire

Suzy Gershman's Born to Shop Guides

Born to Shop: France
Born to Shop: Hong Kong, Shanghai & Beijing
Born to Shop: Italy
Born to Shop: London
Born to Shop: New York
Born to Shop: Paris

Frommer's® Irreverent Guides

Amsterdam
Boston
Chicago
Las Vegas
London
Los Angeles
Manhattan
New Orleans
Paris
Rome
San Francisco
Seattle & Portland
Vancouver
Walt Disney World
Washington, D.C.

Frommer's® Best-Loved Driving Tours

Britain
California
Florida
France
Germany
Ireland
Italy
New England
Northern Italy
Scotland
Spain
Tuscany & Umbria

Hanging Out™ Guides

Hanging Out in England
Hanging Out in Europe
Hanging Out in France
Hanging Out in Ireland
Hanging Out in Italy
Hanging Out in Spain

The Unofficial Guides®

Bed & Breakfasts and Country Inns in:
- California
- Great Lakes States
- Mid-Atlantic
- New England
- Northwest
- Rockies
- Southeast
- Southwest

Best RV & Tent Campgrounds in:
- California & the West
- Florida & the Southeast
- Great Lakes States
- Mid-Atlantic
- Northeast
- Northwest & Central Plains
- Southwest & South Central Plains
- U.S.A.

Beyond Disney
Branson, Missouri
California with Kids
Chicago
Cruises
Disneyland®
Florida with Kids
Golf Vacations in the Eastern U.S.
Great Smoky & Blue Ridge Region
Inside Disney
Hawaii
Las Vegas
London
Mid-Atlantic with Kids
Mini Las Vegas
Mini-Mickey
New England and New York with Kids
New Orleans
New York City
Paris
San Francisco
Skiing in the West
Southeast with Kids
Walt Disney World®
Walt Disney World® for Grown-ups
Walt Disney World® with Kids
Washington, D.C.
World's Best Diving Vacations

Special-Interest Titles

Frommer's Adventure Guide to Australia & New Zealand
Frommer's Adventure Guide to Central America
Frommer's Adventure Guide to India & Pakistan
Frommer's Adventure Guide to South America
Frommer's Adventure Guide to Southeast Asia
Frommer's Adventure Guide to Southern Africa
Frommer's Britain's Best Bed & Breakfasts and Country Inns
Frommer's Caribbean Hideaways
Frommer's Exploring America by RV
Frommer's Fly Safe, Fly Smart
Frommer's France's Best Bed & Breakfasts and Country Inns
Frommer's Gay & Lesbian Europe
Frommer's Italy's Best Bed & Breakfasts and Country Inns
Frommer's New York City with Kids
Frommer's Ottawa with Kids
Frommer's Road Atlas Britain
Frommer's Road Atlas Europe
Frommer's Road Atlas France
Frommer's Toronto with Kids
Frommer's Vancouver with Kids
Frommer's Washington, D.C., with Kids
Israel Past & Present
The New York Times' Guide to Unforgettable Weekends
Places Rated Almanac
Retirement Places Rated